Criminology: A Reader

Criminology: A Reader

Edited by
Yvonne Jewkes and
Gayle Letherby

SAGE Publications
London • Thousand Oaks • New Delhi

SAGE Publications Ltd
6 Bonhill Street
London EC2A 4PU

SAGE Publications Inc.
2455 Teller Road
Thousand Oaks, California 91320

SAGE Publications India Pvt Ltd
32, M-Block Market
Greater Kailash - I
New Delhi 110 048

British Library Cataloguing in Publication data

A catalogue record for this book is
available from the British Library

ISBN 0-7619-4710-8
ISBN 0-7619-4711-6 (pbk)

Library of Congress Control Number available

Typeset by SIVA Math Setters, Chennai, India
Printed in Great Britain by The Cromwell Press Ltd,
Trowbridge, Wiltshire

Contents

Acknowledgements

The editors and publishers wish to thank the following for permission to reprint copyright material:

Part I

Macmillan Ltd for the extract from *Hooligan: A History of Respectable Fears* by Geoffrey Pearson, 1983, reproduced with permission of Palgrave.

Open University Press for 'Perspectives in Criminological Theory' by Sandra Walklate from *Understanding Criminology: Current Theoretical Debates*, 1998.

The Free Press, a Division of Simon and Schuster Inc. for extracts from *Outsiders: Studies in the Sociology of Deviance* by Howard S. Becker, © 1963 by The Free Press; copyright renewed 1991 by Howard S. Becker.

Sage Publications Ltd for 'Ten Points of Realism' by Jock Young from *Rethinking Criminology: The Realist Debate*, edited by Jock Young and Roger Matthews, 1992.

Willan Publishing Ltd for the extract from *Offender Profiling and Crime Analysis* by Peter B. Ainsworth © Peter B. Ainsworth 2001, reproduced by permission of Willan Publishing Ltd.

Open University Press for 'Introduction: the Development of Feminist Perspectives on Crime' by Nicole Hahn Rafter and Frances Heidensohn from *International Feminist Perspectives in Criminology: Engendering a Discipline*, 1995.

Part II

Routledge for 'Crime, Power and Ideological Mystification' by Steven Box from *Power, Crime, and Mystification*, 1983.

Open University Press for the extract from *Understanding Crime Data* by Clive Coleman and Jenny Moynihan, 1996.

Pearson Education Ltd for the extracts from *Corporate Crime* by Gary Slapper and Steve Tombs, 1999, reprinted by permission of Pearson Education Ltd.

Pluto Press for the extract from 'Crime and the Media: a Criminological Perspective' by David Kidd-Hewitt from *Crime and the Media: The Postmodern Spectacle* edited by David Kidd-Hewitt and Richard Osborne, 1995.

Stanley Cohen for the extract from *Folk Devils and Moral Panics: The Creation of the Mods and Rockers,* published by Paladin Press, 1973.

Routledge for 'The Ultimate Neighbour from Hell? Stranger Danger and the Media Framing of Paedophiles' by Jenny Kitzinger from *Social Policy, the Media and Misrepresentation* edited by Bob Franklin, 1999.

Polity Press for the extract from *Crime in Context: A Critical Criminology of Market Societies* by Ian Taylor, 1999.

Part III

Sage Publications Ltd for the extract from *The Penal System: An Introduction*, 3rd edn, by Michael Cavadino and James Dignan, 2001.

Routledge for the extract from *Villains: Crime and Community in the Inner City* by Janet Foster, 1990.

Pearson Education Ltd for the extract from *Crime and Society in Britain* by Hazel Croall, 1998, reprinted by permission of Pearson Education Ltd.

Pluto Press for the extract from *What is to be Done about Law and Order? Crisis in the Nineties* by John Lea and Jock Young, 1993.

Oxford University Press for 'From Scarman to Stephen Lawrence' by Stuart Hall from *History Workshop Journal*, Issue 48, 1999 by permission of Oxford University Press.

Sage Publications Ltd for the extract from *Youth and Crime: A Critical Introduction* by John Muncie, 1999.

The Centre for Crime and Justice Studies for 'The Myth of Girl Gangs' by Susan Batchelor from *Criminal Justice Matters*, 43, February 2001.

Routledge for the extract from *Intimate Intrusions: Women's Experience of Male Violence* by Elizabeth Stanko, 1985.

Routledge for 'When Men are Victims: the Failure of Victimology' by Tim Newburn and Elizabeth A. Stanko from *Just Boys Doing Business? Men, Masculinities and Crime*, 1994.

Part IV

© Robert Reiner 2000. Reprinted from *The Politics of the Police* by Robert Reiner (3rd edition, Oxford University Press, 2000).

Willan Publishing Ltd for 'Policing and the Police: Key Issues in Criminal Justice' by Clive Coleman and Clive Norris from *Introducing Criminology* © Clive Coleman and Clive Norris 2000, reproduced by permission of Willan Publishing Ltd.

Macmillan Ltd for the extract from *Criminal Injustice: An Evaluation of the Criminal Justice Process in Britain* by Frank Belloni and Jacqualine Hodgson, © Frank Belloni and Jacqueline Hodgson 2000.

The Observer Magazine for 'The Injudiciary', 13 December 1992, © Observer.

Blackstone Press for 'Justifications and Purposes of Imprisonment' by Ian Dunbar and Anthony Langdon from *Tough Justice: Sentencing and Penal Policies in the 1990s*, 1998.

Penguin Books Ltd for the extract from *Psychological Survival: The Experience of Long-term Imprisonment* by Stanley Cohen and Laurie Taylor, 1972.

Part V

Sage Publications Ltd for 'Late-modern Criminology: "Late" as in "Dead" or "Modern" as in "New"?' by Nigel South from *Sociology after Postmodernism*, edited by David Owen, 1997.

© Oxford University Press 1997. 'Social Control' from *The Oxford Handbook of Criminology*, edited by Mike Maguire, Rod Morgan and Robert Reiner (2nd edition, 1997) by permission of Oxford University Press.

The Observer for 'Smile, You're on TV', 13 November 1994, © Observer.

The Observer for 'They're Watching You', 29 August 1999, © Observer.

The Guardian for 'Land of the Free', 2 December 2001, © Guardian.

Arnold for 'New Ways to Break the Law: Cybercrime and the Politics of Hacking' by Douglas Thomas from '*Web.Studies: Rewiring Media Studies for the Digital Age*, edited by David Gauntlett © Edward Arnold 2000. Reprinted by permission of the publishers.

Every effort has been made to trace all the copyright holders, but if any has been inadvertently overlooked, the publishers will be pleased to make the necessary arrangement at the first opportunity.

Introduction

The past decade has seen criminology established as one of the fastest-growing subjects for university study. The growth in the undergraduate market has been especially rapid over the past three or four years, with many institutions offering the subject not only as a single honours award, but also in joint or combined forms, or as part of a broader, multi-disciplinary menu of study which might include, for example, criminological components on courses in sociology, general studies and criminal justice studies. Given this continuing development and expansion, the time seems right for the introduction of a Criminology Reader designed to offer a broad introductory base for students coming to the study of crime and deviance for the first time. It is for these students that this volume has been devised.

Our aim in putting together *Criminology: A Reader* is not to provide a collection of 'definitive' readings, which claims to be comprehensive. Rather, we offer a mixture of historical and more recent pieces that are indicative of the issues and perspectives that have shaped the study of crime in the modern period. Consequently, you will not find in this volume only readings that might be described as original or 'classic' theoretical expositions. There are certainly several extracts which fit that description, but had we included only those texts that have shaped the theoretical contours of criminology we would surely have left ourselves open to accusations of selectivity and omission, and could hardly have hoped adequately to reflect the diversity and scope of the subject in a manner appropriate to an introductory text. Instead, we have interspersed our chosen 'classics' with extracts which offer more expansive overviews of the historical, social and theoretical developments of the field with the aim of introducing students to the complexity of definition in relation to lay and professional discourse. In addition, we have included several contemporary readings, some of them newspaper articles, simply because they illustrate an important issue clearly and relevantly. Some of our choices might be deemed idiosyncratic or controversial, but we believe them to be all the more interesting for that, and we hope that they will stir classroom debate.

Overall, we hope to have given a flavour of criminology's varied and frequently conflicting history, as well as its current debates. Our focus lies within the UK, but most of the issues raised are generalizable, and you will find examples from Europe and the United States in the suggestions for further reading, and sometimes in the readings themselves. Although some of the authors represented here do mention issues of method, methodology and epistemology, that is not our main focus. For a consideration of the practical and political aspects of criminological research see, for example, Jupp (1989), Gelsthorpe and Morris (1990), Jupp et al. (2000) and King and Wincup (2000).

Each part of the Reader is discrete and thematic, but the readings have been organized throughout the book in such a way as to develop key themes and ideas, and/or to set up interesting debates between approaches that differ theoretically or methodologically. You may choose to work your way through chronologically or go straight to sections that interest you particularly. Either of these routes is valuable, although we have written our commentaries with the chronological approach in mind and have cross-referenced readings to encourage you to make connections across areas. Clearly, however, there are further connections to be made.

We have heard Readers compared to boxes of chocolates in which some contributions are eagerly devoured, while others are picked up, half eaten, and then discarded or put back in the box – tried, but found wanting. Our own view is that consuming one well-chosen and rewarding reading can, as with chocolates, quickly lead to a desire for more. While we anticipate that many students will wish to pick out those morsels which appear most relevant to a particular course of study or assignment, we hope that our grouping of the thirty-four readings into thematic sections, with theoretical and conceptual links running throughout the entire collection, will result in many of you experiencing this volume as a satisfying whole.

Having said that, we do not anticipate that this will be the only reading that you will do. We certainly do not intend this Reader to limit scholarly endeavour and see it as a springboard to other interesting work in the area. With this in mind we have included at the end of each reading a list of others book and articles which either apply specifically to that particular reading or encourage further thought and interest in related areas. Also, at the end of each reading you will find a list of *Study Questions*. Some of these encourage critical and analytical reflection about the reading; some ask you to think further about the issue in question, perhaps by comparing the main focus in the reading with that of other readings, and some are more activity based. Following up on the *Further Reading* and working on the questions, both alone and in groups, will, we hope, encourage you to develop a critical, reflexive understanding of crime and the victims of crime. In addition, these activities should encourage an interest in and understanding of the responses to crime and the significance of criminology as a discipline. Our aim is to encourage you, the reader, to challenge the stereotypes and the misperceptions of issues that everyone has an opinion about and many misunderstand.

Inevitably we run the risk of upsetting or offending some people because no Reader can hope to represent every aspect of an academic field, least of all one as diverse and eclectic as criminology. Limitations of space have resulted in a number of notable omissions, and our chosen favourites will not be shared by all others working in the area. Furthermore, the vast majority of writers whose extracts we have chosen present their material within a broad sociological framework, which is both a reflection of our own academic backgrounds and of recent influences that have shaped criminology, certainly in the era of developing postgraduate and undergraduate studies in the subject. However, we have tried to include an assortment – to continue the chocolate analogy – of views and perspectives (tastes and flavours!), including some contributions which have had a profound impact on the theoretical development of criminology, and others which have provided the inspiration and model for several generations of empirical research.

In sum, we have attempted to provide a collection of readings which will serve as a broad introduction to the study of crime and criminal justice, and we trust that you will find a surfeit of interesting and useful material in this Reader. While the readings do not have to be read sequentially, a chronological journey through the volume may help you to understand the development of ideas and debates in some areas, and should encourage you to make theoretical and conceptual links between, and across, different readings. You may also find some extracts more challenging, or more relevant to your own particular interests, than others. We hope, though, that *Criminology: A Reader* will inspire you to develop your own tastes and interests, and we trust that none of our choices will be consigned to the status of the half-nibbled marzipan at the bottom of the box!

REFERENCES

Gelsthorpe, L. and Morris, A. (eds) (1990) *Feminist Perspectives in Criminology*, Milton Keynes: Open University Press.

Jupp, V. (1989) *Methods of Criminological Research*, London: Routledge.

Jupp, V., Davies, P. and Francis, P. (eds) (2000) *Doing Criminological Research*, London: Sage.

King, R.D. and Wincup, E. (eds) (2000) *Doing Research on Crime and Justice*, Oxford: Oxford University Press.

Part One

Approaching the Study of Crime: Historical and Definitional Issues

In the first part of the Reader our over-arching theme is that of historical and definitional issues. The authors of some of the readings are concerned with a particular theory or discipline, while others provide critical overviews of theories and approaches to the study of crime and deviance. In many of the readings political issues are also of central concern. Part I opens with a piece by Geoffrey Pearson who focuses on the troublesome youth (the 'hooligan') of the nineteenth century. Pearson challenges historical understandings of hooliganism and his analysis can be compared to similar critiques of so-called 'crime waves' today. In Reading 2 Sandra Walklate provides an overview of many of the theories that have shaped modern criminology. She considers both individualist explanations and approaches that focus on the social. All of these are referred to again either within this part or elsewhere in the book. This reading is followed by an extract from *Outsiders: Studies in the Sociology of Deviance* by Howard S. Becker (Reading 3), which has been highly influential (but not uncriticized), both theoretically and methodologically, within criminology and sociology. In a piece concerned with detailing the contribution of realism to understanding crime, Jock Young (Reading 4) argues that only an approach which is faithful to the nature of crime, and which focuses on lived experience, can hope to offer any adequate explanations. Peter B. Ainsworth (Reading 5) focuses on the contribution that psychology has made, and continues to make, to the study of crime and deviance. This is followed by a reading by Nicole Hahn Rafter and Frances Heidensohn (Reading 6) who identify a distinctive feminist approach which challenges both historical and much contemporary mainstream criminology. When reading through this first part, consider the differences and similarities between the theories and approaches that are represented in these six readings. Overall, the different but sometimes complementary stances that you will encounter provide a theoretical grounding to all other pieces included in this Reader.

1

Victorian boys, we are here!

Geoffrey Pearson

This reading focuses on the troublesome youth – the 'hooligan' – of the nineteenth century. The piece is interesting for several reasons. First, it challenges commonly held misconceptions of the Victorian era as a golden age of stability and moral order. Secondly, it provides a nice example of a moral panic (Reading 11) that is comparable to contemporary panics about 'muggers' (Reading 17), 'yobs' (Reading 19) and 'girl gangs' (Reading 20). Thirdly, the response of the press is also interesting: the 'hooligan' was branded as un-British, and his (and occasionally her) behaviour was presented as a threat to society.

Pearson begins by considering the origins of the word 'hooligan' and outlines the responses of the press, the police and the public. In the late 1890s, when the term 'hooligan' was first used, 'respectable England' felt itself to be 'engulfed by a new rush of crime'. Hooligans then represented an attack on the peaceful, well-ordered way of life and the word began to be associated with gangs in London and used widely and indiscriminately. However, although the hooligan was portrayed as an alien presence, violence and disorder were a familiar part of life in working-class communities, and hostility towards the police was also commonplace. Examples of violence included fights on the streets, in public houses and at football matches, vandalism on the streets and in schools. Attacks on the police were often sparked off by what was perceived to be an unfair arrest but, sometimes, loyalty to the community appeared to be paramount; as the author notes, even murderers frequently evoked the support of the public. Thus, as Pearson comments, suspicion and hostility towards the police in working-class districts of late nineteenth-century London found expression in a broader range of activities than hooliganism alone.

The word 'hooligan' made an abrupt entrance into common English usage, as a term to describe gangs of rowdy youths, during the hot summer of 1898.

SOURCE: From *Hooligan: A History of Respectable Fears* (London: Macmillan, 1983), 74–90.

'Hooligans' and 'Hooliganism' were thrust into the headlines in the wake of a turbulent August Bank Holiday celebration in London which had resulted in unusually large numbers of people being brought before the courts for disorderly behaviour, drunkenness, assaults on police, street robberies and fighting. One of the more alarming aspects of these Bank Holiday disturbances was that they highlighted fierce traditions of resistance to the police in working-class neighbourhoods, so that not uncommonly policemen attempting to make street arrests would be set upon by large crowds – sometimes numbering two or three hundred people – shouting 'Rescue! Rescue!' and 'Boot him!'[1]

At first it was not entirely clear where the word 'Hooligan' had sprung from – and it remains unclear to this day – or exactly what it meant, other than some kind of novel reference to street violence and ruffianism. It seems most likely, however, that it was a word like 'Teddy Boy' or 'Mod' or 'Skinhead' which, coming out of the popular culture of working-class London, had been adopted by youths in some localities in order to describe themselves and what they took for their common identity. A Music Hall song from [the] 1890s, introduced by the Irish comedians O'Connor and Brady, had probably first popularised the word:

> Oh, the Hooligans! Oh, the Hooligans!
> Always on the riot,
> Cannot keep them quiet,
> Oh, the Hooligans! Oh, the Hooligans!
> They are the boys
> To make a noise
> In our backyard.[2]

How it came to be adopted by, and applied to, youthful street gangs is something of a mystery.[3] But whatever its humble origins, when the new word was picked up by the newspapers in August 1898 it was quickly transformed into a term of more general notoriety, so that 'Hooligan' and 'Hooliganism' became the controlling words to describe troublesome youths who had previously been known more loosely as 'street arabs', 'ruffians' or 'roughs'. And once they were christened, as we might expect, the 'Hooligans' were understood as an entirely unprecedented and 'un-British' phenomenon: indeed, we must allow that it was most ingenious of late Victorian England to disown the British Hooligan by giving him an 'Irish' name.

In other ways, too, the phenomenon was located within a scale of alien values and temperaments, thus stamping it as foreign and 'un-English'. When *The Times* (17 August 1898) first turned its attention to the August disorders, describing them as 'something like organised terrorism in the streets', it struck the key-note in an editorial on 'The Weather and the Streets':

> It is curious that simultaneously with reports of excessive heat should come the record of an unusual number of crimes of lawless violence ... Does the great heat fire the blood of the London rough or street arab, with an effect analogous to that of a southern climate upon the hot-blooded Italian or Provencal? ... Or is the connexion between heat and lawlessness not so much one of cause and effect as coincident circumstances – heat generating thirst, and thirst a too frequent consumption of fiery liquor unsuitable for a tropical climate?

A couple of years later, asking 'What are we to do with the "Hooligan"? Who or what is responsible for his growth?' *The Times* (30 October 1900) would harp on the same theme, announcing that 'Every week some incident shows that certain parts of London are more perilous for the peaceable wayfarer than the remote districts of Calabria, Sicily, or Greece, once the classic haunts of brigands'. In the heat of the immediate events of 1898, however, while denouncing the excessive leniency of the law, *The Times* (17 August 1898) had boomed out an even more momentous possibility that 'un-English' violence might have to be curbed by un-English methods:

> In Continental cities, or in the free Republic of America, they have very little scruple about calling out troops and shooting down organised disturbances of the peace … But if we do not adopt Continental methods of dealing with street lawlessness … if we do not wish our police to be formidable as an armed force, we must not grudge an increase in their numbers.

HEADLINE NEWS

If the 'Hooligans' were regarded as an un-English phenomenon, they were also understood as an entirely unprecedented development and respectable England felt itself to have been suddenly engulfed in a new rush of crime. A pattern of trouble quickly came to be associated with the street gangs. The Hooligans fought pitched battles among themselves – Chelsea Boys against Fulham Boys, or Chapel Street against Margaret Street – and they were said to take great pride in their famous victories over rival neighbourhoods. The Hooligans were also said to hunt in cowardly packs, however, and news reports regularly featured them smashing up coffee-stalls and public houses, assaulting staff in pubs and cheap eating-houses, robbing and assaulting old ladies, attacking foreigners such as Italian ice-cream vendors or 'Froggy' cafe owners, and setting upon policemen in the streets with savage howls of 'Boot 'em!' Because, if the supposedly traditional habit of respect for the law was not much in evidence here, then frequent headlines such as '"Boot 'em" at Waterloo', 'They Play Football with a Man' and 'Kick a Man like a Football' serve to remind us that the English 'fair play' tradition of fighting with the fists – and not with the feet – had also gone into eclipse. In South London, for example, it was said that the gangs wore 'boots toe-plated with iron, and calculated to kill easily'.[4] […]

A TOUR OF THE QUIET STREETS

Before looking in more detail at who the 'Hooligans' were, and in order to place the controversies that surrounded them in perspective, it will be helpful to make an imaginative effort to reconstruct the kind of social world in which the original 'Hooligans' moved. On so many occasions, the way in which 'Hooliganism' was greeted implied a sudden, alien interruption of a peaceful and well-ordered way of life. But what did this way of life look like at street level? And what were the habits of the Hooligans' gentle neighbours and families and friends? A brief tour of inspection of London's streets at the time that the Hooligans were publicly christened will help us to see something of what these quiet streets were made of.

In some localities trouble had undoubtedly been expected at the time of the Bank Holiday, and it was reported in Lambeth police court that plainclothes men had been specially stationed 'for the purpose of dealing with cases of street ruffianism'.[5] The newspapers were particularly impressed by the appearance in Marylebone court of 88 people in a single day, 70 of whom were charged with disorderliness of some sort, although *The Times* (16 August 1898) observed that 'the majority of cases were of a very ordinary kind'. The troubled signs of this 'ordinary' street life were very much in evidence, however, and press reports were packed with accounts of assaults and robberies, 'dipping' gangs at race meetings, gang fights and stabbings, vandalism, punch-ups and 'free fights'. The 'free fight' must have been sometimes quite an occasion: a Bank Holiday bust-up in the Old Kent Road, for example, consumed the energies of 200 people.[6]

In the foreground of the Bank Holiday outrages were the 'Hooligan' gangs themselves. In one disturbance that received wide publicity, a policeman had stumbled across a gang of about twenty youths, said to be known as the 'Chelsea Boys' who 'armed with sticks and stones were fighting a contingent of similar young ruffians from Battersea' at Cheyne Walk by the river.[7] A 17-year-old paper-stainer, James Irons, was brought before the magistrate – described by the police as a ring-leader and by his mother as 'a good boy' – where it was said that he had 'used disgusting language, and discharged a number of stones larger than walnuts from a powerful catapult'. Charged with disorderly conduct and with discharging stones from a catapult to the common danger, he was found to have four previous convictions against him for gambling, disorderly behaviour and stone-throwing. Regretting 'that he had no power to send him to prison without the option of a fine', the magistrate imposed a fine of 40 shillings (probably amounting to more than a month's wages) or twenty-one days' hard labour.

Another typical Bank Holiday incident of the kind that brought such infamy to the Hooligans involved four young men, described as 'larrikins' aged between 17 and 20 years, who were charged with damaging an ice-cream feeder belonging to an Italian ice-cream vendor, and assaults on police and a park-keeper.[8] There had been an argument and the youths had overturned the ice-cream barrow, and after a chase there was a scuffle with the police. Identified by police witnesses as the 'Somers Town Boys', the two youths charged with assault received six weeks' hard labour and a month's hard labour. According to one witness, as they ran away across a park they were heard to shout, 'Look out for the Hooligan gang.'

After these incidents the look-outs were certainly posted in the press, and the word 'Hooligan' began to be used widely, if at first somewhat indiscriminately. More to the point, if 'Hooliganism' was an entirely novel outburst as was usually supposed, then a tropical growth of gang life must have sprouted overnight. From August onwards the newspapers were over-flowing with the exploits of the various gangs in London: the 'Lion Boys' from the Lion and

Lamb in Clerkenwell; the so-called 'Clerkenwell "Pistol Gang"': the 'Girdle Gang' which took its name from Thomas, alias 'Tuxy', Girdle; the 'Somers Town Gang' who were said to be the pests of Euston Road and Gower Street; the 'Pinus Gang' who infested Leather Lane and Clerkenwell; the 'Drury Lane Boys'; the notorious 'Waterloo Road Gang'; the 'Pickett Gang'; 'McNab's; the 'Rest Gang'; the 'Fulham Boys'; the 'Chelsea Boys'; the 'Velvet Cap Gang'; the 'Plaid-Cap Brigade' from Poplar; the gangs who romped around King Street and Great Church Lane in Hammersmith and who were said to be 'not "Hooligans" but worse'; and many others, including a band of youngsters who had adopted the dare-devil title of the 'Dick Turpin Gang'.[9]

At first the press were inclined to brand anything as the newly named 'Hooliganism'. When the Girdle Gang appeared in court for an assault on a man whom, it was said, they had kicked 'like a football', *The Daily Graphic* described them as 'a gang of the Hooligan type'. Mr Girdle's solicitor, on the other hand, complained that 'the "Girdle Gang" did not really exist, except in the imagination of a "needy paragraphist"'.[10] But although 'Tuxy' Girdle may not have been a youthful Hooligan, it did emerge that he had been running whores and he received a substantial sentence of penal servitude for the assault on the man whom the gang had suspected of being a police spy.

The new word quickly settled down, however, as a regular pattern began to emerge in the trouble associated with the London Hooligans. They cluttered up the streets in noisy gatherings, swearing at passers-by, spitting on them, and sometimes assaulting and robbing them. *The Daily Graphic* (15 August 1898) reported the antics of the 'Velvet Cap Gang' from Battersea: 'Some dozen boys, all armed with sticks and belts, wearing velvet caps, and known as the "Velvet Cap Gang", walking along ... pushing people off the pavement, knocking at shop doors, and using filthy language.' And then, a few days later there was a similar story from another part of London: 'A gang of roughs, who were parading the roadway, shouting obscene language, playing mouth organs, and pushing respectable people down. The young ruffians were all armed with thick leather belts, on which there were heavy brass buckles' (*The Daily Graphic,* 25 August 1898).

There were innumerable accounts of a similar character, describing 'larking' in the streets. The frequent reports of people being hustled, or pushed off the pavement, probably derived from the practice among working-class youths known as 'holding the street'. This violent ritual of territorial supremacy, as described by Walter Besant in 1901, sounds remarkably like the modern practice at football grounds of 'holding the End': 'The boys gather together and hold the street: if anyone ventures to pass through it they rush upon him, knock him down, and kick him savagely about the head; they rob him as well ... the boys regard holding the street with pride.'[11]

Fights and disturbances in pubs were also commonly reported. One 18-year-old youth appeared in court after throwing glasses at a publican's head, while in another pub case that ended in court a landlord had refused to serve Bank Holiday revellers whereupon they 'Knocked him down, and kicked him in the eye and about the body'.[12] Back in the open street things were no better. We hear of 'an elderly woman … set upon by a gang of young ruffians who knocked her down and stole a bag of provisions she was carrying', and in another case a 17-year-old youth was charged with assaulting an elderly woman on Bank Holiday night: 'Both her eyes were blackened and there was an abrasion on her nose.'[13]

These kinds of incidents could be repeated time and time again, and nor were black eyes and bruises the only injuries sustained. Arriving home late one Sunday night on a railway excursion from Herne Bay, a bottle-fight broke out among the holiday-makers as a result of which a man was killed. But what must astonish us, I think, more than the details of violence is that the only charges brought as a result of this death were against three men who were charged with assault and punished with a 20 shillings' fine, with the additional requirement that they should pay the doctor's bill on the dead man.[14]

In another case, headlined as 'The Alleged Hooligan Tragedy', a man died after a street-fight and it was reported that on arrival at hospital he had made a statement to the effect that, 'I got my injuries in the Borough through being kicked to death by Hooligans.' Eye-witnesses denied this, however, saying that he had been engaged in a 'fair' stand-up fight, but that when other people joined in he had fallen and struck his head on a tramline.[15] There were other cases of deaths in the streets which could not be cleared up, except as 'accidents', and reluctance to give evidence must be counted as an important aspect of popular hostility towards the law.

It was assaults on the police, however, together with fierce resistance to street arrests, that provided the most vivid illumination of popular feeling. In one almost comic instance, a man described as a 'wooden-legged ruffian' who was well known for drunk-and-disorderly offences had kicked a policeman with his wooden leg. In a violent struggle, the policeman found it necessary to unscrew the man's wooden leg as he wrestled him to the ground, striking him across the head with his truncheon. A crowd then assembled and threw pepper at the police, causing such a commotion that it was only possible to get the one-legged prisoner to the police station with the assistance of twelve constables.[16]

In a more typical case, when attempting a street arrest 'a hostile mob raised the cry of "Boot them" against the police'; in another, police attempting to separate a man and woman who were quarrelling were 'set upon by a crowd of 200 persons, who called out "Boot them", and they were assaulted and kicked'. On yet another occasion at Alexandra Park Race Day in 1898, which was said to be 'infested with a crowd of scoundrels and ruffians of the worst race-course stamp', when police arrested a pick-pocket 'the constables were surrounded by a crowd, who kicked them and brutally ill-treated them, and released the prisoner'.[17] There were repeated instances, in fact, of assaults on policemen who then found it necessary to draw their truncheons and fight their way out of a crowd. In a 'desperate struggle in a drunken crowd' a police officer had been stabbed to death in Wilmer Gardens, Hoxton, said to be 'a low neighbourhood infested by a very dangerous class'.[18] While at the height of the Bank Holiday disturbances there was what was described as a 'Midnight Riot' in the vicinity of Euston Road when a policeman attempted to deal with a disorderly woman who 'began to shriek, and … screamed that she was being choked'. Surrounded by a hostile crowd who began to hiss and hoot, the policeman blew his whistle for assistance. 'Unfortunately for the constable', we were told, 'this only had the effect of bringing reinforcements to the mob.' A roar went up of 'Rescue! Rescue!' and among those who joined in were the notorious Somers Town Boys.[19]

'Hooliganism' was invariably portrayed as a totally alien presence, but here we see Hooligans acting in concert with their neighbours, reflecting the fact that in many working-class neighbourhoods hostility towards the police was a remarkably cohesive force. Typically sparked off by what might have been seen as an unfair arrest or an arbitrary use of police power, resistance to arrest on this scale was such an entirely common feature of working-class life before the Great War that it constitutes the most articulate demolition of the myths of deep-rooted popular respect for law and authority in England. A report by Robert Blatchford of a visit to a Music Hall in the 'Gay Nineties' offered a vivid portrait of how these feelings expressed themselves in everyday life. Blatchford did not reckon much to the artistic qualities of the old-fashioned melodrama presented on the stage, but he thought the audience 'were human enough for anything'. Amidst the banter of the assembly of dockers, costers, labourers and mechanics, with their wives and sweethearts and babies – the lads at the back whistling improvised mood music to the events on stage, some pelting those in the pits below with orange pips, and all howling with laughter at their own jokes – he considered that 'very significant were the marks of popular interest and favour':

> 'When the police arrested the hero in the streets and a rescue was attempted by the denizens of the Boro', the audience became quite excited, many of them stood up, and all fell into the spirit of the scene – sympathy being manifestly against the law; and when the stage was darkened and the fortunes of the combat could not be distinguished, open resentment was displayed by the gods, one of whom yelled out to the gasman to 'turn up them bloomin 'glims an' let's see the bloomin 'scrappin'.[20]

Attacks on the police touched on complex structures of loyalty and tradition which cut across simple-minded notions from on high about obedience and civility. Even murderers could be the object of local sympathy. An attempt was made to rescue William 'Fatty' Gould, for example, the accused in the Redcross Court murder case, when he appeared at the inquest: 'assailed by a savage mob' outside the court who shouted their encouragement, 'You will be all right, Bill!' and 'Don't give way, Fatty!'[21] In another murder case, after a 19-year-old youth had been found guilty of a stabbing murder in Oakley Street, a woman who had given crucial evidence against him was ill-treated by neighbours and eventually turned out of her Oakley Street home amidst 'a terrible scene'.[22] Raphael Samuel has also reported an instance of a suspected police informer in the East End who was visited by a mob who expressed their displeasure by burning effigies.[23] We can perhaps only guess at what exactly lay behind such incidents, although these kinds of details begin to add up to something more than a fringe resentment of the police by a marginal 'criminal element'. Suspicion and hostility towards the law in working-class London at the turn of the century drew on much deeper funds of popular feeling than can be usefully or relevantly summed up as the work of 'Hooligan' gangs or 'Hooliganism'.

'The constable in certain districts', *The Pall Mall Gazette* (19 February 1901) observed, 'is apparently looked upon as the common enemy whom it is right to kick and beat whenever that can be done with safety.' 'When he attempts to arrest disorderly persons who have the active sympathy of a crowd of roughs', it added, 'a policeman's lot is not a happy one.' Of that we can be sure. Some idea of how badly the police were treated is given by the reports of the Metropolitan Police Commissioner which show that roughly one-in-four of London's policemen were assaulted each year – 3,444 cases were reported in 1899, for example, when the constabulary strength was 13,213 men and 1,949 sergeants – as police authorities pressed for firmer measures in assault cases.[24] It seems likely, moreover, that the police deliberately avoided mixing it in the more perilous districts. We have already heard complaints against the apathy of the police, and publicans who complained about violence were said to have 'got the name among the police of being "fussy"'.[25] It would have been a disappointed reader, however, who turned to *The Daily Mail's* titillating headline 'HE ATE A POLICEMAN' at the high pitch of the Bank Holiday alarm in 1898 for more news of the monstrous Hooligans, because the story thankfully described the exploits of a truculent crocodile.[26]

Against this background of a bustling, potentially violent and effectively unpoliced street life, we can point to a wide variety of other kinds of rowdyism and misbehaviour at this time in history. There are stories of gangs of roughs waylaying cyclists and pelting them with stones, and in one case a South London cowboy was brought before Lambeth court for lassoing cyclists – 'a kind of horseplay that must be stamped out at once' said the magistrate, with good reason.[27] The police were also being urged to take action against the practice of 'throwing coloured lights' from coaches that were returning from holiday excursions, and there was a growing concern about a wave of incidents in which obstacles – sometimes quite large ones – were placed on railway lines by people described as 'wreckers'.[28] Throughout the late 1890s the police had been bothered by complaints about young boys throwing stones or spitting from the London bridges on to boats and their passengers below. In 1896 while sculling at Putney, an oarsman had been sunk by a stone-throwing youth, and in the following year there was a complaint that a yacht's skylight had been broken at Lambeth Bridge and then 'a shower of horse dung greeted us at Chelsea'. 'I find the spitting this year worse than ever', complained a gentleman in 1900. And although the names given of some of the boys arrested for these offences – David Stones and Arthur Gobbing, for example – suggest the possibility of a hoax, police reports repeatedly referred to 'this dangerous practice' and that 'the danger to the public seems sufficiently marked to warrant some special steps'. Indeed, from 1896 plainclothes men had been deployed to patrol the bridges.[29]

We read in the newspapers of other cases of vandalism. Gas-lamps that are broken, and night-watchmen assaulted when they complain. A case comes to hand of two children, a boy of 8 years and a 10-year-old girl, who broke into their local school and 'then completely wrecked the school furnishings', and this was not the only instance of vandalism and arson in schools.[30] In one Southwark neighbourhood attempts had been made to prevent children from using the drying area on the roof of a block of model dwellings as a playground. Doors and bolts had been fixed, but in a three-month period it was said that '14 dozen locks' had been broken, the children had burned down the door, and even iron gates had not stopped them from gaining access to the roof and throwing stones on people below.[31] There are graffiti, too, and commenting on the improvements in children's drawings since the advent of the Board Schools, the *Westminster Budget* (12 August 1898) described for us how these 'wall sketches' commonly depicted 'the little disagreements which are natural to healthy children'. Here is an example of this Board School artistry: 'This [pointing to a drawing of a girl] is Fanny Ives and she is going to have a smack in the Jaw for hitting Nellie Western.'

Smacks in the jaw between little girls are one thing, perhaps, but there were more formidable indications that all was not well with the gentle sex. A brawl among three women, for example, resulted in one of them 'scoring her face with a door key' because the other woman 'tore her hair and beat her with a poker'. Elsewhere, three girls aged 15 and 16 years were brought to court for robbing a woman of 9s 2½d after they had hustled her. Described by the police as a well-known gang of 'expert pick-pockets', the news headlines identified them as 'Girl Hooligans'.[32] There were other mentions of 'Hooligan Girls' and 'Female Hooligans' and their 'hooliganesque' behaviour. Young women, for example, who were 'arm-in-arm right across the pavement, and kept pushing people off', or another court report which described how 'a respectably-dressed young girl was set upon by four factory girls and unmercifully beaten'. She said that she had 'accidentally brushed against one of the four girls who were standing on the pavement', whereupon 'all four caught hold of her, and beat her in a most savage manner, using fearful language' and left her on the ground bleeding profusely from the nose and mouth.[33]

NOTES

1   *South London Chronicle*, 15 October 1898; *Reynolds's Newspaper*, 2 October 1898; and notes 15–26 below.
2   *Music Hall and Theatre Review*, 26 August 1898.
3   Clarence Rook tells us in *The Hooligan Nights* (Grant Richards, 1899) that the gangs took their name from Patrick Hooligan who lived in 'Irish Court' in the Elephant and Castle, 'a leader among men' who 'established a cult'. Earning his living as a chucker-out, and famed for his lawless daring, Mr Hooligan is said to have died in prison after killing a policeman. Rook likens his career to 'the lives of Buddha and Mahomet' (pp. 23–4). *The Hooligan Nights* is a skilful journalistic portrayal of the life and times of the original Hooligans, but if 'Patrick Hooligan' was a legend in his own time, then it is odd that no one other than Clarence Rook seemed to have heard of him. The press, for example, while using the word 'Hooligan' freely enough, were totally bemused about its origins.

Other stories in circulation suggested that the name had been taken from a comic character in *Nuggets*; or from a music hall turn called 'Brother Hooligan' or 'The

Hooligans', although the music hall trade magazine had never heard of any acts by these names. 'Like many other things', it said, 'the word comes from America.' The word's similarity to the American 'hoodlum' was noted elsewhere, and Australia was also mentioned as its birth-place. Yet another story said that the word had been derived from two brothers named Hoolehan who were prize-fighters, and that in a court case involving them a foolish policeman had mispronounced their name as 'Hooligan'. The policeman's famous mispronunciation also figured in accounts which gave it as a corruption of 'Hooly's gang' or 'Hooley's gang' which is the version accepted by the *Oxford English Dictionary*. Cf. *Music Hall and Theatre Review*, 26 August 1898; *The Daily Mail*, 18 August 1898; *South London Chronicle*, 20 August 1898; J. Trevarthan, 'Hooliganism', *Nineteenth Century*, January 1901, p. 84; E.J. Urwick, *Studies of Boy Life in our Cities* (Dent, 1904) p. 300; *Notes and Queries*, 9th Series, no. 2, 17 September 1898, p. 227 and 15 October 1898, p. 316; 9th Series, no. 7, 19 January 1901, p. 48.

There was indeed a Mr Hooley in the headlines at the same time as the Hooligans in August 1898, but he was not a 'Hooligan'. Mr Edward Terah Hooley was a high-class villain and bankrupt who had been paying 'slush money' to bicycle manufac-turers, and in the course of an absorbing corruption scandal he seemed hell-bent on implicating almost the entire ruling class of England as beneficiaries in his schemes. Mr Hooley's enterprise earned him even more column inches in the press than the terrible Hooligans, and numerous jokes contrived to link the two news stories. So that we hear of 'Hooleyans', Hooleyism', 'Hooleybaloo' and 'Hooleyiana', with 'Mr. Terah Boom-de-Ay Hooley' himself described by *Punch* as a 'Hooley-gan'. Cf. *Bicycling News*, 3 August 1898 and 24 August 1898; *The Daily Mail*, 18 August 1898; *Punch*, 6 August 1898 and 12 November 1898; and a *News of the World* (7 August 1898) cartoon, 'Hooley's Game of Skittles', which shows him bowling down the House of Lords with his evidence in the bankruptcy hearing.

It is a fair guess that it was these long-forgotten jokes which helped to secure the authority of 'Hooley's gang' as the origins of 'Hooligan'. There certainly were street gangs who took their name from a local hard man in such a way, but the Hooligans were not a local gang. Rather, as I will show, they were a well-established 'youth culture' in working-class London, with affinities with similar subcultures in other cities, and we find youths from many parts of London adopting the title of 'Hooligans'. If it had not been for the energies of the press in promoting the new word, however, then no doubt 'Hooligan' would have passed into obscurity along with the unfortunate Mr Hooley and much else of late nineteenth-century London slang.

4 *The Daily Graphic*, 31 August 1898; The Sun, 7 August 1898; *South London Chronicle*, 27 August 1898, 3 September 1898 and 15 October 1898; *News of the World*, 2 October 1898.

5 *The Times*, 2 August 1898.

6 *The Times*, 16 August 1898; *Reynolds's News*, 2 October 1898; *Manchester Evening News*, 15 August 1898.

7 'Hooligans: Street Fights in Chelsea', *The Daily Graphic*, 18 August 1898.

8 *The Times*, 16 August 1898; *News of the World*, 21 August 1898.

9 *The Daily Graphic*, 23 August 1898, 26 August 1898, 27 August 1898, 26 September 1898; *The Daily Mail*, 1 August 1898 and 15 August 1898; *The Sun*, 6 August 1898; *News of the World*, 25 September 1898.

10 *South London Chronicle*, 24 September 1898.

11 W. Besant, *East London* (Chatto and Windus, 1901), p. 177.

12 *Reynolds's News*, 7 August 1898; *South London Chronicle*, 20 August 1898.

13 *South London Chronicle*, 20 August 1898; *Reynolds's News*, 7 August 1898.

14 *South London Chronicle*, 27 August 1898.

15 *The Daily Graphic*, 6 October 1898; *South London Chronicle*, 1 October 1898 and 8 October 1898.

16 *Illustrated Police News*, 9 July 1898.

17 *South London Chronicle*, 15 October 1898; *Illustrated Police News*, 1 October 1898; *Reynolds's News*, 2 October 1898.

18 *News of the World*, 9 October 1898. This is probably the killing remembered by Arthur Harding in R. Samuel, *East End Underworld* (Routledge and Kegan Paul, 1981), pp. 13, 292.

19 *The Daily Mail*, 15 August 1898; *News of the World*, 14 August 1898; *The Evening News*, 13 August 1898.

20 R. Blatchford, *Dismal England* (Walter Scott, 1899), p. 37.

21 *News of the World*, 24 July 1898; *Illustrated Police News*, 30 July 1898.

22 *South London Chronicle*, 5 November 1898. *News of the World* (30 October 1898) described the convicted murderer as 'a youth of the Hooligan type'; but *The Evening News* (21 July 1898 and 26 July 1898) thought the incident arose out of gang rivalries and reprisals against a 'copper's nark'.

23 R. Samuel, 'East End Crime', Conference on Sociology and History, University of Essex, December 1979.

24 *Report of the Commissioner of Police of the Metropolis* 1899, Cd. 399 (HMSO, 1900); *Royal Commission on the Duties of the Metropolitan Police*, vol. 2, Cd. 4260 (HMSO, 1908) qu. 79; Public Record Office, MEPO 2/531 and MEPO 2/570.

25 *The Sun*, 3 August 1898.

26 *The Daily Mail*, 13 August 1898.

27 *News of the World*, 9 October 1898; *The Daily Mail*, 19 August 1898; *Bicycling News*, 10 August 1898.

28 *Reynolds's News*, 9 October 1898; *Manchester Evening News*, 10 September 1898 and 13 September 1898; and 'RAILWAY OUTRAGES ... WHO IS THE WRECKER?', *News of the World*, 11 September 1898.

29 Public Record Office, Metropolitan Police, MEPO 2/362.

30 *South London Chronicle*, 13 August 1898 and 15 October 1898; Public Record Office, MEPO 2/467.

31 *Illustrated Police News*, 16 July 1898.

32 *South London Chronicle*, 13 August 1898 and 3 September 1898.

33 *South London Chronicle*, 27 August 1898; *Illustrated Police News*, 20 August 1898; *The Evening News*, 26 July 1898.

STUDY QUESTIONS

1 If we removed the dates from the newspaper reports that Pearson considers, how similar are they to contemporary media representations of crime in the public sphere? What other, more recent, crime waves have been characterized as 'alien' or 'un-British'?

2 Was hooliganism in the nineteenth century a male phenomenon?

3 In what ways was the social construction of the 'hooligan' racist?

FURTHER READING

For further texts that raise similar issues to those in the reading above, see Pearson, G. (1976) *Working Class Youth Culture*, London: Routledge; Humphries, S. (1981) *Hooligans or Rebels: An Oral History of Working Class Childhood and Youth 1889–1939*, Oxford: Basil Blackwell; and Dunning, E., Murphy, P. and Williams, J. (1988) *The Roots of Football Hooliganism: An Historical and Sociological Study*, London: Routledge and Kegan Paul. For further work on the history of police and public relations, see Storch, R.D. 'The plague of blue locusts: police reform and popular resistance in Northern England, 1840–57'; and Cohen, P. 'Policing the working-class city', both in Fitzgerald, M., McLennan, G. and Pawson, J. (eds) (1981) *Crime and Society: Readings in History and Theory*, London: Routledge in association with Open University Press. Scraton, P. (ed.) (1997) *Childhood in 'Crisis'?*, London: University of Central London Press, provides an interesting account of the demonization of young people today (see also Reading 19). For a critique of 'Victorian values', see Abbott, P. and Wallace, C. (1992) *The Family and the New Right*, London: Pluto.

2

Perspectives in criminological theory

Sandra Walklate

The development of criminology has been characterized by influences from a vast and diverse range of competing theoretical perspectives. In the extract that follows, Sandra Walklate outlines some of the most prominent theories that have shaped modern criminology, arguing that they can be broadly divided into three main categories: a concern with the behaviour of criminals; a concern with the criminality of behaviour; and a concern with the criminality of the state. In the first category, she shows how the classical and positivist schools, although separated by over a century, set up some of the key debates that are still contested by criminologists today – not least the question of whether people freely and rationally choose to commit crime, or whether they are propelled into crime through circumstances beyond their control. As Walklate notes, this fundamental issue is not only crucial for understanding the causes of crime, but it is also of profound importance when considering our responses to crime, and implementing policy.

Following her discussion of individualistic explanations for the behaviour of criminals, Walklate goes on to consider some of the theoretical approaches that have sought social, or sociological, explanations for the criminality of behaviour, focusing on the theories of: social disorganization; 'strain'; and labelling (the last of which is also represented by an extract from the original text by Howard S. Becker in Reading 3). Finally, in her analysis of theories that have directed attention to the criminality of the state, Walklate discusses some of the so-called 'radical' criminologies: Marxism; the 'new criminology'; and critical criminology, each of which extends and develops the thinking of its predecessor. Three other perspectives which are often categorized as 'radical' are left realism and feminism, which are included later in this part (Readings 4 and 6) and postmodernism, which is referred to in Reading 10 and represented in Reading 29.

SOURCE: From *Understanding Criminology: Current Theoretical Debates* (Buckingham: Open University Press, 1998), 16–32.

[…] It is possible to identify three recurrent themes within criminological theory which will be labelled here as a concern with the *behaviour of criminals*, a concern with the *criminality of behaviour*, and a concern with the *criminality of the state*. Each of these themes has been more or less popular at different historical moments and each directs the criminological agenda, in theory and in practice, in quite different ways. We shall discuss each of them in turn.

THE BEHAVIOUR OF CRIMINALS

[…]

Classical Criminology

The key feature of classical criminology is its central presumption that individual criminals engage in a process of rational calculative decision making in choosing how to commit crime. This view is underpinned by two further assumptions: one that individuals have free will; the other that individuals are guided by hedonism, the maximization of pleasure and the minimization of pain. These ideas, in their initial formulation, were important in that they shifted attention towards punishing the offensive behaviour rather than 'punishing' the individual's social or physical characteristics in and of themselves. This shift consequently had an enormous influence on changing attitudes towards punishment and towards the purpose of the law and the legal system.

Classical ideas about crime and punishment can be found in the works of a number of different writers. The writings of Beccaria (1738–94) and Bentham (1748–1832), however, were especially influential. Of the two, Beccaria is frequently cited as being most influential in the subsequent development of the criminological agenda.

Put simply, Beccaria argued that there was a contractual relationship between the individual and the state. This relationship existed to prevent chaos. As a part of this contractual relationship individuals gave up some of their liberties in the interest of the common good with the purpose of the law to ensure that these common interests were met. For Beccaria, this meant that the law should be limited in scope and written down so that people could make decisions on how to behave. Importantly punishment was to fit the crime, not the individual, and was to be certain and swift. Offenders were to be seen as reasonable people with the same capacity for resisting offending behaviour as non-offenders. The guiding principle of the criminal justice process, it was argued, was the presumption of innocence; and in this general framework punishment was to be seen as a deterrent to criminal behaviour. The central concern of the law and the criminal justice process was therefore the prevention of crime through this deterrent function.

These ideas were very influential in reforming criminal codes and informing legislative changes in a number of different social contexts. They were particularly influential in France at the time of the French Revolution and, it is argued, informed the formulation of the American Constitution. However, despite the significant ways in which these ideas underpinned major changes in different legal frameworks, these changes did not accommodate the issue of children's criminal behaviour and did not solve the rising crime rate. Crime was still becoming increasingly problematic. Consequently, as social conditions worsened for many sections of different societies subsequent to the Industrial Revolution, the idea of individuals being motivated by hedonism and free will lost some of its popularity. In its place a more determined image of the human being was constructed. This image reflected one of the ideas which contributed to the birth of positivism within criminology.

Positivist Criminology

Many reviews of the development of criminology begin with reference to the influence of positivism. While the specific meaning to be attached to this term is open to some debate, in the context of criminology it is usually used to refer to a scientific commitment to the gathering of the 'facts' which cause crime. It is this search for 'facts' which most clearly delineates one of the differences between this version of criminology and classical criminology. The other main difference between these two different versions of the criminal individual was the commitment of the early positivists especially to search for the cause of crime within individual biology rather than individual free will. Lombroso (1853–1909) is frequently considered to be the Founding Father of this version of criminological thought.

Lombroso's ideas about crime are clearly influenced by the work of Darwin. The ideas of evolution, which so challenged religious principles of the nineteenth century, are embedded in the work of Lombroso. Most easily identified as an anthropologist, Lombroso embraced what was referred to as the law of biogenetics. This law articulated a particular view of evolutionary development in which it is posited that every individual organism revisits the developmental history of its own species type within its own individual history. The phrase 'ontology recapitulates phylogeny' captured this view of the developmental process and introduced an important concept, that of recapitulation, to Lombrosian criminology. The idea that every living organism, as it develops, undergoes each stage of its own species history, provided a mechanism for explaining both the normal and the abnormal (the pathological). This was achieved through the related concept of atavism.

It was clear, even to those committed to Darwin's ideas, that every individual member of a species type did not always possess all the characteristics of that species type; in other words, abnormalities were produced from time to time. These abnormalities, it was argued, were a product of that individual member being a throwback to an earlier stage of the developmental history of the species: that is, atavistic. In this way the concept of atavism permitted the law of biogenetics to retain its universal status; aberrations were explained as being reversions to an earlier species type. The idea of atavism appealed to the criminal anthropologists, especially Lombroso.

Lombroso assumed that the process of recapitulation usually produced normal individuals. Someone who became criminal, therefore, must constitute a throwback to an earlier stage of biological development – an atavistic degeneration. For Lombroso, such biological degenerations manifested themselves in the peculiar physical attributes possessed by criminals: sloping foreheads, receding chins, excessively long arms, unusual ear size, and so on, resulting in the view of the 'born criminal'.

This commitment to the biological origin of criminal behaviour led Lombroso to construct a fourfold typology of criminals: the born criminal (true atavistic types); the insane criminal (including those suffering from a range of mental illnesses); the occasional criminal (opportunist criminals who commit crime because they possess innate traits which propel them in that direction); and criminals of passion (who commit crime as a result of some irresistible force). For all of these criminal types, their behaviour is a result of their abnormality, that is determined by forces out of their control, rather than the consequence of freely chosen action.

The legacy of Lombrosian criminology has been profound. While the notion of the 'born criminal' might appear somewhat simple and naive in the late twentieth century, Lombroso's commitment to a science of the criminal, and the search for a universal explanation of crime located within the individual, laid the foundation for much of the criminological work which came after. Moreover, the search for the cause of crime within the individual and individual differences continued albeit focusing on different biological and or psychological factors. This has ranged from work on heredity (Goring, 1913), to body type (Kretschmer, 1926), to the notion of a criminal personality (Eysenck and Gudjonnson, 1990).

Latterly, this way of thinking about crime has become theoretically more sophisticated in the form of the biosocial theory of Wilson and Herrnstein (1985) […], and has become technologically more complex in the increasingly controversial world of neuroscience. Here, using advanced technology to construct images of the brain, the view that individuals are merely negatives waiting to be developed, is beginning to reopen the whole debate about whether or not human beings possess free will and where and how an understanding of criminal behaviour might be situated within that debate. Thus the tension remains between classical and positivist views on the nature of human beings.

Each of these versions of focusing on the behaviour of the criminal carries with them different policy implications. As was suggested earlier for the classical criminologist, if individuals had a calculative, hedonistic approach to crime, then the purpose of the criminal justice system was to punish in order to deter them from committing crime. For the positivist, on the other hand, if an individual's criminal behaviour was to be understood as being determined by their biological and/or psychological make-up the purpose of the criminal justice system is either to incapacitate them or, if appropriate, offer them treatment until they were no longer a threat to society. In more current policy debate the influence of these different ways of thinking about and using the criminal justice system are still evident, standing as some testimony to the importance of these ideas.

Positivistic approaches to explaining crime were to be found not only within the search for the individual roots of criminal behaviour, but also in much more sociologically informed approaches to criminology. These approaches take as their focus of concern the wider socio-economic and cultural conditions which may or may not propel individuals into criminal behaviour and it is these more sociologically informed approaches we shall consider under our next thematic heading: a concern with the criminality of behaviour.

THE CRIMINALITY OF BEHAVIOUR

A concern with the criminality of behaviour focuses attention on factors external to the individual which might result in their behaviour either being lawbreaking or being defined as lawbreaking. These ways of thinking about crime have also been influenced by positivism in the sense that they are approaches which have been equally concerned to identify the 'facts' which result in criminality. The way in which that concern has been addressed can be discussed in a number of different ways. For the purposes of this discussion three central ideas can be identified: the concept of social disorganization, strain theory and its derivatives, and labelling theory.

Social Disorganization

The concept of social disorganization emanates from the Chicago School of sociology of the 1920s and 1930s. It reflects one of two main strands of theoretical work coming out of Chicago which were to influence quite profoundly the later development of both criminology and the sociology of deviance, namely, social ecology and symbolic interactionism. [...] The concept of social disorganization is associated with those theorists concerned to understand the social ecology of the city.

Social ecologists drew parallels between the way in which it was thought living organisms maintained themselves and the maintenance of social life. In other words, just as it was possible to identify patterns in the processes of development and adaptation to the environment in the animal and plant world so it was possible to identify similar patterns in the growth and development of the city. This led theorists to suggest that it made sense to think of the city as a series of concentric zones radiating from the city centre: with each zone having different social and economic characteristics and the people living in those different areas differently adapting to those social circumstances. These general presumptions, when overlaid on the substantive data available about city life, led to a much more detailed appreciation of these differing patterns of adaptation. In particular, attention was focused on the 'zone of transition', the area nearest the city centre.

The 'zone of transition' became the focal concern since this was the area in which new immigrants to the city settled (as it was inexpensive and near to places of work), but it was also the area which appeared to manifest more social problems (according to official statistics) from incidences of ill health to crime. The manifestation of problems such as these is explained by the social ecologists as being the result of the breakdown of primary social relationships in this area, with the highly mobile and transitory nature of social life breeding impersonality and fragmentation.

In general terms, then, this theoretical perspective is suggesting that the processes of industrialization and urbanization create communities in which, as a result of immigration and subsequent migration, there are competing norms and values, the consequence of which is the breakdown of traditional norms and values: social disorganization. It is within this general context that crime is most likely to occur. Through the notion of cultural transmission it was also argued that these modes of adaptation to different social conditions in the city were likely to be passed on from one generation to the next as new immigrants enter that part of the city and adapt to those social conditions.

This way of thinking about and explaining the patterning of criminal behaviour (as it was officially recorded) was one of the first to consider the social origins of criminality as opposed to the individual roots of crime. As a result, it not only influenced subsequent generations of sociologically informed criminological work, but also carries with it clear policy implications. In theoretical terms, the concept of social disorganization led later theorists to work in different ways with the interaction between social structure and the social production of norms and values. In policy terms, it has led to a focus on how to reorganize socially disorganized communities, to understanding the ways in which the environment might contribute to crime (designing out crime), and to a concern with how general neighbourhood decline (rising incivilities) might contribute to the crime career of a community, to name several recurring and contemporarily relevant policy themes. It is clear that the focus on the way in which social conditions produce social pathology is a common thread between the social ecologists and those who took up the ideas of strain theory.

Strain Theory

Strain theory emanates primarily from the work of Robert Merton (1938, 1968). His theoretical work was concerned more with the way in which the tensions between the legitimate and illegitimate means of acceding to the norms and values of a particular society resulted in deviant (rather than just criminal) behaviour. The influence of these ideas on criminology have been profound. Merton's ideas can be situated within the theoretical tradition of functionalism. Largely informed by the work of Émile Durkheim and Talcott Parsons, functionalism views society rather like a finely tuned biological organism. In order for society to work effectively its component parts must be in balance and there must be some consensus or agreement concerning the appropriateness of that balance. Put simply, this balance produces social order. Any imbalance results in social disorder.

Merton's work endeavoured to address the social and cultural norms and values which underpinned social order and/or disorder. Centrally he was concerned to identify the circumstances in which, while there might be socially approved ways of achieving success, not everyone by definition had access to those socially approved means, so how did those who lacked such opportunities adapt to the strain which that produced?

In order to understand the conflict generated between acceptance of the norms and values of mainstream society and the ability to succeed within those norms and values, Merton constructed a fivefold typology. This typology was intended to capture, schematically, those people who accepted the cultural norms and values and the institutionalized means of achieving those norms and values (the conformists) to those people who rejected both and put new ones in their place (the rebellious). This schema was intended to convey the ways in which the structure of society in and of itself produced deviant behaviour, some of which would also be criminal behaviour, at all levels in the social structure.

However, the primary implications of this schema resulted in a focus on those in the lower classes since, given the strains of their structural location, it was presumed that they were the most likely to engage in non-conformist behaviour. There are two important theoretical developments which arguably follow on from Merton's concern with the production of deviant behaviour: Cohen's notion of the delinquent subculture and Cloward and Ohlin's concept of differential opportunity. This focus on the lower classes constitutes one of the common strands between Merton's theoretical work and those who came after. We shall discuss each of these in turn.

Cohen's book *Delinquent Boys* was published in 1955. Drawing on both Merton's work and the notion of cultural transmission embedded within social disorganization theory, Cohen developed a framework in which to understand why delinquent subcultures seemed to be formed primarily within deprived inner city areas. Cohen's argument, following Merton, was that lower class youth strove to embrace the norms and values of mainstream society but lacked the means to achieve success. They thus suffered from status frustration: they were denied the status of respectability because they did not have the means to achieve such respectability. Delinquent subculture provided an alternative, sometimes oppositional, means of achieving such status. So the strains produced as a consequence of social disorganization result in the formation of norms and values through which lower class youth can achieve status and success.

One question, however, remained unanswered within this framework; how was it that not all lower class youth embraced the delinquent subculture nor chose the same kind of deviant solution despite being subjected to similar strains of social disorganization? It is at this point that the notion of differential opportunity structures associated with the work of Cloward and Ohlin (1960) became important.

Again embracing Mertonian strain theory, Cloward and Ohlin argued that there is more than one way in any society to achieve success. There are both legitimate and illegitimate pathways. In their view the upper and middle classes have greater access to the legitimate opportunity structure, with the lower classes having greater access to the illegitimate opportunity structure. In a community where these two different kinds of opportunity structures are poorly integrated, there tends to be greater social disorganization. The greater the social disorganization, the more likely that the illegitimate opportunity structure, especially organized criminal gangs, will become dominant. This kind of opportunity structure, it was suggested, provides an alternative route for status and success for those who join it.

Cloward and Ohlin's theory facilitates an understanding of the ways in which different kinds of delinquent subcultures come to be prevalent in different kinds of urban locations; from the retreatist gang (those primarily engaged in drugs), to the conflict gang (those most concerned with violence), the variable factor which predicts which outcome being the level of integration between the different opportunity structures. Thus rather like Cohen, Cloward and Ohlin were endeavouring to weave together the work of the Chicago School on social disorganization with the strain theory of Robert Merton.

What strain theory, and its derivatives, achieved was to centre the importance of structural variables, external to the individual, as a way of understanding the nature of criminal behaviour. What Cohen and Cloward and Ohlin were concerned to address was the question of subculture. They accepted the Mertonian proposition that some people were disadvantaged in their efforts to achieve success and what required explanation was the resulting deviant behaviour. These conditions were mediated by the formation of different subcultural responses. This focus on the interrelationship between structural condition and subcultural response still has current resonance. Some would argue that the ultimate testing ground for this relationship lies within the more current concerns and debates on the underclass [...]. Understanding the relevance of subculture is not solely the preserve of those on the right. It is also a concern of those on the left [...]. In the 1960s this work certainly laid the groundwork for the further development of a second strand of thought emanating from the Chicago School. That work, largely associated with symbolic interactionism, placed much greater emphasis on the social processes involved in becoming deviant and came to be called labelling theory.

Labelling Theory

Labelling theory returns us to the second school of thought which characterized the Chicago School of sociology during the 1920s and 1930s: symbolic interactionism. Originating with the work of George Herbert Mead, symbolic interactionists were concerned to understand the processes underpinning social life and the mechanisms by which meanings are assigned to those processes. As a theoretical perspective, symbolic interactionism centres the creative capacities of human beings and their ability to share understandings with one another. These general propositions direct attention towards the quality of the interactions which take place between people, how those interactions are understood, and how they become modified, refined and developed. This perspective, then, shares common concerns with strain theory in addressing the general question of how behaviour comes to be understood as deviant (rather than criminal) and the role of shared norms and values in that process. In this latter respect the work of Howard Becker, with what came to be called labelling theory, has been particularly influential.

There are two strands to Becker's (1963) labelling theory: a concern to address how it is that a particular behaviour is labelled as deviant, and a concern to understand the impact of that labelling process. As Becker states:

> Social groups create deviance by making the rules whose infraction constitutes deviance, and by applying those rules to particular people and labelling them as outsiders. From this point of view, deviance is not a quality of the act the person commits, but rather a consequence of the application by others of rules and sanctions to an 'offender'. The deviant is one to whom that label has been successfully applied; deviant behaviour is behaviour that people so label. (Becker, 1963: 9)

In understanding deviance, then, importance lies with the reaction to the behaviour not the behaviour itself. This led Becker to construct a fourfold typology of possible labels (reactions) to perceived deviant behaviour: the falsely accused, the pure deviant, the conformist, and the secret deviant.

This focus on the labelling process led criminologists and sociologists to think about criminal behaviour in quite a different way. For instance, while officially recorded crime data identified young, lower class males as the key criminal group, labelling theorists wanted to explore what it was about the criminal justice agencies that led them to focus attention on this particular group of people (as opposed to others who might be secretly deviant, that is, not publicly labelled as deviant). Others became more concerned with the impact of being labelled deviant and explored the notion of a deviant career.

Labelling theory had a major impact on criminology, questioning the discipline's primarily middle class assumptions about the processes surrounding crime and criminal behaviour which led to a closer examination of the way in which the criminal justice system operates and processes individuals. In policy terms, it connects most directly with diversionary policies and initiatives of decriminalization; that is with those policies concerned to divert (potential) offenders from crime and/or the criminal justice system.

But, both in theory and in practice, labelling theory has its limitations, perhaps best summarized by Sumner:

> it is equally problematic that 'labelling theorists' (1) never specified in detail the ideological constitution of the moral and criminal categories, (2) never fully explored the links between these categories and the social structure, and (3) only dealt with the relationship between moral/legal condemnation and 'interest' in an instrumental way. (Sumner, 1990: 23)

The key problem which is embedded in these observations made by Sumner is the question of power and power relationships.

Underpinning the theoretical strands of thought discussed here is a common image of society. That image presumes, for the most part, the normatively predominant view of society as comprising a democratic and consensual process. Largely as a consequence of this presumption, attention is implicitly focused on those who deviate from this normative view, which for the most part results in a concern with the deviant and/or criminal behaviour of the lower classes. There is, however, an alternative way of thinking about the nature of society, which results in quite a different focus in relation to thinking about crime. That view is subsumed in the third theme to be discussed here – the criminality of the state.

THE CRIMINALITY OF THE STATE

There is a clear connection between a critical analysis of labelling processes and their impact and the development of a close interest in those who have the power to label. However, once theorists were moved to consider the question of power and power relationships, it also became clear that the implicit view of society previously held could not accommodate these newer concerns. In theoretical terms it made much more sense to turn to Marx and a view of society as rooted in conflicting interests than to retain the Parsonian image of consensus.

General Marxist presumptions about the nature of society direct attention to the way in which the powerful in society use the various resources available to them (including the law) to secure and maintain their dominant position. In particular, then, this means that the law and the processes which underpin the formation of the law are placed under scrutiny, alongside the way in which the law is used to criminalize particular social groups in the interests of the powerful. Consequently the law, and its enforcement, are seen as particular sites where the legitimized powers of the state are exercised. Those powers, it is argued, express themselves especially along class, race and gender lines.

There are a number of different writers whose work can be located under this general heading of concern with the criminality of the state. Here particular attention will be paid to three varieties of this interest: Marxist criminology, radical criminology, and critical criminology. While these labels certainly are not mutually exclusive, the ideas associated with each of them will be discussed in turn.

Marxist Criminology

Strands of Marxist theorizing can be found in the writings of various criminologists. Arguably the work of Chambliss (1975) and Quinney (1977) has been particularly influential.

Chambliss' work is a clear attempt to use Marxist theorizing to construct a political economy of crime. Marx himself had little to say about crime or the law, but the general tenor of his views on society and social relationships can be translated into the criminological context. As Chambliss argues, capitalism creates the desire to consume and it has to be recognized that not all members of society are able to earn enough to match the levels of consumption induced by the capitalist process. There are the owners and the non-owners, the bourgeoisie and the proletariat, all of whom have different priorities at different points in time both to produce and to consume.

Moreover, the underlying logical development of the capitalist process, it is argued, inevitably results in more and more situations where those who have and those who do not are put in conflict with one another. Sometimes that conflict is violent; more often it results in the behaviour of those who do not have being labelled as criminal. Thus for Chambliss

> The criminal law is thus not a reflection of custom … but a set of rules laid down by the state in the interests of the ruling class, and resulting from the conflicts that inhere in class structured societies; criminal behaviour is, then, the inevitable expression of class conflict resulting from the inherently exploitative nature of economic relations. (Chambliss, 1975, abridged in Muncie et al., 1996: 225)

In this sense, then, crime is to be understood as a reaction to the general life conditions in which individuals find themselves as a result of their social class position.

Within this general framework, of course, there is no necessary presumption that only the relatively powerless are likely to engage in criminal activities. Indeed the general proposition would be that all people in all social classes are capable of committing crime. What is central to this argument is understanding why only some behaviours are so targeted as criminal. To quote Chambliss (1975) again

> Criminality is simply not something that people have or don't have; crime is not something some people do and others don't. Crime is a matter of who can pin the label on whom, and underlying this socio-political process is the structure of social relations determined by the political economy. (abridged in Muncie et al., 1996: 228)

So for Chambliss the underlying cause of crime lies not with individuals, or their greater or lesser acceptance of cultural norms and values, it lies with the state and the political and economic interests which are necessarily served by the law and its implementation.

In some respects, there is still a rational image of the human being embedded in this theoretical framework offered by Chambliss. Crime is to be seen as a rational response to social conditions for some individuals. It is a way of managing the material reality of their lives. This is a variation on the observation made by Marx, that men make choices but not in circumstances of their own choosing. This rationality is consequently circumscribed. It is not the rationality of free will but that which is rationally dictated by the political economy of social relations. As Chambliss argues, 'The state becomes an instrument of the ruling class enforcing laws here but not there, according to the realities of political power and economic conditions' (abridged in Muncie et al., 1996: 230). A similar theoretical feel is found in the work of Quinney (1977).

It can be argued that Quinney's ideas were equally influenced by the work of the phenomenologists as they were by Marx. Consequently different readings of his work can and do emphasize these different theoretical inputs. In general terms, however, Quinney talked about the 'politicality of law' and the 'politicality of crime'. By the politicality of law, Quinney was referring to the extent to which social relations are reflected in the law and the lawmaking process. Social relations which rendered some issues visible and ensured that others remained invisible, in other words, reflected political interests.

In talking about the politicality of crime, Quinney was referring to criminal behaviour as a 'conscientious' activity; not the produce of poor socialization or a deficient personality, but a political expression. In other words, it is not the behaviour which is criminal but the action which is taken against it which renders it criminal.

There is a particular view of society which underlies these twin concerns. This view of society emphasizes the social construction of social reality. In its extreme form, this view of society presumes that social reality is simply a reflection of an individual's state of mind. In its milder versions it is intended to draw attention to the way in which our understanding of social, political and criminological issues (to name a few) are constantly subject to changing perceptions and interpretations. This latter theme links Quinney's general theoretical framework with that of critical criminology [discussed below].

In this particular context, however, Quinney was endeavouring to draw attention to the ways in which definitions of what is and what is not problematic become taken for granted and embedded in social relations, a process which serves the interests of the powerful much more readily than it serves the interests of the powerless. This, he argued, was a structural rather than a conspiratorial relationship.

Quinney went on to construct a typology of crime which could form the central focus of a criminology informed by these ideas. In this typology he talks of crime of domination (police brutality, white collar crime, governmental crimes), crimes of accommodation and resistance (theft and homicide produced by the conditions of capitalism) and terrorism (a response to the conditions of capitalism). Essentially this position reflects a view of the causality of crime as being an expression of the desire for social change, that is, as a political act.

Both of these versions of criminology have two themes in common. Put simply, they both see crime as a product of the behaviour of the authorities rather than as a product of individuals. In other words, this kind of Marxist theorizing endeavours to further the labelling perspective's concern with the power to label. In addition, they both see crime as a relative phenomenon rather than an absolute one. In other words, there is nothing inherently wicked or sinful in criminal behaviour; it is simply behaviour that is so targeted.

The policy implications of work informed in this way are clearly neither simple nor straightforward. They ultimately imply a different social and economic order. Indeed in many respects little practical work ensued from these theoretical developments as a consequence. However, these ideas were valuable in drawing criminological attention to the role of the law in defining the criminality that is seen and not seen and in establishing a much sharper critical focus on those processes. Moreover, these general ideas were also influential in contributing to what has been called here radical criminology, the next theme to be discussed here.

Radical Criminology

The radical criminology of Taylor et al. (1973), which will form the basis of the discussion here, did not emerge in a vacuum. Though largely taken as the starting point of more radical work in the UK, the ideas contained within *The New Criminology* had their origins in the work of earlier labelling theorists as well as versions of Marxist criminology (discussed above). This work remains influential largely because it was one of the first to offer a wide ranging critique of the (then) dominant form of criminology. This dominant form was peopled mostly by psychologists and psychiatrists, concerned with the behaviour of the criminal, looking for the cause of crime within the individual.

Taylor, Walton and Young not only provided a thoroughgoing critique of criminology, but also endeavoured to offer a theoretical perspective to replace this focus on the individual with a focus on the social construction of crime. In so doing they offered a theory synthesizing labelling theory with Marxism as a means of retaining a concern with the value of appreciating individual meaning and action (the question of authenticity) alongside the power of state agencies to control and define (the question of the role of the state). It will be valuable to examine this framework in a little more detail.

The New Criminology has seven elements to it. The first argues that in order to understand a crime (or a deviant act) it is important to locate that act within wider social processes. In other words, individual behaviour must be placed in a wider social, political and economic context. There must be a political economy of crime. Second, having situated a behaviour in this way, sight should not be lost of the immediate circumstances and origins of criminal behaviour. In other words, how and why individuals choose to respond to their structural location in the way that they do, which is expressed as a requirement for a social psychology of crime. Third, people may choose to behave in a particular way, but may for various reasons not carry out their choices or their choices may become modified in the process of interaction. Recognition of these processes means that it is necessary to offer an account of the social dynamics of crime; what were the interactive processes which led to one outcome rather than another?

Fourth, people may behave in a range of different ways, some of which may be labelled deviant, some of which may not be, irrespective of the behaviour itself. In other words, it is important to understand the social reaction to crime. That social reaction may be rooted in the social psychology of what passes between the witnesses to a particular behaviour but it may also be located in a wider audience. That wider audience will include professionals working in the criminal justice agencies as well as other people significant to the offender. Their response to different behaviours requires an understanding of what Taylor et al. call a political economy of social reaction – the fifth proposition. The sixth concern is with the relationship between the social reaction to the deviant and/or criminal behaviour and the impact of that social reaction. In other words, how might this impact or not on their future criminal careers?

The final characteristic or proposition of what these authors call a fully social theory of deviance constitutes an implicit acceptance of the dialectical nature of social reality.

> The central requirement of a fully social theory of deviance, however, is that these formal requirements must not be treated simply as essential factors all of which need to be present (in invariant fashion) if the theory is to be social. Rather it is that these formal requirements must all appear in the theory, as they do in the real world, in a complex, dialectical relationship to one another. (Taylor et al., 1973, abridged in Muncie et al., 1996: 237)

This last requirement demands that account be taken of the nature of the criminal process as a whole and how its component parts produce the whole.

Thus this version of talking about the criminality of the state, while offering a differently nuanced theoretical emphasis from that which was to be found in Marxist criminology *per se*, certainly shares in some of its concerns. In particular, as a result of the emphasis that these theoretical concerns placed on understanding the processes of criminalization, it certainly served to challenge the individualistic correctional stance of earlier criminologies. It also laid the foundation for later theoretical developments, particularly from those wishing to pursue the differing ways in which the power associated with the political economy of the state asserts itself. This is the central focus of the last of the themes to be discussed here – critical criminology.

Critical Criminology

The use of the label 'critical' is employed by different writers intending to invoke differing frames of analysis. It is used here to identify those who have concerned themselves with the multiplicity of way in which the state deploys its use of power. The work of Foucault has been very influential in encouraging a more careful and detailed analysis of the concept of power and how power is asserted. Foucault was particularly interested in the ways in which knowledge and power are constituted in each other, and especially interested in the ways in which this mutual interdependence effectively exercised social control (Foucault, 1977). In some respects, then, critical criminology is concerned to unravel the ways in which taken for granted talk about social problems both simultaneously serves to define those problems and control them. In this sense its focus stems not only from the work of Foucault but also from those of a more traditional Marxist persuasion for whom the state is more explicitly implicated in rendering some issues visible and others invisible. Critical criminology seeks to develop this concern in a more subtly nuanced fashion.

Put simply, critical criminology seeks to explore the ways in which the variables of class, race and gender are played out in the criminal justice system. This version of criminology argues that each of these variables differently articulate a different structural relationship with the interests of the state. This is more than just a concern with the (potential) for discriminatory practices. It reflects a concern with the ideas which underpin discriminatory practices and consequently contribute to their perpetuation: how they become institutionalized. As Scraton and Chadwick state:

> Once institutionalised, however, classism, sexism, heterosexism, and racism become systemic and structured. They become the taken for granted social histories and contemporary priorities which constitute state institutions, informing policies and underwriting practices, and which provide legitimacy to interpersonal discrimination. Through the process of institutionalisation, relations of dominance and subjugation achieve structural significance. (Scraton and Chadwick, 1991: 168)

This position, therefore, not only reflects a concern with the myriad of mechanisms whereby the state reaffirms its power and the underlying structural relations which support that power; as the quote above implies, in its more recent affirmation critical criminology also centres the relationship between structure and agency as found in the work of Giddens (1984). In the same article, Scraton and Chadwick [also] state that

> What this discussion has pursued is the central argument that critical criminology recognises the reciprocity inherent in the relationship between structure and agency but also that structural relations embody the primary determining contexts of production, reproduction and neocolonialism. (Scraton and Chadwick, 1991: 166)

These contexts do not determine outcome. That is the product of the complex interplay between structure and agency in which neither are human beings seen as the sole determiners of what it is that they can and cannot do or how it is that they are seen and not seen. This use of the term critical is certainly redolent of the way in which it has been used in more recent victimological concerns [...].

Critical criminology, then, is concerned to unpick the ways in which ideas which support the state and state practices serve to marginalize and consequently criminalize some groups and not others. In addition it represents a set of theoretical ideas designed to situate the significance of history to these processes. Of particular importance is the way in which this theoretical perspective centres the questions of not only class but also race and gender. In this latter respect it constitutes an important development from the radical criminology of Taylor, Walton and Young of 1973.

As can be seen, the notion of the criminality of the state shifts the criminological agenda away from seeing society as essentially consensual towards seeing society as essentially rooted in conflict. This fundamental shift not only locates the explanation of crime squarely in the social domain, it also centres the practices of the powerful, both the seen and the unseen, as legitimate concerns for the criminological agenda.

This shift in concern also seriously challenges the previously unchallenged presumption contained within much criminological work: the fundamental belief in the objectivity of knowledge. One common thread between those seeking to address the criminality of the state is the implied critique of this view of knowledge and the knowledge production process. In general terms within this perspective, knowledge is understood much more meaningfully as ideology – ideology which more or less supports the state and its practices. This view of knowledge seriously challenges the hold of positivism on criminology. It is a hold which is nevertheless still present and still significant in the criminological debates which have followed. [...]

REFERENCES

Becker, H. (1963) *The Outsiders*. New York: Free Press.
Chambliss, W.J. (1975) Towards a political economy of crime. *Theory and Society* 2: 149–70.
Cloward, R. and Ohlin, L. (1960) *Delinquency and Opportunity: A Theory of Delinquent Gangs*. New York: Free Press.
Cohen, A.K. (1955) *Delinquent Boys*. London: Free Press.
Eysenck, H. and Godjonnson, G.H. (1990) *The Causes and Cures of Crime*. New York: Plenum.
Foucault, M. (1977) *Discipline and Punish*. Harmondsworth: Penguin.
Giddens, A. (1984) *The Constitution of Society*. Cambridge: Polity Press.
Goring, C. (1913) *The English Convict*. London: HMSO.
Kretschmer, E. (1926) *Physique and Character*. New York: Harcourt Brace Jovanovich.
Merton, R.K. (1938) Social structure and anomie. *American Sociological Review* 3: 672–82.
Merton, R.K. (1968) *Social Theory and Social Structure*. New York: Free Press.
Muncie, J., McLaughlin, E. and Langan, M. (eds) (1996) *Criminological Perspectives: A Reader*. London: Sage.
Quinney, R. (1977) *Class, State and Crime: On the Theory and Practice of Criminal Justice*. New York: McKay.
Scraton, P. and Chadwick, K. (1991) The theoretical and political priorities of critical criminology, in K. Stenson and D. Cowell (eds) *The Politics of Crime Control*. London: Sage.
Sumner, C. (1990) *Censure, Politics and Criminal Justice*. Milton Keynes: Open University Press.
Taylor, I., Walton, P. and Young, J. (1973) *The New Criminology*. London: Routledge and Kegan Paul.
Wilson, J.Q. and Herrnstein, R. (1985) *Crime and Human Nature*. New York: Simon and Schuster.

STUDY QUESTIONS

1 What are the causes of crime according to each of the theoretical perspectives outlined by Walklate? To what extent does each theoretical model complement or contradict the others? What are the significant areas of 'overlap' between them?
2 What are the policy implications of each of the broad theoretical approaches? Do they advocate punishment (and, if so, what form should it take) or some other response to dealing with criminality?

3   Positivism's commitment to objective and scientific methods of analysis is
    sometimes criticized for being too deterministic and narrowing the field of
    enquiry, yet it remains a significant influence within criminology and its influ-
    ences can be discovered in many popular and lay discourses about crime, and
    sometimes in the responses of the criminal justice system (Readings 14 and 26).
    What examples can you think of from contemporary discussions about crime
    and criminals that might be said to be positivist in essence?

FURTHER READING

Definitions and explanations of all the theories outlined above can be found in
McLaughlin, E. and Muncie, J. (eds) (2001) *The Sage Dictionary of Criminology*,
London: Sage. Other criminology texts that offer overviews of the theoretical
developments that have shaped the subject include Coleman, C. and Norris, C.
(2000) *Introducing Criminology*, Cullompton: Willan; Jones, S. (1998) *Criminology*,
London: Butterworths; and Tierney, J. (1996) *Criminology: Theory and Context*,
Harlow: Pearson, Another useful overview is provided by David Garland in
'Of crimes and criminals: the development of criminology in Britain', in
M. Maguire, R. Morgan and R. Reiner (eds) (1997) *The Oxford Handbook of
Criminology*, 2nd edn, Oxford: Oxford University Press, and, in the same hand-
book, Paul Rock's 'Sociological theories of crime'. For extracts from many of the
original texts in which these theories were espoused, see Muncie, J.,
McLaughlin, E. and Langan, M. (eds) (1996) *Criminological Perspectives: A
Reader*, London: Sage.

3

Definitions of deviance

Howard S. Becker

As Walklate indicates in Reading 2, Howard S. Becker's *Outsiders* is considered to be one of the 'classic' pieces of modern criminology. In choosing to include an extract from it, it is not our intention to privilege Becker's work above all others. However, it is significant in being among the first to challenge (both within and outside sociological criminology) biological and social determinism by providing a relativistic explanation of deviance and crime. For Becker, deviance and crime are not the product of either a 'sick individual' or a 'sick society', but 'deviant behavior is behavior that people so label'. Deviance is historically and culturally specific and is created by society, not in a deterministic way, but because powerful 'social groups create deviance by making rules whose infraction constitutes deviance'. The process by which labelling occurs is all important, as rules tend to be applied to some people more than others, and it is possible for some to be incorrectly labelled. Furthermore, deviance is not 'a quality that lies in behavior itself, but in the interaction between the person who commits an act and those who respond to it'. Thus, the rules created by 'society', and the associated labelling of some behaviours as deviant, are not universally shared.

Becker's work has been of importance within and outside the study of crime and deviance, both substantively and methodologically, and you will see the influence of his ideas in many of the readings that follow. His work has also been subject to considerable debate and challenge, not least because of the lack of an analysis of social structure and power (see, for example, Taylor et al., 1973, in *Further Reading*).

From our vantage point at the beginning of the twenty-first century it is worth noting Becker's use of language. His unproblematic description of the sociologist/criminologist as a scientist is outdated, and his use of the pronoun 'he' and generic term for black people is now

SOURCE: From *Outsiders: Studies in the Sociology of Deviance* (New York: The Free Press, 1963), 8–18.

unacceptable. With reference to sexist language, we find the response of Belloni and Hodgson (Reading 25), who, throughout their piece, refer to judges, solicitors and solicitors' clerks as 'she', no solution. There are ways of writing that do not exclude or demean anyone.

[…] The sociological view […] defines deviance as the infraction of some agreed-upon rule. It then goes on to ask who breaks rules, and to search for the factors in their personalities and life situations that might account for the infractions. This assumes that those who have broken a rule constitute a homogeneous category, because they have committed the same deviant act.

Such an assumption seems to me to ignore the central fact about deviance: it is created by society. I do not mean this in the way it is ordinarily understood, in which the causes of deviance are located in the social situation of the deviant or in 'social factors' which prompt his action. I mean, rather, that *social groups create deviance by making the rules whose infraction constitutes deviance*, and by applying those rules to particular people and labeling them as outsiders. From this point of view, deviance is *not* a quality of the act the person commits, but rather a consequence of the application by others of rules and sanctions to an 'offender.' The deviant is one to whom that label has successfully been applied; deviant behavior is behavior that people so label.[1]

Since deviance is, among other things, a consequence of the responses of others to a person's act, students of deviance cannot assume that they are dealing with a homogeneous category when they study people who have been labeled deviant. That is, they cannot assume that these people have actually committed a deviant act or broken some rule, because the process of labeling may not be infallible; some people may be labeled deviant who in fact have not broken a rule. Furthermore, they cannot assume that the category of those labeled deviant will contain all those who actually have broken a rule, for many offenders may escape apprehension and thus fail to be included in the population of 'deviants' they study. Insofar as the category lacks homogeneity and fails to include all the cases that belong in it, one cannot reasonably expect to find common factors of personality or life situation that will account for the supposed deviance.

What, then, do people who have been labeled deviant have in common? At the least, they share the label and the experience of being labeled as outsiders. I will begin my analysis with this basic similarity and view deviance as the product of a transaction that takes place between some social group and one who is viewed by that group as a rule-breaker. I will be less concerned with the personal and social characteristics of deviants than with the process by which they come to be thought of as outsiders and their reactions to that judgment. […]

Whether an act is deviant […] depends on how other people react to it. […]

The degree to which other people will respond to a given act as deviant varies greatly. Several kinds of variation seem worth noting. First of all, there is variation over time. A person believed to have committed a given 'deviant' act may at one time be responded to much more leniently than he would be at some other time. The occurrence of 'drives' against various kinds of deviance illustrates this clearly. At various times, enforcement officials may decide to make an all-out attack on some particular kind of deviance, such as gambling, drug addiction, or homosexuality. It is obviously much more dangerous to engage in one of these activities when a drive is on than at any other time. [...]

The degree to which an act will be treated as deviant depends also on who commits the act and who feels he has been harmed by it. Rules tend to be applied more to some persons than others. Studies of juvenile delinquency make the point clearly. Boys from middle-class areas do not get as far in the legal process when they are apprehended as do boys from slum areas. The middle-class boy is less likely, when picked up by the police, to be taken to the station; less likely when taken to the station to be booked; and it is extremely unlikely that he will be convicted and sentenced.[2] This variation occurs even though the original infraction of the rule is the same in the two cases. Similarly, the law is differentially applied to Negroes [sic] and whites. It is well known that a Negro believed to have attacked a white woman is much more likely to be punished than a white man who commits the same offense; it is only slightly less well known that a Negro who murders another Negro is much less likely to be punished than a white man who commits murder.[3] This, of course, is one of the main points of Sutherland's analysis of white-collar crime: crimes committed by corporations are almost always prosecuted as civil cases, but the same crime committed by an individual is ordinarily treated as a criminal offense.[4]

Some rules are enforced only when they result in certain consequences. The unmarried mother furnishes a clear example. Vincent[5] points out that illicit sexual relations seldom result in severe punishment or social censure for the offenders. If, however, a girl becomes pregnant as a result of such activities the reaction of others is likely to be severe. (The illicit pregnancy is also an interesting example of the differential enforcement of rules on different categories of people. Vincent notes that unmarried fathers escape the severe censure visited on the mother.)

Why repeat these commonplace observations? Because, taken together, they support the proposition that deviance is not a simple quality, present in some kinds of behavior and absent in others. Rather, it is the product of a process which involves responses of other people to the behavior. The same behavior may be an infraction of the rules at one time and not at another; may be an infraction when committed by one person, but not when committed by another; some rules are broken with impunity, others are not. In short, whether a given act is deviant or not depends in part on the nature of the act (that is, whether or not it violates some rule) and in part on what other people do about it.

Some people may object that this is merely a terminological quibble, that one can, after all, define terms any way he wants to and that if some people want to speak of rule-breaking behavior as deviant without reference to the reactions of others they are free to do so. This, of course, is true. Yet it might be worthwhile to refer to such behavior as *rule-breaking behavior* and reserve the term *deviant* for those labeled as deviant by some segment of society. I do not insist that this usage be followed. But it should be clear that insofar as a scientist uses 'deviant' to refer to any rule-breaking behavior and takes as his subject of study only those who have been *labeled* deviant, he will be hampered by the disparities between the two categories.

If we take as the object of our attention behavior which comes to be labeled as deviant, we must recognize that we cannot know whether a given act will be categorized as deviant until the response of others has occurred. Deviance is not a quality that lies in behavior itself, but in the interaction between the person who commits an act and those who respond to it.

WHOSE RULES?

I have been using the term 'outsiders' to refer to those people who are judged by others to be deviant and thus to stand outside the circle of 'normal' members of the group. But the term contains a second meaning, whose analysis leads to another important set of sociological problems: 'outsiders,' from the point of view of the person who is labeled deviant, may be the people who make the rules he had been found guilty of breaking.

Social rules are the creation of specific social groups. Modern societies are not simple organizations in which everyone agrees on what the rules are and how they are to be applied in specific situations. They are, instead, highly differentiated along social class lines, ethnic lines, occupational lines, and cultural lines. These groups need not and, in fact, often do not share the same rules. The problems they face in dealing with their environment, the history and traditions they carry with them, all lead to the evolution of different sets of rules. Insofar as the rules of various groups conflict and contradict one another, there will be disagreement about the kind of behavior that is proper in any given situation.

Italian immigrants who went on making wine for themselves and their friends during Prohibition were acting properly by Italian immigrant standards, but were breaking the law of their new country (as, of course, were many of their Old American neighbors). Medical patients who shop around for a doctor may, from the perspective of their own group, be doing what is necessary to protect their health by making sure they get what seems to them the best possible doctor; but, from the perspective of the physician, what they do is wrong because it breaks down the trust the patient ought to put in his physician. The lower-class delinquent who fights for his 'turf' is only doing what he considers necessary and right, but teachers, social workers, and police see it differently.

While it may be argued that many or most rules are generally agreed to by all members of a society, empirical research on a given rule generally reveals variation in people's attitudes. Formal rules, enforced by some specially constituted group, may differ from those actually thought appropriate by most people.[6] Factions in a group may disagree on what I have called actual operating rules. Most important for the study of behavior ordinarily labeled deviant, the perspectives of the people who engage in the behavior are likely to be quite different from those of the people who condemn it. In this latter situation, a person may feel that he is being judged according to rules he has had no hand in making and does not accept, rules forced on him by outsiders. [...]

[...] [P]eople are in fact always *forcing* their rules on others, applying them more or less against the will and without the consent of those others. By and large, for example, rules are made for young people by their elders. Though the youth of this country exert a powerful influence culturally – the mass media of communication are tailored to their interests, for instance – many important kinds of rules are made for our youth by adults. Rules regarding school attendance and sex behavior are not drawn up with regard to the problems of adolescence. Rather, adolescents find themselves surrounded by rules about these matters which have been made by older and more settled people. It is considered legitimate to do this, for youngsters are considered neither wise enough nor responsible enough to make proper rules for themselves.

In the same way, it is true in many respects that men make the rules for women in our society (though in America this is changing rapidly). Negroes find themselves subject to rules made for them by whites. The foreign-born and those otherwise ethnically peculiar often have their rules made for them by the Protestant Anglo-Saxon minority. The middle class makes rules the lower class must obey – in the schools, the courts, and elsewhere.

Differences in the ability to make rules and apply them to other people are essentially power differentials (either legal or extralegal). Those groups whose social position gives them weapons and power are best able to enforce their rules. Distinctions of age, sex, ethnicity, and class are all related to differences in power, which accounts for differences in the degree to which groups so distinguished can make rules for others.

In addition to recognizing that deviance is created by the responses of people to particular kinds of behavior, by the labeling of that behavior as deviant, we must also keep in mind that the rules created and maintained by such labeling are not universally agreed to. Instead, they are the object of conflict and disagreement, part of the political process of society.

NOTES

1 The most important earlier statements of this view can be found in Frank Tannenbaum, *Crime and the Community* (New York: McGraw-Hill, 1951), and E.M. Lemert, *Social Pathology* (New York: McGraw-Hill, 1951). A recent article stating a position very similar to mine is John Kitsuse, 'Societal Reaction to Deviance: Problems of Theory and Method', *Social Problems*, 9 (Winter, 1962), 247–56.
2 See Albert K. Cohen and James F. Short, Jr, 'Juvenile Delinquency', in Robert K. Merton and Robert A. Nisbet (eds), *Contemporary Social Problems* (New York: Harcourt, Brace and World, 1961), p. 87.
3 See Harold Garfinkel, 'Research Notes on Inter- and Intra-racial Homicides', *Social Forces*, 27 (May, 1949), 369–81.
4 Edwin H. Sutherland, 'White Collar Criminality', *American Sociological Review*, 5 (February, 1940), 1–12.
5 Clark Vincent, *Unmarried Mothers* (New York: The Free Press of Glencoe, 1961), pp. 3–5.
6 Arnold M. Rose and Arthur E. Prell, 'Does the Punishment Fit the Crime? A Study in Social Valuation', *American Journal of Sociology*, 61 (November, 1955), 247–59.

STUDY QUESTIONS

1   Can you think of any examples of behaviour that are *universally* defined as 'deviant'?
2   From Becker's perspective it is not the act itself but the labelling of the act by particular groups of people, and the successful application of the label, that is important. What groups does he identify as having particular power and what groups does he consider to be particularly vulnerable? Are these distinctions still relevant today?
3   Make a list of behaviours that were considered deviant in the UK 50 years ago and are not considered deviant now. Do the same for behaviours that once were not, but are now, labelled as deviant (include non-criminal deviant behaviour in your list). How do you account for the changes?

FURTHER READING

For an introduction to, and definitions of, labelling, McLaughlin, E. and Muncie, J. (eds) (2001) *The Sage Dictionary of Criminology*, London: Sage, is a very good new text. The many sociology dictionaries can also be quite useful, for example Abercrombie, N., Hill, S. and Turner, B. (2000) *The Penguin Dictionary of Sociology*, 4th edn, London: Penguin; or Jary, D. and Jary J. (1992) *The Collins Dictionary of Sociology*, London: Collins. See Taylor, I. Walton, P. and Young, J. (1973) *The New Criminology: For a Social Theory of Deviance*, London: Routledge and Kegan Paul, for a critique of labelling. Other relevant texts include Fitzgerald, M., McLennan, G. and Pawson, J. (1981) *Crime and Society: Readings in History and Theory*, London: Routledge in association with Open University Press; Downes, D. and Rock, P. (1998) *Understanding Deviance: A Guide to the Sociology of Crime and Rule-breaking*, 3rd edn, Oxford: Oxford University Press; and Rock, P. (1997) 'Sociological theories of crime' in M. Maguire, R. Morgan, and R. Reiner (eds) *The Oxford Handbook of Criminology*, 2nd edn, Oxford: Oxford University Press. Becker's methodological stance is outlined in 'Whose side are we on?' *Social Problems* 14 1967, pp. 239–47 which has been influential within criminology, sociology and feminism. For guides to non-sexist and non-racist language see, for example, the British Sociological Association website (www. britsoc.org.uk).

4

Ten points of realism

Jock Young

In this reading Jock Young suggests that realists are critical of both positivism and what Young calls the 'new administrative' criminology. He suggests that the realist approach to studying crime and deviance is different because a fundamental aspect of realism is that criminology should be faithful to the nature of crime. He argues that this involves an acknowledgement of the form, social context and shape of crime, as well as attention to its trajectory through time and its enactment in space. Crime rates are a product of changes in the numbers of punitive offenders, the numbers of potential victims and the changing levels of control exercised by the official agencies of control and the public. Young argues that explanations which do not embrace all of these factors cannot explain crime rates. Realism, he suggests, focuses on lived experiences, not abstract generalizations, and is concerned with the material problems which people face. Attention to realism demands the development of an approach where deviance and control cannot be studied independently of each other, and where the specific relevance of culture and history need to be acknowledged. Thus, from this perspective, sociological and criminological explanations of any kind which do not consider crime in relation to the social context have little chance of success.

[···] The most fundamental tenet of realism is that criminology should be faithful to the nature of crime. That is, it should acknowledge the *form* of crime, the *social context* of crime, the *shape* of crime, its trajectory through *time*, and its enactment in *space*.

The form consists of two dyads, a *victim* and an *offender*, and of *actions* and *reactions*: of crime and its control. This deconstruction gives us four definitional

SOURCE: From *Rethinking Criminology: The Realist Debate*, ed. J. Young and R. Matthews (London: Sage, 1992), 24–68.

POLICE,
MULTI-
AGENCIES

OFFENDER

SOCIAL
CONTROL

THE
CRIMINAL
ACT

THE PUBLIC

VICTIM

Figure 4.1

elements of crime: a victim, an offender, formal control and informal control. Realism, then, points to a square of crime involving the interaction between police and other agencies of social control, the public, the offender and the victim (see Figure 4.1).

Crime rates are generated not merely by the interplay of these four factors, but as *social relationships* between each point on the square. It is the relationship between the police and the public which determines the efficacy of policing, the relationship between the victim and the offender which determines the impact of the crime, the relationship between the state and the offender which is a major factor in recidivism, etc. I shall return to this later, but suffice it to say that the relationship between the four points of the square (offender, victim, state agencies and the public) varies with differing types of crime […]. Indeed, a hallmark of critical criminology is its pinpointing of the irony of the frequent symbiotic relationships between control agencies – whether formal or informal – and crime. For example, the way in which the burgled public create the informal economy which sustains burglary, or the police create, through illegalities, a moral climate which spurs delinquents into crime.

Secondly, it should be stressed that, in pinpointing to the fact that crime rates are produced by such an interaction, one is merely describing the process. It does not involve acceptance of the existing patterns of criminalization.

Crime rates are a product, therefore, of changes in the number of putative offenders, the number of potential victims, and the changing levels of control exercised by the official agencies of control and the public. No explanation which does not embrace all these four factors can possibly explain crime rates. Let us focus quite simply, for the moment, on the relationship between social control in all its manifestations, and the criminal act consisting of the dyad of victim and offender.

If we examine changes over time: realists would point to these *necessarily* being a product of changes in criminal behaviour *and* changes in the sensitivity to crime. The increase in the rate of violent crime *by definition* must involve changes in violence. None of this makes it any the less 'real': for this is exactly what crime rates *really* are. This being said, the exponential increases in crimes

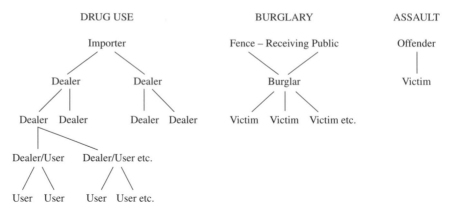

Figure 4.2

occurring in most western countries cannot merely be a product of increased sensitivity to crime. Any dark figure of the crime unknown to the police would have been taken up long ago by the rise in crimes known to the police, and other indices, such as homicide rates and serious property crimes, indicate rises even if we use earlier thresholds as our measure. Thus present rises in rates of violence in countries such as England may well be a product of an increased sensitivity to violence *and* a rise in violent behaviour.

Realist criminology indicates that crime rates are a product of two forces: changes in behaviour and changes in definitions of what is seriously criminal. These two social dimensions are not necessarily covariant. It is quite possible, for example, for vandalism to increase but people to become less concerned and more tolerant about litter, graffiti, etc. It is possible for acts of violence in a behavioural sense to decrease, yet people become more sensitive to violence.

The social context consists of the immediate social interaction of these four elements and the setting of each of them within the *wider* social structure. Such an agenda was set out within *The New Criminology* (Taylor et al., 1973), namely, that the immediate social origins of a deviant act should be set within its wider social context and that such an analysis should encompass both actors and reactors. Realism takes this a stage further, insisting not only that actions of offenders and the agencies of the state must be understood in such a fashion, but that this must be extended to the informal system of social control (the public) and to victims (see Young, 1987).

To turn to the shape of crime: crime is a series of relationships. Each type of crime presents a different network of relationships; if we compare illegal drug use, burglary and assault we note markedly different structures (see Figure 4.2).

Drug dealing has a well-known pyramidal shape; burglary involves numerous victims and regular fences; assault may well be a one-off case of victimization. Furthermore, the natural history of crime involves differences in the content of these relationships. Crime involves both cooperation and coercion.

In the case of drug use, every step of the pyramid is consensual; in the case of burglary, dealing in stolen goods is consensual and the actual act of stealing coercive; in the case of assault, it is a purely coercive act.

The temporal aspect of crime is the past of each of the four elements of the square of crime and their impact on each other in the future. A realist approach sees the development of criminal behaviour over time. It breaks down this trajectory of offending into its component parts and notes how different agencies interact. Thus we can talk of (1) the *background causes* of crime; (2) the *moral context* of opting for criminal behaviour; (3) the *situation of committing crime*; (4) the *detection of crime*; (5) the *response to the offender*; (6) the *response to the victim*. Criminal careers are built up by an interaction of the structural position the offender finds him or herself in and the administrative responses to his or her various offences. These involve both material changes in the offender's structural position and the exchange of ideas (or 'rationalizations') for offending (Matza, 1964; Cohen, 1965). But, of course, such moral careers are not confined to the offender. Other points of the square of crime change over time. Policing practices change in their interaction with offenders, the public's fear of crime in the city creates patterns of avoidance behaviour which consciously and unconsciously develop over time, victims – particularly repeated victims such as in cases of domestic violence – change the pattern of their life as a consequence of such an interaction.

The spatial dimension of crime is the material space in which this process enacts itself. All crime has a spatial dimension, and the geography of crime varies widely in terms of the specific crime. Drug dealing has an international dimension, a national distribution and a focus on specific areas of the city. Burglary occurs widely across a locality and subsists on a hidden economy which is locally based. Assault has no wider spatial dimension. It occurs, however, frequently in specific areas. For example, in terms of assault by a stranger, it has a pronounced geographical focus which is made evident, both in the incidence of assault and the fear of victimization, manifest in the avoidance of certain areas. Just, then, as specific crimes involve differing structures of relationships, they also involve particular structures in space.

Crime occurs privately and publicly and specific crimes are private at certain points of their structure and public at others. In the case of drug dealing, all aspects of the crime, apart from street level, are extremely private transactions. At the level of the opportunistic user, it is quasi-public: people must know who the dealers are, and they must, like any other 'shopkeepers', be relatively open to the public. In the case of burglary, the act itself is, apart from the brief circumspect act of breaking in, a private act; it occurs usually when the owner is out of his or her house, and when neighbours can see no suspicious activities. Subsequently the sale of stolen goods is quasi-public: it occurs publicly in shops which fence wittingly or unwittingly stolen goods or, in terms of direct public purchase, it occurs in the public areas of the pub or workplace. Assault in a public place is, by its very nature, an open event. Unlike domestic violence, it is coercion in the street, in a public house, or in some other public venue.

THE PRINCIPLE OF MULTIPLE AETIOLOGY

If we examine the square of crime, it is obvious that crime rates involve a fourfold aetiology. If involves the causes of offending (the traditional focus of criminology), the factors which make victims vulnerable (e.g. lifestyle analysis, Felson and Cohen, 1981), the social conditions which affect public levels of control and tolerance, and the social forces which propel the formal agencies such as the police. It is impossible to explain crime rates in terms of one of these causal sequences, although it is commonplace in criminological theory that such *partial* explanations are attempted. And, of course, such explanations must involve an *aetiological symmetry*: it is inadmissible, for example, to grant the police a different aetiological status than that of the delinquent. Such an explanatory scheme must detail the *immediate signs* of behaviour and set this within the *wider social origins* (Taylor et al., 1973).

The present period in criminology is characterized by a retreat from a discussion of wider social causes of offending. With a few notable exceptions (Braithwaite, 1979; Currie, 1985), the social democratic tradition of making the link between social structure and offending is severed. In part, this is a response of establishment criminology to new right governments, which, quite clearly, wish to embrace theories which disconnect their policies from uses in the crime rates. The abandonment of interest in crime causation has been complex and manifold. Precisely because it covered a wide spectrum of politics and theory it was extremely effective. The British school of administrative criminology was doubtful about the validity of causes of 'dispositions' altogether. The realists of the right, such as James Q. Wilson, did not deny that there were causes of crime. Indeed, they outlined a plethora of causes (Wilson and Herrnstein, 1985). Rather, they point to the few 'causes' which can be altered without making social changes which would be politically unacceptable, which stresses the individual rather than the social causes of crime. Travis Hirschi (1969), in his influential 'control theory', abandons causation to the extent that it is identified with motivation. Cause metamorphoses from active desire into absence of restraint.

The question of aetiology was, therefore, not abandoned. What were played down were the causes of offending: the traditional focus of criminology. Other aetiologies took its place: the causes of lack of informal controls (control theory), the causes of changes in exposure to victimization (Felson and Cohen's emphasis on lifestyle), the causes of ineffective formal sanctions (Wilson's emphasis on the inadequacy of punishment). That is, the partial causality rooted in the offender characteristic of positivism, in all its varieties, became replaced by other partial causalities focused on other dimensions of the square of crime: informal social control, the victim or the formal system.

Top-down and Bottom-up Explanations

Such a partiality is apparent, not only in criminology of the right, but in criminology of the left. This is seen clearly in the tendency to explain changes in crime and differences in the crime rate between groups, either in terms of *top-down explanations* (changes in the administration of justice), or *bottom-up explanations* (in terms of changes in criminal behaviour). Yet if we are to have a fully developed criminology, we must logically have both a sociology of action and reaction. How can we explain, for example, the rise in the official rate of crimes of violence in the majority of advanced industrial countries in this century if we do not explain both changes in violent behaviour and changes in sensitivity to violence? A one-sided approach – so common – which focuses on one or the other is patently inadequate.

Deviance and control cannot be studied independently of each other. You cannot study changes in policing without changes in patterns of crime, the social control of women without changes in the behaviour of women, the impact of drug legislation without changes in drug use. Systems of social control profoundly affect deviance and changes in deviance patterns of control. The two items are necessary parts of the equation and both variables interact with each other. […]

[…] Realism sees a major cause of criminal behaviour as relative deprivation. Crime can, therefore, occur anywhere in the social structure and at any period, affluent or otherwise – it is simply not dependent on absolute levels of deprivation or the level in the social structure of the offender […]. This being said, it is clear that parts of the poor, particularly the lower working class and certain ethnic minorities who are marginalized from the 'glittering prizes' of the wider society, experience a push towards crime that is greater than elsewhere in the structure (Lea and Young, 1984).

To put an emphasis on relative deprivation as a cause of crime is not to retreat into monocausality. Of course, there are many causes of crime. Even within the tradition of anomie theory, subcultural theorists have tended to give undue emphasis to relative deprivation, the disjunction of aspirations and opportunities, over anomie as a lack of limits, a product of an individualism, where 'From top to bottom of the ladder, greed is aroused without knowing where to find its ultimate foothold. Nothing can colour it since its goal is far beyond all it can attain' (Durkheim, 1952: 256). And certainly one can contrast the anomie of the disadvantaged, which is largely concerned with relative deprivation, from the anomie of the advantaged, which is often a product of a limitless pursuit of money, status and power (Young, 1974; Simon and Gagnon, 1986; Taylor, 1990). This being said, relative deprivation is an extremely potent cause of crime, for it is:

1   not limited to lower working-class crime because relative deprivation can, and does, occur throughout the social structure […];
2   not merely concerned with economic crime because subcultures of violence among the poor and the violence of better-off men occur precisely as a response to relative economic deprivation;
3   not concerned with absolute poverty, and thus pinpoints the paradox of those crimes of the poor which focus on status goods. As Elizabeth Burney pointed out in her study of street robbery: 'Poverty is, nevertheless, not the immediate motive for street crime, since most offenders do not lack necessities: rather, they

crave luxuries. The outstanding characteristic of young street offenders is their avid adherence to a group "style", which dictates a very expensive level of brand-name dressing, financed by crime' (1990: 63; see also Currie, 1990).

The implications of this understanding of causality are of vital importance. Specifically, we have in our cities conditions of unemployment with no fore-seeable future for young people, and where the concept of 'youth' merely extends itself into those aged 30 and beyond. In such a situation relative depri-vation is manifest, in the contrast with the increasingly wealthy strata of those in work, and is underscored by the gentrification of our large cities which allows comparison to be easily available and, indeed, unavoidable.

THE PRINCIPLE OF SPECIFICITY

Both positivism and the new administrative criminology seek generalizations which are independent of culture. A discussion of whether maternal depriva-tion leads to crime, or if beat policing is effective, would be typical endeavours. Left idealism, with its sense of the obviousness of criminological generaliza-tion, enters the field of general laws with an abandon which would alarm the most staunch positivist. Of course unemployment leads to crime; it is self-evident that the recession has led to the rise in heroin use among young people, and so on. Such a mechanistic relationship between objective conditions and human behaviour is absurd. It is central to a realist position that objective con-ditions are interpreted through the specific subcultures of groups involved. This is the nature of human experience and social action. Generalization is pos-sible, but only given specific cultural conditions and social understanding. Thus, absolute deprivation (poverty, unemployment, etc.) is no guide to the genesis of crime. This is the central failure of positivism, both in its aetiology and its policy making. Relative deprivation, experienced injustice in certain limited political situations, is at the root cause of crime.

The utter vacuity of the general 'law': unemployment leads to crime, is displayed when one considers the majority of the human race: women, who have a very high rate of unemployment (in terms of non-domestic labour) and extremely low crime rates. But unemployment *does* give rise to crime in certain circumstances. The failure of such positivism is seen in the Home Office study of the relationship between race and crime (Stevens and Willis, 1979). Here they found a positive correlation between white unemployment and the *white* rate of crime. But for blacks, the relationship was puzzling: for there was a negative correlation between black unemployment and certain sorts of black crime and 'somewhat surprisingly' the white unemployment rate was found to correlate highly with the *black* crime rate. 'A plausible inter-pretation', they note, 'seems hard to find' (p. 23). For, from the point of view of positivism, it is as if one pushed one table and the table next to it moved! But as John Lea and I have argued elsewhere, such a finding is by no means strange:

> As we have argued, there are no *direct* relationships between objective factors and behaviour. The experience of blacks in areas of high white unemployment may well be that of racial discrimination and scapegoating. Such an alienated sub-culture would have a considerable reason to break its lawful bonds with the wider society; it might also experience the demoralisation which is the basis of much criminality. In areas where there is massive black unemployment, there may be less basis for a comparison with whites and thus a relative lack of the frustration that leads to criminality. (Lea and Young, 1984: 160)

Such an analysis can be applied to generalization in a wide variety of areas. For example, in the field of drugs research I have argued for a socio-pharmacological approach. This rejects both the notion that the effects of drugs situation and the moral careers of drug users can be read, so to speak, positivistically from the pages of a pharmocopoeia or relativistically, that drug use is a mere function of culture alone. Rather, specific drugs have effects in particular cultural set-ups: the psychotropic nature of the drug both structures and is structured by the culture (Young, 1971). And in the field of subculture theory, Ward and Kassebaum (1966), in their pioneering study of women's prisons, cut through the debate around whether inmate subculture is transmitted on from the outside pre-prison culture of the prisoners, or is a functional product of 'the pains of imprisonment' while within the prison. By adding the crucial variable of gender to the discussion they have shown how the way in which the pains of imprisonment are experienced is a function of the gender subculture of the inmates. The 'same' prison (objective conditions) produces widely different subcultural solutions (human behaviour) dependent upon the subjective assessment of the inmates.

If we are to be wary about sociological generalizations within one nation at one time, then we should be all the more wary about general laws which attempt to cross historical periods and hop from examples in one country to another. A classic illustration of lack of specificity is Scull's decarceration thesis (1977) which empirically assumed that all forms of deviancy involving incarceration would pass through the same sequence (as if the reactions of the powerful would not vary with the specific deviance) and, even more oddly, that the British figures, which did not fully substantiate his thesis, were simply 'lagging behind' those of the United States. Here we see not only a generalization from one country to another, but from one category to another.

Thus, to be more precise, the problem of specificity refers to generalizing about crime, law or victimization from one country or one social group and assuming that one's conclusions apply to all countries or social groups. It is being unable to see how general variables come together in a very specific form in any particular situation. This results in work which is not only inadequate as a generalization, but is lacking in its ability to cope with what is special about the precise constellation of factors which delineate any particular situation. Specificity is a heuristic failure, both on the level of the general and the particular.

The three major problems of specificity which have dominated criminological thinking have operated on the level of both social category and nationality. The first is obviously the fashion in which male, working-class crime has been used to depict all criminality. We have seen how the impact of, first of all, radical and then feminist criminology has sharply dislodged such thinking. The consequences for theory have been enormous. The new empirical dimensions have far from worked themselves out yet through the maze of conventional theory.

The second is the depiction of crime in advanced industrial countries to describe crime in general. Colin Sumner, in a brilliant essay on crime and under-development (1982), rightly castigates those authors such as Clinard and Abbott (1973) who see crime in poor countries as just a replay of what has occurred in the west, and their general economic development as just a delayed natural evolution. He points to the way in which all the traditional criminological equations become overturned when one begins to look at police behaviour, crimes of the powerful, crimes of the poor and of political oppositionists within the context of global imperialism. Such work has only just begun, but it is of the utmost importance that radical criminology makes a committed attempt to tackle the problems. No one else will. Positivism never did and the new administrative criminology sees itself as producing control generalizations which will apply anywhere, from the estates of New England to the streets of Soweto.

The third problem of specificity is a relatively recent phenomenon occurring in the post-1945 period, and that is the Americanization of criminology. It is important to realize the significance of the domination of US criminology on the criminologies of the rest of the world. The central paradox is that the vast output of the United States – often involving the most innovative work in the field – emerges from a country which is extremely atypical in terms of the majority of advanced industrial countries. The homicide rate, for example, is 14 times higher in Los Angeles than in London, and if we are to look for countries which have similar rates of violence to the United States it would be to Latin America, rather than any other industrial country, east or west. There are a series of atypical characteristics of the United States which may well relate to its exceptional crime rate. For example, its lack of social-democratic politics, its extremely high commitment to the American Dream version of meritocracy, its high emphasis on formal legal equality as an ideal, its remarkable ethnic pluralism, the extent and range of organized crime, the extent of ghettoization, etc. (Currie, 1985, 1990). All of these factors are likely to have a profound effect on the theory generated in such a society. The theory of differential association, Mertonian anomie theory, neo-Chicagoan labelling theory, social control theory, are all illuminated if we begin to think how they fit so well such an exceptional state. This is not an argument for theoretical isolationism. There is no doubt that the United States has, in this century, produced by far the most important developments in theoretical criminology. It is to argue, however, that these theories cannot merely be transplanted to, say, a European context; they have to be transposed *carefully*.

The contradiction, then, is that the most influential work in criminology stems from one of the most atypical advanced industrial states. The extent of this paradox can, perhaps, be illustrated if we imagine that Japan became in the 1990s the leading producer of criminological work. Japan is, of course, an extremely atypical capitalist society – and in the area of crime it is the absolute opposite of the United States. Even by European standards the changes in the crime rate are remarkable. For example, from 1948 to 1982 the crime rate in Japan declined by 36 per cent compared to a rise of 348 per cent in England and Wales over the same period. And this was despite dramatic changes taking place in Japanese society: massive industrialization, vast internal movements of population, urbanization and general social upheaval (Government of Japan, 1983).

It would not be difficult to imagine the types of criminological theory which would emerge from Japan if it indeed dominated the field of criminology. At the bottom line one can imagine quite 'reasonable' theories which linked a rise in the standard of living with a drop in crime. And one can visualize, perhaps, with a certain *schadenfreude*, criminologists in Berkeley or New York trying to fit the evidence of their own country in the new dominant paradigm.

To argue for specificity is not to argue against empirical generalization. It is to say that generalization is possible within particular social orders concerning particular groups. Nor is it to argue that cross-cultural theories of crime are impossible – it is to say firmly that these theories find their resolution in specific societies. For example, the notion of relative deprivation as a theory of discontent, which results in crime in certain social and political circumstances, is one of great heuristic value. But there is a big jump between how the form and content of relative deprivation is experienced among boys in the Lower East Side of Manhattan, to how it is structured in terms of girls in Florence, Japanese youth in Tokyo or corporate criminals in Switzerland.

THE PRINCIPLE OF FOCUSING ON LIVED REALITIES

Realism focuses on lived realities. It is concerned with the material problem which particular groups of people experience in terms of the major social axes of age, class, gender and race, and spatially with their locality. It is these structural parameters which give rise to subcultures. Realism has a close affinity with subcultural theory (Cohen, 1965; Willis, 1977). Subcultures are problem-solving devices which constantly arise as people in specific groups attempt to solve the structural problems which face them. The problems are evaluated in terms of the existing subculture and the subculture changes over time in order to *attempt* a solution to those perceived problems ([...] Young, 1974). Crime is one form of subculture adaptation which occurs where material circumstances block cultural aspirations and where non-criminal alternatives are absent or less attractive.

The experiences of the public with regard to crime and policing cannot be reduced to global figures of the average risk rates of particular crimes or the 'normal' citizen's experience of policing. All evidence indicates that the impact of crime and policing is geographically and socially focused: it varies enormously by area and by the social group concerned. The reason the realists tend to select inner-city areas is to enable us to detail such experiences at the sharp end of policing, while comparing this to data derived from wider-based surveys of total cities and the country as a whole. The reason for the use of extremely high sampling is to be able to break down the impact of crime and policing in terms of its social focus: that is, on social groups based on the combination of age, class, gender and race. Such a high social focus corresponds more closely to the lived realities of different groups and subcultures of the population. Thus, just as it is inaccurate to generalize about crime and policing from figures based on large geographical areas, it is incorrect, even within particular areas, to talk in terms of, for example, 'all' young people, 'all' women, 'all' blacks, 'all' working-class people, etc. (Schwartz, 1988). Generalizations which remain on such global levels frequently obfuscate quite contradictory experiences, generating statistics which often conceal vital differences of impact. We have shown in the *Second Islington Crime Survey* (Crawford et al., 1990), for example, how the introduction of age into the analysis of fear of crime by gender changes the usual generality of men having low fear of crime and women high. In fact, older women have a fear of crime rather like men in the middle age group, and younger women have a fear rather like old men. And, in the case of foot-stops by the police, it becomes evident that differentials based on race are much more complicated than the abstraction that blacks are more likely to be stopped than whites. No older black women in our sample were stopped. Young, white, women were over three times more likely to be stopped than older black men. And even the differential between young black men and young white men becomes remarkably narrowed when class is introduced into the equation. Such an approach in realist method is termed an awareness of the specificity of generalization, the need to base analysis firmly grounded in specific areas and social groups. It is in marked contrast to the approaches which try to explain differences in experience in terms of only one of the major social axes: age, class, gender, or race. Such reductionism, as exemplified by radical feminism or fundamentalist class analysis, simply does not fit the reality of social experience. This approach enables us to be more discriminate about generalization with regard to changes in modes of policing and methods of crime control. For example, in the debate about shifts from consensual to more coercive forms of policing (Lea and Young, 1984), it allows us to ascertain whether contradictory forces are at work involving consensual policing of certain areas and groups and more coercive methods with others. Similarly, the probable efficacy of crime control measures such as beat policing or neighbourhood watch must be grounded in specific communities and locations.

Putting Behaviour into Context

Realism involves the invocation of rationality rooted in material circumstances. That is, it places the behaviour of the offender, the police officer, the victim and the public at large, in the actual material circumstances that each individual experiences (Lea and Young, 1984). This is not to say that people do not make mistakes in understanding the world, whether it is the behaviour of the police officer in stop and search, or the fear of crime of the citizen. Indeed, this is *ipso facto* the very nature of rational behaviour. Rather, it sets itself against an idealism which analyses people's beliefs and behaviour, primarily as a product of free-floating ideas and prejudices, whether a product of outside influences such as the mass media, or socially detached group values, or personal psychological attributes.

Realist method relates attitudes and beliefs to actually lived experience of material circumstances. For example, it attempts to explain police behaviour, not in terms of the enactment of a group of people with, say, authoritarian personalities, or a macho culture, or rigid 'them' and 'us' attitudes engendered at training school. All of these things may or may not be true, but they are not the primary determinants of police behaviour. To take a police patrol as an example: it is the actual nature of the police task, the experiences confronted in attempting to achieve objectives in the face of the opportunities and difficulties encountered on the job which is central to understanding the behaviour of patrolling officers. In this instance of police practice it cannot be deduced from legal rules nor from a free-floating 'cop culture' nor the autonomous prejudices of individual police officers. Realism attempts to put police practice, the interpretation of rules, the generation of an occupational culture, and the attitudes of individual officers, in its context. For example, stop and search procedures are largely ineffective at dealing with the crimes to which the legislation was directed: burglary, hard drug use and carrying weapons. Direct information, either gleaned from the public, or by detective work, would be needed in order to have a high yield from such a procedure. In the absence of such information, patrolling officers equipped with stop and search powers, and wishing to have at least some yield from their work, will of necessity, target those groups which have high offending rates, particularly young, working-class males – black and white. As most people stopped will be perfectly innocent, such a trawling of a particular social group will inevitably create a counter-productive hostility in the target groups and accusations of unfairness, selectivity and prejudice. But it is the inadequate tools for the job and an ill-thought-out piece of legislation which creates the working context for the police, not merely the enactment of personal and cultural prejudice.

Social Constructionism, Positivism and Everyday Life

Realism, then, does not deal in abstractions: the principle of specificity demands that explanation be grounded. It is not just that the concept of 'crime' embraces a motley of types of behaviour and varieties of legal regulation; each 'type' of crime and each form of regulation must be specified if we are to make any progress in understanding their interaction. Opiate addiction, for example, can mean many different things in particular subcultures. Burglary can involve the rational calculation of the professional or the opportunism of the young lad. Domestic violence can involve a variety of sub-species, each with its own life cycle. And, turning to social control, beat policing can involve many greatly different activities from the aggressive to the consensual; neighbourhood watch can be a uniting or a divisive intervention. All of this suggests the necessity of typologies which cut across legal or formal definitions, but, going further, that these typologies must be grounded in the particular lived realities of the phenomenon under investigation. It does not exclude generalization, it merely argues that generalization must be socially based and explanations which are abstracted out of context have very little chance of aetiological success because they ignore the very social context which determines them. [...]

REFERENCES

Braithwaite, J. (1979) *Inequality, Crime and Public Policy.* London: Routledge and Kegan Paul.

Burney, E. (1990) *Putting Street Crime in its Place.* London: Centre for Inner City Studies, Goldsmiths' College, University of London.

Clinard, M. and Abbott, D. (1973) *Crime in Developing Countries.* New York: Wiley.

Cohen, A.K. (1965) 'The sociology of the deviant act', *American Sociological Review,* 30: 5–14.

Crawford, A., Jones, T., Woodhouse, T. and Young, J. (1990) *Second Islington Crime Survey.* Middlesex Polytechnic: Centre for Criminology.

Currie, E. (1985) *Confronting Crime.* New York: Pantheon Books.

Currie, E. (1990) 'Crime and market society', paper presented to the Conference on Crime and Policing, Islington, London.

Durkheim, E. (1952) *Suicide.* London: Routledge and Kegan Paul.

Felson, M. and Cohen, L. (1981) 'Modelling crime rates', *Research in Crime and Delinquency,* 18: 138–64.

Government of Japan (1983) *Summary of the White Paper on Crime.* Tokyo: Research and Training Institute, Ministry of Justice.

Hirschi, T. (1969) *Causes of Delinquency.* Berkeley, CA: University of California Press.

Lea, J. and Young, J. (1984) *What is to be Done about Law and Order?* Harmondsworth: Penguin.

Matza, D. (1964) *Deliquency and Drift.* New York: Wiley.

Schwartz, M. (1988) 'Ain't got no class: universal risk theories of battering', *Contemporary Crisis,* 12: 373–92.

Scull, A. (1977) *Decarceration.* Englewood Cliffs, NJ: Prentice-Hall.

Simon, W. and Gagnon, J. (1986) 'The anomie of affluence', *American Sociological Review,* 82: 356–78.

Stevens, P. and Willis, C. (1979) *Race, Crime and Arrests.* London: HMSO.

Sumner, C. (1982) (ed.) *Crime, Justice and Underdevelopment.* Cambridge: Cambridge University Press.

Taylor, I. (1990) (ed.) *The Social Effects of Free Market Policies.* Hemel Hempsted: Harvester Wheatsheaf.

Taylor, I., Walton, P. and Young, J. (1973) *The New Criminology for a Social Theory of Deviance.* London: Routledge and Kegan Paul.

Ward, D. and Kassebaum, G. (1966) *Women's Prison.* London: Weidenfeld and Nicolson.

Willis, P. (1977) *Learning to Labour.* Farnborough: Saxon House.

Wilson, J.Q. and Herrnstein, R. (1985) *Crime and Human Nature.* New York: Simon and Schuster.

Young, J. (1971) *The Drugtakers*. London: Paladin.
Young, J. (1974) 'New directions in subcultural theory', in J. Rex (ed.) *Approaches to Sociology*. London: Routledge and Kegan Paul.
Young, J. (1987) 'The tasks of a realist criminology', *Contemporary Crisis*, 11: 337–56.

STUDY QUESTIONS

1   Young argues: 'Realism involves the invocation of rationality rooted in material circumstances. That is, it places the behaviour of the offender, the police officer, the victim and the public at large, in the actual material circumstances that each individual experiences.' According to Young, why is 'aetiological symmetry' important?
2   With reference to Young's discussion of the 'shape' of crime, represent 'laundering illegally imported tobacco', 'embezzlement' and the 'fixing of sporting events' diagrammatically.
3   From Young's perspective, why is generalization dangerous?
4   What do you see as the similarities and differences between Young's and Becker's (Reading 3) arguments?

FURTHER READING

Other relevant books by the same authors as the one that this extract is taken from, and which outline the need for a radical realism, include Matthews, R. and Young, J. (eds) (1986) *Confronting Crime*, London: Sage; and Matthews, R. and Young, J. (eds) (1992) *Issues in Realist Criminology*, London: Sage. Limitations of space prevented us from including an extract on 'right realism', which is an orthodox conservative view that locates crime predominantly in poor 'underclass' neighbourhoods and urban ghettoes. For a representative account of right realism, see Murray, C. (1990) *The Emerging British Underclass*, London: Institute of Economic Affairs Health and Welfare Unit. Overviews of both left and right realism can be found in Walklate, S. (1998) *Understanding Criminology: Current Theoretical Debates*, Buckingham: Open University Press.

5

Psychology and criminal behaviour

Peter B. Ainsworth

Since the early 1960s, British criminology has been dominated by sociological thinking and approaches. Two different strands of academic enquiry combined to inspire and influence British criminologists seeking a new direction after several decades dominated by psychological and psychoanalytic explanations of crime. The first was the legacy of European founders of sociology such as Weber and Durkheim; the second was the American Chicago School, where researchers such as W.I. Thomas and G.H. Mead developed new theories of socialization, which included researching patterns of criminal behaviour. Since the early 1960s it has been the sociological enterprise that has continued to dominate criminology as a subject of academic study, as reflected in the vast majority of courses offered in the subject at UK universities. However, given that one of the most salient questions in criminology remains 'what makes a criminal?', it is unsurprising to find that many people look to psychology to try to find answers for criminal behaviour. In this extract, which is taken from a wider analysis of offender profiling, Peter B. Ainsworth considers a broad range of theoretical approaches that can be generally described as emanating from psychology, although some combine psychological and sociological approaches. What distinguishes these perspectives is that they tend to look for a single variable, as opposed to multiple factors, when seeking explanations for crime. Some of the theorists mentioned by Ainsworth have also been discussed in previous readings in this part (e.g. Reading 2).

[...] One of the longest-running debates in psychology is whether genetic or environmental factors are more influential in shaping behaviour. The debate has

SOURCE: From *Offender Profiling and Crime Analysis* (Cullompton: Willan Publishing, 2001), 23–37.

concerned itself with many aspects of human behaviour, including intelligence, personality and criminal behaviour. The debate is not just a sterile or academic one as different viewpoints have very different consequences. If it were found to be the case that a rapist behaved the way that he did purely because of his genetic make-up then little would be achieved by providing therapy for this individual.

Psychologists offering explanations for many aspects of human behaviour today rarely talk about 'heredity versus environment' as if the two were mutually exclusive categories. [...] [A]ll human behaviour is a result of an interaction between a large number of factors, some of which reside within the individual, and some of which are to be found in the external environment. Thus the debate today is not so much about which aspect is the more important, but rather is concerned with the relative influence of various factors and, most importantly the way in which the factors interact.

Nevertheless a brief discussion of some possible genetic influences might be helpful. Our understanding should perhaps start with a consideration of the early views of Cesare Lombroso (1876). Lombroso studied a number of well known criminals in Italian society and formed the view that criminals were of a different genetic type from other law-abiding citizens. His view was that one could see the difference in the physical make-up of criminals and that this suggested that such individuals were a throwback to a period when man was of a more primitive form. He labelled such people atavistic and pointed to a number of abnormal physiological features including their smaller brains. Lombroso went even further than this and suggested that different types of criminal had different physical make-ups. Thus murderers were typically described as having a number of identifiable features including cold, glassy and bloodshot eyes, masses of curly hair, thin lips and long ears. By contrast those convicted of sexual offences typically had, according to Lombroso, glinting eyes, and thick lips.

It is easy to ridicule such simplistic notions today, yet at the time Lombroso's views attracted a massive amount of interest from people in both Europe and the USA. This was despite the lack of good scientific evidence to support his theory. One of the appeals of Lombroso's work was that it used observation and measurement rather than merely relying upon speculation. As such it was seen at the time as a 'scientific' approach to understanding criminal behaviour. In reality many of the methods used by Lombroso were fundamentally flawed and, in hindsight, were anything but scientific.

From a modern perspective Lombroso's views appear simplistic and unsound yet they are not that far removed from the way in which sections of the media portray some criminals today. Labelling certain offenders as 'evil' or describing them as 'fiends', 'animals' or 'monsters' seeks to draw a dividing line between such people and other 'normal' members of society. There is a presumption that such a distinction is easy and appropriate to make. However this is certainly not the case. It might also be argued that Lombroso's was the first attempt to establish a typology which could differentiate between different types of people. [...]

As we discover more and more about genetics, it would be perhaps unsurprising to learn that some researchers have looked to such factors as a possible explanation for criminal behaviour. Work on these notions gained momentum in the 1960s following the discovery of a number of genetic abnormalities, in particular the identification of some males as XYY. Such individuals were portrayed as having twice as much 'maleness' as normal human males and indeed the condition was labelled by some as the 'supermale syndrome'.

Interest in this genetic abnormality increased significantly when some researchers claimed that it was associated with the commission of violent crime (Price et al. 1966; Jarvik et al. 1973). This early work suggested that XYY males were over-represented in the population of prisons and special hospitals and that such individuals appeared to have a high propensity towards extreme violence. The finding that a few infamous prisoners possessed this genetic abnormality only added to interest in the condition. Unfortunately this early work lacked scientific rigour and later, more carefully controlled research failed to substantiate many of the early claims. [...]

[...] This should not, however, be taken to mean that genetics are irrelevant to an understanding of criminal behaviour. Whilst genes rarely appear to have a single, simple or directive effect on behaviour, any individual's genetic make-up will interact with environmental conditions to produce a certain effect. Genetic factors might also be relevant, not so much because they have a direct effect on the propensity towards criminal behaviour, but rather because they have an effect on individual variables such as personality or intelligence. Thus people with a certain genetic make-up may be more likely to develop certain personalities, and it is then these personalities which might be found to be associated with criminal behaviour. [...]

If one wishes to argue that there is a genetic component to criminal behaviour then one obvious starting-point would be to consider whether criminality appears to run in families. Many police officers may hold the view that there are criminal families, i.e. those in which almost all family members have little regard for the law and adopt a criminal lifestyle. It would be easy to argue that genetic factors must have a role to play if criminal parents invariably produce offspring who also become criminals.

In one piece of research, Osborn and West (1979) found that some 40 per cent of sons born to fathers with a criminal record also went on acquire a criminal record themselves. However this finding does not in itself prove that there is a genetic link. Sons of criminal fathers may, for example, receive different forms of socialisation than would the sons of non-criminal fathers. Thus in the former case a son may be praised and rewarded for having committed his first criminal offence, whereas in the latter case the son's behaviour would be disapproved of and perhaps punished. It should also be borne in mind that while 40 per cent of the sons of criminal fathers go on to become criminals themselves, this means that 60 per cent do not do so.

There may be another way in which the figures might be partly explained which has more to do with police practices than genetic transmission. If the police have a local family labelled as 'trouble' they are perhaps more likely to focus on members of that family when trying to solve petty crime. Thus a visit to the family home may turn up some evidence to implicate a youngster's involvement in criminal behaviour and result in a conviction. However, if the same act had been committed by a youngster from a family which was not known to the police, the finger of suspicion might never fall on that person and they might never be identified. This point is also relevant in terms of profiling. Although a profiler may be able to specify a number of attributes which an offender is likely to possess, the police are more likely to focus on those eligible individuals who are already known to them in terms of having a criminal record.

It appears that more proof is needed before we can accept the basic premise that crime does have a large and significant genetic component. Some researchers have turned to a study of twins in an effort to accumulate further proof. We will consider some of this work next.

TWIN STUDIES

[…] The reason why identical twins are of such great interest to psychologists is that, being genetically identical, they might provide some valuable information with regard to the genetic transmission of certain attributes and traits. The human reproduction system ensures that there are no two individuals in the world who are genetically identical – with the exception of identical twins. Thus in order to understand whether criminal behaviour has a genetic component, one might start by looking at pairs of identical twins and examining the number of cases in which one twin's criminal lifestyle is mirrored by that of his or her twin. One could thus obtain a measure of the 'concordance rate', i.e. the proportion of twin pairs in which the behaviour of one twin in a pair is similar to that of the other.

Some early work produced some interesting results. For example, Lange (1931) found that in the case of criminality, the concordance rate for identical twins was 77. However, for non-identical twins it was only 12. Similarly Christiansen (1977) found that the concordance rate for identical twins was around 60, while that for non-identical twins was only half this. Such large differences have not, however, been found in all studies. For example, in his early work, Kranz (1936) found that the concordance rate was 65 for identical twins, but 53 for non-identical twin pairs.

The fact that the majority of studies have shown a much higher concordance rate for identical than for non-identical twins might lead one to conclude with some justification that criminality does appear to have a large genetic component. In reality, however, there may be a number of reasons why these results are as they are and may not 'prove' the theory of genetic transmission of criminal behaviour. For example, we must bear in mind the fact that the vast majority of twins will have been raised together in the same home by the same parents and with the same siblings. As such the environment which they share will be very similar if not identical. Thus if twin pairs do have high concordance rates with respect to criminality, this may partly be accounted for by the similarity of their environment. It is, for example, highly unlikely that parents would encourage one twin to engage in criminal behaviour and discourage the other from doing so.

However, this does not totally account for the fact that identical twins raised in the same home are more likely to be similar in terms of criminal tendencies than are non-identical twins raised together. One possibility is that identical twins are likely to experience an almost identical environment whilst non-identical twins may have slightly different experiences. In addition we know that males are much more likely to have a criminal record than are females. Thus we would expect that pairs of male twins would be more likely to show a high concordance rate in respect of criminality than would male–female pairs.

Before moving on we should also bear in mind that identical twins appear more likely to develop an intense personal relationship with each other than is the case with non-identical twins. In such cases we would hardly be surprised to find that one twin's wish to commit criminal acts was copied by the other's.

In an attempt to try to unravel some of these confounding variables, researchers have sought out identical twin pairs who have been raised separately. The argument here is that if identical twins reared apart still show high concordance rates then this must be explained by reference to genetic factors. Unfortunately (for research purposes) there are very few twin pairs who are separated at birth and of those who are, relatively few will have developed criminal records. Even if large-scale studies of the criminal records of separated twins had been carried out, these would not necessarily provide conclusive proof of a genetic component to criminality.

Some researchers claim that if separated twins show similarity in intelligence, personality or criminality, this proves that there is a strong genetic link. But such a conclusion rests on a somewhat dubious presumption, i.e. that twins reared separately will be raised in environments which share no common elements. In reality this is unlikely to be the case. In most instances each twin will have been raised in an environment which shares many common features with the other's environment. Even if twins are put up for separate adoption, they will tend to be allocated to adoptive parents with largely similar personal and demographic characteristics. We should thus be aware that even twins who are reared in different environments and who may never even meet each other will share many similar experiences while growing up. It would perhaps be naive to presume that any similarities between separated identical twins must be due entirely to their genetic make-up.

One other way in which researchers have tried to disentangle the effects of genetics and the environment is through the study of adopted children. The issue here would be to establish whether children who are adopted early in life end up being more similar (in terms of their criminality) to their natural or to their adoptive parents. In one meta-analysis of some 13 such studies, Walters (1992) suggested that there did appear to be some link between the criminal records of natural parents and their offspring, but that this relationship was not a particularly strong one. Further, Bohman (1995) has pointed out that any tendency towards criminal behaviour may only manifest itself if the individual is exposed to certain environmental conditions. Even if adoption studies do appear at first glance to show a genetic link with criminality, we should be aware that such studies suffer from the same methodological problems outlined earlier with regard to identical twins separated early in life, i.e. that 'separate' environment does not mean environments which share no common features.

Most researchers today would not accept that a genetic link with criminality has been proved conclusively. Having said that, there are some (e.g. Mednick et al., 1987) who still believe strongly in such a link. It is difficult to imagine just how genes might turn one individual into a criminal while ensuring that another avoids committing any criminal acts. Whilst our knowledge of genetics is advancing rapidly it seems unlikely that researchers will one day find a single gene which can explain the transmission of criminal tendencies from a parent to a child. [...]

FAMILY INFLUENCES

[...] Perhaps the best research which has examined family influences on criminal behaviour is the longitudinal study carried out by Farrington and colleagues (Farrington, 1991, 1997). Farrington studied a total of 411 boys who were born to working-class families in London in 1953. Farrington and his colleagues have been able to follow the boys' progress through childhood, adolescence, and adult life. By comparing boys who did develop a criminal record with those who did not, Farrington was able to identify a number of important factors in the development of delinquency. Amongst these were low family income, a large family, parental criminality and poor child-rearing practices.

Interestingly, Farrington has suggested that those individuals who became chronic offenders showed some symptoms of antisocial behaviour quite early in life. Many were identified as troublesome or dishonest in their early years at primary school and by age 10 had been identified as being of low intelligence, impulsive, hyperactive and unpopular. At age 14, most were described as being more aggressive than their peers, and to have friends who shared their delinquent tendencies. By age 18, these same boys also showed a number of differences from the norm, being likely to drink, smoke and gamble more and to be associated with gangs. The longitudinal nature of Farrington's study allowed researchers to check on these individuals' progress into adulthood. Many members of this delinquent group were found in adult life to be living in poor conditions, to have experienced a marital breakdown and/or psychiatric illness and to be having problems dealing with their own children. [...]

PERSONALITY THEORIES

[...] Perhaps the best known theory linking personality with criminal behaviour is that put forward by Hans Eysenck (Eysenck, 1977). Eysenck's early research led him to believe that there were two important personality dimensions along which people varied, i.e. *Extraversion–Introversion* and *Neuroticism–Stability*. The former is characterised by individuals', tendency to seek out stimulation from others (i.e. their sociability) but was also linked with impulsiveness. The neuroticism–stability dimension is concerned with elements such as proneness to anxiety and depression, poor self-esteem, and negative affectivity.

It should be recognized that Eysenck did not attempt to categorise individuals as being of either one personality 'type' or another. Rather, he derived measures by which an individual's score on these two dimensions could be judged in relation to the general population. Most importantly for our present purposes was Eysenck's claim that those who scored higher than average in terms of both extraversion and neuroticism were more likely to become criminal. Eysenck claimed that a large proportion of a person's personality (and indeed other aspects including intelligence) was determined by genetic factors. He believed that genetics largely determine the nature of an individual's cortical and auto-nomic nervous systems and it is these systems which govern an individual's interactions with the outside world. The person scoring highly in terms of extra-version is seen as generally under-aroused and is thus impulsive and constantly seeking stimulation. Furthermore extraverts are more difficult to condition and thus less likely to respond appropriately to the use of rewards and punishments.

In the case of the neuroticism–stability dimension, Eysenck believed that individuals with high neuroticism scores had autonomic nervous systems which were labile and that such people reacted strongly to unpleasant stimuli. However, Eysenck also claimed that such individuals' moodiness and high anxiety made them difficult to condition. According to Eysenck, a combination of high extraversion and high neuroticism produced an individual who constantly sought stimulation and excitement but who was not easily socialised or conditioned and appeared not to learn from their mistakes. Many such individuals would, according to Eysenck, become criminals.

In his later writings, Eysenck claimed to have identified a third important personality dimension, *psychoticism*. A person who scored highly on this dimension was said typically to be solitary, uncaring, cold, cruel and imper-sonal, and tough-minded and aggressive. Whilst not all high extraversion/ high neuroticism individuals also had high psychoticism scores, those who did were more likely to engage in violent and aggressive crimes in which a victim's suffering appeared to be a form of stimulation for the perpetrator.

Eysenck's views have been the subject of considerable debate and a number of authors have questioned many of the basic tenets of his theory. (See Ainsworth, 2000: 76 for a recent review.) It would appear that Eysenck's claim that certain personality types are invariably associated with criminal behaviour is a rather simplistic notion. Many of his claims have not been substantiated, nor supported by other researchers. However, before we relegate Eysenck's views to the scrap heap we should perhaps consider whether it is appropriate to dismiss any notion that personality is relevant to an understanding of criminal behaviour.

To say that Eysenck has failed to prove a causative link between certain personality dimensions and criminal behaviour is not the same as claiming that personality is completely irrelevant. In the same way that genetics is relevant to an understanding of why some people commit crime, personality may be another related piece in a complex jigsaw. [...] [M]any profilers believe that the way in which individuals commit their crimes is in part a reflection of their underlying personality. For this reason it may be important for aspiring profilers to gain some understanding of personality theory.

From what we know about personality it appears that certain personality types are more likely to interact with the world in certain ways, and that in some cases this may be linked with criminal behaviour. For example, we know that some people are more likely to be 'sensation seekers' than are others. Some individuals who are so described may seek out the stimulation which they appear to need by gambling, riding dangerous theme park rides or driving racing cars. However, others may seek to satisfy their need for excitement by embarking upon a life of crime during which they are constantly trying to stay one step ahead of the police. [...]

Similarly some personality types may be more predisposed to develop addictions to alcohol or illegal drugs than are others. In this case it is the addiction which may lead to the adoption of a criminal lifestyle with personality serving only as an intervening variable. Interestingly some recent writers have suggested that certain individuals might become addicted to the commission of criminal acts in themselves, in much the same way as some become addicted to drugs. Hodge et al. (1997) suggest that this fact may partly explain why some young offenders go on to become 'career criminals' while most others desist from offending once they reach adulthood.

Before moving on from a discussion of personality we should also consider that some individuals do appear to possess a type of personality which is almost guaranteed to bring them into conflict with the authorities. Thus those labelled as 'psychopathic' or defined as having an 'antisocial personality disorder' will, by virtue of the way in which these conditions are defined, have shown a propensity towards criminal behaviour, often from an early age (Ainsworth, 2000: Ch. 5). There is no doubt that a number of serial killers would be defined today as psychopathic.

SOCIAL LEARNING THEORIES

Both genetic and personality theories might well be described as psychological in that they appear to presume that the reasons why a person commits crime can be found by looking within the individual themselves. However, there are other theories which take a more sociological, or at least social psychological approach, in examining factors which are external to the individual. Some such theories are described as social learning theories in that they claim that behaviour stems more from an individual's social learning experiences than being the result of genetic predisposition or personality.

Most such theories can be traced back to the writings of E.H. Sutherland who introduced a theory known as differential association (Sutherland, 1939; Sutherland and Cressey, 1970). Sutherland claimed that most people who choose to behave in criminal ways do so because of their association with others, especially in the form of membership of small groups or gangs. Sutherland claimed that such individuals will, as a result of interactions with certain others, learn both new attitudes towards the commission of criminal acts and new criminal techniques. Sutherland claimed that certain individuals may be exposed to a higher ratio of criminal (as opposed to non-criminal) learning opportunities and it is these differential associations which best explain why some individuals turn to a life of crime while others do not do so.

The notion that people behave in certain ways because of their social learning experiences has been developed by a number of other writers, including some psychologists. Perhaps best known is the work of Albert Bandura (Bandura, 1977) who carried out a number of pioneering studies demonstrating the potentially powerful nature of social learning experiences. His best known work is that which involved exposing young children to an adult model who behaved in certain predetermined ways. Some children were shown an adult playing with a large inflatable Bobo doll in a violent and aggressive way, whereas other children were shown an adult behaving in a much less violent way. Having observed the adult's behaviour the children were then allowed to play with the inflatable doll themselves and their behaviour was observed. Bandura reported that there were large differences in the behaviour of the two groups of children, in that those who had been exposed to the aggressive model were much more likely to behave in a similar manner themselves, whereas those who had been shown the less aggressive model were much more likely to indulge in non-violent play.

Following the publication of Bandura's findings, many writers sought to support his views by providing evidence of the powerful effects of social learning. While it does appear to be the case that children will often imitate behaviour which they see others performing, social learning theory is also concerned with the way in which others react to what the child does. For example some parents may react to their son's aggression with condemnation while others may actively encourage their child's apparent attempt to 'stand up for himself'. This knowledge may again be important to a profiler wishing to understand the behaviour of individuals who perpetrate serious criminal acts.

Some advocates of social learning theory have used its basic tenets to argue for a reduction in the amount of violence portrayed on television and in films and videos (see Ainsworth, 2000: 79–82). Whilst there are some documented cases of individuals having imitated the actions of those they have seen on screen, the vast majority of people choose not to copy the (illegal) actions of even the most revered screen heroes. Whilst screen violence may offer a partial explanation for why some people choose to commit some crimes, it would be naive to presume that such an explanation can account for the majority of criminal acts. Thus even if it can be shown that one individual did apparently choose to imitate the actions of some character shown on the screen, one would still need to ask why the vast majority of people who also saw the same video chose not to behave in such a manner.[...]

REFERENCES

Ainsworth, P.B. (2000) *Psychology and Crime: Myths and Reality.* Harlow: Longman.

Bandura, A. (1977) *Social Learning Theory.* Englewood Cliffs, NJ: Prentice-Hall.

Bohman, M. (1995) 'Predisposition to criminality: Swedish adoption studies in retrospect' in *Genetics of Criminal and Antisocial Behaviour.* Ciba Foundation Symposium 194. Chichester: Wiley.

Christiansen, K.O. (1977) 'A preliminary study of criminality among twins' in S. Mednick and K.O. Christiansen (eds) *Biological Bases of Criminal Behaviour.* New York: Gardner Press.

Eysenck, H.J. (1977) *Crime and Personality*, 3rd edn. London: Routledge and Kegan Paul.

Farrington, D.P. (1991) 'Anti-social personality from childhood to adulthood', *The Psychologist*, 4, 389–94.

Farrington, D.P. (1997) 'Human development and criminal careers' in M. Maguire, R. Morgan and R. Reiner (eds) *The Oxford Handbook of Criminology*, 2nd edn. Oxford: Oxford University Press.

Hodge, J.E., McMurran, M. and Hollin, C.R. (1997) *Addicted to Crime?* Chichester: Wiley.

Jarvik, L.F., Klodin, V. and Matsyama, S.S. (1973) 'Human aggression and the extra Y chromosome', *American Psychologist*, 28, 674–82.

Lange, J.S. (1931) *Crime as Destiny.* London: Allen and Unwin.

Lombroso, C. (1876) *L'Uomo Delinquente.* Turin: Fratelli Bocca.

Mednick, S.A., Moffitt, T.E. and Stack, S.A. (eds) (1987) *The Causes of Crime: New Biological Approaches.* Cambridge: Cambridge University Press.

Osborn, S.G. and West, D.J. (1979) 'Conviction records of fathers and sons compared', *British Journal of Criminology*, 19, 120–33.

Price W.H., Strong, J.A., Whatmore, P.B. and McClemont, W.F. (1966) Criminal patients with XYY sex-chromosome complement', *The Lancet*, 1, 565–6.

Sutherland, E.H. (1939) *The Professional Thief.* Chicago: Chicago University Press.

Sutherland, E.H. and Cressey, D.R. (1970) *Criminology*, 8th edn. Philadelphia, PA: Lippincott.

Walters, G.D. (1992) 'A meta-analysis of the gene-crime relationship', *Criminology*, 30, 595–613.

STUDY QUESTIONS

1   Having read Ainsworth, and the other readings in this part, do you think that it is possible to prove conclusively whether criminals are born or made?

2   Carry out an analysis of crime news from a selection of newspapers. Do newspaper reports and editorials tend to support one view or the other, i.e. that offenders are inherently 'bad' or that they are 'made' criminal by their social environments?

3   Ainsworth quotes a study claiming that approximately 40 per cent of criminal fathers produce criminal sons. In the light of your reading of this and other extracts in Part I, what alternative explanations to that of genetic predisposition might you put forward to explain this statistic?

FURTHER READING

Peter B. Ainsworth has also written (2000) *Psychology and Crime: Myths and Reality*, Harlow: Longman, which is a good introduction to the subject and covers much of the same ground as is presented in the reading above. Among the introductory textbooks which include sections on psychological explanations of crime are Coleman, C. and Norris, C. (2000) *Introducing Criminology*, Cullompton: Willan; and Jones, S. (1998) *Criminology*, London: Butterworths. The section 'Explaining crime' is also useful in chapter 2 of Davies, M., Croall, H. and Tyrer, J. (1998) *Criminal Justice: An Introduction to the Criminal Justice System in England and Wales*, 2nd edn, Harlow: Pearson. The psychology of criminal behaviour is the subject of Blackburn, R. (1993) *The Psychology of Criminal Conduct: Theory, Research and Practice*, Chichester: Wiley.

6

The development of feminist perspectives on crime

Nicole Hahn Rafter and Frances Heidensohn

Not only did the 1960s mark the beginning of the dominance of criminology by sociological methods and perspectives, but it was also significant in being the decade in which feminist academics began to question the male bias (androcentrism) of criminology. In the extract that follows, Nicole Hahn Rafter and Frances Heidensohn briefly consider the histories of both 20th-century feminism and Western academic feminism. They also consider the relationship between the two and the impact of feminism on mainstream criminology within the academy and outside it, both in the West and globally. Feminism has raised many uncomfortable questions for criminologists, and has been critical of mainstream criminology for its gender-neutral focus and its exclusion of women. Significantly, the feminist critique has not just focused on the substantive concerns of criminology but also on the methods, methodologies and epistemologies favoured by mainstream criminologists. Thus, feminist work provides a critique of positivism and emphasizes the importance of the researchers' standpoint (see also Gelsthorpe and Morris, 1990, in *Further Reading*). Feminist work focuses on the lived experience of women (and men) as offenders and victims; and has provided a new criminological agenda that includes many issues not previously considered (see, for example, Readings 21 and 22). As Rafter and Heidensohn suggest, like other 'new' approaches to criminology, feminism is overtly political as its primary aim is to improve not criminology but people's lives. They also suggest that feminism's impact has been particularly profound, a view which is supported not least by the rest of the book from which

SOURCE: From *International Feminist Perspectives in Criminology: Engendering a Discipline*, ed. Nicole Hahn Rafter and Frances Heidensohn (Buckingham: Open University Press, 1995), 1–14.

this extract is taken. The book includes chapters which focus on the relationship between feminism and criminology in many parts of the world but also includes attention to differences other than gender. The extract we've chosen ends with a consideration of the future for academic criminology and for the place of feminism within it. Although they outline the questions and concerns that they believe should be central in the future, Rafter and Heidensohn suggest that these issues will not easily be resolved.

[…] In this [chapter] we trace the trajectories of twentieth-century feminism and Western academic criminology and then turn to the much-discussed issue of the results of their encounter, a debate we attempt to reframe and broaden. Next we identify factors that have fostered the recent globalization of feminist criminological analyses. We conclude by specifying key issues that those concerned with gender, crime and social control – however far-flung geographically or diverse in their immediate concerns – are likely to grapple with during the next twenty-five years.

FEMINISM IN THE LATE TWENTIETH CENTURY

We begin with Western academic feminism, partly because it has been the international leader in feminist analyses of crime and criminology, partly because it is the territory with which we, as American and British academics, are most familiar. […]

The immediate roots of twentieth-century Western feminism lie in the liberation movements of the 1960s: the European and American student movements and, in the United States, the civil rights movement as well. Idealistic young women were shocked to realize that male colleagues in these egalitarian movements regarded them as no more than secretaries or sexual playmates. Shock gave birth to indignation, indignation to a resolve to promote the liberation not only of others but of women themselves.

For guidance, newborn feminists turned to *The Second Sex*, Simone de Beauvoir's (1952) analysis of women's ubiquitous treatment as Other. Beauvoir made it painfully clear that this was a world in which the chief interpreters of women were men. Soon the new feminists were producing analyses and manifestos of their own (Friedan, 1963; Millet, 1970). And so began a new 'women's movement' (actually a group of interlocking movements) focused, initially, on issues that were political (reproductive rights), economic (equal wages), social (equal household responsibilities) and relational (equal status). Throughout the Western world, especially in countries with strong democratic traditions, women challenged discrimination (for example, the assumption that the best jobs would go to men), exclusion (for example, the assumption of masculinity as normative) and representation (for example, the lack of women's history). Simultaneously, they began campaigning around issues such as abortion rights and childcare. The personal (as one of their most effective slogans put it) became political.

The new feminists gave a name to what they saw as the underlying problem: *sexism*. As they grasped the consequences of marginalization and negation, silences became matters to fight against. Through the collective efforts that were such a striking characteristic of the early phase of the women's liberation movement, a crucial distinction was made between *sex* (often defined biologically, in terms of female and male) and *gender* (often defined socially, in terms of feminine and masculine). It became clear that gender subordination was neither inborn nor inevitable. Once made, the sex–gender distinction enabled feminists to break free of crippling roles and eventually to imagine cultures in which sexual and gender identities might be mixed, matched and even multiplied.[1]

In the United States and to a lesser extent other countries, the movement carried women on to campuses, where they demanded more opportunities for female scholars and students, together with courses in women's studies. Female students increased in number; in some North American departments, women scholars became regular faculty members, eligible (at last) for tenure and promotion; and the colleges and universities began to approve subjects such as women's history. But the victories were costly, and they remain contested to this day.

Crucial though the contribution of academics was to the development of feminist criminological analyses, other activists contributed with equal force. In fact, much of the original impetus for Western scholars to focus on crime issues came from *outside* university settings, from grassroots movements to help battered women, rape victims and prisoners (Rafter 1990). Participants in these movements would not necessarily have called themselves 'feminists'. [...] As part of the movement to challenge the gender structures of criminology and social control we might even include people whose primary agendas have little to do with feminism – producers of television shows about female cops, for example, and women who have sued to work in men's prisons.[2] Moreover, although we know that on various continents women are campaigning against domestic violence, forced prostitution, political terrorism and other human rights violations, we don't know the degree to which these campaigns are fuelled by feminist concerns (Papanek 1993). Thus 'feminist' may not be a particularly good way to describe efforts by women and their allies to improve the quality of justice. Arguably, 'feminist' trivializes such movements by conceptually reducing them to the concerns of Westerners who identify as feminists.

Moreover, the meaning of 'feminist' is changing. What began as an egalitarian 'women's liberation' movement expanded to include the recognition of gender as a basic element in social structures throughout the world. The goal of feminism broadened to embrace an understanding of how gender shapes verbal interactions, education, identities, organizations and other aspects of culture, such as crime rates, definitions of crime and social control traditions. What began with concern about 'sexism' grew to include the social construction of femininity and enlarged again to include masculinity (Messerschmidt 1993; Newburn and Stanko 1994). Moreover, [...] feminists now investigate how multiple dimensions of power – age, geographical location, race, sexuality, social class and so on – combine with gender to affect human lives. These investigations have fractured the notion of gender, turning it into one of multiple 'femininities' and 'masculinities' [...]. Feminism has rendered problematic concepts whose meanings not long ago seemed self-evident: gangs, Mafia, rape, victims, violence (even 'feminism' itself). It has also challenged the epistemological status of theories of crime.

LATE TWENTIETH-CENTURY CRIMINOLOGY

'Criminology' too is by no means the straightforward term it may first appear. In Italy, […] criminology has long been a 'clinical' speciality. In Eastern Europe, […] criminology was until recently a tool for extolling socialism's 'crime-free' socie-ties. Australian criminology […] continues to be heavily influenced by law and lawyers; the same is true of criminology in some European nations […]. In South Africa […], Great Britain […] and the United States […], the 1970s brought critiques of traditional criminology, variously called 'critical', 'neo-realist', 'progressive realist' or the 'new' criminology. […]

These diversities notwithstanding, it is still possible to generalize about mainstream Western criminology. This academic discipline was ripe for inter-vention and change at the time of its first encounters with feminism. Having flourished in the late nineteenth and early twentieth centuries, by the 1970s the field had become stagnant. Mainstream or official criminology remained insis-tently positivist in its methods, intent on mapping a straightforward world 'out there', dedicated to measuring crime and criminals. Because the vast majority of crimes were committed by men and men constituted over 90 per cent of all prisoners, criminologists felt justified in ignoring women. On the rare occasions on which they mentioned female offenders, they treated women's low crime rates as the phenomenon to be explained. 'It was women's lack of criminality that was seen as the intellectual problem', Robert Connell (1993: x) quips. Men were taken as the norm and women as departures from it: 'deviants from the deviance, so to speak'. Moreover, as Messerschmidt (1993: 15) observes, 'While criminological theory and research have concentrated on men and boys as the normal subjects, the *gendered* man and boy, like women, has been notoriously hidden from criminological history' (emphasis in original). In addition, crimi-nologists slighted the offences most likely to victimize women: domestic violence, incest and rape. Even labelling theorists and critical criminologists, the self-appointed progressives of the 1960s and 1970s, ignored women.

In fact, late twentieth-century mainstream criminology was the most masculine of all the social sciences, a speciality that wore six-shooters on its hips and strutted its machismo. Political science had to acknowledge women because they could vote. The history profession might not welcome women's history, but it could not deny that women had existed in the past. Even law – another highly gendered field – paid more attention to women, perhaps because they constituted more than a tiny fraction of potential cases. But the gatekeepers of criminology and criminal justice apparently assumed that sexism was inherent in their field.

Unpersuaded, three fledgling feminists began questioning criminology's androcentrism (Bertrand 1967; Heidensohn 1968; Klein 1973). Working separately, in three different countries, they none the less raised related issues. What moti-vated Bertrand, Heidensohn and Klein to produce those foundational texts?

Marie-Andrée Bertrand (1994) reports an evolution through the 1960s, from an initial awareness of the sexual double standard in delinquency proceedings, through her Berkeley dissertation critiquing 'the biases of statistics and the sexism of the criminal law', to her more explicitly feminist work of the late 1960s. Dorie Klein (1994) recalls that she was inspired by the student and other liberation movements of the 1960s. Frances Heidensohn began her researches into women and crime in 1965, before she was influenced by American feminism. Initially she was interested in the criminological questions of why female crime rates are lower than male rates; given this, why conventional criminology had not been interested in this topic; and finally, why this lack of interest was so widespread. But all three pioneers were involved as academics in the study of criminology – Klein as a student at Berkeley, Bertrand as a staff member of the University of Montreal while doing her PhD research at Berkeley, Heidensohn as a lecturer at the London School of Economics – and their work reflected growing feminist interests.

By the mid-1970s, several book-length studies of women and crime had been published (Adler 1975; Simon 1975; Smart 1977). It was becoming possible to talk of a feminist criminological agenda. The agenda's authors, moreover, had passed through their pioneering stage and were now entering a second phase, 'consolidating and expressing key ideas more confidently' (Heidensohn 1994: 1013). Developments occurred most swiftly in the United States, where feminists with degrees in criminology or related topics were joining the academy, doing research on women and crime, and developing the first courses in this area. Courses called for texts; collections of articles on women and crime began appearing (Price and Sokoloff 1982; Rafter and Stanko 1982). Publishers, recognizing a new market, added studies of women and crime to their lists. Simultaneously, more women were entering the traditionally male domains of policing, guarding male prisoners and court work, thus providing new data for researchers (e.g. Martin 1980; Zimmer 1986). And a powerful new branch of feminist work, victimological studies, was starting to flourish (e.g. Dobash and Dobash 1979; Russell 1982; Stanko 1985, 1990).

As yet we know next to nothing about the social organization of criminology on an international scale, but research in this area might help us understand the diffusion of feminist ideas in academic criminology as well as variations in their acceptance. How does criminology's location in the academies of various nations encourage or block the acceptance of feminist analyses of crime and social control? In countries where criminology is an adjunct of law or another entrenched discipline […], criminological studies may be relatively weak and feminist criminological studies more marginal still […]. Where criminology is part of a sociology department (as is often the case in the United States), there is apparently more room for it and, within it, for courses in women and/or gender and crime. In sociology departments where there is great demand for crime-related courses (and again this is often true in the United States) gender-related studies may be particularly likely to thrive. We can hypothesize that departments in which students can take a wide range of crime-related courses without restriction are those in which feminist work is most likely to flourish. These matters call for investigation, but it may be that diffusion and receptivity are even more strongly affected by other factors, such as the general strength of feminist movements within a geographical area or linguistic traditions (English being the dominant language of academic feminist criminology).[3]

The long-term health of Western criminology as both an academic speciality and a tool for social improvement may well lie in its willingness to open its boundaries to feminist analyses, postmodernist ideas and interdisciplinary endeavours (Rafter 1990). Academic specialities are always in a state of flux, but today many are experiencing particularly rapid change: new cross-disciplinary fields are emerging and less flexible specializations are becoming backwaters. For some time the most interesting theoretical developments in the understanding of crime and social control have been occurring in other areas: epistemology, gender studies, history, legal theory. In some countries criminology may be able to assimilate (at least partially) the new currents flowing around it; elsewhere it is likely to remain a rock in the stream, impervious to change. In either case, feminist work on crime and social control will probably continue unabated, for its primary aim has always been to improve not criminology but people's lives.

ANALYSING THE IMPACT

Feminist criminological studies have multiplied remarkably over the past two decades, becoming more sophisticated, extending their range and depth, developing new methods and recognizing diverse standpoints. How has this work affected mainstream criminology?

Feminists divide in their answers to this question. A discouraged response has been given by Americans Kathleen Daly and Meda Chesney-Lind (1988: 498), who argue that 'With the exception of feminist treatments of rape and intimate violence', criminology 'remains essentially untouched' by feminist thought. It is true that whereas feminists began their criminological critique with the neglect of women as *offenders*, their greatest achievement has been in developing new theories about and policies for women (and children) as *victims*. But other evidence contradicts Daly and Chesney-Lind's pessimistic conclusion. As they themselves show, by the early 1980s feminists working in Australia, Canada, Great Britain and the United States had raised two central criminological issues. One was the *generalizability problem:* can supposedly gender-neutral explanations of offending apply to women as well as to men, and if not, why not? Today, the burden of explaining why a theory cannot be generalized to both sexes falls on the theorist; to ignore the female case is usually no longer acceptable. The second key issue, which Daly and Chesney-Lind call the *gender ratio problem*, asks why females are less involved than males in nearly every type of criminal behaviour. Feminist work has moved this issue, too, to centre stage in criminological inquiries.

A second and more positive assessment, this one by British sociologist Pat Carlen (1990), holds that feminists' achievements include: putting women on the criminological map; critiquing traditional criminology's essentialist and sexualized view of women; promoting justice campaigns for women and other victims; exploring the possibilities of founding a feminist criminology; challenging the preoccupation with women as offenders; and investigating the potential of feminist jurisprudence. Like Daly and Chesney-Lind (1988), Carlen describes an international endeavour which, while conducted mainly from the English-speaking world, includes Scandinavia and other parts of Europe. Carlen does go on to explore arguments against feminists studying women and crime, but these [...] may be a particularly British concern.

To answer the impact question we might compare feminism's influence with that of some other body of thought that has affected criminology. The most obvious candidate is the critical or 'new' criminology of the 1970s. Both reform efforts have objected to official criminology's claims to neutrality and objectivity; both have presented a new vision of equality and social justice; and both are overtly political. But as the comparison reveals, feminism's impact has been more profound. Feminists have produced a greater volume and range of work; this work has demonstrated greater staying power; and whereas so-called critical criminologists made no mark outside the academy, feminism has transformed criminal justice practices.

Throughout the world, [...] feminists have challenged other's pronouncements about the nature and causes of crime. They have questioned some basic concepts of the discipline and revitalized others. [...] Although much of their work is empirical, feminists have replaced a threadbare positivism – the scientistic belief in objectivity,[4] reliance on unproblematized concepts such as 'race' and 'crime' – with new methodologies. These emphasize the importance of the researcher's standpoint, stress epistemological issues and sometimes merge victimology with criminology [...].

Moreover, feminists have developed a new criminological agenda that includes child abuse, domestic violence, sex and gender offences, fear of crime and the causal role that prior victimization may play in offending. They are researching the involvement of women in social control through studies of policing (Heidensohn 1992), judging (Rush 1993) and prison management (Zimmer 1986; Hawkes 1994). Some feminists are now reconceptualizing the meanings of criminal justice itself: taking a leaf from feminist legal theorists (Minow 1990; Guinier 1994), they are looking for ways to move beyond simplistic either/ors in which one party wins and the other loses, searching instead for third-type solutions that maximize benefits for all and minimize social costs. For example, the emerging battered women's defence (Browne 1987) would give women the right (one men have had for centuries) to choose self-protection as an alternative to tolerating severe physical abuse or facing homicide charges. The interest in developing new conceptions of justice is evident as well in studies of sentencing leniency for 'familied' defendants (Daly 1987) and arguments for differential sentencing of defendants with dependent children (Rafter 1989). [...]

INTERNATIONAL DEVELOPMENTS

Domestic violence, sexual abuse, rape – these issues cut across national boundaries. Sharing fears of male violence, women around the globe are already bound by strong ties. But recent years have witnessed an internationalization of women's concerns about crime and justice. More than a recognition and acknowledgement of mutual interests, this phenomenon is self-consciously feminist. And it aims explicitly at creating transnational and transcultural alliances that will respect diversity.

One factor encouraging globalization is the collapse of old political orders in Eastern Europe [...], the Balkans and South Africa [...]. In country after country, patriarchal regimes that silenced dissent have been overthrown. Out of the rubble are emerging a host of new minorities – ethnic, feminist, nationalist – contending for participation in the new regimes. Internationalization has also been fostered by the trend toward postmodernism – the fragmentation of old explanatory structures and acceptance of multiple perspectives. Interest in discourses, identities, representations: these facets of postmodernist thought have all contributed to a renewed interest in the origins and effects of cultural difference. Globalization has been further promoted by the simple fact that, throughout the world, feminists and their allies have entered work in criminology and criminal justice, creating a critical mass capable of giving voice to women's concerns. Throughout the world we now find crusades against domestic violence and other forms of victimization of women. Participants in these movements now constitute an international audience for information on gender, crime and social control.

Much as international conferences solidified the global women's movement during the 1980s, a conference on Women, Law and Social Control drew feminists together in the early 1990s, internationalizing concerns about crime and justice. Held at Mont Gabriel, Quebec, in 1991 and organized by an international team,[5] the meeting brought together over sixty delegates from eighteen countries (Bertrand et al., 1992). Follow-up meetings were held at the 1993 British Criminology Conference in Wales and the 1994 American Society of Criminology meeting in Miami. Facilitating the exchange of feminist concerns and agendas across national lines, the conferences also challenged assumptions of an uncomplicated, uniform 'sisterhood'.

COMMON THEMES AND FUTURE DIRECTIONS

[...] Within academic criminology, what can we expect in the years ahead? [...] [T]hree issues will be particularly important. First, *is a 'feminist criminology' possible or rather a contradiction in terms*? This question is raised in part by feminists' mistrust of positivism and of state crime control programmes, which all too often have been thinly disguised women control programmes. The question stems as well from current feminist efforts to keep gender on a par with other aspects of social location and experience, such as race and sexuality. If we aim at 'feminist criminology', are we not giving preference to gender over other dimensions of power? Why not instead label our goal 'anti-racist' or even 'multicultural' criminology? In fact, few feminists would be surprised or distressed if their project lost its current identity by spilling over into others. Inclusiveness has long been a feminist goal, one actively advanced by insistence on the embrace of multiple standpoints and the value of crossing boundaries. [...]

Second, *in the years ahead how will feminists deal with the anglo- and ethnocentrism of current work on crime and justice?* For historical and economic reasons, feminism and criminology are both strongest in Western nations, particularly English-speaking countries (Margolis 1993). As a result, problems have tended to be stated in anglocentric and ethnocentric terms. In other parts of the world women often face more serious crime and justice problems, including genital mutilation and widespread sexual slavery. In some places conditions for women are deteriorating [...] owing to cutbacks in welfare services and the growth of inequality and violence. In theory at least, white Westerners seek a more heterogeneous feminism and would welcome a decentring of their own traditions. But the alternatives are not yet clear, especially as sex-equality movements elsewhere are often weaker and more fragmented (Margolis 1993). What directions will or should feminist efforts in criminology take in future?

Third, in the years ahead feminists will have to confront the question: *to what degree are criminology and crime control policies implicated in the construction of hierarchies based on gender, race, class and sexuality?* Traditional criminology has mainly asked how to achieve crime control. Feminists have asked how crime control achieves gender – how control systems contribute to the maintenance of 'female' as inferiority. And feminists have tended to view criminology itself as a tool for reinforcing inequality. [...] Continuing to turn positivism on its head, feminists will doubtless continue to explore how criminology and crime control policies contribute to and reinforce structures of power and hegemony.

These are difficult questions – harder than many posed by mainstream criminologists. They demonstrate the conflicts and contradictions, the differences and divergences that characterize contemporary feminisms. But they also illustrate the magnitude of the feminist criminological enterprise. Ultimately, this is a project of self-obsolescence, for if the discipline were engendered and crime control policy transformed as feminists recommend, they could retire from the field. But then, the field itself as we now know it would no longer exist.

NOTES

1   For more on the criminological history and significance of the sex–gender distinction, see Heidensohn (1994: 997–8) and Messerschmidt (1995: ch. 10). However, the sex–gender distinction is being challenged.
2   Zimmer (1986) discovered that US women who sued and otherwise struggled to be hired as guards in men's prisons did so primarily because the jobs offered convenience and/or good pay, not out of a sense of feminist mission.
3   Piers Beirne and Jim Messerschmidt contributed ideas to this discussion of diffusion and receptivity.
4   For a critique of the myth of objectivity, see Daly and Chesney-Lind (1988). Feminists are certainly not monolithic in their attitudes towards objectivity, however.
5   The Mont Gabriel conference on Women, Law and Social Control was organized by French-Canadian Marie-Andrée Bertrand and two Americans, Kathleen Daly and Dorie Klein.

REFERENCES

Adler, F. (1975) *Sisters in Crime*. New York: McGraw-Hill.

Beauvoir, S. de (1952) *The Second Sex*. New York: Knopf.

Bertrand, M. (1967) The myth of sexual equality before the law. In *Proceedings of the Fifth Research Conference on Delinquency and Criminality*. Montreal: Quebec Society of Criminology.

Bertrand, M. (1994) Information about my own history. Memorandum to Nicole Hahn Rafter of 11 April.

Bertrand, M., Daly, K. and Klein, D. (eds) (1992) *Proceedings of the International Feminist Conference on Women, Law, and Social Control*. Mont Gabriel, Quebec, 18–21 July 1991.

Browne, A. (1987) *When Battered Women Kill*. New York: Free Press.

Carlen, P. (1990) Women, crime, feminism and realism. *Social Justice*, 17 (4), 100–23.

Connell, R.W. (1993) Foreword to J.W. Messerschmidt, *Masculinities and Crime*. Lanham, MD: Rowman and Littlefield.

Daly, K. (1987) Discrimination in the criminal courts: family, gender, and the problem of equal treatment. *Social Forces*, 66 (1), 152–75.

Daly, K. and Chesney-Lind, M. (1988) Feminism and criminology, *Justice Quarterly*, 5 (4), 497–535.

Dobash, R.E. and Dobash, R.P. (1979) *Violence against Wives: A Case against Patriarchy*. New York: Free Press.

Freidan, B. (1963) *The Feminine Mystique*. New York: Norton.

Guinier, L. (1994) *Fundamental Fairness in Representative Democracy*. New York: Free Press.

Hawkes, M.Q. (1994) *Excellent Effect: The Edna Mahan Story*. Laurel Lakes, MD: American Correctional Association.

Heidensohn, F.M. (1968) The deviance of women: a critique and an enquiry. *British Journal of Sociology*, 19 (2), 160–75.

Heidensohn, F.M. (1992) *Women in Control? The Role of Women in Law Enforcement*. Oxford: Oxford University Press.

Heidensohn, F.M. (1994) Gender and crime. In M. Maguire, R. Morgan and R. Reiner (eds) *The Oxford Handbook of Criminology*. Oxford: Clarendon Press.

Klein, D. (1973) The etiology of female crime: a review of the literature. *Issues in Criminology*, 8 (2), 3–30.

Klein, D. (1994) Twenty years ago ... today. In B. Price and N. Sokoloff (eds) *The Criminal Justice System and Women*, 2nd edn. New York: McGraw-Hill.

Kranz, H. (1936) Lelenschicksale Kriminiller, Berlin: Springer Verlag.

Margolis, D.R. (1993) Women's movements around the world: cross-cultural comparisons. *Gender and Society*, 7 (3), 379–99.

Martin, S.E. (1980) *Breaking and Entering: Policewomen on Patrol*. Berkeley: University of California Press.

Messerschmidt, J.W. (1993) *Masculinities and Crime*. Lanham, MD: Rowman and Littlefield.

Messerschmidt, J.W. (1995) 'From patriarchy to gender: feminist theory, criminology and the challenge of diversity' pp. 167–88. In N.H. Rafter and F. Heidensohn (eds) *International Feminist Perspectives in Criminology: Engendering a Discipline*. Buckingham: Open University Press.

Millet, K. (1970) *Sexual Politics*. New York: Doubleday.

Minow, M. (1990) *Making All the Difference: Inclusion, Exclusion, and American Law*. Ithaca, NY: Cornell University Press.

Newburn, T. and Stanko, E. (1994) *Just Boys Doing Business?* London: Routledge.

Papanek, H. (1993) Theorizing about women's movements globally: comment on Diane Margolis. *Gender and Society*, 7 (4), 594–604.

Price, B.R. and Sokoloff, N.J. (eds) (1982) *The Criminal Justice System and Women.* New York: Clark Boardman Company.

Rafter, N. (1989) Gender and justice: the equal protection issue. In L. Goodstein and D.L. MacKenzie (eds) *The American Prison: Issues in Research and Policy.* New York: Plenum.

Rafter, N. (1990) The social construction of crime and crime control. *Journal of Research in Crime and Delinquency*, 27 (4), 376–89.

Rafter, N. and Stanko, E.A. (1982) *Judge, Lawyer, Victim, Thief: Women, Gender Roles, and Criminal Justice.* Boston: Northeastern University Press.

Rush, S.E. (1993) Feminist judging: an introductory essay. *Southern California Review of Law and Women's Studies*, 2 (2), 609–32.

Russell, D.E.H. (1982) *Rape in Marriage.* New York: Macmillan.

Simon, R.J. (1975) *The Contemporary Woman and Crime.* Rockville, MD: National Institute on Mental Health.

Smart, C. (1977) *Women, Crime and Criminology.* London: Routledge and Kegan Paul.

Stanko, E. (1985) *Intimate Instrusions: Women's Experience of Male Violence.* London: Routledge and Kegan Paul.

Stanko, E. (1990) *Everyday Violence.* London: Pandora.

Zimmer, L. (1986) *Women Guarding Men.* Chicago: University of Chicago Press.

STUDY QUESTIONS

1 In your own words, detail the ways in which academic feminism has offered a challenge to Western academic criminology? In your answer, refer to political, substantive and methodological critiques.

2 Rafter and Heidensohn argue that the primary aim of feminist work on crime and social control 'has always been to improve not criminology but people's lives'. From your reading of this piece, what examples of this can you identify? Look back to Reading 4 by Young and consider the similarities and differences between feminism and realism which also grounds its research and analysis in experience, practice and policy?

3 What are the challenges for academic feminist criminology in the twenty-first century?

4 Many different theoretical approaches have been considered in this Part I. Using a large piece of paper, see if you can represent the historical development of these ideas pictorially or diagrammatically, indicating influences and overlaps between theories. Also consider the relationship between 'theory' and other explanations of crime and deviance in society: i.e. lay, media and political discourses.

FURTHER READING

The whole of the book from which the above extract is taken is worth reading both for its global focus and its attention to the politics of gender and other issues of difference: Hahn Rafter, N. and Heidensohn, F. (eds) (1995) *International Feminist Perspectives in Criminology*, Buckingham: Open University Press. Furthermore, Heidensohn, F. (2000) *Sexual Politics and Social Control*, Buckingham: Open University Press, considers contemporary concerns of gender, law and order; and Naffine, N. (1997) *Feminism and Criminology*, Cambridge: Polity Press, provides an historical review of the history of criminology and argues that, historically, gender has been considered as a specialist topic rather being integral to analyses of crime. Both Walklate, S. (1995) *Gender and Crime: An Introduction*, Hemel Hempstead: Prentice-Hall/Harvester; and Heidensohn, F. (1996) *Women and Crime*, 2nd edn, Hampshire and London: Macmillan, focus on theories and issues relevant to the study of women within the criminal justice system; and Gelsthorpe, L. and Morris, A. (eds) (1990) *Feminist Perspectives in Criminology*, Milton Keynes: Open University Press, is interesting because of its focus on issues of theory, method and epistemology and because of the links made between these issues and empirical research and policy.

Part Two:

'Mythologies' of Crime

The key themes unifying all the readings in Part II are that crime is a constructed concept and that some crimes remain virtually invisible due to their absences from 'official' sources. The part thus explores the myths, stereotypes and misrepresentations about criminal behaviour that circulate and self-perpetuate to create a universal picture of the 'problem' of crime. Steven Box (Reading 7) provides a useful introduction to social, organizational and ideological constructions of crime, and is followed by a series of readings which pick up and develop this theme in relation to a variety of representations of crime. Clive Coleman and Jenny Moynihan (Reading 8) discuss the problems inherent in statistical measurements, and introduce the notion of the 'dark figure of crime', implying that our knowledge of crime and criminality gained from official statistics is simply the tip of the iceberg, and that there is a much larger component that is hidden from view. One element of this invisible expanse of criminal activity is the offences committed by companies and institutions, which Gary Slapper and Steve Tombs argue (Reading 9) is far more dangerous and costly than crimes committed by 'conventional' offenders. As they point out, it is not just that much corporate crime is missing from official statistics. The problem of public ignorance is also compounded by a mass media that plays down or ignores the crimes of the powerful, while over-reporting the offences of those sections of society who don't have a voice or who are already marginalized. David Kidd-Hewitt (Reading 10) continues to explore the ways in which media representations inform and misinform the public about the 'picture' of crime, but highlights the contributions that academics have made to our understanding of crime reporting and notions of 'newsworthiness' in relation to crime. Following this, we have included an extract from *Folk Devils and Moral Panics* by Stanley Cohen (Reading 11), which many readers will be familiar with (so frequently referenced is it) but few may have actually read. 'Moral panics', the concept made famous by Cohen, underpins Reading, 12 by Jenny Kitzinger, although she questions its usefulness and universal applicability in relation to serious issues such as the presence of paedophiles in the community. In Reading 13, Ian Taylor explores – and explodes – some of the myths surrounding drug use, arguing that rather than assuming that drugs are at the margins of young people's everyday lives, it should be recognized that they are an integral and omnipresent component of the leisure and pleasure activities of large numbers of people in Britain. In summary, our aim as you read through Part II is to encourage you to question authorized representations of criminal activity and recognize the importance of deconstructing officially recorded figures, media representations and received wisdom concerning the 'problem' of crime.

7

Crime, power and ideological mystification

Steven Box

To open this part on 'mythologies' of crime, Steven Box examines the relationship between the 'official' picture of criminal behaviour and public fears about it. In an incisive and thought-provoking reading, he argues that politicians, the media and the criminal justice system set the agendas for debate about crime and the implementation of criminal justice. These agendas then shape public perceptions about the types and levels of criminal activity and the likelihood of being a victim of crime. Box suggests that the picture of crime that the public receives is manipulated by those in power, and that there is an over-concentration on the crimes of the young, the black, the working-class and the unemployed, and an under-awareness of the crimes of the well- educated upper and middle classes, the socially privileged and those in power. In a critical examination using two different theoretical approaches – liberal scientism (which shares with 'labelling' a theoretical foundation in the approach known as 'interactionism': see Readings 2 and 3) and radical reflexive ness (a 'structuralist' perspective similar in theoretical origin to Marxism: see Reading 2) – Box 'deconstructs' the problem of crime. He analyses the processes by which the public receives information about crime, and concludes that criminal justice is determined by very narrow legal definitions that tolerate, accept or even applaud the crimes of the privileged, while criminalizing the disadvantaged. Crime may thus be described as an *ideological construct*; it protects the powerful and further marginalizes the powerless. Box thus provides us with a useful overview of the problems associated with seeing the problem of crime through the eyes of those in power, a theme which is developed throughout the readings in the rest of this part.

SOURCE: From *Power, Crime, and Mystification* (London: Routledge, 1983), 1–15.

Murder! Rape! Robbery! Assault! Wounding! Theft! Burglary! Arson! Vandalism! These form the substance of the annual official criminal statistics on indictable offences (or the Crime Index offences in America). Aggregated, they constitute the major part of 'our' crime problem. Or at least, we are told so daily by politicians, police, judges, and journalists who speak to us through the media of newspapers and television. And most of us listen. We don't want to be murdered, raped, robbed, assaulted, or criminally victimized in any other way. Reassured that our political leaders are both aware of the problem's growing dimensions and receptive to our rising anxieties, we wait in optimistic but realistic anticipation for crime to be at least effectively reduced. But apart from the number of police rapidly increasing, their technological and quasi-military capacities shamelessly strengthened, their discretionary powers of apprehension, interrogation, detention, and arrest liberally extended, and new prisons built or old ones extensively refurbished (all with money the government claims the country has not got to maintain existing standards of education, health, unemployment welfare, and social services), nothing much justifies the optimism.

The number of recorded serious crimes marches forever upward. During the decade 1970–80, serious crimes recorded by the police increased for nearly every category: violence against the person rose by 136 per cent, burglary by 44 per cent, robbery by 138 per cent, theft and handling by 54 per cent and fraud and forgery by 18 per cent. These increases were not merely artefacts of an increased population available to commit serious crimes. For even when the changing population size is controlled statistically, crimes continue to rise. Thus in 1950, there were 1,094 per 100,000 population. This rose to 1,742 by 1960, then to 3,221 by 1970, and reached 5,119 by 1980. From 1980 to 1981 they rose a further 10 per cent, to reach an all-time record. Ironically, as 'our' crime problem gets worse, the demand for even more 'law and order' policies increases, even though these are blatantly having no effect on the level of serious crimes. At least not on the level recorded by the police.

The result, so we are told, is that the 'fear of crime' has now been elevated into a national problem. Techniques for avoiding victimization have become a serious preoccupation: more locks on doors and windows, fewer visits after dark to family, friends, and places of entertainment, avoidance of underground and empty train carriages, mace sprays or personal alarm sirens held nervously in coat pockets, a growing unwillingness to be neighbourly or engage in local collective enterprises, furtive suspicious glances at any stranger, and attempts to avoid any encounter except with the most trusted and close friends.

Who are these 'villains' driving us into a state of national agoraphobia? We are told a fairly accurate and terrifying glimpse can be obtained of 'our' Public Enemies by examining the convicted and imprisoned population. For every 100 persons convicted of these serious crimes, 85 are male. Amongst this convicted male population, those aged less than 30 years, and particularly those aged between 15 and 21 years are over-represented. Similarly, the educational non-achievers are over-represented – at the other end of the educational achievement ladder there appear to be hardly any criminals, since only 0.05 per cent of people received into prison have obtained a university degree. The unemployed are currently only (*sic*) 14 per cent of the available labour force, but they constitute approximately 40 per cent of those convicted. Only 4 per cent of the general population are black, but nearly one-third of the convicted and imprisoned population are black. Urban dwellers, particularly inner-city residents, are over-represented. Thus the typical people criminally victimizing and forcing us to fear each other and fracture our sense of 'community' are young uneducated males, who are often unemployed, live in a working-class impoverished neighbourhood, and frequently belong to an ethnic minority. These villains deserve, so 'law and order' campaigners tell us ceaselessly in their strident moral rhetoric, either short, sharp, shock treatment, including death by hanging or castration by chemotherapy – 'off with their goolies' – or long, endless, self-destroying stretches as non-paying guests in crumbling, insanitary, overcrowded prisons constructed for the redemption of lost Christian souls by our Victorian ancestors. If only these ideas were pursued vigorously and with a vengeance morally justified by the offender's wickedness, then 'our' society would be relatively crime-free and tranquil. So 'law and order' campaigners tell us.

It is tempting to call all this hype – but that would be extreme! 'Conventional' crimes do have victims whose suffering is real; steps should be taken to understand and control these crimes so that fewer and fewer people are victimized. A radical criminology which appears to deny this will be seen as callous and rightly rejected. Furthermore, those crimes so carefully recorded and graphed in official criminal statistics *are* more likely to be committed by young males, living in poor neighbourhoods and so on. A radical criminology which appears to deny this will be seen as naive and rightly rejected. Finally, there are very good grounds for believing that the rising crime wave is real – material conditions for large sections of the community have deteriorated markedly. A radical criminology which remained insensitive of this would be guilty of forgetting its theoretical roots and rightly rejected. So the official portrait of crime and criminals is not entirely without merit or truth.

None the less, before galloping off down the 'law and order' campaign trail, it might be prudent to consider whether murder, rape, robbery, assault, and other crimes focused on by state officials, politicians, the media, and the criminal justice system do constitute the major part of our real crime problem. Maybe they are only *a* crime problem and not *the* crime problem. Maybe what is stuffed into our consciousness as *the* crime problem is in fact an illusion, a trick to deflect our attention away from other, even more serious crimes and victimizing behaviours, which objectively cause the vast bulk of avoidable death, injury, and deprivation.

At the same time, it might be prudent to compare persons who commit other serious but under-emphasized crimes and victimizing behaviours with those who are officially portrayed as 'our' criminal enemies. For if the former, compared to the latter, are indeed quite different types of people, then maybe we should stop looking to our political authorities and criminal justice system for protection from those beneath us in impoverished urban neighbourhoods. Instead maybe we should look up accusingly at our political and judicial 'superiors' for being or for protecting the 'real' culprits.

If we do this, we might also cast a jaundiced eye at the view that serious criminals are 'pathological'. This has been the favourite explanatory imagery of mainstream positivistic criminology. It was, however, an explanation that only remained plausible if crimes were indeed committed by a minority of individuals living in conditions of relative deprivation. For whilst this was true it was obvious, at least to the conservative mind, that 'something must be wrong with them'. However, if we look up rather than down the stratification hierarchy and see serious crimes being committed by the people who are respectable, well-educated, wealthy, and socially privileged then the imagery of pathology seems harder to accept. If these upper- and middle-class criminals are also pathological, then what hope is there for any of us! Wanting to avoid this pessimistic conclusion, we might instead entertain the idea that these powerful persons commit crimes for 'rational' – albeit disreputable – motives which emerge under conditions that render conformity a relatively unrewarding activity. Having rescued the powerful from 'abnormality' we might do the same for the powerless. Maybe they too are rational rather than irrational, morally disreputable rather than organically abnormal, overwhelmed by adversity rather than by wickedness.

If these are the lessons of prudence, then standing back from the official portrait of crime and criminals and looking at it critically might be a very beneficial move towards getting our heads straight.

However, there is an agonizing choice to make between at least two pairs of spectacles we might wear to take this critical look. We could wear the liberal 'scientific' pair, as did many young trendy academics during the 1960s and early 1970s when the stars of interactionism and phenomenology were in the ascendant. Or we might wear the radical 'reflexive' pair, whose lenses have been recently polished to a fine smoothness by those same trendy academics who have now entered a middle-age period of intellectual enlightenment! These spectacles do provide quite different views on the official portrait of crime and criminals.

LIBERAL 'SCIENTISM': PARTIALLY BLIND JUSTICE

One way of getting a clear perspective on those crimes and criminals causing us most harm, injury, and deprivation is to excavate unreported, unrecorded, and non-prosecuted crimes. This can be achieved by sifting evidence from numerous self-reported crime studies and criminal victimization surveys. This is undoubtedly an important exercise for it leads us to reconsider the *validity* of official criminal statistics and the more extreme pronouncements made directly and uncritically from them.

What lessons are there to be learnt from the results of these surveys? First, there is much more serious crime being committed than the official police records indicate. The emerging consensus is that one serious crime in three (excluding burglary and car theft) is reported to the police. This knowledge can and does add fuel to the alarmist 'law and order' fire: 'it's even worse than we imagined!' Second, although the official portrait of criminals is not untrue, it is inaccurate. It is more like a distorting mirror; you immediately recognize yourself, but not quite in a flattering shape and form familiar to you. Thus self-report data indicate that serious crimes are disproportionately committed by the young uneducated males amongst whom the unemployed and ethnically oppressed are over-represented, but the contribution they make is less than the official data imply. There are, it appears, more serious crimes being committed by white, respectable, well-educated, slightly older males and females than we are led to believe (Box 1981a: 56–93).

To the liberal 'scientific' mind, there are two problems here of 'slippage', one more slight than the other. Too many people fail to report crimes because they consider the police inefficient; we need to restore police efficiency in order to increase the reportage rate and hence obtain a better more reliable gauge of crime. The second, more important slippage, is that the administration of criminal justice is fine in principle, but is failing slightly in practice. The police pursue policies of *differential deployment* (for example, swamping certain parts of London where the West Indian population is prominent) and *'methodological suspicion'*(that is, routinely suspecting only a limited proportion of the population, particularly those with criminal records or known criminal associates). Coupled with these practices are *plea-bargaining* (negotiating a guilty plea in return for being charged with a less serious offence) and *'judicious' judicial decisions* (which take as much notice of who you are as they do of what you have apparently done). In other words, the police, magistrates, judges, and other court officials have too much discretion. The result is too much 'street-justice', 'charge-dealing', 'plea-bargaining', and 'disparate sentencing'. In these judicial negotiations and compromises, the wealthy, privileged, and powerful are better able to secure favourable outcomes than their less powerful counterparts (Box 1981a: 157–207). This slippage between ideal and practice reveals a slightly disturbing picture. The process of law enforcement, in its broadest possible interpretation, operates in such a way as to *conceal* crimes of the powerful against the powerless, but to *reveal* and *exaggerate* crimes of the powerless against 'everyone'.

Furthermore, because a substantial section of this criminalized population is stigmatized and discriminated against, particularly in the field of employment, its reproduction is secured; many of them, out of resentment, injustice, or desperation, turn to more persistent and even more serious forms of crime. This vicious circle increases the over-representation of the powerless in the highly publicized 'hardened' criminal prisoner population.

The outcome of these processes is that the official portrait of crime and criminals is highly selective, serving to conceal crimes of the powerful and hence shore up their interests, particularly the need to be legitimated through maintaining the appearance of respectability. At the same time, crimes of the powerless are revealed and exaggerated, and this serves the interests of the powerful because it legitimizes their control agencies, such as the police and prison service, being strengthened materially, technologically, and legally, so that their ability to survey, harass, deter, both specifically and generally, actual and potential resisters to political authority is enhanced.

To the liberal 'scientific' mind, a solution of this second and more important slippage would involve a strict limitation on police and judicial discretion and less stigmatizaion either by decriminalizing some behaviours, or imposing less incarceration (Schur 1973). The adoption of these policies would narrow the 'official' differential in criminal behaviour between the disreputable poor and the respectable middle-class so that it approximated more closely the actual differences in criminal behaviour – at least criminal behaviour as defined by the state.

RADICAL 'REFLEXIVENESS': ARTFUL CRIMINAL DEFINITIONS

Although an enormous amount of carefully buried crime can be unearthed by this liberal 'scientific' excavation work, we will still be denied an adequate view of those whose crimes and victimizing behaviours cause us most harm, injury, and deprivation.

Through radical 'reflexive' spectacles, all this excavation work occurs so late in the process of constructing crime and criminals that it never gets to the foundations. Those committed to self-report and victimization surveys do not start off asking the most important question of all: 'what is serious crime?' Instead they take serious crime as a pre- and state-defined phenomenon. But by the time crime categories or definitions have been established, the most important foundation stone of 'our crime problem' has been well and truly buried in cement, beyond the reach of any liberal 'scientific' shovel.

Aware that liberal 'scientists' arrive too late on the scene, radicals resolve to get up earlier in the morning. Instead of merely examining how the law enforcement process in its broadest sense constructs a false image of serious crime and its perpetrators, they suggest we should consider the *social construction of criminal law categories*. This involves not only reflecting on why certain types of behaviours are defined as criminal in some historical periods and not others, but also why a particular criminal law comes to incorporate from relatively homogeneous behaviour patterns only a portion and exclude the remainder, even though each and every instance of this behaviour causes avoidable harm, injury, or deprivation.

Some sociologists have pondered these issues and come to the conclusion that *criminal law categories are ideological constructs* (Sumner 1976). Rather than being a fair reflection of those behaviours objectively causing us collectively the most avoidable suffering, criminal law categories are artful, creative constructs designed to criminalize only some victimizing behaviours, usually those more frequently committed by the relatively powerless, and to exclude others, usually those frequently committed by the powerful against subordinates.

Numerous researchers (Chambliss 1964; Duster 1970; Graham 1972; Gunningham 1974; Hall 1952; Haskins 1960; Hay 1975; Hopkins 1978; McCaghy and Denisoff 1973; Platt 1969; Thompson 1975) have produced evidence consistent with the view that criminal law categories are ideological reflections of the interests of particular powerful groups. As such, criminal law categories are resources, tools, instruments, designed and then used to criminalize, demoralize, incapacitate, fracture and sometimes eliminate those problem populations perceived by the powerful to be potentially or actually threatening the existing distribution of power, wealth, and privilege. They constitute one, and only one way by which social control over subordinate, but 'resisting', populations is exercised. For once behaviour more typically engaged in by subordinate populations has been incorporated into criminal law, then legally sanctioned punishments can be 'justifiably' imposed.

In a society such as ours, populations more likely to be controlled in part through criminalization:

> tend to share a number of social characteristics but most important among these is the fact that their behaviour, personal qualities, and/or position threaten the social relationships of production.... In other words, populations become generally eligible for management as deviant when they disturb, hinder, or call into question ... capitalist modes of appropriating the product of human labour ... the social conditions under which capitalist production takes place ... patterns of distribution and consumption ... the process of socializaion for productive and non-productive roles ... and ... the ideology which supports the functioning of capitalist society. (Spitzer 1975: 642)

However, this argument needs qualification. It does not maintain that all criminal laws directly express the interests of one particular group, such as the ruling class. Clearly some legislation reflects temporary victories of one interest or allied interest groups over others, and none of these may necessarily be identical or coincide with the interests of the ruling class. Yet the above argument does not demand or predict that every criminal law directly represents the interests of the ruling class. It recognizes that some laws are passed purely as symbolic victories which the dominant class grants to inferior interest groups, basically to keep them quiet; once passed, they need never be efficiently or systematically enforced. It also recognizes that occasionally the ruling class is forced into a tactical retreat by organized subordinate groups, and the resulting shifts in criminal law enshrine a broader spectrum of interests. But these victories are short lived. Powerful groups have ways and means of clawing back the spoils of tactical defeats. In the last instance, definitions of crime reflect the interests of those groups who comprise the ruling class. This is not to assume that these interests are homogeneous and without serious contradictions (Chambliss 1981). Indeed, it is just the space between these contradictions that subordinate groups fill with their demands for legal change.

It might be objected that even though *some* criminal laws are in the interests of the dominant class and that others which are obviously not in these interests are ineffectively enforced, thus making them dead-letter laws, it still remains true that laws proscribing those types of victimizing behaviours of which we are all too aware and which set the nerve-ends of neo-classical/conservative criminologists, such as Wilson (1975) and Morgan (1978) tingling with fear and loathing, *are in all our interests*. None of us wants to be murdered, raped, or robbed; none of us wants our property stolen, smashed, or destroyed, none of us wants our bodies punched, kicked, bitten, or tortured. In that sense, criminal law against murder, rape, arson, robbery, theft, and assault are in all our interests, since in principle we all benefit equally from and are protected by their existence. Without them life would be 'nasty, poor, solitary, brutish, and short'.

This is all true, but it is not all the truth. For some groups of people benefit more than others from these laws. It is not that they are less likely to be murdered, raped, robbed, or assaulted – although the best scientific evidence based on victimization surveys shows this to be true (Hindelang et al. 1978) – but that in the criminal law, definitions of murder, rape, robbery, assault, theft, and other serious crimes are so constructed as to exclude many similar, and in important respects, identical acts, and these are just the acts likely to be commited more frequently by powerful individuals.

Thus the criminal law defines only some types of avoidable killing as murder: it excludes, for example, deaths resulting from acts of negligence, such as employers' failure to maintain safe working conditions in factories and mines (Swartz 1975); or deaths resulting from an organization's reluctance to maintain appropriate safety standards (Erickson 1976); or deaths which result from governmental agencies giving environmental health risks a low priority (Liazos 1972); or deaths resulting from drug manufacturers' failure to conduct adequate research on new chemical compounds before embarking on aggressive marketing campaigns (Silverman and Lee 1974); or deaths from a dangerous drug that was approved by health authorities on the strength of a bribe from a pharmaceutical company (Braithwaite and Geis 1981); or deaths resulting from car manufacturers refusing to recall and repair thousands of known defective vehicles because they calculate that the costs of meeting civil damages will be less (Swigert and Farrell 1981); and in most jurisdictions deaths resulting from drunken or reckless people driving cars with total indifference to the potential cost in terms of human lives are also excluded.

The list of avoidable killings not legally construed as murder even in principle could go on and on. But the point should be clear. We are encouraged to see murder as a particular act involving a very limited range of stereotypical actors, instruments, situations, and motives. Other types of avoidable killing are either defined as a less serious crime than murder, or as matters more appropriate for administrative or civil proceedings, or as events beyond the justifiable boundaries of state interference. In all instances, the perpetrators of these avoidable 'killings' deserve, so we are told, less harsh community responses than would be made to those committing legally defined murder. The majority of people accept this because the state, by excluding these killings from the murder category, has signified its intention that we should not treat them as capital offenders. As the state can muster a galaxy of skilled machiavellian orators to defend its definitions, and has, beyond these velvet tongues, the iron fist of police and military physical violence, it is able to persuade most people easily and convincingly.

It may be just a strange coincidence, as Vonnegut often suggests, that the social characteristics of those persons more likely to commit these types of avoidable killings differ considerably to those possessed by individuals more likely to commit killings legally construed in principle as murder. That the former are more likely to be relatively more powerful, wealthy, and privileged than the latter could be one of nature's accidents. But is it likely?

The criminal law sees only some types of property deprivation as robbery or theft; it excludes, for example, the separation of consumers and part of their money that follows manufacturers' malpractices or advertisers' misrepresentations; it excludes shareholders losing their money because managers behaved in ways which they thought would be to the advantage of shareholders even though the only tangible benefits accrued to the managers (Hopkins 1980); it excludes the *extra* tax citizens, in this or other countries, have to pay because: (i) corporations and the very wealthy are able to employ financial experts at discovering legal loopholes through which money can be safely transported to tax havens; (ii) Defence Department officials have been bribed to order more expensive weaponry systems or missiles in 'excess' of those 'needed'; (iii) multinational drug companies charge our National Health Services prices which are estimated to be at least £50 millions in excess of alternative supplies. If an employee's hand slips into the governor's pocket and removes any spare cash, that is theft; if the governor puts his hand into employees' pockets and takes their spare cash, i.e. reduces wages, even below the legal minimum, that is the labour market operating reasonably. To end the list prematurely and clarify the point, the law of theft includes, in the words of that anonymous poet particularly loved by teachers of 'A' level economic history, 'the man or woman who steals the goose from off the common, but leaves the greater villain loose who steals the common from the goose'.

The criminal law excludes most sexual acts achieved by fraud, deceit, or misrepresentation – thus a man may pose as a psychiatrist and prescribe sexual intercourse as therapy to a 'gullible female', because he knows the law will regard this as acceptable seduction rather than rape; it excludes men who use economic, organizational, or social power rather than actual or threatened force to overcome an unwilling but subordinate, and therefore vulnerable female; it excludes the forced insertion of any other instrument, no matter how sharp or dangerous. Thus out of a whole range of 'sexual' acts where the balance of consent versus coercion is at least ambiguous, the criminal law draws a line demarcating those where physical force is used or threatened from those where any other kind of power is utilized to overcome a female's resistance. The outcome is that men who have few resources other than physical ones are more likely to commit legally defined rape, whilst those men who possess a whole range of resources from economic patronage to cultural charm are likely to be viewed by the law as 'real men' practising their primeval arts – and that is something the majesty of the law should leave alone!

The criminal law defines only some types of violence as criminal assault; it excludes verbal assaults that can, and sometimes do, break a person's spirit; it excludes forms of assault whose injuries become apparent years later, such as those resulting from working in a polluted factory environment where the health risk was known to the employer but concealed from the employee

(Swartz 1975); it excludes 'compulsory' drug-therapy or electric-shock treatment given to 'mentally disturbed' patients or prisoners who are denied the civilized rights to refuse such beneficial medical help (Mitford 1977; Szasz 1970, 1977a, b); it excludes chemotherapy prescribed to control 'naughty' schoolboys, but includes physically hitting teachers (Box 1981b; Schrag and Divoky 1981).

The criminal law includes and reflects our proper stance against 'murderous' acts of terrorism conducted by people who are usually exploited or oppressed by forces of occupation. But it had no relevance, and its guardians remained mute ten years ago, when bombs, with the United States' and allied governments' blessing, fell like rain on women and children in Cambodia (Shawcross 1979), or when the same governments aid and support other political/military regimes exercising mass terror and partial genocide against a subjugated people (Chomsky and Herman 1979a, b). The criminal law, in other words, condemns the importation of murderous terrorist acts usually against powerful individuals or strategic institutions, but goes all quiet when governments export or support avoidable acts of killing usually against the underdeveloped countries' poor. Of course there are exceptions – the Russian 'invasion' of Afghanistan was a violation of international law and a crime against humanity. It may well have been, but what about Western governments' involvement in Vietnam, Laos, Cambodia, Chile, El Salvador, Nicaragua, Suez, and Northern Ireland? Shouldn't they at least be discussed within the same context of international law and crimes against humanity? And if not, why not?

Thus criminal laws against murder, rape, robbery, and assault do protect us all, but they do not protect us all equally. They do not protect the less powerful from being killed, sexually exploited, deprived of what little property they possess, or physically and psychologically damaged through the greed, apathy, negligence, indifference, and the unaccountability of the relatively more powerful.

Of course, what constitutes murder, rape, robbery, assault, and other forms of serious crime varies over historical periods and between cultural groups, as the changes and contradictions *within* and *between* powerful interest groups, and the shifting alliances of the less powerful bring about slight and not-so-slight tilts of society's power axis (Chambliss 1981). But it is not justifiable to conclude from this that criminal law reflects a value-consensus or even results from the state's neutral refereeing among competing interest groups. It is, however, plausible to view criminal laws as the outcomes of clashes between groups with structurally generated conflicting interests, and to argue that the legislators' intention, or if that is too conspiratorial, then the law's latent function, is to provide the powerful with a resource to reduce further the ability of some groups to resist domination. Needless to stress the point, it is a resource eagerly used to punish and deter actual and potential resisters and thereby help protect the established social order [...].

NOTHING BUT MYSTIFICATION

Unfortunately for those committed to the radical 'reflexive' view, there is nothing but mystification. Most people accept the 'official' view. They are very aware and sensitized to muggers, football hooligans, street vandals, house-breakers, thieves, terrorists, and scroungers. But few are aware and sensitized to crimes committed by *corporate top and middle management* against stock-holders, employees, consumers, and the general public. Similarly there is only a fog, when it comes to crimes committed by *governments* (Douglas and Johnson 1977), particularly when these victimize Third World countries (Shawcross 1979) or become genocidal (Brown 1971; Horowitz 1977), or by *governmental control agencies* such as the police when they assault or use deadly force unwarrantedly against the public or suspected persons, or prison officers (Coggan and Walker 1982; Thomas and Pooley 1980), or special prison hospital staff when they brutalize and torture persons in their protective custody.

Few people are aware how men, who on the whole are more socially, economically, politically, and physically powerful than women, use these resources frequently to *batter* wives and cohabitees (Dobash and Dobash 1981), *sexually harass* their female (usually subordinate) co-workers, or *assault/rape* any woman who happens to be in the way. But we are very aware of female shoplifters and prostitutes, and those poor female adolescents who are 'beyond parental control' and in 'need of care and protection', even though this is a gross misrepresentation of female crime and though the relative absence of serious female crime contradicts the orthodox view that crime and powerless-ness go hand in hand.

Few people become aware of crimes of the powerful or how serious these are, because their attention is glued to the highly publicized social characteristics of the convicted and imprisoned population. It is not directed to the records, files, and occasional publications of those quasi-judicial organizations (such as the Factory Inspectorate in the UK or the Federal Drug Administration in the US) monitoring and regulating corporate and governmental crimes. Because of this, people make the attractive and easy deduction that those behind bars constitute our most serious criminals. As this captive audience is primarily young males amongst whom the unemployed and ethnic minorities are over-represented, it is believed that they, and those like them, constitute our 'public enemies'. Had the results of self-report/victimization surveys and the investigations of quasi-judicial agencies been publicized as much as 'official criminal statistics', and had the radical jaundiced and cynical view of criminal definitions been widely publicized, then the mystification produced by focus-ing exclusively on the characteristics of the prison population would not be so easily achieved. Instead, there would be a greater awareness of how the social construction of criminal definitions and the criminal justice system operate to bring about this misleading image of serious criminals.

Definitions of serious crime are essentially ideological constructs. They do not refer to those behaviours which objectively and *avoidably* cause us the most harm, injury, and suffering. Instead they refer to only a sub-section of these behaviours, a sub-section which is more likely to be committed by young, poorly-educated males who are often unemployed, live in working-class impoverished neighbourhoods, and frequently belong to an ethnic minority. Crime and criminalization are therefore *social control strategies*. They:

(i)   render underprivileged and powerless people more likely to be arrested, convicted, and sentenced to prison, even though the amount of personal damage and injury they cause may be less than the more powerful and privileged cause;

(ii) create the illusion that the 'dangerous' class is primarily located at the bottom of various hierarchies by which we 'measure' each other, such as occupational prestige, income level, housing market location, educational achievement, racial attributes – in this illusion it fuses relative poverty and criminal propensities and sees them both as effects of moral inferiority, thus rendering the 'dangerous' class deserving of both poverty and punishment;

(iii) render invisible the vast amount of avoidable harm, injury, and deprivation imposed on the ordinary population by the state, transnational and other corporations, and thereby remove the effects of these 'crimes' from the causal nexus for explaining 'conventional crimes' committed by ordinary people. The conditions of life for the powerless created by the powerful are simply ignored by those who explain crime as a manifestation of individual pathology or local neighbourhood friendship and cultural patterns – yet in many respects the unrecognized victimization of the powerless by the powerful constitutes a part of those conditions under which the powerless choose to commit crimes;

(iv) elevate the criminal justice into a 'community service' – it is presented as being above politics and dispensing 'justice for all' irrespective of class, race, sex, or religion – this further legitimates the state and those whose interests it wittingly, or otherwise, furthers;

(v)   make ordinary people even more dependent upon the state for protection against 'lawlessness' and the rising tidal wave of crime, even though it is the state and its agents who are often directly and indirectly victimizing ordinary people.

Not only does the state with the help and reinforcement of its control agencies, criminologists, and the media conceptualize a particular and partial ideological version of serious crime and who commits it, but it does so by concealing and hence mystifying its own propensity for violence and serious crimes on a much larger scale. Matza captured this sad ironic 'truth' when he wrote:

> In its avid concern for public order and safety, implemented through police force and penal policy, the state is vindicated. By pursuing evil and producing the *appearance* of good, the state reveals its abiding method – the perpetuation of its good name in the face of its own propensity for violence, conquest, and destruction. Guarded by a collective representation in which theft and violence reside in a dangerous class, morally elevated by its correctional quest, the state achieves the legitimacy of its pacific intention and the acceptance of legality – even when it goes to war and massively perpetuates activities it has allegedly banned from the world. But that, the reader may say, is a different matter altogether. So says the state – and that is the final point of the collective representation [i.e. ideological construction – author]. (Matza 1969: 196)

For too long too many people have been socialized to see crime and criminals through the eyes of the state. There is nothing left, as Matza points out, but mystification. This is clearly revealed in the brick wall of indignation which flattens any suggestion that the crime problem defined by the state is not the only crime problem, or that criminals are not only those processed by the state. There is more to crime and criminals than the state reveals. But most people cannot see it.

REFERENCES

Box, S. (1981a) *Deviance, Reality and Society*, 2nd edn. London: Holt, Rinehart and Winston.

Box, S. (1981b) 'Where have all the naughty children gone?', in National Deviancy Symposium, *Permissiveness and Control*. London: Macmillan.

Braithwaite, J. and Geis, G. (1981) 'On theory and action for corporate crime control'. Unpublished paper.

Brown, D. (1971) *Bury my Heart at Wounded Knee*. New York: Holt, Rinehart and Winston.

Chambliss, W.J. (1964) 'A sociological analysis of the law of vagrancy', *Social Problem*, 12: 46–67.

Chambliss, W.J. (1981) 'The criminalization of conduct', in H.L. Ross (ed.), *Law and Deviance*. London: Sage.

Chomsky, N. and Herman, E.S. (1979a) *The Washington Connection and Third World Fascism*. Nottingham: Spokesman.

Chomsky, N. and Herman, E.S. (1979b) *After the Cataclysm*. Nottingham: Spokesman.

Coggan, G. and Walker, M. (1982) *Frightened for my Life: An Account of Deaths in British Prisons*. London: Fontana.

Dobash, R.E. and Dobash, R. (1981) *Violence against Wives*. London: Open Books.

Douglas, J.D. and Johnson, J.M. (eds) (1977) *Official Deviance*. New York: Lippincott.

Duster, T. (1970) *The Legislation of Morality*. New York: Free Press.

Erickson, K.T. (1976) *Everything in its Path*. New York: Simon and Schuster.

Graham, J.M. (1972) 'Amphetamine politics on Capitol Hill', *Society*, 9: 14–23.

Gunningham, N. (1974) *Pollution, Social Interest and the Law*. London: Martin Robertson.

Hall, J. (1952) *Theft, Law and Society*, rev. edn. Indianapolis: Bobbs–Merrill.

Haskins, G. (1960) *Law and Authority in Early Massachusetts*. New York: Macmillan.

Hay, D. (1975) 'Property, authority and criminal law', in D. Hay et al. (eds), *Albion's Fatal Tree*. London: Allen Lane.

Hindelang, M.J., Gottfredson, M. and Garofalo, L. (1978) *Victims of Personal Crimes*. Cambridge, MA: Ballinger.

Hopkins, A. (1978) *Crime, Law and Business*. Canberra: Australian Institute of Criminology.

Hopkins, A. (1980) 'Crimes against capitalism: an Australian case', *Contemporary Crises*, 4: 421–32.

Horowitz, I.L. (1977) *Genocide: State-power and Mass Murder*, 2nd edn. New Jersey: Transaction Books.

Liazos, A. (1972) 'The poverty of the sociology of deviance: nuts, sluts and perverts', *Social Problems*, 20: 103–20.

McCaghy, C.H. and Denisoff, R.S. (1973) 'Pirates and politics', in R.S. Denisoff and C.H. McCaghy (eds), *Deviance, Conflict and Criminality*. Chicago: Rand-McNally.

Matza, D. (1969) *Becoming Deviant*. Englewood Cliffs, NJ: Prentice-Hall.

Mitford, J. (1977) *The American Prison Business*. London: Penguin.

Morgan, P. (1978) *Delinquent Fantasies*. London: Temple Smith.

Platt, A. (1969) *The Child Savers*. Chicago: Chicago University Press.

Schrag, P. and Divoky, D. (1981) *The Myth of the Hyperactive Child*. Harmondsworth: Penguin.

Schur, E.M. (1973) *Radical Non-intervention*. Englewood Cliffs, NJ: Spectrum.

Shawcross, W. (1979) *Side Show: Kissinger, Nixon and the Destruction of Cambodia*. London: Andre Deutsch.

Silverman, M. and Lee, P.R. (1974) *Pills, Profits and Politics*. Berkeley, CA: University of California Press.

Spitzer, S. (1975) 'Towards a Marxian theory of crime', *Social Problems*, 22: 368–401.

Sumner, C. (1976) 'Marxism and deviance theory', in P. Wiles (ed.), *Crime and Delinquency in Britain*, vol. 2. London: Martin Robertson.

Swartz, J. (1975) 'Silent killers at work', *Crime and Social Justice*, 3: 15–20.

Swigert, V. and Farrell, R. (1981) 'Corporate homicide: definitional processes in the creation of deviance', *Law and Society Review*, 15: 161–82.

Szasz, T. (1970) *Ideology and Insanity*. New York: Anchor.

Szasz, T. (1977a) *Psychiatric Slavery*. New York: Free Press.

Szasz, T. (1977b) *The Theology of Medicine*. Oxford: Oxford University Press.

Thomas, J.E. and Pooley, R. (1980) *The Exploding Prison*. London: Junction Books.

Thompson, E.P. (1975) *Whigs and Hunters*. London: Allen Lane.

Wilson, J.Q. (1975) *Thinking about Crime*. New York: Basic Books.

STUDY QUESTIONS

1   Describe in your own words what you think Box means by 'mythologies' of crime.
2   What are the key points of comparison and contrast between the 'liberal scientific' and 'radical reflexive' approaches to crime that Box identifies? What are the policy implications of each perspective?
3   Carry out a content analysis of a week's newspapers or television news broadcasts. What examples can you find that support Box's thesis that crime is an ideological construct which serves the interests of the powerful and criminalizes the powerless? Who constitutes the 'powerful' in your view?

FURTHER READING

Box introduces and further develops some of the issues raised in the extract above in Box, S. (1981) *Deviance, Reality and Society*, 2nd edn, New York: Holt, Rinehart and Winston; and Box, S., Hale, C. and Andrews, G. (1988) 'Explaining fear of crime', *British Journal of Criminology*, 28 (3). His broadly Marxist approach is also represented in Chambliss, W.J. (1999) *Power, Politics and Crime*,

Boulder, Colorado: Westview Press; and Christie, N. (1993) *Crime Control as Industry*, London: Routledge. A useful introduction to the notion of crime as a constructed concept can be found in Muncie, J. and McLaughlin, E. (eds) (2001) *The Problem of Crime*, 2nd edn, London: Sage. The first chapter, 'The construction and deconstruction of crime', by John Muncie, is of particular interest in relation to the picture of crime presented in official data and by the media.

8

The social construction of official statistics

Clive Coleman and Jenny Moynihan

Clive Coleman and Jenny Moynihan take up Steven Box's theme and explore in greater detail the processes involved in the construction and compilation of 'official' crime statistics (that is, those compiled from data collected by the police, courts and prisons); namely, the discovery, reporting, recording and 'clearing up' of crime. Like Box, they suggest that the picture that we get from official sources is partial and misleading, highlighting only a fraction of the crime that actually occurs, and representing some groups to a much greater extent than others. They refer to the 'dark figure of crime', by which they mean both the vast number of crimes that go unrecorded, and also the 'conventional' image of the undetected offender. The phrase thus encompasses both quantitative (numerical) as well as qualitative (pictorial) assumptions about undetected crime. In the extract that follows, Coleman and Moynihan also refer to the British Crime Survey (BCS), which is a victim survey that relies on the self-reports of victims, rather than police recorded data which arguably tell us more about the organizational processes and priorities of the institutions recording the data than they do about the actual problem of crime. The BCS, which produces biennial reports on crime in Britain, reveals that less than half of all criminal incidents are reported to the police, and only about 60 per cent of *reported* crime is then *recorded* by the police.

DISCOVERY

In some ways this term is misleading, for it may be taken to imply that all crimes are simply 'out there' and easily recognizable to anyone. In practice, not

SOURCE: From *Understanding Crime Data: Haunted by the Dark Figure* (Buckingham: Open University Press, 1996), 32–9.

only do people differ in their knowledge of what constitutes crime, but there are occasions where there is no victim in the usual sense to discover the offence, and others where the victim is left unaware that a crime has been committed. We know relatively little about this area, but we can say something about who first became aware of those incidents which eventually find their way into the official statistics of crime. Studies in Britain indicate that between 77 and 96 per cent of these are initially discovered by members of the public in various guises (Bottomley and Pease, 1986: 34). One study found that only 14 per cent were initially discovered by the police, while 57 per cent were by personal victims, 23 per cent by representatives of victimized organizations, and 3 per cent by witnesses (Bottomley and Coleman, 1981: 43–8). This pattern does not necessarily apply to all offences. The police role in 'discovery' is far more pronounced in many non-notifiable offences, particularly those without a clear victim who has an interest in bringing the incident to the attention of the police (e.g., some of the offences relating to drugs, prostitution, drunkenness, and public order). Here the police have a far more dominant role in the identification of offences and offenders for possible further action.

REPORTING

The agent who initially discovered the event is very often also the one who reports it to the police. The information of the previous section should therefore make clear that we need to take into account the role of such agents as victims, witnesses, store detectives, caretakers, security staff, managers of private and public organizations, and others in the production of crime statistics. Just to take one example, it is now well known that many stores and shops tend only to report cases of shoplifting where a suspect has been apprehended, but that policies and practices show some variability. In view of the probable extent of shoplifting, such policies and practices are likely to have a very large impact on figures of recorded crime.

Successive sweeps of the British Crime Survey (BCS) have asked respondents whether they had reported an offence to the police, and if not, why not. Only some offences in the official statistics can be compared with the more limited range in the BCS. For those that could be compared, it was estimated in the 1994 sweep (figures refer to 1993) that 41 per cent of BCS 'crimes' overall were reported to the police (Mayhew et al., 1994). However, it was clear, as in other years, that the proportion of different offences apparently reported varied widely, ranging from 32 per cent of instances of vandalism to 97 per cent of motor vehicle thefts. These differences need explanation, and it is often suggested that the seriousness of the offence is the main factor influencing reporting. This certainly seems to be borne out by burglary, in which 87 per cent of instances where loss was experienced were reported, whereas only 53 per cent were reported in cases of attempts and no loss of property. This should not be over-generalized as an explanation. Some cases of physical and sexual abuse, for example, come to light, if they ever do, only after considerable periods of time.

The BCS produces its own figures on reasons for not reporting a crime; those most often given by respondents in the 1992 sweep, for example, were that the offence was too trivial (55 per cent), the police could not do anything (25 per cent), or that it was dealt with privately (12 per cent) (Mayhew et al., 1993). What these global results do not reveal is the way in which crime is such a varied category, with a range of reasons for reporting or not, which are often embedded in particular circumstances and sets of relationships, associated experiences of harm, and assessments about what could usefully be done about it. So statements about seriousness should be supplemented by an analysis of the social and psychological context, in which such aspects as embarrassment, the nature of any relationship to the offender, expectations of police reaction or performance, the implications of any insurance policies held, and fears about any possible consequences of reporting (such as reprisals, incrimination, or simply involvement in criminal justice proceedings) should be considered. Just to give one example, Malcolm Young (1991: 368) writes of the small shopkeeper who avoids reporting offences of shop theft to the police in order to avoid having to close the shop at a later date if required to attend any court proceedings.

RECORDING

The mere fact that an incident is reported to the police (even one which, on the surface at least, appears to qualify as a crime) does not ensure that it will be recorded as a crime. One further step is therefore necessary before it becomes a statistical unit. Information about this stage is again available from the BCS. In the 1994 sweep, for example, there is the kind of varied pattern according to offence type shown in other years, such that only 38 per cent of thefts and robberies from the person that have been reported to the police (according to the BCS), 29 per cent of attempted motor vehicle thefts, but 77 per cent of burglaries with loss and 95 per cent of motor thefts, appear to have been *recorded* as such. Overall it was estimated that only 60 per cent of the type of offences covered by the BCS and apparently reported to the police were recorded by them (Mayhew et al., 1994).

The authors of the report of the earlier 1992 sweep suggested a number of reasons for such 'shortfalls', such as the police not always accepting victims' accounts, their view that a report was mistaken or 'disingenuous', their feeling that there was insufficient evidence for a crime to be said to exist, their view that some items were too trivial to justify formal action, especially if the complainants wanted no further police action, were unlikely to provide evidence, or the incident had somehow been 'satisfactorily resolved' (Mayhew et al., 1993: 16). These are, however, largely speculations and it is important to appreciate that the very large shortfalls in some instances also raise questions about the BCS findings, and should be subject to research to find out more about their explanations. Finally, it is now also possible to discern broad changes in police recording practice over the years since 1981, the year of the first BCS estimates. From a comparison of these with the broadly equivalent official data over the period 1981–91, it appears that police recording of acquisitive crimes reported to them decreased, while recording of offences of violence and vandalism increased significantly (Mayhew et al., 1993: Table A2.6). More impressionistic accounts have suggested that there has been a broad decline in the practice known as 'cuffing' (the deliberate non-recording of offences for various reasons by police officers) over a much longer period (Young, 1991: 323–5).

Although it may be broadly true that 'reported offences that fall by the wayside in the police recording process may not be especially serious' (Mayhew et al., 1989: 12), it seems to us that this is an area, like that of reporting, which is ripe for investigation. Not only are these significant topics of enquiry in their own right (for they are a key stage in the mobilization of the criminal justice process), but they have important implications for the data produced by the police and by the BCS. The *classification* of the offence is also an important element here; one reason for the discrepancies between official and BCS data may be that some offences were classified under different categories in the two sets of figures. The influences on decisions whether and how to record may be grouped according to three broad levels: the *social and political context*, the *organizational context* and the *situational context*.

The Social and Political Context

It is worth noting that crime data are produced in a broader economic, political and social context, from which the recording process is not immune. For example, Malcolm Young (1991: 323) suggests that in the 1950s and early 1960s, when crime was not a political issue, there was little incentive for the police to record large numbers of crimes. No extra finance would have been available from local budgets as a result. In fact, because the efficiency of police forces was largely judged on the basis of clear-up rates, there was little reason or incentive to record as crimes minor offences for which there was little prospect of their being cleared up. All of this was gradually to change in the following decades, as there was a dawning realization that claims for resources could ultimately be mounted on the back of a burgeoning crime rate in a society in which crime had increasingly become a political issue. A number of studies have been conducted in the USA which illustrate the impact of political pressures, often at a local level, on crime recording (see the summary in O'Brien, 1985). Many of these studies were concerned with offences in the areas of drugs, prostitution and gambling; most of these offences are non-notifiable in England and Wales, but the data on those persons processed for them are very sensitive to police activity. Other social changes leading to increased recording could be mentioned, such as the growth of technology, allowing rapid response to scenes and improved contact with the station. Under these circumstances, incidents are less likely to be resolved informally and more likely to be formally recorded, and at an earlier stage.

The Organizational Context

Research in the USA has shown how crime recording can be responsive to organizational factors, such as changes in working practices and personnel

(McLeary et al., 1982), and to the degree of 'professionalization' of a police department, higher levels of which may result in a greater use of record-keeping generally and corresponding increases in crime rates (and lower clear-up rates!) (Skogan, 1976, 1978). In England, Farrington and Dowds's (1985) study suggested that between two-thirds and three-quarters of the difference between the higher crime rate of Nottinghamshire and that of two similar counties in 1981 was due to a greater tendency for the police in Nottinghamshire to record thefts of items of little value, offences originating in admissions, and multiple, continuous or series offences as separate crimes. A report by the Inspectorate of Constabulary in 1994 found 'institutionalised anomalies' and different recording practices across seven divisions of the North West London Metropolitan police area which made it difficult to assess the effectiveness of operational performance on crime, especially burglary (*Guardian*, 14 December 1994). One of these anomalies was that in the past some forces had classified many attempted break-ins as criminal damage rather than burglary. New guidelines were issued to eradicate these anomalies, which had produced significant variations in the politically sensitive burglary figures.

The Situational Context

Decisions to record are ultimately made in particular situations, within the broader context mentioned in the previous two sections. Again we have some evidence from the USA about the factors here. The main influences seem to have been the seriousness of the offence, the complainant's preference, the relational distance between complainant and suspect, and deference to the police on the part of the complainant (Black, 1970). Pepinsky (1976) found that officers were very much affected by whether the dispatcher named an offence when the officer was first dispatched to an incident. Maxfield et al. (1980) suggested that levels of recording were affected by the total demand for police service at the time – but this applied to property and minor crimes only. Block and Block (1980) found that the recording of robberies was much more likely if the incident was serious, if the robbery was completed, and if a gun was used. Not surprisingly, similar results have been obtained for arrests (a type of offender-based data). Smith and Visher (1981) found that arrest decisions were also related to the presence of a bystander, race of the suspect, and an antagonistic demeanour on the part of the suspect, when controlling for a range of factors, including seriousness of offence.

No doubt many of these factors affecting recording apply in the British context, but we do not have the kinds of studies to be sure. We do have a number of valuable, but rather impressionistic accounts of 'cuffing' and the reasons for it (Bottomley and Coleman, 1981; Young, 1991), such as a preference for doing something else, to avoid work, to improve detection rates, or a feeling that to record might be counter-productive in some way, although such decisions are more safely made in those cases where there is unlikely to be any

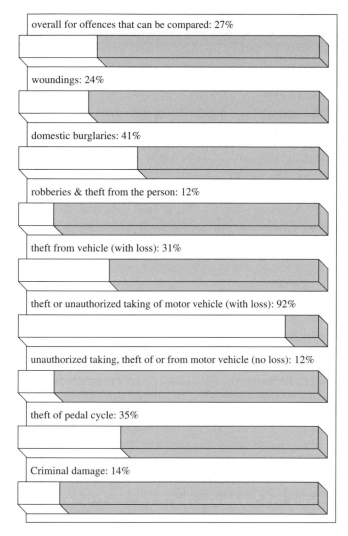

overall for offences that can be compared: 27%

woundings: 24%

domestic burglaries: 41%

robberies & theft from the person: 12%

theft from vehicle (with loss): 31%

theft or unauthorized taking of motor vehicle (with loss): 92%

unauthorized taking, theft of or from motor vehicle (no loss): 12%

theft of pedal cycle: 35%

Criminal damage: 14%

Figure 8.1 Estimates of percentages of BCS offences recorded by the
police: England and Wales, 1993
Source: Home Office (1994: 27)

'comeback'. Such decisions are not always uncontroversial, as police practice in
cases of domestic violence, particularly in the past, illustrates. We also have
other studies of crime recording and writing off incidents as 'no crime' (McCabe
and Sutcliffe, 1978; Bottomley and Coleman, 1981) which reveal some of the
reasoning employed. Finally, we have the fascinating account given by a former
police officer of the various practical techniques adopted to count and record
crime during his service, which included 'the rituals of "cuffing", "creating",
"keepy-backs juggling", "fiddling", and "bending"' (Young, 1991: 377).

Having looked at those three stages in the production of crime data, BCS data can now help us to estimate the proportions of certain 'offences' which end up as recorded crimes. The figures can give some indication of the combined effects of reporting and recording decisions on the resultant statistics. Estimates relating to 1993 of the percentages of BCS offences which were subsequently recorded as crimes are shown in Figure 8.1. Leaving aside any qualifications about these figures [...] it can be seen that, from a 'realist' perspective, different offence groups have very different 'dark figures' of offences. The use of the same kinds of data over time also gives us a different perspective on trends in crime. For example, over the 1981–93 period, officially recorded crime rose by 111 per cent whereas BCS crimes rose by only 77 per cent (Home Office, 1994: 27–8). However, this long-term pattern conceals a reverse trend during 1991–93, when BCS 'crime' rose by 18 per cent, whereas comparable recorded crime rose by only 7 per cent, apparently owing to a fall in reporting.

CLEARING UP CRIME AND THE IDENTIFICATION OF OFFENDERS

Clear-up rates and official offender data must also be understood in terms of the context in which they are produced. It is now fairly well known that few crimes are cleared up in the style of classic detective fiction. Many are solved by a suspect being at the scene when the police arrive, or by the provision of information by members of the public (Bottomley and Coleman, 1981; Burrows and Tarling, 1982). Although the lion's share of clear-ups is produced by charge or summons, a significant number are produced through methods such as TICs and 'prison write-offs', which involve offenders already processed for other offences (Home Office, 1994: Table 2.12). The use of 'secondary' methods of clearing up crime has created some controversy in recent years, such as when Constable Ron Walker went public in alleging that Kent detectives had bloated their detection rates by persuading convicted offenders to admit to crimes that they had not committed (*Observer*, 13 July 1986).

Clear-up rates vary widely between different types of offence (see Home Office Statistical Bulletin [HOSB] 5/95: Figure 10), reflecting the nature of the detection problem facing the police on arrival (e.g., with offences against the person the offender is often well known to the victim, thus producing high clear-up rates). These rates also vary a good deal between police forces, and although often used to compare effectiveness between them, it should be remembered that the rates are influenced by such things as the policing problems faced in particular areas, including the 'offence mix', and practice and policy over the use of 'secondary' clear-ups, which are known to differ between forces (Walker, 1992; Bottomley and Coleman, 1995). For example, some forces have dedicated squads to deal with 'prison write-offs'. Other forces do not have such squads, but may respond to letters from prisoners requesting a visit. These forces might sometimes find their clear-up rates adversely affected as a result, and coming under media and political pressure. If so, the use or threat of 'gate arrests' (the arrest of persons on release from prison) may be used as a way of encouraging prisoners to 'wipe the slate clean' before release. Word soon gets around and more letters are likely to be received. Finally, another key issue concerns the way in which clear-up rates have fallen over recent years – from 35 per cent to 25 per cent between 1985 and 1993, for example (Home Office, 1994: Table 2.12). The reasons for this are complex and clearly require illumination to avoid such statistics being used in a naïve way as simple indicators of police effectiveness. […]

REFERENCES

Black, D. (1970) 'The production of crime rates', *American Sociological Review*, 35: 733–48.

Block, R. and Block, C.R. (1980) 'Decisions and data: the transformation of robbery incidents into official robbery statistics', *Journal of Criminal Law and Criminology*, 71: 622–36.

Bottomley, K. and Coleman, C. (1981) *Understanding Crime Rates*. Farnborough: Gower.

Bottomley, K. and Coleman, C. (1995) 'The police', in M.A. Walker (ed.) *Interpreting Crime Statistics*. Oxford: Clarendon Press.

Bottomley, K. and Pease, K. (1986) *Crime and Punishment: Interpreting the Data*. Milton Keynes: Open University Press.

Burrows, J. and Tarling, R. (1982) *Clearing Up Crime*, Home Office Research Study no. 73. London: HMSO.

Farrington, D.P. and Dowds, E. (1985) 'Disentangling criminal behaviour and police reaction', in D. Farrington and J. Gunn (eds) *Reactions to Crime: The Public, the Police, Courts and Prisons*. Chichester: John Wiley.

Home Office (1994) *Criminal Statistics England and Wales*. London: HMSO.

McCabe, S. and Sutcliffe, F. (1978) *Defining Crime: A Study of Police Decisions*. Oxford: Blackwell.

McLeary, R., Nienstedt, B.C. and Erven, J.M. (1982) 'Uniform crime reports as organizational outcomes: three time series experiments', *Social Problems*, 29: 361–72.

Maxfield, M.T., Lewis, D.A. and Szoc, R. (1980) 'Producing official crimes: verified crime reports as measures of police output', *Social Science Quarterly*, 61: 221–36.

Mayhew, P., Elliott, D. and Dowds, L. (1989) *The 1988 British Crime Survey*, Home Office Research Study no. 111. London: HMSO.

Mayhew, P., Aye Maung, N. and Mirrlees-Black, C. (1993) *The 1992 British Crime Survey*, Home Office Research Study no. 132. London: HMSO.

Mayhew, P., Mirrlees-Black, C. and Aye Maung, N. (1994) *Trends in Crime: Findings from the 1994 British Survey*, Home Office Research Findings no. 14. London: HMSO.

O'Brien, R. (1985) *Crime and Victimization Data*. London: Sage.

Pepinsky, H. (1976) 'Police patrolmen's offence reporting behaviour', *Journal of Research in Crime and Delinquency*, 13: 33–47.

Skogan, W. (1976) 'Crime and crime rates', in W.G. Skogan (ed.) *Sample Surveys of the Victims of Crime*. Cambridge, MA: Ballinger.

Skogan, W. (1978) *Victimization Surveys and Criminal Justice Planning*. Law Enforcement Assistance Administration. Washington, DC: US Government Printing Office.

Smith, D.A. and Visher, C.A. (1981) 'Street-level justice: situational determinants of police arrest decisions', *Social Problems*, 29: 167–77.

Walker, M.A. (1992) 'Do we need a clear-up rate?', *Policing and Society*, 2: 293–306.

Young, M. (1991) *An Inside Job*. Oxford: Clarendon Press.

STUDY QUESTIONS

1   To continue Box's (Reading 7) dual-theoretical approach, a liberal scientist would view crime statistics as outcomes of social and institutional processes rather than valid indicators of actual crimes committed, while a radical reflexive approach would emphasize that such processes are themselves the product of wider social and ideological structures (e.g. class conflict). Thinking back to Young's discussion of realism (Reading 4), how would a left-realist approach view statistical data on crime?

2   Why do certain types of crime (e.g. motor theft) generally get reported, while others (e.g. vandalism) frequently do not? What factors determine whether the police actually record crimes that are reported, and why do some types of crime 'slip through the net' entirely?

3   In general, what are the strengths and weaknesses of statistical sources of crime? To what extent would you expect the BCS to be a more reliable source of information about crime than those statistics that are compiled by criminal justice agencies?

4   What do you understand by the phrase 'the dark figure of crime'? What type of offenders and offences are most likely to go undetected and/or unrecorded?

FURTHER READING

The following texts all offer useful introductions to the measurement of crime: Maguire, M. (1997) 'Crime statistics, patterns and trends: changing perceptions and their implications' in M. Maguire, R. Morgan and R. Reiner (eds) *The Oxford Handbook of Criminology*, 2nd end, Oxford: Oxford University Press; Bottomley, K. and Coleman, C. (1981) *Understanding Crime Rates*, Farnborough: Gower; Bottomley, K. and Pease, K. (1986) *Crime and Punishment: Interpreting the Data*, Milton Keynes: Open University Press; and Walker, M.A. (ed.) (1995) *Interpreting Crime Statistics*, Oxford: Clarendon Press. For a critique of the subject from a left-realist perspective, see Young, J. (1988) 'Risk of crime and fear of crime: a realist based critique of survey-based assumptions', in M. Maguire and J. Pointing (eds) *Victims of Crime: A New Deal?* Milton Keynes: Open University Press.

9

Corporate crime, official statistics and the mass media

Gary Slapper and Steve Tombs

Part of the 'dark figure of crime' that remains largely invisible in statistical representations is the corporate offender. Corporate crime encompasses a huge range of offences, and its costs, according to Gary Slapper and Steve Tombs, far outweigh those associated with ordinary or conventional criminality. The reading that follows comprises two separate extracts from their book, *Corporate Crime* (pp. 54–7 and 91–6 respectively). The first extract considers the question of why corporate offences rarely show up in official measurements of criminal activity, and, when they do, they appear in categories too vague to make any meaningful sense of them. The second extract considers the extent to which the mass media reinforce the socially constructed picture of crime presented in official data. Their argument is that media output as a whole presents a skewed picture of crime which instils fears in the general population. While many of us may take steps to minimize the danger of being the victim of a conventional crime at the hands of a stranger, we are far less vigilant when dealing with businesses and corporations. Read together, these extracts help us to understand how a recognition of corporate offences challenges popular conceptions of the 'problem of crime'.

[...] Quite simply, measures used to indicate the scale of the crime problem do not include reference to measures of corporate offences. As Reiner notes, 'when mention is made of *the* crime statistics what is usually meant is the annual publication by the Home Office Research and Statistics Department of the volume Criminal Statistics: England and Wales, and more particularly ... "Notifiable offences recorded by the police"' (1996: 186). While the categorisation

SOURCE: From *Corporate Crime* (Harlow: Pearson Education, 1999), 54–7, 91–6.

of notifiable offences in Scotland is slightly different (Young 1992), it is equally useless for measuring corporate offences, as it too focuses overwhelmingly upon conventional crimes. Even a cursory examination of the notifiable offences for England and Wales reveals the extent to which they focus upon conventional as opposed to corporate crimes. The first category, *Violent Crime*, consists of violence against the person, sexual offences, and robbery. Second is *Burglary*, which includes burglary in a dwelling and burglary other than in a dwelling. Third is *Theft and Handling of Stolen Goods*, made up of a number of offences, namely: theft from the person; theft of pedal cycle; theft from shops; theft from vehicle; theft of motor vehicle; vehicle crime; and other theft and handling of stolen goods. Three final categories are *Fraud and Forgery, Criminal Damages*, and *Other Notifiable Offences.*

It is clear that the sub-category 'violence against the person' could include some forms of corporate crimes, though does not. Rather differently, the category *Fraud and Forgery* will include some corporate crimes, namely frauds not treated by the Serious Fraud Office. This category is broken down into 'Fraud by company director', 'False Accounting', 'Other Fraud', 'Forgery, or use of false drug prescription' and 'Other Forgery'. Yet this still does not allow us to say anything useful about corporate crime. First, while the two categories 'Other Fraud' and 'Other Forgery' are by far the biggest in terms of numbers of offences, these are also the most general, far too vague to be of any use. Second, there is no means of making the distinction based upon this data between occupational and organisational crime [...].

None of this is to deny the problems with, and inadequacies of, crime statistics for so-called traditional crimes. Yet, whether we like it or not, there is no doubt that one of the key means of defining or representing the seriousness or otherwise of certain forms of criminal activities is through reference to quantitative data, so that 'numbers' remain predominant as a 'descriptive medium' (Maguire 1997: 139) of the scale and distribution of, trends in, and the nature of the crime problem. If, as Maguire notes, 'a salient feature of almost all modern forms of discourse about crime is the emphasis placed upon terms associated with its quantification and measurement' (*ibid.*), then it is hardly surprising that corporate crimes 'do not feature in the debates about the "crime problem"' (Nelken 1994: 355; Green 1990: 27). This is one of the ways in which corporate crimes are organised off crime, law and order agendas [...].

[...] In both academic and political terms, there is far greater scrutiny of corporate crime in the US than is the case for Britain. So it is of relevance to note that in the US, too, official data on corporate crime is grossly inadequate. Almost 20 years ago, a massive and thorough study conducted by Reiss and Biderman for the US Department of Justice pointed clearly to the enormous difficulties of measuring 'white-collar crime' (Reiss and Biderman 1980). The problems that these two researchers pointed to seem no less relevant today, and even more relevant in the context of the UK as compared to the US. Indeed, to attempt to arrive at some overall figure even for the incidence of one group of corporate offences in the UK, namely fraud, would require examination, dissection and re-categorisation of data from a whole range of bodies, including, the Police, the SFO, the European Commission, the British Retail Consortium, the Association of British Insurers, the Association of Payment Clearing Systems, the Credit Industry Fraud Avoidance Scheme, the Audit Commission, the Charity Commission, the Inland Revenue, and HM Treasury (see Levi and Pithouse 1992: 231–2 for a brief list of the bodies involved in regulating fraud in Britain). And if this is the case with fraud […] then the situation with other corporate crimes is even more problematic.

Further, while there are enormous problems with official recording of conventional crimes, a key means of supplementing and correcting these has been the use of self-report or victimisation surveys. The British Crime Survey, for example, has proven an important adjunct to official statistics, to the extent that the Home Office now sponsor such a survey on a biennial basis. Yet while attempts to measure how much corporate crime exists cannot begin from official crime statistics, nor does the BCS attempt to include questions on offences by corporations and other organisations. It is of interest, and a useful indicator of political priorities attached to different forms of offending […], that the Home Office has sponsored a victimisation survey on crimes *against* business in England and Wales (Mirrlees-Black and Ross 1995), while research into such crimes in Scotland is currently being sponsored by the Scottish Office. More generally, there is little attempt to generate more accurate corporate crime data via victim-based reporting. Now, there are some real reasons for this, which relate to the very different relationships between offender and victim that tend to characterise corporate crimes when compared with conventional crimes. In the former, victims are often remote in time and space from the offender; they are frequently diffuse; they are often unaware of their status as victims […]. However, there have been some attempts to measure such victimisation. Most notably, the Second Islington Crime Survey included questions relating to commercial crime, and to health and safety and pollution offences. While we shall not enter into a detailed discussion of these results here (but see Pearce 1990), it is worth noting simply that they do, indeed, indicate widespread victimisation to corporate crime. For example, of those respondents giving definite answers about their experience of buying goods and services during the previous twelve months: approximately 11 per cent had been given misleading information; 21 per cent believed that they had been deliberately overcharged; and 24 per cent had paid for what turned out to be defective goods or services. By way of comparison, the same survey indicated that during the same period, approximately 4 per cent of respondents giving definite answers had a car stolen, 7 per cent suffered from a burglary and 7 per cent from an actual or attempted theft from their person. This indicates that the incidence of commercial crime is high both relatively and absolutely. […]

THE MASS MEDIA

Images of crime, law and order within the mass media both reflect and in turn reinforce dominant social constructions of what constitutes the crime problem in contemporary Britain, within which 'traditional' or street crimes are central. Before entering the detail of our argument around this claim, we should emphasise that we are not claiming that there is no attention to corporate offending. On this point, we should note Levi's words of caution, when he stated that,

> the British and American television viewer or reader of the quality or even some of the 'tabloid' national press might find ample daily evidence to refute the assertion – still repeated in many key criminological texts (Box 1983) – that because of the 24 hours news cycle and the fact that they are owned by 'big business' white-collar crime receives little or no attention in the media. This was an over-simplification even when Box wrote it, but despite the growing concentration of the Press, it is even less true in the mid-1980s. (1987: 11)

He later claims that 'conventional notions of media neglect of white-collar crime and fraud are now *passé*, even if they were ever wholly true' (Levi and Pithouse 1992: 229). Now, Levi is correct to warn against over-simplification here, even if he is rather unfair in his characterisation of Box's own claims on this matter (see Box 1983). But he is, for us, wrong if he is implying that corporate crimes are accurately represented as a phenomenon, or fairly represented alongside conventional crimes. Despite the fact that some corporate crimes are represented via mass media, this does not obviate, and in some ways actually reinforces, the fact that dominant representations of crime, law and order issues within various forms of media have the effect of obscuring or removing corporate crimes from such discussions.

If we examine the treatment of crime, law and order in the broadcast media, the relative invisibility of corporate crimes is immediately clear. A survey of fictional treatments of crime issues across any of the terrestrial or satellite TV channels would reveal a preoccupation with 'cops and robbers', that is, with various aspects of (albeit fictionalised) street crimes. Such is precisely the stuff of classic series such as *Dixon of Dock Green, Z Cars, The Sweeney, Starsky and Hutch* and *Hill Street Blues*, their more contemporary counterparts, such as *The Bill, Homicide, NYPD Blue,* and *Due South,* and the range of crime-based movies shown across TV channels. This is not to imply that there are not occasional treatments of corporate crimes – though where corporate crimes are the subject of fictional broadcasting, these crimes are likely to be financial crimes (*Wall Street* being the famous example; but see Denzin 1990) – but they are extremely rare. In other words, precisely *contra* the claims of Levi, who refers to particular types of programmes 'on abuses of power by business-people or politicians' (Levi 1987: 10; Levi and Pithouse 1992: 239), the issue is one of the overwhelming, reinforcing mass of images rather than particular exceptions. Thus, over 20 years ago, Chibnall documented carefully how discrete areas of crime reporting could converge to produce 'blanket' conceptualisations regarding 'law-and-order' (Chibnall 1977); more recently, Randall has noted that while there is coverage of 'business illegality' in the media, there is relatively little attention to this with the effect that it becomes 'buried' (Randall 1995: 112–13, and passim). As Mathiesen admirably puts it in his recent discussion of the role of the Synopticon in modern capitalist societies, with regard to the media, the total gestalt produced by the messages of television is much more important than the individual programme or even type of programme ... The total message inculcates a general understanding of the world, a *world paradigm* if you like. (1997: 228–30, original emphasis)

Now, one reason for this generalised bias in fictional broadcasting may be the claim that many forms of corporate crime do not make for very interesting television, particularly where the crimes involved are based upon acts of omission: not testing certain hazardous substances; falsifying data required by a regulatory body; meeting to fix markets or prices; not acting upon information about the obvious and serious risks of ferry turnaround times; not meeting standards of maintenance on industrial plant; training pensions sales-staff in the techniques and languages of mis-selling, may not, on the face of it, make for very gripping television. However, we should be aware that traditional crime is just as intrinsically uninteresting, only made worthy of drama through fictionalisation, so that, for example, televisual images of policework bear little or no relation to the ways in which most police officers spend most of their time. In fact, there are no real reasons why dramatised accounts of corporate offending need be any less (or more!) interesting than those of conventional crimes – certainly the documented accounts of 'normalised deviance' within NASA in the lead up to the fatal *Challenger* launch decision (Vaughan 1996) or Goodrich's decision to conceal problems with its aircraft brakes and to proceed on the basis of falsified testing data (Vandivier 1982), or the Heavy Electrical Price-fixing Conspiracy (Geis 1967), or BA's 'Dirty Tricks' campaign against Virgin employees (Gregory 1994), would all make for viewing just as intrinsically interesting as many forms of fictionalised crime drama.

These latter examples are all, of course, drawn from actual case histories. Indeed, if one turns to non-fictional programming, there is perhaps more extensive coverage of corporate crime within the overall diet of crime, law and order issues. Thus there are certainly treatments of corporate crime amongst the classic documentary series such as *Panorama* and *World in Action*, and more latterly *Dispatches, Network First* and *First Tuesday.* Also of note here is the odd coverage of some forms of corporate crime amongst consumer issues programming such as *Watchdog, The Cook Report* and even *That's Life.* Nevertheless, any focus on corporate crime is vastly outweighed by the steady stream of non-fictional treatments of traditional crime issues. More important here than frequent one-off documentaries in the cumulative effect of *Crimewatch, Crimefile, Police Five* and so on. Indeed, amongst the latter it is worth noting that *Crimewatch* attracts a mass audience – and this has an almost exclusive focus upon conventional crimes within a format based around 'documentary reconstruction', using the drama of fiction to represent particular crime events (Schlesinger and Tumber 1994: 248–70). What the latter also illustrates is the media focus upon, and reproduction of, fears around what Stanko has called 'stranger danger'. One effect of the fuelling or production of such fears is at the same time to focus attention away from familiar or other apparently innocuous contexts – thus we tend not to concern ourselves with guarding against victimisation when we visit a local shopping centre, are contacted by a new, privatised water or gas supplier. And corporate executives are equally aware that they are relatively unlikely to be viewed as potential offenders: while it is ironic, it is on one level unsurprising that at the same time as the Chief Executive of Britain's largest private pensions provider – the Prudential – was launching a television and poster advertising campaign featuring himself as the 'trusting face of the man from the Pru', the company was more heavily implicated than any other in the offences related to pensions mis-selling, and was 'named' as one of the most recalcitrant companies in terms of failures to settle urgent cases (*Guardian*, 17 November, 1997).

This imbalance in the coverage of 'crime' in the broadcast media is also reproduced through daily newspaper coverage of crime, law and order issues, where conventional versions of crime, law and order predominate. To claim that corporate crime is not covered in daily newspapers would be inaccurate. But a cursory examination of recent crime, law and order reporting in a number of national newspapers suggests a number of clear, if at this stage highly provisional, conclusions.

First, the sheer volume of coverage of conventional crimes vastly out-weighs that of corporate crimes. Second, where corporate crime *is* treated in mainstream print media, such coverage is less rather than more prominent than treatments of conventional crime. Corporate crime is less likely to be reported within the mass circulation tabloids than it is in the broadsheets; and within broadsheets, corporate crime reporting has a lesser profile than that of conventional crimes, being located in specialist sections rather than in earlier news and features pages. Third, corporate crime is also treated in more specialist rather than popular contexts (a point which Levi himself notes: 1987: 10). Amongst the broadsheets, corporate crime receives by far the greatest volume of coverage in the *Financial Times* (see also Stephenson-Burton 1995) but this is a publication which has a specialist rather than general readership and stands tenth out of eleven in overall circulation tables for national daily newspapers (the circulation of the *Sun*, for example, is about 13 times greater). Fourth, and as should be clear from some of the previous points, where corporate crimes are addressed in the print media, these tend to be financial/economic crimes – that is, those kinds of activities which have been subject to some recent political and regulatory attention (see above) and upon which academics are most likely to focus (see below).

Further, while specialist sections of broadsheets *do* cover aspects of corporate crime, they tend to do so in a way that does not treat these as crime, law and order issues. There are various ways in which this latter effect is produced, and indeed these are common both to print media and the broadcast media considered above. First, representations of corporate crimes tend not to treat them as *corporate* crimes. Most notably, corporate crimes are considered via personalities, and it is the dominance of individual, 'respectable' figures that renders them newsworthy (Levi and Pithouse 1992). Relatedly, such crimes are considered newsworthy for their very abnormality. In other words, they may become individualised, which at the same time has the effect, in many instances, of obscuring their actual causes – beyond individual idiosyncrasy, character or pathology – and thus their normality and routineness. Moreover, to focus upon the individuals involved in such crimes is to obscure the corporations, structures and systems within which, and on behalf of which, they are likely to have offended.

If the corporate origins and nature of corporate crimes are often obscured in their reporting, then so is the fact that they are *crimes* (see Reiner 1997: 196). In support of his claim that there has been a considerable increase since the 1960s in media coverage of 'business crime', Levi himself refers to 'the cult of *expose machismo* in media cycles that favours the making of programmes on abuses of power', not least because 'scandal sells' (Levi 1987: 10, 12). Now, the terms 'scandal' or 'abuse', the latter in particular common currency when referring to corporate crimes (Tumber 1993), are no doubt highly critical; but abuse is a term which carries with it implications of (im)morality rather than legal offence. Moreover, where crimes are treated as scandals (or exposés, and so on), this again serves to emphasise their novelty or rarity. In these ways, the normality of corporate crimes, and their location within (and commission on behalf of) a particular organisational form – the corporation – is again obscured.

The term 'scandal' is one instance of the more general way in which particular forms of language are central to the production and reproduction of crime, law and order issues. Language carries with it particular connotations of causation (and thereby appropriate modes of prevention and regulation) and effects (seriousness). Wells has noted the potency of different forms of language attaching to different types of criminal activity:

> The word 'fraud' is an anaesthetising generic term for a number of offences including theft. If we do not call a white-collar thief a thief then we should not be surprised that it sounds a little odd to talk of a corporation stealing (or wounding or killing). The idea is difficult to contemplate because our image of the thief is of an individual physically taking the property of another. There is a conflict between the images, reinforced by the choice of language, of different types of offence and offender and the possible categories into which they could legally be placed. (1993: 10)

Thus, she continues,

> Through the use of language different messages and meanings are communicated. 'Mugging', 'joyriding', 'shoplifting', 'glassing', 'vandalism' are examples of the many colloquial terms in use for conveying the social meanings of behaviour; each has an equivalent legal term and definition. The social vocabulary for corporate harms is less well-developed. (1993: 12)

Thus if we take as an example occupational safety and health crimes, it is clear that the vast majority of these remain cast as 'accidents', which is likely to mean that there has been little or usually no investigation of their circumstances, nature and relationship to law and legal duties. The language of 'accidents' is one which focuses upon specific events, abstracting them from a more comprehensible context (Scheppele 1991). It evokes discrete, isolated and random events, and carries with it connotations of the unforeseeable, unknowable and unpreventable, despite the fact that any examination of a range of incidents reveals common, systematic, foreseeable and eminently preventable causes and consistent locations of responsibility. Similarly, both the languages of accident and illness invoke events or phenomena in which victims are implicated, via their carelessness, apathy, or lifestyles (bad eating, lack of exercise, alcohol or tobacco use, and so on; Tombs 1991).

Finally, the term 'accident' carries with it implications regarding intentionality, or the lack of it, which are crucial in the context of safety and health crimes. Thus Goldman notes that what she calls 'accidentality terms',

> provide us with an account of the mental element – intention, will, desire, deliberation, purpose, etc. – in some event. When describing some incident or process as an 'accident', or having 'occurred/been done accidentally' rather than 'deliberately' or 'intentionally', we conflate information not just about causation, and perhaps (if pertinent) degrees of culpability and fault to be imputed, but also about the element of consciousness that intruded into the event. (1994: 51–2)

There is no doubt that some of this language is the result of conscious corporate manipulation, both generally and in relation to specific events (Wells 1993: 40). This is hardly surprising given the privileged access to, and indeed the ownership of, all forms of mass media by large corporate interests. The concentration of ownership, the internationalisation of media and communication markets, the role of advertisers and sponsors, and consistent gnawing away at public broadcasting systems by corporate capital all affect the content of various media forms (Bagdakian 1997; Curran and Seaton 1988; Lorimer 1994; McChesney 1997; Tumber 1993). As Wells notes, and as is particularly of relevance given the nature of victimisation in the case of many forms of corporate crimes, the further removed the harms they cause are from the public experience, then the easier is such manipulation (1993: 40).

To say this is of course not to claim that this effect is one that can be characterised as any simplistic determining or controlling; we would not deny that, 'even in the area of business and financial coverage, the mass media, whilst still having a role in reproducing dominant ideology, do at times provide a more open terrain' (Tumber 1993: 347). Levi himself has pointed to the role that the media can and do play in exposing some forms of corporate crime, not least through drawing attention to the plight of victims (see Zedner 1997: 593).

Indeed, the use of particular forms of language need not be understood simply, or perhaps even largely, as the result of conscious manipulation, since 'The social construction of behaviour and events results from a complex interaction between a number of factors, including cultural predispositions, media representations, and legal rules, decisions, and pronouncements' (Wells 1993: 13). What we can conclude is that, all in all, the media both reflect, and help to construct, dominant conceptions of crime, law and order, from which corporate crimes are largely excluded. As Hillyard and Sim have recently stated,

> it is important not to postulate a deterministic position in terms of the relationship between the mass media and popular consciousness but as a range of sociological work has demonstrated that relationship exists and is built on a system of power which has the capability to define in as well as define out what is newsworthy, important and relevant. (1997: 57)

Even academics who tend to deny the obscuring of corporate crime within mass media in fact help to reproduce this. For example, a recent text examining 'The Media Politics of Criminal Justice' contains one half page consideration of 'white-collar crimes', and at least one other one-line reference to these crimes amongst its almost 300 pages (Schlesinger and Tumber 1994). One of these two references was the claim that 'white-collar crimes' had been found to be 'slighted to a lesser degree', that they 'received basically the same display as street crime stories', and that the 'cases concerning fraud and insider dealing in the late 1980s ... [have] given white-collar crime a prominent position in the media' (Schlesinger and Tumber 1994: 185).

REFERENCES

Bagdakian, B.H. (1997) *The Media Monopoly*, 5th edn, New York: Beacon.

Box, S. (1983) *Power, Crime and Mystification*, London: Tavistock.

Chibnall, S. (1977) *Law and Order News: An Analysis of Crime Reporting in the British Press*, London: Tavistock.

Curran, J. and Seaton, J. (1988) *Power without Responsibility: The Press and Broadcasting in Britain*, London: Routledge.

Denzin, N.K. (1990) 'Reading "Wall Street": Postmodern Contradictions in the American Social Structure', in Turner, B.S. (ed.) *Theories of Modernity and Postmodernity*, London: Sage, 31–44.

Geis, G. (1967) 'The Heavy Electrical Equipment Antitrust Cases of 1961', in Ermann, M. and Lundman, R. (eds) (1992) *Corporate and Governmental Deviance: Problems of Organizational Behaviour in Contemporary Society*, Oxford: Oxford University Press, 75–95.

Goldman, L. (1994) 'Accident and Absolute Liability in Anthropology', in Gibbons, J. (ed.) *Language and the Law*, London: Longman, 51–99.

Green, G.S. (1990) *Occupational Crime*, Chicago: Nelson Hall.

Gregory, M. (1994) *Dirty Tricks*, Boston: Little Brown.

Hillyard, P. and Sim, J. (1997) 'The Political Economy of Socio-legal Research', in Thomas, P. (ed.) *Socio-legal Studies*, Aldershot: Dartmouth, 45–75.

Levi, M. (1987) *Regulating Fraud: White Collar Crime and the Criminal Process*, London: Tavistock.

Levi, M. and Pithouse, A. (1992) 'The Victims of Fraud', in Downes, D. (ed.) *Unravelling Criminal Justice*, London: Macmillan, 229–46.

Lorimer, R. (1994) *Mass Communications: A Comparative Approach*, Manchester: Manchester University Press.

McChesney, R.W. (1997) *Corporate Media and the Threat to Democracy*, New York: Seven Stories Press.

Maguire, M. (1997) 'Crime Statistics, Patterns, and Trends: Changing Perceptions and their Implications', in Maguire, M. et al. (eds) *The Oxford Handbook of Criminology*, 2nd edn, Oxford: Clarendon Press, 135–88.

Mathiesen, T. (1997) 'The Viewer Society: Michel Foucault's "Panopticon" Revisited', *Theoretical Criminology*, 1 (2), May, 215–34.

Mirrlees-Black, C. and Ross, A. (1995) *Crime against Retail and Manufacturing Premises: Findings from the 1994 Commercial Victimisation Survey*. Home Office Research Study no. 146, London: Home Office Research and Statistics Directorate.

Nelken, D. (1994) 'White Collar Crime', in Maguire, M. Morgan, R. and Reiner, R. (eds) *The Oxford Handbook of Criminology*, Oxford: Clarendon Press.

Pearce, F. (1990) 'Responsible Corporations and Regulatory Agencies', *Political Quartely*, 61 (4).

Randall, D. (1995) 'The Portayal of Business Malfeasance in the Elite and General Media', in Geis, G. et al. (eds) *White-collar Crime: Classic and Contemporary Views*, New York: The Free Press, 105–15.

Reiner, R. (1996) 'The Case of the Missing Crimes', in Levitas, R. and Guy, W. (eds) *Interpreting Official Statistics*, London: Routledge, 185–205.

Reiner, R. (1997) 'Media Made Criminality: the Representation of Crime in the Mass Media', in Maguire, M. et al. (eds) *The Oxford Handbook of Criminology*, 2nd edn, Oxford: Clarendon Press, 189–231.

Reiss, A. Jnr and Biderman, A. (1980) *Data Sources on White-collar Law-breaking*, Washington, DC: US Department of Justice.

Scheppele, K.L. (1991) 'Law Without Accidents', in Bordieu, P. and Coleman, J.S. (eds) *Social Theory for a Changing Society*, Boulder, CO: Westview Press, 267–93.

Schlesinger, P. and Tumber, H. (1994) *Reporting Crime: The Media Politics of Criminal Justice*, Oxford: Clarendon Press.

Stephenson-Burton, A. (1995) 'Through the Looking Glass: Public Images of White-collar Crime', in Kidd-Hewitt, D. and Osborne, R. (eds) *Crime and the Media*, London: Pluto, 131–63.

Tombs, S. (1991) 'Injury and Ill-health in the Chemical Industry: De-centring the Accident-prone Victim', *Industrial Crisis Quarterly*, 5, January, 59–75.

Tumber, H. (1993) 'Selling Scandal: Business and the Media', *Media, Culture and Society*, 15, 345–61.

Vandivier, K. (1982) 'Why Should my Conscience Bother Me?', in Ermann, M.D. and Lundman, R.J. (eds) *Corporate and Governmental Deviance: Problems of Organisational Behaviour in Contemporary Society*, New York: Oxford University Press, 102–22.

Vaughan, D. (1996) *The Challenger Launch Decision: Risky Technology, Culture, and Deviance at NASA*, Chicago: Chicago University Press.

Wells, C. (1993) *Corporations and Criminal Responsibility*, Oxford: Clarendon Press.

Young, P. (1992) *Crime and Criminal Justice in Scotland*, Edinburgh: The Stationery Office.

Zedner, L. (1997) 'Victims', in Maguire, M. et al. (eds) *The Oxford Handbook of Criminology*, 2nd edn, Oxford: Clarendon Press, 577–612.

STUDY QUESTIONS

1 What do official statistics tell us about the nature of institutional and social power?

2 One of the points made by Slapper and Tombs about our understanding of corporate crimes is that language is used to convey meaning, so that the media frequently describe incidents as 'accidents', 'disasters', 'scandals' or 'negligence', rather than using language which communicates culpability and criminalizes the offence. But in the light of a spate of recent train crashes, there is evidence that this might be changing, and that pressure is mounting for 'accidents' and acts of negligence to be defined, and pursued, as criminal offences. Carry out your own content analysis of a newspaper, TV or radio report of a corporate crime, and analyse the language used in the report, and what meanings it conveys to the reader.

FURTHER READING

Although often considered to be relatively neglected within criminology, the study of white-collar and corporate crime is slowly moving from the margins of criminological enquiry, and there are a number of recent texts which provide helpful introductions to the subject. Hazel Croall has written about it in her 2001 text, *Understanding White Collar Crime*, Buckingham: Open University Press, and in (1998) *Crime and Society in Britain*, Harlow: Pearson (see Reading 16). Gary Slapper has written (1999) *Blood in the Bank: Social Legal Aspects of Death at Work*, Aldershot: Ashgate. One of the few attempts to address the role of the media in reporting white-collar crime is provided by A.E. Stephenson-Brown, 'Through the looking-glass: public images of white collar crime', chapter 7 in D. Kidd-Hewitt and R. Osborne (eds) (1995) *Crime and the Media: The Post-modern Spectacle*, London: Pluto Press. A text which discusses the invisibility of a range of different crimes is Davies, P., Francis, P. and Jupp, V. (eds) (1999) *Invisible Crimes: Their Victims and their Regulation*, Basingstoke: Macmillan.

10

Crime and the media:
a criminological perspective

David Kidd-Hewitt

Having considered the extent to which crime statistics can be said to be socially constructed in the previous three readings, we now continue to explore Gary Slapper and Steve Tombs's suggestion that the mass media also represent crime as socially constructed. In this extract, David Kidd-Hewitt examines the proposition that the media present crime stories (both factual and fictional) in ways that selectively distort and manipulate public perceptions, creating a false picture of crime which promotes stereotyping, bias, prejudice and gross oversimplification of the facts. His argument is that it is not just official statistics that misrepresent the picture of crime, but that the media are also guilty of manipulation and fuelling public fears. One of the television programmes that he singles out as being a significant contributor to false ideas about crime is *Crimewatch UK* (also mentioned by Slapper and Tombs in Reading 9) which, he argues, is guilty of locking its viewers into a terrorizing world of fear reinforcement. Kidd-Hewitt's analysis of the relationship between media and crime centres on a discussion of five key texts which, he argues, were watersheds in the development of sociological understandings of the relationship between crime and the media throughout the 1970s and 1980s, and which remain influential today. An extract from one of these pivotal studies – Stanley Cohen's *Folk Devils and Moral Panics* – is reproduced as Reading 11.

CRIMINAL CAREERS AND THE DRAMATISATION OF EVIL: THE SOCIOLOGICAL TRADITION

The sociological tradition has concentrated primarily on the ways in which the media provide us with perceptions and social constructions about the world we

SOURCE: From *Crime and the Media: The Post-Modern Spectacle*, ed. David Kidd-Hewitt and Richard Osborne (London: Pluto Press, 1995), 9–24.

inhabit. In this area the concern has not been so much whether behavioural role models purveyed by the media are likely to stimulate inappropriate 'copy-cat' behaviour amongst young people or indeed those of mature ages (although this is an important area) – rather it is often the reverse. That is, whether the media tend to engender false and damaging images about particular segments of the populace, for example young people. The accusation is one of stereotyping certain people, perhaps by reason of their age, appearance, ethnicity, gender, family background or geographical location.

Stuart Hall, for instance, refers to the process of manufacturing *public images* by the media and others in positions of power:

> A 'public image' is a cluster of impressions, themes and quasi-explanations, gathered or fused together … the presence of such 'public images' in public and journalistic discourse feeds into and informs the treatment of a particular story. Since such 'public images', at one and the same time, are graphically compelling, but also stop short of serious, searching analysis, they tend to appear in place of analysis – or analysis seems to collapse into the image.[1]

For example, a lead story in *The Sunday Times* of 5 February 1995 is headlined: 'The "savage generation" hits Britain'.[2] This follows the publication of a report by a clinical psychologist who had been looking at official crime rates for violent crime by children aged from 10–13 and 14–16. The story continued: 'Psychologists, magistrates and educationalists say a growing core of aggressive children is to blame, nurtured by the rise in single-parent families, the availability of drugs and violent videos.'[3]

References are then made to the 'public image' of the film *A Clockwork Orange* as indicative of an inevitable truth – that a cult of violence is being enjoyed by young people as young as ten years old. Contextualising the article within a failing criminal justice system, fraught teachers unable to cope, a youngster admitting to smashing car windscreens, the breakup of traditional family life and inadequate parenting skills, there can be little doubt in readers' minds that it is single-parent families that are producing the majority of violent young people who are now termed 'the savage generation'. As a concluding flourish, an author of children's books has the last word: 'Since the Eric Cantona incident I have watched young boys directing kung-fu kicks at people in the streets. Television has brought this type of incident into their homes and made it acceptable.'[4]

A significant role played by contemporary sociologists such as Geoffrey Pearson and Steve Chibnall[5] has been to illustrate how the media regularly feature and fuel concerns about the 'pathological' nature of the younger generation. There is a cycle of media-generated concern that regularly re-visits the younger generation to spell out the gloom and violence likely to come from our disenchanted offspring – the spectacle of the 'youth problem', as is the case with *A Clockwork Orange* – withdrawn from view, yet still used to sustain a post-modern nightmare of youth violence.

Deviants, Labels and Public Reaction

The sociological approach within criminology therefore is concerned with revealing the attitudes that the media might generate or reinforce amongst its viewers or readers as a whole, for example fear, anxiety, terror, hatred, admiration, prejudice, intolerance, bigotry, bias, racism. It is a concern to demystify the processes of media *selection* and media *presentation* in order to expose the simplistic view that the media merely report 'the facts', that they merely reflect society as it is.

The sociological tradition of 'challenging' the media's perception and reporting of deviant and criminal events and of drawing the processes of media production and spectacle into critical academic paradigms is relatively new. It primarily reflects the concerns of young post-war sociologists resolute in their goals to wrest criminology from its well-established pre-war determinist framework of analytical individualism and to turn criminology from the study of mere law infraction to that of law and norm infraction.[6]

> We read of murders and drug-taking, vicars eloping with members of their congregation and film stars announcing the birth of their illegitimate children, football trains being wrecked and children being stolen from their prams, drunken drivers being breathalysed and accountants fiddling the books … indeed, so much space in the mass media is given to deviance that some sociologists have argued that this interest functions to reassure society that the boundary lines between conformist and deviant, good and bad, healthy and sick, are still valid ones.[7]

Stanley Cohen provides a clear account of the agenda that was thus created for a transition into a new British criminology:

1 A re-constitution of criminology: as part of 'the sociology of deviance' and its reintegration into mainstream sociology.
2 An elevation of social control (or 'societal reaction') as a question of central concern and a consequent adoption of a structurally and politically informed version of labelling theory.
3 A determination to 'appreciate' deviance in the senses of granting recognition to the deviant's own subjective meaning and of not taking for granted the conrol system's aim of eradicating deviance.
4 An emphasis on the political nature of defining and studying crime and deviance.[8]

As a result of this 'agenda', much was accomplished in the rethinking of criminology. In the case of crime and the media, the 1970s saw the emergence of the five pivotal studies which have subsequently informed the sociological tradition in this area.

The first study, J. Young's 'The role of the police as amplifiers of deviancy, negotiators of reality and translators of fantasy',[9] developed the key concepts of 'newsworthiness' and 'deviancy amplification'. It demonstrated the relationship that exists between social control agencies and media 'fantasies' that trigger such agencies to over-react and further stereotype deviants – in this case, the marijuana smoker living in West London. It demonstrates that 'moral panics' engendered by media fantasies amplify the deviant act until there is: 'a translation of stereotypes into actuality, of fantasy into reality.'[10]

The respectable image of the police is set against the degenerate image of the bohemian and polarised by the media into a clear-cut account of good versus evil represented thus:

> hippie thugs – the sordid truth: Drugtaking, couples making love while others look on, rule by a heavy mob armed with iron bars, foul language, filth and stench, that is the scene inside the hippies' Fortress in London's Piccadilly. These are not rumours but facts – sordid facts which will shock ordinary decent family loving people.[11]

What becomes clear from Young's study is the speed with which the media can represent or, as claimed in this case, misrepresent an 'outsider life-style' and simultaneously create a social problem; and then develop from that presentation a 'moral panic' which leads to increased social control action from the police, thereby engendering more media coverage of 'sordid druggies' and so on.

The second key study is S. Cohen's *Folk Devils and Moral Panics*.[12] The concepts of 'moral panic' and 'deviancy amplification' have been enshrined in this work that examined the mods and rockers phenomenon of the 1960s.

Cohen is credited by John Muncie as producing the first *systematic* empirical study of media amplification and its public consequences.[13] It certainly strengthened the growing tradition of unpacking the media's role in reporting certain events and revealing how they are able to construct their own version of reality. In doing so, Cohen claimed to demonstrate a 'deviancy amplification spiral'. This builds on Young's concerns at the speed and power the mass media possess to create disquiet, to declare and signal a 'social problem'.

Confrontations *did* occur during Whitsun 1964 at Brighton between youths respectively designated mods or rockers. Cohen notes: 'The Mods and Rockers didn't become news because they were new; they were presented as new to justify their creation as news.'[14] It was the comparison of the 'news' with his own inventory of what occurred and the panic engendered by the way in which the confrontations were reported that Cohen outlines in some detail.

This study began to clarify sociological concern with 'the manufacture of news' as a precursor to the creation of a 'moral panic'. It also pointed to the importance of the symbolic nature of youth cultures. Whether Teddy boys, mods, rockers, punks or skinheads, there is a symbolic threat attached by the media to such perceived uncontrolled autonomy. 'They need to be brought back into line' was the moral crusade mounted by the media and other moral entrepreneurs.

The media therefore were seen initially to 'over-report' the confrontations with regular use of phrases such as 'beat up the town', 'orgy of destruction', 'seige', 'battle', 'screaming mob', 'attack'. The image of innocent holiday-makers struggling to escape from marauding hordes about to take over Brighton was clearly conveyed. The moral panic and subsequent amplification spiral ensued:

> It should be noted throughout, that the amplificatory effects of the control culture were fed back into the mass media, which further exaggerated them, thus producing another link in the sequence. If the policemen did not see themselves as 'the brave men in blue' fighting the evil mob, nor the magistrates themselves as society's chosen mouthpieces for denouncing evil, these polarizations were made in their behalf by others.[15]

It is clear from Cohen's work that sociological concern within criminological studies was now firmly directed towards exposing the media as purveyors of particular social constructions of social reality rather than as objective reporters. The concern is with serious misrepresentation and the control culture impact that flows from such misrepresentations. In other words, 'the manufacture of news'.

In 1973 Stanley Cohen and Jock Young edited a book entitled *The Manufacture of News*.[16] This was a comprehensive attempt to mobilise this growing sociological tradition of demystifying and unpacking the ideological frameworks that inform a range of institutions, the print media in particular. It also symbolises the growing concern with the study of 'deviance' as opposed to merely 'law infraction'. This volume clearly established:

- the mass media as a sociological challenge, that is what explicit or implicit views of society can be ascertained which are generated by media organisations? How do they select and present information?
- notions of deviance and social problems that are manufactured, generated and revealed by the mass media;
- the role of the mass media in moulding and legitimating the shapes and forms of societal control culture. Do they influence control culture and hence control agents, for example the police?

Overall, this was a significant attempt to suggest analytic models of analysis that would aid our sociological understanding of the mass media.

THE MASS MANIPULATIVE AND THE COMMERCIAL LAISSEZ-FAIRE MODELS

These two analytical models should be seen as extremes of a continuum – polarised and opposing. They represent traditions of media operation in the selection, presentation and likely effects of their output on the public. They are *both* capable of encapsulating right and left political positions through which a second structure of selection, presentation and effects flows and can be viewed. 'Selection according to "structured ideological biases" is at the heart of the

Mass Manipulative model but in the Commercial model ... the criteria are seen to be more *intrinsic* to the material.'[17]

Mass Manipulative model	*Commercial Laissez-faire model*
Selection/Presentation/Effects	
• structured ideological biases (*manufactured*)	• locating human interest and the unusual (*discovered*)
• status quo defended, power and interest rule	• competitive enterprise, public demand rules
• concealment of selected news and information	• fact-finding exposes and honest revelations
• high concentration of ownership aids control culture manipulation and consensual models	• concentrated and experienced ownership aids the efficient presentation of the real world and conflict models
• public as an atomised mass (*passive absorbers*)	• public as discerning consumers (*judicious receivers*)

As a means of 'testing' media portrayals of crime and deviance these models provided a critical sociological starting point. In terms of the polarity the models represent the authors comment:

> Our own position ... is at neither extreme. In playing down the more melodramatic effects of the media as portrayed in the Manipulative versions – partly because of a liberal democratic opposition to censorship and control – the Laissez-faire position exaggerates the impotence of the media. Clearly the media must have some influence.[18]

A crucial gap in the literature was filled in 1977 by S. Chibnall's *Law and Order News*.[19] This book is credited as the first to provide a study of crime journalism in Britain.

Apart from its very valuable historical documentation of the growth of 'law and order' news in the press, Chibnall has been able to extract from his study of the working relationships between crime journalists and the police what he refers to as 'the professional news imperatives of journalism.' It is the evaluation of these imperatives that has been important in informing the sociological tradition of crime and media studies since the late 1970s. This also helps to advance Cohen and Young's analysis concerning the selection criteria used for newsworthy items.

Chibnall explains that there are 'at least eight professional imperatives which act as implicit guides to the construction of news stories.'[20] These are

1	Immediacy	(speed/the present).
2	Dramatisation	(drama and action).
3	Personalisation	(culture of the personality/celebrity).
4	Simplification	(elimination of shades of grey).
5	Titillation	(revealing the forbidden/voyeurism).

6   Conventionalism   (hegemonic ideology).
7   Structured access   (experts, power base, authority).
8   Novelty   (new angle/speculation/twist).

Chibnall also provides further professional imperatives that lead to what he terms 'at least five sets of informal rules of relevancy in the reporting of violence … They guide journalists' treatment of violence by asserting the relevance of:[21]

1   Visible and spectacular acts.
2   Sexual and political connotations.
3   Graphic presentation.
4   Individual pathology.
5   Deterrence and repression.

By being aware of these 'journalistic rules of relevancy', the rationales for the selection and treatment of features relating to the coverage of violence, for example, are better understood. As our main source of crime information the mass media need to be revealed as powerful creators and interpreters on our behalf. Chibnall has added significantly to the sociological tradition within criminology that continues to expose this fact.

The last 'watershed' publication of the 1970s which developed the now growing array of *challenges* to the media from sociology, concerning its responsibilities to inform with integrity rather than merely push for sensational portrayal, is that of Hall et al., *Policing the Crisis*.[22] This study can be seen as bridging the 1970s and the first half of the 1980s in several important ways:

1   It advances the sociological debates regarding the media's portrayal of violent crime from the scholarship of the 1970s in a way that begins to inform the new debates about the fear of crimes that have been taking place since the 1980s.
2   It brings in the crucial feature of a comparative framework by siting the moral panic about mugging that occurred in the UK within its American context. Observers in the 1980s and 1990s look towards America far more now in terms of media and crime relationships of all kinds.
3   It includes a clear account of the scapegoating of black youth both here and in the US together with an analysis of the ideological and political frameworks that enabled this to occur, and continue to occur.
4   It clarifies the connections which are seen to exist between the media and control culture agencies and attempts to reveal their power base. It also adds a strong socio-economic context to the debate.

The authors followed 13 months of press and 'official' coverage between August 1972 and the end of August 1973 of the 'new' crime of mugging. They witnessed the 'get tough' ideology emerging from this period and specifically noted how crucial the media's role was in promoting a call to new regimes of law and order. The media had already spent some considerable time during the 1960s covering what was seen as spiralling crime in the US and, as is usually the case, using its horror of the American scene to warn Britain of the tendency for all things American eventually to cross the Atlantic. As Hall et al. pointed out:

When the British Press reported on American cities, the already forged connections between black unrest, inter-racial tension, the spreading ghettoes and crime tended to be reproduced in that form ... It reproduced the idea of American mugging for British consumption.[23]

Their point is that the press had educated the public so effectively that the Pavlovian reaction to a mugging headline was *not* 'a particular kind of robbery occurring on British streets' but rather 'general social crisis and rising crime'.[24] As John Muncie so succinctly puts it: 'Their explanation of the moral panic is firmly placed in the context of deteriorating material conditions in the inner-cities, worsening race relations and the development of a law and order state'.[25]

The longer-term agenda is identified as the stigmatisation of young, black West Indian males as representing the most likely embodiment of '*the mugger*', what Hall et al. refer to as '*a false enemy*'.[26] Through the application of a Marxist analysis they conclude that the symbol of the black mugger becomes part of the capitalist state's transformation of the deprivation of class in general into a specific division involving racial differences:

It provides the separation of the class into black and white with a material basis, since, in much black crime (as in much white working class crime), one part of the class materially 'rips off' another. It provides this separation with its ideological figure, for it transforms the deprivation of class, out of which crime arises, into the all too intelligible syntax of race, and fixes a false enemy: the black mugger.[27]

The media are seen by Hall et al. as integral to sustaining this image of 'a false enemy'.

At another level of crime and media representation, the reality of changed policing roles across the 1970s and into the 1980s in the TV cop shows had slowly but surely replaced the George Dixon figure with a variety of harder, grittier, confrontational police. They were depicted as more adversarial and without illusions about 'the enemy' or that they were engaged in a war.

Keith Ellawell, the Chief Constable for Cleveland, was reported in the *Daily Mail* in 1992 as lamenting the lost bobby in a rather nostalgic fashion: 'People are not as frightened of breaking the law as they were 30 years ago. The rosy-cheeked bobby on his beat is now a thing of the past.'[28] Television had realised the demise of the 'rosy-cheeked bobby' by the 1960s when *Z Cars* took to the small screen, followed by *Softly Softly* and *The Sweeney*.

Similarly in the US, throughout the 1970s in particular, TV portrayed the organisational sophistication of the police through programmes such as *SWAT*, and *Police Story*. Their gritty characters were predominantly undercover cops or at least the non-uniform variety that would have given George Dixon apoplexy – such as *Starsky and Hutch* and *Baretta*. Quirky (unlikely) partnerships such as *McMillan and Wife* and *Cagney and Lacey* provided cosy moments for those missing the Dixon mould. Other, more consensual models using the individual police person were *The Gentle Touch, Police Woman, Get Christie Love,*

Columbo, Kojak, Cannon, Barlow at Large and, for the nineteenth-century buffs, *Sergeant Cork*. Women as the velvet glove against the male iron fist became a clear portrayal into the 1980s.[29] Trow reminisces thus:

> Policemen were nice men … I think it was the friendly comforting face of George Dixon … with his 'Mind how you go', and his 'Look after dear old Mum' which strengthened the security I felt and made sense of the American conviction that our policemen were indeed wonderful.[30]

Sparks feels that moving away from the 'domestic parables' of Dixon to confronting more complex environments in TV crime fiction is functional: 'Television crime fiction brings retribution into the midst of flux and anxiety. In subordinating complex institutional conflicts to the restoration of natural justice it also offers a certain consolation, as Adorno noted.'[31]

THE MEDIA AS PURVEYORS OF FEAR, CONSTERNATION AND DREAD: THE POST-MODERN SPECTACLE

The inner-city disturbances that occurred during 1981 in the UK brought a new dimension to the mass media's ability to bring the spectacle of riot and disorder directly into viewers' homes.

In his report to the Home Office concerning the 'serious disorder in Brixton',[32] Lord Scarman began by commenting on the issue of media spectacle as follows:

> the British people watched with horror and incredulity an instant audio-visual presenta-tion on their television sets of scenes of violence and disorder in their capital city, the like of which had not previously been seen in this century in Britain … the petrol bomb was now used for the first time on the streets of Britain … These young people by their crimi-nal behaviour … brought about a temporary collapse of law and order in the centre of an inner suburb of London.[33]

The significance of this media spectacle was clearly to provide people with eyewitness accounts of more confrontational violence than had ever been seen before. Howard Tumber comments:

> Every day people saw petrol bombs being thrown, fires raging, buildings damaged, and police and youths seriously injured. It was a crisis, and the box in the corner of the room seemed to be bringing the message that civilisation was breaking down and that social order was disintegrating.[34]

Tumber also makes the point that the trivia of local round-up style news programmes were shaken into dealing with a serious analysis of the inner-city phenomenon and providing explanations for what people had witnessed.

It was at this point that the sociological tradition vied for position alongside the psychological. The copy-cat factor was a major feature of debates by psychologists. In addition claims were made that more violent television and films had acted as catalysts. Issues of social deprivation, saturation policing and media amplification spirals were contributed by the sociologists, whilst every politician who wanted publicity was able to obtain it by proffering a cause that damned their political opponents.

However, Tumber reasserted that no change had occurred in the debates concerned with potential links between watching television and committing delinquent acts. Far more evidence exists to identify unemployment as a prime factor in delinquent or violent behaviour. He quoted Halloran's conclusion that:

> most of the psychologists, sociologists and criminologists who have taken delinquency as their main topic of research or study do not appear to regard television or any of the other media as a major cause – or even as an important contributing factor to the development of delinquent behaviour.[35]

What was clearly emerging, however, was a concern about the fear of crime. Selective newspaper reporting and television documentaries, fiction, films and videos stood charged with portraying far more violent crimes, usually on women and the elderly, than are statistically likely to occur. For example, Keith Soothill and Sylvia Walby in their study *Sex Crime in the News* comment: 'The regular presence of the sex fiend on the front page is a phenomenon of the 1970s and 1980s.'[36]

They are not objecting to the news coverage of rape, which they see as a positive move, but the *nature* of that coverage that misdirects women to fear primarily 'stranger-danger' rather than attacks by members of their family or by acquaintances.

Fear of crime information was primarily gathered by successive *British Crime Surveys* during the 1980s. These show a very large gap between people's fear of being a victim and their chances of being that victim.[37] This has engendered a new debate about the 'fear of crime' problem and why there should be such a disparity between, for example, what women fear and the so-called 'reality' of those fears:

> Women's fears are seen variously as a knee-jerk reaction to media coverage of crime; a consequence of their physical and social vulnerability; a generalised response to an underlying, illogical fear of rape and sexual assault; or conversely, a rational reflection of the abuse they experience in the privacy of the home.[38]

Media coverage of crime has certainly been shown to play a significant role in generating such fear.

Schlesinger et al. in *Women Viewing Violence*[39] showed that women identify strongly with the dangers of being physically attacked. *Crimewatch UK*, the foremost 'real' crime reconstruction programme on British television, certainly stands accused of contributing significantly to increasing their audience's fear of personal attack.[40] Indeed, the television presenter of *Crimewatch UK* regularly concludes the programme with the advice: 'Don't have nightmares, do sleep well!'[41] However, the spectacle of violent crime which forms the bulk of the programme's content has rendered this a hollow 'catch-phrase' – a parody of concern.

Crimewatch UK signalled a new television spectacle when, from June 1984, it began to alert the viewing public to a range of crimes that they might help the police to solve. By 1990 the programme claimed it was a direct cause of 251 arrests from 686 cases which resulted in 171 convictions.[42] At the same time, its style of dramatic reconstructions has treated the viewing public to a vast number of portrayals of violent acts in the process of its 'crime solving'.

The programme, however, has been at pains to distance itself from both the tabloid press style of crime reporting and TV cop shows, seeing itself in a responsible partnership with the police to solve crimes and achieve natural justice. Its style of portrayal is nevertheless very close to crime fiction portrayal.[43] For example, in 1985 they reported on 'Mr Cool', so named because of his icy calm and well-turned-out appearance whilst carrying out armed robberies. He threatened to kill people but so far had not done so. He was also a kidnapper. Some of the dialogue of the reconstruction where he held an assistant building society manager under threat of violence ran as follows: 'In a minute we're going back round the front. If you try to run away or say anything I may not kill you, but you won't be able to walk again because I'll shoot you in the back.'[44]

Nick Ross and Sue Cook then recount how:

> An actor named Steve Hodson was chosen to play the part of Mr Cool for our film. Not only did he look very much like the description of the robber, but he could also recreate the silky smooth menacing manner almost perfectly. The resemblance was so striking that, as the Abbey National manager and the Flying Squad team waited for Steve to arrive on the day the filming was to begin, Peter Chapman [the building society manager], who was looking out of the window, suddenly froze. 'That's him', he shouted, pointing to the actor. Steve Hodson was delighted he looked the part until detectives jokingly asked him his movements on certain dates since August 1984. He need not have worried. While we were filming in Brentwood, Mr Cool himself was robbing another building society on the other side of London.[45]

Finally the programme detailed the Mr Cool number to ring if viewers had any information to help in the case.

It is an interesting development, however, that through the medium of such programmes the quantity of violent attacks and deaths that one is likely to witness in non-fiction reconstructions are put into context by the presenters thus: 'each monthly *Crimewatch* features more violence than some police officers will encounter in their lifetimes.'[46]

Taking *Crimewatch UK* as 'real-life' construction leads viewers to a paradigmatic confusion in which Mr Cool, *Reservoir Dogs*, the Yorkshire Ripper, football fans and terrorists all occupy the same pathological universe as they themselves inhabit. The fear of crime and the media's reassurance that something is being done constitute a closed world of threat and reinforcement which imprison the viewer.

This truly signals the era of the post-modern spectacle.

NOTES

1   Hall, S. Critcher, C., Jefferson, T., Clarke, J. and Roberts, B., *Policing the Crisis: Mugging, the State and Law and Order* (London: Macmillan, 1978), p. 118.
2   *The Sunday Times*, 5 February 1995, p. 2.
3   Ibid.
4   Ibid.
5   Pearson, G., *Hooligan: A History of Respectable Fears* (London: Macmillan, 1983) and Chibnall, S., *Law and Order News: An Analysis of Crime Reporting in the British Press* (London: Tavistock, 1977).
6   Taylor, I., Walton, P. and Young, J., *The New Criminology: For a Social Theory of Deviance* (London: Routledge and Kegan Paul, 1973).
7   Cohen, S. (ed.), *Images of Deviance* (Harmondsworth: Penguin, 1971), p. 9.
8   Cohen, S., 'Footprints' on the sand: a further report on criminology and the sociology of deviance in Britain', in M. Fitzgerald et al. (eds) *Crime and Society* (London: Routledge and Kegan Paul, 1981) p. 221.
9   Young, J., 'The role of the police as amplifiers of deviancy, negotiators of reality and translators of fantasy: some consequences of our present system of drug control as seen in Notting Hill', in Cohen, S. (ed.) *Images of Deviance* (Harmondsworth: Penguin, 1971).
10   Ibid., p. 28.
11   Quoted in Ibid., pp. 35–6.
12   Cohen, S., *Folk Devils and Moral Panics: The Creation of the Modes and Rockers* (London: MacGibbon and Kee, 1972).
13   Muncie, J., *The Trouble with Kids Today: Youth and Crime in Post-war Britain* (London: Hutchinson, 1984), p. 2.
14   Cohen, *Folk Devils*, p. 46.
15   Ibid., p. 172.
16   Cohen, S. and Young, J. (eds), *The Manufacture of News. Deviance, Social Problems and the Mass Media* (London: Constable, 1973).
17   Ibid., p. 15.
18   Ibid., p. 339.
19   For details see no. 5 above.
20   Chibnall, *Law and Order*, p. 23.
21   Ibid., p. 77.
22   For details, see no. 1 above.
23   Hall et al., *Policing the Crisis*, p. 21.
24   Ibid., p. 23.
25   Muncie, *The Trouble with Kids Today*, p. 82.
26   Hall et al., *Policing the Crisis*, p. 395.
27   Ibid.
28   *Daily Mail*, 3 March 1992, p. 15.
29   Centre for Research on Criminal Justice, *The Iron Fist and the Velvet Glove*, 2nd edn (California: CRCJ, 1977).
30   Trow, M.J., *Let Him Have It, Chris: The Murder of Derek Bentley* (London: HarperCollins, 1992), p. 82.

31   Sparks, R., *Television and the Drama of Crime: Moral Tales and the Place of Crime in Public Life* (Buckingham: Open University Press, 1992), p. 29.

32   Lord Scarman, *The Scarman Report: The Brixton Disorders 10–12 April 1981* (Harmondsworth: Penguin, 1982), pp. 13–14.

33   Ibid.

34   Tumber, H., *Television and the Riots* (London: British Film Institute, 1982), p. 43.

35   Ibid., pp. 48–9.

36   Soothill, K. and Walby, Sylvia, *Sex Crime in the News* (London: Routledge, 1991), p. 156.

37   *British Crime Surveys*, 1982, 1984 and 1988 (London: HMSO).

38   Painter, K., 'The "facts" of fear', *Criminal Justice Matters*, 19 (Spring 1995), p. 25.

39   Schlesinger, P. et al., *Women Viewing Violence* (London: British Film Institute, 1992).

40   Schlesinger, P. and Tumber, H., ' "Don't have nightmares: do sleep well"', *Criminal Justice Matters*, 11 (Spring 1993), p. 4. See also Schlesinger, P. and Tumber, H., *Reporting Crime: The Media Politics of Criminal Justice* (Oxford: Clarendon Press, 1994).

41   Ross, N. and Cook, S., *Crimewatch* UK (London: Hodder and Stoughton, 1987), p. 158.

42   Schlesinger and Tumber, ' "Don't have nightmares"', p. 4.

43   Schlesinger, P. and Tumber, H., 'Fighting the war against crime: television, police and audience', *British Journal of Criminology*, 33 (1) (Winter 1993), pp. 19–32.

44   Ross and Cook, *Crimewatch UK*, p. 97.

45   Ibid.

46   Ibid., p. 158.

STUDY QUESTIONS

1   Summarize in your own words the reasons why Kidd-Hewitt highlights Young (1971); Cohen (1972); Cohen and Young (1973); Chibnall (1977), and Hall et al. (1978) as the key 'watersheds' in the development of understandings about the relationship between crime and the media.

2   Monitor an edition of *Crimewatch* or a similar show (it would be useful to video it so that you can analyse it in detail). What *kinds* of crimes dominate the programme? What groups of people are most likely to be represented as 'victims', especially in the dramatic reconstruction? Who are most frequently likely to be featured as perpetrators of crime? Does your analysis support the view of Kidd-Hewitt (this reading), Slapper and Tombs (Reading 9), Box (Reading 7) and other critics that such TV programmes are guilty of portraying a partial, distorted view of crime and increasing the fear of personal attack among *certain sections* of their audience?

FURTHER READING

A useful analysis of the work of crime journalists, and the relationship between the mass media, crime and criminal justice professional, is Schlesinger, P. and Tumber, H. (1994) *Reporting Crime: The Media Politics of Criminal Justice*, Oxford:

Clarendon Press, which to a great extent builds on the earlier, but still widely referenced *Law and Order News: An Analysis of Crime Reporting in the British Press* by Steve Chibnall (1977) London: Tavistock. The Schlesinger and Tumber book has a chapter on the origins and subsequent evolution of *Crimewatch UK* (chapter 9: 'Don't have nightmares ...'). The chapter that follows the reading reprinted above is well worth reading: Osborne, R. (1995) 'Crime and the media: from media studies to postmodernism' in D. Kidd-Hewitt and R. Osborne (eds) *Crime and the Media: The Post-modern Spectacle,* London: Pluto Press; as is Reiner, R. (1997) 'Media made criminality: the representation of crime in the mass media', in M. Maguire, R. Morgan and R. Reiner (eds) *The Oxford Handbook of Criminology,* 2nd edn, Oxford: Oxford University Press, which provides a useful overview of the relationship between the media and crime. An interesting contribution from the emerging field of cultural criminology is Ferrell, J. and Sanders, C. (eds) *Cultural Criminology,* Boston: Northeastern University Press (especially chs 1 and 2).

11

Folk devils and moral panics: the creation of the mods and rockers

Stanley Cohen

As noted in the introduction to Reading 10, the book from which this extract is taken is a 'classic' text, extensively referenced in the annals of criminology, sociology, cultural studies and media studies. Its original publication in 1972 coincided with a new concern across all these emerging and developing areas of undergraduate study in the 'sociology of deviance' and a concomitant interest in the impact of the mass media which had enjoyed a rapid expansion over the previous two decades. The extract chosen is interesting for a number of reasons. First, it beautifully encapsulates the mundane 'ordinariness' of the events which gave rise to a moral panic about two rival groups in mid-1960s' Britain. Secondly, Cohen argues that the characteristics that distinguish moral panics from other forms of media reporting are strikingly similar to those which characterize the reporting of physical disasters such as earthquakes or bombings. He supports this idea with an analysis of three different aspects of media reporting: exaggeration and distortion; prediction; and symbolization. The third interesting point which is implicit in this piece is that it tends to be young people who are primarily constructed as social problems. It is not the case that *all* moral panics are concerned with the perceived deviance of youth (recent 'panics' over immigrants and paedophiles are examples of those that target adult 'deviants'), but it is true to say that a large proportion of moral outrage over the years has been directed at children and young people (see Readings 19 and 20). A fourth point of interest is the way in which Cohen describes the news as 'manufactured'. By this he means that

SOURCE: From *Folk Devils and Moral Panics: The Creation of the Mods and Rockers* (St Albans: Paladin, 1973), 30–48.

news is constructed around a series of norms and expectations which define what those who work in the media selectively consider 'newsworthy' and which serve an institutionalized need to 'create' news in order to sell newspapers. As you read the extract, think about the extent to which Cohen's formulation of a moral panic can be applied to recent examples of media concern about crime and deviance.

[…] I am concerned here with the way in which the situation was initially interpreted and presented by the mass media, because it is in this form that most people receive their pictures of both deviance and disasters. Reactions take place on the basis of these processed or coded images; people become indignant or angry, formulate theories and plans, make speeches, write letters to the newspapers. The media presentation or inventory of the Mods and Rockers events is crucial in determining the later stages of the reaction.

On the Monday morning following the initial incidents at Clacton, every national newspaper, with the exception of the *The Times* (fifth lead on main news page) carried a leading report on the subject. The headlines are self-descriptive: 'Day of Terror by Scooter Groups' (*Daily Telegraph*), 'Youngsters Beat Up Town – 97 Leather Jacket Arrests' (*Daily Express*), 'Wild Ones Invade Seaside – 97 Arrests' (*Daily Mirror*). The next lot of incidents received similar coverage on the Tuesday and editorials began to appear, together with reports that the Home Secretary was 'being urged' (it was not usually specified exactly by *whom*) to hold an inquiry or to take firm action. Feature articles then appeared highlighting interviews with Mods and Rockers. Straight reporting gave way to theories especially about motivation: the mob was described as 'exhilarated', 'drunk with notoriety', 'hell-bent for destruction', etc. Reports of the incidents themselves were followed by accounts of police and court activity and local reaction. The press coverage of each series of incidents showed a similar sequence.

Overseas coverage was extensive throughout; particularly in America, Canada, Australia, South Africa and the Continent. The *New York Times* and *New York Herald Tribune* carried large photos, after Whitsun, of two girls fighting. Belgian papers captioned their photos 'West Side Story on English Coast'.

It is difficult to assess conclusively the accuracy of these early reports. Even if each incident could have been observed, a physical impossibility, one could never check the veracity of, say, an interview. In many cases, one 'knows' that the interview must be, partly at least, journalistic fabrication because it is too stereotypical to be true, but this is far from objective proof. Nevertheless, on the basis of those incidents that were observed, interviews with people who were present at others (local reporters, photographers, deckchair attendants, etc.) and a careful check on internal consistency, some estimate of the main distortions can be made. Checks with the local press are particularly revealing. Not only are the reports more detailed and specific, but they avoid statements like 'all the dance halls near the seafront were smashed' when every local resident knows that there is only one dance hall near the front.

The media inventory of each initial incident will be analysed under three headings: (i) Exaggeration and Distortion; (ii) Prediction; (iii) Symbolization.

EXAGGERATION AND DISTORTION

Writing when the Mods and Rockers phenomenon was passing its peak, a journalist recalls that a few days after the initial event at Clacton, the Assistant Editor of the *Daily Mirror* admitted in conversation that the affair had been 'a little over-reported'.[1] It is this 'over-reporting' that I am interested in here.

The major type of distortion in the inventory lay in exaggerating grossly the seriousness of the events, in terms of criteria such as the number taking part, the number involved in violence and the amount and effects of any damage or violence. Such distortion took place primarily in terms of the mode and style of presentation characteristic of most crime reporting: the sensational headlines, the melodramatic vocabulary and the deliberate heightening of those elements in the story considered as news. The regular use of phrases such as 'riot', 'orgy of destruction', 'battle', 'attack', 'siege', 'beat up the town' and 'screaming mob' left an image of a besieged town from which innocent holidaymakers were fleeing to escape a marauding mob.

During Whitsun 1964 even the local papers in Brighton referred to 'deserted beaches' and 'elderly holidaymakers' trying to escape the 'screaming teenagers'. One had to scan the rest of the paper or be present on the spot to know that on the day referred to (Monday, 18 May) the beaches were deserted because the weather was particularly bad. The 'holidaymakers' that *were* present were there to watch the Mods and Rockers. Although at other times (for example, August 1964 at Hastings) there was intimidation, there was very little of this in the Brighton incident referred to. In the 1965 and 1966 incidents, there was even less intimidation, yet the incidents were ritualistically reported in the same way, using the same metaphors, headlines and vocabulary.

The full flavour of such reports is captured in the following lines from the *Daily Express* (19 May 1964): 'There was Dad asleep in a deckchair and Mum making sandcastles with the children, when the 1964 boys took over the beaches at Margate and Brighton yesterday and smeared the traditional postcard scene with blood and violence.'

This type of 'over-reporting' is, of course, not peculiar to the Mods and Rockers. It is characteristic not just of crime reporting as a whole but mass media inventories of such events as political protests, racial disturbances and so on. What Knopf[2] calls the 'shotgun approach' to such subjects – the front page build up, the splashy pictures, the boxscores of the latest riot news – has become accepted in journalism. So accepted in fact, that the media and their audiences have lost even a tenuous hold on the meaning of the words they use. How is a town 'beaten up' or 'besieged'? How many shop windows have to be broken for an 'orgy of destruction' to have taken place ? When can one – even metaphorically – talk of scenes being 'smeared with blood and violence'? Commenting on the way the term 'riot' is used to cover *both* an incident result-ing in 43 deaths, 7,000 arrests and $45 million in property damage *and* one in which three people broke a shop window, Knopf remarks: 'The continued media use of the term contributes to an emotionally charged climate in which the public tends to view every event as an "incident", every incident as a "disturbance" and every disturbance as a "riot".'[3]

The sources of over-reporting lay not just in such abuses of language. There was a frequent use of misleading headlines, particularly headlines which were discrepant with the actual story: thus a headline 'violence' might announce a story which, in fact, reports that *no* violence occurred. Then there were more subtle and often unconscious journalistic practices: the use of the generic plural (if a boat was overturned, reports read ' boats were overturned') and the technique, well known to war correspondents, of reporting the same incident twice to look like two different incidents.

Another source of distortion lay in the publication, usually in good faith, of reports which were later to receive quite a different perspective by fresh evidence. The repetition of obviously false stories, despite known confirmation of this, is a familiar finding in studies of the role of the press in spreading mass hysteria.[4] An important example in the Mods and Rockers inventory was the frequently used '£75 cheque story'. It was widely reported that a boy had told the Margate magistrates that he would pay the £75 fine imposed on him with a cheque. This story was true enough; what few papers bothered to publish and what they all knew was that the boy's offer was a pathetic gesture of bravado. He admitted three days later that not only did he not have the £75 but did not even have a bank account and had never signed a cheque in his life. As long as four years after this, though, the story was still being repeated and was quoted to me at a magistrates' conference in 1968 to illustrate the image of the Mods and Rockers as affluent hordes whom 'fines couldn't touch'.

This story had some factual basis, even though its real meaning was lost. At other times, stories of organization, leadership and particular incidents of violence and vandalism were based on little more than unconfirmed rumour. These stories are important because – as I will show in detail – they enter into the consciousness and shape the societal reaction at later stages. It is worth quoting at length a particularly vivid example from the media coverage of an American incident:

> In York, Pa., in mid-July, 1968, … incidents of rock- and bottle-throwing were reported. Towards the end of the disturbance UPI in Harrisburg asked a stringer to get something on the situation. A photographer took a picture of a motorcyclist with an ammunition belt around his waist and a rifle strapped across his back. A small object dangled from the rifle. On July 18, the picture reached the nation's press. The Washington Post said: 'ARMED RIDER – Unidentified motorcyclist drives through heart of York, Pa., Negro district, which was quiet for the first time in six days of sporadic disorders.' The Baltimore Sun used the same picture and a similar caption: 'QUIET BUT … An unidentified motorcycle rider armed with a rifle and carrying a belt of ammunition, was among those in the heart of York, Pa., Negro district last night. The area was quiet for the first time in six days.'

> The implication of this photograph was clear: the 'armed rider' was a sniper. But since when do snipers travel openly in daylight completely armed? Also, isn't there something incongruous about photographing a sniper, presumably 'on his way to work' when according to

the caption, the city 'was quiet'? Actually, the 'armed rider' was a sixteen-year-old boy who happened to be fond of hunting groundhogs – a skill he had learned as a small boy from his father. On July 16, as was his custom, the young man had put on his ammo belt and strapped a rifle across his back, letting a hunting licence dangle so that all would know he was hunting animals, not people. Off he went on his motorcycle headed for the woods, the fields, the groundhogs – and the place reserved for him in the nation's press.[5]

Moving from the form to the content of the inventory, a detailed analysis reveals that much of the image of the deviation presented was, in Lemert's term, putative: 'that portion of the societal definition of the deviant which has no foundation in his objective behaviour.'[6] The following is a composite of the mass media inventory:

> Gangs of Mods and Rockers from the suburbs of London invaded, on motor bikes and scooters, a number of seaside resorts. These were affluent young people, from all social classes. They came down deliberately to cause trouble by behaving aggressively towards visitors, local residents and the police. They attacked innocent holidaymakers and destroyed a great deal of public property. This cost the resorts large sums of money in repairing the damage and a further loss of trade through potential visitors being scared to come down.

The evidence for the ten elements in this composite picture is summarized below:

1   *Gangs* – There was no evidence of any structured gangs. The groups were loose collectivities or crowds within which there was occasionally some more structured grouping based on territorial loyalty, e.g. 'The Walthamstow Boys'.
2   *Mods and Rockers* – Initially at least, the groups were not polarized along the Mod–Rocker dimension. At Clacton, for example, the rivalry (already in existence for many years) between on the one hand those from London and on the other locals and youths from the surrounding counties, was a much more significant dimension. The Mod–Rocker polarization was institutionalized later and partly as a consequence of the initial publicity. In addition, throughout the whole life of the phenomenon, many of the young people coming down to the resorts did not identify with either group.
3   *Invasion from London* – Although the bulk of day-trippers, young and old, were from London, this was simply the traditional Bank Holiday pattern. Not all offenders were from London; many were either local residents or came from neighbouring towns or villages. This was particularly true of the Rockers who, in Clacton and Great Yarmouth, came mainly from East Anglian villages. The origins of fifty-four youths, on whom information was obtainable, out of the sixty-four charged at Hastings (August 1964) was as follows: London or Middlesex suburbs – twenty; Welwyn Garden City – four; small towns in Kent – nine; Sussex – seven; Essex – four; and Surrey – ten.
4   *Motor-bikes and Scooters* – At every event the majority of young people present came down by train or coach or hitched. The motor-bike or scooter owners were always a minority; albeit a noisy minority that easily gave the impression of ubiquity.
5   *Affluence* – There is no clear-cut information here of the type that could be obtained from a random sample of the crowd. Work on the Brighton Archway Ventures and

all information from other sources suggest that the young people coming down were not particularly well off. Certainly for those charged in the courts, there is no basis for the affluence image. The average take home pay in Barker and Little's Margate sample was £11 per week.[7] The original Clacton offenders had on them an average of 15s for the whole Bank Holiday weekend. The best off was a window-cleaner earning £15 a week, but more typical were a market assistant earning £7 10s 0d. and a seventeen-year-old office boy earning £5 14s 0d.

6 *Classless* – Indices such as accent and area of residence, gathered from court reports and observation, suggest that both the crowds and the offenders were predominantly working class. In the Barker–Little sample, the typical Rocker was an unskilled manual worker, the typical Mod a semi-skilled manual worker. All but two had left school at fifteen. At Clacton, out of the twenty-four charged, twenty-three had left school at fifteen, and twenty-two had been to secondary moderns. All were unskilled; there were no apprentices or anyone receiving any kind of training.

7 *Deliberate Intent* – The bulk of young people present at the resorts came down not so much to make trouble as in the hope that there would be some trouble to watch. Their very presence, their readiness to be drawn into a situation of trouble and the sheer accretion of relatively trivial incidents were found inconvenient and offensive; but if there really had been great numbers deliberately intent on causing trouble, then much more trouble would have resulted. I will make this point clearer when analysing the impact. The proportion of those whom the police would term 'troublemakers' was always small. This hard core was more evident at Clacton than at any of the subsequent events: twenty-three out of the twenty-four charged (ninety-seven were originally arrested) had previous convictions.

8 *Violence and Vandalism* – Acts of violence and vandalism are the most tangible manifestations of what the press and public regard as hooliganism. These acts were therefore played up rather than the less melodramatic effect of the Mods and Rockers which was being a nuisance and inconvenience to many adults. In fact, the total amount of serious violence and vandalism was not great. Only about one-tenth of the Clacton offenders was charged with offences involving violence. At Margate, Whitsun 1964, supposedly one of the most violent events – the one which provoked the *Daily Express* 'blood and violence' report – there was little more recorded violence than two stabbings and the dropping of a man on to a flower bed. At Hastings, August 1964, out of forty-four found guilty, there were three cases of assaulting the police. At Brighton, Easter 1965, out of seventy arrests there were seven for assault. Even if the definition of violence were broadened to include obstruction and the use of threatening behaviour, the targets were rarely 'innocent holidaymakers', but members of a rival group, or, more often, the police. The number of recorded cases of malicious damage to property was also small; less than 10 per cent of all cases charged in the courts. The typical offence throughout was obstructing the police or the use of threatening behaviour. In Clacton, although hardly any newspapers mentioned this, a number of the twenty-four were charged with 'non-hooligan'-type offences: stealing half a pint of petrol, attempting to steal drinks from a vending machine and 'obtaining credit to the amount of 7d by means of fraud other than false pretences' (an ice-cream).

9 *Cost of Damage* – The court figures for malicious damage admittedly underestimate the extent of vandalism because much of this goes undetected. Nevertheless, an examination of the figures given for the cost of the damage suggests that this was not as excessive as reported. Table 10.1 shows the cost of damage at the first four events. It must be remembered also that a certain

Table 10.1   *Cost of Damage to Four Resorts: easter and Whitsun, 1964*

Place	Date	No. of arrests	Estimated cost of damage
Clacton	Easter, 1964	97	£513
Bournemouth	Whitsun, 1964	56	£100
Brighton	Whitsun, 1964	76	£400
Margate	Whitsun, 1964	64	£250

Source: Estimates by local authorities quoted in local press.

amount of damage to local authority property takes place every Bank Holiday. According to the Deputy Publicity Manager of Margate,[8] for example, the number of deckchairs broken (fifty) was not much greater than on an ordinary Bank Holiday weekend; there were also more chairs out on Whit Sunday than ever before.

10   *Loss of Trade* – The press, particularly the local press, laid great emphasis on the financial loss the resorts had suffered and would suffer on account of the Mods and Rockers through cancelled holidays, less use of facilities, loss of trade in shops, restaurants and hotels. The evidence for any such loss is at best dubious. Under the heading 'Those Wild Ones Are To Blame Again', the Brighton *Evening Argus* quoted figures after Whitsun 1964 to show that, compared with the previous Whitsun, the number of deckchairs hired had dropped by 8,000 and the number using the swimming pool by 1,500. But the number using the miniature railway increased by 2,000, as did the number of users of the putting green. These figures make sense when one knows that on the day referred to, the temperature had dropped by 14 °F. and it had been raining the night before. This is the main reason why there was less use of deckchairs and the swimming pool. In Hastings, August 1964, despite a big scare-publiciy build up, the number of visitors coming down by train increased by 6,000 over the previous year.[9] Newspapers often quoted 'loss of trade' estimates by landlords, hotel keepers and local authority officials, but invariably, final figures of damage fell below the first estimates. These revised figures, however, came too late to have any news value.

Although there were cases of people being scared away by reports of the disturbances, the overall effect was the opposite. The Margate publicity department had a letter from a travel agent in Ireland saying that the events had 'put Margate on the map'. Leaving aside the additional young people themselves attracted by the publicity – they would not be defined as commercial assets – many adults as well came down to watch the fun. I was often asked, on the way down from Brighton station,'Where are the Mods and Rockers today?', and near the beaches, parents could be seen holding children on their shoulders to get a better view of the proceedings. In an interview with a reporter during which I was present, a man said, 'My wife and I came down with our son (aged 18) to see what all this fun is at the seaside on Bank Holidays' (*Evening Argus*, 30 May 1964). By 1965 the happenings were part of the scene – the pier, the whelks, the Mods and Rockers could all be taken in on a day trip.

PREDICTION

There is another element in the inventory which needs to be discussed separately because it assumes a special importance in later stages. This is the implicit assumption, present in virtually every report, that what had happened was inevitably going to happen again. Few assumed that the events were transient occurrences; the only questions were where the Mods and Rockers would strike next and what could be done about it. As will be suggested, these predictions played the role of the classical self-fulfilling prophesy. Unlike the case of natural disasters where the absence of predictions can be disastrous, with social phenomena such as deviance, it is the presence of predictions that can be 'disastrous'.

The predictions in the inventory period took the form of reported statements from local figures such as tradesmen, councillors and police spokesmen about what should be done 'next time' or of immediate precautions they had taken. More important, youths were asked in TV interviews about their plans for the next Bank Holiday and interviews were printed with either a Mod or a Rocker threatening revenge 'next time'. The following are extracts from two such interviews: 'Southend and places won't let us in any more. It will get difficult here and so next year we'll probably go to Ramsgate or Hastings' (*Daily Express*, 30 March 1964). 'It could have been better – the weather spoiled it a bit. Wait until next Whitsun. Now that will be a real giggle' (*Daily Mirror*, 31 March 1964).

Where predictions were not fulfilled, a story could still be found by reporting non-events. So, for example, when attention was switched to East Anglian resorts in 1966, the *East Anglian Daily Times* (30 May 1966) headed a report on a play attended by a group of long-haired youths 'Fears When Ton-up Boys Walked in Groundless'. Reporters and photographers were often sent on the basis of false tip-offs to events that did not materialize. In Whitsun 1965, a *Daily Mirror* report from Hastings, where nothing at all happened, was headed 'Hastings – Without Them'. In Whitsun 1966 there was a report (*Daily Mirror*, 30 May 1966) on how policemen on a 'Mods and Rockers patrol' in Clacton could only use their specially provided walkie-talkies to help two lost little boys. Again, headlines often created the impression that something had happened: the *Evening Argus* (30 May 1966) used the subheading 'Violence' to report that 'in Brighton there was no violence in spite of the crowds of teenagers on the beach'.

These non-event stories, and other distortions springing from the prediction theme, are part of the broader tendency which I will discuss later whereby discrepancies between expectations and reality are resolved by emphasizing those new elements which confirm expectations and playing down those which are contradictory. Commenting on this tendency in their analysis of the media coverage of the October 1968 Vietnam war demonstrations, Halloran et al. draw attention to a technique often employed in the Mods and Rockers inventory, 'a phrase or sentence describing in highly emotive terms either the expectation of violence or an isolated incident of violence, is followed by a completely contradictory sentence describing the actual situation'.[10]

The cumulative effect of such reports was to establish predictions whose truth was guaranteed by the way in which the event, non-event or pseudo-event it referred to was reported.

SYMBOLIZATION

Communication, and especially the mass communication of stereotypes, depends on the symbolic power of words and images. Neutral words such as place-names can be made to symbolize complex ideas and emotions; for example, Pearl Harbor, Hiroshima, Dallas and Aberfan. A similar process occurred in the Mods and Rockers inventory: these words themselves and a word such as 'Clacton' acquired symbolic powers. It became meaningful to say 'we don't want another Clacton here' or 'you can see he's one of those Mod types'.

There appear to be three processes in such symbolization: a word (Mod) becomes symbolic of a certain status (delinquent or deviant); objects (hairstyle, clothing) symbolize the word; the objects themselves become symbolic of the status (and the emotions attached to the status). The cumulative effect of these three processes as they appeared in the inventory was that the terms Mods and Rockers were torn from any previously neutral contexts (for example, the deno-tation of different consumer styles) and acquired wholly negative meanings. The identical effect is described by Turner and Surace in their classic study of the Zoot Suit riots,[11] and by Rock and myself in tracing how the Edwardian dress style became transformed into the Teddy Boy folk devil.[12]

In their case study, Turner and Surace refer to this process as the creation of 'unambiguously unfavourable symbols'. Newspaper headlines and inter-personal communication following the initial incidents in Los Angeles, reiter-ated the phobia and hatred towards Mexican American youth. References to this group were made in such a way as to strip key symbols (differences in fashion, life style and entertainment) from their favourable or neutral connota-tions until they came to evoke unambiguously unfavourable feelings. Content analysis showed a switch in the references to Mexicans to the 'Zooter theme', which identified this particular clothing style as the 'badge of delinquency' and coupled such references with mention of zoot-suiter attacks and orgies. Invariably the zooter was identified with the generalized Mexican group. In the same way, the Mods and Rocker status traits were, in later stages of the reaction, to wash off on the generalized adolescent group. Their 'badge of delinquency' emerged as symbols, such as the fur-collared anorak and the scooter, which became sufficient in themselves to stimulate hostile and punitive reactions.[13]

Symbols and labels eventually acquire their own descriptive and explana-tory potential. Thus – to take examples from an earlier folk devil – the label 'Teddy Boy' became a general term of abuse (for example, John Osborne being described as 'an intellectual Teddy Boy'); the devil was seen as a distinct type of personality (drugs were announced to soothe Teddy Boys and make them co-operative for treatment, statements made such as 'some of these soldiers here are just Teddy Boys in army uniform') and the symbols were seen as changing the person ('he was never in trouble before he bought an Edwardian suit'; 'since my son bought this thing a year ago his personality has changed').

Such symbolization is partly the consequence of the same standard mass communication processes which give rise to exaggeration and distortion. Thus, for example, misleading and inappropriate headlines were used to create unambiguously negative symbols where the actual event did not warrant this at all or at least was ambiguous. Accounts of certain events in Whitsun 1964, for example, were coupled with a report of a 'Mod' falling to his death from a cliff outside Brighton. Similarly, in August 1964 there were headlines 'Mod Dead In Sea'. In neither case had these deaths anything to do with the disturbances; they were both pure accidents. A reading of the headlines only, or of early reports not mentioning police statements about the accidents, might have led to a misleading connection. This sort of effect reached its bizarre heights in a headline in the *Dublin Evening Press* (18 May 1964) 'Terror Comes to English Resorts. Mutilated Mod Dead In Park'. The 'mutilated Mod' was, in fact, a man between twenty-one and twenty-five wearing a 'mod jacket'(?) who was found stabbed on the Saturday morning (the day *before* the incidents at the resorts) in a Birmingham park.[14]

Another highly effective technique of symbolization was the use of dramatized and ritualistic interviews with 'representative members' of either group. The *Daily Mirror* (31 March 1964) had 'Mick The Wild One' on 'Why I Hurled That Chisel' and another boy who said, 'I take pep pills. Everybody does here.' The *Daily Herald* (18 May 1964) quoted one boy clutching his injured head as the police bundled him into a van saying, 'Carry on with the plan'; another said, 'We're not through yet. We're here for the holiday and we're staying. Margate will wish it was Clacton when we're finished.' The *Evening Standard* (19 May 1964) found 'The Baron' who hated 'Mods and Wogs' and said, 'I like fighting ... I have been fighting all my life.' The *Daily Mirror* (8 May 1964) found a new angle with 'The Girls Who Follow The Wild Ones Into Battle' and who said about fighting: 'it gives you a kick, a thrill, it makes you feel all funny inside. You get butterflies in your stomach and you want the boys to go on and on ... It's hard luck on the people who get in their way, but you can't do anything about that.'

It is difficult to establish how authentic these interviews are. In some cases they ring so patently absurd a note that they cannot be an accurate transcription of what was actually said; the *Daily Telegraph* (31 March 1964), for example, carried an interview with a Rocker who said, 'We are known as the Rockers and are much more with it.' If any group had a 'with-it' self-image and would even contemplate using such a term, it certainly was not the Rockers. It would be fair to describe these interviews and reports as being composite, not necessarily in the sense of being wilfully faked, but as being influenced by the reporter's (or sub-editor's) conception of how anyone labelled as a thug or a hooligan *should* speak, dress and act. This effect may have occasionally been heightened by a certain gullibility about the fantasies of self-styled gang leaders.[15]

Through symbolization, plus the other types of exaggeration and distortion, images are made much sharper than reality. There is no reason to assume that photographs or television reports are any more 'objective'. In a study of the different perceptions experienced by TV viewers and on-the-spot spectators of another crowd situation (MacArthur Day in Chicago), it was shown how the reporting was distorted by the selection of items to fit into already existing expectations.[16] A sharpening up process occurs, producing emotionally toned symbols which eventually acquire their own momentum. Thus the dissemination of overwhelming public support in favour of MacArthur 'gathered force as it was incorporated into political strategy, picked up by other media, entered into gossip and thus came to overshadow immediate reality as it might have been recorded by an observer on the scene'.[17]

In this study, observers recorded how their expectations of political enthusiasm and wild mass involvement were completely unfulfilled. Through close-ups and a particular style of commentary ('the most enthusiastic crowd ever in our city ... you can feel the tenseness in the air ... you can hear the crowd roar') television structured the whole event to convey emotions non-existent to the participants. This effect explains why many spectators at the Mods and Rockers events found them a slight let-down after the mass media publicity. As Boorstin remarks in discussing the effects of television and colour photography: 'Verisimilitude took on a new meaning ... The Grand Canyon itself became a disappointing reproduction of the Kodachrome original.'[18]

THE INVENTORY AS MANUFACTURED NEWS

The cumulative effects of the inventory can be summarized as follows: (i) the putative deviation had been assigned from which further stereotyping, myth making and labelling could proceed; (ii) the expectation was created that this form of deviation would certainly recur; (iii) a wholly negative symbolization in regard to the Mods and Rockers and objects associated with them had been created; (iv) all the elements in the situation had been made clear enough to allow for full-scale demonology and hagiology to develop: the information had been made available for placing the Mods and Rockers in the gallery of contemporary folk devils.

Why do these sort of inventories result? Are they in any sense 'inevitable'? What are the reasons for bias, exaggeration and distortion? To make sense of questions such as these, one must understand that the inventory is not, of course, a simple sort of stock-taking in which some errors might accidentally creep in from time to time. Built into the very nature of deviance, inventories in modern society are elements of fantasy, selective misperception and the deliberate creation of news. The inventory is not reflective stock-taking but manufactured news.

Before pursuing this notion, let me mention some of the more 'genuine' errors. On one level, much exaggeration and distortion arose simply from the ambiguous and confused nature of the situation. It is notoriously difficult in a crowd setting to estimate the numbers present and some of the over-estimates were probably no more than would have occurred after events such as political demonstrations, religious rallies, pop concerts or sporting fixtures. The confusion was heightened by the presence of so many reporters and photographers: their very presence could be interpreted as 'evidence' that something massive and important was happening.

As I will show when analysing the setting in more detail, it was a problem for everyone present – police, spectators, participants, newsmen – to actually know what was happening at any one time. In such situations, the gullibility effect is less significant than a general susceptibility to all sorts of rumours. Clark and Barker's case study of a participant in a race riot shows this effect very clearly,[19] and in disaster research prospective interviewers are warned, 'People who have discussed their experiences with others in the community can rapidly assimilate inaccurate versions of the disaster. These group versions may quickly come to be accepted by a large segment of the population.'[20]

Important as such errors may be in the short run, they cannot explain the more intrinsic features of deviance inventories: processes such as symbolization and prediction, the direction of the distortions rather than the simple fact of their occurrence, the decision to report the deviance in the first place and to continue to report it in a particular way. Studies of moral panics associated with the Mods and Rockers and other forms of deviance, as well as detailed research on the mass communication process itself (such as that by Halloran and his colleagues) indicate that two interrelated factors determine the presentation of deviance inventories: the first is the institutionalized need to create news and the second is the selective and inferential structure of the news-making process.

The mass media operate with certain definitions of what is newsworthy. It is not that instruction manuals exist telling newsmen that certain subjects (drugs, sex, violence) will appeal to the public or that certain groups (youth, immigrants) should be continually exposed to scrutiny. Rather, there are built-in factors, ranging from the individual newsman's intuitive hunch about what constitutes a 'good story', through precepts such as 'give the public what it wants' to structured ideological biases, which predispose the media to make a certain event into news.

The weekend of the Clacton event was particularly dull from a news point of view. Nothing particularly noteworthy happened nationally or internationally. The fact that the event was given such prominence must be due partly at least to the absence of alternative news. The behaviour itself was not particularly new or startling. Disturbances of various sorts – variously called 'hooliganism', 'rowdyism' or 'gang fights' occurred frequently throughout the late fifties and early sixties in coastal resorts favoured by working-class adolescents. In 1958, for example, Southend police had to appeal for outside support after rival groups had fought battles on the pier. In Whitley Bay, Blackpool and other northern resorts there were disturbances and fighting often more severe than any of the early Mods and Rockers episodes. For years British holidaymakers on day trips or weekend excursions to such European coastal resorts as Calais and Ostend have been involved in considerable violence and vandalism. In Ostend, from the beginning of the sixties, there was a period of the year referred to as the 'English season' during which holidaymakers and members of amateur football clubs caused considerable damage and trouble, rarely reported in the British press. The Mods and Rockers didn't become news because they were new; they were presented as new to justify their creation as news.

It would be facile to explain the creation of the inventory purely in terms of it being ' good news'; the point is simply that there was room for a story at that initial weekend and that its selection was not entirely due to its intrinsic properties. Labelling theorists have drawn attention to the complex nature of the screening and coding process whereby certain forms of rule-breaking are picked out for attention [...]. These are features which relate to social control as a whole and not just the media. The media reflected the real conflict of interests that existed at various levels: for example, between local residents and police on the one hand and the Mods and Rockers on the other. In such situations the media adjudicate between competing definitions of the situation, and as these definitions are made in a hierarchical context – agents of social control are more likely to be believed than deviants – it is clear which definition will win out in an ambiguous and shifting situation.[21]

Once the subject of the story is fixed, its subsequent shape is determined by certain recurrent processes of news manufacture. Halloran et al. refer to the development of an *inferential structure*: this is not intentional bias nor simple selection by expectation, but 'a process of simplification and interpretation which structures the meaning given to the story around its original news value'.[22] The conceptual framework they use to locate this process – and one that is equally applicable to the Mods and Rockers – is Boorstin's notion of the *event as news*. That is to say, the question of 'is it news' becomes as important as 'is it real ?' The argument simply is that:

> events will be selected for news reporting in terms of their fit or consonance with pre-existing images – the news of the event will confirm earlier ideas. The more unclear the news item and the more uncertain or doubtful the newsman is in how to report it, the more likely it is to be reported in a general framework that has been already established.[23]

It is only when the outlines of such general frameworks have been discerned, that one can understand processes such as symbolization, prediction, the reporting of non-events and the whole style of presentation. The predictability of the inventory is crucial. So constant were the images, so stylized was the mode of reporting, so limited was the range of emotions and values played on, that it would have been perfectly simple for anyone who had studied the Mods and Rockers coverage to predict with some accuracy the reports of all later variations on the theme of depraved youth: skinheads, football hooligans, hippies, drug-takers, pro-festivals, the Oz trial. [...]

NOTES

1   Peter Laurie, *The Teenage Revolution* (London: Anthony Blond, 1965), p. 130.
2   Terry Ann Knopf, 'Media Myths on Violence', *Columbia Journalism Review* (Spring 1970), pp. 17–18.
3   Ibid., p. 20.

4   See, for example, Norman Jacobs, 'The Phantom Slasher of Taipei: Mass Hysteria in a Non-Western Society', *Social Problems*, 12 (Winter 1965), p. 322.

5   Knopf, 'Media Myths on Violence', p. 18.

6   Edwin M. Lemert, *Social Pathology* (New York: McGraw Hill, 1951), p. 55.

7   Paul Barker and Alan Little, 'The Margate Offenders: Survey', *New Society* 30 July 1964. This research sample will be referred to subsequently as the 'Bake – Little sample'.

8   Interview (23 November 1964).

9   Estimate by Hastings Stationmaster, quoted in *Hastings and St Leonards Observer* (8 August 1964).

10 James D. Halloran et al., *Demonstrations and Communications: A Case Study* (Harmondsworth: Penguin Books, 1970), p. 112.

11 These riots took place in Los Angeles in 1943. Sailors indiscriminately beat up Mexicans and the 'zoot suit' – the long coat and trousers pegged at the cuffs worn by boys with long, greased hair – became the symbol around which the rioters rallied. In the decade preceding the riots, the treatment of Mexicans in the media gradually became less favourable and concept of 'zoot-suiter' had been built up as a negative symbol, associated with all sorts of crime and deviance. See Ralph H. Turner and Samuel J. Surace, 'Zoot Suiters and Mexicans: Symbols in Crowd Behaviour', *American Journal of Sociology*, 62 (1956), pp. 14–20.

12 Paul Rock and Stanley Cohen, 'The Teddy Boy', in V. Bogdanor and R. Skidelsky (eds), *The Age of Affluence: 1951–1964* (London: Macmillan, 1970).

13 During the inventory period, scooter owners and manufacturers frequently complained about the bad publicity that they were getting. After Clacton, the general secretaries of the Vespa and Lambretta Scooter Clubs issued a statement dissociating their clubs from the disturbances.

14 Newspapers farthest away from the source invariably carried the greatest distortions and inaccuracies. The *Glasgow Daily Record and Mail* (20 May 1964), for example, described Mods as being dressed in short-jacketed suits, with bell bottoms, high boots, bowler or top hats and carrying rolled-up umbrellas.

15 Yablonsky has provided numerous examples of how outside observers accept at face value the fantasies of gang leaders and members. See Lewis Yablonsky, *The Violent Gang* (New York: Free Press, 1962).

16 Kurt Lang and Gladys Lang, 'The Unique Perspective of Television and its Effect: A Pilot Study', *American Sociological Review*, 18 (February 1953), pp. 3–12. Halloran et al., *Demonstrations and Communications*, report an identical process in their analysis of the TV coverage of the 1968 anti-Vietnam war demonstrations.

17 Lang and Lang, 'Unique Perspective', p. 10.

18 Daniel J. Boorstin, *The Image* (Harmondsworth: Penguin Books, 1963), p. 25.

19 Kenneth B. Clark and James Barker, 'The Zoot Effect in Personality: Race Riot Participant', *Journal of Abnormal and Social Psychology*, 40 (1965), pp. 143–8.

20 I.H. Cissin and W.B. Clark, 'The Methodological Challenge of Disaster Research', in G.W. Baker and D.W. Chapman (eds), *Man and Society in Disaster* (New York: Basic Books, 1962), p. 28.

21 The notion of a 'hierarchy of credibility' in regard to deviance is suggested by Howard S. Becker in his paper 'Whose Side Are We On?', *Social Problems*, 14 (Winter 1967), pp. 239–67.

22 Halloran et al., *Demonstrations and Communications*, pp. 215–16.

23 Ibid., p. 26.

STUDY QUESTIONS

1   Although it has become something of an orthodoxy in studies of crime, deviance and the media, Stanley Cohen never intended his conceptualization of

moral panics to be anything other than a discursive case study which might provoke further debate. Consequently, it has recently come in for a great deal of criticism, with some sceptics dismissing it as an idea without substance that is used as a 'catch-all' term to describe *any* widespread concern, from food scares to flu crises (see *Further Reading*, especially Waddington, 1986, and Jewkes, 1999; also Reading 12). What merits do you see in the moral panic thesis, and can it tell us anything useful about the relationship between crime and the media?

2   Cohen describes moral panics as 'manufactured news'. Which elements of the two analytical models outlined by Kidd-Hewitt in Reading 10 – the 'mass manipulative' and 'commercial *laissez-faire*' models – can be found in Cohen's analysis of the Mods and Rockers episode?

3   To what extent do you now think that the mass media contribute to 'mythologies' of crime, as described by Box in Reading 7? How might we distinguish between different media (including new media such as the Internet) when assessing their impact on our thinking about crime?

FURTHER READING

Early attempts to theorize the relationship between the mass media and deviants are found in the collection: Cohen, S. and Young, J. (1971) (eds) *The Manufacture of News*, London: Constable. One of the most comprehensive and well-researched books on moral panics is Goode, E. and Ben-Yehuda, N. (1994) *Moral Panics: The Social Construction of Deviance*, Oxford: Blackwell. Also of interest is Thompson, K. (1998) *Moral Panics*, London: Routledge. A number of texts contain critiques of the moral panic thesis. Among the most vehemently critical is Waddington, P.A.J. (1986) 'Mugging as a moral panic: a question of proportion' pp. 250–6 *British Journal of Sociology*, 37 (2). Also worth a look are Jewkes, Y. (1999) *Moral Panics in a Risk Society: A Critical Evaluation*, Crime, Order and Policing Occasional Paper Series no. 15, Leicester: Scarman Centre; McRobbie, A. and Thornton, S. (1995) 'Rethinking moral panic for multi-mediated social worlds', *British Journal of Sociology*, 46 (4): 559–74 and Watney, S. (1987) *Policing Desire: Pornography, Aids and the Media*, London: Methuen.

12

The ultimate neighbour from hell? stranger danger and the media framing of paedophiles

Jenny Kitzinger

This reading examines a case study – the media reporting of paedophiles – which came to prominence in the late 1990s. In it, Jenny Kitzinger discusses the role of the media in shaping and responding to the problem of releasing sex offenders from prison, and analyses why it became such an emotional issue at this particular time, when convicted sex offenders had been quietly returning to the community from prison for many years previously. Kitzinger's analysis centres on the ways in which the media tapped into existing public fears, presenting the community with an identifiable 'hate figure' on to whom it could project its anxiety and frustration. For Kitzinger, this made the issue something other than (or *more* than) a moral panic, a term which, in her view, reduces the events that she describes to media-generated hysteria, negating the very real and rational responses that the issue provoked. In reducing the story to mere media froth, it also neglects the positive role that the media can play as a forum for public debate. But Kitzinger further argues that the relationship between the media and policy-makers was dangerously intertwined at this time, and it is questionable whether events drove the news agenda or whether the news agenda drove events. According to Kitzinger, one of the legacies of the paedophile crisis is that concerns over children's safety have escalated, but that the domination of the agenda by the shadowy figure of the 'paedophile' – a concept laden with very specific ideas and assumptions – has served to locate dangerousness in a few malfunctioning individuals. In diverting attention to 'stranger danger', and characterizing

SOURCE: From *Social Policy, the Media and Misrepresentation*, ed. Bob Franklin (London: Routledge, 1999), 207–21.

the paedophile as the personification of evil, the media have reinforced the belief that paedophiles are a separate species, a 'breed apart', underplaying the fact that sexual violence exists – indeed, is endemic – in *all* communities, and that sexual abuse of children is more likely to occur within the family than at the hands of an 'evil stranger'.

[...] Child sexual abuse was 'discovered' by the modern media in the mid-1980s. In the UK, this 'discovery' began in 1986 when Esther Rantzen devoted an entire programme called *Childwatch* to the issue and launched the children's helpline 'Childline'. This was quickly followed by a dramatic increase in attention to the issue of child abuse in the rest of the media. Analysis of *The Times*, for example, shows a four-fold increase in coverage of sexual abuse between 1985 and 1987 (Kitzinger 1996) and it became a regular topic for documentaries such as *Everyman* (BBC1, 8 May 1988), *Horizon* (BBC2, 19 June 1989), *World in Action* (ITV, 20 May 1991), and *Panorama* (BBC1, 7 December 1992). By the early 1990s, the issue began to appear in chat shows and drama programmes too. Sexual abuse storylines were incorporated into regular series such as *The Bill* (ITV, 29 January 1993) and *Casualty* (BBC1, 6 February 1993) as well as soap operas such as *EastEnders* and *Brookside* (see Henderson 1998).

Throughout this media attention a constant (but often shadowy) figure lurked in the background: the figure of 'the paedophile'. He appeared in silhouette in Esther Rantzen's original *Childwatch* exposé. He was 'unmasked' in press reports as the Jekyll and Hyde character who posed as a caring priest or committed director of a children's home (Aldridge 1994). He was introduced as 'psycho Trevor' in *Brookside* (Henderson 1998). More recently he even put in a controversial appearance on the chat show *Kilroy* boasting about his offences against children (*The Times* 23 July 1997).[1]

It was not until the second half of the 1990s, however, that public debate began to focus on the dilemmas posed by convicted sex offenders released back into the community. Although sporadic concern, especially around particular individuals, was evident earlier (see Soothill and Walby 1991), it was only in 1996 that media and public outrage focused on these men (and some women) who might invisibly slip back into society free to abuse again.

The origins of this particular focus can be located in 1996. Initial media attention to the 'paedophiles-in-the-community' problem was generated by central government policy initiatives. In March 1996 Michael Howard (then Home Secretary) proposed legislation to monitor sex offenders, details of which were published in June. This led to headlines such as: 'National paedophile register to be set up' (*The Times*, 23 March 1996), 'Paedophiles to be "marked men" on national register' (*The Times*, 18 May 1996) and 'Howard plans paedophile curbs' (*Guardian*, 13 June 1996). The legislation was introduced in December of that year prompting further headlines including: 'Paedophile lists for police' (*The Times*, 19 December 1996) and 'Crackdown on sex offenders unveiled' (*Guardian*, 19 December 1996).

Such reporting followed routine media practice whereby media agendas are traditionally set by high-status official sources (such as government bodies)

(Tuchman 1978). But media coverage and public debate shifted rapidly as particular communities and sections of the media began to agitate for public access to the register and demand that communities be notified when dangerous individuals moved into their neighbourhood. Journalists and pressure groups picked up on similar community notification legislation in the USA known as 'Megan's Law'. Introduced in 1996 this legislation was named after a seven-year-old New Jersey girl, Megan Kanka, who was raped and murdered by a twice-convicted sex offender who lived across the street. Towards the end of 1996, and early 1997, the 'big story' for the media, but the major headache for policy makers, became not government initiatives, but public fear and anger. Headlines in the national press included: 'Parents in dark as paedophiles stalk schools' (*Guardian*, 24 November 1996). 'Paedophile out of prison "fearful for life and limb"' (*Observer*, 15 December 1996), 'Jeering mothers drive paedophile off council estate' (*The Times*, 11 January 1997), 'Stop hiding perverts say protest mums' (*Daily Mail*, 3 February 1997) and 'Town not told of paedophiles' stay' (*The Times*, 12 October 1997).

Protest rapidly spread from one area to another, and concern quickly esca-lated: the role of the local press in voicing these concerns was crucial. Although often ignored when thinking about the media, the local press can play a key role. Indeed, the local media influence many national and international policy-making processes from road building to the disposal of nuclear waste (Franklin and Murphy 1998). The theme of 'paedophiles-within-the-community' received extensive regional media coverage across the UK from Aberdeen to Brighton, from Leicester to Belfast, from Teesside to Lancashire. Indeed, many of the national stories about paedophiles began life on the front page of local papers and some neighbourhood protests were sparked by local press reports rather than vice versa. Headlines from local papers announced: 'Angus mums on alert over local sex offender' (*Press and Journal* (Aberdeen), 17 June 1998), 'Parents besiege abuser's house' (*Press and Journal*, 17 July 1997), 'Residents pledge to continue campaign' (*Leicester Mercury*, 4 July 1998), 'Give us the right to know' (*Torquay Herald Express*, 2 September 1997). 'Parents' paedophile poster campaign' (*Evening Gazette*, (Teesside), 26 January 1998), 'Panic hits town over perverts' (*Belfast Telegraph News*, 22 March 1997) and 'Sex offender's home torched' (*Belfast Telegraph News*, 6 October 1997).

Such articles often included quotes from the host of local residents' groups which formed in response to the 'paedophile' threat: organisations such as 'Freedom for Children', 'People's Power', 'Parents Opposed to Paedophiles' and 'The Unofficial Child Protection Unit'. Reports were also often accompa-nied by photographs of local people marching with banners declaring 'Perverts out' (*Press and Journal*, 9 June 1997) or children carrying placards reading: 'Make me safe' (*Torquary Herald Express*, 2 September 1997). The *Manchester Evening News* published a front-page spread about a local sex offender alongside a photograph of him in his car behind a smashed windscreen after 'a vigilante mob had vented their anger' (cited in Thomas 1997: 68). The tone of some of this reporting was overtly provocative and clearly 'fed the flames' of protest.[2]

Many newspapers adopted a more proactive role rather than merely reporting local unrest with whatever degree of approval or urgings of restraint.

Some papers assumed the role of guardians of public safety, especially in relation to particular dangerous individuals. Robert Oliver, involved in the brutal sexual assault and killing of Jason Swift, was repeatedly pursued by journalists. The *Sun* asked readers to phone an emergency number if Oliver was spotted (*Guardian*, 18 October 1997) and, when he moved to Brighton the local paper, the *Evening Argus*, published his picture on their front page with the headline 'Beware this evil pervert' (*Evening Argus*, 14 October 1997).

In other cases, newspapers alerted people to the presence of 'paedophiles', either through knocking on the doors of neighbours and asking how they felt about living near a sex offender or through 'outing' them on the front page. The *Sunday Express* printed photographs and details of offenders with their last-known address under the headline 'Could these evil men be living next door to you?' (cited in Thomas 1997). The Scottish *Daily Record* produced a similar campaign, devoting the bulk of one issue to asserting a 'Charter for our children' and demanding 'The legal right for communities to be told when a pervert moves into the area' (*Daily Record*, 25 February 1997). Alongside articles headed 'End the suffering', 'Pervert's playground' and 'Monster freed to kill', they published a double-page 'Gallery of shame' with thirty-eight photographs and names of convicted offenders and details of their offences.[3] Four of these were described as 'people power' success stories. One man was 'hounded out of Drumchapel housing scheme because of his sick background' and another 'forced into hiding' while 'people power drove sick child molester, Christie, 50 out of Stirling' (*Daily Record*, 25 February 1997).

'MORAL PANICS' AND 'LYNCH MOBS'?

Such media coverage and the public reactions it reflected, triggered and amplified, presented a major problem for those involved in monitoring and housing convicted sex offenders. The media were accused of whipping up 'hysteria', creating a 'moral panic' and encouraging a 'lynch mob mentality'. Routine community notification and the automatic right of public access to the sex offender' register is opposed by chief constables, chief probation officers and the NSPCC (*Guardian*, 19 February 1997). The main reason for their opposition is the belief that it will not protect children. Instead it may result in vigilante action and drive offenders underground making it less possible to monitor or 'treat' them. Indeed the Association of Chief Officers of Probation (ACOP) documented ten cases where the press had given editorial authority to campaigns to identify and expel offenders, leading to disruption of supervision and, even, to acts of violence (ACOP 1998). Convicted abusers were beaten up and driven from their homes, leaving behind arrangements put in place to monitor them (such as electronic tagging and video surveillance) and often absenting themselves from any treatment programmes. The notorious Robert Oliver was obliged to move from London to Swindon to Dublin to Brighton. Refused hostel accommodation, his location was repeatedly exposed by the media and he finally took refuge in a police station. Ironically, the police and probation services were obliged to protect sex offenders from the public rather than vice versa. The cost of protecting Oliver is estimated at around £25,000 (Adams 1998).

In addition, other people are often caught up in the violence and harassment aimed at 'paedophiles'. Hostels have been attacked (whether or not convicted sex offenders are in residence). The wife and child of one offender were named and driven from their home after it was set on fire. In an earlier case a young girl died after a house in which she had been staying was burnt down (*Guardian*, 10 June 1997). In Brimingham, the 81-year-old mother of a convicted sex offender was forced to move and her home was wrecked when the *Birmingham Evening Mail* twice publicised the address where she lived with her son. In Manchester, a man was badly beaten by a gang who mistook him for a paedophile named by the *Manchester Evening News*.

The panic about paedophiles has also been used to victimise individuals with no known official record of sex offences (and with no connection to convicted offenders). Sometimes it seemed little more than a convenient way of harassing unpopular or minority members of the community (reading between the lines, it appears that gay men and those with mental disabilities are particularly likely to be victimised). The *Sunday Times* documented '30 cases where men wrongly suspected of abusing children have been beaten and humiliated by gangs bent on driving them out of their homes' (*Sunday Times*, 2 November 1997). While writing this chapter, the sensitivity and ongoing nature of some of the controversies was illustrated by reactions to requests I made for information. One newspaper said they would only send out a copy of their exposé on sex offenders if my request was made in writing because of 'the sensitive nature of the material'. A children's charity refused to disclose their policy on this issue over the phone; they would only supply it in print form because 'you have to be so careful'. A media complaints body said they could, at present, release no information beyond saying that they were 'in discussion' and 'looking at' the questions raised by the media 'outing' of offenders.

Clearly the media contributed to the spiral of unrest across the country and some coverage was at the very least counterproductive if not blatantly irresponsible. The media, however, did not create community protests out of thin air and it is fundamentally unhelpful to dismiss media and community reactions as a 'moral panic'. This concept implies that the panic is totally unjustified and that it is state-sanctified; neither could be asserted in this case without qualification. More fundamentally the theory fails to pay attention to the processes through which a 'moral panic' is engendered and therefore offers a way of glossing over rather than truly investigating public reactions (Miller et al. 1998). To accuse the media of whipping up 'hysteria' and creating 'lynch mob' violence is equally inadequate and ignores key sites through which community reactions evolve. (The very term 'lynch mob' is used to signal irrationality in ways which, in addition, obscure the history of lynching and its position in relation to institutional racism.)

Instead of dismissing public and media reactions as proof of their failure to match the rationality and objectivity of the policy makers, it is crucial to give detailed attention to the questions raised by 'the public' and to examine the processes which led to the policy makers and 'the professionals' losing control of the agenda. This is essential if we are to understand the many complex levels on which the media can play a role in social policy issues.

THEORISING COMMUNITY AND MEDIA PROTEST

The 'paedophile-in-the-community' coverage was driven by factors operating on three levels: the first concerns policy and practice initiatives; the second relates to local community responses and the role of local media; the third involves the underlying construction of 'the paedophile' which underpinned the whole debate.

Policy and Practice: Initiatives, Developments and Unanswered Questions

The initial decision to establish a register placed the issue of 'paedophiles-in-the-community' on the public agenda: it begged more questions than it answered. How should these offenders be monitored and who should have access to this information? Policy and practice on this issue were clearly under-developed and often inconsistent. Legal rulings and professional disputes received extensive media coverage. There were, for example, several cases exposing uncertainty about sex offenders' housing rights: 'Town considers banning sex offenders from council houses' (*Guardian*, 9 January 1997) and 'Eviction of paedophile justified, court rules' (*Guardian*, 20 February 1997). Confusion also surrounded probation officers' responsibilities to pass on information about their clients to prospective employers. The Home Office originally advised probation officers not to notify employers of sex crime convictions in case employees were sacked leading to court actions for damages. This advice was quickly withdrawn leading to headlines such as: 'Home Office confusion on paedophiles' (*Guardian*, 5 December 1996).

Policy on notification to the general public seemed to develop in a similar ad hoc fashion. Particularly high-profile cases raised the following questions. If a housing officer takes it upon himself to inform tenants about a released sex offender on their estate should he be disciplined? Should schools be told, but not pass on the information to parents, or did this place headteachers in an untenable position? Should the police inform the public, but only under very special circumstances? One couple in North Wales, for example, was granted legal aid to sue police for publicising details about their sexual offences (*Manchester Evening News*, 9 June 1997). In some cases public warnings were released: 'Police warn of threat to young males: town on paedophile alert' (*Guardian*, 15 October 1997). In other cases communities were not informed, or only provided with information after media exposure. In a graphic illustration of direct interaction between the media and policy decisions one London Council decided to warn parents about a 'very dangerous' convicted abuser who had moved into their area, but only after learning that a television documentary was to name the man (*Guardian*, 27 March 1997). It was not until September 1997 that guidelines came into force clarifying procedures. Police were given the power to warn headteachers, youth group and play-group leaders and local child protection agencies that a convicted sex offender had moved into their area. But these guidelines did not empower the police to broadcast the names of paedophiles generally unless a professional risk assessment said this was necessary. ('Paedophile guidelines expected to end "outing"' *Guardian*, 12 August 1997).

Public fears and critical media interest were also enhanced by the loopholes in the Sex Offenders Act. These loopholes were readily illustrated by high-profile cases such as that of Graham Seddon – a convicted sex abuser, detained by officers in June 1997 carrying a bag containing toys. He was, he said, looking for a child. Seddon was (briefly) detained in a Liverpool hospital but could not be kept against his will. The notorious Robert Oliver (convicted in 1985) also slipped through a loophole. Judged to be neither repentant nor rehabilitated this man was released without any compulsion to comply with supervision; legislation compelling such compliance only applied to those released after a certain date.

Consequently, in the second half of the 1990s there was a confluence of events (such as the release of particular notorious individuals) and the development of policy and procedures which heightened public awareness of this threat. The original highly newsworthy government initiatives set the news agenda, but that agenda was rapidly revised by the questions it posed about obvious areas of uncertainty.

To suggest that events drove the news agenda would be mere tautology. Some events became 'newsworthy' because of existing news hooks (the court case concerning the eviction of a 'paedophile', for example, would not have received so much media coverage outside this time). Minor events quickly become newsworthy because they are 'topical'. Thus 'satellite' reporting included escorted visits of convicted sex offenders to play-parks and fun-fairs and plans for a commercial UK 'paedophile directory'.

In addition, some of the events which generated peak news coverage around this time were also, of course, not official events (such as court cases, government announcements or inquiries); much of the coverage focused on the surrounding community action. In order to understand the extent of local neighbourhood and media protest it is also necessary to look more closely at these responses.

Neighbourhood Reactions: Democracy, Trust and Local Information Exchange and Representation

The local media clearly fed into neighbourhood responses and helped to identify targets for popular anger. Concern about children's safety, however, was certainly not a new phenomenon. 'The paedophile' had already been established as 'public enemy number one' and, long before 1996, fear of the predatory paedophile was etched into the bedrock of parents' anxieties. In focus groups I conducted in the early 1990s, it was clear that fears of child abduction were woven into the fabric of parental experience. Parents talked about the heart-stopping moment when they looked round and realised their young child had disappeared from their side or described the daily pattern of worry every time a son or daughter was late home. One woman summed up her fears and sense of lack of control by stating 'When Andrew goes round the corner he could be off the end of the earth.'

In these focus groups it was also clear that some communities already felt under siege. People spoke about predatory men coming on to the housing estates and, in almost every group, parents described incidents where 'shady' individuals had been seen behaving suspiciously around playgrounds or children had been approached by strangers. Such events inevitably become the topic of conversation (e.g. outside the school gate) and parents felt they had a duty to seek out and share such information. By contrast assaults on children by men within the family were rarely shared with the community (Kitzinger 1998).

Given this background it is hardly surprising that the idea that known sex offenders were to be secretly housed in their neighbourhoods triggered grave concern. The very names of some of the community protest groups express their anger at the restrictions placed upon their lives (e.g. 'Freedom for Children') and their desire to assert their rights (e.g. 'People's Power'). Some protest groups also chose names which encapsulated their disillusionment with official protection and monitoring procedures (e.g. 'The Unofficial Child Protection Unit'). This disillusionment (and some hope and expectations) was vividly articulated by the founder of the (anti-vigilante) 'Scottish People Against Child Abuse'. Speaking to the *Scotsman*, she commented:

> People must be able to sit back and be responsible. If they saw something constructive being done, maybe they would start having trust again in the authorities. The Government is there because we trusted them to look after us and protect our children, but they are not doing that yet. (Scotsman, 16 October 1997)

Official incompetence was a recurring theme both in local discussion and in national coverage. Internationally high-profile cases of multiple sex abusers (from Dutroux in Belgium to Fred and Rosemary West in Cromwell Street) suggested that 'the professionals' could not be trusted to monitor and investigate properly. Dutroux was able to continue his activities even though police were notified that he was building dungeons to imprison abducted children (Kelly 1997). The police were regular visitors to Cromwell Street but the Wests were able to continue to rape and murder their victims. Both these cases served as a backdrop to public concern. In 1997 this concern was underlined, with the murder of Scott Simpson in Aberdeen by a known 'paedophile'. The boy's murderer was under social-work supervision but this did not prevent him committing this crime. The bungling of the Scott Simpson case received extensive coverage (particularly in Scotland). The case was blamed on a failure of social services to follow guidelines and to convey relevant information to the police. The police were also criticised for 'serious corporate failure' in investigating the nine-year-old's disappearance ('Inquiry into blunder as paedophile gets life' *Scotsman*, 11 November 1997). The name of Scott Simpson was evoked by those campaigning for community notification in future cases. His murder suggested the 'experts' and 'professionals' could not provide sufficient protection on their own.

If such cases inspired little faith in 'the authorities', then housing inequalities further exacerbated the crisis. Released prisoners, including convicted sex offenders, tend to be placed in hostels or offered housing in working-class areas and often on council estates. Where offenders were offered social housing, rather than returning to private accommodation, this also raised particular questions about policy. Many protesters expressed anger and frustration at the fact that their fate was to be decided by faceless bureaucrats who rarely lived in such areas themselves. The question often asked in public meetings called to reassure people was: 'How would *you* feel if he was living next door to you and your kids?' Residents often seemed to feel that council tenants were expected to put up with living next to an incinerator, playgrounds built on polluted sites, damp housing or a failing local school. Now they were also expected to tolerate the country's most dangerous predators dumped on their doorsteps. People living on council estates are also, of course, less likely to have access to private transport, or even decent public transport, safe play areas and consistent childcare, all of which may mute concerns about children's safety.

For some protesters it was clear that direct action (ranging from seeking media publicity to vigilante activities) represented the only way of having their voices heard. The local media, for their part, were usually happy to cooperate and have a special remit to respond to local pressure groups and address community reactions. Local newspaper editorials demanding (or in effect providing) community notification presented the papers as standing up for their constituents, asserting a strong neighbourhood identity and fulfilling their functions as representative of 'the people'. While local media have problems representing some local concerns (such as pollution from a factory which is key to providing local jobs), the sex offender presented an apparently clear-cut 'enemy' and 'outsider'. As the *Daily Record* declared: 'the Record believes action must be taken now to confront the plague of abuse that wrecks young lives and disgusts all right-minded Scots' (*Daily Record*, 25 February 1997).

In understanding media and public reactions, therefore, it is important not to be dismissive when 'the public' come into conflict with 'the experts' or when local 'NIMBYISM' seems to come into conflict with the 'wider public good'. Community concern and the conditions under which people are forced to live should not be underestimated. As feminist journalist and author Beatrix Campbell points out, community notification may not be the best way of protecting children, however:

> There is a piety around the notion of 'the mob' which doesn't take responsibility for what some communities endure. A liberal disposition can't cope with what these communities

are facing. There are communities, there are children, who live in a permanent panic about when he's going to get out of prison. That fear, and the dreadful consequences for individuals and communities, don't always infuse the debate. (Beatrix Campbell, conversation with author)

The issue of former neighbours returning from prison to live near their victims has certainly enjoyed considerable media prominence. A housing worker faced with press coverage of such a situation expresses some ambivalence about the media's role. The press focus was unhelpful and resulted in a defensive reaction from parts of the housing authority and generated unnecessary fear on the estate. But media coverage did trigger an official acknowledgement of the problem. Indeed:

> The media were useful in that the tenants had tried telling their housing officer and had not succeeded in persuading her to listen. It is a shame that the council obviously felt inaccessible so that they had to go to the press. There are lessons to be learned from that. But the press made sure that the council reacted. (Housing Officer, interview with author)

In this particular case, local and national media attention also led to further enquiries from tenants about other individuals on this estate. This, in turn, led to the exposure of a further case in which children might be at risk and where there had been a failure in inter-departmental communication. According to the housing officer, this led to 'significant policy shifts about the sharing of professional information and adoption of protocols and guidelines to support that.'

The media then should not be seen as merely 'interfering' in an area best left to 'the experts'. Public debate and involvement in social policy issues is a democratic and practical imperative. Questions from the media and 'the public' (as neighbours, tenants, and citizens) can disrupt important policy initiatives, but they can also be effective in pushing issues onto the policy agenda and refining procedures.

There were far more fundamental problems, however, with the way in which the debate about paedophiles was framed in public discourse, including media coverage and policy making. These problems have far deeper roots than the immediate concerns raised in the second half of the 1990s and this chapter concludes by problematising the way in which 'the paedophile' was constructed as an object of social policy and by identifying some of the problems which were obscured by the media focus on convicted offenders.

Framing Paedophiles: Public, Media and Policy Gaps in Addressing Child Sexual Abuse

Throughout this chapter the word 'paedophile' has appeared in inverted commas: the intention has been to signal the constructed nature of the term.

'The paedophile' has become the dominant way through which sexual threats to children are conceptualised and articulated, but the concept is laden with ideas and assumptions which confine thinking about this issue to a very narrow focus.

'The paedophile' is a concept enmeshed in a series of crass stereotypes which place the child sexual abuser 'outside' society. In the tabloid press abusers are 'animals', 'monsters' 'sex maniacs', 'beasts' and 'perverts' who are routinely described as 'loners' and 'weirdos'. Right across the media it is also implied that paedophiles, far from being 'ordinary family men', are more likely to be gay (for systematic analysis of this see Kitzinger and Skidmore 1995). Such conceptualisations were amply illustrated in the press reporting about 'paedophiles-in-the-community'. The *Daily Record's* 'Gallery of shame', for example, perpetuated all the old stereotypes, highlighting particular words in bold block capitals. Struggling for variety of negative epithets to describe their gallery of thirty-eight sex offenders the paper ran through the usual list warning readers of: 'TWISTED Dickons [who] got eight years for raping two young sisters'; 'WEIRDO Sean Regan 'who 'was dubbed "The Beast"', and 'DEPRAVED paedophile Harley' who preyed on terrified children as young as six.' Other convicted offenders were variously described as: 'EVIL Herriot', 'PERVERT teacher', 'SEXUAL predator', and 'SEX BEAST'. In among these highlighted adjectives one man was simply described as 'BACHELOR Paritt'(with its gay implications) and three of the descriptions highlighted a disability (e.g. 'DEAF Duff posed as a priest as he prowled the street' and 'DEAF MUTE Eaglesham, 66, carried out a series of sex attacks on a 10-year-old girl') (*Daily Record*, 25 February 1997).

Portraits of 'paedophiles' do more than simply stereotype and reinforce prejudice against particular minority groups. They also imply that 'paedophiles' are a separate species, subhuman or 'a breed apart' (Hebenton and Thomas, 1996). The term also singles out the sexual abuse of children, as if there were no connection between the acts of sexual abuse and exploitation perpetrated against children and those perpetrated against adult women. One interesting piece of information released by the Home Office during the height of the paedophile crisis was the fact that, by the time they are forty, one man in 90 has been convicted of a serious sex offence, such as rape, incest or gross indecency with a child (Marshall 1997). This fact, combined with evidence that most perpetrators of sexual assault are never convicted, suggests that every community is likely to have its share of sex offenders. The release of the Home Office statistic received some media attention, but was quickly forgotten and rarely integrated into the narrative of stories about 'paedophiles-in-the-community'. The fact that most 'paedophiles-in-the-community' were undetected and probably well integrated into their neighbourhood was rarely raised. The fact that most people would already know a sex offender was ignored.

To acknowledge that sexual violence was quite so endemic would have undermined the narrative thrust of most 'paedophile-in-the-community' stories. By confining their attention to a minority of convicted multiple abusers and defining those who sexually abuse children as a certain type of person, 'a paedophile', the media were able to focus not on society but on a few dangerous individuals within it. The problem of sexual violence was represented by the newspaper image of the man with staring eyes or the evil smirk, the 'beast' and 'fiend' who could be singled out, electronically tagged, exposed and expelled. If paedophiles are literally 'evil personified', then such evil can be exorcised by exclusion of these individuals from society. This individualised approach fits in with certain strands in criminological discourse (see Hebenton and Thomas 1996); it also fits in with the whole media shift towards 'dumbed down' personalised stories whereby, for example, journalists focus on the noisy and antisocial 'neighbour from hell' rather than examining the problem of 'sink estates' through analysis of employment, recreation facilities and housing condition (Franklin 1997). 'Paedophiles' are, of course, in this sense the ultimate neighbour from hell.

The concept of 'the paedophile' is flawed. It locates the threat of abuse within the individual (rather than in social, cultural or bureaucratic institutions). In the context of abuse in children's homes, for example, attention can be focused on the cunning infiltrator while ignoring the nature of care system, funding and resourcing. In the case of other sites of abuse attention is confined to 'the outsider' and 'the loner' leaving the role of fathers, and the institution of the family unquestioned. 'The paedophile' is presented as a danger which 'prowls our streets' and is used to reinforce the media's and policy makers' disproportionate focus on 'stranger danger' (Kitzinger and Skidmore 1995). Indeed, 'the paedophile' is a creature that embodies stranger danger. He reflects and sustains a focus on abusers as outcast from society rather than part of it. As feminist activist and academic, Liz Kelly, argues, the concept of 'the paedophile' helps to shift attention away:

> from the centrality of power and control to notions of sexual deviance, obsession and 'addiction'. Paedophilia returns us to … medical and individualised explanations…. Rather than sexual abuse demanding that we look critically at the social construction of masculinity, male sexuality and the family, the safer terrain of 'abnormalities' beckons. (Kelly 1996: 45)

If we adopt the word 'paedophile' and see it as synonymous with 'child sexual abuse' then we narrow the policy agenda. The fact that most children are assaulted by someone that they know virtually disappears from the debate and policies which would be deemed unacceptable if applied to 'ordinary men' become allowable. Commenting on government initiatives in relation to 'paedophiles' Kelly draws attention to the fact that 'paedophiles' may be denied the right to work with children or even to approach playgrounds, yet such proposals would cause outrage if applied to fathers (Kelly 1996: 46). Indeed, women are often forced by the courts to allow violent and abusive partners access to their children, even where those children have also been sexually abused by him.

The fundamental critique here is that the notion of 'the paedophile' restricts definitions of 'the problem' and thus limits how we can envisage solutions. The term helps to obscure important aspects of sexual violence and shifts attention 'away from political solutions addressing male power and the construction of masculinity toward a range of "problem-management" solutions [such as] a "long term incarceration" (*Mail*), "risk assessment tribunals for dangerous men" (*Guardian* and *The Times*) and "individual therapy" (*Guardian*)' (McCollum 1998: 37).

NOTES

1   For discussion of the emergence of the child abduction threat (in the USA) see Best (1990); for discussion of the media creation of the popular image of the 'paedophile priest' see Jenkins (1996).
2   Other reports urged caution and restraint. The (Aberdeen) *Press and Journal*, for example, reported efforts to reassure the public and condemn vigilante action: 'Crowd (self) control' (*Press and Journal*, 6 August 1997) 'Police and community condemn vigilantes' (*Press and Journal*, 10 June 1997) and similar reports and editorials appeared in other papers, e.g. 'Sex crime vigilantes not answer' (*Yorkshire Enening Post*, 6 February 1997); 'Have faith in the police to shield our children' (*Express on Sunday*, 10 August 1997).
3   The *Bournemouth Evening Echo's* 'Protect our children' campaign involved setting up a register of convicted sex offenders, compiled from newspaper reports. This was, however, available only to workers with children. Other papers, such as the *Guardian*, adopted a policy of only 'outing' offenders if there was evidence that supervision had broken down and children were at risk.

REFERENCES

Adams, D. (1998) 'The "at risk" business', *Police Review*, 30 January, 16–17.

Aldridge, M. (1994) *Making Social Work News*, London: Routledge.

Association of Chief Officers of Probation (1998) *Recent Cases of Public Disorder around Sex Offenders which have Impeded Surveillance and Supervision*. London: ACOP.

Best, J. (1990) *Threatened Children*, Chicago: Chicago University Press.

Franklin, B. (1997) *Newzak and News Media*, London: Arnold.

Franklin, B. and Murphy, D. (1998) *Making the Local News. Local Journalism in Context*, London: Routledge.

Hebenton, B. and Thomas, T. (1996) 'Sexual offenders in the community: reflections on problems of law, community and risk management in the USA, England and Wales', *International Journal of the Sociology of Law*, 24: 427–43.

Henderson, L. (1998) 'Making serious soaps: public issue storylines in TV drama serials', in Philo, G. (ed.) *Message Received*, London: Longman.

Jenkins, P. (1996) *Pedophiles and Priests: Anatomy of a Contemporary Crisis*, Oxford: Oxford University Press.

Kelly, L. (1996) 'Weasel words: paedophiles and the cycle of abuse', *Trouble and Strife*, 33: 44–49.

Kelly, L. (1997) 'Confronting an atrocity', *Trouble and Strife*, 36: 16–22.

Kitzinger, J. (1996) 'Media representations of sexual abuse risks', *Child Abuse Review*, 5: 319–33.

Kitzinger, J. (1998) 'The gender politics of news production: silenced voices and false memories', in Carter, C., Branston, G. and Allen, S. (eds) *News, Gender and Power*, London: Routledge.

Kitzinger, J. and Skidmore, P. (1995) 'Playing safe: media coverage of child sexual abuse prevention strategies', *Child Abuse Review*, 4 (1): 47–56.

Marshall, P. (1997) *The Prevalence of Convictions for Sexual Offending*, Research Findings 55, London: Home Office Research and Statistics Directorate.

McCollum, H. (1998) 'What the papers say', *Trouble and Strife*, 37: 31–7.

Miller, D., Kitzinger, J., Williams, K. and Beharrell, P. (1998) *The Circuit of Mass Communication: Media Strategies, Representation and Audience Reception in the AIDS Crisis*, London: Sage.

Soothill, K. and Walby, S. (1991) *Sex Crimes in the News*, London: Routledge.

Thomas, T. (1997) 'How could this man go free? Privacy, the press and the paedophile', in Lawson, E. (ed.) *Child Exploitation and the Media Forum: Report and Recommendations*, Dover: Smallwood Publishing Group, 67–9.

Tuchman, G. (1978) *Making News: A Study of the Construction of Reality*, New York: Free Press.

STUDY QUESTIONS

1   Based on this reading and Reading 11 (Readings 13, 17 and 20 also discuss contemporary media scares), what would you say are the defining characteristics of a moral panic? Has this reading changed your view of its usefulness in describing the relationship between deviants and modern media systems?

2   Can you think of any other examples of criminal or deviant activities, the discussion of which has been significantly defined or determined by the media?

3   To what extent do you think that media scares such as the 'paedophile crisis' serve to deflect attention from what are arguably more serious and endemic problems, e.g. that of crime and abuse within the home, or – as Slapper and Tombs highlight (in Reading 9) – crimes committed by businesses and corporations?

FURTHER READING

Interesting contributions to the issues raised by Kitzinger can be found in Aldridge, M. (1994) *Making Social Work News*, London: Routledge; and Soothill, K. and Walby, S. (1991) *Sex Crimes in the News*, London: Routledge. The views of the probation service are represented in Association of Chief Officers of Probation (1998) *Recent Cases of Public Disorder around Sex Offenders which have Impeded Surveillance and Supervision*, London: ACOP. Neil Websdale offers a comparative analysis using case studies from America in 'Predators: the social construction of "stranger-danger" in Washington state as a form of patriarchal ideology' in J. Ferrell and N. Websdale (eds) (1999) *Making Trouble: Cultural Constructions of Crime, Deviance and Control*, New York: Aldine de Gruyter. Stimulating and provocative analysis can be found in Jenkins, P. (1992) *Intimate Enemies: Moral Panics in Contemporary Britain*, New York: Aldine de Gruyter; and Jenkins, P. (1996) *Pedophiles and Priests: Anatomy of a Contemporary Crisis*, Oxford: Oxford University Press.

13

Crime in context: a critical criminology of market societies

Ian Taylor

As the example of paedophiles in the community demonstrates (see Reading 12), it is not unusual for deviant activities to be publicly and politically debated within frameworks set by the popular press. Another issue that has dominated media agendas for several decades, and which periodically emerges as a source of anxiety, is the use of drugs by young people. Whether we wish to use the term 'moral panic' or not, the media's tone when reporting young people's use of recreational drugs tends to be 'hysterical', negating the fact that for large numbers of people, young and not so young, drugs are a 'normal' part of their everyday lives. Furthermore, drugs are compatible with widely varying lifestyles, not all of which conform to the media's stereotypes of junkies, bohemians and the urban underclass. Even when the media reported the story of the Ecstasy-related death of teenager, Leah Betts, they did so in such a way as to suggest that, while anyone's teenage son or daughter could be at risk, drug dealing and drug use was still the preserve of the seedy and subterranean, preying on the innocent and vulnerable. Hence the 'normalization' of drug use among young people is denied and the 'mythology' of drugs is perpetuated. In this extract Ian Taylor comments on the prevalence of drugs and alcohol in everyday social life, and argues that we should recognize their ubiquity, rather than confining them to subcultural analysis which implies that they are the preserve of a minority of marginalized and maladjusted offenders. His analysis is underpinned by a concern with the processes of economic and social change that have shaped crime in free-market societies and the proposition (made famous by Ulrich Beck, 1992; see *Further Reading*) that contemporary society is characterized by 'risk'. Many individuals are highly attuned to the existence and formation of hazards and dangers in almost

SOURCE: From *Crime in Context: A Critical Criminology of Market Societies* (Cambridge: Polity Press, 1999), 81–6.

every aspect of contemporary life and respond by seeking temporary escape from this 'risk society'. The most prized commodities in modern consumer cultures may therefore be those which offer respite from the anxieties and insecurities that beset (post)modern life, e.g. drugs and alcohol. Consequently, Taylor argues, we should seek to understand their role in many people's lives, as a distraction from the pressures of a competitive market society, as well as an expression of the gratifications of consumption. He maintains that it is only when we recognize their cultural omnipresence, and seek to understand *why* they are endemic in contemporary life, that we can begin to confront their relationship to crime and disorder.

One of the most critical issues, substantially ignored by modernist subcultural theory in the 1960s, preoccupied with young people's role in a society of production, is the extraordinary economic significance, in the sphere of consumption, of 'the youth market'. For all that young people as individuals may have been commanding lower wages in the post-Fordist labour markets of the 1990s, the overall size of the market for youth-oriented consumption products (from music and clothing through to new technology products, from CD players to computers) in most Western societies is enormous, and – as audience researchers have regularly confirmed – of vital importance for setting trends within adult consumption markets as well. In a number of powerful interventions, Zygmunt Bauman (1987, 1988, 1993, 1995, 1996) has discussed the inherent logic of this newly liberated market in consumption. It is a market that no longer has to confront the complex web of regulation imposed in the earlier modernist period – for example, regulating the public sale or intrusion of sexual commodities or clearly delimiting the limits of interpersonal violence, for example, in its representation on cinema.[1] This has helped launch the processes which have led commentators on contemporary Russia to identify it as *bespredel*, a 'society without limits' (Handelman, 1994) – that is, a society in which 'everything is for sale'. The most prized commodities in such a society are those which appear to offer a temporary respite or escape from the sense of threat, the turmoil of constant change, the everyday striving and, indeed, the sense of defeat and despair that life in a competitive market society seems often to involve.

Not the least of the connections here is the question of young people's involvement with the use of illegal drugs. In Britain, in the late 1990s, the concern focuses on an apparent renewal of interest in drugs (after what was thought to be some reduction in use reported in the 1980s, after major government campaigns on heroin). The current preference is apparently for so-called dance drugs, sometimes used in combination with cannabis and/or with alcohol.

The market in cannabis and dance drugs for young people 'going out' on the weekend, in British cities like Manchester, or, indeed, the youth cities of 'middle Europe' like Berlin, Budapest or Prague, is enormous. About a quarter of all respondents (aged 16 to 29) in Britain admitted to Home Office Crime Survey researchers in 1994 that they had used prohibited drugs (overwhelmingly, cannabis or one of the dance drugs) in the previous year (Ramsay and Percy, 1996). In the north-west of England further research, based primarily on 'self-report surveys', suggested that six out of ten 14–15-year-olds in the region reported being offered drugs, and 36 per cent admitted to having used drugs in the past month (Measham et al., 1994). The same researchers' interpretation of other evidence on patterns of drug use in the region suggested that over 200,000 young people aged sixteen to twenty-four had used some form of drug – most commonly, cannabis or one of the dance drugs. On the basis of their survey research, they advanced the proposition that consumption of drugs, especially cannabis and Ecstasy, should now be regarded as a 'normal' feature of adolescence, at least in this part of England.

These generalizations about overall prevalence of drug use are contro-versial on various counts.[2] For many commentators, the most important interpretation of the recent return of cannabis use amongst young people and, in particular, the widely publicized explosion in the use of Ecstasy was that which emphasized the anti-depressant qualities of these two drugs (Keane, 1997). It was in this way, in part, that one could begin to understand the *demand-side* of this particular pleasure market – particularly in the light of the depressing realities of the juvenile labour market itself, and the morose mix of authori-tarianism and moralism which accompanied the treatment of the young in the last years of the Conservative administration. This would not be to ignore the presence in particular neighbourhoods or in places of youthful resort of the front-line salespeople (the 'pushers') involved in the trade in drugs (the 'supply-side' in this particular market), but it would be to insist that any adequate explanation of the success of these particular suppliers must first explain the conditions which gave rise to 'demand'. It is important, that is, to approach the analysis of the prevalence of drugs amongst young people in market societies in the late 1990s specifically as a phenomenon of markets: the marketing of pleasure, through purchase of a pleasurable item from a salesperson (albeit, in this instance, in formally illegal exchange). Vitally, as Dorn and South argued in a series of interventions in the late 1980s (Dorn and South, 1983, 1987; Dorn et al., 1991), this particular market is a *mass market*, not just in terms of its overall economic significance but also in terms of its immediate impact on – and its widespread intrusion into – the lives of young people.

Research in the United States, in Britain and in other European societies amongst children of school age has confirmed a widespread acquaintance with illegal drugs, circulating amongst friends or on sale nearby. In this particular sense, of course, the drug markets of the 1990s are more 'democratic' (widely dispersed and available) than those described by Cloward and Ohlin in 1960, where drug-use was explained as the resort of the 'double-failure', moving on into the retreatist subculture. Analysis of the contemporary processes of recruit-ment of young people into drug-using careers, involving one substance or another, or a mix of drugs, would have to follow a different trajectory to that pursued in the 1960s – making sense, in particular, of experimental drug-use as a first resort on the part of young people in market societies. The relationship between experimentation with different kinds of drugs and involvement in other forms of criminality (especially theft) would involve much more complex lines of analysis than the straightforward sequences of career moves identified by either Cloward and Ohlin or Albert Cohen (1955). Certainly, some forms of involvement with addictive drugs are closely linked to serious forms of theft and robbery. A research project in the north-west of England conducted by Howard Parker and his associates in the mid-1990s interviewed a sample of 82 heavy users of cocaine, who reported spending an average of £20,000 each on their cocaine supplies, as against only £6,000 on other domestic expenditures (Parker and Bottomley, 1996). Not least because of its illegal status, but also because, as a mass market, it is concerned with its own survival in a volatile market place, the drug market 'naturally' operates as a supermarket for different tastes. In this fashion, hard drugs become more easily available to young people who might feel 'they have nothing to lose'. It is also important to realize how much of the consumption activity of a youthful generation working for low wages or in insecure employment is, in any case, connected with the illegal market – for example, in the market for replica clothing, running shoes or bootleg CDs and videos – and how drugs, especially when sold as a special deal or a bargain, present themselves as just another commodity on the market (Ruggiero and South, 1997). In a number of other British research reports, significant numbers of young people are reported to be experimenting with combinations or mixes of drugs ('polydrug users'). It may be, indeed, that we need to retrieve at least one of the themes of the subcultural theory articulated by David Matza, in recognizing the existence of a very contemporary version of a 'subculture of delinquency' – that is, a loose and broad-based 'outsider culture', consisting of young people who have taken dance drugs and/or cannabis, or who know of those who do, and who therefore locate themselves outside of any identifiable and dominant moral sphere of strict legality. In some areas of youthful activity – for example, in clubbing – there may be a very close relationship between the commercial youth culture, sceptical of a purely legalistic idea of righteousness, and the broader body of young people as a whole. So we will need to understand that the distribution of 'outsider cultures' per se will not be a direct expression of social position and patterns of economic deprivation.[3]

The developments taking place in these markets in youthful pleasures and style in the late 1990s in Britain make it clear that any adequate explanation of that market has also to take into account the market in alcohol – and offer an explanation both of the demand for, and supply of, alcohol to young people. In 1997, the local and national press in Britain gave extensive publicity to the marketing by breweries and drinks companies of alcoholic soft drinks ('alcopops') in street-corner shops and supermarkets (where they were available for purchase by young people under the age of eighteen). The marketing of these new products to the youth market had actually been initiated (through an advertising campaign costing £190 million) in 1995, and by 1997 amounted to a £275 million.[4] Campaigns to market alcoholic lollipops ('popsicles' in American parlance) to children were also in active preparation (Guardian, 24 June 1997). The launch of these new youth products occurred in a context in which, according to other reports, increasing numbers of young children were starting to drink alcohol at an increasingly early age.[5] Average consumption of alcohol amongst young people as a whole was reported to have risen from 0.8 units per week in 1990 to 1.3 units in 1994 (Alcohol Concern, 1997).

This occurred, it should also be noted, at a time in which alcohol use amongst adults was also significantly on the increase, and in which a significant number of adults (6 per cent of all adult men) were drinking to levels that were likely to damage their health (with 1 in 20 being alcohol-dependent, as against only 1 in 45 who were deemed to be dependent on any other kind of drug, from tranquillizers to Ecstasy), and at a time of increasing concern over the broader social effects of alcohol abuse. A report from the Alcohol Concern organization, *Measures for Measures*, released in 1997, graphically suggested:

> The link between violent crime and alcohol has a long history with recent research suggesting that drink is involved in 65 per cent of murders and 75 per cent of stabbings. Even more injuries and deaths are caused by drink-drive accidents which kill 600 people a year and thousands of injuries. The accidents do not end on the road. About 25 per cent of drownings and 40 per cent of deaths in fire are put down to drink. One in four acute male hospital admissions is related to alcohol. Young men are particularly vulnerable to alcohol-related violence. There are 5,000 'glassings' annually, in which a smashed beer glass is used as a dangerous and disfiguring weapon. All told, there are about 33,000 alcohol-related deaths every year in Britain. (Dean, 1997, summarizing Alcohol Concern)

The involvement of alcohol (and, particularly, of the kinds of strong lager marketed at adolescent young men) in some of the most horrific instances of youth violence in British post-war social history (from the Notting Hill race riots in 1957 to the Heysel disaster in 1986) is a matter of record. The 'excessive' use of alcohol by young British men is now widely recognized throughout many other European Union member-states as a symbol of a seriously problematic cultural adaptation. The challenge to social science and criminology, both politically and analytically, is quite clear, and it is irresponsible for populist commentators to take refuge in familiar mystifications of social scientists – operating within a framework involving a rather mechanical positivism, on the one hand, and relativistic appreciation of all things youthful, on the other – to cavil about the complexity of causal explanation and thereby clear British breweries or alcohol-abusers of any responsibilities in respect of the social consequences of alcohol abuse amongst British youth (Sumner and Parker, 1995; Parker, 1996).

In the general area of drug and alcohol abuse, the discourses of those health professionals and those social service workers who are still involved with personal and familial crises in the broad society speak urgently of the need for national (and, perhaps, international) strategies of *harm-reduction* – activated by a recognition, born of close observation, of the serious consequences of drug and alcohol abuse on individuals' lives, and the lives of their friends, families and (frequently) their neighbours and larger – perhaps already disadvantaged and disorganized – neighbourhood. Elliott Currie (1993a, b), in grappling with the drug dilemma in the United States and the prospect confronting young people in that society, recognizes that the launch of effective campaigns of harm-reduction might involve some of the elements that are currently being advocated by critics of current drug polices in the United States – notably the decriminalization of minor drug-use, particularly, as in the Netherlands, the large-scale decriminalization of marijuana. Such a selective decriminalization of certain drugs could be one dimension in a serious campaign of harm-reduction, not least in disrupting the process of production of 'outsider cultures' of illegal drug-use. However, as Currie continues, in respect of the currently extraordinarily influential calls for the 'decriminalization' – that is, the 'deregulation' – of all drug-use (that is, the 'market solution') Currie observes:

> Proponents of full-scale deregulation of hard drugs also tend to gloss over the very real primary costs of hard drug use – particularly on the American level – and to exaggerate the degree to which the multiple pathologies surrounding drug use in America are simply an intended consequence of a 'prohibitionist' regulatory policy. (Currie, 1993b: 68)

A central obligation of critically minded social commentators working in this area is to explain the 'conditions of existence' of the *apparently escalating demand* for both dance drugs and hard drugs amongst different fractions of the youthful population. In the sphere of alcohol abuse, the task is to explain the centrality of heavy drinking in 'British culture' generally – and, amongst many adolescent young men and 'young adults', the continuing play of the 'Eight pints a night' culture – drinking into oblivion – as a measure of 'the man', and other variations in the use of drink, and their consequences. One key issue here is to explore the reported new forms of transgressive 'excess' with drink, sometimes in combination with other drugs and its relationship to the mass marketing of drink in youth magazines and also of the new 'laddishness'. In other European societies, the issue might be posed differently. For example, in Italy one serious issue is the use, not so much of drink, but of different varieties of drugs by young men, notably in the affluent North, in the course of different forms of 'excess', like the playing of 'chicken-games' on motorcycles on the motorways. The availability of drugs is also closely connected in with the emergence in that country of a range of alternative strategies for survival adopted by new immigrants into Italy – often operating under various degrees of duress in the drug trade as the front-line operatives for organized crime. In this instance, as in some of the heavily marginalized housing estates of Northern Europe, the significance of drugs as an item in the hidden economies of everyday survival is inescapable. But the analysis of the destructive personal effects of the use of such drugs on users, and on the neighbourhoods in which they live, is also a vital challenge.

Calls for the decriminalization of the drug trade – predicated as they are on the belief that 'the market' (unlike the State) has an inherent capacity to solve most social problems – may (contradictorily) forget the broader origins of the demand for drugs or alcohol – in particular, that is, their critical role as distractions from (as well as expressions of) the pressures inherent in competitive market society itself (not least a market society dedicated to the constant marketing of the short-lived pleasures of 'consumption').

NOTES

1 The collapse of this regime of regulation is apparent in both Hollywood (*Reservoir Dogs, Silence of the Lambs, Grosse Pointe Blank*) and British cinema (*Shallow Grave*). In the case of Hollywood cinema, this has resulted in the decision by Dustin Hoffman to direct his energies and talents to other film-making opportunities.
2 The thesis that 'recreational drug use' was now a normal feature of adolescence in north-west England has been challenged by Shiner and Newcombe (1997), for its

exaggerating the numbers of regular users and for trying to generalize from total responses to a large-scale survey to the 'meaning' of sporadic experimentation with drugs use by young people.

3 As Mugford and O'Malley have observed (from a critical perspective), this tendency to link drug-abuse and involvement in one analytical move to patterns of economic deprivation, through a structuralist sociology, is a feature of Elliott Currie's work in the United States, as well as that of Dorn and South in Britain (Mugford and O'Malley, 1991).

4 Luke Harding, 'Straw to Get Tough over Teenage Drinking Craze', Guardian, 17 May 1996.

5 Survey research by the University of Exeter's Health Education Unit, published in 1997, suggested that 3 per cent of boys aged 12–13 admitted to consuming 21 units of alcohol a week, and over 7 per cent of boys aged 14–17 (Guardian, 30 June 1997).

REFERENCES

Alcohol Concern (1997) Alcopops – Research Findings (April).

Bauman, Zygmunt (1987) 'Fighting the Wrong Shadow', New Statesman, 25 September: 20–2.

Bauman, Zygmunt (1988) 'Britain's Exit from Politics', New Statesman, 29 July: 34–8.

Bauman, Zygmunt (1993) Postmodern Ethics. Oxford: Blackwell.

Bauman, Zygmunt (1995) Life in Fragments: Essays in Postmodern Morality. Oxford: Blackwell.

Bauman, Zygmunt (1996) 'The Moth Seeks out the Lamp', New Statesman, 1 November: 21–2.

Cloward, Richard and Ohlin, Lloyd (1960) Delinquency and Opportunity: A Theory of Delinquent Gangs. New York: Free Press.

Cohen, Albert (1955) Delinquent Boys: The Culture of the Gang. Chicago: Free Press.

Currie, Elliott (1993a) Reckoning: Drugs, Cities and the American Future. New York: Hill and Wang.

Currie, Elliott (1993b) 'Towards a Policy on Drugs', Dissent (Winter): 65–71.

Dean, Malcolm (1997) 'Haunted by the Spirits', Guardian (21 March).

Dorn, Nicholas and South, Nigel (1983) Of Males and Markets: A Critical Review of 'Youth Culture' Theory. London: Middlesex Polytechnic, Centre for Occupational and Community Research, Research Paper 1.

Dom, Nicholas, Henderson, S. and South, Nigel (eds.) (1991) AIDs: Women, Drugs and Social Care, London: Falmer.

Dorn, Nicholas and South, Nigel (1987) A Land Fit For Heroin? Drug Policies, Prevention and Practice, Basingstoke: Macmillan.

Handelman, Stephen (1994) Comrade Criminal: The Theft of the Second Russian Revolution. London: Michael Joseph.

Keane, Jonathan (1997) 'Ecstasy in the Unhappy Society', Soundings, 6 (Summer): 127–39.

Matza, David (1969) Becoming Deviant, Englewood Cliffs, NJ: Prentice Hall.

Measham, Fiona, Newcombe, Russell and Parker, Howard (1994) 'The Normalization of Recreational Drug Use among Young People in North-West England', British Journal of Sociology (Summer): 287–312.

Mugford, S.K. and O'Malley, P. (1991) 'Heroin Policy and Deficit Models: the Limits of Left Realism', Crime, Law and Social Change, vol. 15, 19–36.

Parker, Howard (1996) 'Young Adult Offenders, Alcohol and Criminological Cul-de-sacs', British Journal of Criminology, 36 (2), 282–98.

Parker, Howard and Bottomley, Tim (1996) 'Crack Cocaine and Drugs-crime Careers', *Research Findings No. 34* (Home Office Research and Statistics Directorate). London: Home Office.

Ramsay, Malcolm and Percy, Andrew (1996) 'Drug Use Declared: Results of the 1994 British Crime Survey', *Research Findings No. 33* (Home Office Research and Statistics Directorate). London: Home Office (June).

Ruggiero, Vincenzo and South, Nigel (1997) 'The Late-modern City as a Bazaar: Drug Markets, Illegal Enterprise and the "Barricades"', *British Journal of Sociology*, 48 (1), 54–70.

Shiner, Michael and Newburn, Tim (1997) 'Definitely, Maybe Not? The Normalisation of Recreational Drug Use Among Young People'. *Sociology*, 31 (3): 511–30.

Sumner, Maggie and Parker, Howard (1995) *Low in Alcohol: A Review of International Research into Alcohol's Role in Crime Causation*. London: Portman Group.

STUDY QUESTIONS

1 Do you agree with the view, put forward in this reading, that drugs and alcohol are 'just another commodity on the market'; no different, in essence, to clothing, CDs or videos?

2 How would you evaluate Taylor's suggestion that drugs are used as a form of escapism from the anxieties and risks that characterize contemporary life? Could other forms of criminal behaviour be conceptualized similarly?

3 Do you think that the construction of particular drugs as 'dangerous' and illegal actually reflects the chemical properties of the drug and its effect on the human body or symbolic and political definitions of drugs, drug use and drug-users?

4 Are the use of drugs and the construction of drug-users as mad or bad gendered and racialised?

FURTHER READING

A useful review of how theoretical explanations have been used within criminology to explain and account for societal understandings and explanations of drugs and drug use is provided in chapter 10, 'Deviance', by Jock Young in Worsley, P. (ed.) (1987) *The New Introductory Sociology*, Harmondsworth: Penguin. Ecstasy use among young people is examined in Hammersley, R., Khan, F. and Ditton, J. (2001) Ecstasy and the Rise of the Chemical Generation, London: Routledge. The whole edition of *Criminal Justice Matters*, no. 24 (Summer 1996) is devoted to 'Debating drugs' and contains articles on the history of 'the drugs problem'; 'the drugs scene'; 'drug policies' and 'the use of drugs in prisons'. The relative 'normalization' of drugs within some professions is examined in Francis, P. and Wynarczyk, P. (1999) 'Regulating the invisible? The case of workplace illicit drug use' in P. Davies, P. Francis and V. Jupp (eds) *Invisible Crimes: Their Victims and their Regulation*, Basingstoke: Macmillan. The political and policy implications of the drugs industry are explored in Green, P. (1998) *Drugs, Trafficking and Criminal Policy: The Scapegoat Strategy*, Winchester: Waterside. The idea of modern society being characterized by 'risk' is explored most famously by Beck, U. (1992) *Risk Society*, London: Sage; and Giddens, A. (1991) *Modernity and Self-identity*, Cambridge: Polity Press.

Part Three

Crime and Social Stratification

In Part III there are nine readings all of which in some way relate to the social stratification of offenders and victims of crime. The readings collectively suggest that the class, race, age and gender of criminals and victims have an impact on their experience of crime, and on the ways in which they are processed through the criminal justice system. In Reading 14 Michael Cavadino and James Dignan draw on statistical evidence and a large number of empirical studies to consider bias within criminal justice. Their focus is social class, race and gender, and many of the issues raised here are considered elsewhere in this part. The next two readings focus specifically on social class and crime. Janet Foster (Reading 15) concentrates on the prevalence and meanings of working-class crime in south-east London and develops a 'hierarchy of villainy'. On the other hand, Hazel Croall (Reading 16) is concerned with the offences of middle-class 'white-collar' and 'corporate' criminals, their victims and the consequences of their crimes. Moving to the issue of 'race' and crime, John Lea and Jock Young (Reading 17) argue that the responses of the media and the political left to supposed high crime rates amongst ethnic minority groups are inadequate and misleading, while Stuart Hall (Reading 18), who is concerned specifically with police/race relations, considers the impact of the Scarman Report in the 1980s and the Macpherson Report at the end of the 1990s. The next two readings are concerned with youth and crime, but are also interesting for what they tell us about gender. John Muncie (Reading 19) considers the relevance of the term 'criminal career' in understanding youth crime and looks at the relevance of femininity and masculinity to crime and to the debates about it. Susan Batchelor (Reading 20) reports on a study in Scotland which explores girls' experience of violence, and she outlines media responses to the study in the context of their construction of a problem of 'girl gangs'. For the final two readings in this section we shift emphasis and consider in detail the perspective of the 'victim'. Elizabeth A. Stanko (Reading 21) provides a critique of traditional victimology and argues that this approach does not adequately explain and account for the physical and sexual violence in many women's lives. Tim Newburn and Elizabeth A. Stanko (Reading 22) extend this critique with specific reference to the experience of men as victims and demonstrate the need to see men as both oppressors and oppressed. When reading these selections think of how aspects of our identity affect our experience of crime as both perpetrators and victims and reflect on how these pieces challenge your own and other's stereotypical views of 'typical' criminals and victims.

14

Bias in the criminal justice system

Michael Cavadino and James Dignan

This reading focuses on bias in the criminal justice system in relation to social class, 'race' and gender. Drawing on statistical evidence and a large number of empirical studies, Michael Cavadino and James Dignan suggest that bias is not always the result of deliberate discrimination but may stem from prejudicial and stereotypical attitudes. With reference to social class, it is clear that prisoners are overwhelmingly working class, and that unskilled and unemployed people are over-represented in the penal population. Conversely, throughout the processes of investigation, prosecution, sentencing and imprisonment, 'white-collar' criminals are much more likely to be treated leniently. The same can be said more generally of white offenders. A large amount of research indicates that black people are disproportionately the object of police attention and suspicion, are arrested and prosecuted more often than their numbers in the general population would lead one to expect, and are likely to receive more severe sentences (reflected in the fact that, in 1999, although only 5.5 per cent of the population of England and Wales were non-white, 18 per cent of male prisoners and 25 per cent of female prisoners were non-white). When considering gender bias the picture is more complicated. In this case, as Cavadino and Dignan point out, members of the oppressed group – i.e. women – are distinctly under-represented in the criminal statistics, with women and girls accounting for only 5 per cent of the prison population in 1999 despite comprising just over half of the general population. Some writers suggest that women are treated 'chivalrously' by police and courts and therefore the bias is in their favour. However, others suggest that women who break the law are considered 'doubly deviant' because they have also broken accepted codes of femininity, and are treated more harshly as a result.

SOURCE: From *The Penal System: An Introduction*, 3rd edn (London: Sage, 2001), pp. 309–32

Cavadino and Dignan provide a thorough overview of the workings of the criminal justice system and how it affects specific groups of people. The issues raised are relevant to all the other readings in this part. Furthermore, several aspects of Cavadino and Dignan's argument relate to issues raised elsewhere: for example, the definitions and explanations of crime (Part I); the socially constructed nature of crime, criminals and criminal statistics (Part II); the attitudes and practice of criminal justice system workers (Part IV) and the prevalence of social control (Part V).

[…] At any stage, bias can occur for a variety of reasons. It often results, not from deliberate discrimination, but from unconscious prejudices and stereotypes (fixed preconceptions that some kinds of people are more criminal than others) and even as an unintended consequence of *prima facie* reasonable attitudes, practices and decisions. But whatever the causes, such biases add weight to radical critiques which claim that the penal system functions to reinforce the position of powerful sections of society over the less powerful. They also […] suggest that the penal system's crisis of legitimacy may be largely self-inflicted: the system is perceived as unjust because it really is unjust.

The issue of bias in the criminal justice system has received a measure of official recognition. One result has been section 95 of the Criminal Justice Act 1991, which requires the Home Secretary every year 'to publish such information as he considers expedient for the purpose of … facilitating the performance by [persons engaged in the administration of criminal justice] of their duty to avoid discriminating against any persons on the ground of race or sex or any other improper ground', a provision which has led to the issuing of several publications (for example, Home Office, 2000a, b) containing the results of research and monitoring. To some extent this has helped in the identification of biases within the system. But so far there is little sign that it has brought about any diminution in the actual occurrence of bias.

CLASS

Although the regular official series of criminal and penal statistics do not provide data on social class or occupation, it is clear that the penal system's subjects are overwhelmingly working class, and that unskilled and unemployed people are particularly over-represented in the penal population The 1991 National Prison Survey found that 6 per cent of prisoners aged 17 or over had never had a job. Of the rest, 82 per cent had manual occupations (compared with 56 per cent of the general population), and 41 per cent were unskilled (compared with 19 per cent generally). Just prior to imprisonment, one-third of prisoners were unemployed (Walmsley et al., 1992: 10–11, 21). Similarly, Harris and Webb (1987: 115–16) found that almost all of a sample of 971 boys on supervision orders were working class, and fewer than 8 per cent had a parent in a 'white-collar' job. Several surveys of defendants in criminal courts have yielded similar results. One found that only 5 per cent of defendants in Sheffield in 1971 and 1972 (excluding motoring cases) were from social classes I and II, compared with 35 per cent of the general population (Bottoms and McClean, 1976: 75); while a recent study of four magistrates' courts in the North of England in 1993 found that between 75 and 91 per cent of defendants sampled were unemployed (Crow et al., 1995: 46; cf. Crow and Simon, 1987).

This does not in itself demonstrate that there is a class bias operating in the criminal justice system to produce these results, for they could occur without bias if a similar proportion of *crimes* were committed by members of the working class. But 'self-report' research studies (in which respondents are asked in confidence what offences they have committed) suggest that this is not the case. It seems that there is *some* greater tendency for people from lower socio-economic groups to commit offences, or at least the kind of offences which tend to be dealt with by means of the normal criminal justice system. (This is not perhaps surprising when – just to mention the most obvious line of explanation – the vast majority of recorded crime is against property, which is exactly what poorer people lack.) But the class differential in commission of crimes as measured by self-report studies is much smaller than the class differential in officially processed offenders (see, for example, Hood and Sparks, 1970: ch. 2; Rutter and Giller, 1983: 132–7). Gold's (1966: 44) American findings were fairly typical: 'About five times more lowest than highest status boys appear in the official records; if records were complete and unselective we estimate that the ratio should be closer to 1.5 : 1.' Somehow, between the commission of offences and the official responses of prosecution and punishment, the difference between the classes gets vastly magnified.

Such magnification could occur for a variety of reasons, not all of them necessarily connected with bias. Perhaps some misdeeds of middle-class offenders are relatively invisible and hence unlikely to come to official notice. This is probably true of embezzlement and tax dodging compared to burglary and robbery, for example. But there could also be biases operating at the various stages of the criminal process which ensure that middle-class offenders are dealt with more leniently. At many of these stages, there is as yet little research evidence to confirm or deny the existence of class bias in the system. But there are some straws in the wind.

A classic study in the United States in the 1960s by Piliavin and Briar (1964) indicates one way in which unintended class bias could occur at the police stage. The authors found that police officers who came across juveniles committing offences were expected to exercise discretion as to whether to arrest or reprimand the juvenile. The result was that, for nearly all minor violators and for some serious delinquents, it was the police's *assessment of the youth's character* which was the prime determinant of the officers' decisions. Officers decided whether the young person was basically law-abiding and 'salvageable', or an incorrigible 'punk', and made their decisions accordingly. This assessment of 'character' was, however, based on the very limited information available to the officers, notably 'cues' such as the youths' race, dress and – most importantly – their *demeanour*. Those who failed to show the police what was considered to be sufficient respect received negative character assessments and harsher treatment. Since attitudes towards the police vary across socio-economic groups,[1] such a criterion is extremely likely to result in effective class discrimination. It could also be that a 'rougher' demeanour not intended to convey disrespect could be misinterpreted, again to the disadvantage of the suspect from the lower socio-economic group.

Such a bias could occur at a very early stage in the criminal process, before the police have even discovered or decided that an offence has been committed. When police officers encounter members of the public they often have to decide – perhaps instantly – whether this person is a potential criminal or not. There is usually little to go on in making this decision except by using stereotypical 'cues' which mark people as either 'rough' or 'respectable', yet a snap decision of this kind may condition the entire ensuing interaction (Cain, 1971: 81–4; Bottomley, 1973: ch. 2). This suggests that the police may be much less likely to suspect or investigate middle-class people – or, probably equally importantly, people who give the impression of belonging to the stably employed 'respectable working class'. And indeed studies have found that unemployed[2] people are significantly more likely to be stopped on foot by the police than those who have a job (Smith, 1983: 101; Skogan, 1990: 28–9, 61). As a result, the police will be likely to detect or recognize a higher proportion of offences committed by those in lower socio-economic groups.

Subsequent to detection of an offence comes the decision whether or not to prosecute or caution. In England, Bennett (1979) found that middle-class juvenile offenders in London were more likely than their working-class counterparts to be cautioned instead of being prosecuted for minor offences. There could be several factors influencing the police decision which have the effect of creating a class bias. Farrington and Bennett (1981) demonstrated that a juvenile's perceived 'bad attitude' is a potent determining factor of the police decision in London as well as in the USA; other studies have found that the offenders' *parents'* perceived attitudes are influential (Gold, 1966; Bennett, 1979; Fisher and Mawby, 1982). And Landau and Nathan (1983), again in London, found that the police were more inclined to prosecute 'latch-key children', a practice likely to work against low-income families.

It is also the case that, at the investigation and prosecution stages, typically middle-class offences can be dealt with in a radically different manner from 'ordinary crime', often by agencies other than the police. For example, breaches of factory health and safety regulations, including those which threaten or cause serious accidents,[3] are policed by an agency (the Health and Safety Executive) which prefers to warn rather than prosecute. Carson (1971) found that in the 1960s the HSE's predecessor the Inspectorate of Factories prosecuted a mere 1.5 per cent of detected offences. However, when a firm was detected offending three or more times, the rate of prosecution increased – to 3.5 per cent! Even disregarding cases where the Inspectorate took no formal action at all, this made an overall 'cautioning rate' of 98 per cent. This later declined to 84 per cent by 1991/92 (calculated from Health and Safety Executive, 1992) – but it still puts the police's cautioning rate of 33 per cent[4] in the shade. (See further Sanders, 1985; Sanders and Young, 2000: 365–8.) Similarly, the Inland

Revenue very rarely prosecutes tax fraud offenders, although the Department of Social Security is much more likely to prosecute those people (from lower socio-economic groups) who defraud the benefits system (NACRO, 1986a: ch. 10; Cook, 1989: ch. 7).

There is a distinct lack of studies at the sentencing stage which directly compare the sentences received by working-class and middle-class offenders *for the same offences,*[5] although it is (for example) highly plausible that sentencers might perceive a middle-class offender as less incorrigible and therefore deserving of a lesser sentence. Again, sentencers (themselves overwhelmingly middle-class) might well feel that a middle-class offender has already suffered enough through the disgrace of conviction, and sentence leniently as a result. Or richer defendants may be able to afford better lawyers who are more adept at representing their clients' circumstances as mitigating their culpability. There is plenty of anecdotal evidence of apparent leniency towards middle-class offenders, especially those convicted of typical 'white-collar' offences: the £3 million fraudsters in the 1960s whose prison sentences were a fraction of those imposed on the £2 million Great Train Robbers (Morris, 1980: 92); the non-custodial sentences passed on insider dealer Geoffrey Collier in 1987 and (following a much-questioned plea-bargain agreement) fraudulent trader Roger Levitt in 1993; the halving of 'Guinness trial' defendant Ernest Saunders' sentence to 2½ years by the Court of Appeal in 1991 following evidence that he was suffering from pre-senile dementia (which went into remission after his release); and the transfer of a senior doctor from prison to a private clinic better known for treating the addictions of famous celebrities following his conviction for assaulting his wife (*Guardian*, 30 August 2000).

Research does seem to have confirmed that the courts are often much more punitive towards the relatively poor people who fraudulently draw too much social security than towards the relatively well-off people who defraud the Inland Revenue of what may be much greater sums (Cook, 1989: 160–5).[6] Again, this is not the result of intentional class bias, but the effect of the prevailing (Marxists might say 'bourgeois') ideology which holds that the latter method of defrauding the public purse is less reprehensible than the former.

Unemployed people can again get a particularly raw deal at the sentencing stage. Traditionally, the fact that an offender has a job and a steady work record has been regarded as counting in his or her favour, whereas unemployment has been seen as reflecting negatively on the offender's character. Again, sentencers may sometimes decide to pass non-custodial sentences on employed offenders so that they do not lose their jobs although they would imprison a similar but unemployed offender. (An analogous effect can occur when the court decides whether to grant bail or remand in custody.) Finally, unemployment can restrict the sentencing options the court perceives itself as having. In particular, the court may be reluctant to impose a fine or other financial penalty on an unemployed offender, because the sum imposed would seem (to the relatively affluent sentencer) ridiculously small if related to the offender's means, or because it is felt that the offender could not or will not pay up. Research studies have confirmed that unemployed offenders are significantly less likely to be fined than those who are employed. Although some of the unemployed who might otherwise have been fined are given discharges or probation orders, others receive custodial sentences (Softley, 1978; Crow et al., 1989).

Following a sentence of imprisonment, white-collar offenders are much more likely to be allocated to open prisons, where the conditions and régime may be distinctly preferable (Jones et al., 1977: especially 66–70). This fact was highlighted in August 1990 when three businessmen found guilty of dishonesty offences involving millions of pounds in the 'Guinness affair' were transferred instantly from the slum conditions of Brixton Prison to the relatively salubrious Ford Open Prison. It is also possible that white-collar offenders get parole more easily (Levi, 1989: 102–5); certainly this was suggested by the experience of jockey Lester Piggott, who in 1988 was paroled at the earliest opportunity from his (relatively speaking, hardly draconian) three-year prison sentence imposed for evading over £3 million in taxes. [...]

RACE

According to official estimates, 5.5 per cent of the population of England and Wales is of non-white ethnic origin. Yet in 1999 18 per cent of male prisoners and 25 per cent of female prisoners were non-white.[7] The most dramatic discrepancy concerns 'black' (or 'Afro-Caribbean') people,[8] who account for under 2 per cent of people aged 10 and over in England and Wales, but comprised 12 per cent of the male and 19 per cent of the female prison population in 1999. It has been estimated that at this rate nearly one in ten young black men will have received a custodial sentence before their 21st birthdays, double the proportion of their white peers (*New Law Journal*, 30 March 1990; *Guardian*, 27 February 1989). Why do such disproportionately large numbers of black people find their way into custody?

One obvious hypothesis would be that black people are more likely to commit offences than white people. Since racial discrimination (conscious and unconscious, direct and indirect) results in black people being disproportionately disadvantaged in terms of unemployment and homelessness, this would not be surprising. However, there is no real evidence that this is the case. When it has been claimed – notoriously, by the Metropolitan Police in 1982 and again by Metropolitan Police Commissioner Paul Condon in 1995 – that black people are disproportionately involved in crime, the statistics produced to back up these claims have been rightly criticized as unreliable and misleading (Smith, 1982; Crow, 1987: 305). A recent Home Office research study (Graham and Bowling, 1995) found that young Afro-Caribbeans had very similar rates of offending to white youths (see similarly Flood-Page et al., 2000: 20).

However, it is clear from a plethora of research studies that Afro-Caribbean people are disproportionately the object of police attention and suspicion. For example, a national study using British Crime Survey data from 1996 found that 23 per cent of black respondents had been stopped by the police during the previous year compared with 16 per cent of whites and 15 per cent of Asians

(Bucke, 1997).[9] Black people are also more likely to be stopped several times in a year, and to be searched by the police following a stop. Overall, black people are, according to official figures, five times more likely to be searched by the police on the streets than white people.[10]

These results are presumably not unrelated to what the Policy Studies Institute found when invited to survey the work of the police in London in the early 1980s, that 'racialist language and racial prejudice were prominent and pervasive [in the Metropolitan Police] and that many individual officers and also whole groups were preoccupied with ethnic differences' (98 per cent of police officers are white: Home Office. 2000a: 62.) Although this racism did not usually manifest itself on the street, the PSI specifically noted that 'one criterion that police officers use for stopping people (especially in areas of *low* ethnic concentration) is that they are black' (Smith and Gray, 1983: 109–10). It seems that many police officers hold inaccurate, stereotyped views of black people, automatically placing them in the 'rough' (potentially criminal) category, especially when they are seen in areas where they 'don't belong'.[11] Research has found instances of police officers acting on the basis of stereotypes such as 'the assumption that West Indians running or carrying a bag are up to no good' (Southgate and Ekblom, 1986: 11).

The issue of police racism, and of their use of stop and search powers in particular, came to the fore in Lord Scarman's inquiry into the Brixton riots of 1981 (Scarman, 1986) and again on the publication of the Policy Studies Institute research on the Metropolitan Police in 1983. But little seemed to have changed by the time the Macpherson Report was published in February 1999. This was the report of an official inquiry into the case of Stephen Lawrence, a black student who was murdered by a gang of white youths at a south-east London bus stop in April 1993. Macpherson concluded that the bungled police investigation into the murder, as a result of which none of the murderers were brought to justice, was affected by the *'institutional racism'* evident in the Metropolitan Police.[12] This institutional racism, Macpherson thought, was for the most part unintentional and unconscious, but the police were nevertheless infected by 'processes, attitudes and behaviour which amount to discrimination through unwitting prejudice, ignorance, thoughtlessness, and racist stereotyping which disadvantage minority ethnic people' (Macpherson, 1999: 6.34). Macpherson identified stop and search practices as a particular cause of ill-feeling between the police and the black community, and said: 'we are clear that the perception and experience of the minority communities that discrimination is a major element in the stop and search problem is correct' (para. 45.8).

More recently there has been a backlash against the Macpherson Report from some quarters, with claims that the police, especially in London, have become afraid to use their stop and search powers (on black people in particular) and that street crime has risen as a result. The Conservative Leader of the Opposition, William Hague, complained in December 2000 that 'the way in which the Macpherson Report has been used to brand every officer and every branch of the force as racist, has contributed directly to a collapse of police morale and recruitment and has led to a crisis on our streets'

(*Guardian*, 15 December 2000). Such claims are of dubious validity. Although recorded stops and searches did decline significantly following the report's publication, there was a *smaller* decrease in searches of black people than of white suspects.[13] And while street robbery (unlike crime generally) was on the rise at this time, it seems unlikely that a reduced number of stops and searches was a cause of this, since stops and searches rarely produce evidence of robberies and there is no reason to believe that people are deterred from committing robberies by the prospect of being searched. There is now official ethnic monitoring of stops and searches (following a Macpherson recommendation), and senior police officers in London currently claim to be moving towards a more 'targeted' and 'intelligence led' use of stop and search (O'Connor, 2000). Whether any of this will result in any long-term improvement in police practices remains to be seen.

Black people are also *arrested* more often than their numbers in the general population would lead one to expect – four times as often as white people in 1988/99 (Home Office, 2000a: 19). Some of this difference may be explained by the fact that many arrests result from stops, which as we have just seen happen more often to black people (Willis, 1983: 18–19). It is also the case that black people are arrested particularly often for offences 'in which there is considerable scope for selective perception of potential or actual offenders' (Stevens and Willis, 1979: 41).[14] Phillips and Brown (1998: 44–5) found that the evidence against arrested black and Asian suspects was less often sufficient to charge them than in cases of arrested white suspects.

There is also evidence that race can make a difference to the police's decision whether to *caution* offenders or proceed to prosecution. The overall 'cautioning rate' (percentage of known offenders who are cautioned rather than prosecuted) for notifiable offences in 1999/2000 was 16 per cent for whites, 15 per cent for Asians and 11 per cent for black people (Home Office, 2000a: 20). Landau and Nathan (1983) found in London that white juveniles were significantly more likely to be cautioned than their black counterparts. A white juvenile with previous convictions was over four times more likely to be cautioned than a similar black youth.[15] Some other studies have found that black defendants are more likely to have been brought to court for offences which caused no loss, damage or injury (Stevens and Willis, 1979: 37; Crow and Cove, 1984), raising the possibility that similar white offenders might not have been prosecuted. This could, however, be partly due to the actions of victims rather than the police: perhaps similar offences by white people might have gone unreported to the police in the first place (see Shah and Pease, 1992).

Interestingly, research has found that ethnic minority defendants (both black and Asian) are more likely to have the prosecutions against them dropped after being charged by the police, that black defendants are more likely to plead not guilty, and that black and Asian defendants who plead not guilty are more likely to be acquitted in court (Phillips and Brown, 1998; Home Office, 2000a: 37). This suggests that the police may often charge ethnic minority suspects on the basis of a lesser amount of solid evidence than they might require in the case of a white suspect.

Black defendants are more likely than whites to be *committed for Crown Court trial*, according to a number of studies (Fitzgerald, 1993: 19–21; Home Office, 2000a: 38), and [...] defendants who are tried in the Crown Court are likely to receive harsher sentences than those tried by magistrates. The higher committal rate seems to be partly the result of black defendants more often electing to be tried at the Crown Court, but it is at least as often due to magistrates declining jurisdiction. Moreover, black Crown Court defendants are *remanded in custody*, instead of being granted bail, more often than whites: one study found 26 per cent of sentenced black defendants had been remanded in custody compared with 20 per cent of whites and 18 per cent of Asians (Hood, 1992: 146–7). The fact that black defendants who are remanded in custody are much more likely than their white counterparts to be acquitted or not proceeded against (Fitzgerald, 1993: 22) suggests that black and Asian people are often wrongly denied bail.

There is good evidence that race can also play an important part in *sentencing*. Several studies in the United States indicate that black defendants tend to receive more severe sentences (including more custodial sentences and more death sentences; see, for example, Spohn et al., 1981–2; Baldus et al., 1986; 1989), but the evidence from the USA is not entirely consistent (Pruitt and Wilson, 1983). Nor is it consistent in England, with several studies (e.g. McConville and Baldwin, 1982; Crow and Cove, 1984; Moxon, 1988: 59; Walker et al., 1990) having found no evidence of racial bias in sentencing, but a variety of others (see, for example, NACRO, 1986b: ch. 3; Walker, 1988; Hudson, 1989) finding that black defendants are more likely to receive custodial sentences than are comparable white defendants.

The largest and most rigorous study of this question – Roger Hood's *Race and Sentencing* (1992) – provides the best evidence to date of a race effect in sentencing. Hood carefully examined sentencing at five Crown Courts in the West Midlands in 1989, and found that 57 per cent of black male defendants were sentenced to custody compared with 48 per cent of the white men; for women the figures were 29 per cent and 23 per cent. Taking into account all other relevant variables such as the offence charged and the offender's previous record, black men were 5 per cent more likely than white men to be sent to prison (Hood, 1992: 75–9, 163).[16] At one court (Dudley Crown Court), black defendants were 23 per cent more likely to receive custody. Adult black and Asian males also received longer average sentences of imprisonment, and were particularly likely to receive sentences of over three years.

Several studies have found that, although black offenders are to be found disproportionately in prisons, they are *under*-represented in other sectors of the penal system. Notably, black offenders have been found to receive proportionately fewer probation orders; and there have also been claims that young black offenders have been under-represented on intermediate treatment programmes (Taylor, 1981; NACRO, 1986b: ch. 4; Pitts, 1986: 133; Moxon, 1988). These phenomena could well be related: for some reason black offenders are deemed unsuitable for non-custodial supervisory sentences and as a result find their way into custody relatively quickly. This raises questions not only about sentencers, but also about the role of the probation officers and youth justice workers who assess offenders' suitability for these disposals and relay their assessments to the courts in pre-sentence reports (PSRs). Some studies have indeed suggested that PSRs serve to disadvantage black defendants. For example, de la Motta (1984) found that reports on young black defendants in Nottingham were three times as likely as those on whites to make no recommendation as to sentence – usually interpreted by the sentencing court to amount to a veiled recommendation for custody. It has been suggested that 'probation officers may well make fewer recommendations for supervision in the community because they lack the confidence to carry this out successfully' (NACRO, 1986b: 16) (91 per cent of probation staff are white: Home Office 2000a: 64.) However, other studies have found no such differences between recommendations in reports on black and white defendants (Mair, 1986; Moxon, 1988; Hood, 1992: 150–60) – but still fewer black defendants received probation orders than whites. One factor seems to be that PSRs are prepared less often on black defendants (for example, Hood, 1992: 150–1; Flood-Page and Mackie, 1998: 117), which is partly (but only partly) because reports are usually prepared in advance only on defendants pleading guilty, and black defendants are more likely to plead not guilty.[17] The 1994 change in the law allowing courts to dispense with PSRs before sentencing adults to custody could have made matters worse for black defendants.

The overall situation may have altered in recent years. A study of sentencing in the mid-1990s found no difference in custody rates between black and white defendants whether or not other factors were taken into account, although Asian men received more custodial sentences than would have been expected on this basis (Flood-Page and Mackie, 1998: 115–20). Currently, it seems that black offenders are slightly more likely to receive community sentences than white offenders, but not less likely to receive custody (instead they receive fewer discharges) (Home Office, 2000a: 38). Concerns remain about both sentencing and the quality of treatment ethnic minority offenders receive from the probation service. A recent thematic inspection (HM Inspectorate of Probation, 2000) revealed that the quality of pre-sentence reports on white offenders was significantly higher than those prepared for offenders from ethnic minorities. The quality of supervision given to African and Afro-Caribbean probationers also raised significant concerns with regard to risk assessments, the level of contact received and enforcement practice.

Bias against black people in the criminal justice system does not by any means cease at the point of sentence. Black prisoners are less likely than whites to be allocated to open prisons (NACRO, 1986b: 20). Elaine Genders and Elaine Player (1989) have provided substantial evidence of racial discrimination within prisons, finding for example that the best jobs were regularly allocated to white prisoners. Again, inaccurate racial stereotypes (this time held by prison officers) had a lot to answer for. Prison officers (97 per cent of whom are white: Home Office, 2000a: 64) believed that Afro-Caribbean prisoners were arrogant, lazy and anti-authority, had 'chips on their shoulders' and tended to stick together. Although these stereotypes were demonstrably false, they led prison staff to perceive black prisoners as unsuitable for the most desirable jobs.

Genders and Player's findings were perfectly exemplified by the case of John Alexander. Southampton County Court found in May 1987 that the Home Office had unlawfully discriminated against Mr Alexander, a black prisoner whose application to work in the prison at Parkhurst was refused on the basis of an assessment report which stated that 'he displays the usual traits associated with his ethnic background, being arrogant, suspicious of staff, anti-authority, devious and possessing a very large chip on his shoulder'. The Prison Service has had a formal race relations policy since 1983 and has made repeated statements in recent years opposing any discrimination or display of prejudice by prison staff or by prisoners against each other, but racism is of course not so easily eradicated. This was reflected in the findings of the 1991 National Prison Survey (Walmsley et al., 1992: 38) that only 29 per cent of black Caribbean prisoners felt that prison officers treated them well, compared with 43 per cent of white prisoners. Another study (Burnett and Farrell, 1994) found that nearly half of black prisoners reported having been racially victimized by prison staff and over half thought they had been discriminated against over access to facilities and activities.

Even more disturbing was the murder of Zahid Mubarek in March 2000 by a rabidly racist fellow inmate in Feltham Young Offender Institution. The Prison Service inquiry into this incident was reported to have found that Feltham was imbued with institutional racism, with ethnic minority staff and inmates being subjected to overt racist abuse from prison officers (*Guardian* 22 January 2001). The incident also led to the Prison Service inviting the Commission for Racial Equality to carry out a formal inquiry into racism in prisons. Already, in March 2000, prisons minister Paul Boateng had ordered an inquiry into racism among prison officers in Full Sutton Prison near York. The Prison Service Director General Martin Narey has reported receiving hate mail following his own admissions that institutional racism and indeed 'pockets of malicious racism' exist within the Prison Service (*Guardian*, 14 February 2001) It seems clear that racism and racial discrimination remain a potent and undeniable reality in English prisons.

There is a little evidence about the relationship between race and the *parole* decision. A Home Office (1994) study of parole recommendations in 1990 found that the proportions of ethnic minority prisoners recommended for parole were lower than those of white prisoners, but the differences tended to vanish when other factors such as type of offence and length of sentence were taken into account. When the figures were 'normalized' to allow for these factors, 60 per cent of white prisoners who were considered were recommended for parole compared with 56 per cent of those of West Indian or Guyanese ethnic origin. More recent figures for the granting of parole and home detention curfew show little difference between eligible black and white prisoners, Asian prisoners are more likely to be granted early release, probably because they generally represent a lesser risk of reconviction and are less likely to commit offences in prison (Home Office, 2000a: 42). [...]

GENDER

Within the criminal justice system, the dimension of gender differs in one crucial respect from those of class and race: in this case, members of the oppressed group (women) are distinctly *under*-represented in the criminal statistics. Women and girls accounted for a mere 5 per cent of the prison population in 1999,[18] despite comprising just over half of the general population. (Nevertheless, there are currently more women prisoners than ever before – 3,250 in 1999 – and in recent years their numbers have been rising even faster than men's.) Women are also under-represented at previous stages of the criminal justice system, though to lesser extents. In 1999, 16 per cent of those found guilty of indictable offences and 17 per cent of those found guilty or cautioned were female,[19] while only 15 per cent of those arrested in 1999/2000 were female (Home Office, 2000b: 9).

Again the question arises as to whether this difference is due to a real difference in offending behaviour between the two sections of the population (in this case, males and females). With very rare exceptions,[20] commentators agree that females do, in fact, commit fewer offences than do males, although the difference may be much smaller than the official figures suggest. Moreover, female offenders generally commit less serious offences than their male counterparts, and have committed fewer offences previously: the typical detected female offender is 'a young girl, a first offender charged with shoplifting' (Heidensohn, 1985: 11). Explanations for this state of affairs vary. Positivistic explanations exist which claim that differing male and female biologies are the cause: girls may not literally be made out of sugar and spice and all things nice, but their hormones lead them to be more law-abiding. More plausible in our opinion are theories which emphasize the different social experiences of males and females. Girls are socialized to be more passive and conformist than boys, and throughout their lives girls and women may find themselves subject to greater informal social controls; they may also have less opportunity to commit certain types of crime (see, for example, Smart, 1976: 66–70; Heidensohn, 1985: ch. 9).

Whatever the explanation, if we accept that women and girls do in fact commit fewer (and generally less serious) offences than men and boys, then the bare statistics say nothing about whether there is any bias operating in the criminal justice system either in favour of women or against them. Perhaps there would be even fewer women in prison if they were treated the same as comparable male offenders; or perhaps there would be more. There have traditionally been two rival schools of thought on this issue, one holding that female offenders are dealt with more leniently than males and one asserting the reverse.

The first view – the 'chivalry theory' – claims that chivalry leads police and sentencers (who are predominantly male)[21] to afford women less harsh treatment. It is easy to point to incidents which appear to bear this out. Our personal favourite is a case reported in the *Daily Mirror* in January 1978: '*Judge frees "inhuman" mum*. A mother who flogged her eight-year-old son with a belt, gave him cold baths and forced him to stand naked for hours at night … was saved from prison *because she has another child to care for'* (cited by Heidensohn 1985: 51;

our italics). Were the chivalry theory to be correct, this would not of course mean that there is no sexist bias in the criminal justice system, but that the sexism takes the form of a condescending 'chivalry' which may benefit some female offenders but is hardly likely to advance the general cause of female social equality. (It is, however, the kind of view often propounded by anti-feminists of the 'women should stop moaning because they get the better deal as things are' ilk.)

The opposing view, put forward in particular by feminist commentators, has been termed the 'evil woman' theory (Nagel and Hagan, 1983). It asserts that women who offend will receive *harsher* treatment from the criminal justice system. This is because women who commit crimes are seen as 'doubly deviant': they have offended not only against the law, but also against deeply ingrained social norms about how women should be, so they are perceived as being particularly depraved. Rebellious anti-social behaviour on the part of a young man may be reprehensible, but it is less disturbing because such behaviour is after all masculine – 'boys will be boys'. Similar conduct on the part of a young woman is far more unsettling because it is unfeminine. Moreover, there is a tendency for female criminality to be 'sexualized' in a way that male offending is not. Female offenders are assumed to be sexually deviant, or their sexuality is regarded as associated with their offending, assumptions which are not made with male offenders. The result is that women's crime evokes an especially puni-tive response. This punitiveness may be overt, or it may be disguised as pater-nalistic concern for the woman's welfare. The woman's disturbing deviance may be rationalized away as 'sickness', leading to a positivistic 'treatment' measure which could be more intrusive than the sentence a male offender would receive for a similar offence (see generally Heidensohn, 1985: ch. 3).

These theories can be tested against the evidence that exists concerning the different stages of the criminal process. At the first stages of initial contact between the police and possible female suspects, one clearly established fact is that the police stop and search men much more often than women (in fact about twice as often.)[22] A national survey of boys and girls aged 14 and 15, carried out by Home Office researchers in 1983 (Riley and Shaw, 1985; Riley, 1986) casts some light on the phenomenon. Boys were more than twice as likely to have been stopped by the police than girls of the same age (29 per cent compared with 13 per cent in the preceding twelve months). Boys were more likely to be stopped if they and their friends were delinquent, but this was not true for girls. Girls were more likely to be stopped if their lifestyles were 'unfeminine' – if they went around in mixed-sex groups, were relatively more involved with drugs and alcohol, spent more time with their friends and were subject to less parental supervision. These findings do not show that the police treat girls worse than boys, but they do lend some support to the feminist claim that females are dealt with by criminal justice agencies according to different crite-ria from those applied to males, criteria related to traditional female gender-roles, with the result that their femininity is being policed as much as their offending. This is a theme which will recur as we progress through the criminal process.

Moving on to the decision whether to *arrest* a suspect, while there is little directly relevant British research evidence, a study of drug arrests in Chicago between 1942 and 1970 (de Fleur, 1975: 101) found 'a tendency not to arrest females as often as males if they behaved in expected, stereotypic ways. During drugs raids females often cried, claimed to have been led astray by men, or expressed concern about the fate of their children. These behaviors usually were successful.' However, females who were more aggressive and hostile were arrested more often than those who behaved in more traditionally feminine ways.

There is no doubt that detected female offenders are *cautioned* much more often than males. In 1999, 48 per cent of females found guilty of or cautioned for an indictable offence received a caution, compared with 30 per cent of males (Ayres et al., 2000: table 4). Claims have been made that such figures show chivalry operating in women's favour (Walker, 1968: 299–300), and also that they show the reverse (Smart, 1976: 137–8).[23] It is of course necessary to take into account the type of offences involved and the offenders' previous records in deciding whether any bias goes into the creation of the statistical difference between the sexes. Ideally, one should also allow for other variables which may affect the decision whether to caution or prosecute, such as social class and race. Landau and Nathan's (1983) study of juvenile cautioning in London found that, when such other variables were controlled for, the sex of the offender made no significant difference to the decision of the police (see also Landau, 1981). (However, Loraine Gelsthorpe (1989: 106) found evidence that girls were more likely than boys to be cautioned for offences of similar seriousness.) Again, although girls are not overall dealt with more harshly than boys, it may be that they are judged by different, gender-role-related criteria. It has been suggested that police again act more leniently towards female offenders who act in stereotypically feminine ways, such as showing remorse by crying or apologizing (Gelsthorpe, 1985: 3, 1989: 105).[24]

Women are *remanded in custody* less often than men, apparently because they are less likely to have breached bail in the past or to be of no fixed abode (Flood-Page and Mackie, 1998: 121). When women are remanded in custody, they are less likely than remanded males to be subsequently sentenced to custody by the court (35 per cent of female and 47 per cent of male remandees in 1999 – Home Office, 2000b: 15). This could mean that some women are being remanded in custody when comparable male offenders are not;[25] certainly it means that many women offenders are being sent to prison before trial although their actual offence is subsequently not deemed serious enough to warrant deprivation of liberty. 48 per cent of women who are remanded in custody are charged with theft or fraud rather than more serious or violent offences (Home Office, 2000b: 15).

The 'chivalry' and 'evil woman' theories have both been put forward in respect of *sentencing*. The bare statistics show, as one would expect, that women and girls sentenced for indictable offences on the whole receive less severe sentences than males. In 1999, 13.5 per cent of females' sentences were custodial compared with 25 per cent of males' (Ayres et al., 2000: table 11). Sentencing patterns differ in some other respects as well: women are much more likely than males to receive probation orders, and less likely to be fined or ordered to perform community service.[26] Do these figures indicate bias – and if so, in what direction?

Pat Carlen (1983) argues that sexist bias enters into the sentencing decision to the disadvantage of women who offend against the norms of femininity. From her interviews with sheriffs (Scottish judges) she concludes that when sentencers are 'faced with a sentencing dilemma in a case where the offender is female, they mainly decide their sentence on the basis of their assessment of the woman as mother' (Carlen, 1983: 63). All the sheriffs she interviewed said (chivalrously) that they particularly hated sending women to prison. Nevertheless, they admitted that they sometimes imprisoned women in circumstances when they would have fined a man, because women were nor-mally financially dependent on their husbands and often could not afford to pay a fine appropriate to the offence. They would be particularly inclined to send a woman to prison if her children were in care. Carlen quotes sheriffs as commenting: 'If she's a good mother we don't want to take her away. If she's not a good mother it doesn't really matter', and 'One often finds out, when inquiries are made, that the women have left their husbands and their children are already in care. In those cases it may seem a very good idea to send them to prison for three months to sort themselves out' (Carlen, 1983: 67).

Carlen's claim that sentencers make their decisions in this manner receives some support from surveys of women in prison, a disproportionate number of whom seem to have unconventional family backgrounds. Of Carlen's own sam-ple of 20 Scottish women prisoners only one was currently married and living with her husband (Carlen, 1983: 38). In another Scottish sample, 65 per cent of the women prisoners had children under 18, but only half of these had been looking after them immediately prior to being imprisoned (Dobash et al., 1986: 193). In England, Genders and Player found that half of their sample of women prisoners over the age of 30 had a non-conventional background; fewer than half of those with dependent children lived within a 'traditional nuclear family setting' (in which they included living with a long-term cohabitee) (Genders and Player, 1986: 360). The findings of the 1991 National Prison Survey (Walmsley et al., 1992: 17) differed only slightly from this: 49 per cent of female prisoners of 18 or over had been living with a spouse or partner prior to their imprisonment, and nearly a half of those with dependent children were unmarried. Further support for Carlen's thesis comes from a study of magistrates' sentencing in Cambridge by Farrington and Morris. They found that women who were divorced or separated or had a 'deviant family background' were more likely to receive a relatively severe sentence, but these factors made no difference to the kind of sentences which male offenders received (Farrington and Morris, 1983: 244–5). (In the United States, Nagel (1981) made similar findings.)

Overall, Farrington and Morris found that the sentences received by female defendants at the Cambridge City Magistrates' Court were not signifi-cantly heavier or lighter than those passed on men when the relevant factors of offence type and offender's previous record were controlled for. In combination with their findings about the effects of 'deviant family backgrounds', this suggests the possibility that there could be sexist biases in sentencing operating *in both directions* (and, in this study, cancelling each other out). Women who are married and looking after their children may be the beneficiaries of chivalry and receive a lighter sentence than a man, but women who are less acceptably feminine – who are perceived as 'evil women' because they are not good wives and mothers[27] – may be treated more harshly.

However, the same cancelling out of biases was not apparent in two studies of Crown Court sentencing practice (Moxon, 1988; Hood, 1992: ch. 11); chivalry seemed to predominate. (Nagel (1981) has also found this to be true in the USA.) After allowing for factors such as offence and criminal record, women were significantly less likely than men to receive a custodial sentence. For example, Moxon (1988: 54) found that male first offenders charged with theft or fraud were almost twice as likely to receive unsuspended custody as were comparable women. Similarly, Hedderman and Hough (1994) found that in 1992 female first offenders were only half as likely to receive a sentence of immediate imprisonment than were male first offenders, and the pattern was similar for specific offences such as theft and for offenders with one, two or three previous convictions. Flood-Page and Mackie (1998: 121–3) found much the same picture emerging in the mid-1990s. Dowds and Hedderman (1997) found a more mixed picture when they examined a large sample of male and female adult offenders sentenced in 1991 for shoplifting, violence and drugs offences. Taking other factors into account, female shoplifters were less likely than comparable males to receive a prison sentence. Men and women were equally likely to be imprisoned for their first conviction for violence or a repeat drug offence – but women were less likely to receive custody for a *first drug* conviction or *repeated violent* offence.

It is not entirely clear how or whether these findings can be reconciled with those of Farrington and Morris. But it is noticeable that Farrington and Morris divided sentences into two categories, 'relatively lenient' and 'relatively severe', the latter including probation, community service and suspended sentences, whereas the other studies divided sentences into unsuspended custody and non-custodial sentences. Farrington and Morris's finding could therefore be explained by the known tendency for courts to sentence women disproportionately to probation, while the other studies suggest that – as Carlen's sheriffs claimed – courts may often be fairly loath to sentence women (especially mothers) to *custody*.

It is often claimed (for example Mawby, 1977; Fitzgerald and Sim, 1979: 81) that women must be sentenced more harshly because a greater proportion of women who receive prison sentences have no previous convictions compared with imprisoned men: this was true of 38 per cent of women serving prison sentences in 1991 but only 10 per cent of male prisoners (Walmsley et al., 1992: 64). (Similarly, a much smaller proportion of female than male prisoners have been found guilty of a violent offence.)[28] This argument looks convincing at first sight, but it is fallacious. For these kinds of percentages are just what we should expect to find given that the great bulk of the female offender population consists of people with no or few previous convictions, and the figures are perfectly compatible with women receiving sentences which are similar to or more lenient than those passed on comparable male offenders (Walker, 1981). The correct comparison – of how female and male offenders with similar records are actually dealt with at the sentencing stage – was the comparison made by the studies we mentioned in the previous two paragraphs.

There seems to be a particular reluctance on the part of sentencing courts to impose fines on women. This could be partly – though probably not entirely – due to sentencers taking into account the fact that women are less likely to have their own income and more likely to have childcare responsibilities (Dowds and Hedderman, 1997; Gelsthorpe and Loucks, 1997). The result of this seems to be that (like unemployed offenders, whom courts are also reluctant to fine) a woman may end up receiving a less severe sentence than a male offender (such as a discharge rather than a fine) but may also sometimes receive a more intrusive sentence such as probation.

The preponderance of research evidence, however, suggests that women who offend are not on the whole sentenced less severely than comparable males, and that they sometimes receive more lenient sentences, including escaping custody where a male would not. What is not known, however, is to what extent this could be accounted for by arguably relevant differences in the situations of male and female offenders, such as childcare responsibilities. Perhaps a woman with a child to look after does not deserve to escape imprisonment any more than an otherwise comparable male offender without such a responsibility, but does the child deserve to lose its mother? It may well be that such considerations – perhaps rightly – account for the differences between men and women as regards whether they receive custodial sentences. The possibility also remains that some women – perhaps those who are perceived as especially deviant because of their lifestyles or their particular crimes – come off worse than comparable male offenders because of their gender. As Chris Tchaikovsky of the organization Women in Prison has aptly put it: 'Judges tell me all the time that they never send women to prison. The truth is that the woman in the neat white blouse who is sorry and depressed is acceptable, but the girl in the leather jacket with the Mohican haircut and the drug problem is treated very badly' (*Guardian*, 9 February 1994).

Much attention has been focused in recent years on the position of women who kill their violent male partners. The best-known example is Sara Thornton, whose murder conviction was quashed and a retrial ordered by the Court of Appeal in December 1995. It is argued that the legal defence of 'provocation' (which can reduce a charge of murder to manslaughter, with consequent possibilities of a lesser sentence than the mandatory life imprisonment sentence for murder) serves to prejudice women in comparison with men, because it requires a sudden loss of self-control. Men may be more able to avail themselves of this defence because they are more likely to kill women using methods such as strangulation which they can claim resulted from a sudden burst of anger, whereas women's methods of killing their partner may look more premeditated. Moreover, the law has been slow to recognize the effects of 'cumulative provocation' consisting of recurrent violence over a long period (Nicolson and Sanghvi, 1995). These arguments may well be correct, despite the fact that women seem to succeed in pleading provocation in a higher proportion of domestic homicides than do men (Hedderman and Hough, 1994). For it seems very likely that women in such cases are typically subjected to much higher degrees of provocation (and especially of violence) from their partners than the men are. The law of provocation was significantly reinterpreted by the Court of Appeal in the 1990s,[29] giving greater recognition to 'cumulative provocation' but still requiring 'loss of self-control' to establish the provocation defence. It cannot of course be assumed that homicide – one of the rarest of offences – provides a typical picture of the way the legal and penal systems deal routinely with the great bulk of non-violent female offending.

If courts do indeed have a *general* tendency to be relatively lenient with female offenders, especially as regards custody, it could be a leniency bought by exploiting stereotyped notions about women and their crimes, at the price of reinforcing these stereotypes. Defence lawyers' pleas in mitigation and pre-sentence reports might encourage leniency by playing on the positivistic idea that women who offend are sick, or 'mad rather than bad', or by portraying the woman as weak, and led astray by a dominant man. In thus arguing that the women cannot help their actions, lawyers and probation officers could be helping to perpetuate the sexist ideology which holds that women are in general weaker, less rational than men and more driven by their emotions. Mary Eaton (1986) makes the wider claim that mitigation pleas and pre-sentence reports reinforce prevailing ideologies about women's rightful roles within the family by stressing either the normality of the woman's domestic behaviour (and therefore her essential goodness) or else its abnormality (as either a cause or a symptom of the pathology that has led her to offend).

It is doubtless the perception of women who offend as 'mad rather than bad' and in need of help (perhaps combined in some cases with reluctance to impose a fine) which leads to the tendency for female offenders to receive more probation and supervision orders than males.[30] Such paternalism could have the effect of 'up-tariffing' […] some female offenders with comparatively trivial offending records, leading to an increased danger of a more severe sentence if they re-offend subsequently.

When women are sentenced to custody, how does their treatment compare to that of men? At first sight it might seem that they are treated better, since penal establishments for females are on the whole (superficially at least, and with some notable exceptions) physically less unpleasant places than those for males. But in some respects women prisoners are worse off. For example, because women comprise such a small percentage of the prison population, only 17 out of the 130-plus penal institutions in England and Wales accommodate females; this means that women are often held at enormous distances from their homes, in remote locations, making visiting a particular problem. Again, it is probably the case that, for a variety of social and psychological reasons, women find the experience of imprisonment much more traumatic than men do (Heidensohn, 1985: 75–9), leading to a higher incidence of flare-ups and self-mutilation in women's prisons.[31]

It can be argued that women prisoners *should* be treated differently from men because their circumstances and needs are different. Most of them have children under 16, of whom only a quarter are being cared for by the child's father or a spouse or partner;[32] they are more likely to be dependent on opiate drugs, and nearly half report having been physically and/or sexually abused (HM Chief Inspector of Prisons, 1997). And indeed women prisoners are treated differently from men – but whether these differences are appropriate to their needs is another question. Traditionally, the training of female prisoners is directed towards equipping them to perform the work they are thought most likely to do when they are released, namely housework. The general picture has not changed much: the work that women do in prison is still dominated by domestic-type tasks such as cleaning, sewing and cooking, which also figure prominently in the training provided for female prisoners, along with training for traditionally female jobs such as typing, catering and hairdressing (Hamlyn and Lewis, 2000: chs 4 and 5). Genders and Player, who studied female youth custody centres (now called young offender institutions), found this stereotyping of women's work to be combined with psychological rehabilitation theory:

> an important part of the treatment and training of young women serving youth custody relates to the building of self-confidence and self-esteem, the lack of which is deemed responsible for much of the attention- and approval-seeking which causes many girls to come into conflict with the law. The skills which are taught in youth custody centres, however, continue to permit success mainly within the boundaries of stereotypical female roles. The concentration upon personal hygiene and appearance, through training in beauty care and hairdressing, and the development of domestic skills, such as cleaning, cooking and household budgeting, makes clear those areas in which delinquent young women are expected to develop feelings of self-worth. (Genders and Player, 1986: 368)

The positivistic 'mad not bad' stereotype of female offenders has had a particular influence on prison regimes for women. An official Home Office publication of 1977 stated that 'most of the women in prison wish to conform with society but for various reasons are unable to do so. For example, many are in need of medical or psychiatric treatment' (Home Office, 1977: 101). Even if female prisoners are more likely to be mentally ill than male prisoners are, this would only mean that a larger *minority* of female prisoners are in need of psychiatric treatment[33] (Heidensohn, 1985: 73–5; Morris, 1987: 124–5). It seems likely that female prisoners are *treated as* mentally ill to an excessive extent; certainly they seem to be prescribed psychotropic medication to a much greater extent than male prisoners (Morris, 1987: 124). This is not to deny that a great deal of mental *distress* is suffered by female prisoners: as we said before, women prisoners probably do suffer from imprisonment to a greater extent than men do.

In 1968 – roughly at the zenith of the 'rehabilitative ideal' – it was announced that Holloway (by far the largest women's penal establishment in England) was to be redesigned and rebuilt as, in essence, a secure psychiatric hospital. The new design turned out to be disastrous, and in 1981 the prison was given a 'modified brief' by the Home Office, abandoning the notion that all its inmates should be treated according to a medical model. This did not prevent the rebuilt Holloway from suffering severe problems, including over-crowding and low staff morale, compounded by a public scandal which blew up in 1984 about the prisoners' living conditions. Ironically, the most damning publicity was directed at the psychiatric unit (known to inmates as 'the Muppet House'), in which there were three suicides and several outbreaks of self-mutilation. The scandal resulted in a Home Office inquiry, following which the prison improved significantly (HM Chief Inspector of Prisons, 1992). Subsequently, however, conditions deteriorated again, provoking an unprece-dented walkout by Chief Inspector of Prisons Sir David Ramsbotham in December 1995 after inspectors had reportedly found squalid conditions and a heavy-handed, over-zealous security régime in place at Holloway. This was again followed by an apparent improvement in conditions, at least for the time being, but Holloway's problems seem to recur on a regular basis.

In recent years, female prisoners seem to have suffered at least as much as male inmates from the 'security first' atmosphere engendered by the Woodcock (1994) and Learmont (1995) reports into prison security, despite the fact that women generally pose much less of a threat to security. One manifestation of this was a policy introduced in April 1995 that women prisoners (including those in advanced stages of pregnancy) should be handcuffed or chained when being treated in hospitals outside prisons. The outcry which followed a TV news report of a prisoner chained to a prison officer hours before and after giving birth led to a modification of the policy in January 1996, but only to exempt women arriving at hospital to give birth (and most of those attending ante-natal checks) from being cuffed or chained while in the hospital.

Overall, though, it appears that female offenders do not in general receive harsher treatment than their opposite numbers of the opposite sex; and some-times they may receive more lenient treatment, perhaps especially as regards the decision to impose custodial sentences. However, it also seems very likely that *some* women are effectively punished for deviating from conventional feminine norms, and that the system tends to react to female offenders in a manner which is, one way or another, imbued with sexism. To use Althusser's terminology, the penal system can be seen both as part of the 'Repressive State Apparatus' visiting deviant women with punitive sanctions and as an 'Ideological State Apparatus' communicating and reproducing the sexist ideology which structures patriarchal society (Eaton, 1986: 88–9). Or, as a Durkheimian might put it, our social culture is still permeated with sexism, which is bound to find expression in our punitive practices.

Currently women offenders are being punished increasingly harshly for their deviance. Indeed, the female prison population has recently been increasing much more rapidly than the numbers of male prisoners. Between 1993 and 1999 the male prison population increased by a massive 43 per cent, but the numbers of female prisoners more than doubled, from 1,560 to 3,250. This disproportionate rise is probably not because women are now being sentenced more harshly than men, but because the increase in sentence severity since 1993 has in particular meant that a great many more relatively petty offenders have been sent to prison, or sent there for longer. And since as we have seen most female offenders are relatively petty criminals, this shift has affected women disproportionately. [...]

NOTES

1   The Policy Studies Institute (Smith, 1983: 247) found that Londoners in the professional and managerial occupational groups were more critical of the police than others; but it also seemed that unemployed people were significantly more likely to be critical of the police than people in employment. Similarly, results from the national British Crime Survey (Skogan, 1990: 13–14) have shown people who are unemployed, less educated or living in the inner city to be less happy with the police than others.

2   It does not, however, seem to be the case that *employed working-class* people are stopped more often than middle-class people. In fact, if stops in cars are included, professionals and higher earners are more likely to be stopped, because they are more likely to drive cars (Skogan, 1990: 28–9, 61).

3   For evidence that deaths at work which are caused by managers' culpable carelessness are dealt with very differently from other deaths caused by fault, see Bergman (1991). In May 2000 the government announced its intention to introduce a new offence of 'corporate killing' for which *companies* could be prosecuted (Sanders and Young, 2000: 368–71), but this would not affect the criminal liability of the individual managers who might be at fault.

4   This figure is for 1999 (Ayres et al., 2000).

5   For an article attempting the tricky task of comparing the treatment of white-collar and other offenders, see Levi (1989). See also Nelken (1997).

6   Disparity can also be detected in Court of Appeal decisions about the appropriate sentences for these offences, although the gap has narrowed to some extent in recent years. Two fairly typical cases are *R. v. Hayes* (1981) 3 Cr App Rep (S) 205 (nine months' imprisonment for conspiracy to defraud the Inland Revenue of £19,424) and *R. v. Adams* (1985) 7 Cr App Rep (S) 411 (two years' custody for defrauding social security of £7,000).

7   45 per cent of non-white people in English prisons are not of UK nationality, indicating that drug couriers account for some of the racial disparity, especially among females (75 per cent of foreign female prisoners are serving sentences for drugs offences). But only some. When non-UK nationals are excluded from the figures, 14 per cent of male and 15 per cent of female prisoners are of ethnic minority origin (Home Office, 2000a: ch. 7).

8   In this [chapter], we use the term 'black' to refer to people of African or Caribbean ethnic origin only. This chapter concentrates on the most obvious and most disturbing statistical differences between the races in the criminal justice system, which are between white people on the one hand and 'black' people on the other. Comparisons between whites and people of 'Asian' (Indian, Pakistani or Bangladeshi) ethnic origin often yield very different results. For example, the preponderance of research suggests that Asian people are *under*-represented in both

recorded and unrecorded offending (e.g. Stevens and Willis, 1979: 2; Graham and Bowling, 1995) and are stopped by the police less often than Afro-Caribbeans and either less often or about as often as whites (Smith, 1983: 95; Skogan, 1990: 28). Hood (1992: 75–9) found that, unlike black defendants, Asian Crown Court defendants were slightly less likely than whites to be sentenced to custody. Genders and Player (1989) found that, within prisons, Asians were regarded stereotypically by staff as 'model prisoners', in stark contrast to Afro-Caribbeans.

9   See also Willis (1983: 14); Skogan (1990: 27–9; 1994: 25–6, 73); Flood-Page et al. (2000: 49–50).

10   These figures may not be as bad as they seem when different social, demographic and lifestyle characteristics of different ethnic groups are taken into account. The average black person may be more likely to be found on the city streets than the average white person, and the racial differences in stop and search rates sometimes disappear when these factors are controlled for (MVA and Miller, 2000). Nevertheless it seems unlikely that a ratio as great as 5 to 1 can be satisfactorily explained away entirely in this way.

11   'Demeanour' could also be important here. Either stereotyping by the police, or the fact that black people tend to be more critical of the police than whites (Field, 1984: ch. 7; Flood-Page et al., 2000: 54; Mirrlees-Black, 2001; Sims and Myhill, 2001), or both, could lead to the police perceiving black people as having a bad attitude towards them and discriminating against them as a result.

12   Evidence of institutional racism on the part of the Crown Prosecution Service was also reported by an independent inquiry into allegations of racial discrimination against CPS staff (*Guardian*, 11 May 2000).

13   In the year 1999/2000 recorded stops and searches fell by 41 per cent in London and 14 per cent on average elsewhere, but searches of black people fell by only 35 and 10 per cent respectively (Home Office, 2000a: 7–8).

14   This was particularly noticeable for the (now abolished) offence of 'sus', or 'being a suspected person loitering with intent'. Black people were 15 times more likely than whites to be arrested for this offence, a figure which led Home Office researchers to wonder politely whether some of the difference may be accounted for by the possibility that the suspicions of policemen bear disproportionately on blacks' (Stevens and Willis, 1979: 33).

15   See also Commission for Racial Equality (1992). A study in London by Farrington and Bennett (1981) found that race made no significant difference to cautioning rates; but it is possible that their lumping together of blacks and Asians affected their results. In Leeds, Walker et al. (1990) found that 31 per cent of black juveniles cautioned or prosecuted received a caution compared with 41 per cent of whites, a difference which was not statistically significant.

16   This difference was not statistically significant at the 0.05 level conventionally used by statisticians, and in theory there is a 7 per cent chance that it could be attributable to chance. However, in the light of other evidence about the effects of race in criminal justice and the fact that the difference is in the 'expected' direction, Hood (1992: 80–1; 1995) is doubtless justified in taking it as evidence of a genuine 'race effect' in sentencing.

17   Since it appears that more black than white defendants are *acquitted*, or have their cases dismissed by the court for lack of evidence (Walker, 1988; Walker et al., 1990; Phillips and Brown, 1998; Home Office, 2000a: 37), it may be that black defendants deny guilt more often simply because black people are more often wrongly arrested and wrongly prosecuted.

18   Calculated from Cullen and Minchin (2000).

19   Calculated from Ayres et al. (2000: table 4).

20   One outstanding (and notoriously sexist) exception was Otto Pollak (1961), who claimed that women are responsible for vast amounts of crime which go undetected

because of women's more deceitful nature and because chivalrous men do not want to see women prosecuted or punished (see Heidensohn, 1985: 118–21).

21 83 per cent of police officers are male, as are around 90 per cent of Crown Court judges and 51 per cent of magistrates (Home Office, 2000b: ch. 10). Some research suggests that women magistrates deal more severely with female defendants (Farrington and Morris, 1983: 245), which may fit in with the 'chivalry theory'. On the other hand, it could mean that 'good', law-abiding women tend to come down harder on 'evil', law-breaking women than men do.

22 The 1988 British Crime Survey found that 20 per cent of males and 10 per cent of females had been stopped in the previous 14 months, while the 1992 BCS found figures of 28 and 16 per cent over a 12 month period (Skogan, 1990: 28; 1994: 73). See also Flood-Page et al. (2000: 48–9).

23 Walker's claim was based on unrefined statistics which took no account of the seriousness of the offence or the offender's previous record; on the other hand, Smart's claim was based on a statistical fallacy which Walker later refuted (Walker, 1981: 380–1).

24 However, it is not clear that the police are acting in a *directly* sexist manner at this point. Gelsthorpe suggests that boys who showed remorse (which they did less often than girls) were also more likely to be cautioned.

25 It is possible that many sentencers pass a non-custodial sentence rather than a short prison sentence on a woman who has been remanded in custody, reasoning that she has already had 'a taste of custody'. If so, the fact that women's prison sentences are on average much shorter than men's (because their offences are less serious) could explain the gender difference pointed out in the text.

26 In 1999, 22 per cent of females sentenced for indictable offences were placed on probation or supervision orders, 7 per cent given community service orders and 21 per cent fined. The corresponding figures for male offenders were 13, 9 and 28 per cent (Ayres et al., 2000: table 8).

27 The case of Susan Jones is of interest. Mrs Jones's four-year prison sentence for robbing seven building societies was quashed by the Court of Appeal in July 1991 and a probation order with a condition of psychiatric treatment was substituted. The trial judge had referred to her 'wicked crimes' but the Court of Appeal judges stated that she was '*not a wicked woman*' and had only robbed because she had become desperate about her family's debts and was concerned about her twin children but 'did not want to worry her husband' (*Guardian*, 30 July 1991).

28 On 30 June 1999, only 25 per cent of female sentenced prisoners were in prison for violent or sexual offences including robbery, compared with 44 per cent of male prisoners (calculated from Cullen and Minchin, 2000: table 1).

29 In the cases of *R. v. Ahluwalia* [1992] 4 All ER 889 and *R. v. Humphries* [1995] 4 All ER 1008.

30 See above, n. 26.

31 Women prisoners are punished for offences against prison discipline much more often than men: in 1999 there were 213 offences per 100 female prisoners compared with 158 per 100 males (Home Office, 2000b: 32). Part of the reason for this seems to be that, although the governing Prison Rules do not vary, there are generally more unnecessary restrictions placed on women prisoners and the rules are more rigorously enforced against them (Morris, 1987: 121–4; NACRO, 1992).

32 There are four mother and baby units within women's prisons (in Holloway, Askham Grange, Styal and New Hall prisons) with places for 72 women and their babies, who can only stay with their mothers up to the age of 18 months. The Prison Service is currently considering expanding the places available and allowing children up to the age of four. It is a controversial question whether this is the right approach to the needs of mothers and their children, as opposed to ensuring that as few mothers as possible are in prison in the first place.

33   Studies such as Gunn et al. (1991) have only found a very small percentage of women prisoners suffering from psychoses such as schizophrenia, although rather more with neurotic disorders and depression. It is only possible to conclude that a *majority* of female prisoners are mentally disordered by including categories such as drug dependency and 'personality disorder'. The latter is not a treatable illness but essentially a judgment that the individual has an unusual personality, for example by reason of anti-social behaviour. Not surprisingly, many prisoners (both male and female) can be diagnosed in this manner.

REFERENCES

Ayres, M. et al. (2000) *Cautions, Court Proceedings and Sentencing England and Wales*. Home Office Statistical Bulletin 19/00. London: Home Office.

Baldus, D.C., Pulaski, C.A. Jr. and Woodworth, G.W. (1986) 'Arbitrariness and Discrimination in the Administration of the Death Penalty: a Challenge to State Supreme Courts', *Stetson Law Review*, 15: 138–261.

Baldus, D.C., Woodworth, G.W. and Pulaski, C.A. Jr (1989) *Equal Justice and the Death Penalty: A Legal and Empirical Analysis*. Boston: Northeastern University Press.

Bennett, T. (1979) 'The Social Distribution of Criminal Labels', *British Journal of Criminology*, 19: 134–45.

Bergman, D. (1991) *Deaths at Work: Accidents or Corporate Crime?* London: Workers' Educational Association.

Bottomley, A.K. (1973) *Decisions in the Penal Process*. London: Martin Robertson.

Bottoms, A.E. and McClean, J.D. (1976) *Defendants in the Criminal Process*. London: Routledge and Kegan Paul.

Bucke, T. (1997) *Ethnicity and Contacts with the Police: Findings from the British Crime Survey*. Home Office Research Findings no. 59. London: Home Office.

Burnett, R. and Farrell, G. (1994) *Reported and Unreported Racial Incidents in Prison*. University of Oxford Centre for Criminological Research Occasional Paper no. 14.

Cain, M. (1971) 'On the Beat: Interactions and Relations in Rural and Urban Police Forces', in S. Cohen (ed.), *Images of Deviance*. Harmondsworth: Penguin.

Carlen, P. (1983) *Women's Imprisonment: A Study in Social Control*. London: Routledge and Kegan Paul.

Carson, W.G. (1971) 'White Collar Crime and the Enforcement of Factory Legislation', in W.G. Carson and P. Wiles (eds), *Crime and Delinquency in Britain*. London: Martin Robertson, pp. 192–206.

Commission for Social Equality (1992) Juvenile cautioning: Ethnic Monitoring in Practice. London: CRE.

Cook, D. (1989) *Rich Law, Poor Law: Differential Response to Tax and Supplementary Benefit Fraud*. Milton Keynes: Open University Press.

Crow, I. (1987) 'Black People and Criminal Justice in the UK', *Howard Journal of Criminal Justice*, 26: 303–14.

Crow, I. and Cove, J. (1984) 'Ethnic Minorities and the Courts', [1984] *Criminal Law Review*, 413–17.

Crow, I. and Simon, F. (1987) *Unemployment and Magistrates' Courts*. London: NACRO.

Crow, I., Cavadino, M., Dignan, J., Johnston, V. and Walker, M. (1995) *The Impact of the Criminal Justice Act 1991 in Four Areas in the North of England*. University of Sheffield.

Crow, I., Richardson, P., Riddington, C. and Simon, F. (1989) *Unemployment, Crime and Offenders*. London: Routledge.

Cullen, C. and Minchin, M. (2000) *The Prison Population in 1999: a Statistical Review*. Home Office Research Findings no. 118. London: Home Office Research and Statistics Directorate.

Dobash, R.P., Dobash, R.E. and Gutteridge, S. (1986) *The Imprisonment of Women*. Oxford: Basil Blackwell.

Dowds, L. and Hedderman, C. (1997) 'The Sentencing of Man and Women', in C. Hedderman & L. Gelsthorpe (eds.) Understanding the Sentencing of Women, pp. 7–21, Home Office Research Study no. 170, London: Home Office.

Eaton, M. (1986) *Justice for Women? Family, Court and Social Control*. Milton Keynes: Open University Press.

Farrington, D.P. and Bennett, T. (1981) 'Police Cautioning of Juveniles in London', *British Journal of Criminology*, 21: 123–35.

Farrington, D.P. and Morris, A.M. (1983) 'Sex, Sentencing and Reconviction', *British Journal of Criminology*, 23: 229–48.

Field, S. (1984) *The Attitudes of Ethnic Minorities*. Home Office Research Study no. 80. London: HMSO.

Fisher, C.J. and Mawby, R.L. (1982) 'Juvenile Delinquency and Police Discretion in an Inner City Area', *British Journal of Criminology*, 22: 63–75.

Fitzgerald, M. (1993) *Ethnic Minorities and the Criminal Justice System*. The Royal Commission on Criminal Justice, Research Study no. 20. London: HMSO.

Fitzgerald, M. and Sim, J. (1979) *British Prisons*. Oxford: Basil Blackwell.

de Fleur, L.B. (1975) 'Bias Influences on Drug Arrest Records: Implications for Deviance Research', *American Sociological Review*, 40: 88–103.

Flood-Page, C. and Mackie, A. (1998) *Sentencing Practice: An Examination of Decisions in Magistrates' Courts and the Crown Court in the Mid-1990s*. Home Office Research Study no. 180. London: Home Office.

Flood-Page, C., Campbell, S., Harrington, V. and Miller, J. (2000) *Youth Crime: Findings from the 1998/99 Youth Lifestyles Survey*. Home Office Research Study no. 209. London: Home Office.

Gelsthorpe, L. (1985) 'Girls and Juvenile Justice', *Youth and Policy*, 11: 1–5.

Gelsthorpe, L. (1989) *Sexism and the Female Offender: An Organizational Analysis*. Aldershot: Gower.

Gelsthorpe, L. and Loucks, N. (1997) 'Magistrates' Explanations of Sentencing Decisions', in C. Hedderman and L. Gelsthorpe (eds), *Understanding the Sentencing of Women*. Home Office Research Study no. 17. London: Home Office.

Genders, E. and Player, E. (1986) 'Women's Imprisonment: the Effects of Youth Custody', *British Journal of Criminology*, 26: 357–71.

Genders, E. and Player, E. (1989) *Race Relations in Prisons*. Oxford: Clarendon Press.

Gold, M. (1966) 'Undetected Delinquent Activity', *Journal of Research in Crime and Delinquency*, 3: 27–46.

Graham, J. and Bowling, B. (1995) *Young People and Crime*. Home Office Research Study no. 145. London: HMSO.

Gunn, J., Maden, T. and Swinton, M. (1991) *Mentally Disordered Prisoners*. London: Home Office.

Hamlyn, B. and Lewis, D. (2000) *Women Prisoners: A Survey of their Work and Training Experiences in Custody and on Release*. Home Office Research Study no. 208. London: Home Office.

Harris, R. and Webb, D. (1987) *Welfare, Power and Juvenile Justice*. London: Tavistock.

Health and Safety Executive (1992) *Annual Report, 1991/2*. London: Health and Safety Executive.

Hedderman, C. and Hough, M. (1994) *Does the Criminal Justice System Treat Men and Women Differently?* Home Office Research and Statistics Department Research Findings no. 10. London: Home Office.

Heidensohn, F. (1985) *Women and Crime*. Basingstoke: Macmillan.

HM Chief Inspector of Prisons (1992) *HMP Holloway: Report by HM Chief Inspector of Prisons*. London: Home Office.

HM Chief Inspector of Prisons for England and Wales (1997) *Women in Prison: A Thematic Review by HM Chief Inspector of Prisons*. London: Home Office.

HM Inspectorate of Probation (2000) *Towards Race Equality: Thematic Inspection Report*. London: Home Office. Also available on-line (www.homeoffice.gov.uk/newindexs/index_probation.htm).

Home Office (1977) *Prisons and the Prisoner: The Work of the Prison Service in England and Wales*. London: HMSO.

Home Office (1994) *Parole Recommendations and Ethnic Origin, England and Wales 1990*. Home Office Statistical Bulletin 2/94. London: Home Office.

Home Office (2000a) *Statistics on Race and the Criminal Justice System 2000*. London: Home Office.

Home Office (2000b) *Statistics on Women and the Criminal Justice System 2000*. London: Home Office.

Hood, R. (1992) *Race and Sentencing: A Study in the Crown Court* (in collaboration with G. Cordovil). Oxford: Clarendon Press.

Hood, R. (1995) 'Race and Sentencing: A Reply', [1995] *Criminal Law Review*, 272–9.

Hood, R. and Sparks, R. (1970) *Key Issues in Criminology*. London: Weidenfeld and Nicolson.

Hudson, B. (1989) 'Discrimination and Disparity: the Influence of Race on Sentencing', *New Community'*, 16: 23–34.

Jones, H., Cornes, P. and Stackford, R. (1977) *Open Prisons*. London: Routledge and Kegan Paul.

Landau, S.F. (1981) 'Juveniles and the Police: Who is Charged Immediately and Who is Referred to the Juvenile Bureau?', *British Journal of Criminology*, 21: 27–46.

Landau, S.F. and Nathan, G. (1983) 'Selecting Delinquents for Cautioning in the London Metropolitan Area', *British Journal of Criminology*, 23: 128–49.

Learmont, J. (1995) *Review of Prison Service Security in England and Wales and the Escape from Parkhurst Prison on Tuesday 3rd January 1995*. Cm 3020. London: HMSO.

Levi, M. (1989) 'Fraudulent Justice? Sentencing the Business Criminal', in P. Carlen and D. Cook (eds), *Paying for Crime*. Milton Keynes: Open University Press, pp. 86–108.

McConville, M. and Baldwin, J. (1982) 'The Influence of Race on Sentencing in England', [1982] *Criminal Law Review*, 652–8.

Macpherson, W. (1999) *The Stephen Lawrence Inquiry: Report of an Inquiry by Sir William Macpherson*. Cm 4262-1. London: The Stationery Office.

Mair, G. (1986) 'Ethnic Minorities, Probation and the Magistrates' Courts', *British Journal of Criminology*, 26: 147–55.

Mawby, R. (1977) 'Sexual Discrimination and the Law', *Probation Journal*, 24: 38–43.

Mirrlees – Black, C. (2001) *Confidence in the Criminal Justice System: Findings from the 2000 British Crime Survey*. Home Office Research Findings no. 137. London: Home Office.

Morris, A. (1987) *Women, Crime and Criminal Justice*. Oxford: Basil Blackwell.

Morris, T. (1980) 'Penology and the Crimes of the Powerful', in A.E. Bottoms and R.H. Preston (eds.) *The Coming Penal Crisis: A Criminological and Theological Exploration*. Edinburgh: Scottish Academic Press.

de la Motta, K. (1984) 'Blacks in the Criminal Justice System', unpublished MSc thesis, Aston University.

Moxon, D. (1988) *Sentencing Practice in the Crown Court*. Home Office Research Study no. 103. London: HMSO.

MVA and Miller, J. (2000) *Retribution Reconsidered*. Dordrecht: Kluwar Academic Publishers.

NACRO (1986a) *Enforcement of the Law Relating to Social Security: Report of a NACRO Working Party*. London: NACRO.

NACRO (1986b) *Black People and the Criminal Justice System*. London: NACRO.

NACRO (1992) 'Offences against discipline in women's prisons', briefing paper.

Nagel, I. (1981) 'Sex Differences in the Processing of Criminal Defendants', in A. Morris and L. Gelsthorpe (eds), *Women and Crime*. Cambridge: Institute of Criminology, pp. 104–24.

Nagel, I.H. and Hagan, J. (1983) 'Gender and Crime: Offence Patterns and Criminal Court Sanctions', in M. Tonry and N. Morris (eds), *Crime and Justice*, vol. 4. Chicago: University of Chicago Press, pp. 91–144.

Nelken, D. (1997) 'White Collar Crime' in M. Maguire, R. Morgan and R. Reiner (eds.) *The Oxford Handbook of Criminology* (2nd edn.) pp. 891–924. Oxford: Clarendon.

Nicolson, D. and Sanghvi, R. (1995) 'More Justice for Battered Women', *New Law Journal*, 28th July: 1122–4.

O'Connor, D. (2000) 'Stop and Think', *Guardian Society*, 19 January 2000.

Phillips, C. and Brown, D. (1998) *Entry into the Criminal Justice System: A Survey of Police Arrests and their Outcomes*. Home Office Research Study no. 185. London: Home Office.

Piliavin, I. and Briar, S. (1964) 'Police Encounters with Juveniles', *American Journal of Sociology*, 70: 206–14.

Pitts, J. (1986) 'Black Young People and Juvenile Crime: Some Unanswered Questions', in R. Matthews and J. Young (eds), *Confronting Crime*. London: Sage, pp. 118–44.

Pollak, O. (1961) *The Criminality of Women*. New York: A.S. Barnes.

Pruitt, C.R. and Wilson, J.Q. (1983) 'A Longitudinal Study of the Effect of Race on Sentencing', *Law and Society Review*, 17: 613–35.

Riley, D. (1986) 'Sex Differences in Teenage Crime: the Role of Lifestyle', *Home Office Research Bulletin*, 20: 34–8.

Riley, D. and Shaw, M. (1985) *Parental Supervision and Juvenile Delinquency*. Home Office Research Study no. 83. London: HMSO.

Rutter, M. and Giller, H. (1983) *Juvenile Delinquency: Trends and Perspectives*. Harmondsworth: Penguin.

Sanders, A. (1985) 'Class Bias in Prosecutions', *Howard Journal of Criminal Justice*, 24: 176–97.

Sanders, A. and Young, R. (2000) *Criminal Justice*, 2nd edn. London: Butterworths.

Scarman, L. (1986) *The Scarman Report*. Harmondsworth: Penguin.

Shah, R. and Pease. K. (1992) 'Crime, Race and Reporting to the Police', *Howard Journal of Criminal Justice*, 31: 192–9.

Sims, L. and Myhill, A. (2001) *Policing and the Public: Findings from the 2000 British Crime Survey*. Home Office Research Findings no. 136. London: Home Office.

Skogan, W. G. (1990) *The Police and Public in England and Wales: A British Crime Survey Report*. Home Office Research Study no. 117. London: HMSO.

Skogan, W.G. (1994) *Contracts between Police and Public: Findings from the 1992 British Crime Survey*. Home Office Research Study no. 134. London: HMSO.

Smart, C. (1976) *Women, Crime and Criminology: A Feminist Critique*. London: Routledge and Kegan Paul.

Smith, D.J. (1983) *Police and People in London. I: A Survey of Londoners*. London: Policy Studies Institute.

Smith, D.J. and Gray, J. (1983) *Police and People in London. IV: The Police in Action*. London: Policy Studies Institute.

Smith, S. (1982) *Race and Crime Statistics*. London: Board for Social Responsibility, Church of England.

Softley, P. (1978) *Fines in Magistrates' Courts*. Home Office Research Study no. 46. London: HMSO.

Southgate, P. and Ekblom, P. (1986) *Police–Public Encounters*. Home Office Research Study no. 90. London: HMSO.

Spohn, C., Gruhl, J. and Welch, S. (1981–2) 'The Effect of Race on Sentencing: a Re-examination of an Unsettled Question', *Law and Society Review*, 16: 71–88.

Stevens, P. and Willis, C.F. (1979) *Race, Crime and Arrests*. Home Office Research Study no. 58. London: HMSO.

Taylor, W. (1981) *Probation and After-care in a Multi-racial Society*. London: Commission for Racial Equality.

Walker, M. (1988) 'The Court Disposal of Young Males, by Race, in London in 1983', *British Journal of Criminology*, 28: 441–60.

Walker, M., Jefferson, T. and Seneviratne, M. (1990) *Ethnic Minorities, Young People and the Criminal Justice System*. ESRC Project no. E06250023: Main Report.

Walker, N. (1968) *Crime and Punishment in Britain*, rev. edn. Edinburgh: University of Edinburgh Press.

Walker, N. (1981) ''Feminists' Extravaganzas', *Criminal Law Review*, June 1981: 379–86.

Walmsley, R., Howard, L. and White, S. (1992) *The National Prison Survey 1991: Main Findings*. Home Office Research Study no. 128. London: HMSO.

Willis, C.F. (1983) *The Use, Effectiveness and Impact of Police Stop and Search Powers*. London: Home Office.

Woodcock, J. (1994) *The Escape from Whitemoor Prison on Friday 9th September 1994 (The Woodcock Enquiry)*. Cm 2741. London: HMSO.

STUDY QUESTIONS

1　Think again about the explanations and theories of crime considered in Part I. How relevant are these to the workings of the contemporary criminal justice system and the treatment of particular groups of people within it?

2　Does the operation of the criminal justice system assist the development of a public perception of a typical 'criminal type'?

3　Is it possible to challenge the biases that Cavadino and Dignan detail?

FURTHER READING

The social class of those processed through the criminal justice system – especially of defendants on trial – is a much under-researched area in criminology, but discussions of whether people from minority ethnic groups are treated differently within the criminal justice system can be found in many texts. Policing of black people is addressed in Benyon, J. (1986) *A Tale of Failure: Race and Policing*, Coventry: Centre for Research in Ethnic Relations, University of Warwick; Bowling, B. (1998) *Violent Racism: Victimisation, Policing and Social Context*, Oxford: Clarendon Press; and Cashmore, E. and McLaughlin, E. (1991) *Out of Order? Policing Black People*, London: Routledge. The treatment of ethnic minorities by the courts is covered in Gelsthorpe, L. and McWilliams, W. (eds) (1993) *Minority Ethnic Groups and the Criminal Justice System*, Cambridge: Cambridge University Press; and Hood, R. (1992) *Race and Sentencing*, Oxford: Clarendon Press. Issues concerning ethnic-minority prisoners remain understudied, with one notable exception: Genders, E. and Player, E. (1989) *Race Relations in Prisons*, Oxford: Clarendon Press. The notion that women who commit serious crimes are 'doubly deviant' (and therefore 'doubly damned') is explored by Ann Lloyd (1995) *Doubly Deviant, Doubly Damned: Society's Treatment of Violent Women*, Harmondsworth: Penguin. Joan Smith also explores this argument in *Misogynies* (1989) London: Faber and Faber, and in the chapter on 'Unnatural born killers' in her later book, *Different for Girls* (1997) London: Chatto and Windus, where she focuses on the cultural construction of Myra Hindley and Rosemary West as 'evil monsters'. On a similar theme is Helena Kennedy's 1992 text, *Eve Was Framed: Women and British Justice*, London: Chatto and Windus. The best recent overview of gender, crime and criminal justice is Walklate, S. (2001) *Gender, Crime and Criminal Justice*, Cullompton: Willan; and Walklate, S. (1995) *Gender and Crime: An Introduction*, Hemel Hempsted: Prentice-Hall/Harvester, is also useful. Schwartz, M.D. and Milovanovic, D. (eds.) (2000) *Race, Gender and Class in Criminology: the Intersections*, London: Routledge focuses on social stratification as an analytical concept in criminological study. Finally, a comparative analysis of different criminal justice systems in different parts of the world is provided by Nelkan, D. (ed.) (2000) *Contrasting Criminal Justice: Getting from Here to There*, Aldershot: Ashgate.

15

Crime, culture and community

Janet Foster

The relationship between social class and crime is further developed in this reading and the next. As part of a wider study of criminal activity in south-east London, Janet Foster considers the relationship between crime, culture and community. After giving a brief outline of housing development in the area since the Second World War, Foster considers the relevance of these developments to changes in community life, kinship networks and criminal activity. She suggests that, although there was little sense of community, kinship ties remained an important feature of the area. She also argues that here, as in many inner-city areas, crime is ever present and pervasive, and tradition plays an important part in attitudes towards crime and in patterns of offending. With this in mind, crime and criminals, as one chief inspector of police suggested to her, can be divided into a 'league division of villainy'. Within this football analogy the 'real' villains (professional criminals) comprise division one; the 'honest' villains (who begin from the premise that 'there is nothing wrong with crime as long as it don't hurt anybody') division two; and the vast majority of offenders (which includes unsuccessful and inadequate law-breakers – i.e. those who get caught – drug and drug-related offenders and street robbers) division three.

OLD SLUMS TO NEW SLUMS

South East London has to some extent always been regarded as the 'poor relation across the water' (Williams 1949) and did not develop significantly until the industrial revolution (because transport links with the city were extremely poor). As a result the area was for many generations largely isolated from other

SOURCE: From *Villains: Crime and Community in the Inner City* (Lodon: Routledge, 1990), 6–20.

parts of London; even today, many South Londoners never go north of the River Thames (cf. Bartles-Smith and Gerrard 1976). Although the area's geographical isolation and insularity played an important role in its development, the impact of the industrial revolution sealed South East London's fate as 'Huge areas degenerated from meadow to slum in a generation' (Bartles-Smith and Gerrard 1976). Descriptions of the area from the nineteenth century onwards were damning. Williams (1949) described it as 'a bad place, a sink of shadow and sorrow, vice and filth, ignorance and degradation' while Booth (1889) believed it was 'poverty stricken and overcrowded', 'inhabited by thieves, and unfortunates', 'a citadel of outcasts'.

These powerful images of the area as poverty stricken and crime prone remain an important characteristic in the twentieth century. Despite the fact that heavy bombing during the Second World War and the slum clearance programmes which followed changed the face of the area (about 50 per cent of housing is post war; OPCS 1981), many of the old slums were simply replaced by new ones. One police officer called the area 'the arsehole of the world!'; another described it as 'absolute degradation' (Foster 1989). Many share in their condemnation.

The 'utopian' ideals which influenced the erection of the huge system-built council estates that dominate the Stanton and Gorer Lane skylines today are now recognised to have been a dreadful mistake (cf. Coleman 1985; Power 1987). Poor design and construction often combined with extreme social isolation for many of the estates' occupants. Slum clearance programmes disrupted kinship and community ties and although there is some debate about whether it was the effects of slum clearance itself or wider social changes which were taking place at the time that made these policies so unpopular (cf. Mogey 1956; Coates and Silburn 1970; Ungerson, 1971; Parker, 1973) there is little doubt that slum clearance had a devastating impact on the Borough in which Gorer Lane and Stanton are situated. As one local explained:

> When the big development and slum clearance started, these people were picked up and they were moved, most of them quite reluctantly out of their own areas, and although they only moved p'rhaps two or three miles sideways, it really just wasn't the [same].... They moved these people and they were split up and rehoused – very few of 'em actually stayed in the Borough. [Therefore] all the estates were retopped with people from all over the place, the whole community got diluted down. You had a great influx of discontented people that didn't want to be living here anyway, but were rehoused and as a result the whole thing went down hill. Over a ten-year period this enormous movement left very little of the indigenous people of the Borough left, it just went and then you had people from everywhere.

This resident's impressions are given some support by Clarke and Hedges survey of the Borough in 1976. They found that only 17 per cent of those sampled had 'long term personal associations with the area.'

Despite the close geographical proximity of Gorer Lane and Stanton and a similar social and economic profile, post-war changes affected Stanton more severely than Gorer Lane and had a consequent impact on resident profile, ethnic minority settlement, and patterns of crime and offending there.

In Gorer Lane, while slum clearance influenced levels of community relations and neighbourly contact (cf. Clarke and Hedges 1976), it remained a relatively homogenous area, as a police officer brought up there argued:

> The average person from Gorer Lane was probably born and bred in Gorer Lane of stock that were born and bred here. [They] have always done a particular job.... They become road sweepers, they become dustmen, they go into the print. They take largely manual type work, semi-skilled work, because their dad did it and can introduce them.... The council provide the accommodation.

Stanton however was less resistant to change in the decades after the war and the effects of slum clearance itself seem to have been more dramatic there. The three huge council estates which dominate the skyline in East Stanton have become some of the most notorious in the country and experienced difficulties from the outset, as one local explained:

> When [the East Stanton] estate was built, ... people from practically all over London were moving in ... and I do believe East Londoners will not live alongside South East Londoners ... they don't communicate. They were rehousing people from far away on to that estate with people who were local and they didn't hit it off.

Hostility between Londoners was not the only area of conflict, as other immigrant groups like the Scots and Irish discovered. Their experiences were similar to those Stacey (1960) found in Banbury. She wrote:

> it may be said with a fair degree of certainty that working-class families from the north of England or from Scotland are very unlikely to settle on intimate terms as neighbours to Banburians (p. 110).... To the Banburians the immigrants seemed 'foreign' ... because they came with values and customs greatly different from those of the town (pp. 14–15).

The new estates therefore began their existence with considerable difficulties but these almost pale into insignificance alongside the problems which have occurred since their habitation, many of which were due to poor architectural design. One report commissioned by the local council recommended spending £29.6 million to remedy faults on one estate which was only eleven years old. Certain kinds of crimes such as burglary were facilitated by split-level designs (cf. Newman 1972; Brown and Altman 1981; Coleman 1985), whilst the rubberised walkways and badly lit corridors provided adequate opportunity for 'muggings'. All these factors, in addition to the sheer numbers of people in a very small geographical area, soon resulted in the number of tenants requesting transfers far outweighing those wishing to move in. Inevitably they quickly became 'sink estates'. […]

'COMMUNITY' AND KINSHIP IN SOUTH EAST LONDON

Although the effects of post-war changes in East Stanton were more dramatic than those in Gorer Lane, slum clearance did contribute to a weakening of kinship networks and 'community' life in both areas. The old slum neighbourhoods, however poor, were often seen to be supportive environments where most people knew one another and would help each other out. Yet, as Bartles-Smith and Gerrard point out, slum dwellers

> had contrary to popular belief little sense of community involvement and belonging. It was, when it existed, a united sense of common deprivation.... They had no stake in the area. Even in the early twentieth century when the community spirit was strongest, when fewest people had moved and immigration had ceased, the sense of identity was not based on anything they owned,... but on their mutual deprivation. Constantly the best emigrated. Their leaving created a ghetto for those who could not depart. (Bartles-Smith and Gerrard 1976: 25)

Notions of 'community' are often idealised and unrealistic (cf. Pearson 1983). Yet there is a powerful belief that 'community' is a good thing that is often lacking, particularly in anomic and unneighbourly high-rise council estates. Although such images are not always correct (see Foster 1988) there have been significant changes in patterns of kinship and association in the area as a whole. As Clarke and Hedges (1976: 12/158) pointed out in their study of the Borough:

> we were struck by the extent to which people felt that the large-scale post-war redevelopment ... has destroyed what might be called 'community spirit'.... What people mean by community spirit, however, is difficult to pin down. To some older people it is likely to be nostalgia for the past, for a sense of community probably only possible among people facing problems of poverty which were often endurable only when shared. Now what remains in the memory is the closeness engendered by the sharing of hardships, rather than the bitterness of poverty. However, a sense of community does seem to exist in many areas and where it is thought to be declining rapidly much regret is expressed.

Clarke and Hedges found that 'only two in five' residents in the sample felt 'they belonged to a community'. East Stanton was perceived to be the 'least pleasant place in the borough to live' and had the lowest degree of community spirit [...]. Nevertheless kinship ties remain an important feature of the area (cf. Clarke and Hedges 1976) but are rarely characterised by common residence on a particular street or estate [...]. Wallman's observation in South West London is equally appropriate to Gorer Lane.

> It is clear that most of the south London born are well placed in terms of access to kin as a local resource. The elderly have children and special relatives nearby for company and

support. Sons and daughters are able to rely on parents and other relatives for advice and practical help. Their local kin networks include various generations and consequently their knowledge of and information about the area are likely to be extensive and effective. The latter point shows very clearly in relation to acquiring employment. (Wallman 1982: 115)

[...] [I]t is important to emphasise that despite all the changes which have taken place around them, the lives of those described in this [chapter] remained rooted in tradition. For them Young and Willmott's famous characterisation of Bethnal Green remains salient:

> Either length of residence or localized kinship does something to create a network of local attachments, but when they are combined, as they are in Bethnal Green, they constitute a much more powerful force than when one exists without the other. Then people have a number of links, or ways of orienting themselves, to the same person: he was at school, he is a relative by marriage, he lives in a well known neighbourhood. The people can make use of one or the other of their possible approaches to establish a relationship with almost anyone.... In this old established district the relatives are a vital means of connecting people with their community. The family does more than anything else to make the local society a familiar society, filled with people who are not strangers. (Young and Willmott 1957: 116)

THE TRADITIONS OF CRIME IN SOUTH LONDON: A LEAGUE DIVISION OF VILLAINY

[...] The two most celebrated examples of South London villainy in the twentieth century were the Great Train Robbers and the Richardson brothers (Lucas 1969; Parker 1981; Read 1984). The Train Robbers captured the hearts and imaginations of thousands of working-class people when they robbed a mail train in 1963. Read (1984) in his biography of the men argued that their lives must be seen within a context of a 'whole sub-society of working class South London', where 'there is no doubt that there was and is still endemic poverty juxtaposed to conspicious consumption north of the River.' He describes the robbers as showing 'total repugnance for the rules and formalities of the modern state' where 'the only authority recongnised by (them) was the natural authority of a "name" – another criminal who had earned their respect through demonstrable qualities of courage, cunning and ruthlessness' (1984: 321–2).

Organised crime stood at the top of a 'league division of villainy' in the area, which one police officer likened to a football league division table, where involvement in criminal activities occurred simultaneously on a variety of levels.[1] The 'league table' is divided into three basic groups: the 'real' villains (division one); the 'honest' villains (division two); and league division three villainy. These divisions represent highly simplified 'ideal types' and reflect both traditional aspects of crime, which remain an important characteristic of the area, and more recent patterns of offending which have resulted from the dilution of traditional community and kinship networks in Stanton, and other forms of crime, for example drugs, which have become more prevalent. The characteristics of the different leagues are outlined below.

The Real Villains

> I have a certain amount of respect for those who have a life of crime because they hold their own moral codes, and have a concept of a fair cop, which is more than can be said for the slags who kick in the front door and burgle all their neighbours. (Police Officer, Stanton)

Although a large proportion of crime in both Gorer Lane and Stanton was of a relatively petty nature, the area has always attracted a number of professional criminals. As one officer commented:

> There's a lot of good villains living on this ground. You get a lot of yobs who are full of mouth and everything else, but you get a lot of good villains.... They don't do petty burglaries, they'll do armed robberies, like the bullion thing.

It is this professional element who comprise the league division one category. They are characterised by their readiness to use actual or threatened violence in the commission of their crimes. As Read notes:

> When Gill Hussey asked Jim, who she considered so gentle and controlled, how he had come at the age of 18 to beat up a police inspector he had simply replied, 'It's the name of the game'. Buster's defence of the coshing of Mills, was that he did 'what had to be done'. It is the logic of the profession which in criminal careers leads to cruelty and death. (Read 1984: 325)[2]

While it is often assumed by law-abiding elements that those who engage in crime have no morality, it would be misleading to suggest that the violence of 'professionals' is totally arbitrary. One of Hebdige's respondents aptly summarises the situation.

> Straight people say that the people who are beneath the law live in the jungle. But there's a law of the jungle. It's like a religious code. If you are involved in the twilight zone there are certain rules laid down and you abide by them. (Hebdige 1977: 30)

This was illustrated to some extent by the activities of the Richardsons, who headed the South London underworld during the 1950s and early 1960s.

Parker, in his excellent biography of the brothers, wrote of the violence which led to the famous 'Torture Trials':

> To most people, these attacks were brutal. In terms of the south London code and sub-culture, they were not much out of the ordinary. Both men were villains anyway, both had had their share of fighting and violence. They had taken a liberty and they deserved what they got.... 'It was just one of them things,' says Roy Hall today, 'They took a liberty. We got the hump. They got a whack.' (Parker 1981: 198)

Parker rightly points out that, although such codes exist, we must not fall into the trap of believing that they are always applied; rather they are general guide-lines which are breached from time to time. Parker highlights the contradictions between theory and practice in the trial of Charlie Richardson.

> The saddest thing about it is that Charlie really felt he was innocent. The Old Bailey trial had dealt solely with the cases of the few men who had been beaten. To Charlie, they had deserved what they had got. They were con-men who had tried to take him on. Their beat-ings were permitted in the underworld code by which he lived. But even if some of his victims were con-men – some in fact had not taken Charlie on at all – they were not men of violence. Neither had Charlie's violence been spontaneous. It had been premeditated, almost savoured in its anticipation. (Parker 1981: 337) [...]

Honest Villains

The second league division of villainy involved the 'Honest Villains' who operated according to similar codes of conduct to the professionals but began from the premise 'there is nothing wrong with crime as long as you don't hurt anybody'. Violence in this instance was more a threat than an actuality and where it did occur tended to be restricted to summary justice. This was an important characteristic of working-class life in general. Distrustful of the police and feeling that summary justice often had much more impact (in terms of personal satisfaction and a greater deterrent value) it was a regular occurrence in the area. As a detective constable pointed out:

> Gorer Lane's ground still has a lot of real old South London people that 'sort out their own problems'. If you went to a fight the victim signed a statement saying that they didn't want the police to investigate the incident. Later the person responsible for the assault got a pasting and the same reply would come. 'Don't worry Guvnor, no police – we'll deal with it in our own way.'

The influence of the area and its local employment structure had an impor-tant effect on crime where certain trades (for example in second-hand cars and scrap metal) offered ample opportunities for dealing in stolen goods (cf. Hebdige 1977). The Richardsons, for example, used their Peckford Scrap Metal company as a front for many of their illegitimate activities (see Lucas 1969; Parker 1981), and in this study, Del, the most successful person with whom I had contact, was a scrap metal dealer who bought and sold stolen goods [...]. Offences which fell into the 'honest villainy' category included fraud, fencing, certain types of burglary, theft, and shoplifting.

Whilst the first two categories of villainy encapsulate some of the traditions of the area and its crime, the third includes elements of change which were perceived to be increasingly threatening by both police and criminals alike.

League Division Three Villainy

> 40 per cent within the Borough you could almost class as league division threes or potential league division threes and drugs is largely responsible for it…. Twenty years ago you didn't have a drugs problem. (Police Officer, Gorer Lane)

The third division represents the vast majority of offenders and includes three distinct types of offending: the unsuccessful and inadequate law breakers who were without skills and persistently got caught; drugs and drug-related offences; and finally street robberies ('muggings') and other activities identified as 'black crime'.

The proliferation of both drugs and mugging in recent years was a threatening development because it created instability and unpredictability in certain parts of the area – East Stanton in the case of 'black crimes' [...], and the large white estates in Gorer Lane in the case of serious drugs such as heroin. Both these forms of offending tampered with the relationship which existed between the police and the criminal fraternity, as one officer explains:

> The average villain in this area had a lot of respect for us. We're on the other side of the fence, but it's a game…. They're honest in as much as you know where you stand with them. League division three criminals you have problems with. They are the types who hit back, the ones who will never accept nothing … you don't know where you stand, you've gotta watch yer back the whole time. If I know where I stand that makes all the difference. Funny thing to say about a villain but it's the only way I can adequately describe it.

Although both offenders and law enforcers recognised the existence of a 'game' in some of their interactions, offenders were always at a competitive disadvantage and often had little choice but to participate in it (cf. Carlen 1976). Nevertheless the existence of this understanding between the police and the criminal fraternity involved a degree of negotiation and acceptance of each side's position (cf. Parker and Allerton 1962).

Although I have described these different divisions as being mutually exclusive, there is of course movement within the hierarchy. Juveniles, for example, would begin in league division three but might progress into the top division, although this avenue was restricted to a reasonably small number of people. Many more negotiated an existence between the semi-legitimate and illegitimate spheres available in both 'honest' and league division three crime. [...]

NOTES

1   I would like to thank Chief Inspector Davies for this league division analogy, which I have expanded and developed.
2   There is some controversy about the exact definition of a professional criminal. Mack (1964) suggests that violence need not be an integral aspect of professional crime, while Taylor (1985) argues that only a very small number of criminals (possibily 500) throughout Britain actually possess 'professional' status. This title is reserved for those involved in serious and organised crime, for example armed robbery.

REFERENCES

Bartles-Smith, D. and Gerrard, D. (1976) *Urban Ghetto*, London: Guildford.

Booth, C. (1889–91) *Life and Labour of the People of London*, 3 vols, London: Williams and Norgate.

Brown, B. and Altman, I. (1981) 'Territoriality and Residential Crime: a Conceptual Framework', in Brantingham, P. and Brantingham, P. (eds) *Environmental Criminology*, Beverly Hills, Calif.: Sage.

Carlen, P. (1976) *Magistrates' Justice*, London: Martin Robertson.

Clarke, P. and Hedges, B. (1976) *Living in Southwark*, London: Social and Community Planning Research.

Coates, K. and Silburn, R. (1970) *Poverty: The Forgotten Englishman*, Harmondsworth: Penguin.

Coleman, A. (1985) *Utopia on Trial: Vision and Reality in Planned Housing*, London: Hilary Shipman.

Foster, J.A. (1988) 'Crime and Community: an Ethnographic Evaluation of Two London Housing Estates', unpublished report for Home Office, London: Research and Planning Unit.

Foster, J.A. (1989) 'Two Stations: an Ethnographic Study of Policing in the Inner City', in Downes, D. (ed.) *Crime and the City: Essays in Honour of John Mays*, London: Macmillan.

Hebdige, D. (1977) *Subcultural Conflict and Criminal Performance in Fulham*, Occasional paper, Sub and Popular Culture Series, no. 25, Centre for Contemporary Cultural Studies, Birmingham.

Lucas, N. (1969) *Britain's Gangland: Violence is their Way of Life*, London: Pan.

Mack, J. (1964) 'Fulltime Miscreants, Delinquent Neighbourhoods and Criminal Networks', *British Journal of Sociology*, 15: 38–53.

Mogey, J. (1956) *Family and Neighbourhood: Two Studies in Oxford*, Oxford: Oxford University Press.

Newman, O. (1972) *Defensible Space: Crime Prevention through Urban Design*, New York: Macmillan.

OPCS (1981) *Census Results: Small Area Statistics*. London: HMSO.

Parker, B.J. (1973) 'Some Sociological Implications of Slum Clearance Programmes', in Donnison, D. and Eversley, D. (eds) *London: Urban Patterns, Problems and Policies*, pp. 248–73. A study sponsored by the Centre for Environmental Studies, London: Heinemann.

Parker, R. (1981) *Rough Justice*, London: Fontana.

Parker, T. and Allerton, R. (1962) *The Courage of his Convictions*, London: Hutchinson.

Pearson, G. (1983) *Hooligan: A History of Respectable Fears*, London: Macmillan.

Power, A. (1987) *Property Before People: The Management of Twentieth Century Council Housing*, London: Allen and Unwin.

Read, P. P. (1984) *The Train Robbers: Their Story*, originally published 1978, London: W.H. Allen.

Shaw, C. and McKay, H. (1942) *Juvenile Delinquency and Urban Areas*, Chicago: University of Chicago Press.

Stacey, M. (1960) *Tradition and Change: A Study of Banbury*, London: Oxford University Press.

Taylor, L. (1985) *In the Underworld*, originally published 1984, Oxford: Blackwell.

Ungerson, C. (1971) 'Moving Home: a Study of the Redevelopment Process in two London Boroughs', *Occasional Papers on Social Administration 44*, London: Bell.

Wallman, S. (1982) *Living in South London: Perspectives on Battersea 1871–1981*, Aldershot: published for the LSE by Gower.

Williams, H.W. (1949) *South London*, London: Robert Hale.

Young, M. and Willmott, P. (1957) *Family and Kinship in East London*, London: Routledge and Kegan Paul.

STUDY QUESTIONS

1 Having read Foster's piece, how important do you think the links between crime, culture and community are?

2 Some writers have been critical of the 'romanticization' of working-class crime by middle-class academics. How else (other than romantic) might we describe Foster's graphic description of life and crime in the inner city?

3 What do you understand by the phrases 'real villains', 'honest villains' and 'league division three villainy'? How useful do you think they are in describing police and public perceptions of crime? (You may find it helpful to refer to Reading 23.) How do the mass media perpetuate these hierarchies of villainy in factual and fictional accounts?

FURTHER READING

For examples relating to the status of crimes and criminals in working-class communities, see McVicar, J. (1974) *McVicar by Himself*, London: Hutchinson; and Robins, D. and Cohen, P. (1978) *Knuckle Sandwich: Growing up in the Working*

Class City, Harmondsworth: Penguin. It is worth noting that crime at work is not always a 'white-collar' activity (see Readings 9 and 16), but is also a feature of 'blue-collar' workplaces. See Ditton, J. (1977) *Part Time Crime: An Ethnography of Fiddling and Pilferage*, London: Macmillan; and Mars, G. (1982) *Cheats at Work: An Anthropology of Workplace Crime*, London: Allen and Unwin, for empirical work on crime in 'working-class occupations'. See also *Further Reading* for Reading 14.

16

White collar and corporate crime

Hazel Croall

Following Slapper and Tombs's broad discussion of the invisibility of corporate crime in official statistics and the media (Reading 9), we now turn our attention to the specific definitions and scope of white-collar and corporate crime. Further to Foster's account (Reading 15), this extract by Hazel Croall (like others in this book, e.g. Readings 7, 9 and 14) supports the view that, while working-class crime is perceived as 'real' or 'conventional', white-collar and corporate crime is not, even though it is likely that the latter exceeds the costs of the former. In this piece Croall attempts to answer the questions: 'Who are the offenders?' and 'Who are the victims?' She argues that white-collar and corporate crime is not only 'under-policed' and 'under-prosecuted' but that it is small businesses, rather than large, wealthy corporations, who are most likely to be prosecuted and least likely to be able to pay for expert advisers to negotiate with enforcers and contest cases in court. The victims of white-collar and corporate crime include consumers and employees, and most people are probably the victims of this type of criminal activity several times a month. The effects of such crimes are frequently invisible, and may be regarded as trivial or acceptable. Yet the results of white-collar and corporate crime may be physical injury or even death. Croall ends the extract by examining the organizational aspects of offences. She asks why white-collar and corporate crime is treated differently from conventional crime, and considers how to challenge this orthodoxy.

[...] The definition of white collar crime has always been contentious (Croall 1992; Langan 1996; Nelken 1997). It was first defined by Edwin Sutherland in 1941 as 'crime committed by persons of high social status and respectability in the course of their occupations' (Sutherland 1949: 9). He questioned the

SOURCE: From *Crime and Society in Britain* (London: Longman, 1998), 269–87.

existing focus on lower-class offenders by pointing to the illegal activities of those involved in business and commerce, sparking off a long debate about the definition and status of white collar crime. [...]

Research Problems

[...] Official statistics are particularly unreliable as so few offences are detected, reported and prosecuted. They do not fit legal offence categories and regulatory offences, being non-indictable, are not all listed separately. These are dealt with by a vast range of enforcement agencies and Inspectorates including those dealing with, for example, financial, customs and excise, health and safety, consumer protection and pollution regulations, whose records, which are not all widely available, do not always indicate numbers of known and detected offences. [...] [V]ictim surveys do not cover white collar and corporate crime although some surveys, such as the third Islington Crime Survey, have included questions on commercial and health and safety at work offences (Pearce 1992), and others have carried out surveys of institutional victims (Levi 1988). These are inevitably limited to offences of which many victims are aware but [...] some are not.

Other forms of research are also difficult. Samples of offenders are difficult to obtain and, as so many offences are hidden in occupational routines, can only be studied by participant observation or in-depth interviewing (see, for example, Ditton 1977; Mars 1982). Researchers, however, are rarely in a position to carry out such research, especially in financial and commercial enterprises. The complexity of offences also means that considerable financial, scientific or legal expertise is required to fully analyse them (Levi 1987). Enforcement agencies are more approachable and have been the subject of many revealing studies which have explored how offences and offenders are typified and how enforcement decisions are made (see, for example, Carson 1971; Hawkins 1984; Hutter 1988; Cook 1989). As is the case for professional and organized crime, a variety of other sources are used including individual case studies, investigative journalism, court observation and reports, cases reported in the mass media, and interviews with enforcers.

The Nature and Extent of Offences

Given all these difficulties it is virtually impossible to estimate the extent of white collar crime, although many so-called 'guesstimates' argue that it probably exceeds the costs of conventional crime. Levi (1987), for example, estimated that in 1985 the total cost of fraud reported to fraud squads amounted to £2,113 million, which was twice the cost of theft, burglary and robbery in that year. In a survey of 56 large corporations he also found that almost 40 per cent reported at least one fraud costing over £50,000. As will be seen below, major frauds involve billions of pounds, and the BCCI case was initially estimated to have involved £5–15 billion (*Sunday Times* 14/7/91). Recent publicity has also surrounded the high cost of frauds on the National Health Service with the Healthcare Financial Management Association having recently estimated that 'tens of millions of pounds' are being lost by prescriptions frauds and false claims of payment by doctors, dentists, pharmacists and opticians (*The Guardian* 24/6/97: 8). [...]

It has also been argued that white collar crime has increased in recent years, with the high-profile cases referred to above and many other smaller pensions and financial frauds. While, as Nelken (1997) points out, it is impossible to estimate if white collar crime has increased as its extent has never been established, a number of factors have been associated with a possible increase. Punch (1996) argues, for example, that the deregulation and globalization of financial markets in the 1980s increased opportunities for crime, the declining power of trade unions and the climate of deregulation which curtailed the resources of enforcement agencies hindered detection and the growth of the 'spirit of enterprise' created a moral climate encouraging the prioritization of profits at the expense of consumers and workers.

Offenders

As so few offenders are prosecuted it is difficult to determine their characteristics, although there are some indications that they are not from such high-status backgrounds as is often assumed (Croall 1989; Langan 1996). For example, Levi (1987) argues that prosecutions for fraud more often involve 'mavericks' than 'elite insiders' and Clarke (1989) found that businesses resorting to arson as a form of insurance fraud were mainly small businesses with financial difficulties. Cook (1989) found that the Inland Revenue tend to prosecute moonlighting builders and small video stores whose offences are cheap and easy to investigate, and in a study of consumer protection legislation, the majority of convicted offenders were small rather than large businesses – butchers, bakers, grocers and corner shops – rather than large multi-national corporations who formed only a small minority (Croall 1989) Other studies have also found many offenders whose businesses lie on the margins of legality and illegality – often described by enforcers as 'rogues' or 'cowboys' – who are more akin to 'shady operators' (Sutton and Wild 1985; Croall 1989).

This, as with other forms of crime, can reflect the activities of enforcement agencies and the vulnerability of different kinds of offenders to detection and prosecution. It was pointed out above that enforcement agencies tend to prosecute only a small number of known offenders and deal with others by persuading them to comply or negotiate out-of-court settlements. 'Rogues', 'cowboys' and other small businesses may be perceived to be either unwilling or unable to change their operations and therefore more 'deserving' of prosecution. Their offences are more visible as they are more often involved in selling directly to the public – the white collar equivalent of street crime – whereas large organizations can more easily conceal their operations (Hutter 1988; Croall 1989). Small businesses may also be vulnerable in that their operations are less complex and the proprietor is more readily identifiable as the responsible person (Croall 1989).

Wealthy offenders or large corporations can more easily avoid breaking the law as they can employ expert advice on how to stay within the 'letter' of the law while flouting its 'spirit' (McBarnet 1988). Tax accountants specialize in finding legal loopholes for clients to avoid paying taxes, and legal, scientific, financial and technical advisers may be employed to find ways around the law (McBarnet 1988). Smaller businesses are less able to afford this advice. If larger businesses do break the law, they may also use expert advisers to negotiate with enforcers and to contest cases in court – producing more lenient outcomes (Croall 1989). As with other forms of crime, there is therefore no simple relationship between social status and offending although the relative absence of wealthy and powerful offenders does not imply that they are intrinsically more law abiding.

Far less is known about the age, gender and 'race' of offenders although [...] it is reasonable to assume that white collar offenders are older as some degree of age and experience is necessary to commit offences. The race or ethnicity of offenders has not been systematically explored, although as with other forms of crime offences may be associated with 'outsiders' and 'mavericks', with immigrants and foreigners whose commercial ethics are assumed to be inferior. There is little evidence, however, to substantiate this. It has also been seen that white collar and corporate offending is assumed to be male dominated. While women's share of fraud is higher than for other crimes, this is attributable to non-white collar forms of cheque and credit card fraud (Levi 1994). In very general terms there have been few 'notorious' female white collar offenders to compare with the male defendants in the *Guinness* trials, the BCCI executives, or the managing directors of firms who have been charged with corporate manslaughter (Levi 1994). This may be because women are less often found in positions with so many opportunities to commit high-profile white collar or corporate offences. Nonetheless women are convicted for white collar offences and a small proportion of small business offenders were female proprietors and employees (Croall 1989). More research is needed, however, to establish whether women do, as is sometimes suggested, have more business integrity (Levi 1994).

Patterns of Victimization

There has been less systematic exploration of victimization from white collar than from other forms of crime and [...] it is not easy to capture in victim surveys. Some offences, such as insider trading or corruption, are seen as victimless although the former adversely affects investors and lack of trust in financial markets or standards in public life can adversely affect business and government (Croall 1992). Institutional victims such as the government or companies may be seen as 'able to afford it' although the public pays higher prices and taxes to make up for losses from white collar crime. White collar crime also involves power. It was seen earlier that offences often involve an abuse of an occupational role, involving scientific, technical or professional expertise. Thus some offences involve the power of the knowledgeable seller, producer or service provider over the less knowledgeable client or consumer. This need not imply a class relationship – the employer who lacks computer skills may be powerless in the face of the computer expert and the middle-class car owner powerless in the face of the garage mechanic. On the other hand, as for other forms of crime, the more affluent may more easily avoid risks as they can choose not to work in dangerous workplaces, live near polluting industries and are less likely to employ 'cowboy' builders (Croall 1998). In addition, poorer victims may suffer disproportionately.

Victims of organizational crime are generally described as consumers, workers or the general public, but other forms of inequality [...] can be involved. While some offences do affect people indiscriminately, others affect specific groups. Producers and sellers design and 'market' products for specific groups and, for example, cheap, substandard and often counterfeit goods will most often be targeted at poorer consumers. Gender is involved as many products and services, reflecting idealized images of masculinity and femininity, are targeted specifically at men or women. Some of the most notorious examples of corporate crime have involved products designed to alter women's bodies either through cultural representations of 'beauty' or through controlling their reproductive capacities (Szockyj and Fox 1996). The notorious Dalkon Shield contraceptive was marketed world wide on the basis of falsified test results, and led to many deaths, infertility and illness. Current concerns include 'cosmetic surgery' and the use of silicone breast implants which can cause permanent damage and whose side effects are not emphasized (Croall 1995; Szockyj and Fox 1996). Many women follow intensively marketed diets, many of which do not work and some of which carry health risks (Croall 1995). While these latter are not 'criminal' offences, there have been calls to subject some of the worst abuses to the Trade Descriptions Act as they are inherently misleading (Croall 1995).

Workers [...] are victimized by occupationally related diseases contracted from the substances they work with, by being paid low wages or by being endangered, killed or injured through neglect of safety regulations. Many fatalities and injuries are associated with traditionally male-based industries, and in such 'man's work' 'accidents' are often attributed to the intrinsic risks and dangers rather than to the neglect of safety precautions which may be the immediate cause of the 'accident' (Carson 1981). Women, on the other hand, can be the victims of long-term health risks in, for example, the food industry. They are also particularly vulnerable to low pay, harassment and illegal discrimination (Croall 1995; Szockyj and Fox 1996). Women's assumed financial or technical incompetence may make them vulnerable to, for example, car repair and service and financial frauds (Croall 1995). Age is also relevant, as illustrated by the abuse of the elderly or young in institutions and the exploitation of the middle aged and elderly by pensions frauds, the most dramatic example being the plundering of the pension funds of Maxwell employees (Punch 1996).

Victimization by white collar crime can compound victimization from other forms of crime and can also be repeat victimization – most people are probably the victims of several white collar offences each month. It can also have widespread and often devastating effects on local communities – as happens, for example, in major pollution incidents or so-called 'disasters'. This illustrates the point made by Box that, while the effects of corporate crime are often seen as trivial, or economic rather than physical, corporate crime can kill and injure (Box 1983). […]

UNDERSTANDING WHITE COLLAR AND CORPORATE CRIME

It has been more difficult to apply many of the traditional theories of crime to white collar crime, particularly as so many focused on the lower-class offender. Pathological theories are particularly limited – as Sutherland (1949: 257–8) commented, criminologists

> Would suggest in only a jocular sense that the crimes of the Ford Motor Company are due to the Oedipus complex, those of the Aluminium Company of America to an inferiority complex, or those of the US Steel Corporation to frustration and aggression, or those of du Pont to traumatic experience.

Similarly anomie theory was more difficult to apply, with greed, rather than need, often seen to be at the heart of white collar offending (Box 1983; Punch 1996). The cultural tolerance of many offences also made subcultural theory appear less appropriate and, as offenders are by and large not seen as deviant, labelling perspectives were similarly not applied (Box 1983; Croall 1992). Radical and critical criminologists focused less on offenders and offences than on the relationship between business power and the law implied in the lesser criminalization of white collar crime […]. Recent work on white collar and corporate crime reflects a variety of perspectives, some informed by earlier theories and others looking at the organizational aspects of offences.

Criminogenic Organizations?

As white collar and corporate crime rely on occupational and organizational roles, attention has turned to the organization, which has often been characterized as 'criminogenic' (Croall 1992; Punch 1996). To Punch, the organization is the offender, the means, the setting, the rationale, the opportunity and also the victim of corporate deviance (Punch 1996). The diffusion of responsibility can […] assist offending by distancing individuals from responsibility and thereby from guilt. In addition, the source of much corporate crime lies, as indicated in the P&O case, in organizational systems and standard operating procedures which should ensure the prevention of law breaking. These may not be fully enforced, and in some organizations the prioritization of profits or, in non-profit-making organizations, efficiency has often been seen to lead to systems being ignored in the face of, for example, competitive pressure or the pressure for increasing output or sales (Croall 1992).

Occupations and organizations also provide different kinds of 'illegitimate opportunity structures'. Not all employees have the opportunity to evade taxes or handle cash and some occupations are particularly criminogenic or 'fiddle prone' (Mars 1982). These include those relying on the use of specialist knowledge where the 'ignorant' consumer or employer is particularly vulnerable. Professional occupations who have the power to 'diagnose' problems and suggest solutions are particularly criminogenic, as are occupations like car sales and services (see, for example, Croall 1992). Other occupations are fiddle prone because workers have autonomy in their work, are not closely overlooked and handle money – thus the sales representative has more opportunities for fiddling than the supermarket cashier (Mars 1982). 'Gatekeepers', a category which includes actual gatekeepers and occupations such as brokers, are responsible for introducing clients to service providers, which provides many opportunities for corruption (Mars 1982).

The economic environment within which organizations operate can also be related to offending. Some forms of white collar crime increase during recessions where the need to prioritize profits or to survive can take precedence over compliance with regulations. This can increase costs and crimes may be committed to raise necessary cash, or desperate business proprietors may burn their premises to gain the insurance money. In this situation businesses face a form of anomie – with opportunities for success being blocked and crime being an 'innovative' response (Box 1987). Other forms of offending flourish in boom times – insider dealing, aggressive takeovers and many financial crimes may expand with the increasing opportunities offered by a buoyant market (Box 1987). The law and its enforcement also form a key part of the business environment. A 'rational' decision to offend may be affected by calculations of how great the chances are of being caught, prosecuted and sentenced. The small chance of prosecution and the scarce resources of enforcers have been seen to provide a favourable regulatory environment (Box 1987; Croall 1992).

This can also be affected by economic policies which [...] have been dominated by 'free market' principles discouraging intervention in the industrial sphere. This, along with the 'spirit of enterprise', arguably provided an ideal moral climate for many forms of business crime as the aggressive pursuit of profits became morally acceptable (Punch 1996). It also led to what has been described as 'deregulation', which constrained the powers and resources of law enforcers. In respect of tax evasion, Cook points to the conflict of values between *laissez-faire* and welfarism. Under *laissez-faire* values taxation is seen as unfair and over-taxation is resisted. In this climate, 'beating' the Inland Revenue becomes a legitimate 'sport' whereas taking from what is 'given' by the state is seen as a serious crime (Cook 1989). Economic priorities may also be important. In his work on health and safety in the North Sea oil fields, Carson argues that a 'political economy of speed', in which governments were eager to maximize the revenues from oil, made them reluctant to subject oil companies to tougher regulation (Carson 1981).

Criminalization and White Collar and Corporate Crime

This latter example points to the complex issue of criminalization in relation to white collar and corporate crime. To what extent does the criminal status of offences reflect the power of business groups over the law? It could alternatively be argued that white collar and corporate crime are treated differently because they are different and pose different problems for control. This can be seen by looking at the development of laws and law enforcement.

While business groups do exert considerable influence over the laws regulation their activities, it is difficult to substantiate any 'conspiracy theory'. Some business activities are criminalized, thus business groups are not always successful in resisting regulation. Moreover, business groups do not always represent a cohesive set of interests (see, for example, Croall 1992). Work on the origins of nineteenth-century legislation like the early Factory and Food and Drugs acts suggests that some business groups agreed to regulation as it was seen as being in their best interests to do so. Larger manufacturers, for example, calculated that smaller competitors might be priced out of the market by regulation. In the first instance laws were often 'symbolic', making few provisions for enforcement. The eventual form of law emerged out of a long process of negotiation between government, industry and enforcers in which different industrial groups represented their own interests, and in which stricter enforcement was accepted but the status of offences was differentiated from other forms of crime (Carson 1971; Paulus 1974). In his work on North Sea oil referred to above, Carson also found that the state, enforcers and businesses, which might have all been seen to represent 'establishment interests', often disagreed (Carson 1981).

Law enforcement has also been seen to be a crucial part of the process of criminalization, and the enforcement of white collar and corporate offences has often been characterized as lenient. To enforcers and some commentators, however, the compliance strategies outlined above are a more cost-effective way to protect the public than prosecution (Hawkins 1990; Pearce and Tombs 1990). It has been argued, for example, that as prosecution is expensive and may often fail and often leads only to a small fine, advice, persuasion, negotiation and out-of-court settlements are cheaper and more effective. Agencies may have a continuous relationship with regulated businesses and taking an overly tough stance could antagonize them, reducing the chances of compliance (Hawkins 1984). On the other hand, this can be challenged. How, for example, is cost effectiveness to be measured in relation to crime? Is it cost effective to prosecute a burglar? Or, as Steven Box once asked, would it be seen as appropriate to write several letters to a burglar asking that burglar to desist from breaking into people's houses? (Box 1983). Moreover, it can also be asked why enforcement agencies so often proceed against 'easier' targets instead of the 'richer pickings' to be gained from, for example, more affluent tax payers – which might also be more cost effective (Cook 1989). To some, therefore, arguments about cost effectiveness reflect ideological constructions. [...]

REFERENCES

Box, S. (1983) *Power, Crime and Mystification*. London: Tavistock.

Box, S. (1987) *Recession, Crime and Punishment*. London: Macmillan.

Carson, W.G. (1971) 'White Collar Crime and the Enforcement of Factory Legislation', in Carson W.G. and Wiles P. (eds) *Crime and Delinquency in Britain*. London: Martin Robertson.

Carson, W.G. (1981) *The Other Price of British Oil*. London: Martin Robertson.

Clarke, M. (1989) 'Insurance Fraud', *British Journal of Criminology*, 29 (1), 1–20.

Cook, D. (1989) *Rich Law, Poor Law: Different Responses to Tax and Supplementary Benefit Fraud*. Milton Keynes, Open University Press.

Croall, H. (1989) 'Who is the White Collar Criminal?', *British Journal of Criminology*, 29 (2), 157–74.

Croall, H. (1992) *White Collar Crime*. Buckingham: Open University Press.

Croall, H. (1995) 'Target Women: Women's Victimisation from White Collar Crime', in Dobash, R., Dobash, R. and Noaks, L. (eds) *Gender and Crime*. Cardiff: Cardiff University Press.

Croall, H. (1998) 'Business, Crime and the Community', *International Journal of Risk, Security and Crime Prevention*. Vol. 3 (4): 281–92.

Ditton, J. (1977) *Part Time Crime: An Ethnography of Fiddling and Pilferage*. London: Macmillan.

Hawkins, K. (1984) *Environment and Enforcement: Regulation and the Social Definition of Pollution*. Oxford: Clarendon Press.

Hawkins, K. (1990) 'Compliance Strategy, Prosecution Policy and Aunt Sally – A Comment on Pearce and Tombs', *British Journal of Criminology*, 30 (4), 444–67.

Hutter, B. (1988) *The Reasonable Arm of the Law?* Oxford: Claredon Press.

Langan, M. (1996) 'Hidden and Respectable: Crime and the Market', in Muncie, J. and McLaughlin, E. (eds) *The Problem of Crime*. London: Sage.

Levi, M. (1987) *Regulating Fraud: White Collar Crime and the Criminal Process*. London: Tavistock.

Levi, M. (1988) *The Prevention of Fraud*. Crime Prevention Unit, Paper 17. London: HMSO.

Levi, M. (1994) 'Masculinities and White Collar Crime', in Newburn, T. and Stanko, E. (eds) *Just Boys Doing Business?* London. Routledge

McBarnet, D. (1988) 'Law, Policy and Legal Avoidance: Can Law Effectively Implement Egalitarian Strategies?', *Journal of Law and Society*, 15 (1).

Mars, G. (1982) *Cheats at Work: An Anthropology of Workplace Crime*. London: George Allen and Unwin.

Nelken, D. (1997) 'White Collar Crime', in Maguire, M., Morgan, R. and Reiner, R. (eds) *The Oxford Handbook of Criminology*, 2nd edn. Oxford: Clarendon Press.

Paulus, I. (1974) *The Search for Pure Food: A Sociology of Legislation in Britain*. London: Martin Robertson.

Pearce, F. (1992) 'The Contribution of "Left Realism" to the Study of Commercial Crime', in McLean, B. and Lowman, J. (eds) *Realist Criminology: Crime Control and Policing in the 1990s*. Toronto: University of Toronto Press

Pearce, F. and Tombs, S. (1990) 'Ideology, Hegemony and Empiricism: Compliance Theories and Regulation', *British Journal of Criminology*, 30 (4), 423–43.

Punch, M. (1996) *Dirty Business: Exploring Corporate Misconduct*. London: Sage.

Sutherland, E. (1949) *White Collar Crime*. New York: Holt, Rinehart and Winston.

Sutton, A. and Wild, R. (1985) 'Small Business: White Collar Villains or Victims?', *International Journal of the Sociology of Law*, 13: 247–59.

Szockyj, E. and Fox, J.G. (eds) (1996) *Corporate Victimization of Women*. Boston: Northeastern University Press.

STUDY QUESTIONS

1   Croall suggests that the policing of white-collar and corporate crime reflects wider ideological constructions of crime and criminals. Why are these types of crimes 'under-policed' and how do you account for differences within these categories?

2   Are there any theoretical explanations that are particularly useful when studying white-collar and corporate crime?

3   Make a list of offences that would come under the heading of 'corporate crime'. How would you evaluate the assessment of both Croall (this reading) and Slapper and Tombs (Reading 9) that the economic, physical and social costs of such offences are far greater than those associated with conventional crime?

FURTHER READING

The most comprehensive recent overview of corporate crime can be found in Croall, H. (2001) *Understanding White Collar Crime*, Buckingham: Open University Press (a revised and updated replacement to her previous 1992 text, *White Collar Crime*). Another good place to start your reading in this area is Langan, M. (2001) 'Hidden and respectable: crime and the market', in J. Muncie and E. McLaughlin (eds) *The Problem of Crime*, 2nd edn, London: Sage. A classic piece of work in this area, which interestingly was largely ignored within criminology for over 20 years, is Sutherland, E. (1949) *White Collar Crime*, New York: Holt, Rinehart and Winston. More specific studies focusing on white-collar and corporate offences in particular industries include Bergman, D. (1991) *Deaths at Work: Accidents or Corporate Crime?* London: WEA; and Braithwaite, J. (1984) *Corporate Crime in the Pharmaceutical Industry*, London: Routledge. The problems of researching corporate offending are discussed by Whyte, D. (2000) 'Researching the powerful: towards a political economy of method?' in R. D. King and E. Wincup (eds) *Doing Research on Crime and Justice*, Oxford: Oxford University Press.

17

The race and crime debate

John Lea and Jock Young

In considering the relationship between 'race' and crime, John Lea and Jock Young begin with a six-part critique of an early 1980s tabloid newspaper article 'BLACK CRIME SHOCK: *Blacks carried out twice as many muggings as whites in London last year.*' They argue that the article was inaccurate (based as it was on simplistic, misleading statistics) and an example of 'blatant moral hysteria' which encourages racist attitudes. Writing from a 'new realist' perspective, Lea and Young go on to argue that much of the left's previous criticism of this kind of reportage and opinion is also simplistic and damaging. They suggest that it is misleading to argue that any link between high crime rates and ethnic-minority background is solely the result of police prejudice. They argue that the recorded rates for a range of offences committed by Asians is consistently lower than the rates for white offenders, and that the argument for higher crime rates among black people is only applicable to certain types of crime. Lea and Young further suggest that most crime is *intra*-class and *intra*-racial in that it takes place *within* communities; yet, they argue, both the media and the left operate within ideological frameworks which highlight *inter*-racial rather than intra-racial crime and pay little attention to the real problems facing working-class communities.

The repeated issue by the Metropolitan Police of crime statistics involving ethnic distinctions for a particular type of street crime, commonly called mugging, has once again raised the question of race and crime. The overwhelming response from the left has been, correctly, to deplore the one-sided, political nature of these statistics and to see them as consistent with an attempt to fuel an atmosphere of moral panic in which the issues raised by the Scarman Report and

SOURCE: From *What is to be Done about Law and Order? Crisis in the Nineties* (London: Pluto Press, 1993), 105–12.

the Greater London Council's campaign for a democratic police authority can be safely ignored. It has given rise to an extreme reaction in the gutter press; for instance, the *Sun* ran a headline BLACK CRIME SHOCK and carried *without* inverted commas the statement: 'Blacks carried out twice as many muggings as whites in London last year' (23 March 1983). Let us state now the extremely strong objective reasons for being highly sceptical about statements such as that out of 19,258 cases of robbery and violent theft in London, 10,960 were carried out by blacks.

(1)   They focus on only one type of crime out of a whole catalogue of serious offences. Robbery and violent theft only account for about 3 per cent of all serious crime. They ignore the fact that whites are more likely to commit the vast majority of serious crimes and present us with the image of the 'black criminal'.

(2)   Many of these crimes are of an amateurish and minor nature, but the phrase 'robbery and violent theft' suggests something of a more extreme nature. In a Home Office Research Study of mugging, for example, it was found that 54 per cent of those mugged suffered minor injuries such as cuts and bruises, and only 3 per cent needed to stay in hospital for longer than twelve hours (*New Society*, 25 March 1983).

(3)   The category 'robbery and violent theft' is a very flexible one and blends with other offence categories such as 'theft of personal property'. By allocating crimes from the latter to the former, inflated figures can easily occur. The exercise of police discretion can quite easily alter the amount of a particular crime by changes in recording practices. A recent study, for example, suggests that precisely such a manipulation occurred in the claim that there was a dramatic rise in street crime in Brixton in 1981 (Blom-Cooper and Drabble, 1982).

(4)   They ignore the fact that mugging is a very indistinct category and that only about one-third of all robbery and violent theft fits the conventional notion of it. This was put well in a Runnymede Trust Bulletin:

> Mugging is not, however, an offence known in law and the term is not normally used by police. To the public it usually means a theft, in the street, which is accompanied by violence. But the Metropolitan Police category of robbery and other violent thefts includes 'snatches' where the victim is neither threatened nor injured (7,330), robberies from business premises open to the public (2,684), and 'other robberies' which are not street robberies (2,860). This leaves 5,889 robberies which would fit in with the popular meaning of 'mugging', only 31 per cent of the figure bandied about in the press, and only 0.9 per cent of the total recorded serious offences. (No. 143, p. 8)

(5)   It does not present us with the ethnic origins of the victims of crime, thus serving to feed the illusion that black crime is predatory upon white. Of course, most crime is intra-racial and intra-class.

(6)   It does not allow for the fact that police statistics *are in part* a function of police prejudices. It presents the figures on ethnic divisions as objective reflections of reality.

All in all, we have an extremely slanted portrayal of the crime problem which, no doubt, contributes considerably to the build-up of racial fears in the non-black community. It is a blatant example of the type of moral hysteria about crime which has occurred throughout the century. The main preoccupation during the fifties and sixties was the crime of lower-working-class youth, and now attention has been shifted on to young blacks.

Even if the figures were totally accurate – and we have seen that this is an impossibility – it is a priority that they be presented in context, to allow the audience to understand their true significance. Figures do not speak for themselves and there are plenty of racist 'contexts' into which they will inevitably be slotted if the presenters of the statistics 'naively' inform us that they are only giving the public 'the facts'. It is vital, therefore, that we debunk this strategy and provide accurate interpretations to counter the moral panic over crime which serves to fuel racism.

But a common reaction on the left and among liberal commentators has been significantly different from this. Instead of scrutinizing the figures impartially and providing a context in which they can be understood, they have engaged in a wholesale dismissal of the evidence, often in a very contradictory fashion. They have either questioned the validity of any connection at all between race and crime (e.g. Bridges and Gilroy, 1982), or argued that the problem is irrelevant as such crime is insignificant by comparison with the 'crimes of the powerful' (e.g. Harman, 1982). Bridges and Gilroy suggest that any link between crime rates and ethnic background is purely a function of police prejudice and that any discussion to the contrary gives 'intellectual support to racist stereotypes of the black community as socially and politically disorganized' (p. 35). Such a position, quite apart from the vacuous definition of racism involved, appears to associate critical discussion with silence. As if silence can eliminate the fear of crime, or blank denial rid us of racial prejudice! It is precisely such silences that have placed the left continually on the defensive and guaranteed the hegemony of the right over the terrain of law and order. A challenge to this long established domination by the right must begin with the simple recognition that crime is a pressing problem for the poor and for the black community, and that the control of crime is a vital issue for socialists.

As we have argued, in all industrial societies a small minority of the oppressed sections of society are brutalized into criminality. But because crime is produced by the system, it does not follow that crime is some sort of crypto-political struggle against the system. Bridges and Gilroy (1982) refer evasively to the 'social and political character' of working-class black crime (p. 35). One might as well argue that dying of asbestos poisoning, undoubtedly a disease produced by industrial capitalism, is some sort of political activity. The notion of crime as a kind of politics rests on a few myths that need to be dispelled. Working-class crimes are predominantly intra-class and intra-racial. A poor person is more likely to rob a poor person than a rich person, a black is more likely to assault another black than a white, and a white more likely to attack a white than a black. Eighty per cent of crimes of violence involving serious injury and 62 per cent of those causing slight injury are intra-racial (see Stevens and Willis, 1979).

The high crime rate of certain minority segments of the black community is directed to that community. Street culture is, on the one hand, expressive and liberative, and on the other, individualistic, macho and predatory. Hustling is not a pursuit of angels; only the most unmitigated romantic would believe this. 'Hyenas and wolves of the street' was how Malcolm X referred to street criminals, and George Jackson in his prison letters wrote to his mother about intra-racial crime in his community:

> The men can think of nothing more effective than pimping, gambling and petty theft. I've heard men brag about being pimps of black women and taking money from black women who are on relief. Things like that I find odious, disgusting.

And as a matter of fact, socialists ever since Engels have consistently viewed the vast majority of crime as serving to destroy the community, as something that has to be resisted. Yet these idealists tend merely to invert the imagery of the mass media. If the mass media say that crime is a danger then it obviously is not!

Both the mass media and the left share one thing: they overwhelmingly concentrate on inter-racial crime. Inter-racial crime is a minor, albeit very serious, phenomenon; within this category a substantial proportion occurs because of overtly racist reasons. Thus a recent Home Office study attributes one-quarter of all inter-racial crimes to racist motives. In absolute terms these represent only a 0.25 per cent of recorded crime, but what is of significance is the victimization rate for minority groups. The rate for Asians was fifty times that for white people, and that for blacks thirty-six times (see *Racial Attacks*, Home Office, 1981). We have no doubt that this is a gross underestimation and that the police response to racial persecution is severely inadequate. What we must note, however, is that the criminal victimization rates *as a whole* are considerably greater. Furthermore, the left, although correctly focusing on racist incidents, seems, quite incorrectly, unable to see the existence of crime outside this category.

A startling illustration of this shortsightedness is the following quote from *Policing London*, commenting on the Metropolitan figures and the study we have just mentioned:

> Though they posses the information, the Met did not publish at the same time figures which show what proportion of the victims of these crimes are also black. The Home Office report on Racial Attacks (November 1981) indicated that, with regard to offences such as violence against the person and robbery: 'The incidence of victimization has been much higher for the ethnic minority populations, particularly the Asians, than for white people. Indeed the rate for Asians was 50 times that for white people and the rate for blacks was over 36 times that for white people.' (Policing London, No. 1, July–August 1982, p. 3)

Now, to any reader this remark could only be read as suggesting that serious criminal victimization was fifty times greater for Asians, and thirty-six times greater for blacks, than for whites. This is precisely what has been repeated in several other articles. Of course, these figures do not refer to the total extent of criminal victimization by ethnic groups. They do not even refer to inter-racial attacks. What they do refer to, as we have already noted, is inter-racial attacks where there is 'strong evidence or some indication' of a racist motive. As a matter of fact, the criminal victimization of blacks in the very restricted category of robbery and violent theft alone (about 3 per cent of all serious crime) is over ten times greater than for *all* serious crime against blacks of an overtly racist nature; for Asians the figure is fourteen times. This is not to deny the problem of racist attacks. *On the contrary*, police inactivity with regard to such outrages is a scandal. Our point here is simply that the left, while quite rightly pressing for police involvement in combating such crime, turns a blind eye towards the existence of a massive amount of crime against blacks and the working class.

Inter-racial crime, involving blacks against whites, is a minor phenomenon. Mugging is far from being an exclusively black crime – yet it is also one of the *few* crimes where there is some evidence of a substantial, if still minor, racial component (Pratt, 1980). The mass media have picked upon an atypical black crime and portrayed it as the *typical* crime, while at the same time grossly over-estimating its seriousness. It is, in fact, largely without serious violence, involves small sums of money and it is the amateurish crime of young boys and adolescents. But its impact should not be underplayed. £5 stolen from an old age pensioner is of far greater significance than £500 stolen from Woolworths, which is why the former, rightly, creates more alarm and disgust than the latter. Mugging, regardless of whether the perpetrator or victim is white or black, is a despicable crime but one which must be seen in perspective. It must neither be exaggerated, in an alarmist fashion, nor ignored as a matter of petty importance.

Intra-racial crime and intra-class crimes are of massive proportions, but because much of the left is locked in a debate with the mass media they are simply not seen. Thus, for ideological reasons, real problems facing the community are quite simply ignored and a ground-swell of anxiety allowed to build up. Both intra-racial and inter-racial crime are demoralizing and divisive within the black community and the working class. The fact that most working-class crime and black crime is directed against the working-class and black communities, coupled with the situation where such communities are less likely to receive adequate police protection than the rich, should be the starting-point for the left. The need is surely for more efficient police protection responsive to the needs of the working class and the groups within it.

If unemployment and deprivation brutalized into criminality a minority of the poor in certain cultural and political circumstances, why is there such a problem for writers on the left to accept the proposition that the accentuation of such deprivation through the additional mechanisms of racial discrimination results in higher crime rates? The claim that the higher recorded rate for certain types of crime for young blacks is purely and simply a product of police prejudice is open to a number of objections [...] but the following four points form an incontestable basis:

(1) Such a claim makes the assumption that the 'real' crime rate for all social groups is the same. This is tantamount to the suggestion that the black community does not in reality suffer any additional ill-effects from racial discrimination.
(2) The recorded rate for a range of Asian crimes is consistently lower than the white rate (Stevens and Willis, 1979). Police racism would have to manifest very strangely indeed to be entirely responsible for such results.

(3) The crime rate for the first generation of West Indian in immigrants recorded in the 1960s was lower than the general rate (Lambert, 1970). Either real changes in the crime rate within the black community have occurred or the police were exercising positive discrimination for over a decade in favour of the black community!

(4) The argument for higher crime rates for black youth is only made for certain types of crime. The police do not claim, for example, that blacks have a higher rate for burglary than whites, or for bank robbery. The issue centres around street crime (see Scarman Inquiry Minutes, Day Two).

REFERENCES

Blom-Cooper, L. and Drabble, R. (1982) 'Police Perception of Crime', *British Journal of Criminology*, Vol. 22 (1) Jan 1982 pp. 184–7.

Bridges, L. and Gilroy, P. (1982) 'Striking Back', *Marxism Today*, Vol. 26(6), June 1982 pp. 34–5.

Harman, C. (1981) 'The Summer of 1981: a Post-riot Analysis', *International Socialism*, 2: 1–41.

Harman, C. (1982) 'The Law and Order Show', *Socialist Review*, 82. 04/18 pp. 18–21.

Lambert, J. (1970) *Crime, Police and Race Relations*, Oxford: Oxford University Press.

Pratt, M. (1980) *Mugging as a Social Problem*, London: Routledge and Kegan Paul.

Stevens, P. and Willis, C. (1979) *Race Crime and Arrests*, Home Office Research Study no. 58, London: HMSO.

STUDY QUESTIONS

1 What do you understand by the terms 'intra-class' and 'intra-racial' crime?

2 In your own words detail the problems with the *Sun* article. From Lea and Young's perspective, why are the responses of the left to high crime rates among ethnic-minority groups also inadequate?

3 What explanations, other than police and court prejudice, can you give for high crime rates among some ethnic-minority groups?

FURTHER READING

There are many texts that discuss the relationship between police and ethnic minority groups, e.g. Hall, S., Critcher, C., Jefferson, T., Clarke, J. and Roberts, B. (1978) *Policing the Crisis: Mugging, the State and Law and Order*, London: Macmillan; Holdaway, S. (1996) *The Racialization of the British Police*, Basingstoke: Macmillan; Chan, J. (1997) *Changing Police Culture: Policing in a Multi-cultured Society*, Cambridge: Cambridge University Press; Fitzgerald, M. (1999) *Stop and Search*, London: New Scotland Yard; and Bowling, B. and Phillips, C. (2002) *Racism, Crime and Justice*, Harlow: Longman; see also *Further Reading* for Reading 18.

18

From Scarman to Stephen Lawrence

Stuart Hall

The issue of police/race relations is considered in detail by Stuart Hall who, in this reading, focuses on racism within the police force and in society in general. He does this through a consideration of racialized violence, rioting and public disorder in the streets of the UK in the early 1980s (and the resultant Scarman Report of 1981) through to the inquiry into the death of Stephen Lawrence (and associated Macpherson Report of 1999). Hall suggests that there is some evidence to suggest that over the past 20 years those already opposed to multiculturalism feel more, and not less, oppressed by changes in society. This is characterized by a growing sense of 'defensive embattlement', particularly among some English people, in pursuit of a so-called distinctive traditional 'British way of life'. Hall suggests that 'English cultural nationalism' has paved the way for a revised type of 'cultural racism' to add to other, previous, versions of racism. The murder of Stephen Lawrence and subsequent murder inquiry occurred within this context, and the Macpherson Report is distinctive in characterizing the conduct of the Metropolitan Police not only as professionally incompetent but also as an example of institutional racism. Hall considers the positive and not so positive aspects of the report and the responses to it. In his 1981 report Lord Scarman wrote 'the standards we apply to the police must be higher than the norms of behaviour prevalent in society as a whole' yet, two decades later, there is still no way to hold officers directly accountable. Thus, Hall concludes that those expecting Macpherson to usher in a new dawn in relations between black people and the police need to think again.

Nearly two decades separate the Report by Lord Scarman which brought the race riots of 1981 to some sort of official conclusion,[1] from the Report by

SOURCE: From *History Workshop Journal*, 48 (1999), 187–97.

Sir William Macpherson which in 1999 concluded the Official Inquiry into the death of the black teenager, Stephen Lawrence.[2] These have been momentous decades in the history of race and the future of Britain as a multicultural society. The routine way to assess this period is to ask whether, taking one thing with another, things haven't gotten better on the race-relations front? This way of framing the question assumes not only that some simple answer can be given, but that the verdict will be positive. The question, however, is not amenable to such simplistic optimisms.

[...] The attack, at 10.30 in the evening of 22 April 1993, on Stephen Lawrence and Duwayne Brooks [took place] as they waited at a bus-stop in Well Hall Road, Eltham, South London, by five white youths chanting: 'What, what, nigger?' Within sight of several witnesses, Stephen Lawrence was stabbed twice in the chest and died shortly after. The police refused to view the incident as a racial attack, treating Duwayne Brooks, who narrowly escaped with his life, as a suspect: and they failed to arrest anyone for weeks, despite considerable hearsay evidence. Instead, they pursued for several days the wholly unsubstantiated belief that there must have been a fight, somehow involving the two black boys. When five white youths were finally arrested, the identification collapsed and charges were abandoned. Following two internal reviews (the first, which exonerated the Metropolitan Police's handling of the original affair, later described by Macpherson as 'effectively indefensible'),[3] the Inquiry found that the Met's handling of the affair 'was marred by a combination of professional incompetence, institutional racism and a failure of leadership by senior officers'.[4] The incompetence – exposed, day after day, as the whole police construction of the events collapsed before the eyes of press and public – was indeed staggering. But, Macpherson insisted in 1999, the incompetence could only be explained by 'pernicious and persistent institutional racism'.

[...] From the early race riots of Nottingham and Notting Hill in 1958, through the 1970s campaigns against 'sus' laws (permitting arbitrary stop-and-search), the death of Blair Peach from a police baton at a 1979 demonstration in Southall, the uproar following the death of Colin Roach in Stoke Newington police station in 1983 and the lack of explanation for many other black deaths in police custody, the Deptford Fire and the arson of Asian shops and homes, the 1980s 'disorders' in Brixton and at Broadwater Farm, Tottenham, to Stephen Lawrence's murder in 1993 or the flaming body of Michael Menson falling unheeded into the Thames in 1997, black people have been the subject of racialized attack, had their grievances largely ignored by the police, and been subjected to racially-inflected practices of policing. Each of those events was followed by a campaign, unofficial inquiries (I sat on two), recriminations from the authorities, promises of reform. Very little seems to have changed. Relations between black communities and police have continued to be a catalogue of disasters, marked by mistrust, prejudice and disrespect, often leading to tragedy.

Of course, the whole 'race-relations' situation in Britain cannot be accurately assessed from the perspective of black/police relations alone. But these do have a symptomatic value. The basis of the constitutional state is that the citizen, whatever his/her race, colour or creed, has the right to the full protection of the law – if necessary from 'the law' itself. Until recent governments began privatizing justice and policing as if this had no bearing on the question of the state's arbitrary power over the citizen, it was assumed that only the state had the power to deprive citizens of their liberty, and then legitimately only by due process. Consequently, how the police treat the citizen has become a litmus test of liberty in all free societies; and the question 'Who guards the guards?' one which cuts to the very heart of fundamental civic liberties and human rights. The excuse, which successive Chief Police Officers have peddled for twenty years, that since British society is 'racist' we must expect a proportionate number of police officers to be racists too is not only cynical but constitutionally unacceptable. As Scarman himself observed, 'the standards we apply to the police must be higher than the norms of behaviour prevalent in society as a whole'.[5] A similar argument (popularly known as the 'rotten apples' theory) – that, since society contains a lot of villains, the police too will necessarily have its 'normal ration' of corrupt officers – could not be legitimately advanced; and when some such charge has been laid in the past, senior police have mobilized extraordinary manpower and resources to stamp it out. Racism, however, continues to be subject to a different logic.

This double standard is a testimony to the stubborn persistence of racial thinking as part of the deep, unconscious structure of British common sense, often crystallized in institutional cultures. It testifies to the pervasive disavowal and double-talk which across the years has covered over the yawning gaps between policy and practice in these institutions. The state of black/police relations thus gives us an unwelcome glimpse into how racialized difference is actually being negotiated at a deeper level, where unreconstructed attitudes find a sort of displaced but systematic expression in places which the utopian language of 'multicultural Britain' cannot reach.

The Scarman Report was the official response to an unprecedented level of racialized violence, rioting and public disorder in the streets, which erupted first in April 1980 in the St Paul's district of Bristol and spread, during 1981, to Brixton and Southall, Toxteth in Liverpool, Manchester Moss Side, Handsworth in Birmingham, Sheffield, Nottingham and other cities. It culminated with further rioting on 15 July 1981, following an aggressive police swoop on houses around the Railton Road area of Brixton, which the Police Complaints Board subsequently said showed 'an institutional disregard for the niceties of the law', and which resulted in extensive damage to property for which the Met paid compensation.[6] As is customary in such circumstances, contingent events sparked off the rioting, against the background of racial disadvantage, fears about rising crime and drug use, growing black youth unemployment and deepening despair amongst the black communities, compounded by the looming spectre of the Thatcherite assault on the structures of welfare support.

Lord Scarman's Report was no panacea, but it was distinctive for at least three reasons. First, it broke the prevailing law-and-order consensus by firmly locating the sources of unrest in 'insecure social and economic conditions and in an impoverished physical environment' – a 'set of social conditions which create a disposition towards violent protest'.[7] Scarman argued that the problem of policing 'deprived, inner-city, multiracial localities' was framed by 'the social, economic and related problems … faced by all residents of such areas' and 'the social and economic disadvantages which are suffered particularly by black residents, especially young blacks'.[8] The Report was 'a strong argument in favour of a historical and social explanation of the riots'.[9]

Secondly, Scarman put his trust in a much-expanded programme of police training on community and race issues as a way of trying to get to grips with the racialization of routine police work. Many aspects of Racism Awareness Training were controversial from the start: and the reform was so patchily introduced (many Chief Constables exercising their discretion to take no action at all), the trainers so inadequately prepared, the programme so lacking in senior managerial authority or integration into wider policing practices, as to be grossly inadequate on the ground to the liberal purpose intended.

His third strand was the statutory establishment of community consultative committees, designed to give the community an augmented voice and 'help to provide an agenda for a continuing dialogue between the police and the public about the nature of policing in today's society'.[10] These committees had some educational value, but they had no way of resolving the deep conflicts and intense hostilities which frequently surfaced, could not represent the diversity of community opinion with one voice and had no power to influence policing policy when it really mattered.[11]

Some parts of Scarman's reforms of policing were implemented, though inadequately. The wider social and economic reforms, however, were seriously out of key with the political temper of the times and triggered no significant political or policy response. In retrospect, Scarman was to bewail the 'lack of implementation of the social and economic recommendations' and to acknowledge that he should have been 'more outspoken about the necessity of affirmative action to overcome racial disadvantage'.[12]

Racial disorder flared again in 1985, first in Handsworth, where two Asian men died; it spread to Brixton, where a police officer's shot paralysed Mrs Cherry Groce during a house search for her son; thence to Toxteth, Peckham and Tottenham, where Mrs Cynthia Jarrett collapsed and died during a house search for evidence against her son (subsequently acquitted). In the rioting around the Broadwater Farm Estate, in Tottenham, PC Keith Blakelock was stabbed to death. Two features distinguished this period of unrest (in which incidentally both white and black youth were heavily involved). First, the violence was preceded by a much-increased, pro-active programme of police raids, aimed at drugs, drug pushers and concealed weapons. No effort was made to forewarn the very active Broadwater Farm community group until too late.[13] Secondly, the police response to urban unrest was notably vigorous. For the first time para-military policing tactics (including full riot-gear, plastic bullets and CS gas) were deployed on British streets in the effort, apparently, not to contain the violence but to 'win' the public-order 'war'.

This appeared to signal some sort of climacteric – or nadir – in black/police relations, which, as we've said, always have wider significance; and was followed by dire warnings of further unrest and violence. Yet, in fact, there were no parallel explosions in the subsequent decade. What, then, has been happening in the interim? Have black/police relations substantially improved? Have the policing reforms finally begun to bite? […]

Racial attacks on the homes and shops of Asian families have continued unabated. The stop-and-search and school-exclusion figures for blacks have been soaring again. The criminalization of areas of high immigrant settlement coupled with pervasive involvement in drugs have sharpened confrontations between a so-called 'villainous' minority and the police, which spill over into and infect general police/community relations.

Seen in this context, the Stephen Lawrence affair does not appear so aberrant as it did at first glance. There has been no slow, steady, evolutionary 'rise and rise' of a new multicultural spirit in Britain. There has been change – but racism just as deeply persists. Indeed, there is some evidence to suggest that, as multicultural drift has become increasingly a sort of tolerated norm, those opposed to it feel more, not less, threatened, as the tide imperceptibly shifts against them. This is compounded by the astonishing social diversity which has overtaken the so-called 'majority' population. We know that what is called 'the British way of life' is really a euphemism for the stabilized pattern of differences and inequalities which has come to be accepted as the natural order of things in Britain. But in almost every feature of that settled pattern, over the past two decades, change and diversity have intervened. Social, economic, cultural, technological and moral shifts, unsettling established patterns and norms, have combined with Britain's relative economic decline, the unrequited loss of imperial destiny and the onset of globalization, which relativizes the power of the nation-state and national culture, to produce nothing short of a crisis of British, and especially English, identity. What does it mean to be 'British' in a world in which Britain no longer rules the waves?

There is thus a growing sense of defensive embattlement, particularly amongst some of the English, in response to what that minority sees as the erosion of a distinctive and 'historic' (that is, a traditional) British way of life: especially – first – by the encroachment of the demonized 'Europe' – Euroscepticism has undoubtedly helped to strengthen the defensiveness of English culture against (all) 'the others'; and, secondly, by devolution, and the new constitutional settlement. The latter has allowed Scotland, Wales and – if all goes well – Northern Ireland to slip away into greater autonomy, weakening, the ties (deeply uneven as they have always been) which bound the four kingdoms (sic) into an entity which could plausibly be represented as one 'United Kingdom'. For all its toying with the slogans of 'New Britain' and 'Cool Britannia', New Labour's highly-tempered modernism has rendered it incapable of voicing these subterranean resentments. On the other hand, the Conservatives cannot decide whether their plight is desperate enough to oblige them to throw all caution to the winds and become the party of a new 'Little Englandism'.

On all three fronts, then – the multicultural, the European and the devolved kingdom – what passes for an 'English' nationalism feels deeply threatened and beleaguered. A spirit of what has properly, in the post-globalization sense, to be called an English cultural nationalism – an English 'fundamentalism' – has been slowly emerging into the light of day. This is the precondition for a revived – and transformed – type of 'cultural racism', to add to and to compound the other garden varieties. The small overtly-fascist political groupings have so far been able to politicize only a very small proportion of this subterranean sentiment (they have been much less successful at invading the political mainstream than Le Pen's blue-suited shock troops in France). However, they have touched the hearts of a small, dedicated band of converts amongst a section of white working-class young men, living in some of Britain's most depressed and forgotten corners. They have few employment or educational prospects, feel a deep sense of national shame and dispossession, practise their manoeuvres in the context of international sport (last bastion of territoriality in an increasingly de-territorialized world). They are the small seedbed of that form of violent collective projection which follows the classic logic – 'We are poor because the blacks are here'.

Against that background, the Inquiry into Stephen Lawrence's death was a remarkable affair. The murder occurred in precisely such an area as described above: one with a long history of racialized violence around schools, playgrounds and sports-fields (including incidents involving the five white suspects)[14] – and near Plumstead, where a police Racial Incident Unit had been established as early as December 1990, because of the high level of racial incidents. The Inquiry referred to several cases of black boys beaten up by white gangs between 1991 and 1993 'to highlight both the regularity of such offences and the lack ... of coordinated information about them'.[15] The area is also a well-known stamping-ground of the British National Party and of Combat 18.

The Inquiry would not have happened without the stubborn persistence of Stephen's parents, Neville and Doreen Lawrence, and the small campaign group which supported them. Liaison with the parents throughout the five-year investigation was, however, pathetic. They were sidelined, rarely informed about or kept in touch with developments, the construction being put about by the police that they had been 'nobbled' by anti-police political agitators. Duwayne Brooks, who had to run for his life from the attackers, and was wandering around at the scene of the crime distraught and agitated because of the lack of police follow-up to his leads and the ambulance delay, was treated by them as a hysterical and unreliable witness, rather than as a victim. Macpherson judged that he was 'stereotyped as a young black man' and that this played a part in 'the collective failure of those involved to treat him properly'.[16] The Metropolitan Police were obliged to apologize to all three unreservedly for their conduct.

Whatever else happened when the police arrived on the scene – and the Report's view is that 'Anybody who listened to the evidence of the officers involved in the initial police action after the murder would ... be astonished at the lack of command and lack of organization that took place'[17] – the suspects were not pursued; the search was fitful, disorganized, misdirected and fruitless. The police assumed – 'without any basis for such a conclusion',[18] and despite Brooks's testimony – that there had been a fight in which Lawrence and

Brooks were somehow implicated. Despite the long history of racial incidents in the area, and the clear guidance from the Association of Chief Police Officers that the word of a participant involved in an incident who alleges that there was a racial motive must be believed until evidence to the contrary emerges,[19] no one took Duwayne Brooks seriously; and experienced officers, up to and during the Inquiry, persisted in denying that racism had been involved.[20] There was an implicit, collective, 'institutional' refusal to define the incident as a racialized attack.

This is the point at which gross and systematic professional incompetence by the police began to slide imperceptibly into the question of institutional racism. Thereafter, even when the five white suspects had been widely named and police attention was finally turned on them, both incompetence and racism remained in evidence. Two of the suspects, leaving home with something unusual in black binliners, were not followed nor the contents examined. Records of statements by local people naming the five suspects, including a lengthy and detailed account (Message 40) by a 'James Grant' (supposed to be a police informer), were not passed on. Some vital notes and notebooks, briefing documents, records of meetings, minutes of strategic decisions whether to arrest or not, have all gone missing – disappeared (despite almost continuous uproar about the case between 1993 and the Inquiry and two formal internal inquiries) down a very black hole.

The Report itself is a curious document. It fails altogether to place the event in the broader historical context of black/police relations and disconnects it from the local contexts of racial violence. On the other hand, its minute recording of evidence given at the Inquiry in painstaking sequence has its own impact, since the slow-motion unravelling in public of the justificatory narratives offered by the police constituted a drama of its own (the dramatized version which played to packed houses at the Tricycle Theatre needed only a carefully-edited transcript). The facet which has captured public attention is, of course, the issue of 'institutional racism', which thrust its way, 'unwittingly', into the centre of the Report. The issue remains controversial. Critics of the Report do not like it because, they say, its emphasis on 'unwitting' and 'unconscious' racism lets racists in general, and the police in particular, off the hook. They want a more moralized definition which forces racists to take responsibility for their actions. It is also said to be so general (applying equally to all institutions) that it leaves things where they are: if every institution is racist, then there is nothing to do but destroy them and start again – a recipe for inaction.

Though these dangers do exist, I would argue that the official use of the term 'institutional racism' to characterize the conduct of the Metropolitan Police, from the lowest to the most senior ranks, is a real advance, in a long campaign which is unlikely to have many short-term or any total victories. Moreover, the idea of 'institutional racism' strikes at the heart of one very English kind of racism, which thrives, not against, but cosily inserted within, liberalism. Lord Scarman muddied the waters by suggesting the phrase could mean 'knowingly, as a matter of policy' – a wobble on which Sir Paul Condon, the Metropolitan Police Commissioner, then constructed a veritable mountain of prevaricating apologetics. Macpherson's definition accepts 'unwitting' and 'unconscious' and adds 'unintentional.'[21] Of course, there is a great deal of 'witting, conscious and intentional' racism about. But there is also a great deal which arises

> because of lack of understanding, ignorance or mistaken beliefs … from well-intentioned but patronising words or actions, … from unfamiliarity with the behaviour or cultural traditions of people … from ethnic minorities … from racist stereotyping … out of uncritical self-understanding born out of an iniflexible police ethos of the 'traditional' way of doing things [which] thrive in a tightly knit community.[22]

The first part of that definition is weak – powerful racist stereotypes of 'the other' can hardly be effectively described as 'lack of understanding, ignorance or mistaken beliefs.' But it gets better as the sentence goes on. The idea could be much more sharply and succinctly expressed than it is in Macpherson, but the broader discussion in the Report does begin to capture its salient features […].

The key points to bear in mind here are as follows. First, institutional racism does not require overtly racist individuals: it conceives racism as arising through social processes – a difficult idea for the English imagination since (as a former Prime Minister, Mrs Thatcher, once gloriously observed) the latter has no concept of 'the social' which cannot be reduced to 'individuals and their families'. Second, institutional racism has clearly taken the argument that *culture* regulates *conduct*. These behavioural norms are carried within the occupational culture of an organization, and transmitted by informal and implicit ways through its routine, everyday practices as an indestructible part of the institutional *habitus*. Racism of *this* kind becomes routine, habitual, taken for granted. It is far more effective in socializing the practice of officers than formal training or regulations. (The arduous reporting of racial incidents or domestic violence, by contrast, is defined, in the occupational culture, as 'rubbish' policing.) And it blocks a professional reflexivity from ever coming into operation. Far from being seen as exceptional, this 'unwitting' type of racism becomes part of the very working definition of 'normal police work'. It is perfectly possible for young officers – whose promotion up the ranks and acceptance as 'regular cops' depends on imbibing as an unreflected practice this folk-wisdom of 'how to be a good copper' – to love reggae, eat Vindaloo curry every Saturday night, have a few black friends, and still think that 'good policing' requires them to act on the assumption that a young black man carrying a holdall at a bus-stop after dark almost certainly just committed a robbery and should be 'sussed' – stopped and searched. This is certainly not the *only* kind of racism which operates in our institutions, but it is one, distinct variety and, precisely because of its institutional embeddedness, one of the most difficult to identify and dismantle.

It is not clear that the Macpherson recommendations can deal effectively with it. Sir William did try to put Sir Paul Condon on the spot by noting the latter's stubborn resistance, conducted as a war of attrition throughout the Inquiry ('I acknowledge the danger of the institutionalization of racism.

However, labels can cause more problems than they solve').[23] Macpherson remarked that 'Any Chief Officer who feels unable so to respond [to the problem of institutional racism] will find it difficult to work in harmony and co-operation with the community in the way that policing by consent requires.'[24] What then are we to deduce from the fact that the Home Secretary chickened out and Sir Paul remained in office, successfully riding out the post-Lawrence Inquiry storm on the way to a happy retirement?

The police and press counter-campaign effectively diverted public attention to the two most questionable of Macpherson's seventy recommendations: number 38, proposing a review of the court's power to prosecute after acquittal if 'fresh and viable' evidence emerged, and number 39, constituting racist language or behaviour in private a prosecutable offence. This tactic, together with pervasive denials and disavowals, has served to obscure other more significant proposals, such as subjecting the police to extensive performance indicators on racial matters, bringing the Met under a proper police authority, opening the police to a Freedom of Information Act and to the Race Relations Act, from which they are currently exempt, granting disclosure of evidence by right to parties represented at an inquest, improving the monitoring and recording of racist incidents, underlining the witness's priority in defining a 'racist incident', and 'ensuring that serious complaints against officers are independently investigated.'[25] What has not been tackled is how to hold officers directly accountable in terms of preferment, and how to make the 'cost' of proven racist behaviour by police officers, witting or unwitting, directly impact on their careers, pay, promotion prospects and indeed job retention and retirement rewards. There is no other way to begin to drive reform up and down through the ranks to the levels of actual practice by professional officers and denizens of the 'canteen culture' alike, where former strategies have failed to reach. That this is to be left, once again, to internal police and cosy Home Office 'review', and that accountability and independent investigation of complaints have not been ranked higher or strengthened by the Government's response to the Macpherson Report, does not bode well. A few Racism Awareness Training films are no doubt at this very moment being prepared, and beleaguered desk sergeants once more to be put in charge of organizing 'the training' – with the laughably ineffectual results about which we already have overwhelming evidence.

Those expecting Macpherson to usher in a new epoch in black/police relations had therefore better think again. [...]

NOTES

1 Lord Scarman, *The Brixton Disorders 10–12 April 1981: Report of an Inquiry by the Rt. Hon. The Lord Scarman, OBE*. Cmnd 8247. HMSO, London, 1982.
2 Sir William Macpherson of Cluny, *The Stephen Lawrence Inquiry Report*, Cm 4264–1, TSO, London, 1999.
3 Ibid., para 28.14, p. 197.
4 Ibid., para 46.1, p. 317.
5 Scarman Report, 1981, para 4.64, p. 64, quoted in Macpherson 6.9 p. 21.

6 *Report of the Police Complaints Board 1982*, HC 278, HMSO, London, 12 April 1983, p. 1, quoted in John Benyon and John Solomos (eds), *The Roots of Urban Unrest*, Pergamon Press, Oxford, 1987, p. 5.
7   Scarman Report, para 2.3.
8   Ibid., paras 2.1–2, p. 38.
9   John Solomos, *Race and Racism in Contemporary Britain*, Macmillan, Houndmills, 1989, p. 116.
10 Scarman Report, p. 99, quoted in Simon Holdaway, *The Racialization of British Policing*, Macmillan, Houndmills, 1996, p. 128.
11 See the analysis of consultative committees in Michael Keith, 'Squaring circles', *New Community* 15: 1, pp. 63–77.
12 Lord Scarman, 'The Quest for Social Justice', in Benyon and Solomos (eds), *Roots of Urban Unrest*, p. 128.
13. See *The Broadwater Farm Inquiry: Report of an Independent Inquiry into Disturbances of October 1985 at the Broadwater Farm Estate, Tottenham*, chaired by Lord Gifford Q.C., Broadwater Farm Inquiry, 1986.
14 Macpherson Report, para 7.15, p. 38.
15 Ibid., para 7.23, p. 39.
16 Ibid., para 5.12, p. 16.
17 Ibid., para 11.1, p. 62.
18 Ibid., para 11.13, p. 63.
19 Ibid., para 19.37, p. 146.
20 Ibid., paras 19.34–19.44, pp. 145–8.
21 Ibid., para 6.34, p. 28.
22 Ibid., para 6.17, p. 22.
23 Sir Paul Condon's letter to Inquiry of 2 Oct. 1998, cited in Macpherson Report, para 6.25 p. 24.
24 Macpherson Report, para 6.48, p. 31.
25 Ibid., p. 333.

STUDY QUESTIONS

1   What do you understand by the term 'institutional racism'? How is it different from – and similar to – racism by individuals?
2   Do you think that the police/race relations situation got better or worse between 1981 and 1999?
3   In your opinion, does Hall's account support or challenge the arguments of Lea and Young (Reading 17)?

FURTHER READING

See *Further Reading* for Reading 17, but for specific information relating to the two reports referred to in the extract from Hall, see Scarman, Lord (1981) *The Brixton Disorders 10–12 April 1981: Report of an Inquiry*, Cmnd 8427, London: HMSO; Benyon, J. (ed.) (1984) *Scarman and After*, Oxford: Pergamon Press; Macpherson, Sir W. (1999) *The Stephen Lawrence Inquiry: Report of an Inquiry by Sir William Macpherson of Cluny*, London: Home Office, CM 4262–1; and Bland, N., Miller, J. and Quinton, P. (2000) *Upping the PACE: An Evaluation of the Recommendations of the Stephen Lawrence Inquiry on Stops and Searches*, London: Home Office.

19

Youth and crime

John Muncie

Having considered issues of social class and race, this reading and the next focus on the relationship between youth and crime, although attention is also given to gender differences. While Reading 20 is concerned specifically with girls' experience of violence, in the extract that follows John Muncie explores the differences *between* male and female criminal activity. Muncie provides a critique of the 'criminal career' as an explanation of youth crime and considers various explanations of, and reactions to, youth crime within criminology, by the media, and by the Home Office. As Muncie suggests, one of the strongest predictors of non-offending seems to be that of gender, as only one in six of all known young offenders is a young woman. Muncie considers the explanations for the crimes that women and girls *do* commit, and also the explanations that aim to account for the lower rates of offending by women and girls. (It is interesting to cross-reference Muncie's comments with Cavadino and Dignan's observations about crime and gender in Reading 14.) Since the 1970s, and following feminist influence within criminology, one explanation for the differential crime experiences of women/girls and men/boys that has gained favour is that the dominant ideologies of femininity encourage conformity in women and girls. More recently (since the early 1990s), the (associated) 'threat' of masculinity has also become part of discussions of crime both within and outside academia. As well as considering issues of gender, Muncie looks at the relevance of class to understanding young people's involvement in crime. Elsewhere in the book from which this extract is taken he takes this further in relation to youth subculture where he also considers race and ethnicity.

PATTERNS OF OFFENDING AND NON-OFFENDING

Despite the shortcomings of official statistics, self reports and victim surveys, it remains widely assumed that age is a major indicator of involvement in crime.

SOURCE: From *Youth and Crime: A Critical Introduction* (London: Sage, 1999), 23–34.

Because proportionately more ethnic minority and working-class youth and fewer female youth are dealt with by the youth justice system it is also believed that the crime problem is predominantly a problem of young males from lower social class and ethnic minority communities. This focus on youth has also encouraged research into how criminal careers are formed and developed. In popular idiom, the 'truant of today' will eventually be the 'criminal of tomorrow'. And for a small number, offending will not be transient, but will be both frequent and persistent. This section provides a critical assessment of these 'taken-for-granted' notions.

Criminal Careers

The 'criminal career' approach suggests that offending is part of an extended continuum of anti-social behaviour that first arises in childhood, persists into adulthood and is then reproduced in successive generations (Farrington, 1994). Whilst offending by the vast majority of young people is believed to be widespread, much of this is transient and minor, arising from 'having fun' and rowdyism rather than from any calculated decision to engage in criminality. Nevertheless the chance of acquiring at least one criminal conviction during a lifetime affects four out of 10 males and one in 10 females. But according to Farrington (1996) a relatively small number – about 5 per cent of males – become 'chronic offenders' who then go on to account for about a half of all known offending. One of the most ambitious projects to investigate why delinquency begins and to assess how far criminality can be predicted was the Cambridge Study in Delinquent Development. In 1961 a sample of 411 working-class boys aged eight was selected from six primary schools in Camberwell, London. Girls were not included. Only 12 were from ethnic minorities. They were contacted again when aged 10, 14, 16, 18, 21, 25 and 32 to examine which of them had developed a 'delinquent way of life' and why some had continued a 'life of crime' into adulthood. About a fifth of the sample had been convicted of criminal offences as juveniles and over a third by the time they were 32. But half of the total convictions were amassed by only 23 young men – less than 6 per cent of the sample. Most of these 'chronic offenders' shared common childhood characteristics. They were more likely to have been rated as troublesome, impulsive and dishonest at primary school. They tended to come from poorer, larger families and were more likely to have criminal parents. They had also experienced harsh or erratic parental discipline. Six variables were eventually suggested by the researchers as predictors of future criminality (Farrington, 1989):

- socio-economic deprivation (e.g. low family income/poor housing);
- poor parenting and family conflict;
- criminal and anti-social families;
- low intelligence and school failure;

- hyperactivity/impulsivity/attention deficiency;
- anti-social behaviour (e.g. heavy drinking, drug taking, promiscuous sex).

In addition those convicted at an early age (10–13) tended to become the most persistent offenders. On this basis Farrington (1994: 566) contends that future 'chronic offenders' could have been identified with reasonable accuracy at the age of 10. He argues that

> children from poorer families are likely to offend because they are less able to achieve their goals legally and because they value some goals (e.g. excitement) especially highly. Children with low intelligence are more likely to offend because they tend to fail in school. Impulsive children … are more likely to offend because they do not give sufficient consideration and weight to the possible consequences. Children who are exposed to poor child rearing behaviour, disharmony or separation on the part of their parents are likely to offend because they do not build up internal controls over socially disapproved behaviour, while children from criminal families and those with delinquent friends tend to build up anti-authority attitudes and the belief that offending is justifiable. The whole process is self-perpetuating. (Farrington, 1994: 558–9)

Using the same sample Farrington, Barnes and Lambert (1996) subsequently maintained that if children had a convicted parent by the time they were 10 then that was the 'best predictor' of them becoming criminal and anti-social themselves. Criminal behaviour, it was argued, was transmitted from parents to children: crime runs in the family.

Using an ethnographic, rather than statistical and personality measurement approach, Foster's (1990) study, which spanned the generations in one area of south-east London in the early 1980s, also found that parental attitudes to education, street life and crime were replicated (through subtle processes of parental reinforcement) by their children. Youth crime served as an apprenticeship to adult offending when, for example, techniques could be learnt to minimize the risks of detection and arrest. But all this occurred in a context whereby many of their illegal activities were not considered as crime: 'these were not criminal "careers", just ordinary people whose everyday world took for granted certain kinds of crime' (Foster, 1990: 165). As a result, whilst the Cambridge study is a good example of the degree to which various social and personality factors correlate statistically with 'known' offending, it fails to capture the broader context in which such offending takes place. It assumes that legal definitions of crime are shared by all communities. Foster's analysis shows clearly that this is not the case. The issue becomes not simply one of lawbreaking, but of conflicting cultural and moral values embedded in different material realities. Moreover, the Cambridge study substantiates public concern about lower-class criminality, but only because the range of other types of criminal activity typically associated with white collar and corporate crime are not identified as problematic. It may be able to shed some light on the characteristics of those offenders who are recorded in the official statistics, but tells us little about the extent, causes and meaning of offending *per se*.

From a different theoretical perspective, Craine and Coles (1995) used the concept of 'career' to explore how young people in inner city Manchester coped with unemployment and social deprivation in the 1980s and the realization that the prospect of a traditional 'career' in the formal labour market had largely disappeared. The alternative 'careers' that were developed included market trading and social security fraud (working and claiming), 'fencing' stolen goods, unlicensed street trading, acting as 'lookouts', 'touting' and 'hustling'. As with Foster's (1990) informants, these 'edge of crime' activities were regarded as quite legitimate. For some this ethos may have heralded a progression to organized shoplifting, robbery and drug dealing whereby crime came to be a major means of earning a living. But, above all, the 'drift into crime did not involve a major moral dilemma for the young people concerned. Rather it was the result of a series of incremental choices to access the alternative opportunity structures around them' (Craine and Coles, 1995: 20). The picture of 'crime careers' painted by the Cambridge study is one of inadequate and morally damaged individuals. For Craine and Coles it is a matter of young people reacting rationally to the (lack of) opportunities available to them.

Persistent Offending

one-boy crime wave (Daily Mail, 10 September 1992)

Hardcore child super crooks are bringing fear to Britain's streets … they are our number one crime problem … they account for 90 per cent of offences. (Daily Star, 30 November 1992)

ratboy: a 14 year old becomes a byword for trouble. (Independent, 9 October 1993)

criminial mastermind, 14, mocks police force (Times, 3 September 1995)

1,000 burglaries by teenage gang (Daily Telegraph, 23 March 1997)

From mid 1991 onwards stories appeared regularly in the press about some young people who it was argued were so involved in crime that they seemed to account for much of the crime in the areas where they lived (Newburn, 1996: 69). The epitome of this was 'Ratboy'. Alleged to have committed 55 offences by the time he was 14, one boy in north-east England first came to the notice of the police, when he was 10, for burglary. After two cautions his parents volunteered him for local authority care, from which he absconded 37 times. In February 1993 he was found hiding in a ventilation duct. A local newspaper could not print his name, so invented the nickname Ratboy. Next day he was front page national news. With the construction of images of sewers, of a hidden underworld and of secret tunnels running beneath the urban landscape, the boy became a symbol of all juvenile crime against which the police and courts were 'impotent' to act (despite the existence of local authority secure units). But in many other respects the boy did not live up to the prevailing stereotypes of dangerous and outcast youth. He did not come from a broken home ... he was not violent ... he did not grow up in some 'urban wasteland' ... he became a 'symbol surrounded by clichés' (*Independent*, 9 October 1993).

Again it is worth noting that such fears are not new. In the mid 1970s the Magistrates' Association had warned of 'a minority of tough, sophisticated young criminals ... who deride the powerlessness of the courts to do anything effective' (cited by Rutherford, 1986: 61).

Such clichés once more fed into a growing public and political concern about *persistent* young offenders in the 1990s. In July 1992 a Home Affairs Committee was established to inquire into all aspects of juvenile crime and the youth justice system, looking in particular at the 'problems of persistent offenders' (HAC, 1993: vii). Noting conflicting evidence from the Association of Chief Police Officers (ACPO) which claimed that the rate of juvenile offending had *increased* by 54 per cent during the 1980s and Home Office statistics which had recorded a 37 per cent *decrease*, the Committee tentatively concluded that

> one possible explanation ... is a growth in the numbers of persistent offenders ... If there is a small but growing number of juvenile offenders responsible for many offences, it is possible to reconcile the indisputable fact that the number (and rate, to a lesser extent) of known juvenile offenders has fallen over time with the more speculative assertion that the number of offences committed by juveniles has risen. (HAC, 1993: xii)

Asked to provide specific numbers, ACPO suggested it was 'a very, very small handful'. A survey of all police forces eventually came up with the number of 106 (HAC, 1993: xiii).

In March 1993 the Home Secretary announced his intention to introduce a new sentence, the secure training order, and a new institution, the secure training centre, to deal with those children aged 12, 13 or 14 identified as seriously persistent juvenile offenders. It was notable that this commitment was made some time before Home Office sponsored researchers into the issue had had time to report. Hagell and Newburn (1994) assessed the extent of 'persistence' by sampling all those 10–16 year olds arrested three times or more in 1992 in one Midlands county and two London boroughs. Of a total of 531, 74 were also eventually interviewed. Fourteen per cent were girls. The most common offences were traffic, non-residential burglary, theft from shops and car theft. Violent offences were exceedingly rare, as was offence *specialization* (such as burglary and car theft). The mean number of offences per reoffender was 5.6, with the majority committing three 'known' offences. Only two had committed more than 40. On the basis of such data Hagell and Newburn (1994) further query the possibility of arriving at some objective definition of 'persistence'. They compared three definitions:

1   those top 10 per cent of 10–16 year olds who were arrested and known to have committed offences or alleged to have committed offences in one year;
2   those 10–16 year olds who were known or alleged to have committed 10 or more offences in three months;

3   those 12–14 year olds who had committed three or more offences punishable by imprisonment, one of which having been committed whilst subject to a supervision order (the secure training order criteria).

Inevitably, no two definitions of 'persistence' produced similar figures and in particular they often did not identify the same individuals. The first two definitions led to the identification of 30 'persistent offenders', but 15 identified by definition 1 did not appear in definition 2. Twenty-five offenders met the third definition. Only eight were identified by all three. Similarly, Crowley's (1998) study of three local authorities found only 10 young offenders who would meet the secure training order criteria and that whilst the vast majority had experienced disrupted educational histories and were already 'known' by the social services, it was impossible to define these offenders as being of a particular 'type'. Most young reoffenders are not 'hard core' in the sense of being continually engaged in serious crime, but are more likely to be repeated minor offenders. Hagell and Newburn (1994: 122) concluded that 'a discrete group of persistent offenders cannot be identified' and that 'any definition of persistence will inevitably be arbitrary'.

Moreover, interviews with the most persistent offenders revealed stories of chaotic and disruptive lives, time spent in children's homes, school exclusions and psychological intervention or counselling: 'what they hoped for in the future was to settle down, have families and find work. What they saw in the future was usually less rosy' (Hagell and Newburn, 1994: 130; Crowley, 1998). Nevertheless the image of a 'persistent hard core' of 'superpredators' (*Sunday Times*, 16 February 1997) continued to feed popular and political debates throughout the 1990s. Despite widespread criticism from agencies and organizations working with young offenders (Children's Society, 1993), the secure training centres proposed by the Conservatives were first condemned and then supported by the New Labour government of 1997. The first opened in 1998.

The question of persistence has also been tackled from another angle: that is that intervention at an early age – particularly in the form of secure institutions – is unlikely to prevent reoffending and may only succeed in cementing 'criminal careers'. In Crowley's (1998) sample more than a half had spent time in institutional care. Bailey et al. (1994) found that of all those sent to a secure unit 80 per cent had previously been in local authority care. Only 7 per cent had had no previous psychological or psychiatric contact. Similarly Boswell (1995) found that 91 per cent of all 10–17 year olds who had committed the most serious offences had experienced abuse or loss in their earlier life. Criminal convictions can have substantial long-term consequences, not only in terms of gaining access to housing or employment, but also in informing the courts' attitude to dealing with further offences. Reoffending rates on leaving secure units are also high – estimated by NAJC (1993) to be between 70 and 80 per cent.

This suggests that some types of intervention are not only inappropriate, but may also encourage the kinds of behaviour that they are designed to treat or deter.

Young Women as Non-offenders?

Farrington (1996) contends that those factors that are known to protect young people against offending include having a resilient temperament, an affectionate relationship with at least one parent, parents who provide effective and consistent discipline and maintain a strong interest in their children's education. However, one of the strongest predictors of non-offending seems to be that of gender. Only one in six of all known young offenders is a young woman. In general their crimes are also less serious, with theft and handling stolen goods by far the most common. Such data have led Newburn and Stanko (1994: 1) to observe that 'the most significant fact about crime is that it is almost always committed by men'. Nevertheless some reservations about the validity of such a bald statement should be noted. Self report studies, for example, suggest that although fewer girls than boys do break the law, the difference is not marked. Anne Campbell (1981: 22) notes that whilst official statistics in 1976 produced a ratio of male to female offending of 8.95 : 1, results from self reports of 16 year old schoolgirls showed a ratio of 1.33 : 1. She argues that when young women commit crime they follow the same pattern as young men in terms of which acts they commit. In contrast, Walklate's (1995: 6) review of the statistical data concludes that while 'men and women commit similar crimes albeit at different rates, women appear to commit the more serious crimes at a much lesser rate than men'. This is even more the case when the largely hidden crimes of domestic violence are taken into consideration. Moreover as Graham and Bowling's self report study (1995: 28) found, the rate of offending for young women peaks earlier and recedes at an earlier age than that of young men. So although at ages 14–17 the male : female ratio of offending may be just 1.4 : 1, by the ages of 22–25 it is 11 : 1.

It is clear then that even though it would be misleading to view young women as non-offenders, significant gender based differences in rates and frequency of offending still need to be explored. Until the 1970s the most common form of explanation of female crime was firmly tied to biology. For example, Cowie et al. (1968) linked female delinquency to abnormal 'hormonal balance' and argued that 'sex chromosome constitution is one of the basic factors determining liability to delinquency'. West (1967) accounted for girls' deviance in psychodynamic rather than social terms: wayward girls are likely to show neurotic symptoms and 'psychopathic traits', he argued. The dominance of such biologically based analyses is reflected again in the widespread assumption that the delinquency of young women is related to 'deviant' sexuality, promiscuity and/or prostitution.

Thus delinquent girls are viewed as doubly deviant: delinquent for breaking the law and abnormal for contradicting dominant feminine roles. In court, they are much more likely to be declared in need of 'care, protection and control' than boys [...]. Their behaviour continues to be judged differently, and by different standards. Much of this is a hangover from a psychological approach to youth developed at the turn of the century. Traditionally adolescent boys have been seen primarily as ambitious, and in need of mental growth and challenge, while adolescent girls were viewed as emotional, prone to weepiness, flirtatious and in need of social protection (Frith, 1984: 50).

Since the 1970s many of these assumptions have been challenged by a feminist critique of both traditional and contemporary youth studies. Such a critique has pointed out not only that issues of female deviance have generally been neglected (most studies are of boys) but also that the prevalence of psychological interpretations has led to some gross distortions of patterns of young women's conformity and deviance (McRobbie, 1978, 1980; Heidensohn, 1985). The new feminist studies have argued in particular that gender roles are socially constructed rather than biologically determined, and have revealed the key role played by dominant ideologies of femininity in shaping the differential experiences and responses of young women to their position of structured subordination. In accounting for lower rates of offending, recent enquiries have focused on questions of culture, ideology and social control. For example, Sue Lees (1986) has detailed how masculine and feminine behaviours are subject to different social rules and operate according to different norms. Characteristically these act to constrain girls' behaviour to a much larger degree than boys'. For instance, girls' potential income and spending power is lower than that of boys. Parents guard girls' leisure time much more closely. Through a variety of informal means of control emanating largely from a sexual division of labour, girls' behaviour outside the home is carefully constrained. In turn, such controls are linked to dominant ideologies about women's natural place being in the home, revolving around a culture of domesticity rather than street based leisure or employment. A key element in the construction of these gender related opportunities is the different ways in which male and female sexuality is defined. While it is expected that boys will 'sow their wild oats', the implications for girls of becoming known as receivers of the 'wild oats' is often drastic and irreversible. A long list of derogatory labels – slag, slut, scrubber, whore, easy lay – awaits the independent or promiscuous girl, terms for which there are no male alternatives. To remain 'respectable', young women must suppress their sexual desire. This double standard of sexual morality is central to explaining women's subordination within a 'natural career' of marriage, home and children, and continually acts to restrict young women's freedom of movement (Lees, 1986: 82).

There is indeed a continuity of control in women's offending and non-offending lives (Heidensohn, 1985). Small rises in the recorded crime rate for young adult women may be enough to spark off a moral panic about girl gangs menacing the streets, targeting other groups of women, as indeed did happen in 1993–4 (*Guardian*, 25 November 1994). The predictable result was that the numbers of young women in prison increased from 140 in 1992 to 223 in 1994 and 252 in 1997. All were held in wings of adult prisons. In 1997 there were no separate young female offender institutions in England and Wales. Young women, it seems, are not immune to authoritarian state responses: indeed custody 'lays them open to the pains of adult imprisonment before their time' (*Youth Justice Newsletter*, no. 6, 1997).

Violent Crime: 'Yobs' and Aggressive Masculinity?

As we have noted, violent crimes against the person account for approximately 10 per cent of all recorded young offending. In 1995 15,000 14–20 year old males were found guilty or cautioned for such offences, compared to 3,600 young women. Overall men account for nearly nine out of every 10 people found guilty of indictable offences and are responsible for 92 per cent of convicted cases of violence against the person. Statistics such as these have long been available, but it is only in the past decade that it has seriously been suggested that the problem of crime may indeed be a 'problem of men'; or perhaps more precisely termed a problem of 'maverick masculinities'. This academic interest coincided with increasing public and political concern about the apparently growing anti-social behaviour of the young urban male which the Prime Minister referred to in 1994 as a 'yob culture'. As Ros Coward (1994: 32) recalls:

> yob is a species of young white working class male which if the British media is to be believed, is more common than ever before. The yob is foul mouthed, irresponsible, probably unemployed and violent. The yob hangs around council estates where he terrorises the local inhabitants, possibly in the company of his pit-bull terrier. He fathers children rather than cares for them. He is often drunk, probably uses drugs and is likely to be involved in crime, including domestic violence. He is the ultimate expression of macho values: mad, bad and dangerous to know.

Such images pervaded the crime discourse of the early 1990s; they captured the real and imaginary fears of the time. And as Coward (1994: 33) argues, the yob came to carry the 'weight of a masculinity' which was deemed to be unacceptable. Not that such images were at all new. The 'yob' has been regularly demonized since Victorian times and has most recently been found in the black-leathered bike rider of the 1960s 'rocker', in the 'mindless mentality' of the 1970s football hooligan and in the 'boorish' lager lout of the 1990s. But in the 1990s images of the 'yob', as Coward (1994) contends, were to a degree legitimized by right-wing notions of a dangerous underclass (Murray, 1990) and by feminist critiques of masculinity (Campbell, 1993). For Murray, unmarried and unemployed men are akin to primitive beasts lacking any civilizing influence. For Beatrix Campbell the 'threat' of masculinity is more complex. Her analysis of the various riots of 1991 in Britain's working-class housing estates draws attention to what was 'self-evident' but publicly rarely acknowledged: they were perpetuated in the main by young men. While public debate circulated between unmarried mothers failing to exercise control over their male offspring, and unemployment and urban deprivation creating legions of the dispossessed, Campbell (1993) stresses how the abandonment of certain communities by the state has not caused a crisis of masculinity, but unleashed it in extreme forms. Young men on council estates became engaged in a militaristic culture of crime: celebrating war and force as ways of sorting things out

(Campbell, 1993: 323). Unemployment had denied men access to legitimate masculine status. Joyriding, drugs, ram raiding, burglary or rioting on the streets became the key means by which *young men* in economically deprived areas could assert themselves as men. In contrast, Campbell argues, *young women* responded to the same circumstances of deprivation by forging self help and constructive solidarities and provided the only means through which their communities could be sustained. Moreover, she contends that on the streets, and particularly in the context of car crime, joyriding and police chases, it is a similar display of masculinity that is being expressed by the perpetrators and the law enforcement agencies alike.

Indeed crime, rather than being abnormal, can provide an avenue to express some socially revered values. Stan Cohen was one of the first to note that 'we must realise that some of our most cherished social values – individualism, *masculinity*, competitiveness – are the same ones that generate crime' (Cohen, 1973: 622, italics added). Or as Connell (1995) contends, violence and crime are key contexts in which a particular collective conception of masculinity is 'made'.

Such notions have also been applied to youth crime through the study of football hooliganism. Dunning et al. (1988) argue that 'aggressive masculinity' is not only tolerated in some lower-working class communities, but is positively sanctioned as an 'important source of meaning, status and pleasurable emotional arousal' (Dunning et al., 1988: 210). This is not to deny that male violence does not exist elsewhere, indeed it is a common characteristic of all social classes, but it takes on a particularly visible form in those groups who are excluded from the status to be found in educational and occupational success. However, openly violent behaviour is rarely uncontrolled or random. It takes place in specific places and in culturally approved contexts, to the degree that perpetrators of indiscriminate violence are liable to be labelled 'nutters' by their peers (Dunning et al., 1988: 212).

Trying to find 'violent crime' predominantly in 'masculinity' remains a vexed issue. Coward (1994: 35), for example, notes how the equation has simply 'become a way of attacking the least powerful men in our society'. Indeed demonizing the 'yob' can serve to hide the continuities between their behaviour and that of other men (Walklate, 1995: 179). Similarly Stanko (1994) argues that the discourse of male violence is fixated on the predatory crimes of the street. Not only does this tend to overlook the fact that working-class male youth are likely to be both the perpetrators *and* victims of such crime, but it detracts from the hidden violence used by men against women in the home. A focus on *masculinity* denies that there may be many and varied masculinities (Connell, 1995). It also ignores female violence. Campbell's (1981) study of 251 16 year old schoolgirls, for example, found that 89 per cent of them had been involved in at least one physical fight. The key variable may ideed not be gender alone, but, as Segal (1990: 27) contends, how gender and class combine to reflect back the 'increased barbarism' created by the social divisions and inequalities of contemporary capitalism.

REFERENCES

Bailey, S., Thornton, L. and Weaver, A. (1994) 'The first 100 admissions to an adolescent secure unit', *Journal of Adolescence*, vol. 17, pp. 207–20.

Boswell, G. (1995) *Violent Victims*, London, Prince's Trust.

Campbell, A. (1981) *Girl Delinquents*, Oxford, Blackwell.

Campbell, B. (1993) *Goliath: Britain's Dangerous Places*, London, Methuen.

Children's Society (1993) *A False Sense of Security*, London, Children's Society.

Cohen, S. (1973) 'The failures of criminology', *The Listener*, 8 November, pp. 622–5.

Connell, R.W. (1995) *Masculinities*, Cambridge, Polity Press.

Coward, R. (1994) 'Whipping boys', *Guardian Weekend*, 3 September, pp. 32–5.

Cowie, J., Cowie, V. and Slater, E. (1968) *Delinquency in Girls*, London, Heinemann.

Craine, S. and Coles, B. (1995) 'Alternative careers: youth transitions and young people's involvement in crime', *Youth and Policy*, no. 48, pp. 6–27.

Crowley, A. (1998) *A Criminal Waste: A Study of Child Offenders Eligible for Secure Training Centres*, London, Children's Society.

Dunning, E., Murphy, P. and Williams, J. (1988) *The Roots of Football Hooliganism*, London, Routledge.

Farrington, D. (1989) 'The origins of crime: the Cambridge study of delinquent development', Home Office Research and Planning Unit, Research Bulletin, no. 27, London, HMSO, pp. 29–33.

Farrington, D. (1994) 'Human development and criminal careers', in Maguire, M., Morgan, R. and Reiner, R. (eds) *The Oxford Handbook of Criminology*, Oxford, Clarendon.

Farrington, D. (1996) *Understanding and Preventing Youth Crime*, Social Policy Research Findings, no. 93, York, Joseph Rowntree Foundation.

Farrington, D., Barnes, G. and Lambert, S. (1996) 'The concentration of offending in families', *Legal and Criminological Psychology*, vol. 1, pp. 47–63.

Foster, J. (1990) *Villains*, London, Routledge.

Frith, S. (1984) *The Sociology of Youth*, Ormskirk, Causeway.

Graham, J. and Bowling, B. (1995) *Young People and Crime*, Home Office Research Study no. 145, London, HMSO.

HAC (Home Affairs Committee) (1993) *Juvenile Offenders*, Sixth Report, London, HMSO.

Hagell, A. and Newburn, T. (1994) *Persistent Young Offenders*, London, Policy Studies Institute.

Heidensohn, F. (1985) *Women and Crime*, London, Macmillan.

Lees, S. (1986) *Losing Out: Sexuality and Adolescent Girls*, London, Hutchinson.

McRobbie, A. (1978) 'Working class girls and the culture of femininity', in Centre for Contemporary Cultural Studies, *Women Take Issue*, London, Hutchinson.

McRobbie, A. (1980) 'Settling accounts with subcultures: a feminist critique', *Screen Education*. no. 34, pp. 37–49.

Murray, C. (1990) *The Emerging Underclass*, London, Institute of Economic Affairs.

NAJC (1993) *Creating More Criminals*, Briefing Paper no. 1, June, London, New Approaches to Juvenile Crime.

Newburn, T. (1996) 'Back to the future? Youth crime, youth justice and the rediscovery of "authoritarian populism"', in Pilcher, J. and Wagg, S. (eds) *Thatcher's Children*, London, Falmer.

Newburn, T. and Stanko, E. (eds) (1994) *Just Boys Doing Business?* London, Routledge.

Rutherford, A. (1986) *Growing out of Crime*, Harmondsworth, Penguin.

Segal, L. (1990) *Slow Motion: Changing Masculinities, Changing Men*, London, Virago.

Stanko, E.A. (1994) 'Challenging the problem of men's individual violence', in Newburn, T. and Stanko, B. (eds) *Just Boys Doing Business?*, London, Routledge.

Walklate, S. (1995) *Gender and Crime: An Introduction*, Hemel Hempstead, Prentice-Hall/Harvester.

West, D. (1967) *The Young Offender*, Harmondsworth, Penguin.

STUDY QUESTIONS

1   How would you define the term 'deviant career'? Is this a useful way to account for and explain crime by young people?

2   Why are 'delinquent girls' (and criminal women) seen as 'doubly deviant'? How do you account for lower rates of offending among girls and women?

3   From your reading of this piece and others (e.g. Readings 1 and 11) would you say that the 'threat' of masculinity is a new concern?

FURTHER READING

The subcultural affiliations of young people, and their involvement in crime and deviance, provide the subject for a wide array of studies. Among the 'classics' are Hall, S. and Jefferson, T. (1976) *Resistance through Rituals: Youth Subcultures in Post-war Britain*, London: Hutchinson; and Willis, P. (1977) *Learning to Labour*, London: Saxon House. Phil Cohen's extensive body of work on the subject has been collected together in Cohen, P. (1997) *Rethinking the Youth Question*, Basingstoke: Macmillan. A comprehensive study of juvenile delinquency, incorporating sociological and psychological approaches, can be found in Rutter, M., Giller, H. and Hagell, A. (1998) *Antisocial Behaviour by Young People*, Cambridge: Cambridge University Press. Other good texts in this area are Furlong, A. and Cartmel, F. (1997) *Young People and Social Change*, Buckingham: Open University Press; Brown, S. (1998) *Understanding Youth and Crime: Listening to Youth?* Buckingham: Open University Press; and, for an 'official' assessment with policy recommendations, The Audit Commission (1996) *Misspent Youth: Young People and Crime*, London: Audit Commission.

20

The myth of girl gangs

Susan Batchelor

Susan Batchelor reports on a study concerned to explore violence and
violent behaviour from the perspective of girls which was undertaken in
Scotland by herself and colleagues. In this reading Batchelor also reports
on the media interest in, and response to, the study. The findings from the
study support the view that violence by girls is *not* a major social problem.
The study focuses on violence perpetrated by girls, violence experienced by
girls and violence witnessed by girls. Despite this, the press characterized
the project as 'a study of violent girls' and some newspapers went so far
as to misquote the research to support their assumption that violence by
girls (especially within 'gangs') is on the increase.

Headlines about 'girl gangs' roaming the streets and randomly attacking
innocent victims have been a recurring feature of the pages of our newspapers.
In such reports, 'girl violence' has been presented as becoming commonplace. Yet
the everyday experience of girls presents a very different picture of the nature
and extent of violence in girls' lives. Drawing on press coverage of a recent study
of 'ordinary' girls' views and experiences of violence, this [chapter] will examine
the main differences between media and real life images of girls and violence.

WHAT THE RESEARCH SAID

A View from the Girls: Exploring Violence and Violent Behaviour (ESRC funded)
was a study developed within the context of a perceived increase in violent and
aggressive behaviour by girls, fuelled by considerable media attention. In spite
of this attention, we knew very little about the nature and extent of violent
behaviour by girls, or the impact of violence in their lives. There are several reasons for this lack of knowledge, but the main one is that violence is overwhelmingly committed by men. Violence by women is rare: in Scotland in 1998,
only seven-and-a-half per cent of those found guilty of non-sexual crimes of
violence were female – a total of 412 women (Scottish Executive, 1999).

SOURCE: From *Criminal Justice Matters*, 43 (2001), 26–7.

The findings from the girls and violence study support the view that violence by girls is not a major social problem. We found little evidence to suggest that girls are using physical violence to any great extent, since only a very small proportion of girls (five per cent) reported being routinely physically violent towards others. Perhaps most notably, we did not find any evidence of the existence of girl gangs. Not one of the 800 teenage girls that took part in the research claimed to be in a girl gang, nor did they know of anyone else who was a member. (Most researchers believe that a 'gang' must have a name, identifiable 'colours', a formal authority structure, and, perhaps most importantly, endurance over time. See Campbell, 1995, for further discussion.)

What our research did find was that girls' ideas about 'what counts' as violence did not correspond with adult or legal views. A common understanding of violence is of an intentionally harmful, interpersonal physical act, such as punching or kicking. This was challenged by many of the girls that we spoke to, who maintained that verbal behaviours (such as name-calling, threats and intimidation) were often intended and experienced as potentially more hurtful and damaging than physical violence.

Girls also considered the context in which a particular act occurs as important. Physical fights between brothers and sisters within the home were not seen as 'violent' in the same way as fights taking place between other young people outside the home, no matter how serious. Such fighting (between siblings) was reported as a frequent occurrence, accounting for 59 per cent of the violence reported by girls.

Witnessing physical violence was another common experience. The vast majority of girls reported having witnessed some form of interpersonal physical violence at firsthand, and nearly two-thirds knew someone who had been hurt by physical violence. In the majority of cases, such incidents involved young people from their local neighbourhood.

WHAT THE PAPERS SAID

Long before fieldwork began, the girls and violence study attracted an immense amount of media interest, and this continued throughout its duration. At times, we were fielding up to 25 media enquiries per week. Newsworthiness is the key to understanding the intensity of media coverage. British national newspapers have always looked towards crime, particularly violent crime, to generate a strong supply of 'good stories'. The problem is that much crime is mundane. Newspapers get round this problem by focusing on atypical and dramatic cases. 'Girl violence' is newsworthy because of the gender of the offender, not the crime she has committed. It epitomises everything that challenges the way in which 'nice girls' behave. This is in stark contrast to the presumed naturalness of men's aggression: nowhere is the violence of young men reported as 'boy violence'.

Press coverage consistently depicted the project as a study developed in response to the 'problem' of violence by young women ('Concern at girls and violence – Study investigates female aggression', *The Herald*, 20/10/98). High profile cases were cited as evidence of a growing trend of girl thugs and these were spuriously linked to the research project ('Teen project looks at torture case', *Greenock Telegraph*, 4/5/98). Coverage of these cases typically consisted of a brief account of isolated incidents, with little or no detail or background information.

Following the launch of the findings, newspapers took a range of 'angles' on the key messages of the research. Some focused on girls' fear of sexual assault ('Girls live in fear of sexual attack', *The Herald*, 30/9/00), the impact of verbal abuse and fall outs between friends ('Girls fear losing their friends more than rape', *Sunday Herald*, 24/9/00), and girls' everyday experience of violence ('Violence is just a fact of life say teenage girls', *Daily Telegraph*, 7/10/00). It could be argued that these headlines broadly represent the key findings outlined above. However, a closer reading indicates an over-reliance on existing media templates (e.g. the threat of sexual violence and the escalation/normalisation of physical violence) and careless use of 'hard' quantitative data. For example, one report claimed that 'four out of ten [girls] had been beaten up'. Whilst our findings did report that 41 per cent of girls from the self-report survey had been the victim of physical violence, we were careful to explain that this meant they had been hit, kicked or punched by someone on at least one occasion. This finding has to be considered in light of the qualitative data, which suggests that the majority of such incidents occur between siblings in the home.

Newspaper reports also used horror stories and unusual case studies to illustrate the research findings. One newspaper claimed that 'One girl said she was too scared to leave the house for fear of being attacked. Another described how a girl gang member had held a knife to the throat of her best friend'. Not only were these two incidents reported inaccurately (one girl told us she was afraid to leave the house for fear of being sexually attacked and another told us of a friend who had a knife held to his throat by another young man), they were atypical events and by no means represented the common experience of girls. This suggests a difficulty on the part of journalists, who are working to tight deadlines and strict word limits, in engaging with crucial contextual information.

MISQUOTING RESEARCH

Another 'angle' adopted by the press involved misquoting the research to back up the girl gang story ('Deadly as the males – Experts probe explosion of violence by girl gangs', *Daily Record*, 30/9/00). The report appearing in the *Daily Record*, Scotland's biggest selling newspaper, claimed that: 'The shocking extent of violence among teenage girls in Scotland was revealed yesterday. A study found girl gangs taking part in unprovoked attacks is now commonplace'. The article went on to allege that 'The number of violent crimes committed by girl thugs in Scotland has almost doubled in the last decade'. Unsurprisingly, the reporter did not cite the source of this data. If we look at the official figures for the last eleven years (1987–1997), we can see that the number of women convicted of violent offending in Scotland has increased, but only by 15 per cent (that is, 38 additional cases). The comparable figure for men is an increase of 26 per cent, or 818 cases (Scottish Executive, letter, 21 April 1999). It is worth noting that, because the number of violent crimes committed by women is so low, a very small number of cases can make a great deal of difference in terms of percentage rises.

SO WHAT?

Whenever I tell people about the subject of my research, they virtually always respond with an urban myth about a friend of a friend who was the victim of a girl gang, or alternatively they put forward the 'common-sense' view that girls are becoming more violent. The main problem with misrepresenting the reality of girls' lives is that it can contribute to unrealistic public attitudes, which in turn can create misdirected public policy. The media fondness for relying on simplified statistics and atypical cases precludes any discussion of the complex sociospecific contexts of violence in girls' lives. As young women are demonised by the media, their genuine problems can be marginalised and ignored. Indeed, it is the girls who have become the problem.

REFERENCES

Campbell, A. (1995) 'Creating a Girl Gang Problem', *Criminal Justice Matters*, 19: 8–9.
Scottish Executive (1999) *Criminal Proceedings in the Scottish Courts, 1998* (CrJ/1999/8). Edinburgh: Scottish Executive.

STUDY QUESTIONS

1 Why do you think the Scottish media were so interested in the issue of 'girl gangs'?
2 How does the press coverage in this case compare to that of the nineteenth-century 'hooligan' discussed by Pearson in Reading 1?
3 To what extent does this reading support the notion (expressed in Readings 7, 11 and 12) that crime news is 'manufactured'?
4 How does Batchelor et al.'s study challenge our ideas of 'what counts as violence'?

FURTHER READING

The best-known texts on girls and youth cultures are McRobbie, A. (1978) 'Working class girls and the culture of femininity', in Centre for Contemporary Cultural Studies, *Women Take Issue*, London: Hutchinson; McRobbie, A. (1991) *Feminism and Youth Culture*, London: Macmillan; Campbell, A. (1981) *Girl Delinquents*, Oxford: Blackwell; and Campbell, A. (1984) *The Girls in the Gang*, Oxford: Blackwell, the latter about girl gang members in New York. Two articles that demonstrate some of the same myths and stereotypes encountered by Batchelor et al. appeared in *Criminal Justice Matters*, vol. 19, in 1995: 'Creating a girl gang problem' by A. Campbell; and 'Troublesome young women' by A. Worrall. Sue Lees (1993) *Sugar and Spice: Sexuality and Adolescent Girls*, Harmondsworth: Penguin, is interesting for its focus on the sexualization of young boys and girls. See Ditton, J. and Duffy, J. (1983) 'Bias in the newspaper reporting of crime news', *British Journal of Criminology*, vol. 3, no. 2, for further attention to bias in the press. Further suggestions for reading in this area are made by Muncie, J. (1999) *Youth and Cime: A Critical Introduction*, London: Sage (see Reading 19).

21

Ordinary experiences

Elizabeth A. Stanko

So far in Part III we have focused mostly on the differential rates of offending and non-offending by different groups of people, and the responses of law-enforcement agencies and the wider society. However, some attention has also been given to the perspective and experience of victims. In this reading and the next, the concern is with both victims and perpetrators of crimes of sexual and physical violence. Although the focus here is on gender differences, it is also important to consider other groups within society that may be vulnerable to this kind of attack. For example, as Furlong and Cartmel (1997: 93; see *Further Reading* for Reading 19) note, 'the concentration on young people as the perpetrators of crimes has left us blind to the extent to which young people are victims...'.

In this extract, Elizabeth A. Stanko argues that, within male-dominated society, women's experience of sexual and physical violence at the hands of men can appear normal and 'ordinary', and she suggests that a common theme throughout women's descriptions of everyday encounters with men is that of powerlessness. Stanko considers some of the explanations for this and also outlines some of the reasons why it is hard for women to resist and challenge this treatment. She provides a critique of victimology, an approach which has traditionally examined the psychological characteristics and social circumstances or lifestyles of those most likely to find themselves the victims of crime. Stanko argues that this approach often implies 'victim culpability' and denies the commonality and possibility of sexual and/or physical assault within the lives of *all* women.

To be a woman – in most societies, in most eras – is to experience physical and/or sexual terrorism at the hands of men. Our everyday behaviour reflects our precautions, the measures we take to protect ourselves. We are wary of

SOURCE: From *Intimate Intrusions: Women's Experience of Male Violence* (London: Routledge and Kegan Paul, 1985), 9–19.

going out at night, even in our own neighbourhoods. We are warned by men and other women not to trust strangers. But somehow they forget to warn us about men we know: our fathers, our acquaintances, our co-workers, our lovers, our teachers. Many men familiar to us also terrorise our everyday lives in our homes, our schools, our workplaces.

Women's experiences of incest, battering, rape and sexual harassment become the sources for documenting all women's actual and potential experiences. Physically and/or sexually assaulted women speak in similar voices; much of what they say describes what it means to be female: the child who finds she is treated as sexually available at 9, the battered woman who is embarrassed by her black eyes, shamed by her failed marriage; the raped woman who is grateful to survive, only to live with nightmares; the sexually harassed woman who is humiliated by the pornographic pictures she finds every day on her desk. In each case, a woman endures an invasion of self, the intrusion of inner space, a violation of her sexual and physical autonomy.

Cast in a mould constructed within male-dominated society, women's experiences of sexual and physical violation take on an illusion of normality, ordinariness. Through an assumption of normality, many characterise male physical and/or sexual aggression as linked to biological make-up, sparked by an innate, at times uncontrollable, sexual drive. After all, boys will be boys, we sigh. While we acknowledge that not all men publicly display this uncontrollable biological predisposition, we further believe its display is generally aroused by deserving, provoking women. We consequently ignore what is assumed to be typical male behaviour directed toward provoking women. At the same time, though, we recognise that some male aggression is not sparked by provocative women. These, we reassure ourselves, are the rarest of situations. Above all, we retain traditional assumptions about women who experience sexual and/or physical assault; some women are alluring, masochistic and provoke the uncontrollable responses of some men, and some women are pure, proper but unfortunately come across some men who are uncontrollable. When we try to account for women's experiences of male violence, explanations of it centre around the naturalness or unnaturalness of male aggression in relation to women's behaviour.

As a result, women's experiences of male violence are filtered through an understanding of *men's* behaviour which is characterised as either typical or aberrant. If it is considered typical, men's physical and sexual aggression toward women is left, to a large extent, unfettered. The sexual advance by a male professor toward a young female student, the 'rough sex', the slapping of one's wife, the wolf whistle on the street, the comments about women's physicality, the man's brushing up against a female secretary's body in the xerox room (and on and on) are, most people accept, natural expressions of maleness. These expressions are assumed to be non-threatening to women, even, some would say, flattering. The vicious rape, the brutal murder of a woman, the cruel physical torture of a girlfriend are, we feel, the aberrant examples of maleness. These examples, most would agree, are threatening to women. In the abstract we easily draw lines between those aberrant (thus harmful) and those typical (thus unharmful) types of male behaviour. We even label the aberrant behaviour as potentially criminal behaviour.

What becomes lost, though, in this commonsensical separation between 'aberrant' and 'typical' male behaviour is a woman-defined understanding of what is threatening, of what women consider to be potentially violent. Often, women themselves are confused – sometimes defining male behaviour as typical, other times as aberrant – but none the less feel threatened by some displays of either. Women who feel violated or intimidated by typical male behaviour have no way of specifying how or why typical male behaviour feels like aberrant male behaviour. Essentially, the categories *typical* and *aberrant* are not useful for understanding women's feelings about, and thus women's experiences of male intimidation and violence. Confusing though they may be, women's experiences point to a potential for violence in many of women's ordinary encounters with men. One important study, by Jalna Hanmer and Sheila Saunders, surveyed a Yorkshire, England community querying women about their experiences of male violence.[1] Of the 129 adult women interviewed, 59 per cent reported some form of 'threatening, violent or sexually harassing behaviour' toward them in the past year. It is unlikely that women, when threatened, wait to categorise potentially threatening behaviour toward them as either typical (thus unthreatening) or aberrant (thus threatening) male behaviour. Women not only define a whole variety of male behaviour toward them as potentially violent, but male behaviour toward other women is seen as potentially threatening as well. The interviewed women of Hanmer and Saunders's study also reported incidents of male violence they witnessed or overheard happening to other women. Hence, the *daily* possibility of being threatened by male behaviour is one message women constantly receive.

A common theme throughout the women's descriptions of everyday encounters with men, report Hanmer and Saunders, is powerlessness: women are unable to predict, and thus unable to control, men's behaviour or anticipate when it might lead to violence. It doesn't matter whether men themselves read their own behaviour as typical or aberrant. Women read a great deal of male behaviour as threatening. For example, while many think 'flashing', exposure of the male genitals, is a non-threatening event, the women who were interviewed interpreted these events as potentially violent. 'Exposure of the male genitals ... to a woman on her own in an isolated part of an open space or deserted street,' state Hanmer and Saunders, 'may engender fears of injury and death because of the uncertainty about what may happen next.'[2] Women's uncertainty, their inability to predict what is supposed to be typical (and thus not threatening) or what is aberrant (and thus threatening) male behaviour opens up an ever-present fear and makes women uneasy about their safety on the street, in the home, or in the workplace. Women's fear reflects a recognition of their vulnerability *as women* to men's behaviour and thus to the possibility of male violence.

In what have come to be called criminal victimisation studies, evidence of women's fear has in fact been found in studies focusing on the incidence of crime. Conducted in both the United States and Britain, these surveys attempt to measure the prevalence of criminal behaviour and the extent to which these criminal incidents are reported to the police. (Not surprisingly, not all criminal incidents are reported to the police. In fact less than one half of all serious incidents come to police attention in both US and Britain.) Researchers also ask whether the interviewed person feels safe walking alone at night in their own neighbourhood. Women's fear about their safety on the street, according to these surveys, is *overwhelmingly* higher than men's fear.[3] According to these same surveys, women are less likely than men to be subjected to serious criminal incidents. Why is there such a difference between women's reported fear and women's reported experiences of criminal behaviour? Why are more women than men afraid to walk alone in their own neighbourhoods after dark? It is the Hanmer and Saunders study which provides the clues. First, women's experiences of threatening or sexually harassing male behaviour, feeding directly into their inability to predict when male intimidating behaviour will lead to violence, remind women that they are vulnerable. Second, [...] many women are reluctant to report criminal incidents when they feel they should have predicted when a man would act violently toward them. Consequently, women's fear stems from their powerless and precarious position: being vulnerable to men's threatening, sexually harassing or violent behaviour and unable to predict when the threatening behaviour will turn to violence.[4]

Vulnerability, also commonly assumed to be an inherent gender trait of women, has connotations other than those related to the probability of criminal attack. Women's vulnerability takes on additional meaning; for women, it is, above all, sexual vulnerability. As Catharine MacKinnon correctly recognises, 'Vulnerability means the appearance/reality of easy sexual access, passivity means receptivity and disabled resistance, enforced by trained physical weakness; softness means pregnability by something hard.'[5]

It is women's vulnerability that makes women's sexuality and the ever-present potential for sexual violation a 'material reality of women's lives, not just a psychological, attitudinal, or ideological one.'[6] This reality rings clear in account after account of women who experience sexual and/or physical assault. Its potential reality is experienced by many other women. Those women whose houses have been burgled, for example, where there is no confrontation between assailant and the woman, report feelings of sexual violation.[7] The reality of physical and/or sexual vulnerability is part of women's experience of being in the world.

Yet vulnerability for women has another, more insidious side. It also has connotations about the 'invitation' to be physically and/or sexually violated. Any attempt to label men's behaviour as threatening or sexually harassing raises additional myths surrounding women's sexuality as the *cause* for men's actions. 'She asked for it', 'she considers it flattery', as the myth goes, the woman is to blame. A woman who labels behaviour as sexually harassing, for instance, is accused of reading into 'perfectly innocent' behaviour. Or she is accused of encouraging men's behaviour in the first place. It is assumed a woman's very presence is what introjects sexuality into the workplace or street – an assumed asexual territory. So, too, women are expected not to acknowledge any advances as sexual for fear they might be suspected of being 'wise' to all other forms of sexuality.[8] Suddenly, it is the woman who is misinterpreting the event, according to traditional thinking, only 'whores' can recognise the street cues of sexualised behaviour, and the responsibility for 'sexualising' encounters rests solely with the woman.

Not surprisingly, academic as well as legal orientations toward women's experiences of sexual and/or physical violence incorporate a concept of vulnerability into general explanations of criminal violence. In the last forty years, within American and European criminology, there has emerged a focus on the 'victim' of crime, a focus which theoretically includes an explanation for women's experiences of male violence. [...] Victimology, often deemed to be a separate discipline in its own right, explores the relevance of victims to the phenomenon of crime. The term 'victim' is applied by various theorists to those who experience traditional crimes, such as murder, rape, assault, robbery, burglary and so forth, as well as to groups of individuals who experience high rates of or distinct forms of crime, like, for example, physically boundaried communities or the elderly. In applying the term 'victim', though, one implicitly separates victim from non-victim. Accordingly, victim characteristics are then explored by theorists for their contribution to patterns of criminal behaviour.[9] Women – as a special group – are considered worthy of study; men are not.

Women and their vulnerability fit neatly into the theoretical focus of victimologists.[10] Suspicions regarding a woman 'victim's' behaviour – what led the man to attack the woman? – have foundations in the assumptions about typical and aberrant male behaviour. A woman 'victim' is thus seen as separate from women who are not victims of male violence.

Benjamin Mendelsohn, who in 1956 proposed the term 'victimology', studied the victim–criminal relationship, essentially to examine the 'potential of victimal receptivity'. He established victim typologies along the lines of victim 'culpability'. Categories such as the 'completely innocent victim', 'victim with minor guilt' due to 'ignorance', the 'provoker victim', or the 'simulating victim' (one who feigns victimisation in order to punish another person) are included in Mendelsohn's list.[11] These particular categories were constructed so as to be applicable to both male and female victims. When, however, these categories are placed within the context of many traditional assumptions about women, we can see how certain categories can be more readily applied to women as a whole. Pointing to the probable participation of women in their own sexual and/or physical violation, traditional characteristics of women match those of a 'victimised' populace. Some of these – that women are passive, easily led, vulnerable, sexually unmanageable, impulsive, unpredictable – continue to have power over the way women who have experienced male violence are viewed by criminal justice decision makers and how 'victimised' women are viewed by their neighbours and relatives, all of whom make judgments about the nature of male violence to women. From these traditional characteristics, we get the idea that women are *by nature* 'victims'.

Von Hentig, the influential European theorist, in his 1940s' analysis of sexual crimes, did just that. 'The female', one of von Hentig's types of victims, places women in the 'born victim' category. Being female, according to him, is yet 'another form of weakness',[12] women have less strength, thus are easy prey to men. Furthermore, women occupy a biologically determined status in sexual crimes. Von Hentig's typology is rather blatantly rooted in assumptions about women. I am not, however, arguing that women have the same strength as men and that is why von Hentig's typology is faulty. It is more a problem of omission: what does women's weakness have to do with 'sexual' crimes? Should not the inquiry be directed to the reasons why women, who are physically weaker than men, are subjected to attack from them? The1960s' theorists in victimology, who began to question biologically based explanations, did not address this question. Instead, they constructed another, perhaps more subtle process of categorisation, one that focuses on 'victim' responsibility for criminal behaviour. Some victims precipitate or provoke criminal behaviour. It is not difficult to characterise women as 'precipitative' or 'provocative' in situations of men's sexual and/or physical aggression. Both these categories focus attention on the woman's behaviour, away from that of the male aggressor.

Just as women are, according to some theorists, biologically predisposed to being 'victims', their experience of male violence, according to another group of theorists, becomes rooted in social explanations derived from 'independent' assessments of women's provocation and participation. Precipitative victims are those

> who have done nothing specifically against the criminal (as opposed to the provocative victims), but whose thoughtless behaviour instigates, tempts, or allures the offender to commit a crime against the enticing victim … *an overly revealing dress of a female may allure to rape*. Naturally, a perfectly socialized person [if there is such a thing at all] is not supposed to be tempted or enticed to the extent of violating the rules of the criminal law…. Yet, the characteristics of the criminal's personality are often bent by the characteristics of the victim's behaviour toward committing the crime.[13]

Here we see how the typical male becomes an aberrant male: women cause it. (This thinking does not work in reverse. Just for a moment imagine why an over-revealing pair of trousers doesn't allure a woman to rape a man. Sexual precipitation or for that matter sexual provocation means women arouse men.) Provocative victims, on the other hand, have done something to incite the aggressor; the responsibility for any criminal action is heavily shared by both offender and the abused woman. (I'm not sure which category is better for women: born victims or socially responsible victims. Each are equally insidious, easily rooted in a male view of women's behaviour, and equally important, a male view of men's behaviour. Once biology is challenged as an explanation for behaviour, it seems, behaviour becomes socially learned. In both, however, females are targets of male violence. Regardless, traditional stereotypes just carry on in another form.) These typologies – victim as provocative or as precipitative – fit neatly with existing stereotypes about women: they are sexually unmanageable and thus they 'ask for' it; they are nagging and thus they deserve the punch in the mouth.

In essence, Western criminologists have adopted theoretical explanations characterising women's experiences of male violence through what Kathleen Barry terms the 'rape paradigm'.[14] In many ways, academics and policy makers do not merely passively incorporate traditional stereotypes about women; they frequently create new forms of them. Rather than look to any explanations of male violence in social forces or in masculinity, academics, criminal justice decision makers, and men and women alike look instead to women's supposed behaviour – before, during and after men's actions. As we examine in more detail women's own reactions to male behaviour which they experience as violent, we see that it too rests in seeing women themselves 'as driven by their own needs into abusive situations and enslavement'.[15]

Creating a category 'victim' is one way of dealing with women's experiences of male violence. The role and status of 'victim' is separate from that of all women. 'Victimism', the practice of objectifying women's experiences of male violence, serves to deny the commonality among sexually and/or physically assaulted women and their oneness with all women.[16] [...] We can then easily separate victims from all women. We even have academic and institutional explanations to assist us.

Yet women *know* to read situations as potentially threatening, sexualised, or violent. It is a form of protection, a way of hoping to avoid the blame placed upon them for any sexual and/or physical attack. Comments, glances, physical touching can be felt as either sexual or not. Sometimes those comments, glances or touching are acknowledged, some are returned willingly, but many others, unwelcomed, serve as intrusions. It is assumed, at least from a male point of view, that men honour or flatter women by acknowledging their sexuality, and that women are to trust that men will protect them from threatening behaviour. And sexuality – tacitly understood as heterosexual sexuality – is, after all, a taken-for-granted part of life, purportedly pleasurable, welcomed at all times – at least from a male point of view.[17]

For women to label male behaviour as 'aberrant' – that is to report sexually and/or physically violent male behaviour to the official authorities (in most instances women call the police, the authority invoked is the authority of the criminal law) – is to characterise it outside the parameters of typical, normal or inevitable. Many women too believe that men's aberrant (thus criminal) behaviour is supposedly distinct from men's typical behaviour toward women. The category 'crime' – the only official category which exists within society to define aberrant behaviour – emerges as the standard against which women have to measure aberrant male behaviour toward them. It is a standard which does not arise from women's experiences of male violence. 'As women's experience blurs the lines between deviance and normalcy (aberrant and typical), it obliterates the distinction between abuses *of* women and the social definition of what a woman *is*.'[18] To be a woman is to be potentially sexually and/or physically assaulted by men. Is there a difference between typical and aberrant male behaviour? Is there a difference between women who have experienced male violence and those who have not? How do we, as women, distinguish between typical male physical and sexual aggression (thus not harmful?) and aberrant male aggression or between women who have experienced male aggression and those who have not? We must turn to women's experiences to find the parameters or to find that the parameters are not really distinguishable.

Women do define instances of male behaviour as abusive, threatening, violent or potentially violent – many more than we have ever known before. But because women experience the world through male perceptions of it, they question their own feelings and perceptions of the world. Their voices crack of qualification and self-doubt because they know, a powerful lesson of growing up in a male-dominated world, that their private assessment and the public assessment of their experiences of sexual and/or physical violation are likely to be at odds.[19] Women also learn to define their worlds and thus their experience as less important than men's. In the social hierarchy of value, they are less. Women therefore internalise and silence many of their experiences of sexual and/or physical intimidation and violation. That is why many of their experiences do not show up in surveys counting criminal incidents. Only 'bad' girls get hurt, we've been told. Rather than being exposed as 'bad', women stay quiet. As a consequence, women feel shame, humiliation, and self-blame for men's sexual and/or physical aggressive behaviour toward them. Women's experiences of physical and/or sexual intimidation and of male violence and their own reactions to it are thus welded to male dominance in Western society which rests upon women's secondary position.

To understand women's experiences of men's physical and/or sexual intimidation and violence is also to understand that society allows for, and on many levels encourages, male intimidation and violence to women, and, in particular, intimidation and violence which is directed at women as sexual beings.

By separating women's experiences of sexual and/or physical assault from women's experiences of sexual and/or physical intimidation, as many are likely to do, we see each assault as an aberration or a random occurrence – a 'personal' problem. Alternatively if we link them together, we can create new information on the overall treatment of women by men. What emerges is not random or isolated. What emerges is a flood of common experiences. Women are likely to experience some form of men's intimidating or violent behaviour in their lifetimes, often many times over. It is irrelevant to women whether this behaviour is, for men, conscious or unconscious, intended or unintended, typical or aberrant.[20] It is experienced by women as intimidating, harassing and violent.

Women, no longer afraid of their feelings, of sharing those daily instances of humiliation, and of hearing women speak of physical and sexual assault, break the pattern of men's intimidation and violence. It is a way of gaining power over our awareness of our condition as women. At its very heart says Susan Griffin, is that

> the whole issue [of understanding men's power over women seems] ... to revolve around whether or not one could trust a woman's word; and behind this questioning of our word, whether one could trust a woman's being, whether we could trust our own being.[21]

[...] Women do resist, persistently and tenaciously, the effects of male violence. Women are survivors. They have done so for hundreds and hundreds of years. Many have developed scar tissue, but survive they do and continue to struggle for autonomy. Women are not, as some would have us believe, masochistic, addicted to violence, prone to seeking it out, or in any way defeated by violence directed toward them. Our survival is our strength, our experiences the reminders that there is much more work to do.

Understanding the process of women's responses to men's intimidating, threatening, or violent behaviour can enable us to uncover the reasons why women remain silent. This silence, contrary to popular thinking, does not mean tacit acceptance. Silence is a way for the powerless to cope with very real situations.

Silence is a *declaration*. Factors such as concern for others, situational helplessness, fear and terror, and perhaps even immobilising depression encourage silence. This exploration into women's experiences with men's intimidating or violent behaviour, then, is meant to articulate the process of making sense of women's lives and the role male violence plays in it. This very discussion breaks the silence and begins to transform it into a deafening roar, for it is through sharing and understanding men's power in our own lives that we also share the courage, laud the resistance, and help other women continue to resist it in their own lives.

NOTES

1   Jalna Hanmer and Sheila Saunders, 'Blowing the cover of the protective male: a community study of violence to women', in Eva Gamarnikow, David Morgan, June Purvis and Daphne Taylorson (eds), *The Public and the Private*, London, Heinemann, 1983, pp. 28–46. For information about the methodology and a practical 'how to' guide for conducting studies of women's experiences of male violence, see Jalna Hanmer and Sheila Saunders, *Well Founded Fear: A Community Study of Violence to Women*, London, Hutchinson, 1984.

2   Hanmer and Saunders, 'Blowing the Cover', p. 30.

3   See, for example, Mike Hough and Pat Mayhew, *The British Crime Survey; First Report*, London, HMSO, no. 76, 1983. Data released to me by the Home Office indicate that over 50 per cent of women as opposed to 14 per cent of men reported they felt a 'bit' to 'very' unsafe on their neighbourhood streets alone after dark. The United States Department of Justice, Law Enforcement Assistance Administration, *Criminal Victimization in the United States* (many volumes), summary findings on fear reporting differences in men's and women's fear in the *LEEA Newsletter*, March 1974, p. 15, 6 out of 10 women, versus 2 out of 10 men, report fear on the street within a mile of their homes.

4   See Margaret T. Gordon, Stephanie Riger, Robert K. LeBailly and Linda Heath, 'Crime, women, and the quality of urban life', in Catharine R. Stimpson, Elsa Dixler, Martha J. Nelson and Kathryn B. Yatrakis (eds), *Women and the American City*, Chicago, University of Chicago Press, 1980, pp. 141–57.

5   C.A. MacKinnon, 'Feminism, marxism, method, and the state: an agenda for theory', *Signs*, vol. 7, no. 3, 1982, p. 530.

6   Ibid., p. 539.

7   Mike McGuire, *Burglary in a Dwelling*, Cambridge Studies in Criminology, XLIX, London, Heinemann, 1982.

8   For a discussion of the 'wise', see Erving Goffman, *Stigma*, Englewood Cliffs, New Jersey, Prentice-Hall, 1963. See also Florence Rush, 'Freud and the sexual abuse of children', *Chrysalis*, no. 1, 1977, pp. 31–45, for an interesting analysis of how Freud's theorising set women up for the blame for abuses to their own sexuality.

9   See, for example, Hans von Hentig, *The Criminal and his Victim*, New Haven, Connecticut, Yale University Press, 1948; Israel Drapkin and Emilio Viano (eds), *Victimology: A New Focus*, Lexington, Massachusetts, D. C. Heath and Co., 1975 (5 vols); Stephen Schafer, *The Victim and his Criminal*, New York, Random House, 1968.

10 For a feminist critique of victimology, see Lorenne Clark and Debra Lewis, *Rape: The Price of Coercive Sexuality*, Toronto, Canada, The Women's Press, 1977, pp. 147–58; Nicole H. Rafter and Elizabeth A. Stanko, 'Introduction', in N.H. Rafter and E.A. Stanko (eds), *Judge, Lawyer, Victim, Thief: Women, Gender Roles and Criminal Justice*, Boston, Massachusetts, Northeastern University Press, 1982, pp. 1–28; and Kurt Weis and Sandra S. Borges, 'Victimology and rape: the case of the legitimate victim', *Issues in Criminology*, vol. 8, Fall 1973, pp. 71–115.

11 Benjamin Mendelsohn, 'The origin of the doctrine of victimology', *Excerpta Criminologica*, vol. 3, May–June 1963, pp. 239–344.

12 Von Hentig, *The Criminal and his Victim*, pp. 404–38, for his categories of victims.

13 Stephen Schafer, 'The beginning of victimology', in Burt Galaway and Joe Hudson (eds), *Perspectives on Crime Victims*, St Louis, Missouri, C.V. Mosby Company, 1981 p. 21, my emphasis.

14 Kathleen Barry, *Female Sexual Slavery*, New York, Avon Books, 1979, pp. 40–2.

15 Ibid., p. 42.

16 Ibid., pp. 43–6.

17 MacKinnon states, 'Sexuality, if noticed at all, is like "everyday life", analysed in gender-neutral terms, as if its social meaning can be presumed the same, or coequal, or complementary, for men and women', *Signs*, vol. 7, no. 3, 1982, p. 526. For an enlightening discussion of the male point of view with regard to male violence, see Catharine A. MacKinnon, 'Feminism, marxism, method, and the state: toward feminist jurisprudence', *Signs*, vol. 8, no. 4, 1983, pp. 635–58.

18 MacKinnon, *Signs*, vol. 8, no. 4, 1983, p. 532.

19 See, for example, Carol Gilligan, *In a Different Voice*, Cambridge, Massachusetts, Harvard University Press, 1982; and Jessie Bernard, *The Female World*, New York, Free Press, 1981.

20 Susan Brownmiller, *Against our Will: Men, Women and Rape*, New York, Bantam Books, 1975, p. 5, states that rape is 'nothing more or less than a conscious process of intimidation by which *all men* keep *all women* in a state of fear' (emphasis in original). I disagree. Not all men consciously threaten women with rape. But men, by virtue of their membership in the category 'men', are potentially threatening to women because of women's knowledge about and fear of rape. Men, however, do acknowledge women's fear of rape. See Timothy Beneke, *Men on Rape*, New York, St Martin's Press, 1982.

21 Susan Griffin, *Rape: The Power of Consciousness*, San Francisco, Harper and Row, 1979, p. 24.

STUDY QUESTIONS

1   The public sphere (the streets) has traditionally been considered a dangerous place, whereas the home is usually characterized as 'a safe haven'. How does Stanko's argument challenge this view? What connections can you see between Stanko's argument and that of Kitzinger (Reading 12)?

2   From your reading of Stanko's extract what would you say are the problems with victimology explanations?

3 Towards the end of the reading Stanko introduces the term 'survivor'. Is this a more appropriate term than victim? Why?

FURTHER READING

Approaches to victimology from different parts of the world are included in Crawford, A. and Goodey, J. (2000) *Integrating a Victim Perspective within Criminal Justice: International Debates*, Aldershot: Ashgate. Masculine violence towards women, children and towards other men is discussed in several chapters in the edited collection by Bowker, L.H. (ed.) (1998) *Masculinities and Violence*, Thousand Oaks, CA: Sage. Women's experience of male violence is discussed by Hester, M., Kelly, L. and Radford, J. (eds) (1995) *Women, Violence and Male Power*, Buckingham: Open University Press; Hoyle, C. (1998) *Negotiating Domestic Violence: Police, Criminal Justice, and Victims*, Oxford: Oxford University Press; Radford, J., Friedberg, M. and Harne, L. (eds) (1999) *Women, Violence and Strategies for Action: Feminist Research, Policy and Practice*, Buckingham: Open University Press; and Stanko, E.A. (1990) *Everyday Violence*, London: Pandora. The historical and theoretical evolution of victimology and victimization are discussed in Tierney, J. (1996) *Criminology: Theory and Context*, Harlow: Longman. Sandra Walklate explores the subject of victimization in relation to 'positivist victimology', 'radical victimology' and 'critical victimology' in Walklate, S. (1998) *Understanding Criminology: Current Theoretical Debates*, Buckingham: Open University Press, and she addresses victimology in relation to masculinism in Walklate, S. (2001) *Gender, Crime and Criminal Justice*, Cullompton: Willan.

22

When men are victims:
the failure of victimology

Tim Newburn and Elizabeth A. Stanko

In this, the final reading in Part III, the issue of 'the victim' – this time the male 'victim' – is revisited by the author of the previous reading and a colleague. Tim Newburn and Elizabeth A. Stanko present an overview of the feminist critique of 'conventional' victimology and then consider victimology from the perspective of left realism (see Reading 4) with specific reference to the experience of men as 'victims'. Newburn and Stanko suggest that left realism has an oversimplified view of victimization, not least because it relies on the concept of 'hegemonic masculinity' (where all men benefit from the fact that they are men), and is unable successfully to dismantle the binary view of victims and offenders as mutually exclusive 'ideal types'. Thus, from this perspective, men (the oppressors) cannot also be classified as 'victims'. Contrary to this, as Newburn and Stanko suggest, there is evidence to suggest that men not only victimize women but they also victimize each other in ways which cause significant trauma, so it is necessary to deconstruct how power is managed between and among men. There is a lack of research in this area and Newburn and Stanko argue that more is needed so that we can understand how men experience violence and how their sense of self may be affected. Furthermore, additional work in this area may help our understanding of the relationship between personal experiences of victimization and offending. Overall, Newburn and Stanko's argument is that it is necessary to 'take victimization seriously' and consider the experience of men as victims as well as oppressors.

Whilst once it was realistic to argue that 'the victim' was not only the forgotten party in the criminal justice process but also in criminology, the development both of victim services and of academic victimology have drawn attention to

SOURCE: From *Just Boys Doing Business: Men Masculinities and Crime*, ed. Tim Newburn and Elizabeth A. Stanko. (London: Routledge, 1994), 153–65.

this significant oversight. A veritable industry of 'services' has developed and a wide range of academic studies have focused upon these developments and the range of victims that they are designed to support. Indeed, so strong have these developments been, that a number of authors have referred to the emergence of an all-encompassing 'victims movement' (see Pointing and Maguire 1988).

Yet, the criminal justice system remains far from being victim-friendly, and whilst uncovering new areas (see Morgan and Zedner 1992 on child victims), the study of crime victims appears to have reached something of a plateau. One of the reasons that this sub-discipline is fairly stagnant is, we suggest, that, in at least one important respect, criminologists continue to treat the notion of 'the victim' as if it were a 'given', i.e. as if it were unproblematic. More particularly, insufficient attention is paid to the complexity of criminal victimisation; all too often the use of the label 'victim' is underpinned by the assumption that it may only be applied to members of relatively powerless social groups, or that it describes a state of being which itself induces powerlessness. Though we have moved some way from the more or less explicit victim-blaming characteristic of von Hentig's (1948) view of victim as perpetrator and Wolfgang's (1958) concept of 'victim precipitation', there is some danger that we have moved so far in the other direction that victims are conceptualised as individuals who have no experience of crime as offenders, and/or as people who have little understanding of threat and harm other than being victims of random crime. Indeed, in much recent victimological literature, victims are characterised as helpless and vulnerable, and in need of advice so that they may avoid such misfortune in the future.

Such descriptions fail to tackle the complexity of relationships between 'offenders' and 'victims'. As far as the realities of the lives of some – especially young – males are concerned, such a dichotomy is hard to sustain. Young men, who according to crime surveys report the largest proportion of personal crime, are also the population which are most likely to be offenders. [...]

[...] Beginning with von Hentig in the late 1940s and Marvin Wolfgang in the 1950s, early studies concentrated on the role of the victim in the aetiology of crime. At this point, criminologists were still searching for 'grand theories' that would explain crime, and victims of crime became, in part, another focus of that concern. For von Hentig and others, the specific focus was upon the role of the victim in the precipitation or perpetration of the crime.

It was not until the mid-1960s and the early 1970s, however, that victims 'attracted any serious public attention' (Pointing and Maguire 1988). The mid- to late 1960s saw the first murmurings of the nascent victims' movement and in its wake academic victimology, which was about to be radically transformed by the utilisation of large-scale survey techniques, moved its focus to the victim population rather than the individual (Fattah 1992). This gave rise to what one author has characterised as a 'lifestyle' approach to victimology or, alternatively, as 'conventional victimology' (Walklate 1989). In this approach, which is associated primarily with Hindelang et al. (1978) and Cohen and Felson (1979), it is argued that there is a link between routine daily activities and exposure to circumstances in which the risk of victimisation is high. Whilst this constituted a significant advance on the work of von Hentig, its dependence upon survey methodologies meant that such an approach failed (indeed was unable) to take account of those structural constraints which were not easily observable or measurable. Furthermore, in its concentration on the public domain and its avoidance of the private, it merely reinforced conventional views of victimisation and through its policy emphasis on individual lifestyle engaged in, at least implicit, victim-blaming once more.

The shortcomings of 'conventional' victimology were thrown into sharp relief, however, by the re-emergence of feminism and its impact on criminology generally. Feminists were critical of both the theory and methodology associated with the lifestyle approach, and they stressed the importance of the experience of victimisation. Focusing in particular on rape and domestic violence, a number of authors were able to illustrate the limitations of the social survey as a method of uncovering either the incidence of these forms of victimisation or the reality of the experience of victimisation. Central to their account was the issue of power for as Stanko, for example, has argued: 'unless policing and crime survey researchers lend credence to the concept and reality of gender stratification, violence against women will, on many levels, remain a hidden, but all too real part of women's lives' (1988: 46).

Crucially, feminism challenged not only the methodological basis of such work but also its implicit philosophy of knowledge. The claims to objectivity made by conventional victimologists were challenged, and suggestions that such survey-based work constituted 'science' were attacked for systematically excluding women's experiences and interests. From the feminist perspective,[1] *experience* constituted the epistemological basis of much feminist knowledge. The work of feminists, and particularly activists rather than academics was crucial to the transformation in understanding about the frequency and impact of rape, sexual assault and domestic violence. One simple but important historical lesson, therefore, is that certain forms of victimisation only become visible when they do, because of the campaigning work of representative groups. The victim categories that go with these forms of victimisation are not givens: not only would it be wrong to argue that they have always been visible to us, but also to suggest that they were there waiting to be uncovered. Certainly, attention has been drawn to certain forms of victimisation at specific points in history, but the victim categories that we use as a result are also historically specific. Specific forms of crime need to be understood within the cultural and historical context which gives them meaning.

Despite this far-reaching critique, much of criminology has managed to remain relatively impervious to feminist concerns and, in a recent paper, Smart (1990) concluded by suggesting that criminology had little to offer feminism. In recent years, however, there has emerged a victimological perspective – left realism – that claims to take the feminist critique seriously. It is worth looking in some detail at what left realism offers, if anything, by way of an alternative perspective, before moving on to consider the victimisation of men.

LEFT REALISM

Although the new realism is presented as a broad criminological enterprise (Matthews and Young 1992; Young and Matthews 1992), there are reasonable grounds for arguing that it is their 'victimology' that is the central plank of the perspective (Walklate 1992), and indeed Young has argued such 'realism necessitates an accurate victimology' (Young 1986: 23) . Furthermore, in taking on board a feminist critique, this realist victimology was, we were told, going to put 'experience' centre-stage:

> Realism starts from problems as people experience them. It takes seriously the complaints of women with regard to the dangers of being in public places at night, it takes note of the fears of the elderly with regard to burglary, it acknowledges the widespread occurrence of domestic violence and racist attacks. It does not ignore the fears of the vulnerable nor recontextualise them out of existence by putting them into a perspective which abounds with abstractions such as the 'average citizen' bereft of class or gender. (Young 1986: 24)

Ironically, however, the preferred methodology of the new realists is based on large-scale, though locally focused, surveys, that are in many respects barely distinguishable from the tools used by the administrative criminologists that the realists are so critical of. Local crime surveys are defended on the basis not only of their geographical focus, but also their sampling procedures which are held to map better what is already known about patterns of victimisation (Jones et al. 1986: appendix 2; Young 1988: 169). This is a neat bit of footwork for it allows left realism to claim that it has taken the lessons of feminism on board whilst clinging to the tailcoats of a positivistic model of scientific discovery.

There are, however, a number of significant ways in which realism has failed in its attempt to 'take victimisation seriously' and, in the main, these are related to the difficulties that realism has in dealing with the variety and plurality which characterises victimisation in modern society. Indeed, Walklate suggests that realist victimology, like its administrative counterpart, focuses on crime as it is commonly understood and that therefore it 'neither tackles the question of victimisation by corporations or by implication the victimisation of children' (1992: 112). Crucially, she accuses realism of failing to incorporate fully an understanding of power relationships into its theoretical framework and therefore of being unable to help us understand how individuals actively resist their structural powerlessness. Once again, this is a shortcoming that it shares with the conventional victimology it has been at pains to distance itself from. We are surely left pondering whether realism and conventionalism are really so different.

Methodologically and ontologically then there are distinct parallels between realism and conventional victimology. However, it is the political underpinnings of the two positions that separates them most clearly. Administrative criminology in its eschewal of interest in aetiology and its association with social control theories clearly has an affinity with the political right, whereas realism is explicit in its espousal of vaguely 'left' politics. This comes out quite clearly in the agenda of realist victimology and, it will be argued, is central to its inability to take the complexity of victimisation seriously. The political agenda in realist victimology can be seen clearly in the quote from Young earlier in which he sets out those areas of victimisation which realism is keen to take seriously: women, the elderly, victims of racist attacks, crimes against the least powerful. Few would wish to take exception to any of this, one assumes, except on the grounds that it is significantly incomplete. Uncomfortable though it may be, the reality of the world in which we live is that it is not just the 'least powerful' or even always the 'less powerful' who suffer criminal victimisation. Moreover, it is the articulation of the ways in which power is manifest in individual interactions, especially amongst those who have the benefits of structured privilege because they are men in a gender-stratified society. Men differ in economic flexibility, race, education, sexual orientation, and so forth, and men negotiate power and privilege amongst themselves as well as with women.

The central problem for realist victimology is that it is unable to wrench itself from a simple binary view of victims and offenders; a view which treats these categories as if they are not only mutually exclusive, but also characterised by uniform relations of power in which the victim is portrayed as 'weak, helpless, defenceless and unsuspecting' (Fattah 1992). The processes of criminal victimisation are not that simple, nor their politics that convenient. As Ruggiero has pointed out,

> some crimes confirm the existing distribution of power, but some do not. It is not enough for criminologists to assume the relations of dominance in victim–offender relations nor simply to present themselves as defenders of the weak. Their task is to uncover and explain the complex processes through which 'victims' and 'offenders' are reproduced.[2] (Ruggiero 1992: 129)

We suggest that this complexity also sheds light on how the notion of power is interpersonally negotiated, and how 'hegemonic masculinity', as conceptualised by Connell (1987), obscures our ability to deconstruct how power is managed between and amongst men.

As a consequence of this oversimplified view of the nature of victimisation, realism is unable to be realistic about the position of men. This stems from the desire of realists to remain steadfastly on the side of the underdog. Whilst not wishing to take issue with such political sympathies, we do wish to argue that the uncritical application of such sympathies to models of victimisation results in a unidimensional picture of social relations which divides the world into oppressors and oppressed. Thus, all men are oppressors unless they can be located in another oppressed group (elderly men perhaps, victims of racist or/and homophobic attacks certainly, male victims of child sexual abuse probably).

In the passage quoted earlier, Young talked of the importance of avoiding abstractions like 'average citizen' bereft of class or gender. The step forward made possible by this insight is only limited, however, if the theory of gender on which it is based is largely undifferentiated or even 'essentialist'. In a somewhat similar manner to their idealised view of the homogeneous working-class community (see the critical comments in Gilroy and Sim 1985), the realists continue to talk of men and women as if they too were largely homogeneous categories. However, as Scraton (1985) has noted, such assumptions about social cohesion are perhaps overly optimistic. Though, in this instance he is critical of their presentation of working-class community, his comments could just as easily be applied to their presentation of gender, for 'Just as it is probable that men from all classes see street violence as a "problem" for them, they would not see most actions of sexual harassment as a "problem" at all' (1985: 168).

One of the problems with realist victimology is that its underlying philosophy – 'that crime really is a problem for the working-class, ethnic minorities, for all the most vulnerable members of capitalist societies' (Young 1986: 29) – is too simplistic to allow for a properly realistic understanding of the scope of victimisation. More particularly, it is unable to confront the reality in which men (and not just working-class men) not only victimise women, but also victimise each other, and that such victimisation may have a significant impact upon those who experience it. What, then, do we know about the impact of crime upon men?

MEN AS VICTIMS OF CRIME

The first point to be made is that there have been relatively few studies of male victims of crime. The bulk of early victimological literature focused on victims as a group largely undifferentiated by gender and, more recently, attention has been directed at uncovering and detailing the impact of violence by men against women (*inter alia* Dobash and Dobash 1979, 1992). One of the results of this has, quite rightly, been to raise awareness of the frequency with which men *victimise*, especially within the 'home'. Adult men are rarely the *victims* in this context (although when they are, they are likely to meet with disbelief and disregard for their situation). Outside the home men are not only more likely to offend, but especially where 'public' violence is concerned, men – particularly young men – are most likely to seek police or medical assistance for personal crime, and report such incidents to crime researchers (Hough and Mayhew 1985; Shepherd 1990). However, little is known about men's experience of victimisation, even where violence is involved.

Much of this neglect is based upon a widely held but largely untested assumption that a central element of masculinity involves an unwillingness to talk about or admit 'weakness'. Thus, in the study of the fear of crime, of which gender is the most significant feature (LaGrange and Ferraro 1989), there is considerable discussion of the disparity between women's and men's reported levels of fear. In much of the literature, it is seemingly quite unproblematically assumed that men are reticent to disclose vulnerability (Maxfield 1984; Crawford et al. 1990), thus reinforcing the tendency to focus almost exclusively on women's experiences of physical and sexual assault.

A second but related point is that the evidence that is available, whilst indicating often major differences between men's and women's reactions to criminal victimisation, nevertheless indicates that a proportion of men are significantly affected by crime. Research by Maguire and Corbett (1987) on support schemes for victims of crime provides a good illustration of this point. Using data from the 1984 British Crime Survey, excluding vehicle theft and miscellaneous personal theft, a significantly higher proportion of female than male respondents reported themselves or their households being 'very much' affected, though the authors did continue to speculate 'whether this represents a "real" difference, or is caused by a greater reluctance among men to admit to being emotionally upset ... is difficult to state with any certainty' (1987: 50). In one sense, of course, it is not the fact that there is a difference that is important. For the purposes of the argument here, the point to bear in mind is that this research, like other research of a similar nature (Shapland et al. 1985), shows that a proportion of men – albeit a proportion that is smaller than that of women – *do* admit to having been profoundly affected by crime.

Nevertheless, the differences between men's and women's reactions to crime ought not to be allowed to obscure the fact that a considerable number of men *were* willing to admit to being severely emotionally affected by crime. Furthermore, in the case of assault or robbery, over half of all victims reported intense fear and

> 'shaking or shivering' and feeling 'dazed, confused or unreal', symptoms associated with shock as well as fear, were at high levels among ... both sexes in the case of assault. This latter finding, together with the fact that there was no significant difference in these reactions by age in the case of male victims, helps to underline one of the key points to emerge from this exercise: *the effects of violent crime are severe for a high proportion of men, as well as for women*. (Maguire and Corbett 1987: 56)

A properly 'realist' victimology therefore, would have to confront the inescapable fact that men not only victimise women, but they also victimise each other, and in ways which may cause severe short-term and significant long-term trauma.

In a recent small-scale study of male victims of sexual assault, King (1992) explodes many of the myths about the impact of crime upon men. He was able to conclude that despite its limitations: 'the results of this study demonstrate that male sexual assault is a frightening, dehumanising event, leaving men who have been assaulted feeling debased and contaminated, their sense of autonomy and personal invulnerability shattered' (King 1992: 8). There are a number of issues here which it is worth unpicking slightly. First, men are often extremely frightened by such events. They are, as such, emotional beings capable of feeling vulnerable, capable of expressing feelings and capable of asking for support. Second, in relation to the sexual assault of males, there is a further point that complicates the experience of victimisation, and that is the consequences that such an assault may have for the victim's view of himself as a man. Such attacks strike at the heart of stereotypical 'hegemonic masculinity' (Connell 1987) in which men are in control, are invulnerable and are heterosexual. Sexual assault potentially problematises such a view of masculinity, leading to a sense of loss of self. As Adler has argued:

> Where the victim is male, any claim that he consented projects onto him a homosexual identity. Where the victim is homosexual, this can lead to considerable feelings of guilt, which tend to act as a deterrent to reporting. Where the victim is heterosexual, the very fear of being thought a homosexual may well stop him from reporting. Indeed, the reasons for not reporting for male victims are much the same as they are for female victims, and include shock, embarrassment, fear, self-blame, and a high degree of stigma. (Adler 1992: 128)

Thus, King (1992) found that although there were many similarities between the reactions of male victims and those reported for women, 'the stigma for men may be even greater, however, in a society which expects its male members to be self-sufficient physically and psychologically' (1992: 10).[3]

There are significant parallels between the experience of sexual assault as described by men and women. This is not to suggest that the social context within which such assaults occur is the same for women and men – of course it is not – merely to say that the *experience* may be similar on other levels. Whilst men's sense of 'invulnerability' may be shattered by such events, this in itself may be a misreading. It is surely part of the same ideology of masculinity that presents men as uniformly powerful, controlling and non-emotional, which leads us to believe that men behave as if they *were* invulnerable. The available evidence suggests that at least some men feel vulnerable some of the time, though some of these are unlikely to admit feeling so. For at least some of the men in King's sample the experience of victimisation is more likely to have increased their sense of vulnerability rather than destroyed some sense of invulnerability. The most important lesson from this, however, is that we have 'discovered' a series of empirical questions: do men feel vulnerable? Which men? Under what circumstances? And so on.

We may also find clues to understanding some links for some men between experiences of victimisation as children and offending. For those sexually abused as young boys, the longer-term impact on their sexual identity/ masculinity may have significant consequences for others as well as for the victim. There is considerable debate over the strength of the evidence in this regard (see Finkelhor 1986) though a recent review (Watkins and Bentovim 1992: 47) concluded that 'the sexual abuse of boys in childhood is an important contributory but not a necessary factor in the development of a perpetrator'. What does seem clear, however, is that sexual victimisation of boys at a young age – and the anger at the sense of powerlessness that this involves – frequently leads them to attempt to reassert a controlling and powerful masculinity, often through hostile and aggressive behaviour (Rogers and Terry 1984). It would appear then that the dominant model of masculinity that we hold is a crucial mediating factor in the short- and longer-term outcomes for male victims of (sexual) assault.

Recent work by Stanko and Hobdell (1993) reinforces the point that the impact of assault (though in this study non-sexual assault) on men is an area that has for too long been neglected by criminologists. They conducted a study of thirty-three male victims of assault by other men, many of whom reported fear, phobias, disruption to sleep and social patterns, hypervigilance, aggressiveness, personality change and a considerably heightened sense of vulnerability. The authors suggest that masculinity is not only an important factor in helping make sense of the consequences of victimisation for these men, but that the ways in which offers of support were offered, together with the victim's ability to look for, or accept, help and support was also crucially affected by the ways they and others perceived them as 'men', within a context of what masculinity means more generally. This work raises many questions about how men cope with violence, how they order their lives as a result of violence, how criminal justice professionals and support organisations view male victims. In all of this there is the issue of whether male victims of crime require help and support and, if so, how it might be offered and what might help. One of the consequences of the centrality of the 'hegemonic' model of masculinity, within both victimology and criminal justice, has been that the 'needs' of male victims of crime have remained largely unconsidered.

To an extent this position is reflected by the services that are provided for victims of crime. Although it is clear that men may be profoundly affected by crime, that some at least will be open to offers of help and support, relatively little thought has been given to providing services to this group of victims. This is not in any sense to suggest that the needs of men should be prioritised in some way or, indeed, that they should be singled out, but simply to point out that they should be recognised. Services which assume that men do not need help or will not accept help merely collude in the reproduction of an ideology which places the traits of 'strength', 'resilience' and 'emotional independence' at the centre of the dominant conception of masculinity. On the basis of the brief review above of research on the impact of assault on men it would be hard not to agree with Maguire and Corbett's conclusion in relation to Victim Support that: 'The findings strongly suggest that the low priority given by some schemes to young male victims of violence may be a mistaken policy' (1987: 56).

Finally, the neglect of masculinity also obscures other crimes against men: racist attacks, homophobic attacks, domestic violence between gay men (Island and Letellier 1991), men's experiences of attack by women (although it constitutes the smallest proportion of men's assault, an analysis focusing how power and safety are negotiated is essential). The small literature which addresses racist violence often neglects to articulate how being male is part of the way racist violence works. No doubt, many black and minority women and children are targets of such violence, but so too are adult and adolescent men. How do such men make sense of such violence within climates of racial hatred? So too, gay men confront homophobic violence (Herek and Berrill 1992). Thus, the frame of masculinity aids our understanding of men's reactions to crime and fear of crime as well. Maxfield (1984) for instance locates men's anxiety over crime as a concern for others, a concern which he characterises as 'altruistic' fear of crime. So too this frame contributes to a more holistic account of men's offending. What is now needed is some research to explore what impact victimisation has upon offenders' sense of themselves, and the harm they potentially do to others.

MASCULINITY, MALE VICTIMS AND THE SHORTCOMINGS OF VICTIMOLOGY

From this evidence we may speculate – as this is basically all that is possible given the paucity of empirical evidence – that all forms of (violent) victimisation may provide a threat to the well-being of some men in some circumstances. It is therefore, at the very least, an area of victimisation that needs to be taken seriously. All men will not experience or respond to violence in the same way or even in similar ways. Some, perhaps even the large majority, will remain largely unconcerned or lastingly affected by such experiences, whilst others may suffer long-term trauma not just as victims of crime, but as *male* victims of crime. Their experience will be directly mediated by their views of themselves as men, their socially located understanding of what men *are* and the consequences of the experience may well be visible in a changed understanding of self.

Both conventional and left realist victimologies utilise a model of masculinity that is akin to what Connell (1987) has described as 'hegemonic masculinity', and therefore tend to avoid dealing with the issue of the victimisation of men. The promise by left realists to 'take victimisation seriously' is limited by its politics which has difficulty with any social relationships that do not fall neatly into dichotomic categories of 'oppressor' and 'oppressed'. The world in which we live is just not that simple or that comfortable. The amount of effort that has been put into studying victims of crime over the past twenty years should have convinced us by now that, at least where men are concerned, there is frequently no easy distinction between offender and victim. In order to think about the victimisation of men we have to confront some difficult political questions. Accepting that men also suffer as a result of criminal victimisation is not to deny that men continue to occupy an advantaged position in relation to women, or that women are 'unequal' victims of crime. However, what it requires us to do is to give up our essentialist models of gender which undifferentiatedly present women as victims and men as oppressors, and confront the social reality in which men not only routinely victimise women, but also victimise each other.

NOTES

1   What Harding (1986, 1987) has referred to as 'standpoint feminism'.
2   The use of this argument here should not in any sense be taken to imply some denial of the basic reality of the power structure within which violence against women and men takes place – the collective oppression of women by men.
3   As Stanko (1990) suggests: 'a "real" man is a strong, heterosexual male protector, capable of taking care of himself and, if necessary, guarding his and others' safety aggressively. He is the man who will stand up in a fight, but will not abuse his power by unnecessarily victimising others. And, according to the mythology of the "real" man, he will do so fearlessly' (1990: 26–7).

REFERENCES

Adler, Z. (1992) 'Male victims of sexual assault – legal issues', in Mezey, G.C. and King, M.B. (eds) *Male Victims of Sexual Assault*, Oxford: Oxford University Press.

Cohen, L. and Felson, M. (1979) 'Social change and crime rate trends: a routine activity approach', *American Sociological Review*, 44: 588–608.

Connell, R.W. (1987) *Gender and Power: Society, the Person and Sexual Politics*, Cambridge: Polity Press.

Crawford, A., Jones, T., Woodhouse, T. and Young, J. (1990) *Second Islington Crime Survey*, Middlesex Polytechnic: Centre for Criminology.

Dobash, R.E. and Dobash, R.P. (1979) *Violence against Wives: A Case against Patriarchy*, New York: Free Press.

Dobash, R.E. and Dobash, R.P. (1992) *Women, Violence and Social Change*, London: Routledge.

Fattah, E.A. (1992) *Towards a Critical Victimology*, London: Macmillan.

Finkelhor, D. (ed.) (1986) *A Sourcebook on Child Sexual Abuse*, Beverly Hills, CA: Sage.

Gilroy, P. and Sim, J. (1985) 'Law, order and the state of the left', *Capital and Class*, spring.

Harding, S. (ed.) (1986) *The Science Question in Feminism*, Milton Keynes: Open University Press.

Harding, S. (ed.) (1987) *Feminism and Methodology*, Milton Keynes: Open University Press.

Von Hentig, H. (1948) *The Criminal and his Victim*, New Haven, Conn: Yale University Press.

Herek, G., and Berrill, K. (1992) *Hate Crimes*, Beverly Hills, CA: Sage.

Hindelang, M.J., Gottfredson, M.R. and Garofalo, J. (1978) *Victims of Personal Crime: An Empirical Foundation for a Theory of Personal Victimisation*, Cambridge, Mass.: Ballinger.

Hough, M. and Mayhew, P. (1985) *Taking Account of Crime: Key Findings from the 1984 British Crime Survey*, London: HMSO.

Island, D. and Letellier, P. (1991) *Men who Beat the Men who Love Them*, London: Harrington Park Press.

Jones, T., Maclean, B. and Young, J. (1986) *The Islington Crime Survey*, Aldershot: Gower.

King, M.B. (1992) 'Male sexual assault in the community', in Mezey, G.C. and King, M.B. (eds) *Male Victims of Sexual Assault*, Oxford: Oxford University Press.

LaGrange, R. and Ferraro, K. (1989) 'Assessing age and gender differences in perceived risk and fear of crime', *Criminology*, 27 (4), 697–719.

Maguire, M. and Corbett, C. (1987) *The Effects of Crime and the Work of Victim Support Schemes*, Aldershot: Gower.

Matthews, R. and Young, J. (1992) *Issues in Realist Criminology*, London: Sage.

Maxfield, M. (1984) *Fear of Crime in England and Wales*, London: HMSO.

Morgan, J. and Zedner, L. (1992) *Child Victims: Crime, Impact and Criminal Justice*, Oxford: Oxford University Press.

Pointing, J. and Maguire, M. (eds) (1988) *Victims of Crime: A New Deal?*, Milton Keynes: Open University Press.

Rogers, C.N. and Terry, T. (1984) 'Clinical interventions with boy victims of sexual abuse', in Greer, J.G. and Stuart, I.R. (eds) *Victims of Sexual Aggression: Treatment of Children, Women and Men*, New York: Reinhold.

Ruggiero, V. (1992) 'Realist criminology: a critique', in Young, J. and Matthews, R. (eds) *Rethinking Criminology: The Realist Debate*, London: Sage.

Scraton, P. (1985) *The State of the Police*, London: Pluto.

Shapland, J., Willmore, J. and Duff, P. (1985) *Victims in the Criminal Justice System*, Aldershot: Gower.

Shepherd, J. (1990) 'Violent crime in Bristol: an accident and emergency department perspective', *British Journal of Criminology*, 30 (3), 289–305.

Smart, C. (1990) 'Feminist approaches to criminology or postmodern woman meets atavistic man', in Gelsthorpe, L. and Morris, A. (eds) *Feminist Perspectives in Criminology*, Milton Keynes: Open University Press.

Stanko, E.A. (1988) 'Hidden violence against women' in Pointing, J. and Maguire, M. (eds) *Vicitims of Crime: A New Deal?*, Milton Keynes: Open University Press.

Stanko, E.A. (1990) *Everyday Violence: How Women and Men Experience Sexual and Physical Danger*, London: Pandora.

Stanko, E.A. and Hobdell, K. (1993) 'Assault on men: masculinity and male victimisation', *British Journal of Criminology*, 33 (3), 400–15.

Walklate, S. (1989) *Victimology: The Victim and the Criminal Justice Process*, London: Unwin Hyman.

Walklate, S. (1992) 'Appreciating the victim: conventional, realist or critical victimology?', in Matthews, R. and Young, J. (eds) *Issues in Realist Criminology*, London: Sage.

Watkins, B. and Bentovim, A. (1992) 'Male children and adolescents as victims: a review of current knowledge', in Mezey, G.C. and King, M.B. (eds) *Male Victims of Sexual Assault*, Oxford: Oxford University Press.

Wolfgang, M.E. (1958) *Patterns in Criminal Homicide*, New York: Wiley.

Young, J. (1986) 'The failure of criminology: the need for a radical realism', in Matthews, R. and Young, J. (eds) *Confronting Crime*, London: Sage.

Young, J. (1988) 'Risk of crime and fear of crime: a realist critique of survey-based assumptions', in Pointing, J. and Maguire, M. (eds) *Victims of Crime: A New Deal?*, Milton Keynes: Open University Press.

Young, J. and Matthews, R. (eds) (1992) *Rethinking Criminology: The Realist Debate*, London: Sage.

STUDY QUESTIONS

1   In what ways can this mid-1990s piece be seen as a development of Stanko's mid-1980s ideas (see Reading 21)?

2   What do you understand by the term 'hegemonic masculinity'? With reference to the work of Newburn and Stanko, why is it unhelpful when studying crimes of sexual and physical assault?
3   Having read Readings 21 and 22 on violence, what kind of support do you think is important for victims of sexual violence?

FURTHER READING

The social construction of 'masculinity' as a subject of academic study emerged in the 1970s with the publication of Tolson, A. (1977) *The Limits of Masculinity*, London: Routledge, which was arguably the first work to analyse in detail relationships between powerful and (relatively) powerless men, as opposed to simply the domination of men over women. A number of writers have since continued the deconstruction of masculinity, notably Connell, R.W. (1987) *Gender and Power*, Cambridge: Polity Press; Connell, R.W. (1995) *Masculinities*, Cambridge: Polity Press; and Hearn, J. and Morgan, D. (eds) (1990) *Men, Masculinity and Social Theory*, London: Allen and Unwin, all of which explore the notion of 'hegemonic masculinity' – as does *The Sage Dictionary of Criminology* (2001), edited by McLaughlin, E. and Muncie, J. London: Sage. The question 'can men be victims?' is addressed by Sandra Walklate (2001) *Gender, Crime and Criminal Justice*, Cullompton: Willan; and is further discussed in relation to hegemonic masculinity in men's prisons by Yvonne Jewkes (2002) *Captive Audience: Media Masculinity and Power in Prisons*, Cullompton: Willan.

Part Four

The Criminal Justice System

T he six readings in Part IV focus on various aspects of the criminal justice system. The first two readings are concerned with police and policing. In the first, Robert Reiner (Reading 23) considers the occupational culture of the police force ('cop culture'). He explores how subcultural values are developed, and considers their significance in understanding relationships within the force, and the personal relationships that police officers have with the public. Clive Coleman and Clive Norris (Reading 24) are also interested in the occupational culture of the police and explore the relationship between this and police discretion and discrimination through a consideration of the 'over-policing' of black people and the 'under-policing' of domestic violence. In the first of two readings on courts Frank Belloni and Jacqueline Hodgson (Reading 25) discuss research on magistrates' courts and the Crown Court and argue that the workings of both are affected by ideological and financial constraints resulting too often in miscarriages of justice. This is illustrated further by Andrew Billen (Reading 26) who focuses on the figure of the judge and, using examples, demonstrates that as a group, judges are out of touch with the lives and concerns of most people. The final two readings in this part focus on imprisonment. The first, by Ian Dunbar and Anthony Langdon (Reading 27), considers the question: 'why do we punish?' The authors argue that the answer is twofold: punishment is seen to have 'expressive functions' and 'practical objectives'. They then consider the specific aims of imprisonment and argue that these are confused and frequently conflictual. Stanley Cohen and Laurie Taylor (Reading 28) draw on covert research that they undertook at HMP Durham and describe the day-to-day experience of incarceration in the prison's maximum-security wing. Overall, and following on from Part III, the readings in this section are concerned with different aspects of the criminal justice system and the experience of some of those – as workers, offenders or victims – within it.

23

Cop culture

Robert Reiner

The first two readings in this part on the criminal justice system focus on the police and policing. Robert Reiner is concerned specifically with the occupational culture of the police: 'cop culture'. In this extract, he concentrates on what he sees as the five elements of cop culture, namely: mission–action–cynicism–pessimism; suspicion; isolation/solidarity; conservatism; and machismo. Reiner argues that police work is seen as challenging and exciting, and purposeful in the sense that it is not 'just a job' but a 'way of life'. However, although police work can be seen as a mission, this in itself often leads to feelings of cynicism and pessimism as order and stability are overly valued. Police training encourages suspiciousness as socialization into the force is structured by patterns of power and privilege in society. So police officers are likely to be more suspicious of the marginalized and the powerless (see Reading 8). This suspiciousness is likely to spill over into everyday life and, together with the effects of unsociable working hours, difficulty in switching off from both the tension of the job and aspects of the police discipline code, many officers find that their work can affect relationships outside the police force and lead to social isolation. Internal solidarity, though, is not just the product of social isolation but also related to the need to support colleagues, both when 'in action' and from public criticism. Conservatism is partly a function of the job, as the majority of the 'clients' of the police are drawn from the lower socio-economic classes and the police are routinely pitted against organized labour and the left. Also, the force is both hierarchical and tightly disciplined. Machismo is characterized by over-use of alcohol and sexual indulgence and is a product of the masculine ethos of the force and the tension built up by the work. At the end of the extract Reiner does briefly mention the difficulties that women police officers have in being accepted in the force. Overall, though, his analysis does not account for gender differences (for example, in relation to issues of 'mission', 'isolation' and so on) and at times he writes

SOURCE: From *The Politics of the Police*, 3rd edn (Oxford: Oxford University Press, 2000), 89–98.

of 'the policeman' unproblematically. This is a shame as all aspects of 'cop culture' are likely to be experienced differently by police*women* – and others who do not fit the white, heterosexual, masculine hegemonic 'norm'.

MISSION–ACTION–CYNICISM–PESSIMISM

A central feature of cop culture is a sense of mission. This is the feeling that policing is not just a job but a way of life with a worthwhile purpose, at least in principle. 'It's a sect – it's like a religion, the police force' (constable, cited in Reiner 1978: 247). The purpose is conceived of not as a political enterprise but as the preservation of a valued way of life and the protection of the weak against the predatory. The core justification of policing is a victim-centred perspective. As a constable put it to me: 'Speaking from a policeman's point of view it doesn't give a damn if we oppress law-breakers, because they're oppressors in their own right' (Reiner 1978: 79).

The mission of policing is not regarded as irksome. It is fun, challenging, exciting, a game of wits and skill. Many commentators have stressed the hedonistic, action-centred aspects of cop culture (notably Holdaway 1977, 1983; Policy Studies Institute 1983, iv: 51–6; Skolnick and Fyfe 1993; Geller and Toch 1996; Crank 1998). They are undoubtedly very strong and of central importance. The main substance to which the police are addicted is adrenalin (Graef 1989). But the thrills of the chase, the fight, the capture, the 'machismo syndrome' (Reiner 1978: 161), although rare highlights of the work, are not merely a sport. They can be so uninhibitedly and delightedly engaged in because they are also seen as worthwhile. In a policeman's own eyes he is one of the 'good guys' and it is this which gives him the licence for action. He is not just a racing-driver or boxer in a blue uniform.

This moralizing of the police mandate is in many respects misleading. It overlooks the mundane reality of everyday policing, which is often boring, messy, petty, trivial and venal. It permits the elision of the universally approved elements of the police task (apprehending a murderer, say) and the political role of policing in upholding a specific state and social order. Certainly the 'sacred canopy' (Manning 1997: 21) often drawn over police work can be a tool of the organization, protecting and advancing its interest in gaining more resources, power, and autonomy from independent scrutiny. Nevertheless, it is important in understanding police work that it is seen as a mission, as a moral imperative, not just another job. This makes its established practices much more resistant to reform than if they were merely self-serving.

The elements of mission in the police perspective are reflected in their sense of themselves as 'the thin blue line', performing an essential role in safeguarding social order. The myth of police indispensability, of their essential social function 'to protect and serve', is central to the police worldview. Even much police wrongdoing has been attributed to arguably misguided pursuit of a 'noble cause', the 'Dirty Harry' dilemma of achieving essential ends by tarnished means (Klockars 1980; Waddington 1999a: 112–14; Morgan 2000).

Nevertheless, police officers tend to acquire a set of views which have been rightly described as 'cynical', or 'police pessimism' (Niederhoffer 1967; Vick 1981). Officers often develop a hard skin of bitterness, seeing all social trends in apocalyptic terms, with the police as a beleaguered minority about to be overrun by the forces of barbarism (Reiner 1978: ch. 11). This pessimistic outlook is only cynical in a sense – in the despair felt that the morality which the police officer still adheres to is being eroded on all sides. It is not a Wildean cynicism which knows the price of everything and the value of nothing. Rather it resembles a Marxian account of commodity fetishism: price has sadly masked value. The very strength of the hardboiled outlook of policemen derives from the resilience of their sense of mission. Cynicism is the Janus face of commitment.

The salience of a sense of mission obviously varies between police officers. It was much more evident in the type I labelled the 'new centurions' (after the title of Joseph Wambaugh's seminal 1971 police novel) than those the argot calls 'uniform-carriers', who shirk the work as much as possible (Reiner 1978: ch. 12). But many (if not most) 'uniform-carriers', with their quintessentially cynical views ('It's the survival of the fittest … You've got to look after No. 1 … The policeman should exploit his job to the full advantage'), became that way precisely because of the effects of career disappointment destroying a prior sense of mission.

Undoubtedly many policemen see their combat with 'villains' as a ritualized game, a fun challenge, with 'winning' by an arrest giving personal satisfaction rather than any sense of public service. But this cynical view may well function as a self-protecting shield to reduce the anxiety that the thief-taker's many failures would otherwise induce.[1] One constable advised me:

> All police work's a game. You get the people who do wrong and the people that try and catch them. Sometimes the wrong-doers get caught, sometimes they don't. If they get caught and copped, if they get nicked and weighed-off, fair enough. If they don't there's no point getting emotionally involved.

Cynicism about thief-taking as a game is thus functionally analogous to the role of humour as tension-release, expressed in the motto 'If you can't take a joke you shouldn't have joined this job' (Reiner 1978: 216–17; Holdaway 1983: 138–54; Young 1995; Waddington 1999a: 114–16).

The core of the police outlook is this subtle and complex intermingling of the themes of mission, hedonistic love of action and pessimistic cynicism. Each feeds off and reinforces the others, even though they may appear superficially contradictory. They lead to a pressure for 'results' which may strain against legalistic principles of due process. *Pace* Skolnick's account, this pressure for 'efficiency' is not primarily derived externally but is a basic motivating force within police culture. It does, however, relate to the other facets of cop culture – suspicion, isolation/solidarity, conservatism – in the way Skolnick suggests.

SUSPICION

Most police officers are aware that their job has bred in them an attitude of constant suspicion that cannot be readily switched off. Suspicion is a product of the need to keep a lookout for signs of trouble, potential danger and clues to offences. It is a response to the danger, authority, and efficiency elements in the environment, as well as an outcome of the sense of mission. Police need to develop fine-grained cognitive maps of the social world, so that they can readily predict and handle the behaviour of a wide range of others, in frequently fraught encounters, without losing authority (Rubinstein 1973: chs. 4–6; Holdaway 1983: chs. 6–7; Kemp et al. 1992; Waddington 1999a: 101–2). Police stereotyping has been the subject of many critiques. They suggest that stereo-types of likely offenders become self-fulfilling prophecies as people with those characteristics are disproportionately questioned or arrested, leading to a vicious cycle of deviance amplification (Young 1971). However, stereotyping is an inevitable tool of the suspiciousness endemic to police work. The crucial issue is not its existence but the degree to which it is reality-based and helpful, as opposed to categorically discriminatory in a prejudiced way – and thus not merely unjust but counter-productive for the police force's own purposes (Banton 1983).

Suspicion does not only develop out of the intrinsic conditions of police work; it is deliberately encouraged by training. Skolnick cited an American manual giving detailed guidance for field interrogations which begins, 'Be suspicious. This is a healthy police attitude.' Among the Catch-22 tips for signs of the 'unusual' subject who should be stopped are: '7. Exaggerated unconcern over contact with the officer. 8. Visibly "rattled" when near the policemen' (Skolnick 1966: 45–6). A similar guide to the 'abnormal', embracing most of the population, was found in an English field manual by David Powis, a former Metropolitan assistant commissioner. Powis included in his list of suspicious types political radicals or intellectuals who 'spout extremist babble', or people in possession of a 'your rights' card (Powis 1977: 92).

While police suspiciousness and stereotyping are inescapable, the particu-lar categories informing them tend to be ones that reflect the structure of power in society. This serves to reproduce that structure through a pattern of implicit discrimination.

ISOLATION/SOLIDARITY

Many commentators have emphasized the marked internal solidarity, coupled with social isolation, of police officers (Clark 1965; Westley 1970: ch. 3; Cain 1973; Reiner 1978: 208–13; Graef 1989; Skolnick and Fyfe 1993; Crank 1998: ch. 15; Waddington 1999a: 99–101, 117). They have been referred to as 'a race apart' (Banton 1964), 'a man apart' (Judge 1972), 'a beleaguered minority' (Alex 1976).

Certainly, many police officers report difficulties in mixing with civilians in ordinary social life. These stem from shift-work, erratic hours, difficulties in switching off from the tension engendered by the job, aspects of the discipline code, and the hostility or fear that citizens may exhibit to the police. Social isolation is the price to be paid for Peel, Rowan, and Mayne's policy of elevating the British police as symbols of impersonal authority, and was to an extent a direct product of recruitment policies aimed at severing officers from their local communities (Miller 1999: 26–8). Internal solidarity is a product not only of isolation, but also of the need to be able to rely on colleagues in a tight spot, and a protective armour shielding the force as a whole from public knowledge of infractions. Many studies have stressed the powerful code that enjoins officers to back each other up in the face of external investigation (Stoddard 1968; Westley 1970: ch. 4; Shearing 1981b; Punch 1985; Skolnick and Fyfe 1993; Kleinig 1996; Newburn 1999). The offences that colleagues shield are not necessarily major infractions to be protected from external eyes. Rank-and-file solidarity is often aimed at concealing minor violations (what Cain 1973: 37 called 'easing behaviour') from the attention of supervisory officers.

This points to a misleading aspect of the emphasis on solidarity and isolation. First, it neglects the importance of conflicts inside the police organization. Some of these are structured within the rank hierarchy and the force division of labour, say between uniform and detective branches. It is true that internal conflicts may often be overridden by the need to present a united front in the face of external attacks. But this is not always so. The fundamental division between 'street cops' and 'management cops' can be reinforced in the face of external investigation (Ianni and Ianni 1983). 'Management cops' are derided by the 'street-wise' operational officers. The depth of the gulf is due to the different, often contradictory, functions of the two levels. The 'management' have to project an acceptable, legalistic, rational face of policing to the public. This may mean complicity with misconduct in some circumstances, deliberately hearing, seeing and saying nothing. But when reform pressures become intense, the 'management' may be forced into confrontation with the street level. To an extent, however, the apparent gulf and conflict between 'street' and 'management' orientations is functional for the organization itself (Grimshaw and Jefferson 1987). It allows presentational strategies to be adopted by management levels in real ignorance of what these might cover up, while at the same time the sacrifice of some individuals as 'bent' ratifies the effectiveness of the disciplinary process as a whole.

The 'them' and 'us' outlook which is a characteristic of police culture makes clear distinctions between types of 'them' (as well as of 'us'). The police perspective on social divisions in the population clearly reflects the structure of power as filtered through the specific problems of police work (Reiner 1978: ch. 11; Lee 1981; Shearing 1981a, c; Holdaway 1983: ch. 6; Young 1991).

The social structure as perceived by the police is one in which the hard class distinctions of the past have been eroded. Many policemen subscribe to an ideal of egalitarianism (epitomized by remarks such as 'nothing would give me greater pleasure than being able to nick the Lord Mayor'). At the same time they are acutely aware of the status distinctions which do exist (and their need to be finely tuned to them in giving and expecting the appropriate level of deference):

'You deal with everybody here. From the basic form of human life in the jungle conditions of the bad areas, to the elite of the town. The posh dinner parties that go on. You have to handle them all' (uniformed constable). Society does not bestow fair and equal chances. As one constable remarked to me: 'It's hard for a kid if his mother's tomming it, and his dad's always in the boozer.' [...]

POLICE CONSERVATISM

The evidence we have of the political orientations of police officers suggests that they tend to be conservative, both politically and morally. Partly this is due to the nature of the job. The routine 'clients' of the police are drawn from the bottom layers of the social order. But control of the lumpen elements is not necessarily something which even politically conscious members of the working class would be averse to. However, in their public order role, and even more so in the work of their specifically political 'high policing' sections, the police have been routinely pitted against organized labour and the Left (Lipset 1969; Skolnick 1969; Bunyan 1977; Brodeur 1983; Morgan 1987; Della Porta and Den Boer 1988; Reiner 1998; Weinberger 1991, 1995: ch. 9; Vogler 1991; Gill 1994, 1997a, b; Brewer et al. 1996; Mazower 1997; Huggins 1998). Furthermore, the force has from the start been constructed as a hierarchical, tightly disciplined organization. Thus the police officer with a conservative outlook is more likely to fit in. Processes of selection and self-selection lead police officers to be conservative. [...]

[...] When I attempted to interview police in the 1970s about their political attitudes this was prohibited by the Home Office, as it was claimed that it would impugn the traditional notion of the police as outside any form of politics (Reiner 1978: 11, 283; 1997). I have seen an unpublished 1977 dissertation by a police officer who interviewed a sample of colleagues in a northern city force, using the questions I had been prohibited from asking. He found that 80 per cent described themselves as Conservative – 18 per cent of whom were to the right of the party. The remainder were evenly divided between Labour, Liberal, and 'don't know'. Of his sample, 80 per cent had voted in all recent elections. A slight rightward shift was indicated by the fact that 9 per cent had moved from Labour or Liberal to Conservative between 1974 and 1977, with no movement in the opposite direction. Despite this, 64 per cent affirmed that the police should remain politically neutral at all times, 21 per cent wished for the right to join a political party without taking an active role, while 12 per cent wished to be able to take an active part in politics.

More recently, a survey was conducted of 286 serving Metropolitan Police officers which included questions on voting patterns and intentions (Scripture 1997). This found that of those who had voted in the 1979, 1983, 1987, and 1992 general elections the overwhelming majority had supported the Conservatives (respectively 79 per cent, 86 per cent, 74 per cent, and 74 per cent: Scripture 1997: 172). However, only 44 per cent intended to vote Conservative at the next general election (the survey was conducted before the 1997 election). This was probably a result of police disenchantment with the Conservative government's reform package aimed at subjecting the service to market disciplines, embodied in the 1993 Sheehy Report and the Police and Magistrates Courts Act 1994 (Loveday 1995a, b; McLaughlin and Murji 1996, 1997; Rose 1996: ch. 6; Reiner 1997: 1030–9).

The trend in the 1970s towards more open involvement in political debate of chief constables and the Police Federation has already been described (Judge 1994; McLaughlin and Murji 1998; Loader and Mulcahy 2000). It clearly expressed views which were symbiotically related to Conservative Party policies, and echoed (at a less explicit level) the American 'blue power' political campaigning of the 1960s and 1970s.

Apart from specific party politics, the police tend to hold views on moral and social issues which are conservative. 'Cops are conventional people....' [...].

MACHISMO

Despite this moral conservatism, in many respects police culture departs from puritanism. The police world is one of old-fashioned machismo (Fielding 1994; Crank 1998: ch. 14). Sexism in police culture is reinforced by discrimination in recruitment and promotion (Graef 1989: ch. 6; Hanmer et al. 1989; Young 1991: ch. 4; Heidensohn 1992, 1994, 1998; Halford 1993; Martin 1996; Walklate 1996; Brown 1997). The contempt exhibited for such sexual deviance as homosexuality and paedophilia is accompanied by routinized 'sexual boasting and horseplay', often at the expense of women colleagues (Policy Studies Institute 1983, iv: 91–7). Policemen are not notorious for their aversion to illicit heterosexual activities. As one constable told me, 'Policemen have one of the highest divorce rates in the country. There's always a bit of spare round the corner, because of the glamour of the job' (Reiner 1978: 212).[2] Nor are policemen notably abstemious from alcohol, for all their contempt for users of other drugs. One hazard of police research is the taking of mental notes while sinking under a bar as the consumption of pints mounts. Police alcoholism has been a perennial problem since the early days of the force. The alcoholic and sexual indulgences of police are a product both of the masculine ethos of the force and of the tension built up by the work. Their significance in this regard is brought out best by the novels of Joseph Wambaugh, in particular *The Choir-boys* (1976), with their central theme of policing as a morally (even more than physically) dangerous occupation. The decidedly non-puritanical ethos about heterosexual behaviour, drinking and gambling can expose the police officer to strains, tensions and charges of hypocrisy when enforcing laws in these areas. This factor helps explain the greater propensity for police corruption in the specialist enforcement of vice laws.

It has always been tough for women police officers to gain acceptance. The establishment of employment for policewomen in the first place came only after a protracted campaign (Carrier 1988). Despite formal integration, they continue to experience discrimination (Bryant et al. 1985; Jones 1986, 1987; Dunhill 1989; Heidensohn 1989, 1992, 1994, 1998; Walklate 1992, 1996; Brown et al. 1993; Brown 1997). The difficulties they face in achieving higher rank were illustrated by the highly publicized action claiming sex discrimination brought by Alison Halford, former assistant chief constable in Merseyside (Halford 1993). However, since then a number of women chief officers have been appointed. […]

NOTES

1   It also serves to resolve the 'Dirty Harry' problem, whereby 'policing constantly places its practitioners in situations in which good ends can be achieved by dirty means.' This is 'a genuine moral dilemma … from which one cannot emerge innocent no matter what one does' (Klockars, 1980: 33). Cynicism is a clearly possible psychological result.
2   I remember well the experience in 1971 (soon after I began research on the police) of attending a conference where, after the learned seminars a local officer took me, two other sociologists, and two out-of-town policemen to a local drinking club. There were about fifty men there, and just three women – two strippers and the barmaid. To the amazement of the observing but not participating sociologists, at the end of the evening the three policemen managed to walk off with the three women, whom they had been assiduously chatting up while fending off earnest discussions of police sub-cultural normative patterns.

REFERENCES

Alex, N. (1976) *New York Cops Talk Back*. New York: Wiley.

Banton, M. (1964) *The Policeman in the Community*. London: Tavistock.

Banton, M. (1983) 'Categorical and Statistical Discrimination', *Ethnic and Racial Studies*, 6 (3) (July).

Brewer, J.D., Guelke, A., Hume, I., Moxon-Browne, E. and Wilford, R. (1996) *The Police, Public Order and the State*, 2nd edn. London: Macmillan.

Brodeur, J-P. (1983) 'High Policing and Low Policing: Remarks about the Policing of Political Activities', *Social Problems*, 30 (5) (June): 507–20.

Brown, J. (1997) 'Equal Opportunities and the Police in England and Wales: Past, Present and Future Opportunities', in P. Francis, P. Davies, and V. Jupp (eds), *Policing Futures*. London: Macmillan.

Brown, J., Maidment, A. and Bull, R. (1993) 'Appropriate Skill–Task Matching or Gender Bias in Deployment of Male and Female Police Officers', *Policing and Society*, 3 (1), 121–36.

Bryant, L., Dunkerley, D. and Kelland, G. (1985) 'One of the Boys', *Policing*, 1 (4), 236–44.

Bunyan, T. (1977) *The Political Police in Britain*. London: Quartet Books.

Cain, M. (1973) *Society and the Policeman's Role*. London: Routledge and Kegan Paul.

Carrier, J. (1988) *The Campaign for the Employment of Women as Police Officers*. Aldershot: Avebury.

Clark, J.P. (1965) 'Isolation of the Police: a Comparison of the British and American Situations', *Journal of Criminal Law, Criminology and Police Science*, 56 (3), 307–19.

Crank, J.P. (1998) *Understanding Police Culture*. Cincinatti: Anderson Publishing.

Della Porta, D. and Den Boer, M. (eds) (1988) *Policing Protest*. Minneapolis: University of Minnesota Press.

Dunhill, C. (ed.) (1989) *The Boys in Blue: Women's Challenge to Policing*. London: Virago.

Fielding, N. (1994) 'Cop Canteen Culture', in T. Newburn and E.A. Stanko (eds), *Just Boys Doing Business: Men, Masculinity and Crime.* London: Routledge.

Geller, W. and Toch, H. (eds) (1996) *Police Violence: Understanding and Controlling Police Abuse of Force.* New Haven, Conn.: Yale University Press.

Gill, P. (1994) *Policing Politics: Security Intelligence and the Liberal Democratic State.* London: Frank Cass.

Gill, P. (1997a) 'Making Sense of Police Intelligence: the Use of a Cybernetic Model in Analysing Information and Power in Police Intelligence Process', *Policing and Society*, 8 (3), 289–314.

Gill, P. (1997b) 'Police Intelligence Processes: a study of Criminal Intelligence Units in Canada', *Policing and Society*, 8 (4), 339–66.

Graef, R. (1989) *Talking Blues.* London: Collins.

Grimshaw, R. and Jefferson, T. (1987) *Interpreting Policework.* London: Unwin.

Halford, A. (1993) *No Way up the Greasy Pole.* London: Constable.

Hanmer, J., Radford, R. and Stanko, E.A. (eds) (1989) *Women, Policing and Male Violence.* London: Routledge.

Heidensohn, F. (1989) *Women in Policing in the USA.* London: Police Foundation.

Heidensohn, F. (1992) *Women in Control: The Role of Women in Law Enforcement.* Oxford: Oxford University Press.

Heidensohn, F. (1994) ' "We Can Handle it out Here": Women Police Officers in Britain and the USA and the Policing of Public Order', *Policing and Society*, 4 (4), 293–303.

Heidensohn, F. (1998) 'Women in Policing', *Criminal Justice Matters*, 32: 13–14.

Holdaway, S. (1977) 'Changes in Urban Policing', *British Journal of Sociology*, 28 (2), 119–37.

Holdaway, S. (1983) *Inside the British Police.* Oxford: Basil Blackwell.

Huggins, M. (1998) *Political Policing.* Durham, NC: Duke University Press.

Ianni, E.R. and Iaani, R. (1983) 'Street Cops and Management Cops: the Two Cultures of Policing', in M. Punch (ed.), *Control in the Police Organization.* Cambridge, MA: MIT Press.

Jones, S. (1986) 'Caught in the Act', *Policing*, 2 (2), 129–40.

Jones, S. (1987) *Policewomen and Equality.* London: Macmillan.

Judge, A. (1972) *A Man Apart.* London: Barker.

Judge, A. (1994) *The Force of Persuasion.* Surbiton: Police Federation.

Kemp, C., Norris, C. and Fielding, N. (1992) *Negotiating Nothing: Police Decision-making in Disputes.* Aldershot: Avebury.

Kleinig, J. (1996) *The Ethics of Policing.* Cambridge: Cambridge University Press.

Klockars, C. (1980) 'The Dirty Harry Problem'. *The Annals*, 452 (November): 33–47.

Lee, J.A. (1981) 'Some Structural Aspects of Police Deviance in Relations with Minority Groups', in C. Shearing (ed.), *Organizational Police Deviance.* Toronto: Butterworth.

Lipset, S.M. (1969) 'Why Cops Hate Liberals, and Vice Versa', *Atlantic Monthly*; Reprinted in W. Bopp (ed.), *The Police Rebellion.* Springfield, IL: C.C. Thomas, 1971.

Loader, I. and Mulcahy, A. (2000) 'The Power of Legitimate Naming: Pt. I: Chief Constables as Social Commentators in Post-war England; Pt. II: Making Sense of the Elite Police Voice'. *British Journal of Criminology*, 41(1) winter: 41–55.

Loveday, B. (1995a) 'Contemporary Challenges to Police Management in England and Wales: Developing for Effective Service Delivery', *Policing and Society*, 5 (4), 281–302.

Loveday, B. (1995b) 'Reforming the Police: From Local Service to State Police', *Political Quarterly*, 66 (2). 141–156.

McLaughlin, E. and Murji, K. (1996) 'Time Change: New Formations and Representations of Police Accountability', in C. Critcher and D. Waddington (eds), *Policing Public Order*. Aldershot: Avebury.

McLaughlin, E. and Murji, K. (1997) 'The Future Lasts a Long Time: Public Police-work and the Managerialist Paradox', in P. Francis, P. Davies and V. Jupp (eds), *Policing Futures: The Police, Law Enforcement and the Twenty-first Century*. London: Macmillan.

McLaughlin, E. and Murji, K. (1998) 'Resistance through Representation: "Storylines", Advertising and Police Federation Campaigns', *Policing and Society*, 8 (4), 367–99.

Manning, P. (1997) *Police Work*, 2nd edn. Prospect Heights, IL: Waveland Press.

Martin, C. (1996) 'The Impact of Equal Opportunities Policies on the Day-to-day Experiences of Women Police Constables', *British Journal of Criminology*, 36 (4): 510–28.

Mazower, M. (ed.) (1997) *The Policing of Politics in the Twentieth Century*. Providence, RI: Berghahn Books.

Miller, W. (1999) *Cops and Bobbies*, 2nd edn. Columbus, OH: Ohio State University Press.

Morgan, J. (1987) *Conflict and Order: The Police and Labour Disputes in England and Wales 1900–1939*. Oxford: Oxford University Press.

Morgan, R. (2000) 'The Utilitarian Justification of Torture', *Punishment and Society*, 2 (2), 181–96.

Newburn, T. (1999) *Understanding and Preventing Police Corruption: Lessons from the Literature*. London: Home Office Policing and Reducing Crime Unit.

Niederhoffer, A. (1967) *Behind the Shield*. New York: Doubleday.

Policy Studies Institute (1983) *Police and People in London*: i, D.J. Smith, *A Survey of Londoners*; ii, S. Small, *A Group of Young Black People*, iii, D.J. Smith, *A Survey of Police Officers*; iv, D. J. Smith and J. Gray, *The Police in Action*. London: Policy Studies Institute.

Powis, D. (1977) *The Signs of Crime*. London: McGraw-Hill.

Punch, M, (1985) *Conduct Unbecoming. The Social Construction of Police Deviance and Control*. London: Tavistock.

Reiner, R. (1978) *The Blue-coated Worker*. Cambridge: Cambridge University Press.

Reiner, R. (1997) 'Policing and the Police', in M. Maguire, R. Morgan, and R. Reiner (eds), *The Oxford Handbook of Criminology*, 2nd edn. Oxford: Oxford University Press.

Reiner, R. (1998) 'Process or Product? Problems of Assessing Individual Police Performance', in J-P. Brodeur (ed.), *How to Recognise Good Policing*. Thousand Oaks, CA: Sage.

Rose, D. (1996) *In the Name of the Law: The Collapse of Criminal Justice*. London: Jonathan Cape.

Rubinstein, J. (1973) *City Police*. New York: Ballantine.

Scripture, A. (1997) 'The Sources of Police Culture: Demographic or Environmental Variables?', *Policing and Society*, 7 (3), 163–76.

Shearing, C. (1981a) 'Subterranean Processes in the Maintenance of Power', *Canadian Review of Sociology and Anthropology*, 18 (3), 283–98.

Shearing, C. (ed.) (1981b) *Organisational Police Deviance*. Toronto: Butterworth.

Shearing, C. (1981c) 'Deviance and Conformity in the Reproduction of Order', in C. Shearing (ed.), *Organisational Police Deviance*. Toronto: Butterworth.

Sheehy, P. (1993) *Report of the Inquiry into Police Responsibilities and Rewards*, 2 vols. London: HMSO. Cm. 2280.

Skolnick, J. (1966) *Justice without Trial*. New York. Wiley.

Skolnick, J. (1969) *The Politics of Protest*. New York: Bantam.

Skolnick, J. and Fyfe, J. (1993) *Above the Law: Police and the Excessive Use of Force*. New York: Free Press.

Stoddard, E.R. (1968) 'The Informal Code of Police Deviancy: a Group Approach to Bluecoat Crime', *Journal of Criminal Law, Criminology, and Police Science*, 59 (2), 201–13.

Vick, C. (1981) 'Police Pessimism', in D. Pope and N. Weiner (eds), *Modern Policing*. London: Croom Helm.

Vogler, R. (1991) *Reading the Riot Act*. Milton Keynes: Open University Press.

Waddington, P.A.J. (1999) *Policing Citizens*. London: UCL Press.

Walklate, S. (1992) 'Jack and Jill Join up at Sun Hill: Public Images of Police Officers', *Policing and Society*, 2/3: 219–32.

Walklate, S. (1996) 'Equal Opportunities and the Future of Policing', in F. Leishman, B. Loveday and Savage, S. (eds), *Core Issues in Policing*. London: Longman.

Wambaugh, J. (1971) *The New Centurions* London: Sphere/New York: Dell.

Wambaugh, J. (1976) *The Choir-boys*. London: Futura/New York: Dell.

Weinberger, B. (1991) *Keeping the Peace? Policing Strikes in Britain 1906–1926*. Oxford: Berg.

Weinberger, B. (1995) *The Best Police in the World*. London: Scolar Press.

Westley, W. (1970) *Violence and the Police*. Cambridge, MA: MIT Press.

Young, J. (1971) 'The Role of the Police as Amplifiers of Deviancy', in S. Cohen (ed.), *Images of Deviance*. London: Penguin.

Young, M. (1991) *An Inside Job: Policing and Police Culture in Britain*. Oxford: Oxford University Press.

Young, M. (1995) 'Black Humour: Making Light of Death', *Policing and Society*, 5 (2), 151–68.

STUDY QUESTIONS

1   What do you understand by the phrase 'cop culture'? How do you think socialization into these subcultural attitudes may affect a police officer's work?

2   What is the likely effect of the 'machismo-syndrome' on the recruitment, drop-out rate and experience of women and/or non-white police officers?

3   How accurate are fictional and media representations of the police and 'cop culture'?

FURTHER READING

Robert Reiner has written extensively on the origins, history and role of the police. Among his best-known works on the subject are *The Blue-coated Worker*

(1978) Cambridge: Cambridge University Press, and *Chief Constables* (1991) Oxford: Oxford University Press. His chapter on 'Police research' in R.D. King and E. Wincup (eds) (2000) *Doing Research on Crime and Justice*, Oxford: Oxford University Press, is also of interest, as is his broad overview of policing in M. Maguire, R. Morgan and R. Reiner (eds) (1997) *The Oxford Handbook of Criminology*, 2nd edn, Oxford: Oxford University Press. Finally, he is one of the contributors to N. Morris and M. Tonry (eds) (1992) *Modern Policing*, Chicago, Ill: Chicago University Press. Another relevant text is Morgan, R. and Newburn, T. (1997) *The Future of Policing*, Oxford: Oxford University Press. An interesting collection of first-hand accounts of police work, including 'cop culture', is provided in Graef, R. (1990) *Talking Blues: The Police in their own Words*, London: Fontana. The whole edition of *Criminal Justice Matters* no. 17 (Autumn 1994) is dedicated to 'Policing.' For accounts of the role and experience of women in the police service, see Heidensohn, F. (1992) *Women in Control: The Role of Women in Law Enforcement*, Oxford: Clarendon Press; and Jones, S. (1986) *Policewomen and Equality: Formal Policy versus Informal Practice*, London: Macmillan; while Halford, A. (1994) *No Way up the Greasy Pole*, London: Constable, provides a first-hand account of the difficulties faced by one senior policewoman. The experience of gay and lesbian police officers is discussed in Burke, M. (1993) *Coming out of the Blue: British Police Officers Talk about their Lives in 'the Job' as Lesbians, Gays and Bisexuals*, London: Cassell; and Leinen, S. (1993) *Gay Cops*, New Brunswick, NJ: Rutgers University Press.

24

Policing and the police: key issues in criminal justice

Clive Coleman and Clive Norris

In this second reading about the police and policing, Clive Coleman and Clive Norris extend the discussion about the occupational culture of the police force and consider the relationship between this and police discretion and discrimination when 'upholding' and 'applying' the law. Discretion can involve doing or not doing something and, with this in mind, Coleman and Norris suggest that the police are not 'slaves to the law' but use the law to restore order and impose symbolic justice. They focus on the complex relationship between discretion and discrimination through a consideration of the 'over-policing' of black people and the 'under-policing' of domestic violence. Coleman and Norris suggest that, although the policing of each of these issues may be related in some ways to subcultural police attitudes (i.e. racism and sexism respectively), discrimination may occur for other reasons: for example, transmitted discrimination and institutional practices. Further, there is evidence to suggest that police officers' expression of prejudicial attitudes is not always transmitted into prejudicial practice. Thus, Coleman and Norris argue that the concept of police culture is only one possible contributor to an understanding of police discretion.

The police are by far the most visible institution of the criminal justice system. While most people will have had little or no contact with prisons, probation or the courts, there must be few who by the age of majority have not come into personal contact of one kind or another with the police. Indeed, for the most part, the police want to be seen. Their distinctive uniforms with helmets fashioned to elevate their stature, and their clearly marked patrol cars equipped with sirens and flashing blue lights are clearly designed to draw attention to themselves. This is, of course, no accident; the police are the visible presence of the state in civil society.

SOURCE: From *Introducing Criminology* (Cullompton: Willan, 2000), 116–17, 130–39.

From the establishment in London of the New Police in 1829 by Sir Robert Peel, visibility was the order of the day. There were originally to be no detectives who could move freely among the citizenry in plain clothes, for this would resemble a continental model of policing which, as one parliamentary committee of the time declared, 'would be odious and repulsive' to the British idea of liberty. Nor were the police to be attired in the fashion of the military, for one of the prime justifications for the setting up of the New Police was the failure of the army to maintain order without recourse to gross and excessive force. This had occurred with some frequency in the preceding fifty years and most tragically at Peterloo, when in 1819 a demonstration was set upon by the army and hundreds were injured and eleven people killed.

When, therefore, on 29 September 1829 the citizens of London beheld the spectacle of groups men being marched to their beats dressed in 'blue-tail coat, blue trousers ... and a glazed black top-hat strengthened with a thick leather crown' (Critchley 1978: 51), they were witnessing the birth of a new institution. It was an institution that was symbolically differentiated from both the military and continental models of policing through its distinctive uniform (modelled on civilian business dress of the day), and effectively differentiated by its mandate, which was first and foremost preventative. This was to be achieved by providing a visible deterrent to acts of crime and disorder. As the new Commissioners wrote in their first force instruction: 'It should be understood that at the outset the principal object to be obtained is the prevention of crime.' [...]

DISCRETION AND DISCRIMINATION

As Waddington (1999: 31) has rightly observed: 'Prior to the revisionism of the 1960s, the prevailing assumption was that policing was little more than the application of law.' [...] [M]uch criminological attention has been aimed at challenging this assertion. But what in practice does it mean 'to uphold' or to apply the law? Does it mean that whenever a law is broken the police must enforce it? If this were true, the police would merely be puppets of the legal system, blindly enforcing the law regardless of context or consequence. What we know from detailed studies of police work in Britain (Banton 1964; Cain 1973; Holdaway 1983; Waddington 1993), America (Black 1980; Rubinstein 1973; Van Maanen 1978; Bayley 1994) and Canada (Ericson 1982) is that this could not be further from the truth. The police use law, among a number of other resources, in order to restore order and impose symbolic justice. They are not slaves to law but law is their servant. This realisation is of profound importance because it signals the centrality of discretion to understanding police work. In this next section we want to examine the nature, consequences and importance of discretion.

Discretion

What is police discretion? Drawing on Davis's (1969) seminal, but general definition of discretion, Klockars proposed the following:

A police officer or police agency may be said to exercise discretion whenever effective limits on his, her or its power leave them free to make a choice amongst possible courses of action or inaction. (Klockars 1985: 93)

We can note three salient points about this definition. First, Klockars does not use the word 'law', but the words 'effective limits'; this is because even where the law may insist on a course of action (in America there are 'full enforcement' statutes), if there is no mechanism for ensuring that officers comply, they are 'effectively' able to choose. In the context of police this is very important, since one of the most striking aspects of the police organisation is that the degree of discretion is greatest at the lowest level of the hierarchy, partly because much police work outside the station is of such low visibility to managerial oversight (Goldstein 1960).

Secondly, discretion is not just a property of individual police decisions in dealing with particular incidents, but of departmental policies, structures and organisation which frame those individual decisions. For instance, the setting up of a local robbery squad to tackle a recent rise in street crime is a discretionary decision, albeit one taken at a managerial or organisational level. Discretion at this level has been reduced in England and Wales since the Police and Magistrates Courts Act 1994. This enables the Home Secretary to set national policing objectives, and police authorities must produce annual local policing plans and set performance targets to measure the achievement of objectives.

Thirdly, the exercise of discretion can involve doing something or not doing something. This is important because the term 'discretion' has sometimes been equated with a questionable decision not to arrest someone where there were legal grounds for doing so. The important thing to note is that, in English law at least, the decision to arrest is itself discretionary.

Let us take a simple example to illustrate this point. Imagine that a police officer is called to the scene of two men fighting on a street corner. They are still fighting when the police arrive. The officer could:

- break it up with an informal warning to both participants and take no other action
- break it up, inquiring into the cause and attempting to conciliate and mediate between the two parties
- formally caution one or both parties
- attempt to find the cause of the fight and arrest the person they believe to be the most blameworthy
- arrest both parties on any appropriate public order or assault charges. (Lustgarten 1986: 10)

As Lustgarten has rightly argued, 'all the suggested options are within the range of a constable's legal powers. To say therefore that he must uphold the law, or is responsible to the law, is in practical terms meaningless' (Lustgarten 1986: 11).

If discretion is so subversive to our notion of the rule of law, why do the police have it? In general there have been four major justifications for the existence of police discretion:

- the finite resources available to perform police work
- the need for interpretational latitude in applying law
- the need to preserve legitimacy
- the need for efficiency.

We will examine each in more detail below.

Resources

Given that the police have finite resources, they have to make choices about how to deploy them and this inevitably means prioritising some activities over others. Moreover, if the police were rigorously to enforce some high volume offences like speeding, the capacity of others within the criminal justice system to process them, such as the Crown Prosecution Service and the courts, would soon be exceeded. As already noted, however, the scope for discretion in setting priorities has been lessened by the Police and Magistrates Courts Act 1994.

Interpretational Latitude

The law as it is written in the books purports to be clear and unambiguous, but the messy reality of life rarely falls easily into the neat categories of the law. All criminal statutes in England and Wales say that 'a police constable may arrest...'. Police officers have to interpret what they find to find a fit between the events and the law, and they need to temper the law with notions such as justice/fairness and appropriateness. As Klockars (1985: 98) notes, the law 'overreaches' itself and criminalizes more than it intends. For instance, would the interests of justice be served by prosecuting a surgeon for travelling at ten miles an hour over the speed limit, on her way to perform life saving surgery, or the driver of a vehicle which due to his own carelessness had swerved off the road resulting in the death of his wife and daughter? Probably not.

Legitimacy

Full enforcement would lead to an undermining of the basis for police legitimacy. One of the advantages of under-enforcement is that the police can build up credit with a citizenry who, in acknowledgement that they have been dealt with more favourably in the past, are more likely to cooperate with police requests for help in the future. 'Policing by consent' is a key concept in this context. At the extreme, some have argued that full enforcement would completely undermine the social fabric: 'Any society that committed the energy, resources and personnel to root out and punish all wrongdoers would set off enough mass paranoia, violent conflict and savage repression to become a charnel house, and pass into oblivion' (Blumberg 1970, cited in Rock 1973: 179).

Efficiency

A policy of full enforcement would not allow the police to differentiate between important and trivial crimes, and between cases where some productive outcome can be achieved and those where this is unlikely. Where resources are finite (see above), decisions need to be made about the most efficient or effective use of them. Full enforcement would also make it impossible for the police to 'trade' the threat of sanction for information. One of the key investigative strategies, especially in 'victimless' crimes, of letting the little fish go, in exchange for information so that bigger fish can be caught, would be unworkable (see Dunnighan and Norris 1999).

Criminologists have, then, recognised the inevitability of discretion, that police work is only partially concerned with law enforcement, and even when there are clear infractions of law, there is no guarantee that arrest and prosecution will follow. This realisation has had two major implications for criminology.

First, that recorded crime statistics cannot be treated as an accurate or reliable measure of the nature, distribution and extent of criminality. As Kitsuse and Cicourel noted, crime rates should be 'viewed as indices of organisational processes rather than as indices of the incidence of certain forms of behaviour' (Kitsuse and Cicourel 1963: 135). This insight led to a number of important studies documenting how crime statistics were a social construction (McCabe and Sutcliffe 1978; Bottomley and Coleman 1981; Young 1991), and the development of alternative measures of crime and victimisation which are not reliant on police processing, such as self-report studies and victimisation surveys (see Coleman and Moynihan 1996, for a review).

Second, if the law does not provide the full answer as to what police officers should do in a situation, attention shifts to what else influences their decisions. As Klockars points out, this issue strikes at the heart of democratic governance, with its emphasis on 'the rule of law'. As he writes:

> Under a government of laws police should not be allowed to make what amounts to their own laws, amend laws that have already been made, or decide that some people should have certain laws enforced on them while allowing others to violate the same laws with impunity. The whole idea of the police enjoying some broad discretionary power seems to open the door to arbitrariness, favouritism and discrimination. (Klockars 1985: 95)

For this reason, much criminological attention has been focused on what, given such discretion, shapes police decision-making and the extent to which this leads to policing which is *discriminatory*, in the sense that the law is unevenly applied in relation to different social groups in a way that is 'unjustified by legally relevant factors' (Reiner 1992: 162).

Discrimination

There is little doubt about the existence of what Reiner calls differentiation – that the exercise of police powers falls disproportionately upon some groups rather than others. Police enforcement activity largely falls upon the young rather than the old, the poor rather than the affluent, men rather than women, the urban rather than the rural, public rather than the private domains, and so on. Whether and to what extent differentiation involves discrimination are more difficult questions to answer. For illustrative purposes, we will briefly concentrate on two areas: the 'over-policing' of black people and the 'under-policing' of incidents of domestic violence.

The 'over-policing' of black people

The 'over-policing' of black people has been consistently documented by a range of studies at the level of stops, arrests and post-arrest decisions:

Stops: studies have consistently found that black people are more likely to be stopped than whites, with estimates ranging from between two and four times what one would expect on the basis of their presence in the population. Not only is the rate of stops greater, but a black person is more likely to be repeatedly stopped during the course of a year (PSI 1983; Willis 1983; Norris et al. 1992; Skogan 1994; Macpherson 1999).

Arrests: studies by Stevens and Willis (1979), PSI (1983), Walker et al. (1990) and Phillips and Brown (1998) have all found evidence of a higher black arrest rate than one would expect from their presence in the population. For instance, one of the most recent surveys, Phillips and Brown (1998), found that in eight out of the ten police stations they studied, black people were between two and eight times more likely to be arrested than whites.

Post-arrest decisions: studies have also revealed how other areas of police discretionary decision-making also seem to disadvantage black people, such as in the choice of charge (Blom-Cooper and Drabble 1982), the decision to caution rather than commence formal proceedings (Landau and Nathan 1983; Jefferson and Walker 1992; Phillips and Brown 1998) and the decision to recommend bail (see FitzGerald 1993, for a review).

Of course, one possible explanation for these differences is that black people actually do commit certain types of crime more than whites and are therefore more likely to be targets of police action. In this case, it could be argued that the differentiation is justified on the basis of differential offending profiles of the black and white communities. Despite this issue being hotly debated amongst criminologists (see Reiner 1992; Lea and Young 1993), there is no easy resolution to it. For example, we do not in this instance have enough satisfactory studies of relative crime rates that are independent of police practice. There have been few self-report studies of offending behaviour that have looked at ethnic differences, although one of the few to have been conducted in this country (Bowling et al. 1994; Graham and Bowling 1995) found no significant differences between black and white self-reported offending. However, this study has been criticised on methodological grounds (Coleman and Moynihan 1996). As FitzGerald (1993: 4) wrote in her report to the Royal Commission on Criminal Justice, 'it is impossible to know the precise extent of ethnic differences in offending rates once all other relevant factors are taken into account [such as age, employment status, area of residence, etc.]; and this makes for uncertainty in interpreting ethnic differences at the point of entry.' The broad consensus amongst many criminologists is that while differences in offending behaviour may explain some of the over-representation of black people in the criminal justice system, they only explain *some* of it (Lea and Young 1993; Smith 1997).

For some commentators (see particularly Gilroy 1982; Bridges 1983), the over-enforcement of law against black people can be explained by the informal norms, values, attitudes and beliefs which they see as comprising the occupational police sub-culture. In particular they draw on the findings of a raft of ethnographic studies, which document the use and prevalence of racist language by the police and a range of negative attitudes towards black people in general. From this it is argued that it is easy to see how police discretion produces over-enforcement: it is the result of officers' prejudice and discriminatory behaviour.

However, following Reiner (1992), we would argue that the pattern of differentiation cannot be seen as simply a product of higher rates of offending or as simply arising from attitudes found in the police sub-culture; the process is far more complex and multi-layered than this. Taking the evidence from various observation studies (including James 1979; Holdaway 1983; PSI 1983: vol. 4), Reiner (1992: 157) argues that categorical discrimination (i.e. action against members of a particular group only on the basis that they are members of that group) is probably the least important form of discrimination that may be operating. If discrimination does occur, it is more likely to be operative because of other practices which are outside of the purview of the individual police officer, or not related to his or her attitudinal values. These additional forms of discrimination Reiner terms transmitted, interactional, institutionalised and statistical discrimination (Reiner 1992: ch 4).

- *Transmitted discrimination* operates because the police are heavily dependent on calls from the public and, thus, differential enforcement rates may result. If the public are more likely to call the police to incidents involving members of ethnic groups, then it is discrimination by sections of the public rather than the police that is operative. Furthermore, in their role as dispute settlers, the police are often dependent on the preference of the complainant as to what action to take and a higher arrest rate for ethnic groups may be the result of public prejudice.
- *Interactional discrimination* results from the officer using discretion, not on the basis of legally relevant criteria, but on aspects of the interaction between the suspect and the officer, such as the level of respect accorded by the suspect to the officer. The greater the disrespect shown, the more likely that an arrest will follow. Given relationships between some young black people and the police, such groups may thus be more likely to have formal action taken against them. As Reiner (1992: 167) notes, while 'contempt of cop' is not a valid reason for arrest, it may provide a possible basis for a valid booking of a suspect who would otherwise have been let off.
- *Institutionalised discrimination* can arise, for example, from the more intensive policing of particular areas with high rates of crime and deprivation (which may also be areas of greater black residence). Thus, particular sections of the community living in those areas are disproportionately stopped, searched and arrested. Thus police policies and procedures at an organisational level 'may

work out in practice as discriminatory because of the structural bias of an unequal society' (Reiner 1992: 158).

* *Statistical discrimination* can be a predominant factor in proactive policing, especially in stop and search operations. If the lifestyle of a group is thought to involve a legally proscribed activity, such as New Age travellers or Rastafarians using marijuana, those identified as a member of that group can become a target for police attention. An attempt has been made to rule out stop and search on the basis of such things as appearance and apparent lifestyle by the Police and Criminal Evidence Act 1984. However, such practices may perhaps be one reason why black people are more likely to be arrested as a result of proactive policing strategies (see Phillips and Brown 1998: 38–9). Even so, it should be remembered, as Reiner points out, that the basis for such actions is a misguided concern with effectiveness – by targeting those thought to be the most 'likely' suspects. The Stephen Lawrence Inquiry (Macpherson 1999) concluded that 'institutional racism' was apparent in a number of areas; in its view, despite the complexities involved in the interpretation of the evidence, there remained 'a clear core of racist stereotyping' (para 6.45) in stop and search.

The 'under-policing' of incidents of domestic violence

If the police appear to over-enforce the law in relation to black people, then conversely it has been shown that in relation to domestic violence, the law is under-enforced. Detailed empirical studies, mainly carried out in the 1970s and 1980s, have shown how the police were reluctant either to arrest or prosecute perpetrators of domestic violence, even when there was clear evidence of an offence having been committed (Pahl 1982; Edwards 1989). Moreover, even when the police did arrest, it was often for an offence of less seriousness than the evidence would warrant, such as for 'breach of the peace' rather than 'assault occasioning actual bodily harm'. As Kemp et al. (1992: 119) concluded:

> Our research indicates that police officers as a matter of course tend to decriminalise domestic disputes where there is evidence of a criminal infraction. Even when there is a *prima facie* case for arrest and charge they under-utilise their legal powers in order to achieve an informal resolution, recommend civil proceedings or make an arrest on resource [usually lesser] charges.

In a similar way to that in which the over-policing of black people has been attributed to the values and beliefs of officers transmitted through the occupational culture, so too has the under-enforcement of laws relating to domestic violence. Again some commentators note the prevalence of sexist language, stereotypical attitudes towards women in general, the marginalisation and harassment of women police officers, and a generalised belief in the inappropriateness of police intervention in domestic affairs, consigning it to the status of 'rubbish' work. From this it is argued that it is easy to see how police discretion produces a pattern of under-enforcement; again it is seen as a result of prejudiced attitudes and values contained within the occupational culture (Stanko 1985; Edwards 1989). There have been concerted attempts to change police policy and attitudes in this area in the last decade or so since these studies were conducted.

There are, however, problems with academic accounts and policy initiatives which see a simple translation of attitudes into behaviour. For instance, Hoyle's (1998) study of the policing of domestic violence found that a general open-ended question to police officers about domestic disputes elicited a whole range of negative responses, but these generalised attitudes were often belied by how they said they handled specific disputes. As she reported:

> The initial comments were indicators of how domestic disputes are still, to some extent, trivialised by officers within a canteen culture discourse, whilst the response to questions about what officers actually did in practice indicate the divide between certain negative cultural attitudes and behaviour. (Hoyle 1998: 76)

This gap between attitudes and behaviour was similar to that reported in relation to 'race' some years ago by the PSI study *Police and People in London* (1983):

> Our first impression … was that racialist language and racial prejudice were prominent and pervasive and that many individual officers and also whole groups were preoccupied with ethnic differences. At the same time, on accompanying these officers as they went about their work, we found that their relations with black and brown people were often relaxed and friendly … we are fairly confident that there is no widespread tendency for black or Asian people to be given greatly inferior treatment by the police. (PSI 1983: 109 and 128)

This possibility of a gap between what officers say and what they do undermines the simplistic use of a concept of occupational culture (usually based on what officers say) as guide to, and explanation for, actual police behaviour (usually that considered undesirable).

A number of criminologists (Manning 1977; Holdaway 1983; Norris 1989; Hoyle 1998; Waddington 1999) have adopted a more complex view of police culture, which recognises that while police culture may have negative and undesirable traits, in itself that culture has to be understood as embracing far more than just negative attitudes. Police culture may still be used to help explain the difference between law in action and the law in the books, but that culture is seen as arising from the common problems that officers face in the course of their work. It not only contains attitudes and beliefs, but a stock of recipe knowledge on how to achieve the policing task: a set of working rules for managing the vicissitudes of the job (Manning 1982). And here it should be remembered that the job is not primarily about the prevention of crime or the enforcement of laws but about reproducing order by providing authoritative intervention and symbolic justice. As Chatterton (1983: 208) has argued:

> The decisions and actions taken at incidents reflect the concern to control relationships between themselves and the various publics on a division, to maintain their capacity to intervene authoritatively in any incident and to preserve their own and others' beliefs that they were 'on top of the area'.

Moreover, officers are also concerned with satisfying organisational demands that incidents are satisfactorily terminated: for example, that once a police officer has dealt with an incident they are not called out again, for this would suggest that the officer failed to negotiate or enforce an effective closure to the incident in the first place, raising questions about his or her competence (see Chatterton 1983: 201).

It should be stressed that such issues as over- and under-enforcement and discrimination and differentiation cannot be understood in terms of the police culture alone, but have to be seen in terms of the complex inter-relationships between the individual officer, suspects, the public, the occupational culture, the police organisation, the law, and the police role.

Thus the ideal of law is of even and equal enforcement and therefore that similar offences should be treated in similar ways. The patrol officer, on the other hand, is not primarily concerned with such abstract notions in individual encounters, but with authoritatively intervening to reproduce order. Meanwhile, the occupational culture provides a set of 'recipe rules' for determining how this should be achieved, such as that disrespectful and uncooperative suspects deserve to be arrested, and about the extent to which victims' preferences should be taken into account (Hoyle 1998; Waddington 1999). Simultaneously, the police organisation, as represented by the shift sergeant and inspector, is less concerned with the specific outcome of any individual incident than with its speedy termination on the ground and bureaucratic resolution at the station. Dealing with incidents quickly and effectively and 'clearing the message pad' so that an officer is free to deal with the next potential emergency becomes a primary goal in reactive policing (Fielding et al. 1989). In this context arrest, which will take an officer away from routine policing, may be seen as an undesirable outcome; on the other hand, targets in policing plans may encourage arrests to be made, so a balance has to be struck. Finally, we should add that the officer also brings to any incident their own individual norms and values, which make the individual officer the 'final arbiter and mediator' of the legal, organisational and cultural influences (Fielding, 1988: 60). In this context, the concept of police culture can only be one possible contributor to our understanding of police discretion. […]

REFERENCES

Banton, M. (1964) *The Policeman in the Community*. London: Tavistock.

Bayley, D. (1994) *Police for the Future*. New York: Oxford University Press.

Black, D. (1980) *The Manners and Customs of the Police*. London: Academic Press.

Blom-Cooper, L. and Drabble, R. (1982) 'Police perceptions of crime', *British Journal of Criminology*, 22, 184–7.

Blumberg, A. (1970) *The Scales of Justice*. Chicago: Aldine.

Bottomley, K. and Coleman, C. (1981) *Understanding Crime Rates*. Farnborough: Gower.

Bowling, B., Graham, J. and Ross, A. (1994) 'Self-reported offending among young people in England and Wales', in J. Junger-Tas, G. Terlouw and M. Klein (eds)

Delinquent Behaviour among Young People in the Western World. Amsterdam: Kugler.

Bridges, L. (1983) 'Policing the urban wasteland', *Race and Class* 24 (2): 31–48, Autumn.

Cain, M. (1973) *Society and the Policeman's Role.* London: Routledge and Kegan Paul.

Chatterton, M. (1983) 'Police work and assault charges', in M. Punch (ed.) *Control in the Police Organisation.* Cambridge, Mass.: MIT Press.

Coleman, C. and Moynihan, J. (1996) *Understanding Crime Data: Haunted by the Dark Figure.* Buckingham: Open University Press.

Critchley, T. (1978) *A History of the Police in England and Wales.* London: Constable.

Davis, K. (1969) *Discretionary Justice.* Urbana, Ill.: University of Illinois.

Dunnighan, C. and Norris, C. (1999) 'The detective, the snout, and the Audit Commission: the real costs in using informants', *The Howard Journal,* 38, 67–86.

Edwards, S. (1989) *Policing 'Domestic' Violence.* London: Sage.

Ericson, R. (1982) *Reproducing Order: A Study of Police Patrol Work.* Toronto: University of Toronto Press.

Fielding, N. (1988) 'Competence and culture in the police', *Sociology,* 22, 45–64.

Fielding, N., Kemp, C. and Norris, C. (1989) 'Constraints on the practice of community policing', in R. Morgan and D.J. Smith (eds) *Coming to Terms with Policing.* London: Routledge.

FitzGerald, M. (1993) *Ethnic Minorities and the Criminal Justice System,* Royal Commision on Criminal Justice Research Study no. 20. London: HMSO.

Gilroy, P. (1982) 'The myth of black criminality', *Socialist Register.* London: Merlin.

Goldstein, J. (1960) 'Police discretion not to invoke the criminal process', *Yale Law Journal,* 69, 543–94.

Graham, J. and Bowling, B. (1995) *Young People and Crime,* Home Office Research Study no. 145. London: HMSO.

Holdaway, S. (1983) *Inside the British Police.* Oxford: Blackwell.

Hoyle, C. (1998) *Negotiating Domestic Violence: Police, Criminal Justice and Victims.* Oxford: Clarendon Press.

James, D. (1979) 'Police–black relations: the professional solution', in S. Holdaway (ed.) *The British Police.* London: Edward Arnold.

Jefferson T. and Walker, M. (1992) 'Ethnic minorities in the criminal justice system', *Criminal Law Review* 81 (140): 83–95.

Kemp, C., Norris, C. and Fielding, N. (1992) *Negotiating Nothing: Police Decision-making in Disputes.* Aldershot: Avebury.

Kitsuse, J. and Cicourel, A. (1963) 'A note on the uses of official statistics', *Social Problems,* 11, 131–9.

Klockars, C. (1985) *The Idea of Police.* Beverly Hills, CA: Sage.

Landau, S. and Nathan, G. (1983) 'Selecting delinquents for cautioning in the London Metropolitan area', *British Journal of Criminology,* 23, 128–49.

Lea, J. and Young, J. (1993) *What is to be Done about Law and Order?* 2nd edn. London: Pluto Press.

Lustgarten, L. (1986) *The Governance of Police.* London: Sweet and Maxwell.

McCabe, S. and Sutcliffe, F. (1978) *Defining Crime.* Oxford: Basil Blackwell.

Macpherson, W. (1999) *The Stephen Lawrence Inquiry.* London: The Stationery Office.

Manning, P. (1977) *Police Work*. Cambridge, Mass.: MIT Press.

Manning P. (1982) 'Organisational work: structuration of the environment', *British Journal of Sociology*, 33, 118–139.

Norris, C. (1989) 'Avoiding trouble: the patrol officer's perception of encounters with the public', in M. Wetheritt (ed.) *Police Research: Some Future Prospects*. Aldershot: Avebury.

Norris, C., Fielding, N., Kemp, C. and Fielding, J. (1992) 'Black and blue: an analysis of the influence of race on being stopped by the police', *British Journal of Sociology*, 43, 207–24.

Pahl, J. (1982) 'Police response to battered women', *Journal of Social Welfare Law*, 5, 337–43.

Phillips, C. and Brown, D. (1998) *Entry into the Criminal Justice System: a Survey of Police Arrests and their Outcomes*, Home Office Research Study no. 185. London: Home Office.

Policy Studies Institute (PSI) (1983) *Police and People in London*, vol. IV: D. J. Smith and J. Gray, *The Police in Action*. London: PSI.

Reiner, R. (1992) *The Politics of the Police*, 2nd edn. London: Wheastshef.

Rock, P. (1973) *Deviant Behaviour*. London: Hutchinson.

Rubinstein, J. (1973) *City Police*. New York: Ballantine.

Skogan, W. (1994) *Contacts between Police and Public: Findings from the 1992 British Crime Survey*, Home Office Research Study no. 134. London: HMSO.

Smith, D. (1997) 'Ethnic origins, crime and criminal justice', in M. Maguire, R. Morgan, and R. Reiner (eds) *The Oxford Handbook of Criminology*, 2nd edn. Oxford: Clarendon Press.

Stanko, E. (1985) *Intimate Intrusions*. London: Routledge and Kegan Paul.

Stevens, P. and Willis, C. (1979) *Race, Crime and Arrests*, Home Office Research Study no. 58. London: HMSO.

Van Maanen, J. (1978) 'The asshole', in P. Manning and J. Van Maanen (eds) *Policing: A View from the Street*. Santa Monica, CA: Goodyear.

Waddington, P. (1993) *Calling the Police*. Aldershot: Gower.

Waddington, P. (1999) *Policing Citizens*. London: UCL Press.

Walker, M., Jefferson, T. and Seneviratne, M. (1990) *Ethnic Minorities, Young People and the Criminal Justice System*. Sheffield: Centre for Criminological and Sociolegal Studies, University of Sheffield.

Willis, C. (1983) *The Use, Effectiveness and Impact of Police Stop and Search Powers*, Research and Planning Unit Paper no. 15. London: Home Office.

Young, M. (1991) *An Inside Job*. Oxford: Clarendon.

STUDY QUESTIONS

1 From your reading of Coleman and Norris's piece how would you define and justify police discretion?

2 Having read this piece have you revised your view of the relationship between 'cop culture' and police work? Now re-read Hall's piece (Reading 18). Do the three readings (18, 23 and 24) support or challenge each other?

3 What other crimes can you think of that are 'over-' or 'under'-policed? What explanations can you give for this?

FURTHER READING

Introductory overviews of policing can be found in Coleman, C. and Norris, C. (2000) *Introducing Criminology*, Cullompton: Willan; Davies, M., Croall, H. and Tyrer, J. (1998) *Criminal Justice: An Introduction to the Criminal Justice System in England and Wales*, 2nd edn, Harlow: Pearson; McLaughlin, E. and Muncie, J. (eds) (2001) *Controlling Crime*, 2nd edn, London: Sage; and Newburn, T. (1995) *Crime and Criminal Justice Policy*, Harlow: Longman. The over-policing of black people is discussed most famously in Hall, S., Critcher, C., Jefferson, T., Clarke, J. and Roberts, B. (1978) *Policing the Crisis: Mugging, the State and Law and Order*, London: Macmillan and more recently in Bowling, B. and Phillips, C. (2002) *Racism, Crime and Justice*, Harlow: Longman. The response of the police to incidents of domestic violence is addressed in Hoyle, C. (1998) *Negotiating Domestic Violence: Police, Criminal Justice, and Victims*, Oxford: Oxford University Press; and Hanmer, J., Radford, J. and Stanko, E.A. (eds) (1989) *Women, Policing and Male Violence: International Perspectives*, London: Routledge. Police culture is further addressed by Young, M. (1991) *An Inside Job: Policing and Police Culture in Britain*, Oxford: Oxford University Press.

25

The trial

Frank Belloni and Jacqueline Hodgson

Having considered the role and culture of the police within the criminal justice system we now turn to the court, the place where the guilt (and punishment) or innocence of those who have been accused of crime is decided. In the first reading Frank Belloni and Jacqueline Hodgson detail the role of lawyers, magistrates and judges within both the magistrates' courts and the Crown Court. Belloni and Hodgson draw on data from their own empirical research and that of others and suggest that the protection of the accused against wrongful conviction is *not* the highest priority in either the magistrates' courts or the Crown Court. Evidence suggests that magistrates are pro-police, prosecution-orientated, and assume that most defendants are guilty. Furthermore, research indicates that some defence lawyers in both the magistrates' courts and the Crown Court also have a negative view of the accused. Belloni and Hodgson further suggest that financial considerations affect case preparation and court proceedings and, again, this is often detrimental to defendants. Not only is much of the preparation of cases delegated to staff with little or no experience, but it is often cheaper and easier for busy lawyers to persuade their clients to plead guilty. The worst case scenario here is the wrongful conviction of innocent people. Yet, as Belloni and Hodgson point out, poor advocacy and court experience is very difficult to challenge and correct.

The goal of the trial is to determine whether the accused person is guilty as charged. This requires a decision on the basis of evidence put before the court by the prosecution, and on the countervailing arguments of the defence. In the Crown Court, which tries indictable offences,[1] the presiding judge is educated in the law and has acquired considerable trial experience before being appointed to the bench. She [sic] regulates the proceedings, determines the admissibility of evidence, and ensures that the trial is conducted fairly. Following presentation of evidence by the prosecution and the response of the

SOURCE: From *Criminal Injustice: An Evaluation of the Criminal Justice Process in Britain* (Basingstoke: Macmillan, 2000), 147–58.

defendant, the judge sums up the case and charges a jury (whose members are randomly selected)[2] with the task of determining, on the facts of the case, whether the accused has been proven guilty beyond a reasonable doubt.

Proceedings in the magistrates' courts, where more than 93 per cent of all cases are processed, differ from those in the Crown Court. First, whereas the accused in Crown Court trials must be present to plead to the indictment, and should normally be in court throughout her trial, summary trials may take place in the absence of the accused.[3] Secondly, some safeguards for accused which apply to Crown Court trials do not apply to summary trials. For example, prosecution disclosure is required in Crown Court, but in the magistrates' courts the accused have no legal right to have the prosecution case disclosed prior to trial;[4] and while Code E, PACE (Police and Criminal Evidence Act) requires that all police station interviews with persons suspected of indictable offences must be tape-recorded, this does not apply to summary offences. Thirdly, summary court trials are less formal and more hurried, and the magistrates who process them generally lack formal legal training.[5] Thus they are less schooled in due process rights than judges. 'Such training as the magistrates get', observed a solicitor-advocate,

> is organised by either the courts or the prosecution [who] are predominantly telling them about how to convict … [and] the courts have a liaison judge … who comes down to tell them about sentencing. They aren't telling them about the importance of seeing that the rights of the accused are protected, and there is no equal balancing act with a defence lawyer telling them about their problems. So all the training is biased towards the prosecution, and that's a problem.[6]

As a result, trials in magistrates' courts are likely to be less attentive to procedural safeguards aimed at protecting accused persons against wrongful conviction.[7] Finally, in contrast to Crown Court, where verdicts are decided by juries,[8] in summary court the issue of guilt is resolved by the magistrates, who are seen as pro-police and prosecution-oriented.[9] This perception is widely shared by both defendants and solicitors.[10]

A number of factors shape the magistrates' perspective. In addition to the historical tie between magistrates and the police, a close and positive relationship exists between them as a result of their frequent and mutually respectful interaction in the courts. Magistrates identify the police as trusted allies in the task of processing persons accused of criminal offences. In contested cases, for example, police testimony was found to account for 53 per cent of those which depended upon direct evidence, and 70 per cent of those involving circumstantial evidence. (McConville et al., 1994: 213–15). Given the determining role of police testimony in most summary court trials, the magistrates' acceptance of the credibility of police evidence, as against that of the accused, is essential. As Wundersitz et al. (1991: 201) argue, 'In … direct contests between the defendant and the police, the magistracy itself, as a representative of the state, has a vested interest in upholding the reputation of the police, who also represent the state, by accepting their side of the story. In addition to the legitimacy accorded to the police per se, their testimony is assumed to be credible because its presentation is practiced, assertive and depersonalized (supported by the "objective" testimony of other police witnesses)'.

Conversely, given the hiatus in socioeconomic status between the magistrates (who are appointed by the Lord Chancellor) and those whom they must judge, together with the tilt in the political profile of most lay justices,[11] it is difficult for magistrates to identify or empathize with those accused of criminal offences. Rather, they are inclined to disbelieve defendants and to be predisposed to assume their guilt.[12] Thus while the underlying perception that the accused are guilty may begin with the police, it is carried forward to those on the bench and reflected in their decisions. And while the magistrates are said to be less inclined than previously to accept without question what the police do, officers' testimony against the defendant (explained a solicitor with 30 years of summary court experience) still weighs heavily with the magistrates. The latter remain 'predisposed to convict the accused. There is still a "no smoke without fire" syndrome of thought: "The guy wouldn't be in the dock unless he'd done this." And this contributes to the very high rate of conviction in summary court.'[13] The effect of the foregoing is that the burden of proof is reversed in the magistrates' courts: it is now up to the defendant to establish her innocence (McConville et al., 1994: 227).

The perception held by lawyers that the magistrates believe most defendants are guilty, and that this may affect their ability to make judgments based on the facts of a case, is confirmed in other interviews. In reference to the high conviction rate of accused persons in summary court (98.2 per cent), another solicitor stated frankly: 'Well, in the last analysis 90 per cent of them are guilty. We know that, they know that.'[14] Thus the notion that 'this person wouldn't be here if they weren't guilty',[15] continues to be shared in varying degrees by those of like mind – the police, magistrates and some solicitors.

The overarching objective of cutting costs, which is ceaselessly pursued by those who manage the criminal justice system, also influences proceedings in summary court. The constraints now imposed on magistrates by the Treasury create pressures to process cases as quickly as possible – whatever the consequences for the defence. The magistrates, explained a defence solicitor,

> [have] got to get through so many cases per day in order to qualify for funding. The magistrates' clerks have to make sure that their lists are moving quickly, not delayed by adjournments, even when there is good cause – as when a witness may be needed. No one wants proper preparation. The defence may have a very difficult time in the face of all that. He's put under pressure because he knows that he is going to be [seen as] irritating if he holds things up in any way.[16]

Financial considerations also influence case preparation in summary court. The introduction of fixed fees has contributed to a diminished defence, and to an increased number of convictions, by discouraging lawyers from doing more than the minimum required.

> One of the factors accounting for the ever higher conviction rate in the magistrates' court is that the Lord Chancellor introduced fixed fees for contested trials. In the past you were paid by the hour, but now there are fixed fees for a trial. And while the fee for a plea of guilty, which takes very little time, is about £200, the fee for a fully contested defence in a summary trial is only about £500 – no matter how many hours you work. So the incentive to prepare cases is gone. Many of my colleagues … have adapted by developing practices which just pile it high and sell it cheap. They just take their fee and run. They do one interview with the client and then defend him. There is no incentive to do anything more. No one wants proper preparation. The courts don't want it, the Lord Chancellor doesn't want it.[17]

The attitude of magistrates toward the accused is shared by some defence lawyers who represent defendants in the magistrates' courts and in the Crown Court. The findings of McConville et al. (1994), that defence lawyers are pre-disposed to a belief in the guilt of their clients, are confirmed by a number of our own interviews. They suggest that a number of lawyers have a negative, or at least equivocal, attitude toward their role as defender of the accused. Among solicitors, this is reinforced as a consequence of very high conviction rates in summary court. Like the magistrates, they become increasingly inclined to assume the guilt of those who are charged by the police, and to empathize with the latter's desire and effort to convict them. This is illustrated in the remarks of a Birmingham duty solicitor, who is intended to serve as the frontline defender of a person suspected of a criminal offence:

> My personal view is that a lot of those people, perhaps most of them, have in fact committed the offence for which they are brought to the police station. Now my job should not be to allow people who've committed offences to get off. I say this shouldn't be my job, but in a sense it is my job … [B]ut looking at it from the viewpoint of the population as a whole, that's not right, is it?[18]

An attempt to explain why some solicitors harbour a cynical attitude toward their clients, as well as a high degree of ambivalence about their own role in the criminal process, was made by a former Assistant Secretary General of the Law Society.

> People do get case-hardened. Most people … are charged with a standard set of offences: thefts, shop-lifting, burglaries, etcetera. Therefore, solicitors see the same kind of case happening time and time again; and you can't exactly blame them for thinking: 'I have seen many of these cases before and it will surprise me greatly that this person is going to be somebody who didn't actually do it.' So the fact that defence lawyers can jump to that sort of conclusion fairly early on in a case is hardly surprising.[19]

The guilty-plea orientation of most defence lawyers is reflected in the way solicitors' firms are structured and in the approach adopted in preparing cases (McConville et al., 1994). Widespread delegation of responsibilities to non-solicitors is common. It is clear also that they do very little proactive defence work for their clients. They do not seek to find evidence to support their client's case, nor do they attempt an independent investigation of the evidence of the prosecution.[20] In fact, observed Roger Ede,

> it strikes me as odd here that in preparing cases for the magistrates' court, you don't actually go out and try to find out whether what the prosecution witness is saying is true, or … whether they can shed any other light on matters [which might] point you to other witnesses or to other inquiries you can make.[21]

Instead, what is done by way of case preparation reflects a strategy largely limited to trying to shoot down the prosecution case: typically taking a proof of evidence to affirm or rebut the prosecution case.

The inadequacy of trial preparation is not limited to solicitors in summary court cases; it applies equally to barristers and to the Crown Court, where the pre-trial preparation of solicitors may be aggravated by the poor advocacy of counsel. In 1989, Marcel Berlins described the standard of performance of barristers as 'competently mediocre'; and this assessment was endorsed in 1996 by Helga Drummand. Having observed the performances of 60 advocates in court, both prosecuting and defending, she concluded that while roughly one-third of the presentations were good, the remainder were shot through with faults of one kind or another. Thus, 'for every confident presentation, there are at least two advocates floundering' (1996: 656). In her view, advocacy involves telling a story in a systematic fashion,[22] and she noted that those who performed best were armed with well-filled, hand-written notebooks. She suggested that many of the faults observed were due to inadequate preparation followed up by attempts to disguise such inadequacy. However, neither inadequate pre-trial preparation by defence solicitors nor the poor advocacy of counsel at the trial are considered grounds for appealing against conviction.

Part of the weakness of the defence in court is traceable to the last-minute receipt of briefs: the less time a barrister has to prepare a case, the longer it takes to present it in court and the poorer the performance. But it is equally clear that barristers are not helped by the inadequate pre-trial preparation of solicitors. Moreover, the division of labour that exists in the legal profession introduces a 'moving part' to the criminal justice system; and moving parts increase the need for liaison and coordination – which is notable largely for its absence. The result too often is a lack of critical information at trial, which cripples the process. Drummand (1996) cites one court session concerned with bail applications in which half the cases were adjourned, as counsel were unable to produce vital evidence because communication with the solicitors had broken down. Each party had assumed that the other would take the initiative. The judge was quite displeased, especially as this was the second time in one week that the system had failed to work.

Overall, the failures of defence lawyers may contribute to the wrongful conviction of innocent persons. Yet the harmful consequences to defendants of poor advocacy have been especially difficult to correct because of the clear reluctance of judges to question the performance of defence lawyers, particularly that of barristers. Although defence lawyers may inadequately prepare or otherwise perform poorly in either the pre-trial or trial stages, the Court of Appeal has been strongly averse to consider this matter as grounds for over-turning a conviction.[23] This was unambiguously stipulated in the remarks of Taylor J in the case of *R* v. *Gautam*: 'It should be clearly understood that if defending counsel in the course of his conduct of a case makes a decision, or takes a course which later appears to have been mistaken or unwise, that generally speaking has never been regarded as a proper ground for appeal.'[24]

Nor has the Court indicated much flexibility on the issue in more recent cases: incompetency of counsel as the grounds for a criminal appeal still remains very limited.[25] In *R* v. *Swain*,[26] the Court held that if it had a lurking doubt that the defendant might have suffered some injustice as the result of 'flagrantly incompetent advocacy' by his counsel, then it would quash the conviction. This was reiterated in *R* v. *Ensor*,[27] where the Court held that counsel's errors may constitute valid grounds for appeal *only* in the case of 'flagrantly incompetent advocacy' and affirmed in *R* v. *Wellings*.[28] Again the Court was unsympathetic to an appeal grounded only on a mistaken decision by counsel at a trial. It is only when counsel's conduct could be described as flagrantly incompetent advocacy, observed Lord Lang CJ, that the court would be minded to intervene.

However, exceptional conditions may be taken into account. Thus, in *R* v. *Clinton*,[29] Rougier J said that where counsel had made decisions in good faith after proper consideration, and where appropriate after due discussion with the client, her decisions could not possibly be said to render a subsequent verdict unsafe or unsatisfactory. But where it was shown that the decision was taken either in defiance, or without proper instructions, or when all the prompting of reason and good sense pointed the other way, it might be open to an appellate court to set aside the verdict. These *exceptional* conditions were found in *Clinton*: the Court held that a positive defence had never been presented to the jury; and that the nature of the case, and of the prosecution evidence, made it essential for the appellant to be advised to give evidence, and the failure of his counsel to call him as a witness had been a grave error. The verdict was found unsafe and unsatisfactory, and the conviction was quashed.

In contrast to the equivocal posture of the appellate court, JUSTICE has long been concerned about miscarriages that flow from errors in defence strategy leading up to and during the trial. In Anne Owers' view, this is a major problem:

> You're talking about a solicitor who has not been sufficiently robust in protecting his client at the police station; or a solicitor or a barrister who, under pressure at trial has just made the wrong decision, or has decided not to call evidence that should be called or not to challenge some evidence when it should have been challenged. [I]t's our view that if those decisions go to the safety of the conviction then they should be arguable grounds for

quashing. But the Court of Appeal is particularly suspect in the way in which it deals with defence errors at trial. Some courts will accept it, some won't. You can feel the profession kind of clamming up together, particularly if it's a barrister that you're talking about. The courts are now readier to criticize solicitors, but where barristers are involved the judges are more closed.[30]

The RCCJ joined JUSTICE in criticizing the Court for ignoring the harmful consequences for the defendant that may flow from the incompetency of defence lawyers, and for the perpetuation of the harm resulting from the unwillingness of the appellate court to take corrective action. Its Report pointedly noted that:

> wrong jury verdicts of guilty may be the result of errors by the lawyers – whether of judgement or of performance – which do not amount to 'flagrantly incompetent advocacy'. It cannot possibly be right that there should be defendants serving prison sentences for no other reason than that their lawyers made a decision which later turns out to have been mistaken. (RCCJ, 1993: 174)[31]

In expressing disapproval of the Court's routine dismissal of appeals made on the grounds of incompetent advocacy, the Commission signalled their awareness that the quality of defence provided in the Crown Court often falls far short of what is necessary to ensure adequate protection for the accused. However, as already indicated, the problem begins with the split in the legal profession between solicitors and barristers, and with the division of functions assigned to the two types of lawyers. Solicitors may represent defendants in the magistrates' court, but most must instruct barristers to represent their clients in the Crown Court.[32] This discontinuity of representation ill-serves the interests of clients of the legal profession, especially in criminal cases. Under the prevailing regime, responsibility for the preparation of the defence's case is assigned to a solicitor; but once the preparation is complete, the brief (containing copies of documents relevant to the case) must be passed to an advocate who has the task of representing the defendant in court. As a result, in cases involving indictable offences most solicitors are prevented from representing their client in court.[33] Thus, the brief is passed to counsel, and the accused suddenly finds her fate is in the hands of a barrister with whom she has had no prior contact. Nevertheless, from that moment the determination of whether the accused is acquitted or found guilty will depend in part upon counsel's knowledge of the case, her skills, and her posture toward possible outcomes for the case.

    This truncated role encourages the solicitor to disengage from a case as quickly as possible, and with the least amount of involvement. Thus less time and care is spent on case preparation than might be were she to bear an ongoing responsibility for the fate of her client. The resulting harm to the interests of the accused is considerable. According to an experienced solicitor:

The most serious indictment of the system in many ways is the disincentives it gives to lawyers on both sides of the fence to prepare cases properly ... [T]here is no incentive for the solicitor to prepare it. He's not going to be facing the judge in court. The judge is not going to tear him up for having failed to produce this or that witness; it's the barrister who is going to get it in the neck ... So the solicitor says to himself, 'Well I don't know what some barrister is going to advise so I'll just prepare the papers in some sort of bog standard way: that is, put in a client's statement, witness statement, wrap it up and send it off to the barrister.' Consequently, briefs are all inadequately prepared.

Nor is there any incentive to take any major decisions, because once counsel gets the case he's going to assert his authority about how it should be run. So the solicitor will say, 'Well, what's the point in me doing any more work on this case – like trying to make some deal with the prosecution by pointing out that they don't have any evidence on this or that charge? What's the point in my doing all that if the barrister might take a different view? So I'll leave all that.'[34]

These factors contribute to the disinclination of solicitors to commit effort to the preparation of cases for Crown Court. However, other factors are at work. McConville et al. (1994) argue that financial considerations strongly influence the attitude of solicitors in other respects. In looking at the operation of the majority of firms, they found that much of the preparation associated with Crown Court cases – such as investigations, conferences with counsel, pre-trial discussions and court appearances – is delegated to staff who are non-qualified, have little experience or both. The reason: their services cost less. Thus, it is the primacy of profit which underpins the operations of many firms, including their willingness to devolve all important decisions to counsel (McConville et al., 1994). However, they found exceptions: operating within the same financial limits, some firms are able to provide substantial solicitor input into the preparation of Crown Court cases, whilst others employ non-legally qualified but experienced staff. These exceptions (as in police station work) demonstrate that it is not only financial constraints, but the ideological commitment of lawyers which in part governs their practice (McConville et al., 1994: 239–43).

Despite the solicitor's early disengagement from a Crown Court case she is none the less deeply implicated in the result, for the quality and thoroughness of the brief she passes to counsel very likely influences the latter's view and reaction to the case. Thus, faced with a poorly prepared brief, counsel may seek to avoid trial by persuading the defendant to plead guilty to the charge or to some (negotiated) lesser offence, with the promise of a lesser sentence. Under the worst scenario, an innocent person may be convicted for want of adequate defence. Meanwhile, the barrister can move on to a new brief.[35]

Case preparation by the solicitor should not, although it often does, stop with the handing over of the brief. After discussion of the case with counsel, or on receiving additional information from the prosecution, further investigation may be required, such as following up on witnesses, taking statements or instructing forensic experts. In some firms, in fact, experienced and legally qualified staff handle Crown Court work, carrying out detailed investigation and legal research as well as liaising closely with counsel (McConville et al., 1994). However, in many practices Crown Court work is considered routine, requiring only the 'attendance' of someone to 'sit behind counsel' who will take notes and report back on the case outcome; thus, inexperienced staff with little or no knowledge of the case are employed; typically this may be a clerk or secretary, and in some instances even friends or family. Moreover, having transmitted the brief to a barrister, the solicitor relinquishes responsibility.

Apart from relieving the solicitor of a sense of responsibility, the introduction of counsel as the defendant's new representative serves other purposes. The barrister is presented as 'the expert' who has been 'specially chosen' for the client, and as someone who can provide a further independent and dispassionate opinion on the case. However, rather than having the benefit of a second legal adviser in the construction of their defence, defendants may find themselves ambushed into pleading guilty. Most do not meet their barrister until the day of trial, and conferences held prior to the trial date may often form a part of that 'ambush' strategy. Thus, despite expressing personal commitment to the client, doubts are raised by counsel about the way in which the court would view the evidence and the credibility of the witnesses, as well as how the defendant's story might look to the jury. This paves the way for further pressure to be applied on the day of trial, when the defendant is at her most vulnerable.

In instances where this ambush strategy runs counter to the instructions in the brief, the presence of a solicitor's clerk is often ineffectual. She may have little or no prior involvement and be in possession of insufficient information about the case to raise any objections, as well as being generally overawed by the whole process and so unable to resist counsel's actions. Lesser charges are negotiated by defence counsel with the prosecution on the day of the trial and then sold to the client and clerk as a good deal which the barrister has fought hard to secure (McConville et al., 1994: 256–61). Defendants are in no position to contradict the 'professional' (who claims access to the personal views of the judge, together with insider knowledge of the daily workings of the court), least of all in the emotionally charged setting at the door of the court.

One reason counsel might encourage the defendant to plead guilty is the pressure felt by the barrister herself. Because of the unpredictability of the 'list system' used in Crown Court, barristers may confront conflicting case responsibilities on a given court day which necessitate the hurried passing of a brief to another barrister. This is reportedly a very common occurrence and it means that the barrister to whom the brief is passed must prepare herself to represent the case on the shortest possible notice – perhaps on the afternoon before the case is to be heard, if not on the trial date itself. Zander and Henderson (1993) found that there were barrister changes before trial in 48 per cent of cases, and 25 per cent of barristers received their brief only in the afternoon before trial. Thus on scant notice and without ever having met the client, the barrister must review the evidence and somehow be prepared to defend 'her' client in court. Not surprisingly, some barristers might look for an easy way out by persuading the client to plead guilty, accept a negotiated sentence, and thus avoid the trial. The results of counsel having received a late brief in terms of the consequences for her client were explained by a solicitor as follows:

> Most of the barristers I see will come straight into court to see a client they've never met before. They will arrive at the courtroom, three-quarters of an hour before the case starts, and meet the client for the first time with a bundle of papers that they would have read the night before. And the barrister will almost immediately start saying to the client 'Look, I've read all your papers; your solicitor is a wonderful man, but I can tell you that you really haven't got a chance ... I know you thought you might be plead-ing not guilty, but having looked at everything there's no way that you are going to get acquitted ... If you plead not guilty and you contest this sort of thing, you will almost certainly go to jail. And I can see exactly why you don't want to plead guilty, but this is what you are going to do. But don't worry old fellow, because we're going to stop you going to jail.'[36]

The RCCJ acknowledged that last-minute changes of counsel lead to hurried reviews of evidence, and to efforts to encourage defendants to plead guilty to avoid severe sentence and/or to secure a lesser negotiated sentence. Their response was to propose changes to limit the number of late or 'returned' briefs, backed up by judicially imposed sanctions in the form of costs, or referral to the Professional Conduct Committee of the Bar, who should make and enforce the appropriate rules to ensure effective pre-trial preparatory work (1993: 108–9). However, failing a drastic change in the courts' list system, it is unlikely that anything will be done about returned briefs.

The RCCJ acknowledged that things go wrong in court as a result of incompetent and poorly prepared barristers, and that 'action is seldom taken to put them right or to prevent a recurrence' (1993: 139). Accordingly, they pro-posed (i) measures to ensure that barristers are adequately trained and fully competent; (ii) the creation of a code of practice for the conduct of advocates in court; (iii) compulsory training in forensic science and psychiatry for lawyers involved in criminal work; and (iv) the enforcement of professional standards and sanctions for incompetent performance of lawyers.

However, despite the Commission's stated commitment to increasing the fairness of trials, they appeared to be far more preoccupied with their cost and efficiency. Thus, in addition to proposals for preparatory hearings, plea bargaining and sentence discounts, they also recommended (pp. 120–2) that: indictments be drafted more precisely (no more than a listing of offences and the briefest of facts to support the allegations); the prosecution's opening speech be shortened to 15 minutes; judges be allowed to cut the presentation of irrelevant or repetitive evidence and to punish 'time-wasting counsel' by order-ing a cut in their fees; and, wherever possible, the reduction of evidence to written statements. All of these proposals, whatever the RCCJ claims to the con-trary, may be seen as designed more to streamline and cut the cost of trials than to make trials fairer. [...]

NOTES

1 These involve serious offences, ranging from treason and murder (Class 1) to grievous bodily harm, robbery and all 'either-way' offences (Class 4).

2 However, ethnic minorities have been under-represented (Baldwin and McConville, 1979: 97–8); and the government has taken steps which have increased the prosecution's potential to influence the jury's composition (Jackson, 1993: 133–4) while decreasing those of the defence (s. 118, Criminal Justice Act 1998).

3 Under, s. 12 of the Magistrates' Courts Act 1980. In the cases examined by Phillips and Brown (1998), two per cent of all defendants processed by the magistrates were proven guilty in their absence (p. 157).

4 However, the CPS may voluntarily provide advance information if the offence charged is summary only; moreover, the defence may also provide information, but only on a voluntary basis.

5 Some cases are heard by stipendiary magistrates who are formally trained in the law, and whose powers were increased in the Crime and Disorder Act 1998. However, they constitute only a tiny fraction of magistrates (for instance, in 1991 there were only 76 compared to appoximately 28,000 lay magistrates: Jackson, 1993: 148).

6 Interview, May 1995.

7 While the protections afforded defendants tried in the Crown Court were acknowledged by the RCCJ [Royal Commission onCriminal Justice], the lack of similar protections in summary court was not a matter of concern to the Commission. Thus in discussing proposals to protect against false confessions, they stated that while 'the risk of a false confession may not increase in proportion to the seriousness of the offence the consequences for the suspect [in either way and indictable only cases] are greater and therefore the suspect should arguably be given greater protection in such cases against a wrongful conviction' (RCCJ, 1993: 59).

8 However, Parliament has reduced the opportunity of defendants to elect trial by jury by reclassifying serious offences as summary; and the RCCJ (1993) proposed the elimination of the accused's automatic right to elect trial by jury [...]. This was abandoned in the face of criticism, only to be resurrected by the government in 1998. While supported by the Lord Chief Justice, it has been sharply criticized by Lord Steyn, one of Britain's most senior judges, who called it a 'bad proposal', whose 'purpose is to cut costs. It has nothing to do with justice' (quoted in Dyer, the *Guardian*, 14 October 1998).

9 In 1997, in cases in which defendants had pleaded not guilty, less than a fourth of cases were dismissed by the magistrates (Home Office, 1997: 134), whereas 60 per cent were acquitted in the Crown Court (LCD, 1998: 66).

10 Hedderman and Moxon (1992); see also [...] Phillips and Brown (1998: 164).

11 The Lord Chancellor's Department reported the following figures on the political affiliation of magistrates in England: Conservative (7,892), Labour (3,242), Liberal Democrat (2,694) and Independent (1,375). Those for Wales were: Conservative (715), Labour (664), Liberal Democrat (345), Plaid Cymru (117) and Independent (201); see LCD, December 1995: 'Political Profile of Benches' (document provided to authors).

12 Cf. Hedderman and Moxon (1992). This was also expressed to us in a number of interviews – for instance, Chris Mullin, MP, Home Affairs Committee (July 1995), and Roger Ede, Law Society (May 1995).

13 Interview, March 1995.

14 Interview with solicitor-advocate, February, 1995. Similar statements were made by other defence solicitors.

15 Interview with Anne Owers of JUSTICE, April 1995.

16   Interview with John Davis, solicitor-advocate, June 1995.
17   Interview with solicitor, June 1995.
18   Interview, February, 1995; original emphasis.
19   Interview, February, 1995.
20   It is claimed that this is due, in part, to a concern that lawyers will be accused of having perverted the course of justice. To do so, explained the Law Society's Roger Ede, would violate the unwritten rules that govern the conduct of the roles of defence and prosecution. Thus 'solicitors will very, very rarely interview prosecution witnesses. It's just not done' (Interview, May 1995).
21   Interview, May 1995.
21   See also Wagenaar et al. (1993), who describe advocacy as narrative. Yet they found that many advocates are poor storytellers.
23   See also *McCarrol* v. *HM Advocate* (1949) SLT: 74.
24   (1978) *The Times*, 4 March.
25   For discussion of other relevant cases, see Gow, *NLJ*, 29 March 1996.
26   [1988], Crim LR, 109.
27   [1989] 1 WLR 497.
28   20 December 1991; unreported CA.
29   [1993] 2 All ER 998.
30   Interview, April 1995. See also JUSTICE (1989: 3 and 51).
31   See the Court of Appeal's reluctance to take account of the defence lawyer's advice to her client in custody when drawing adverse inferences from silence under s. 34 CJPOA (Criminal Justice and Public Order Act, 1994). [...]
32   Provisions in the Courts and Legal Services Act 1990 make it possible for experienced solicitors to qualify for rights of audience in the higher courts (which include the Crown Court). However, a veto given to four senior judges over the extension of rights beyond barristers in private practice has frustrated the aim of the 1990 Act. Thus only a small percentage of solicitors have done so. In 1998, the Lord Chancellor proposed plans to scrap the veto in order to facilitate extension of higher court rights to a broader segment of the legal community (Dyer, *the Guardian*, 14 October 1998).
33   However, a solicitor may appear in Crown Court in an appeal against a summary court judgment, or on a committal for sentence, provided the solicitor (or a partner or assistant member of her staff) appeared on behalf of the client in the lower court. Further, except for trials of more serious cases, solicitors have advocacy rights in criminal proceedings in the Crown Court in certain locations (Lord Chancellor's 1972 Practice Direction). Finally, under provisions of the Courts and Legal Services Act 1990, more than 500 solicitors have been granted rights of audience in the Crown Court.
34   Interview, February 1995.
35   And there are other benefits to the barrister: 'By delivering a guilty plea, defence lawyers can ... increase their credibility with both prosecutor and judge (thereby strengthening their hand in the occasional contested case)' (McConville and Baldwin, 1981: 194).
36   Interview, February 1995. The respondent served on the Philips Commission (which led to PACE 1984), and presently serves as an officer of the Law Society. Other examples may be found in McConville et al. (1994).

REFERENCES

Baldwin, J. anmd McConville, M. (1979) *Jury Trials*. Oxford: Clarendon Press.
Berlins, M. (1989) 'Counsels of despair', *Spectator*, 25 November.

Drummand, H. (1996) 'Stands of advocacy revisited', *New Law Journal*, 3 May: 656.

Hedderman, C. and Moxon, D. (1992) *Magistrates' Courts or Crown Court? Mode of Trial Decisions and Sentencing*. Home Office Research and Planning Unit Report no. 125. London: HMSO.

Home Office (1997) *Review of Delay in the Criminal Justice System: A Report* (The Narey Report). London: Home Office.

Jackson, J. (1993) 'Trial procedures' in C. Walker and K. Starmer (eds) *justice in Error*, pp. 130–62. London: Blackstone.

JUSTICE (1989) *Miscarriages of Justice*. London: JUSTICE Education and Research Trust.

Legal Action Group (1993) *Police Misconduct*. London: LAG Education and Service Trust Ltd.

Lord Chancellor's Department (LCD) (1998) *Judicial Statistics, 1997*. London: HMSO.

McConville, M. and Baldwin, J. (1981) *Courts, Prosecution, and Conviction*. Oxford: Clarendon Press.

McConville, M., Hodgson, J., Bridges, L. and Pavlovic, A. (1994) *Standing Accused: The Organisation and Practices of Criminal Defence Lawyers in Britain*. Oxford: Clarendon Press.

Mansfield, M. and Wardle, T. (1993) *Presumed Guilty: The British Legal System Exposed*. London: Heinemann.

Phillips, C. and Brown, D. (1998) *Entry into the Criminal Justice System: A Survey of Police Arrests and their Outcomes*. Home Office Research Study, no. 185. London: Home Office.

Royal Commission on Criminal Justice (RCCJ) (1993) *Report*, Chaired by Viscount Runciman of Doxford, Cmnd 2263. London: HMSO.

Wagenaar, W., van Kopper, P. and Crombag, H. (1993) *Anchored Narratives*. Hemel Hempstead: Harvester Wheatsheaf.

Wundersitz, J., Naffine, N. and Gale, F. (1991) 'The production of guilt in the juvenile justice system: the pressures to "plead"', *Howard Journal*, 30 (3), 192.

Zander, M. and Henderson, P. (1993) *The Crown Court Study*. Royal Commission on Criminal Justice Research Study no. 19. London: HMSO.

STUDY QUESTIONS

1   From your reading of Belloni and Hodgson's piece, how important do you think preparation of a case is for a 'fair trial'? Does the model that represents justice as weighted in favour of the defendant operate in practice?

2   Belloni and Hodgson suggest that defendants sometimes find themselves 'ambushed' into pleading guilty. What do you understand by this and why does it happen?

3   Can you think of any examples of miscarriages of justice?

FURTHER READING

Several relevant chapters on courts, trials and sentencing can be found in Davies, M., Croall, H. and Tyrer, J. (1998) *Criminal Justice: An Introduction to the*

Criminal Justice System in England and Wales, 2nd edn, Harlow: Pearson. A similar introductory review is provided by Loraine Gelsthorpe in her chapter, 'Critical decisions and processes in the criminal courts', in E. McLaughlin and J. Muncie (eds) (2001) *Controlling Crime*, 2nd edn, London: Sage. The pre-trial process (including the reasons underlying miscarriages of justice) is examined comprehensively by Andrew Ashworth (1998) *The Criminal Process: An Evaluative Study*, 2nd edn, Oxford: Oxford University Press. John Baldwin provides a first-hand account of conducting research in courts in 'Research on the criminal courts', chapter 8 in R.D. King and E. Wincup (eds) (2000) *Doing Research on Crime and Justice*, Oxford: Oxford University Press. Also worth a look are Gibson, B. and Cavadino, P. (1995) *Introduction to the Criminal Justice Process*, Winchester: Waterside Press; Galligan, D.J. (1996) *Due Process and Fair Procedures: A Study of Administrative Procedures*, Oxford: Clarendon Press; and Baldwin, J. and McConville, M. (1997) *Negotiating Justice: Pressures to Plead Guilty*, London: Martin Robertson.

26

The injudiciary

Andrew Billen

Andrew Billen's newspaper article on the judiciary demonstrates very well the gulf between judges and the majority of their defendants. Indeed, in terms of background, education, salary, lifestyle, attitudes and interests it does appear that 'Judges are out of touch with ordinary people and everyday life.' In introducing the case studies at the end of the article (just a few of which are presented here), Billen suggests that these examples of inappropriate judicial comments exemplify the weaknesses of the profession as a whole. For similar examples of problematic judicial commentary read Joan Smith's 1989 book *Misogynies* (details in *Further Reading*) where, in a chapter entitled 'M'Learned Friends' she cites an example of a case in the mid-1980s where a man who killed his wife, butchering and cooking her, and depositing bags of her body throughout London, was given a six-year prison sentence by a judge who said 'I will deal with you on the basis you were provoked, you lost your self-control, and that a man of reasonable self-control might have been similarly provoked and might have done what you did.' See also Reading 14 by Cavadino and Dignan who consider court-sentencing practice in relation to issues of social class, 'race' and gender. Interestingly, almost a decade on from Billen's article, judges are still appointed from the Lord Chancellor's Office and interest groups are still advocating change.

What a piece of work is a judge! Though we have the right to be tried by a jury of our peers, the judge presiding over us appears, from the wig on his head (£690) to the court shoes and buckles on his feet (£135), as something very remote from most of our lives. Indeed, often he does not appear to live in the same world as us, let alone share the same cultural assumptions.

This remoteness manifests itself in a variety of ways, of which one of the most popular is the display of judicial ignorance. For example, in 1990, the year of the World Cup, Mr Justice Harman (q.v.) asked: 'Who is Gazza? Isn't there an operetta called *La Gazza Ladra?*' (Indeed there is.) He was following in the

SOURCE: From the *Observer* magazine, 13 December 1992.

great footsteps of Mr Justice Cantley, who, in 1978, midway through a case involving the Football Association, asked a barrister: 'Kevin Keegan, does he play for England or Scotland?' Twenty years before, trying a libel action about three Labour politicians alleged to have been drunk at a conference in Venice, Lord Goddard asked why the offending article was called 'Death in Venice': 'Who had died there?' None of this is so very far from A.P. Herbert's Mr Justice Snubb, who asked: 'What is a crossword?'

However, it is not just judges' throw-away remarks that have earned them a growing reputation for being eccentric and out of touch. There are also their summings-up, which are too often seen to be biased (the 'has-she-not-fragrance?' factor). Sentencing can look arbitrary, varying wildly from courtroom to courtroom. Ageing male judges often seem to take sexual assaults against women less seriously than the rest of society.

Worst of all, perhaps, there has been until very recently the repeated refusal of the Court of Appeal to overturn patently unsafe convictions such as those of the Birmingham Six. A recent survey, published in *Solicitors Journal*, found that 65 per cent of people in Britain agree with the statement 'Judges are out of touch with ordinary people and everyday life'. This is hardly surprising.

The judiciary is drawn from a narrow band of life. To state the obvious first, all judges are lawyers. A circuit judge must have been a barrister of 10 years' standing or have held the office of recorder for five years. High Court judges are drawn more selectively from the same pool, while the Lord Justices of Appeal must either be judges already or barristers of 15 years' standing. The Legal Action Group, for one, wants the legal system to take in Cinderellas like the industrial and social security appeal tribunals. By bringing their chairmen and women within the older legal apparatus a new generation of judges might be persuaded to emerge, many of them female, some of them black and Asian.

This might avoid the (fortunately increasingly rare) occasions when a judge himself seems to share practically pre-war assumptions about race. Famously, Judge McKinnon, hearing a case of incitement to racial hatred in 1978, commented that he had been nicknamed 'Nigger' at school and it hadn't done him any harm.

The present system of appointing judges by recommendation of the Lord Chancellor is obscure. Judges appear to emerge from a charmed circle of club-bable barristers. Last October, Lord Williams QC, chairman of the Bar Council, called the appointment system 'farcical' and added that there was 'lamentably scanty' training and a failure to monitor performances. 'We all know', he said, 'that some judges are slow, incompetent, rude and arrogant.' Justice, the all-party independent law reform group, has called for the appointments system to be demystified and opened up.

Nor is it a fallacy that judges come mainly from public school and Oxbridge backgrounds. A recent survey by Stephen Byers, Labour MP for Wallsend, showed that 84 per cent of the 27 judges appointed to the Lords, the Court of Appeal and the High Court between 1989 and 1991 had been to public school, and 77 per cent to either Oxford or Cambridge. If anything things are getting narrower: a 1974 study of appointments to the same posts between 1951 and 1968 showed 72 per cent had been educated at public school and 83 per cent at Oxbridge.

Only one of the 1989–91 intake was a woman, Dame Joyanne Bracewell, who was appointed to the High Court Family Division in 1990. Yet it is precisely on issues of particular concern to women that our judges, as the case-studies [below] show, are most vulnerable to charges of insensitivity. The liberal lawyer Helena Kennedy pointed out in 1988 that the only woman judge at the Old Bailey, Judge Nina Lowry, was 'one of the few members of the judiciary who recognise the seriousness of rape and give it its proper place at the double-figure end of the sentencing range'.

Judges have been so criticised for failing to appreciate the seriousness of rape that in September a videotape of a 1990 BBC *Everyman* programme about Jill Saward, the victim of the Ealing Vicarage Rape [...] was shown to some 70 circuit judges at a refresher seminar organised by the police. The hope was that the judges 'might understand the trauma better'.

The assumptions about rape that offend Ms Kennedy are not just male, but old-fashioned male. This should not be so much of a surprise given the greying, balding, sagging features of so many of our judges.

None of those whose more interesting moments are recorded on these pages is much under 60. The campaign group Justice has asked for the retirement age, at present 75 but soon to fall to 70, to be reduced still further to 65. The *Solicitors Journal* survey found that 86 per cent of people felt that judges should retire earlier.

Judges are also removed from most of us by reason of their salaries. A circuit judge is paid £65,912, a High Court Judge £87,620 and a Lord of Appeal £103,790. Yet there is an argument gaining currency that we do not pay enough to attract the best lawyers to the bench.

When Sir Roger Parker retired as an Appeal Court judge in July, he called his annual salary of £87,620 'peanuts' – and warned that the bench, unless it increased its rates, would attract monkeys. Judges, he said, were having to sell their homes in order to remain on the bench. This may be putting the case rather too strongly, yet it is customary for the Chairman of the Bar, almost always a top QC, to be offered a High Court judgeship after his year of office. In the past seven years, four have either not taken up the offer or let it be known beforehand that they were not interested. The present chairman, Lord Williams, has already made it clear that he does not want to be a judge. Much of the reluctance is financial: a top QC in commercial law can earn at least £300,000, going up to £800,000. Even in less rewarding fields an annual salary of £250,000 is not unusual.

But it is easier to suggest that our judges may be becoming monkeys from within the profession than from without. When it parodied the summing up in Jeremy Thorpe's trial for conspiracy to murder [...] *Private Eye* was playing with fire. Aside from the question of contempt of court, which normally applies only to material published during a case, judges, like anybody else, can sue for libel. Only last month, a news agency admitted liability for, quite wrongly, accusing

High Court Judge Mr Justice Popplewell of falling asleep during a murder trial. The judge was paid undisclosed damages.

Judges are beginning to feel got at. In a letter to *The Daily Telegraph* last July, Judge Jarlath Finney criticised those who said judges should not speak out on legal matters: 'I have long felt, though, that much of the hatred directed towards the judiciary these days is motivated not by any rational process of thought but by envy of the power entrusted to us; rather like Peter Cook's marvellous E.L. Wisty in *Beyond the Fringe* with his rambling moan that "but for the Latin" he could have been a judge.'

In fact, gathering ammunition against a judge is difficult. No records are kept of how many of their cases are overturned when retried in the Appeal Court. The feisty magazine *Legal Business* carried out a survey earlier this year but admitted that even its statistics were likely to be misleading: the better a judge the more complex the cases he is likely to be given to try, and so the greater likelihood of an appeal. And verdicts can be over-ruled because of new evidence or the incompetence of a defendant's counsel, as well as because of the way a judge has handled the case. Somewhere in the library of the Court of Appeal there is a folder stuffed full of reports of appeals upheld because of judicial error but, this being Britain, it is not open to examination by the public.

The names that appear here do not belong to incompetent judges. We would, however, suggest they belong to judges who perhaps for the only time in their careers made an injudicious comment or showed a moment of injudiciousness that exemplified for many the weaknesses of the profession as a whole.

In saying even this we are aware we may be in danger of constituting a gross *scandulum magnatum,* or even a breach of the time-honoured principle of *homo obstat justitia ruat coelum.* Suffice to say that, as you read these pages, it is important to remember that justice must not only be done – but be seen to be believed. […]

JUDGE RAYMOND DEAN

The judge who told a jury that when a woman says no she doesn't necessarily mean it

In April 1990 Judge Dean told an Old Bailey rape trial jury: 'As the gentlemen on the jury will understand, when a woman says no she doesn't always mean it. Men can't turn their emotions on and off like a tap like some women can.'

An hour later, jurors cleared a property consultant of rape. The judge […] said he agreed with their verdict.

Afterwards he defended his comments: I said sometimes, and I underline the word sometimes, even if the woman says no she may not really mean no. I didn't intend to suggest that this is something that happens frequently. If that remark, as it seems to have done, has upset certain people, I regret it. In saying that, I was simply repeating something I have heard over the last 40 years.'

Audrey Wise, the Labour MP for Preston, called his comments 'appalling' and 'an invitation to rape'. […]

JUDGE GABRIEL HUTTON

The judge who hoped a rapist would keep his well-paid job

Born in 1932, a circuit judge since 1978, Judge Hutton [...] is an understanding man. In 1988 he tried the case of a man who broke into the home of a 42-year-old nurse, exposed himself and then attempted to rape her. This, the judge decided, merited a two-year sentence. However, he decided to suspend all but a month of it. He told the rapist: 'I hope you'll be able to keep your well-paid job and the couple of weeks you spend in prison will be treated by employers as part of your holidays.'

Another time he gave a two-year suspended sentence to a convicted child molester who subjected an eight-year-old girl to a year-long series of sexual assaults. 'It seems, on the evidence', said Judge Hutton, 'that this child has not suffered as a result of these offences.'

In 1990 he gave two years' probation to a man who sexually assaulted a nine-year-old boy. The man, said Judge Hutton, needed a chance 'to get over his problems'.

SIR KENNETH JUPP

The judge who preferred rape to be kept in the family

Three years before Sir Kenneth retired in 1990 after 15 years as a High Court judge, he gave a man who raped his ex-wife a two-year suspended sentence. The judge [...] observed: 'This was a rare sort of rape. It is not like someone being jumped on in the street. This is within the family and does not impinge on the public.' [...]

SIR JAMES MISKIN

The judge who told a 'nig-nog' joke

Sir James, the Recorder of London from 1975 until he retired in July 1990, once entertained a Mansion House dinner to a story about 'a nig-nog'. On the same occasion he joked that he was engaged on the trial of 'murderous Sikhs'. The Sikh in question had yet to be found guilty. Sir James was publicly rebuked by Lord Lane, the Lord Chief Justice.

JUDGE ARTHUR MYERSON

The judge who praised a rapist for practising safe sex

Arthur Myerson, 64, has been a circuit judge since 1978. In April last year, at York Crown Court, he gave a rapist a lighter sentence of three years. The reason was that the rapist, who had attacked a teenage prostitute, had worn a condom as he raped her. Myerson [...] said: 'You showed concern and consideration by wearing a contraceptive.'

The judge's reasoning was attacked by the Women Against Rape group. Labour MP Robert Cryer said the sentence was 'entirely in line with the erratic behaviour of the British judiciary'. [...]

STUDY QUESTIONS

1   Does the judiciary represent a real cross-section of society? What measures could be taken to improve the representativeness and/or training of magistrates and judges?
2   Spend a day in a court and observe what happens. From your experience how accurate would you say is the research of Belloni and Hodgson (Reading 25) and the reporting of Billen (this reading)?

FURTHER READING

As suggested above, Smith, J. (1989) *Misogynies*, London: Faber and Faber, is an interesting and informative read. Lees, S. (1997) *Ruling Passions: Sexual Violence, Sexual Reputation and the Law*, Buckingham: Open University Press; and Smart, C. (1989) *Feminism and the Power of the Law*, London: Routledge, are also relevant here. The role of the judiciary is explored in Malleson, K. (1999) *The New Judiciary: The Effects of Expansion and Activism*, Aldershot: Ashgate. See also *Further Reading* for Belloni and Hodgson (Reading 25).

27

Justifications and purposes of imprisonment

Ian Dunbar and Anthony Langdon

The question 'Why do we punish?' is one of the most frequently asked in academic criminology and, as Ian Dunbar and Anthony Langdon note in the following reading, the answer lies in two directions. First, there is the 'expressive' function of punishment: it is a means by which society draws together in social solidarity and expresses blame. Secondly, punishment is a way of securing particular objectives, namely reducing or preventing crime. A further, more focused, question is 'What is prison for?' the answers to which have important consequences for the kinds of daily regimes that prisons adopt (Bottoms, 1990; see *Further Reading*). Both these questions underpin Dunbar and Langdon's critique. They argue that the aims of imprisonment are imperfect and confuse attempts at serious and coherent policy-making precisely because they contain ideas of both punishment (the social, expressive function) and crime control (which is policy-oriented and directed at offending in terms of its violation of laws). Although Dunbar and Langdon devote some attention to the theme of retribution, they focus mainly on the three issues on which imprisonment can be empirically tested: deterrence, rehabilitation and incapacitation.

Nobody asks why we need schools or hospitals, or what their functions are supposed to be. Prisons, however, are something else again. There are not many important jobs where the entire rationale of the work is, rightly, under such recurrent scrutiny, and someone going to work in the prison service for the first time will feel this quite acutely. Before one can say anything much about prison issues it is necessary to address the basic questions and at least indicate the purposes that imprisonment is supposed to fulfil. What follows is a very compressed account of the propositions that are conventionally cited, but we

SOURCE: From *Tough Justice: Sentencing and Penal Policies in the 1990s* (London: Blackstone Press, 1998), 7–20.

think that the considerations that should govern rational policy-making on this subject do boil down to a few essential issues, and we believe that what follows is a fair summary.

There is a distinction between seeing punishment as the way in which a society expresses blame, and seeing it as a way to secure particular objectives (always the reduction of crime) by changing offenders' behaviour or circumscribing their freedom of action. There are various sub-plots within these major themes – such as the argument that a credible system of State punishment is required to divert victimised individuals from feeling the need to exact their own vengeance. In an influential book[1] H.L.A. Hart drew a distinction between the 'general justifying aims' for having a system of punishment and the principles of distribution that should determine how punishment is allocated to individual offenders. Hart argued that the general aim is the prevention and control of crime, while individual distribution should be according to the principle of desert.

In practice, there is a consensus that the main justifications for punishment boil down to the following four aspects:

(a) deterrence (both 'specific' to the individual offender and 'general' to exert a deterrent influence on the population at large);
(b) rehabilitation (to reform the offender's character, rather than frightening him into good future behaviour);
(c) incapacitation (preventing the offender from committing crimes in society – normally by locking him up, though banishment and capital punishment are also incapacitating penalties to which we shall make no further reference);
(d) retribution (making offenders suffer punishment because they deserve it).

It is obvious that the first three of these concepts are forward-looking, with the aim of reducing crime, and that it is therefore possible to make a meaningful effort to estimate their success in meeting that aim. There is, in fact, a large research literature by people who have tried to measure the effect of punishment on offenders' behaviour.

Retribution, however, is free-standing and not susceptible to empirical testing, except that a punishment system justified on retributive grounds should be internally proportionate and coherent, so that self-evidently lesser offences do not receive greater punishment than more serious ones and vice versa. It is, however, just as possible to have a coherent and moderate punishment system as a coherent and severe one. The overall severity of a punishment system is rooted deep in a society's culture.

In addition to the classic justifications of punishment set out above there is the alternative approach that offenders should compensate their victims and/or wider society for the wrong they have done. That principle is represented in our law by compensation orders, which require the offender to make a payment to the victim or the victim's relatives, and which courts have to consider ordering in every case involving death, injury, loss or damage. Community service orders are a way of punishing an offender by making him do useful work for the community as a whole. At the present time a debate is developing on restorative justice, which seeks to move away from the conventional analysis we have described here, and into new areas of mediation and involvement of victims and offenders. This approach offers new ways of making offenders face up to their crimes, and it is potentially a very hopeful development. [...]

The penalty of imprisonment, by its nature, spreads across the categories of justification in a way that other forms of punishment do not. An offender who is given a prison sentence that is primarily chosen on grounds of retribution will inevitably also be incapacitated from committing offences (outside prison, at least) during the duration of his sentence; an optimist might hope that the prison experience would reform him; and a disciplinarian might believe that the experience and knowledge of the punishment would act as a deterrent to the offender and/or others.

This pooling and blurring of the aims of imprisonment – involving ideas both of punishment and crime control – makes the subject extremely hard to explain to the public, though better public understanding is essential. Most of the public probably see the two things as so closely connected as to be identical. In fact, the fit between the two is a very imperfect one, as we shall try to summarise.

The confusion of rationales has always bedevilled the pursuit of a rational sentencing and imprisonment policy. It has in the past meant that policy-makers have slid from one rationale to another as empirical analysis has undermined previous justifications; it still means that politicians can lump together different justifications in a way that confuses serious analysis; and it has been one of the factors that have enabled sentencers to adopt what has been called a 'cafeteria' approach from a menu of competing rationales to find the justification that most supports their gut feeling about the sentence they sense to be appropriate. One of [our] main themes [...] is, in fact, that a great increase in the use of imprisonment has been encouraged and planned in the last few years on the ostensible basis that it is a necessary part of an effective crime control strategy, whereas the truth is that it has been an exercise in retribution that has demonstrably had little to do with crime control.

Nevertheless, there is plenty of evidence available on the first three of the possible aims of imprisonment listed above, and [below] we summarise the main points that we think a disinterested adviser should be reporting to policy-makers at the present time.

DETERRENCE

The idea of specific deterrence is that the experience of a punishment is so unpleasant that the offender alters his behaviour to reduce the risk of being punished again. Most offenders on leaving prison would probably say – and indeed believe – that they will try to avoid another unpleasant experience of prison, but the well-known fact is that, when allowance is made for the differences between the groups, reconviction rates are essentially the same for ex-prisoners as for those given various kinds of non-custodial sentences.[2] There are doubtless prisoners who are deterred by their experience of prison, just as there are probationers who are deterred by their experience of probation, but imprisonment, as such, does not appear to be an especially effective type of sentence from the point of view of deterring subsequent criminal behaviour by those who experience it. Attempts have been made in this country and others to subject prisoners to regimes that are so unpleasant that they exert a special deterrent effect, but these appear to be a blind alley. Thus, the 'short, sharp shock' detention centre regime that was experimentally established in the early 1980s following the 1979 Conservative election manifesto proved to have no better post-release reconviction scores than centres operating the normal regime. Whether the last Conservative government's experimental 'boot camp' regime should be seen as primarily deterrent or reformative in intention is a nice question, since it was presented as a cocktail of both principles, as were some of its exemplars in the USA. Certainly, American 'boot camp' regimes of the aggressive kind have not been shown to be at all effective in discouraging reoffending.

If punitive regimes are not the answer, though, surely longer sentences must have a potent effect in deterring the individual from reoffending? Once again, the research literature indicates otherwise. While there is some evidence that the prospect of long sentences is among the factors that weigh with mature recidivists who decide to give up a life of crime, this seems to be part of a general ageing development, and the evidence does not support the idea that long sentences in themselves are generally effective deterrents to those who experience them.

The question of general deterrence is, perhaps, more complex. First of all, there is empirical evidence that the very existence of a system of law enforcement does have a general deterrent effect on crime, just as one would expect. The classic case that is quoted is the removal for some months of the Danish police force by the occupying Germans in the Second World War, and the subsequent vivid rise in offences of theft and robbery.

The question that is relevant to policy-making, however, is the relationship between increases of penalty levels and the incidence of the relevant offending behaviour, and here there appears to be simply no sufficient evidence of linkage to support deterrence-based arguments for increasing penalties for particular offences. (There may, of course, be perfectly good reasons for such adjustments on other grounds.) Beyleveld's comprehensive study in 1980[3] brought out very clearly the extreme rarity of instances in which changes in levels of offending could confidently be attributed to fear of a particular penalty as opposed to other considerations. It also stressed that the key factor in deterrence is not the objectively demonstrable risk of punishment but the individual potential offender's perception of the risk of being caught, about which it is extremely unsound to generalise from the basis of one's personal experience. This is not to say that deterrent effects are never obtainable, but simply that there is no reliable basis for assuming them. There is, for example, some evidence, such as Harding's study of Canadian robbers' attitudes towards carrying firearms,[4] that offenders of particular categories who are prone to plan ahead may tend to be influenced by special penalties. On the other hand – and this is particularly relevant to current political argument – there is specific research[5] on burglars that shows them to be predominantly feckless people with a short-term focus, who put out of their minds while committing a crime the possibility of being detected. According to this research, they see themselves as having little choice but to commit burglaries as the only way they know in which to relieve overwhelming immediate needs (usually for money, but sometimes also for self-esteem).

The behavioural psychologists' views on deterrence theory chime in with the above, and boil down to the following.

First, most people have internalised moral scruples about offending. Those who do not have such scruples are deterred much more by informal social control mechanisms such as the opinion of their friends, neighbours and family than by the threat of formal sanctions.[6] As for those who are not inhibited by their own code of values or by informal social control mechanisms, punishment may indeed be an effective agent of change, but only if it scores highly on the following long-recognised features.

(a) *Certainty*. Punishment should be the inevitable and unavoidable consequence of the offending behaviour.
(b) *Immediacy*. Punishment should follow the offending behaviour rapidly, so as to impress the connection upon the individual.
(c) *Severity*. If punishment is not applied with great intensity, its effects are uncertain.
(d) *Comprehensibility*. The reason and justification for the punishment should be understood by the individual on whom it is inflicted.

In addition, James McGuire, whose *What Works*[7] summarises the research evidence, argues that a further necessary criterion is the availability to the individual of alternative means for the achievement of the goals otherwise sought through offending behaviour.

It is immediately obvious how enormously far all these requirements are from the daily reality of the criminal justice processes. Above all, with police clear-up rates at around 25 per cent and with less than 3 per cent of the crimes that are actually committed leading to formal caution or prosecution, the likelihood of punishment for much crime is a very long way from being a certainty. The great criminologist Beccaria is still generally thought to have been absolutely right in his maxim that certainty, rather than severity, is the test of an effective antidote for crime.

Looking beyond the paramount requirement of certainty, the current realities do not score well on the other characteristics of an effective deterrent punishment system. As the Labour government has recognised in respect of youth crime, the delays that have become endemic in our criminal justice mean that the commission of an offence and any eventual punishment for it are widely separated in time. As for severity, we shall be arguing that imprisonment is indeed a harsher sanction than it has recently been fashionable to acknowledge, but many people who go to prison already have very damaged lives, and their perception of risking imprisonment has to be seen in that context.

The conclusion of all this must be that there is no sound evidence for believing that, in the real world, changes in sentencing policy should have any appreciable general deterrent effect on the incidence of crime. If immediate execution was the penalty that was routinely enforced for parking offences then we would no doubt be more careful where we left our cars, but that is a fantasy situation and not a real-world one.

REHABILITATION

The idea of imprisonment having a beneficial reformative effect in itself has had an extraordinarily long history. When modern-style imprisonment took shape at the turn of the eighteenth and nineteenth centuries as a replacement for earlier corporal punishment systems, the dominant theme was one of enforced monastic isolation in which the offender should contemplate his sins and his need for redemption. The very words 'penitentiary', 'reformatory', 'corrections' say as much – as well as reminding us how much of our penal thinking in this country has been influenced by agendas set in the USA, by no means always to our advantage.

Throughout the nineteenth century the rhetoric of reformation coexisted with the harshest penal regimes, and it comes as an astonishing breath of fresh air to read the following reply by Sir Godfrey Lushington, the Permanent Secretary (i.e., the head civil servant) of the Home Office in evidence to the reforming Gladstone Committee in 1895:

> I regard as unfavourable to reformation the status of a prisoner throughout his whole career; the crushing of self-respect, the starving of all moral instinct he may possess, the absence of opportunity to do or receive a kindness, the continual association with none but criminals … the forced labour and the denial of all liberty. I believe the true mode of reforming a man or restoring him to society is exactly in the opposite direction to all these. But of course this is a mere idea. It is quite impracticable in a prison. In fact, the unfavourable features I have mentioned are inseparable from a prison life. All that I care to insist on is that this treatment is not reformatory. I consider that a mediaeval thief who had his right hand chopped off was much more likely to turn over a new leaf than a convict who has had 10 years penal servitude.[8]

That critique was levelled against a system of prison treatment that now appears unbearably cruel, rigid and coercive. In the event, the Gladstone Committee set deterrence and reformation as the simultaneous aims of imprisonment, and the new emphasis on reformation did lead to a change for the better in the prison system. Yet even today anyone who really knows about prisons must still read Lushington's words with the deeply uncomfortable recognition that much of what he had to say is inherently true of imprisonment by its very nature.

In the twentieth century the reformative ideal reinvented itself in terms of behavioural science rather than religious imperatives and Victorian paternalism. It reached its high point in the 'medical' or 'treatment' model that was widely accepted in the USA in the 1960s, before spectacularly crashing in the 1970s. What then brought it down was the combined onslaught of empirical analysts who demonstrated that exposure to prison regimes of whatever duration did not of itself have a reformative effect in terms of reconviction rates, and civil libertarians who demonstrated that the indeterminate sentencing that went with the treatment model led to capricious post-sentence decision-making, including inbuilt bias against ethnic and other groups. What is nowadays virtually universally accepted is that imprisonment of itself does not have a reformative effect, but that certain kinds of treatment programme can have a significant effect in reducing offending behaviour among certain groups of individuals, and that programmes of these kinds can be administered in prison.

The current state of the art in this area is conveniently summarised by James McGuire in *What Works*.[9] McGuire argues that, while more research is needed, the technique of meta analysis (which involves aggregating and re-analysing the results of different research projects) has clearly indicated the general characteristics of treatment programmes that are successful. The statistical level of success, measured against control groups, is claimed to be of the order of 10 per cent, with treatment programmes in the community being about twice as effective as those within penal institutions. Successful programmes are focused on the factors that caused individuals to offend, and those that employ cognitive behavioural methodology are found to work best. Effective programmes rely on clear aims and explicitly defined methods; they require well-trained and properly resourced staff; and it is essential that the objectives underpinning the work should be adhered to (i.e., the programme should deliver what has been undertaken to the participants). There needs to be managerial support, a commitment to evaluation, and mechanisms for feeding the results of evaluation back into the conduct of the programme.

People involved with prisons have often been tempted in the past to claim more for their rehabilitative role than the system can actually deliver. Claims of that sort make their originators feel better about the machine with which they are involved and they are very understandable. Nevertheless, they blur a clear focus on the nature of imprisonment, and they have sometimes led to mistaken policies. Modern offending behaviour programmes are one of the most important developments now going on in the prison world, and their recent establishment throughout the English prison system has been a very positive step. While rehabilitation programmes of this kind are a very necessary and worthwhile thing to pursue within prisons, however, they do not overturn the generally accepted proposition that people should not be sent to prison simply for rehabilitation.

INCAPACITATION

It has always been blindingly clear that, whatever prisons cannot do, the one thing that they can achieve is to keep people locked up so that they cannot commit crimes outside in society. Nevertheless, incapacitation as a general theory of imprisonment has historically been given less attention than deterrence and rehabilitation. It has only been as those justifications for imprisonment have been eroded that the study of incapacitation has moved into the forefront, first in the USA and now in this country.

Imprisonment on grounds of incapacitation involves detaining (and, if done in prison, inevitably punishing) people not for what they have done but for what it is thought they might do if they were at liberty. It manifestly involves both the technical issue of prediction and the ethical issue of what degree of predictive certainty is required to justify an individual's continued detention. In practice, elements of incapacitatory thinking have always been likely to be involved in the sentencing of the 'dangerous offender' and the 'persistent offender', though the incapacitation element may well exist alongside and be submerged by other rationales.

The problem with the 'dangerous offender' is that grave violent offences are rare occurrences that are difficult to predict, so that even the best developed methods only reach an accuracy of 50 per cent, with one 'false positive' for each 'true positive'. To the extent that 'dangerous offenders' bring themselves into that category by grave offences in the first place, long sentences will usually be merited on straightforward grounds of proportionality, and it has always been the case that this may mask an element of public protection. Difficult decisions then have to be made, however, in considering the release of a life-sentence prisoner or the early release of a fixed-sentence one, since conduct in prison may be no reliable indication of behaviour on release. The most problematic cases are those of people whose immediate offence is not especially grave, but who give cause for genuine concern about their dangerous propensities. There is, of course, a mental health element in virtually all such cases, and the particular problem of the so-called psychopath (whose behaviour is not normal, but who is generally not treatable and hence within the ambit of restraint authorised on medical grounds) has been an unresolved matter of concern for at least the last 25 years.

The persistent (but not dangerous) offender also will merit a long sentence if his immediate offence is a grave one. The question to which sentencers and politicians have constantly reverted, however, is what to do about persistent non-violent property offenders, who constantly reoffend, but who never commit crimes that are big enough in themselves to justify long imprisonment. One answer is simply to punish them in proportion to what they have done and to accept with resignation that they are quite likely to do something similar again until they give up crime. But if that measure of political and judicial acceptance is jettisoned, the only alternative is specially long confinement for such offenders, which has been the central feature of many failed policies in English penal history. One example from the nineteenth century is the 'cumulative principle' advocated by a Gloucestershire magistrate, Barwick Lloyd Baker, in 1863.[10] This principle required that the punishment for a first felony conviction should be a week or so's imprisonment on bread and water, for the second a year's imprisonment, for the third seven years' penal servitude, and for the fourth life imprisonment. With a tone of hermetic certainty that has uncanny echoes of some current political attitudes, Baker calmly asserted that 'if you tell a man clearly what will be the punishment of a crime before he commits it, there can be no injustice in inflicting it', though his approach proved highly controversial and was disowned by the Lord Chief Justice of the day. Later, the Prevention of Crime Act 1908, enabled courts to impose a supplementary sentence of preventive detention, in addition to the current sentence, on convicted felons with three previous felony convictions. Churchill, when Home Secretary, was enraged to find these powers being used against petty pilferers and he issued a circular demanding that the additional sanction should only be invoked against offenders who were 'a serious danger to society'. After that, the use of the power withered away, but it was only to be resuscitated in a different guise by the Criminal Justice Act 1948, which authorised sentences of preventive detention between five and 14 years for persistent offenders. Preventive detainees serving enormous sentences for trivial offences are well within the memory of the present authors (one chronic pilferer comes to mind who, in the early 1960s, was serving 14 years for stealing a chicken). Eventually the judges themselves turned against this sort of thing and the power was repealed, only to be replaced by the extended sentence provisions in the Criminal Justice Act 1967, which never caught on.

What the 'cumulative principle' and the various statutory provisions for preventive confinement do seem to show is, first, that there is nothing new under the sun so far as penal policy is concerned and, second, that institution-alised attempts to protect society from the non-violent persistent offender have always foundered on the inherent tendency of such arrangements to suck in less serious offenders, whose disproportionately heavy punishment becomes unacceptable. Alongside the structured policy initiatives, however, there exists the informal courtroom practice of 'sentencing on record' (i.e., simply sentenc-ing multiple recidivists more severely than their current offence justifies) and this is harder to pin down, though the practice is probably still alive and well. 'Sentencing on record' was at the bottom of one of the policies in the Criminal Justice Act 1991 that was abruptly reversed in 1993.

Setting aside all considerations of proportionality and fairness, the basic questions faced by incapacitation theory are how to select the offenders to be given the preventive confinement, and how to quantify the crime that is prevented by taking them out of circulation. Since the sole justification of incapa-citation policy is to prevent crime, policy-makers taking this path should have an accurate assessment of the amount of crime reduction that is bought by imprisonment programmes that inevitably involve high resource costs (together with less easily quantifiable human costs).

One approach to crime control by incapacitation would simply be greatly to increase sentence lengths across the board, on the proposition that the offending behaviour of many criminals is known to range across a variety of offence categories, and that the more criminals in prison, the less crime would necessarily be committed. A smarter, more cost-effective, approach would be one that tried to exploit the fact that a disproportionate amount of crime is committed by a comparatively small number of high-rate offenders. Such an approach would try to home in on the defining characteristics of the high-rate offenders and put away those people who corresponded to the resulting descriptive profile. If that kind of approach was found not to be workable, one might try to obtain at least some of its benefits by defining a profile of previous offending, which is known to be a very significant indicator of future offending, and giving long preventive sentences to people who clocked up the necessary qualifying convictions. All these approaches have had their proponents in the last few decades and they have, in fact, been given the distinguishing names of collective, selective and categorial incapacitation, respectively.[11]

There is a persuasive feel of simplicity about the idea of dealing with crime by putting the high-rate offender out of action, but in practice the proposition tends to fall apart. This is primarily because crime is something that is done by a surprisingly large part of the population, and most criminal careers are fairly short. No less than 34 per cent of males and 8 per cent of females will have a conviction for a 'standard list' offence[12] before the age of 40 (though more than half of that number will only have been convicted once). Crime is also a young person's game, predominantly being carried out by young males during a comparatively short period in their lives. The peak age for known offending is 18 for males and 14 for females.[13]

Crime is, therefore, not an activity that is mainly conducted by an easily identifiable and finite group of special people called criminals but is, rather, the product of a very large and volatile pool, constantly being both replenished and diminished as individuals move into and out of criminal activity. At no time can one know with certainty how large that pool is, or what is the rate of offending by the individuals within it. Neither can one know what would be the rate of offending by the imprisoned and incapacitated population if it was at liberty, though incarcerated individuals who are well advanced in their criminal careers (as many will tend to be if they have had time to clock up qualifying convictions) must be expected to reduce and desist from offending under the normal process of maturation and settling down. Two highly relevant considerations are the fact that many offences are carried out as joint enterprises, so that the incapacitation of one individual will not necessarily have much effect on offence rates if his criminal colleagues remain active, and the fact that some criminal activities (drug dealing is the example that is usually given) reflect market principles, so that the place of one incapacitated supplier is likely to be promptly taken by a new recruit. Additionally, all prison populations are already skewed towards persistent and high-rate offenders, so any expansion of them is bound to represent diminishing margins of improvement in crime prevention.

The distinguished criminologists Franklin Zimring and Gordon Hawkins, in their respected book *Incapacitation*,[14] warn against attempting to make global estimates of the amount of crime prevention that is obtainable by incapacitation, saying 'the amount of crime prevented by incapacitation is both variable and contingent, varying in relation to different social circumstances and under different criminal justice policies'. That is a wise health warning, especially in the context of the USA, where so many different criminal justice systems and policies operate simultaneously at federal and state level. In the context of a single jurisdiction such as England and Wales we believe that it is possible to arrive at a meaningful estimate of the incapacitatory effect, as an essential aid to policy-makers. So far as we are aware, the fullest examination in the United Kingdom of the crime-reduction effects of incapacitation remains the work published in 1993[15] by Roger Tarling, then head of the Home Office Research and Planning Unit. Tarling concluded that there was little ground for thinking that sentences could efficiently be targeted on groups that were particularly likely to reoffend, and his key conclusion was that 'a change in the use of custody of the order of 25 per cent would be needed to produce a 1 per cent change in the level of crime'. In other words, doubling the prison population would reduce crime by just 4 per cent, which is a figure that is well within the fluctuations of the rate at which people report crimes to the police and the rate at which the police record the crimes that are reported to them.

One of the unsatisfactory features of the Parliamentary discussion of the Crime (Sentences) Act 1997 was the slight attention that was given to exploring the crime-reduction effect of those very costly proposals, though Tarling's findings were mentioned by some critics of the legislation. We have absolutely no reason to suppose that further research would come to conclusions very different from Tarling's or that his 25-to-one gearing between the crime rate and the size of the prison population would be moved into a different ballpark. We believe that this is the line that a disinterested adviser should be putting to policy-makers at the present time. Nevertheless, as part of the rationalisation and demystification that is so much needed, it would be desirable for the government to consider if further research could establish more facts about rates and patterns of offending.

The gearing that we have indicated between prison populations and crime rates, together with the high resource costs of imprisonment, means that expanding the prison population of a country that already has a high rate of imprisonment is inherently unlikely to represent a very effective way of responding to crime. Nevertheless, when incapacitation is presented as the only option it has a simplicity and clarity of aim that gives it great political potency. Zimring and Hawkins put this perfectly in *Incapacitation* when they wrote:

> Just as locking up more offenders must reduce criminal activity by some amount, releasing large numbers of offenders or allowing them to remain outside prison must produce some increase in the number of crimes experienced by the community that receives them. Support of decarceration is thus the moral equivalent of approving higher crime rates, entailing a high risk of political extinction for anyone sufficiently naive to endorse the policy.[16]

We would only add that the fear of political extinction seems now to extend well beyond the topic of reducing prison numbers: it would be more accurate to say that it inhibits any questioning of the need to go on increasing the scale of imprisonment.

CONCLUSIONS

[...] It is perfectly true to say that the existence of the prison sanction is a deterrent, but there is no sound basis for claiming much for the deterrent effects of sentencing changes. Some kinds of rehabilitation programmes in prison have some effect with some kinds of offenders (though less successfully than in a non-penal setting) but offenders should not be sent to prison simply for rehabilitation. As for incapacitation, nobody doubts the need to protect the public from genuinely dangerous offenders (with all the issues of identification, procedural justice and risk assessment that this involves), but enormous numbers of people would theoretically have to be imprisoned to have an appreciable effect on the general crime rate.

All this kind of crime control argument can very easily turn out to be irrelevant since the political decision-maker can always claim to be articulating what is 'right' by way of retribution pure and simple, and then the need for more punishment is likely to be put to the public as something that is self-evident.

Punishment has a powerful symbolic function. Inflicting punishment has always been one of the main ways in which a State projects itself as powerful and effective (and the less confident a government is, the more need it probably sees for such props). These aspects are similar to the theme of nationalism in foreign policy. People do need to feel that they are properly protected and that criminals are punished, just as they need to feel that the government is protecting national interests. If the public are constantly told that punishment is inadequate and that much more of it is easily available, then of course they will want to see it delivered. Once confidence is undermined and the genie of punishment as the answer to crime is let out of the bottle, it is extraordinarily difficult – perhaps impossible – to get it back in again.

NOTES

1   Hart, H.L.A., *Punishment and Responsibility* (Oxford: Clarendon Press, 1968).
2   Lloyd, C., Mari, G. and Hough, M., *Explaining Reconviction Rates: A Critical Analysis* (Home Office Research Study No. 136) (London: HMSO, 1994); Kershaw, C., 'Reconvictions of those commencing community penalties in 1993, England and Wales', *Home Office Statistical Bulletin* 6/97 (London: Home Office, 1997).
3   Beyleveld, D., *A Bibliography on General Deterrence Research* (Westmead: Saxon House, 1980).

4   Harding, R., 'Rational choice gun use in armed robbery', 1 *Criminal Law Forum* 427 (1990).

5   Bennett, T. and Wright, R.T., *Burglars on Burglary* (Aldershot: Gower, 1984); Wright, R.T. and Decker, S.H., *Burglars on the Job* (Boston: North Western University Press, 1994).

6   Willcock, H.D. and Stokes, J., *Deterrents and Incentives to Crime among Boys and Young Men Aged 15–21 Years* (London: HMSO, 1968).

7   McGuire, J. (ed.), *What Works: Reducing Reoffending* (Chichester: Wiley, 1995).

8   Evidence to Home Office Departmental Committee on Prisons 1895, Q.11482.

9   See note 7.

10 The cumulative principle arguably combined specific deterrence and incapacitation.

11 See, for example, Von Hirsch, A., *Past or Future Crimes* (Manchester: Manchester University Press, 1986).

12 The 'standard list' includes all indictable offences and some of the more serious summary ones.

13 All the figures in this paragraph are taken from Barclay, G.C., Tavares, C. and Prout, A., *Information on the Criminal Justice System in England and Wales* (London: Home Office, 1995).

14 Zimring, F. and Hawkins, G., *Incapacitation* (New York: Oxford University Press, 1995).

15 Tarling, R., *Analysing Offending: Data, Models and Interpretations* (London: HMSO, 1993).

16 Zimring and Hawkins, *Incapacitation*.

STUDY QUESTIONS

1   To what extent do the four functions of imprisonment identified by Dunbar and Langdon overlap, and in what ways do they appear to conflict with each other? To what extent is each of the four goals concerned with the rights of the offender, and to what degree do they seek to protect the rights of the public and of victims of crime?

2   Former Conservative Home Secretary, Michael Howard, is famous for saying that 'prison works'. In the light of your reading of this extract, would you agree or disagree with him? What are the main arguments for and against this statement and how can they each be supported with reference to the justifications for imprisonment highlighted in the reading?

FURTHER READING

Justifications for imprisonment are further discussed in Bottoms, A.E. (1990) 'The aims of imprisonment' in D. Garland (ed.) *Justice, Guilt and Forgiveness in the Penal System*, Edinburgh: University of Edinburgh Centre for Theology and Public Issues, Occasional Paper 18; Davies, M., Croall, H. and Tyrer, J. (1998) *Criminal Justice: An Introduction to the Criminal Justice System in England and Wales*, 2nd edn, Harlow: Pearson; Hudson, B. (1996) *Understanding Justice: An Introduction to Ideas, Perspectives and Controversies in Modern Penal Theory*, Milton Keynes: Open University Press; and Newburn, T. (1995) *Crime and Criminal*

Justice Policy, Harlow: Longman. Also of interest are Matthews, R. (1999) *Doing Time: An Introduction to the Sociology of Imprisonment,* Basingstoke: Macmillan; Morgan, R. (1997) 'Imprisonment: current concerns and a brief history since 1945' in M. Maguire, R. Morgan and R. Reiner (eds) *The Oxford Handbook of Criminology,* 2nd edn, Oxford: Oxford University Press; and Player, E. and Jenkins, M. (eds) (1994) *Prisons after Woolf: Reform through Riot,* London: Routledge.

28

The closed emotional world of the security wing

Stanley Cohen and Laurie Taylor

Having considered, in Reading 27, the 'official' justifications for imprisoning offenders, we now turn to the actual *lived* experiences of those behind bars. The reading that follows describes the day-to-day experience of incarceration in one of England's most notorious prisons. Cohen and Taylor's book, from which the extract is taken, has become a 'classic' text on the deprivations that long-term prisoners face, and has achieved a certain amount of infamy as well as critical and commercial acclaim. Originally denied access to the prison by the Home Office, Cohen and Taylor conducted their study of men in Durham's E-wing in the 1960s covertly, while running an adult education class. Capital punishment had recently been abolished and there were widespread fears among politicians and the public that the prison system was now having to cope with what the newspapers called 'a new breed of prisoner with nothing to lose' (*The Sunday Times*, 23 January 1977). Anxiety was fuelled by a media peddling stories about the emergence of a new 'super-criminal', and the fact that Cohen and Taylor's students included some of the most newsworthy felons of the time (in the late 1960s Durham housed the 'Great Train Robbers' and the Kray twins, among other well-known inmates), together with the researchers' covert and arguably unethical means of access, partly accounts for the study's continuing notoriety and longevity thirty years after it was published. The reading provides a detailed description of the severities of life in a maximum-security wing, and graphically illustrates not only the hardships of everyday life in prison, but also the assaults that are inflicted on prisoners' self-identities. Furthermore, despite having been written some thirty years ago, many prisoners, prison staff and prison researchers believe that Cohen and Taylor's account is still relevant and meaningful to the experiences of inmates today. However, it should be remembered that

SOURCE: From *Psychological Survival: The Experience of Long-term Imprisonment* (Harmondsworth: Penguin, 1972), 60–82.

> such experiences are not universal: in particular, those who are serving
> short sentences or who serve their sentences in low- category – especially
> categories 'C' or 'D' – institutions may experience prisons as rather less
> austere places. It is likely, however, that most inmates, whatever their
> sentence or security classification, would find points of familiarity and
> resonance in the following account.

'It's like living in a submarine.'
Paul, one of the prisoners, on life in the wing

The atmosphere in Durham maximum security wing differs from that in other
parts of the prison. There are no long lines of prisoners moving in and out of
the building, no sudden bursts of sound, no crowded rooms, no clanking
machinery. This building is designed for no other purpose than successfully to
contain its inmates. Its success is measured exclusively by its impregnability.

After going through the three sets of gates which admit you to the main
prison, it takes approximately ten minutes to get into the wing. You are led
between the dogs by an officer, then scrutinized through a peep-hole before the
first double-locked door of the actual wing is opened from the inside. This admits
you to an antechamber in which you wait until more routine signals are
exchanged by officers on both side of another double-locking door. Once through
this, you find yourself standing on the specially thickened concrete ground floor
of the block. Above tower the familiar metal cat-walks. Your walk along the
ground floor arcade to the metal stairs which lead to the first landing is further
scrutinized from a spy-hole in a door at the far end of the block; each corner on
the way up to the meeting room on the second floor is controlled by an officer.

After all these elaborate precautions, it comes as a surprise to find the
building so empty. There are no prisoners to be seen. Although there are nearly
sixty cells in the wing, only a few are occupied. It is rather like the lions' cage
at Whipsnade: after all the wire and spikes and notices, it is slightly absurd to
find that the objects of all this attention are not readily visible. The analogy is
not one that escapes the prisoners. During the 1968 riot when the prisoners
seized their own records and read the reports which had been written about
them, one found that a chaplain had referred to him as an animal. On his next
pastoral visit to the man's cell he was greeted by a savage roar.

In fact the four floors of the security wing we studied rarely housed more
than twenty prisoners at any one time. There were nevertheless always plenty of
prison officers to be seen, peering through glass windows in doors, sitting in their
office cells, leaning over the landing rails and exchanging words with their mates
on other levels through the anti-suicide netting. The officers always outnum-
bered the prisoners by about two-to-one, a staffing requirement which meant that
officers were regularly called upon to remain inside the wing after their normal
working day, or night, was over. Shifts of up to fifteen hours were not unusual. It
was overtime which their economic situation hardly allowed them to refuse.

The relative emptiness of the place, the open landings, the high ceiling above the 'fours', were not enough to relieve the sense of claustrophobia experienced by staff, prisoners and visitors to the wing. It was not just the presence of so many locks and keys which created this feeling – these are after all a standard element in all prisoners' and prison officers' lives and had become a familiar aspect of life inside for many of the recidivists in E-Wing – but rather the completely lifeless atmosphere of the entire building. This was the claustrophobia of the tomb, rather than the crowded lift. The lighting was completely uniform, there were no shadows or pools of light (although at least at Durham the neon uniformity was not too intense – in another security wing, where closed circuit television is constantly used, the lighting has to be permanently maintained at a higher level of brightness). There were no colour variations in the wing at all, no distinctive clothes, merely two sets of uniforms (a move to allow lifers to wear some of their own clothes brought questions in the House and a swift indication from the Home Office that such liberalization was not intended).

There were no windows which opened in this building to let in any air, so the great concrete and steel vault throbbed day and night, winter and summer, to the rhythm of an inadequate ventilation system. The outside world was totally excluded. Even the suggestion that an additional fan might be installed to cool one particularly oppressive room was rejected for a long time on the grounds that even the smallest air chink in the wall would allow external enemies to introduce poisoned gas into the wing. This was then a lifeless cavern of railings and landings and pipes. 'It's like living in a submarine,' as Paul said. And, of course, for these prisoners the voyage was measured in decades, not months.

Long-term prisoners did not spend their entire time in the wing. An exercise yard had been attached to the building, a small round, high-fenced compound. At the top of the wire fence, the barbed wire curved inward and down to make escape by climbing impossible. We were told that professional soldiers had been used to test the security precautions here. Their failure to escape had meant that the prisoners were allowed to walk through a low concrete corridor from E-Wing and emerge rather like Roman gladiators into the barbed wire arena outside.

The environment at Durham was by no means unique. The special security wing at Leicester is regarded as even more claustrophobic by inmates. It consists of one floor, approximately twenty-five yards long and five yards wide. At times there have been fourteen officers and two T.V. cameras to watch over seven inmates.

Particular social and physical environments, however extreme, do not have automatic consequences for the social-psychological life of their inhabitants [...]. One may rather talk of them placing certain general limits upon patterns of daily life. They raise questions about matters which are taken for granted in other contexts. [Here] we particularly consider the problems of sociability and privacy, the problems of friendship and loneliness in the type of environment we have described.

RELATIONSHIPS INSIDE

When we are in trouble, when we experience anxiety or disturbance in our normal life, we look around for other people who are similarly placed in order that we can modify the distressing effects by collectively constructing reassuring accounts. The presence of an intimate also opens up the possibility of a distraction, of a reduction in the saliency of the distressing circumstances. It has even been shown by social psychologists that anxious people derive some comfort from the mere physical proximity of others, even if communication is prohibited. In the maximum security wing therefore, the circumstances which normally impel one to seek an intimate or friend are heightened. But the usually taken-for-granted nature of friendship is surrounded with problems in this environment.

In the first place there is the difficulty of actually finding a companion. There are usually only twenty other prisoners to choose from and there are certain restrictions upon choice even within this limited number. These men have nearly all been imprisoned for extreme acts of deviance, and the prospect of association with some of them may induce as much anxiety as does the prospect of facing life in the security wing alone. These prisoners, like most people, have a fear of being contaminated by certain sorts of deviance, a fear of being personally affected through contact with other individuals. As the American sociologist, Gresham Sykes, remarks in his discussion of a much larger security prison: 'While it is true that every prisoner does not live in the constant fear of being robbed or beaten, the constant companionship of thieves, rapists, murderers and aggressive homosexuals is far from reassuring.'[1]

Even this qualified comment is an overstatement in relation to the situation we studied. The prisoners we met were worried about contamination but only by one other type of inmate – the sex offender. The criminal careers of the other men – robbery, protection, murder – were not divisive factors, they did not provide a basis for either friendship or enmity. This is not to say that these men are not aware of each other's distinctive derelictions or that old gang loyalties or personal feuds are forgotten, but only that there is a self-conscious decision to play down such matters in the interest of group solidarity.

But all these men distinguish themselves sharply from sex offenders. The distinction is physically marked in the wing by the segregation of the sex offenders on a separate landing. This top landing can only be reached by negotiating another locked gate. We spent some time on this top floor although our regular class initially disapproved of such visits. The 'ordinary' prisoners had little contact with the men on the 'fours' although there were opportunities for them to meet each other. We were completely unsuccessful in our attempts to invite men from the top floor down to our classes on the lower. The 'lower' class objected declaring that the others were 'monsters' or 'animals', although they recognized the hypocrisy or at least the irony involved in the application of such crude labels. As David said: 'We know it's a prejudice, but we just have to differentiate ourselves from them.' Gradually, however, we became aware that this was not an absolute differentiation. Some softening of the rejection takes place over time. Some sex offenders are eventually admitted to limited interaction, although not chosen as intimates, whilst others are still rigidly excluded. A sexual offender, whose 'madness' is regarded as passive, for example, and who displays a certain pathetic quality is more easily tolerated than an offender who has committed a similar crime but who exhibits a certain sense of self-consciousness about what he has done or displays an ideological arrogance about his pre-prison deviant life style.

If the offender's behaviour can be seen as a variation on a recognizable perversion then he may also have his humanity partially restored. Buggery, bestiality and rape can all be encompassed. But Paul's attempt on one occasion to justify a particularly aberrant piece of sexual behaviour on the grounds of its similarity to normal sexual practice, broke down when he tried to allow the deviant a degree of self-consciousness about his 'perverted' behaviour. It could only be acceptable as long as the individual 'did not know what he was doing'. (Not that this preference for particular motivational accounts is confined to long-term prisoners. Its existence amongst middle-class magistrates has been described by one of us in a piece of research which was very much influenced by group discussions on the normality of 'sexual deviance' in the wing.)[2]

This anxiety about close relationships with sex offenders means that there are a reduced number of prisoners from whom to select a companion. The average short-term prisoner can find friends from amongst his cell-mates, or from the hundreds of men in his block; he may select a companion from his workplace, or from the library. In the security wing there is no alternative but to choose from the small group of notorious prisoners who share every minute of his daily life. The short-term prisoner may even manage without close friends, having little anxiety about the length of his sentence to dissipate and enjoying regular visits from a family or wife to whom he will return within a few years.

Standard texts on prison life are often reassuring about social relationships within the prison, not just because they are typically describing larger prisons where there is more choice available, but also because of their assumptions about the possibilities of interaction between staff and inmates. Sykes (1958: 33) observes that: 'Guards and prisoners are drawn from the same culture and they hold many of the same values and beliefs. They share a common language and a common historical experience.'

In their pioneering study of a large English maximum security prison, Pentonville, Terence and Pauline Morris illustrate in detail the common predicaments of the staff and prisoners and their cultural affinities. In terms of social aspirations and achievements, they are heir to a common culture, the urbanized working class.

> Their speech is punctuated by the same idioms, they employ the same swear words, they both carry little tins of tobacco and cigarette papers. In behaviour and attitudes they also exhibit marked cultural affinity; they have strong views about women going to work, about sex and about the colour question; they read the same newspapers and have

similar tastes in entertainment ... It was striking how in the matter of eating habits, some officers were indistinguishable from prisoners.[3]

In E-Wing very few of these similarities applied. The prisoners might have had the same socio-economic origins as the prison officers, but they shared very little in later experience and contemporary culture or language. They go out of their way to differentiate themselves from the officers on the landing. It would not be going too far to say that they felt in some danger of being contaminated by what they regard as the dull, prejudiced, lumpen-proletarian nature of their guards. Their jokes were often at the officers' expense. When David was asked by an officer about what he had learnt in class that night, he explained carefully that they had been discussing a report which showed that prison officers were predominantly 'authoritarian psychopaths'. The officer's cheery satisfaction with the reply was a source of amusement amongst many of the men for several weeks. It was not that the prisoners simply felt intellectually superior, but also that they felt culturally distinct. They were predominantly from London, they had a metropolitan smartness which they contrasted with the dull peasant mentality of their provincial guardians. The only sign of feeling for the officers had a patronizing quality. The most sympathetic and at the same time the most revealing comment came from Roy, one of the better-known members of the wing. He observed that 'screws not only had to spend as many waking hours in the wing as the inmates, but also that when they got home at night and got into bed, their wives turned to them and said: "Darling, did you speak to Roy today?"'

This awareness of their public image also set them apart from the officers. They all know the truth about famous murders and robberies, whilst their guards, despite their proximity to the agents of such enterprises, have to rely upon mass media interpretations. Prisoners in the security wings have a strong sense of personal status; they are still frequently referred to in newspapers and on television, and they rigorously dissociate themselves from petty criminals – the 'gas meter bandits' – of the rest of the prison. This sense of status is quite strong enough to exclude the screw from being chosen for social relationships. The Governor or the Assistant Governor are more likely to be viewed as potential colleagues. At least they are accorded intelligence and their motives are presumed to be honourable. They are not, like the screws, doing the job because there is nothing else they could do. But long-term relationships with Governors are just as impossible as those with fellow prisoners. Promotion and transfer of administrative staff break down relationships as insensitively and suddenly as do routine arbitrary movements of men from wing to wing.

RELATIONSHIPS OUTSIDE: LETTERS AND VISITS

It is not just inside contacts which are a problem; the long-termer is also gradually losing his outside contacts. Old gang loyalties quickly disappear once the leader or lieutenant has been inside a few years and there is a growing problem involved in retaining contact with wives and children. You suddenly realize as

Roy said that 'you want *their* letters more than they want *yours*'. There are occasional passages in outsiders' letters which suggest that they have not read the prisoners' letters too carefully, or that other events have forced the contents out of their minds. Either way, a sense of the unilateralism of the relationship grows upon the lifer. A concern about how long it will last begins to undermine the reassurance which accompanied the initial separation.

This concern is undoubtedly realistic. It is just not possible for many prisoners to believe that wives or friends will wait for twenty years. There is already enough anxiety in the prospect of half a life in prison without the additional worry which is involved in anticipating a 'Dear John' letter. There may almost be some fatalistic relief in reducing the emotional reliance upon outsiders. It increases the individual's autonomy; it ensures that the absence of visitors or letters is not a recurrent worry, and that such absences do not provide opportunities for patronizing sympathy by officers. [...]

What the Category A prisoners lack in the way of correspondence with the outside world cannot be made up for by visits. Officially, visits may only be made by wives and blood relations and are limited to periods of thirty minutes every eight weeks. However, Governors and the Home Office can show some flexibility in the enforcement of these regulations. Visits by 'approved' friends with no criminal records may be allowed and the frequency of visits may be increased, so that, in some cases, a visit every fortnight is granted. Nevertheless the restrictions upon the length of visits and upon who may visit are still harsh. Wives who have to travel several hundred miles every fortnight if they are to keep any contact with their husbands are hardly satisfied with the thirty-minute conversation to which they may be limited when they arrive.

All visitors are extensively vetted. Their special status is underlined by the fact that they have to submit a photograph of themselves to prevent imper-sonation occurring. Any person may be excluded from visiting for no stated reason. One member of our class – Ray – was denied a visit from his wife for nearly a year because she had a criminal record. (Her crime consisted of harbouring Ray after he had committed an offence of which she declared herself to have no knowledge.) The prisoners particularly resent the way in which departures from the rules can be presented by governors as examples of official liberality. Their only means of contacting the outside world become a matter of negotiation with the authorities and therefore dependent upon good behav-iour.[4] Even when visits do take place, they are inevitably closely monitored by prison officers and personal contact is minimized (for example, children are not allowed to sit on their father's lap). The conduct of the prisoner during the visit is considered an important indicator of his progress and is noted in the daily diary which is kept on every Category A man.

We have itemized only a few of the frustrating elements in the area of visiting and correspondence. Most prisoners could describe many more. Such matters become a constant source of anxiety and concern. In these circum-stances it is not surprising that contacts with outside breakdown or are con-sciously reduced by the prisoners. There is some pattern in the way in which this breakdown occurs.

Nearly thirty years ago Maurice Farber produced a highly sensitive account of life in an American prison, which describes the problems of outside relationships in terms of the amount of suffering that the presence of such relationships produces. His long and intimate interviews with prisoners revealed that the relationship between suffering and contact with the outside was curvilinear. Those who had few contacts with the outside through letters and visits were low in suffering, those who had medium contact suffered a great deal, while those who had high contact were again found to be low in suffering. Farber's interviews were with long and short-term prisoners, so generalization is difficult. But he found clear evidence of prisoners who cut off all contact in order to reduce suffering. As one said: 'I don't do hard time. It's much easier if you get the outside off your mind and just forget about your family, your folks and your wife.'[5]

The curvilinear relationship suggests that prisoners take an 'all or nothing-at-all attitude'. Either one attempts to keep everything going, to continue to live vicariously with wife and children and friends, or one abandons oneself to the prison community. The middle state in which relationships are only tenuously maintained seems least bearable. It is difficult to see how, over very long periods, high outside contact can be consistently maintained given the restrictions on writing and visiting which we have described. We predict that those few – and they are very few – who maintain high outside contact at the moment will have to suffer considerably over the years until their links become so tenuous that they are led towards the more popular and less worrying position of low contact. Of course there are those who do not have to face this dilemma. An American prisoner writes:

> One of the reasons I always did easy time was I had nobody who would write or visit me. Also, I had no life outside. My mind was usually always in the here and now. I lived a day at a time and had no thoughts of the streets or getting out. Most of the dudes I knew had a family or friends who would write to them and sometimes they got a visit. Every night if they didn't get a letter, they would pace the floor worrying about why their people didn't write. It was the same way with visits. If they didn't get an expected visit they would bug out?[6]

Some indication of the way relationships break down is provided by data obtained from our Eccleston sample. We asked eighteen Category A prisoners who had served approximately one third of their sentence about visits and letters. Half the men had not been visited for three years. For the majority of the men, visits were now less regular and their attempts to make new contacts in the outside world had either failed or been suppressed. Only half the men received letters as frequently as when they arrived and most of them said they felt more isolated. There was some evidence here that men had deliberately severed all contacts early in their sentence.[7]

There is another factor which influences the cutting down on outside contacts. This is the awareness of personality changes which tend to make previous outside relationships less viable. These prisoners have not only developed themselves physically while they have been in jail, they have also developed mentally. They are engaged in educational courses of varying complexity; if permission were granted there are several who would have little difficulty in obtaining degrees from correspondence courses or from the Open University. Many of the men we know write extensively. Jock recently produced a 20,000-word paper for us on his life in the army, David regularly writes a thousand words of a novel every day, while Alec turns out short essays about his childhood. The amount of reading done by these prisoners is also impressive. Three or four books are read in a week, the complete works of Freud or Dickens may be read at a stretch. David wrote to tell us that: 'Louis is at the moment reading the works of William Shakespeare (the complete works by the sound of it) and we exchange terribly literary letters about the sonnets with which I'm familiar.'

Such intellectual work undoubtedly allows the men a chance to realize certain goals in an otherwise relatively undifferentiated future but it also offers them a chance of finding some sophisticated articulations of their predicament. The work is far from being a mere endurance exercise – a shallow ritual. The men refer to the dramatic changes that this or that book has produced in their view of life. They talk of their personality as changing as a result of what they have read, and they recognize the cumulative nature of these changes.

Not all long-term prisoners share these literary concerns but such intellectual involvement provides another reason for the gradual moving away from reliance upon outsiders as friends. Relatives do not know how it is inside in quite the same way that Serge or Solzhenitsyn know. The importance of their sympathy may be gradually undermined by their failure to keep pace with changes in the prisoner's perception of his environment and of himself. Visiting hours are too short, the length of letters too restricted, to allow any adequate communication of these matters to outsiders. This is important for we do not mean to say that prisoners independently or naturally in the course of time move away from outside contacts.

Perhaps the significance of visiting is not apparent to those who are well away from the actual situation in the wings. 'A visit' sounds a casual matter – it sounds dispensable in the interests of security if one defines it in orthodox social terms. But these are not just brief intrusions from the outside world; when this link breaks the individual must rely completely upon the inmate culture or upon his own resources. There are no other directions available.

To summarize: in a situation where friends are particularly needed there are special difficulties placed in the way of making or maintaining them. The small number of inmates, the presence in this number of certain undesirables and the alien character of the prison officers, combine to make inside choice of companions difficult, while at the same time links with outside intimates become tenuous because of difficulties over visits and letters, changes in the personality and sensibility of the inmates, and because of the impossible prospect of twenty years' physical separation.

THE DILEMMA OF FRIENDSHIP

All these restrictions upon choice of contacts mean that one remains friendless or that typically just one other person is selected as a companion. There is also a good social-psychological reason why close dyadic relationships develop. For these men, who are forced to restrict their friends by the circumstances of the wing would, in any case, have difficulty in maintaining a network of friends in the way in which we normally do outside.

In everyday life we typically have several friends, several other people whom we rely upon for reassurance about our intellectual, ethical or sexual attributes. We may go to our wife or girl-friend for reassurance about our sexual ability, we will make use of another friend for career advice, and perhaps another for intellectual reassurance. The fact that we have several friends whom we use on different occasions and before whom we can strike different poses does not make any of them dispensable. Indeed, there is a considerable anguish felt at losing 'someone with whom we can really talk', or 'someone with whom we can have a good night out', even though we may not regularly avail ourselves of these opportunities for talking or carousing.

In the security wing one cannot have someone to talk to at work, someone to laugh with at leisure, for the audience is always the same and the choice of companions the same. There is one set of characters and one stage – the typical shifting from place to place and group to group which is common in outside life and even in larger prison populations is not possible. There is little role segregation, little opportunity for the presentation of different selves in different contexts. In such circumstances, a single personal relationship may be called upon to sustain the various functions which would be spread across several other friends in outside life. One's friend in the security wing is not simply there for sex, or intellectual chats, or discussion of personal anxieties, or humour, or solidarity against alien forces – but for *all* these things. Inevitably the relationship is very close. But such intense relationships are not likely to last very long. Home Office policy in relation to the maximum security wings involves moving inmates from one wing to another without warning. To quote from a recent letter: 'As you may have seen from the press Louis has left us. I am a "bit sick" because he was a close friend. In these places, you get to know people really well and Louis was one of the best ...'

When a man loses his friend in these conditions, there is no point in trying to maintain the relationship. Letters between the divided men are unlikely to be allowed, and if one gets out of prison before the other, he cannot visit his friend because of his criminal record. Under these circumstances, friends have to be quickly dropped following a move and new alliances sought. As the letter went on to say: 'Louis was my close friend and constant companion for over a year yet now he has gone to Parkhurst and I accept, almost without thinking, that I will not see him again.'

The intensity of relationships between men, an intensity which is often reinforced by sexual concerns in these deprived circumstances, and the suddenness of the break which occurs in the relationship make for a highly charged emotional atmosphere in the wings. 'The place is like a girls' school,' complained one of the men. This is certainly an incestuous setting; the men wish they could go to a bigger prison and object to the present dispersal system on the grounds that it forces them to live in highly charged emotional enclaves.

The following extract from an interview describes the situation.

Martin: At least in a bigger prison, it's closer to normal. If you get angry with someone, or he gets on your nerves, you can always get away from him for a while; go to another wing or another landing till it blows over. But here it's impossible, there's no escape, you can't get more than twenty feet away from anyone.

Stan: So you think that most people in these wings would like to move to bigger places?

Martin: Yes, even though that might mean giving up some of the physical facilities we have here.

Not that these problems will necessarily be resolved when the men move to larger wings. We asked the men in Eccleston to describe the difficulties which they found in making friends in prison. These men – in this case our sample was made up of forty-two long-termers – did not of course have many of the restrictions upon making friends which were present in E-Wing. They were nevertheless in relatively confined security conditions and obviously found that the making of friends in these circumstances was a very real problem.

Nearly one half of the group described the chief difficulty about friendship in prison in terms of the deep involvement it entailed. They talked about getting 'too close for safety' and referred to the way in which one could easily get hurt by completely confiding in one other person. Complete involvement with one other person was said to be dangerous because of the hurt which could then be produced by his being moved away ('you wake up and they are gone') or by his decision to adopt another prisoner as a companion. A majority of the prisoners said that they quite deliberately avoided the complexities which could result from such a close relationship, although at the same time they admitted the especially great need for friends which prison induced.

One Eccleston prisoner described the interpersonal situation in the following way:

> One is subject to intense pressures by virtue of one's imprisonment and one tends to regress to childhood, to the stage where little things mean a great deal. As our feelings are linked directly to external influences over which we have no control, people tend to be hypersensitive, and as with children take it out on those closest to them, i.e. their close friends, i.e. a letter arrives late or doesn't arrive and this is enough to cause murder.

Although Eccleston is larger than E-Wing, it is clearly not big enough to eliminate the possibilities of highly charged interpersonal relationships. The comments made by the prisoners on the questionnaire echoed the more extended statements we collected in Durham.

The strains induced on friendship by physical proximity in a confined space are sensitively portrayed by Richard Byrd, writing specifically about two-man relationships under such conditions as an isolated camp:

> once the simple tasks of the day are finished, there is nothing else to do but take each other's measure. Not deliberately. Not maliciously. But the time comes when one has nothing left to reveal to the other; when even his unformed thought can be anticipated, his pet ideas become a meaningless drool, and the way he blows out his pressure lamp or drops his boots on the floor or eats his food become a rasping annoyance ... In a polar camp, little things like that have the power to drive even disciplined men to the edge of insanity ... There is no escape anywhere. You are hemmed in on every side by your own inadequacies and the crowding pressures of your associates.[8]

PRIVACY

The continual surveillance by another (which Byrd talks about) should attune us to another problem which exists alongside the special nature of friendships in the wing. It is not just that friends are limited, that they have to be selected from inside, that they will tend to serve several functions, and that they will be suddenly lost for ever – this is only one aspect of the abnormal social situation of the long-term prisoner. In addition to this perversion of normal social relationships, he is faced with a complete lack of privacy.

Again, as in the case of friendship, this word needs to be taken apart in order that the assumptions involved in its everyday use can be made clear. Superficially we may not be particularly impressed when we hear that prisoners lack privacy; it sounds very much like a condition that those outside prison frequently experience and which has no serious psychological implications.

But when we look at the concept of privacy carefully we can start to make distinctions which have serious implications for long-term prisoners. Following an analysis made by the American political scientist A.F. Westin, we can distinguish four basic states of privacy: solitude, intimacy, anonymity and reserve.[10] Solitude refers to the state in which the person is alone and unobserved by others – a state of complete isolation. This never obtains in the maximum security wing. There are 'Judas holes' in every cell door and in one wing electronic devices under the floor enable prison officers to monitor the actual movements of the prisoners in their cells.

In addition there may be closed circuit television cameras which necessitate the use of strong light in all areas of the wing and from whose eyes not even the prison officers can escape. We have been given examples of officers who justify the enforcement of petty restrictions by reference to the camera. 'Don't blame me. It's the camera's fault.' One prisoner described the paranoia induced by such continuous observation in the following way.

This tomb, this electronic torture chamber bound with eyes … camera eyes … and the dead unfeeling eyes of the state's cossacks.

And another wrote to describe his wing:

> It is very claustrophobic here, very small wing, if you can imagine a world of twenty-five yards long by five yards wide. This is where we spend most of the day except for two one-hour exercise periods in the yard. You would never believe the microscopic surveillance that takes place here with television camera eyes and the eyes of warders. It literally is a dehumanizing chamber.

Solitude is typically required in everyday life that we can go out of play for a while. Complete isolation from observation, and from sudden intrusion are necessary conditions for indulgence in private fantasies, for obtaining a sense of individuality. Attempts to find solitude – and the related states of privacy – are a central feature of what Goffman in *Asylums* calls 'the underlife of a total institution'. He describes in detail how inmates try to obtain protection from official surveillance through going to *free places* (places shared with any other inmate) and *group territories* (places shared with a few selected inmates). Here, in corners of the hospital garden or out-of-the-way work places, the inmates withdraw temporarily from authority. Such withdrawal is rarely possible in E-Wing. Though the prisoners have some private territory in the form of their own cells the structure and size of the building, together with the security measures, hardly allow for any free places.

But if there is no opportunity for solitude, there is even less for the second state of privacy – intimacy. This refers to the type of privacy sought by two or even more people who wish to achieve maximum personal affinity. This again sounds a minor matter until we reflect upon the energy that most of us put into its achievement. Typically it involves not merely freedom from the presence of others but also the exclusion of distracting noises and sounds, an exclusion which we often effect in domestic and social situations by the use of gentle lighting, soft music and the removal of the telephone from its hook. We might think of this sort of privacy as expendable until we imagine a life in which the opportunity for the construction of such an intimate environment never existed.

The third state of privacy, which Westin describes as anonymity, refers to the seeking and achieving of freedom from identification and observation in public places. It is the presence of such anonymity which allows one to relax in different settings. One can switch off, drop out and not be a subject of comment for so doing. This type of anonymity is often available for offenders in large prisons. But in the maximum security wing everyone is known to everyone else. In such circumstances anonymity for even a few moments is impossible.

This predicament is shared with physically stigmatized persons, who are continual objects of public attention.[10] The prisoners have a dual lack of anonymity: not only are they open to being approached and addressed by anyone in the wing, but their identities are public knowledge and therefore anything they do or say can be transformed into a story.

The remaining private state of reserve is defined by a person's ability not to reveal certain aspects of himself that are particularly personal or shameful. The security wing is not conducive to reserve. Every prison officer knows in detail the lives of the men he observes. Their mail is read, their visitors' conversations overheard, their life histories are available on record for general inspection. Their health problems are matters for public discussion. They are watched during the performance of intimate toilet functions. Their domestic problems become public troubles. As Jock said:

> being locked up with small groups of six to ten can be unbearable at times. One of our number only has to have trouble with family or be out of sorts and everybody suffers with him – where one could get away from this kind of poisonous atmosphere in a larger unit.

It may seem long-winded to draw out all these aspects of privacy, but it is important to stress that whilst we may intermittently endure the absence of one or other states – we may for example regret the lack of solitude on our holiday, the absence of intimacy in our office, the impossibility of anonymity in the town's only night spot or the lack of reserve which is possible at the golf club – we do not have to face continually the absence of all four states of privacy. In other institutions which resemble the security wing in certain aspects, large prisons, monasteries, convents, mental hospitals, there is usually some recognition given to these requirements of privacy even if the allowances which are made are still insufficient to prevent some suffering on the part of the inmates.

The lack of privacy of all kinds, and the particular nature of the friendship patterns which exist in the wing have serious consequences for the men. There are few opportunities to assert individuality, to show personal autonomy, or to engage in orthodox types of emotional release. [...]

NOTES

1   Gresham Sykes, *The Society of Captives: A Study of a Maximum Security Prison* (Princeton, NJ: Princeton University Press, 1958), p. 77.
2   Laurie Taylor, 'The Significance and Interpretation of Motivational Accounts: the Case of Sex Offenders', *Sociology* (January 1972).
3   Terence and Pauline Morris, *Pentonville: A Sociological Study of an English Prison* (London: Routledge and Kegan Paul, 1963), p. 99.
4   It is significant that the recently formed prisoners' union, P.R.O.P. (Preservation of the Rights of Prisoners), considers it of central importance to transform the 'privileges' relating to visits and letters into *rights*.
5   Maurice Farber, 'Suffering and Time Perspective of the Prisoner', Part IV of Kurt Lewin (ed.) *Studies in Authority and Frustration* (University of Iowa, *Studies in Child Welfare*, vol. XX, 1944), p. 176.
6   'One Who's There', *County Time* (San Francisco: Connections), p. 10.
7   Further confirmation – of a somewhat different order – of this pattern can be found in Timothy Leary's semi-mystical Joycean ramblings about his prison experience: 'Letters very important to prisoner who has outside love tie. But outside love ties are impossible and sensible inmate immediately detaches from his ex-mate (Go wild crazy berserk).' Timothy Leary, *Jail Notes* (New York: Douglas Books, 1970), p. 60.

8   Richard Byrd, *Alone* (London: Putnam, 1938), pp. 16–17.
9   A.F. Westin, *Privacy and Freedom* (London: Bodley Head, 1970).
10 Erving Goffman, *Stigma* (Harmondsworth: Penguin, 1968).

STUDY QUESTIONS

1   In Reading 27, the primary purposes of imprisonment were identified as deterrence, rehabilitation, incapacitation and retribution. Having read this account of life in a maximum-security prison, which of these rationales for incarceration are being most successfully achieved? Which are being least successfully met and with what consequences?

2   Think back to Foster's analysis of a 'league division of villainy' (Reading 15) and Croall's argument that white-collar and corporate crime are often seen as trivial or acceptable (Reading 16). Which types of criminals – e.g. professional criminals, drug-related offenders, embezzlers etc. – do you think are likely to go to which type of prison? And thinking back to the reading by Cavadino and Dignan (Reading 14), what might be the most difficult problems that women face in prison?

3   According to Cohen and Taylor, what are the particular problems that face long-term prisoners which might militate against their chances of coping with, and adapting to, a life of confinement and eventual reintegration back into the community?

4   Since Cohen and Taylor wrote their book, prisons have seen a number of significant improvements in standards of living (for example, the end of 'slopping out', better visiting rights, and the introduction of personal television sets for many inmates). Given what you have read in this extract, do you think that such improvements are likely to have had any significant impact on the experience of incarceration for long-term prisoners, or are they likely to be viewed as cosmetic and superficial in relation to the 'bigger picture' of loss and deprivation?

FURTHER READING

The problems of carrying out research in prisons is further addressed by Cohen, S. and Taylor, L. (1977) 'Talking about prison blues' in C. Bell and H. Newby (eds) *Doing Sociological Research*, London: Allen and Unwin; and King, R. (1999) 'Doing research in prisons' in R. King and E. Wincup (eds) *Doing Research on Crime and Justice*, Oxford: Oxford University Press. A poignant insight into the life of a long-term prisoner is provided by Shannon, T. and Morgan, C. (1996) *The Invisible Crying Tree*, London: Doubleday. Good introductions to prisons and prison life can be found in Coyle, A. (1994) *The Prisons We Deserve*, London: HarperCollins; and Stern, V. (1994) *Bricks of Shame: Britain's Prisons*, 2nd edn, Harmondsworth: Penguin. The particular problems facing long-term and life-sentence inmates are addressed in Bottoms, A.E. and Light, R. (1987) *Problems of Long-term Imprisonment*, Aldershot: Gower; and Sapsford, R. (1983) *Life Sentence Prisoners: Reaction, Response and Change*, Milton Keynes: Open University Press. For women's experiences of imprisonment, see

Padel, U. and Stevenson, P. (1988) *Insiders: Women's Experience of Prison*, London: Virago. The 'classic' text by Ward, D. and Kassebaum, G. (1965) *Women's Prison: Sex and Social Structure*, London: Weidenfeld and Nicolson, is well worth a look, although it resorts to categorizing women prisoners in crude and unhelpful behavioural typologies, in the same way that most prison sociologies of male inmates do. Other frequently referenced texts include Carlen, P. (1983) *Women's Imprisonment: A Study in Social Control*, London: Routledge; Carlen, P. (1992) *Alternatives to Women's Imprisonment*, Milton Keynes: Open University Press; and Dobash, R., Dobash, R. and Gutteridge, S. (1986) *The Imprisonment of Women*, Oxford: Blackwell. Angela Devlin has written a fascinating account, combining descriptive detail of her own experiences conducting research in women's prisons with broader theoretical and conceptual themes of imprisonment, in (1998) *Invisible Women*, Winchester: Waterside Press. For a slightly different perspective from the 'norm' – that of a middle-class, middle-aged, professional woman behind bars – see Peckham, A. (1985) *A Woman in Custody*, London: Fontana.

Part Five

Crime, Control and the Future

art V addresses a key challenge facing criminology in its current phase; that is, to understand the complex and diverse forms of social control that are not only creeping into the logic of punishment, but are increasingly characterizing general life. One writer whose influence is evident in many of the following readings is Stanley Cohen whose theories about 'dispersed discipline' (an idea developed from the work of Foucault) are referred to by Nigel South (Reading 29) and by Barbara A. Hudson (Reading 30). Cohen's impressive body of work is well represented elsewhere in this volume; put simply, his vision of social control is that alternatives to custody are being developed, not out of any moral or humanitarian consideration for offenders, but as a practical response to the financial constraints that governments operate within. Furthermore, Cohen argues that the use of informal and alternative forms of social control has not reversed the numbers of offenders receiving custodial sentences, and 'actually causes an overall system expansion which might not otherwise have occurred' (1985; see *Further Reading* for Reading 29). South and Hudson are just two among many writers who have taken up and developed Cohen's thesis, exploring the ways in which discipline, surveillance and regulation are being extended beyond prisons and dispersed throughout the community as a whole. His rather pessimistic vision is brought to life in two of the readings that follow, taken from the *Observer* newspaper. John Naughton (Reading 31) considers the impact of surveillance technologies on responses to crime and discloses some of its more sinister applications, while Martin Bright (Reading 32) continues to interrogate our generally benevolent attitude towards methods of surveillance in an exposé of company 'snoopers'.

A more optimistic version of social control is provided by Gary Younge (Reading 33) in an article from the *Guardian*, which describes a successful penal policy in Finland that has seen the prison population reduced dramatically. This reading then provides a counter to Cohen's pessimistic thesis, although it should be noted that Finland's pioneering approach is currently under extreme public and political pressure from those who believe it to be too liberal. In the final reading, we continue our exploration of power and social control, but change tack slightly to consider one of the ways in which advances in communication and information technologies are enabling some individuals and groups to find new ways of breaking the law. The extract by Douglas Thomas (Reading 34) argues that cyberspace is presenting new challenges to those who seek to govern and regulate the behaviour of others. The subject of the extract – computer hacking – is just one of the ways in which authority is being challenged and traditional relations of power and control are being undermined and subverted. When reading Part V, think back to what you have read elsewhere in this book and consider how social control operates differently for different groups in different social contexts. As you read, try to reflect on whether these pieces offer any suggestions for the future of criminology.

29

Crime, control and the future: some theories and speculations

Nigel South

Nigel South provides a thought-provoking account of crime and criminology as seen through a 'postmodernist' lens. Of all the criminological theories running through the readings in this volume, postmodernism is the most recent attempt to conceptualize crime and theorize about appropriate responses to it. The extract reproduced here is part of a wider discussion, reflecting on the current state and possible future directions of criminology early in the new millennium. In it, South discusses the increased use and diversification of forms of social control and surveillance, which many writers, whose work South draws on, regard as one of the most insidious features of contemporary crime control. He then moves on to consider what – if anything – postmodernism can add to our knowledge of social conflict, crime and social problems. His analysis embraces a wide range of behaviours and activities which, he suggests, are emerging as post-traditional responses to the control of crime and deviance. The commentary that South provides assumes a fairly advanced degree of familiarity with the contours of sociological and criminological debates about social control and, consequently, you may find it quite challenging. But persevere, as the extract offers a fascinating insight into the questions that dominate the debates about social control; debates which we, as criminologists, will be addressing and shaping over the next few years.

What might future patterns of crime look like? Commentators of left, liberal and right persuasions might agree that the increasing growth of socially excluded, marginal groups in society, will lead to more street crime and, in response, more – and more diversified – social control and surveillance. The

SOURCE: From 'Late-modern Criminology: "Late" as in "Dead" or "Modern" as in "New"?', in D. Owen (ed.) *Sociology after Postmodernism*. (London: Sage, 1997), 89–102.

explanations and recommended interventions might, of course, differ (although, increasingly, they may not). Drug-related crime will continue to increase, the related profits generating significant developments in criminal organization, and expansion into legitimate commerce (Ruggiero and South, 1995). Some trends in crime suggest that business organizations are increasingly both targets for and perpetrators of criminality, related to who has access to organizational resources or is responsible for corporate success – the crimes of the middle and managerial classes. Relatedly, at various international levels the blurring of crimes committed by criminal organizations and corporate organizations will be significant (Punch, 1993; Ruggiero, 1996); while changes in global finance and trade will mean more fraud against governments, trade alliances (e.g. the European Union) and corporations. Crimes against the environment such as pollution, and resulting problems such as public health dangers, will increasingly be matters for international crime and control agendas.

In terms of future political and social control *responses* to future crime trends, there are various visions we could sample. One important criminological review of 'future trends emerging in the present' is Cohen (1985). Cohen's thesis and concerns are elaborate and expansive but one of the key metaphors he employs has been particularly influential. This is his suggestive portrayal of the growing social control system as one 'catching-up' more and more citizens in ever-larger nets of ever-finer mesh, as the spectrum of punishment extends from the prison through the community, and the variety and type of sanctions and penalties multiply.

Cohen's 'visions of social control' are bleak and pessimistic and find echoes in other dystopian predictions of the future of urban control.[1] At the same time, there are other writers who seek to map out the viability of future reformist agendas in a more hopeful spirit. To consider the former view first.

SEGREGATION AND SURVEILLANCE IN THE LATE MODERN CITY

In a more recent work, Cohen (1994: 70–4) has updated his review of trends in social control. Among these, perhaps particular significance should be attached to the emergence of 'the actuarial regime' and the 'risk society' (1994: 73; cf. Feeley and Simon, 1992):

> Instead of altering individual behaviour, actuarial, surveillance and compliance regimes alter the physical and social structure in which individuals behave. This policy ... [it is argued] is both easier to implement than the old 'disciplinary regimes' and, ultimately, more effective.

> these trends ... grafted onto new technologies and the increased surveillance capacity of modern organisations ... – have led sociologists of social control to some grim characterisations: the age of surveillance, the classified society, the managed society, the engineered society, the suspicious society, the self-monitored society, the transparent society, the maximum-security society etc.

Writing on the future of Los Angeles, Davis (1994) outlines the application of such technological and surveillance developments in practice, and speculates on where the ongoing process of segregation in the city will lead.

In contemporary metropolitan Los Angeles a new species of special enclave is emerging in sympathetic synchronization to the militarization of the landscape. For want of a better generic appellation, we might call them 'social control districts' (SCDs). (pp. 8–9)[2]

post-riot Southern California seems on the verge of creating yet more SCDs. On the one hand the arrival of the Federal 'Weed and Seed' program, linking community development funds to anti-gang repression, provides a new set of incentives for neighborhoods to adopt exclusion and/or enhancement strategies. As many activists have warned, 'Weed and Seed' is like a police-state caricature of the 1960s War on Poverty with the Justice Department transformed into the manager of urban redevelopment. The poor will be forced to cooperate with their own criminalization as a precondition for urban aid. (p. 11)

Generally, it can be argued that the interface between architecture (e.g. planning secure pathways through the dangerous city) and the directing of human action is becoming ever more significant. Again Davis's (1994) explorations of 'urban control and the ecology of fear' in post-riot Los Angeles offer a window on one future of social control. Here a strategy of segregation and surveillance has made its impact on the city. Or rather, first, it has created 'a city within a city'.

It is not only the riots of the post-Rodney King assault and trial that Davis refers to here. After rioting in 1965 and fears of greater ethnic conflict, the city's redevelopment agency began to physically segregate the new core business areas from the ghetto areas: palisades, concrete pillars, freeway walls were built, traditional pedestrian connections between the poor district and the new business district were removed, 'foot traffic in the new financial district was elevated above the street on pedways whose access was controlled by the security systems of individual skyscrapers'. All of this has, as Davis observes, 'ominous racial overtones' (p. 4).

Similarly, the extensive and comprehensive surveillance of all these areas

constitutes a virtual scanscape – a space of protective visibility that increasingly defines where white-collar office workers and middle-class tourists feel safe.... Inevitably the workplace or shopping mall video camera will become linked with home security systems, personal 'panic buttons', car alarms, cellular phones and the like, in a seamless continuity of surveillance over daily routine. Indeed, yuppies' lifestyles soon may be defined by the ability to afford electronic guardian angels to watch over them. (Davis, 1994: 5; original emphasis)

DEPRIVATION, REFORMISM AND REALIST OPTIMISM

Alternatively, from a perspective that can be seen as a form of American 'left-realism', Elliott Currie has offered a more hopeful scenario and agenda for America's inner cities and, in particular, its drug problems:

Given the extent of the devastation inflicted on the cities and the poor by the unleashing of the strategy of inequality, there is a sense in which almost anything we do to improve the conditions of life for those most at risk could help to reduce drug abuse. But we need to make more specific choices. ... Here then are five crucial elements of a long-term strategy ... all of which are also both economically sustainable and congruent with a larger vision of the society we wish to achieve. (Currie, 1993: 283–4)

Currie's agenda is then outlined under the following headings: 'Expanding the opportunity structure', 'Revitalizing public health care', 'Supporting families', 'Assuring shelter' and 'Rebuilding the infrastructure' (pp. 284–323), with a following evaluation of funding viability and an assertion of the realistic benefits of such programmes. Unsurprisingly, a similar spirit is present in a recent essay by Young (1996) on criminology and late-modernity:

> Crime occurs when citizenship is thwarted, its causes lie in injustice, yet its effect is, inevitably, further injustice and violation of citizenship. The solution lies not in the resurrection of past stabilities, based on nostalgia and a world that will never return, but in a new citizenship, a reflexive modernity which will tackle the problems of justice and community, of reward and individualism, which lie at the heart of liberal democracy. (Young, 1996: 33)

Britain does not (yet?) have social problems on the same scale as those evident in the inner cities of the USA. However, as debates around the 'under-class' thesis (Morris, 1994; Morrison, 1994: 148–51; Byrne, 1995) indicate, since the riots of the 1980s and early 1990s there has been a growing 'authoritarian' fear that the problems of the inner city are only just being 'contained' (Keith, 1991; Young, 1992). It is clearly arguable that sceptics and pessimists may sometimes exagger-ate 'Doomsday' visions of the future; none the less, the everyday reality of the pre-sent does not seem short of indicators of the fragility of society. Whether justifiably or not, 'anxieties' about crime, control and social order are commonplace. With paramilitary policing (Jefferson, 1990) and privatization of law enforcement services (South, 1994) being among the high-profile policing and policy responses to such urban anxieties, we may yet move ever closer to the 'Robocop scenario' – the age of the 'postmodern cop' as 'urban cowboy' (Burke, 1989). […]

POSTMODERNISM

Postmodernism was first associated with changes in architecture, art and design – away from the uniformity of modernism and toward a mixing of styles and materials, pastiche and irony; a challenge to the straightforwardness and conventions of modernism (TCS, 1988; Smart, 1990: 74–5). It celebrates frag-mentation and the plurality of cultures; a greater playfulness, humour and scepticism; a world of consumerism and global communications. For some authors, the future (postmodern) image of social control is one of soft and sedating seduction by a world of consumerism and fantasy – life in Disney World (Shearing and Stenning, 1987). The future social order as envisaged by Aldous Huxley in *Brave New World* is a more accurate reflection of trends in social control than Orwell's nightmare of a totalitarian, repressive *1984*. Yet, for other commentators, one vision of postmodernity may actually be much closer to the *1984* image. Ironically, society may end up here, not because of triumphs of positivism or utilitarianism but as the result of a backlash against boundless deconstructionism. In this dystopian postmodernity, rather than the embrace of autonomy and plurality, we encounter after all, demands for the reassertion of the certainties of authority and penality. Thus Morrison has argued that

The possibilities of postmodernism, openness, powers and freedoms, are also the possibilities of a postmodern nightmare. Lost in the midst of postmodern disjointedness, of processes so varied that no centre can be dreamt of, the process of ruling becomes authoritarian. The demands of a populace searching for meaning prioritizes basic certainties, walls, divisions, demarcations and territories to control temporal space in the void of non-meaning. (Morrison, 1994: 144)

Beyond speculations on the future of control, overlaps between criminology and cultural studies should also provide spaces for exploration of postmodern ideas and theories. To take just two examples, Redhead (1991) argues that past theories of *youth culture and deviance* are no longer useful. These theories claimed to

look beneath or behind the surfaces of the shimmering mediascape in order to discover the 'real', authentic subculture, apparently always distorted by the manufactured press and television image, which in turn becomes 'real' as more and more participants act out the media stereotypes. This 'depth model' is no longer appropriate – if it ever was – for analysing the surfaces of the (post)-modern world, a culture characterised by shallowness, flatness and 'hyper-reality'. (Redhead, 1991: 94)

Perhaps then, what is needed is a 'Cultural Criminology' (Ferrell and Sanders, 1996), sensitive to postmodern style and practices yet remaining 'a criminology', even if transgressively so:

Bending or breaking the boundaries of criminology to construct a cultural criminology in this sense does not undermine contemporary criminology as much as it expands and enlivens it. Cultural criminology widens criminology's domain to include worlds conventionally considered exterior to it: gallery art, popular music, media operations and texts, style. In the same way, it introduces criminology into contemporary debates over these worlds, and defines criminological perspectives as essential to them. (Ferrell and Sanders, 1996: 17)

Representation, media and discourse would naturally be central to such a criminology:

For good or bad, postmodern society exists well beyond ... discrete, linear patterns of action and reaction. Rather, ... criminal events, identities, and styles take life within a media-saturated environment, and thus exist from the start as moments in a mediated spiral of presentation and representation. (Ferrell and Sanders, 1996: 14)

But – can *postmodernism* say anything *constructive* about *responding* to social conflict, crime and social problems?

Postmodernism can be seen as conservative: rejecting modernist agendas for reform and progress. Yet intellectually, postmodernism is also characterized as liberating, precisely *because* it challenges assumptions about historical inevitabilities, the march of progress and 'Grand Narrative' views of history. Postmodernism allows that different perspectives involve different interests and different criteria of significance.[3]

The US cultural commentator Todd Gitlin (1989) has developed an optimistic and useful perspective on postmodernity and social issues, which suggests that we do not have to retreat from aspiration but that there *can* be an agenda for social and political action in the postmodern world. He asks 'how then can we develop a workable political point of view for the post modern era?' With regard to a form of social intervention that is a control of 'excesses', Gitlin suggests we need a 'politics of limits' rooted in three 'protections'.

1   The Ecological – the earth must be protected against exploitation and damage caused by humanity's activities.
2   The Pluralist – the social group must be protected against domination by other social groups whether by cultural exclusion, economic power or social marginalization; pluralism is encouraged.
3   The Libertarian – the individual must be protected against domination by larger groups.

A politics of limits respects multiplicity over hierarchy and difference over deference. Or, as Morrison (1994: 144) similarly argues, 'the attainment of solidarity in the context of diversity and difference demands a new metaphysics, an awareness in which a generality is struggled for which embraces plurality.[4]

So – what might a postmodern concern with post-traditional-criminology issues look like?

Morrison (1994: 143) argues that, 'the problematic of postmodern criminology will be how to create and sustain a social solidarity which takes pragmatism as its epistemology and plurality and contingency as its foundational ontology'. To apply Gitlin's version of postmodernism, *limits* and *protections* must be respected even within a postmodern world of diversity. Only if these *are* respected can individuals be free to express self-identity/ies, enjoy freedom of movement, rights of participation and citizenship. It follows that, in some way, these limits must be consensually and pragmatically enforced. This could therefore represent a new shift in the history of regulation and punishment: from the 'spectacle of punishment' in the age of the sovereign power, to the individualized penal servitude of the bureaucratic criminal justice system of modernity – to a postmodern mix of lifestyle, cultural and penal censures and sanctions.[5] For example: electronic tagging (your home is your prison); financial regulation (the extra-legal policing of consumerism); the medieval past resurrected in the present, e.g. 'Parish Constables' and Citizen Watch patrols, and the return of the chain-gang in Alabama alongside the building of a new generation of 'ultimate security' prisons. A postmodern image of social control might also have a *global character*: consider the ways in which the role of the United Nations has changed in recent years and disappointment over its inability to be a successful international peacekeeping, 'police force' (Fisas, 1995), as in the conflicts in former-Yugoslavia and Rwanda. Global environment problems and global crimes such as money laundering washed through the 24-hour a day banking system (South, 1992) also need global coordination of laws and other responses.

Domestically, continuing trends in 'decentralization' and 'privatization' reflect Conservative government policy to distance the state further from the administration of punishment and control (e.g. privately run prisons, private security policing; South, 1988, 1994; Johnston, 1992; Ryan and Ward, 1992). In such a context, traditional appeals to state law via the national courts may no longer be adequate and appeals for justice may increasingly need to invoke international principles of human rights and see appellants turning to *supranational* human rights courts (Turner, 1993). Conservative, bourgeoise notions of justice are outmoded, and in a post-Marxist world we cannot appeal to socialist ideals, so the ideologies and institutions of modernity have had their chance and failed (Morrison, 1994; 150–1). Regard for international human rights (1) would reflect diversity, (2) is not tied to the sovereignty of individual nations, (3) is a global standard breaking away from national histories of exploitation, colonialism and nationalism.[6]

There is a small but growing literature on postmodernism and criminology (substantial critical responses are Hunt, 1991; Lea, 1996). My own speculations are merely suggestive of issues for debate between those who would strengthen and argue a future for late-modern criminology and those who would postmodernize in order to deconstruct the subject.

NOTES

1 For readers who like a good detective story but need some academic justification for such enjoyment, Kerr (1992) is a powerful fictional speculation on various enforcement and other social trends into the next century, also managing to embrace feminism, the Frankfurt School, a nice joke on the resurrection of Lombrosian positivism and much else.
2 Davis nicely 'remodels' the Chicago School's 'zonal model of the city' as it might apply to late-modern Los Angeles.
3 Thanks to David Owen for this point.
4 Note, amidst all this celebration of the 'newness' of postmodernism, remarkable echoes of symbolic interactionism (pluralism, anti-essentialism etc of Plummer, 1990) and Young's (1975: *passim* and p. 91) manifesto for a 'working class criminology': 'Forms of deviancy occur as attempts to create unhampered and livable space .... a tenderloin of the city where a sense of "the possible" breaks through the facticity of what is.'
5 Thanks here to Nicholas and Dorn for shared discussions and speculations on postmodernism and policing some years ago; and see also Sumner, 1994.
6 Ideas suggested in an unpublished talk on 'postmodernism' by Bryan Turner, Essex Postgraduate Conference, Clacton 1990.

REFERENCES

Burke, F. (1989) 'Panic killing (cops)', in A. Kroker, M. Kroker and D. Cook (eds), *Panic Encyclopedia*. London: Macmillan.

Byrne, D. (1995) 'Deindustrialisation and dispossession: an examination of social division in the industrial city', *Sociology*, 29 (1), 95–155.

Cohen, S. (1985) *Visions of Social Control*. Cambridge: Polity Press.

Cohen, S. (1994) 'Social control and the politics of reconstruction', in D. Nelken (ed.), *The Futures of Criminology*. London: Sage.

Currie, E. (1993) *Reckoning: Drugs, the Cities and the American Future*. New York: Hill and Wang.

Davis, M. (1994) *Beyond Blade Runner: Urban Control – the Ecology of Fear*. Open Magazine Pamphlet series. New York: The New Press.

Feeley, M. and Simon, J. (1992) 'The new penology: notes on the emerging strategy of corrections and its implications', *Criminology*, 30 (4), 452–74.

Ferrell, J. and Sanders, C. (1996) *Cultural Criminology*. London: Northeastern University Press.

Fisas, V. (1995) *Blue Geopolitics: The United Nations Reform and the Future of the Blue Helmets*. London: Pluto.

Gitlin, T. (1989) 'Postmodernism defined, at last!', *Utne Reader*, Summer, 34: 52–61.

Hunt, A. (1991) 'Postmodernism and critical criminology', in B. Maclean and D. Milovanovic (eds), *New Directions in Critical Criminology*. Vancouver: Collective Press.

Jefferson, T. (1990) *The Case against Paramilitary Policing*. Milton Keynes: Open University Press.

Johnston, L. (1992) *The Rebirth of Private Policing*. London: Routledge.

Keith, M. (1991) ' "Policing a perplexed society"?: No-go areas and the mystification of police–black conflict', in E. Cashmore and E. McLaughlin (eds), *Out of Order? Policing Black People*. London: Routledge.

Kerr, P. (1992) *A Philosophical Investigation*. London: Chatto and Windows.

Lea, J. (1996) 'Criminology and postmodernism', in P. Walton and J. Young (eds), *The New Criminology Revisited*. London: Macmillan.

Morris, L. (1994) *Dangerous Classes*. London: Routledge.

Morrison, W. (1994) 'Criminology, modernity and the "truth" of the human condition: reflections on the melancholy of postmodernism', in D. Nelken (ed.), *The Futures of Criminology*. London: Sage. pp. 134–53.

Plummer, K. (1990) 'Staying in the empirical world: symbolic interactionism and postmodernism', *Symbolic Interaction*, 13 (2), 155–60.

Punch, M. (1993) 'Bandit banks: financial services and organized crime', *Journal of Contemporary Justice*, 9 (3), 175–96.

Redhead, S. (1991) 'Rave off: youth, subcultures and the law', *Social Studies Review*, 6 (3), 92–4.

Ruggiero, V. (1996) *Organized and Corporate Crime in Europe: Offers that Can't be Refused*. Aldershot: Dartmouth.

Ruggiero, V. and South, N. (1995) *Eurodrugs: Drug Use, Markets and Trafficking in Europe*. London: UCL Press.

Ryan, M. and Ward, T. (1992) 'From positivism to postmodernism: some theoretical and strategic reflections on the evolution of the penal lobby in Britain', *International Journal of the Sociology of Law*, 20: 321–35.

Shearing, C. and Stenning, P. (1987) 'Say cheese!: from the Panopticon to Disney World', in C. Shearing and P. Stenning (eds), *Private Policing*. Beverly Hills, CA: Sage.

Smart, C. (1990) 'Feminist approaches to criminology or postmodern woman meets atavistic man', in L. Gelsthorpe and A. Morris (eds), *Feminist Perspectives in Criminology*. Buckingham: Open University Press. pp. 70–84.

South, N. (1988) *Policing for Profit: The Private Security Sector*. London: Sage.

South, N. (1992) 'Moving murky money: drug trafficking, law enforcement and the pursuit of criminal profits', in D. Farrington and S. Walklate (eds), *Offenders and Victims: Theory and Policy*. London: British Society of Criminology/Institute for the Study and Treatment of Delinquency.

South, N. (1994) 'Privatizing policing in the European market: some issues for theory, policy and research', *European Sociological Review*, 10 (3), 219–33.

Sumne, C. (1994) *The Sociology of Deviance: An Obituary*. Buckingham: Open University Press.

TCS (1988) *Postmodernism*. Double issue of *Theory, Culture and Society*, 5 (2/3): June.

Turner, B. (1993) 'Outline of a theory of human rights', *Sociology*, 27 (3), 489–512.

Young, J. (1975) 'Working class criminology', in I. Taylor, P. Walton and J. Young (eds), *Critical Criminology*. London: Routledge.

Young, J. (1992) 'Riotous rage of the have-nots', *Independent on Sunday*, 19 July.

Young, J. (1996) 'Writing on the cusp of change: a new criminology for an age of late modernity', in P. Walton and J. Young (eds), *The New Criminology Revisited*. London: Macmillan.

STUDY QUESTIONS

1   What predictions does South make for future patterns of crime? To what extent are we already witnessing the emergence of some of the crimes he highlights? How are the criminal justice agencies and criminologists responding to these new threats?

2   What forms does social control take in contemporary life? What are the consequences (positive and negative) of these initiatives for the lives of those who are subject to them? How are they variously characterized by those who adhere to the 'dispersal of discipline' thesis (e.g. Cohen); by those who adopt a reformist, optimistic approach (left realists); and by those who abandon traditional approaches in favour of a postmodernist perspective?

3   What do social-control strategies of the type highlighted by South tell us about the nature of power in modern Western societies? How might class/gender/racial inequalities be conceptualized in the light of such measures?

FURTHER READING

The starting-point for any research into social control should probably be Stanley Cohen. His two most famous works on the subject are his 1985 book *Visions of Social Control: Crime Punishment and Classification*, Cambridge: Polity Press, and the 1979 paper, 'The punitive city: notes on the dispersal of social control', *Contemporary Crisis*, 3 (4), reproduced in Muncie, J., McLaughlin, E. and Langan, M. (eds) (1996) *Criminological Perspectives: A Reader*, London: Sage. You may, however, wish to consult the wider context in which Cohen's work is located, and, if this is the case, you should read the defining work on the disciplinary society, Michel Foucault's (1977) *Discipline and Punish*, Harmondsworth: Penguin. A valuable contribution which builds and develops the insights provided by Cohen and Foucault, is that of Shearing, C.D. and

Stenning, P.C. (1985) 'From the panopticon to Disney World: the development of discipline' in A. Doob and E. Greenspan (eds) *Perspectives in Criminal Law*, Ontario: Canada Law Book Inc., which in its critique of the disciplinary methods employed by the Disney Corporation takes us well within the realms of postmodern analysis that Nigel South highlights in the reading. Two of the references contained in the reading are also well worth a look in this respect: Gitlin, T. (1989) 'Postmodernism defined at last!', *Utne Reader*, Summer, 34: 52–61; and Morrison, W. (1994) 'Criminology, modernity and the "truth" of the human condition: reflections on the melancholy of postmodernism', in D. Nelken (ed.) *The Futures of Criminology*, pp. 134–53, London: Sage.

30

Social control

Barbara A. Hudson

This reading begins by referencing some of the great writers who have charted the penal system's central role in the emergence of capitalism. Their common theme is that imprisonment became favoured over torture and execution as a form of punishment during the period of industrialization that began in the late eighteenth century, in a programme of institutional expansion that encompassed schools, workhouses, factories and asylums, as well as prisons. One of the primary original functions of imprisonment, according to Foucault, Rusche and Kirchheimer, and others, was to regulate the behaviour of, and discipline, the least powerful strata of society. However, in the 1960s and 1970s a new approach emerged, shifting the focus of attention to punishment, regulation and control within communities. The issues raised by this new approach are examined by Hudson, who considers the moves towards community corrections that have been central to a thirty-year period of 'decarceration'. Her focus is the diverging responses to the social control of two different forms of deviancy: mental illness and criminality. While decarceration policies aimed at those with mental illnesses have been successful – in de-institutionalizing people, if not in caring for them effectively – policies that provide alternatives to custody have paradoxically been accompanied by increasing numbers of offenders being institutionalized in prison. Furthermore, Hudson concurs with the proposition raised by South (Reading 29) that Cohen's notion of an ever-widening, ever-strengthening net of social control is evident in the forms of surveillance, monitoring and restriction that we all now experience in everyday life. Specific examples of this 'net' will be explored in the two readings which follow this one and, read together, the first four extracts in Part V suggest that the principles of imprisonment are no longer confined to particular kinds of institutions such as prisons. The principles of incarceration stretch across time and space, with new modes of control – such as CCTV and the emergence of electronic databases – that do not distinguish or

SOURCE: From *The Oxford Handbook of Criminology*, ed. M. Maguire, R. Morgan and R. Reiner (Oxford: Clarendon Press, 2nd edn, 1997), 460–72.

discriminate between the criminal and non-criminal, the guilty and innocent. Consequently, we are all now subject to some of the principles of imprisonment as we go about our daily lives, and social control has re-emerged as a problem for discussion and debate.

[...] Durkheim, Rusche, and Kirchheimer, Melossi and Pavarini, and Foucault were writing about the rise of imprisonment. They took as their subject the transformation of control from torture and execution to imprisonment; from the whim of individuals to the performance of scheduled procedures by state officials; from exclusion by death or banishment to inclusion through reform and rehabilitation. What was common to the control of different dimensions of deviance in the period of rapid industrialization in the late eighteenth and nineteenth centuries was the building of institutions to segregate and then to socialize recruits to the labour force and to isolate or normalize the deviant: schools, workhouses, and asylums were institutions which had much in common, both architecturally and socially, with prisons.

The period in which these works appeared and became influential in criminology, however, was a period in which the institutional response to deviance was subject to sustained critique, and during which total institutions appeared to be becoming less central to social control. Mental hospitals, for example, had begun to close following the 1959 Mental Health Act in England and Wales; the 1969 Children and Young Persons Act introduced supervision orders for young people, which was meant to lead to fewer young people being committed to children's homes for either delinquency or welfare reasons; community service and suspended sentences were introduced as alternatives to custody for offenders, and the use of probation was extended.

Three of the key writers on control in the era of decarceration are David Greenberg (1975, 1977), Andrew Scull (1977, 1983), and Stanley Cohen (1979, 1985). These authors have produced critiques of the move away from institutional corrections to community corrections that have used many of the ideas and theoretical perspectives of the historians of the prison-building era.

During the 1960s and early 1970s, community corrections such as work with adolescents designed to prevent the onset of delinquency (alternative schooling; neighbourhood projects in high-delinquency areas; placement of 'at risk' youngsters on social work caseloads; removal of children of single-parent, or supposedly inadequate, parents to children's homes; treatment of 'hyperactive' children with drugs and/or counselling, in much the same way that children are being diagnosed as having Attention Deficit Disorder and prescribed ritalin today) proliferated to general approval. Similarly, in the field of mental illness, it was taken as axiomatic that treatment in the community was preferable to treatment in hospital. To proponents of such policies, community corrections and treatments were regarded as incontrovertibly both more humane and more effective than institutional measures.

In a pioneering paper, David Greenberg (1975) challenged some of the assumptions behind community corrections, saying that they were not necessarily more humane, more effective, or less costly than institutional sanctions. Andrew Scull (1977) extended a similar analysis to the treatment of the mentally ill. Greenberg's and Scull's thesis was that community treatment often amounted to malign neglect, with people left to fend for themselves, unsupported or inadequately supported in a rejecting, uncaring environment; receiving patchy, untested treatment/corrections; and that the move from the institution to the community might represent cost savings for the central state, which paid the costs of care in institutions, but represented additional costs to local authorities or voluntary agencies, who paid for community corrections and care. Only if central state institutions were closed down, and income transferred from central to local government, might there be cost savings. There was usually, it was pointed out, a trade-off between humanity, effectiveness, and cheapness: the provision of benign, effective community control and care is expensive.

Greenberg and Scull wrote in Marxist terms, restating the link between forms of control and the imperatives of the economy. They identified an apparent 'decarceration era' of the 1970s. What had occurred, they argued, was that the expanding demand for labour of the prosperous 1960s, which had encouraged the spread of rehabilitative sanctions designed to fit offenders and other deviants for the labour market, had encountered the fiscal crisis of the 1970s, triggered off by rises in world oil prices. As states were trying to rein back their public expenditure, recession led to mounting unemployment, so that the imperative of reducing money spent on deviant populations became stronger than the need to fit as many people as possible for the labour force.

A paradox of the decarceration period was that although there appeared to be a reduction in the incarceration of deviants, more and more people were being brought into the social control net. The paradox may have been more apparent than real: although the case for decarceration is supported by statistics for declining numbers of mentally ill patients institutionalized in hospitals at least in the USA and UK, evidence was much more equivocal in the case of incarceration of the criminal and delinquent (Scull, 1977; Matthews, 1979; Hudson, 1984). This apparent paradox has been explored most comprehensively by Cohen (1977, 1979, 1985), who demonstrated that the extension of community corrections seemed to fit Foucault's model of 'dispersed discipline'. Foucault had argued that the objective of the disciplinary control strategy that he depicted was:

> to make of the punishment and repression of illegalities a regular function, coextensive with society; not to punish less, but to punish better; to punish with an attenuated severity perhaps, but in order to punish with more universality and necessity; to insert the power to punish more deeply into the social body. (Foucault, 1977: 82)

Cohen documented the increasing number of people cautioned and convicted; he chronicled the strengthening of supervisory punishments; he observed the recruitment of friends, relatives, and neighbours into surveillance, the development of contracts and curfews. Phrases such as net-widening (more people subject to control); net-strengthening (sanctions such as probation and social work supervision having added requirements); blurring of the boundaries (between liberty and confinement, friend and controller) became part of the academic discourse of criminologists and the professional discourse of criminal justice practitioners. Prison came to be seen not just as a building but as a principle, the coercion of time and space (Hudson, 1984); a principle of disciplinary surveillance which could be most fully realized in the prison and the asylum, but which was present to varying degress in most of the innovations of contemporary control. The probation office, the day hospital, the attendance centre, the clinic, are all places where offenders or patients are required to be for certain periods of time, and where they are assessed and observed.

Cohen also incorporated the ideas of the social historians of the rise of imprisonment that new strategies of control could not simply be interpreted as the putting into practice of humanitarian reforms. His analysis (Cohen, 1985) of the development of strengthened and widened control networks incorporated Rothman's (1980) idea that when the conscience of reformers met the convenience of administrators, convenience was usually the winner; that good intentions often had bad unintended consequences; that whatever appeared to be taking place by way of loosening and thinning the networks, the 'deeper structures' of control meant that whatever might seem to be happening in the direction of greater tolerance of diversity, normalization through the established mixture of socialization and repression would continue.

By the late 1980s decarceration of the criminal seemed to be going into reverse, whilst deinstitutionalization of the mentally ill and of other 'problem populations' is still proceeding (children's homes and homes for the elderly continue to close, for example). Reformers and workers in the so-called caring professions, the very people who had been in the forefront of calls for the shift from institutional to community care in the 1950s and 1960s, began to complain of lack of institutional accommodation. Instead of following the same trajectories as the meta-analyses of control such as those of Cohen and Foucault had anticipated, the control of crime and of other forms of deviance seemed to be reversals of each other. In the case of crime and delinquency, the criticism of reformers and others today is that the mechanisms of community control have proliferated whilst the number of prisons and young offender institutions has also expanded; in the case of the mentally disordered, the criticism is that hospitals and asylums have closed, but have not been replaced by community care facilities (Hudson, 1993). Scull, in the first (1977) edition of his book *Decarceration*, had expected the deinstitutionalizing trends of the care and control of mental illness to be followed by similar trends in the response to crime and delinquency; by the time of his revised edition (1984), he saw that this was not the case, that the response to these two forms of deviancy was diverging rather than converging. [...]

POST-SOCIAL CONTROL

From the mid-1980s onwards, criminology seemed to have retreated from concern with wider fields of deviancy and control, and once again to be focusing more exclusively on crime and punishment. The emergence of the 'left realist' paradigm, associated in England with the work of Jock Young (1986, 1987, 1988) and his colleagues and in America with the work of Elliott Currie and others (1985), is illustrative of this reconcentration in relation to the separation of crime from deviancy; Garland (1990) has produced a powerful analysis of punishment which, whilst paying appropriate regard to the wider context of control, foregrounds punishment as a discrete social institution. Whilst those who urged the restriction of the field to crime and punishment produced strong critiques of the control theorists, it can be held that the insights of feminist criminologists, especially, mean that crime and punishment cannot be understood without *transgressing* criminology into wider fields (Cain, 1989). Similarly, writers who are raising questions about the criminalization of the kinds of drugs taken most commonly by minority ethnic groups and the much more restrained campaign against other drugs (Tonry, 1985), as well as people who are investigating the expansion of penal policy to fill the void left by restriction of economic and social policy (Hall, 1980; Gamble, 1988) must look beyond the parameters of realist criminology (Hudson, 1993).

Social control is re-emerging as an important problem, not only because of these analytic requirements, but because of the appearance of new modes of control, which appear to dissolve some of the distinctions between coercive and non-coercive, penal and social, control. Closed-circuit television in city centres; security patrols in shopping malls; strengthened asylum and immigration policies; expansion of electronic data collections, catch in the control net the innocent as well as the guilty, and operate on distinctions such as member/ non-member, resident/non-resident, creditworthy or non-creditworthy, as much as on criminal/non-criminal. In the venues of late-twentieth century England and America, the dress-code is as important as the criminal code (Shearing and Stenning, 1985).

Much of the emerging analysis of these new modes of control is utilizing the Foucauldian framework to ask whether the ubiquitousness of the electronic eye denotes the arrival of the *panopticon society*, where social control is everywhere, and becomes so pervasive that the distinction between external control and self-control disappears (Poster, 1990; Lyon, 1994). It would appear that these developments signify further progress in the dispersal of discipline, but that the essential project of the technologies of power identified by Foucault – that of normalization – has been abandoned. The objective of the new strategies of control is identification of the different and the dangerous in order to exclude: from the club, from the apartment building, from the estate, from the shopping mall, from the country.

These new control strategies have been described as forming an 'actuarial regime', by Jonathan Simon. Changing people, which is difficult and expensive, he says has been abandoned in favour of the simpler task of restricting people's possibilities of movement and action, through exclusion from general and particular locations and from opportunities to obtain goods and services, and through their exclusion from participation in various activities:

> Disciplinary practices focus on the distribution of behavior within a limited population ... This distribution is around a norm, and power operates with the goal of closing the gap, narrowing the deviation, and moving subjects towards uniformity .... Actuarial practices seek instead to maximise the efficiency of the population as it stands. Rather than seeking to change people ('normalize them', in Foucault's apt phrase) an actuarial regime seeks to manage them in place. (Simon, 1988: 773).

REFERENCES

Cain, M. (ed.) (1989) *Growing Up Good: Policing the Behaviour of Girls in Europe.* London: Sage.

Cohen, S. (1977) 'Prisons and the Future of Control Systems', in M. Fitzgerald et al., (eds), *Welfare in Action.* London: Routledge and Kegan Paul.

Cohen, S. (1979) 'The Punitive City: Notes on the Dispersal of Social Control', *Contemporary Crises*, 3: 83–93.

Cohen, S. (1985) *Visions of Social Control: Crime, Punishment and Classification.* Cambridge: Polity Press.

Currie, E. (1985) *Confronting Crime: An American Challenge.* New York: Basic Books.

Foucault, M. (1977) *Discipline and Punish: The Birth of the Prison.* London: Allen Lane.

Gamble, A. (1988) *The Free Economy and the Strong State: the Politics of Thatcherism.* Basingstoke: Macmillan.

Garland, D. (1990) *Punishment and Modern Society.* Oxford: Oxford University Press.

Greenberg, D. (1975) 'Problems in Community Corrections', *Issues in Criminology*, 19: 1–34.

Greenberg, D. (ed.) (1977) *Corrections and Punishment.* Beverly Hills, CA: Sage.

Hall, S. (1980) *The Drift to a Law and Order Society.* London: Cobden Trust.

Hudson, B.A. (1984) 'The Rising Use of Imprisonment: the Impact of "Decarceration" Policies', *Critical Social Policy*, 11: 46–59.

Hudson, B. (1993) *Penal Policy and Social Justice.* Basingstoke: Macmillan.

Lyon, D. (1994) *The Electronic Eye: The Rise of the Surveillance Society.* Cambridge: Polity Press.

Matthews, R. (1979) '"Decarceration" and the Fiscal Crisis', in B. Fine, R. Kinsey, J. Lea, S. Picciotto, and J. Young (eds), *Capitalism and the Rule of Law.* London: Hutchinson.

Poster, M. (1990) *The Mode of Information.* Cambridge: Polity Press.

Rothman, D. (1980) *Conscience and Convenience: The Asylum and its Alternatives in Progressive America.* Boston: Little Brown.

Scull, A. (1977) *Decarceration: Community Treatment and the Deviant – A Radical View.* Englewood Cliffs, NJ: Prentice-Hall (rev. edn, 1984).

Scull, A. (1983) 'Community Corrections: Panacea, Progress or Pretence?', in D. Garland and P. Young (eds), *The Power to Punish.* London: Heinemann.

Shearing, C.D. and Stenning, P.C. (1985) 'From the Panopticon to Disney world: The Development of Discipline', in A.N. Doob and E.L. Greenspan (eds), *Perspectives in Criminal Law*. Aurora, Ontario: Canada Law Books.

Simon, J. (1988) 'The Ideological Effects of Actuarial Practices', *Law and Society Review*, 22 (4), 772–800.

Tonry, M. (1995) *Malign Neglect: Race, Crime and Punishment in America*. New York: Oxford University Press.

Young, J. (1986) 'The Failure of Criminology: the Need for a Radical Realism', in R. Matthews and J. Young (eds), *Confronting Crime*. London: Sage.

Young, J. (1987) 'The Tasks of a Realist Criminology', *Contemporary Crises*, 11: 337–56.

Young, J. (1988) 'Radical Criminology in Britain: the Emergence of a Competing Paradigm', *British Journal of Criminology*, 28 (2), 289–313.

STUDY QUESTIONS

1   One of the key points that Hudson makes in this reading is that alternatives to imprisonment emerged amid hopes that they would reduce the need for prisons, and provide cheaper and more effective ways of punishing offenders. However, the evidence suggests that, far from replacing prisons, alternatives to custody have in fact developed alongside a continually spiralling prison population. To what extent do you think that alternatives to prison support Cohen's notion of a widening and strengthening 'net' of social control?

2   How is the net of surveillance and social control extended to 'ordinary' citizens in the population at large?

3   Towards the end of the reading Hudson alludes to Bentham's 'panopticon', a centrally located prison tower designed to allow a small, unseen few to monitor and control the lives of large numbers of prisoners. (The question often raised by this scenario is 'But who guards the guards?' – a point that you should bear in mind as you read the next two readings.) The concept of the panopticon is frequently applied to new communication technologies. In your opinion, what particular information, surveillance or monitoring techniques might be said to be extensions of the panoptic model?

FURTHER READING

In addition to the work of Cohen (referenced in the suggestions for *Further Reading* for Reading 29), Hudson's analysis of community corrections as alternatives to custody draws on Greenberg, D. (1975) 'Problems in community corrections', *Issues in Criminology*, 19, and Scull, A. (1977) *Decarceration: Community Treatment and the Deviant – A Radical View*, Englewood Cliffs, NJ: Prentice-Hall, which share a Marxist commitment to linking forms of control with economic cycles and, like Cohen, are profoundly sceptical of the liberal rhetoric behind decarceration strategies. For alternative views and criticisms of the 'dispersal of discipline' approach, two texts are well worth a look: Bottoms, A.E. (1983) 'Neglected features of contemporary penal systems', in D. Garland and

P. Young (eds) *The Power to Punish: Contemporary Penality and Social Analysis*, London: Heinemann; and Matthews, R. (1987) 'Decarceration and social control: fantasies and realities', in J. Lowman, R.J. Menzies and T.S. Palys (eds) *Transcarceration: Essays in the Sociology of Social Control*, Aldershot: Gower. For a challenging but wide-ranging theoretical treatise on the complexities of crime and control in late-modern society, embracing and revising traditional notions of citizenship, difference, risk and reflexivity, read Young, J. (1999) *The Exclusive Society*, London: Sage.

31

Smile, you're on TV

John Naughton

As has been illustrated in the last two readings, social control can take many forms. One of the most contested areas of political and social debate over recent years has been the social control of populations as they go about their everyday lives at work, at home and in public places such as streets, shopping centres and football stadiums. Closed-circuit television (CCTV) cameras have become a familiar part of Britain's landscape, although few of us are aware of the extent to which we are being monitored as we go about our daily lives. Many of us have embraced the new technology, grateful for its role in cutting crime, especially in city centres. Some have even invested in relatively cheap, do-it-yourself CCTV kits to monitor our homes and cars. However, the following two readings raise the question of whether we should be so benign towards surveillance technologies, and so unconcerned about who operates them. Furthermore, while most people remain relatively unbothered by the presence of TV cameras in city centres, they might be more troubled by the surveillance of their telephone calls or e-mails by their employer. The following two articles both examine the pros and cons of new technologies designed to reduce unlawful activities, but each raises a number of questions in relation to who has control over them and how they exercise their powers.

On a street somewhere in King's Lynn, a group of teenagers, on mountain bikes cluster, aimlessly riding up and down a set of steps. One of them decides to fill in the time with a spot of impromptu graffiti artistry. This completed, he rides off with his mates – straight into the arms of a local policeman, who knows exactly which one to stop even though he has not seen the offence being committed. He escorts the boy to the scene of the crime and makes him repair the damage, after which cop and miscreant go their separate ways. As he resumes his beat, the policeman looks up to the top of a building and waves.

SOURCE: From the *Observer Life* magazine (13 November 1994).

He's waving to a rooftop video camera, and through it to the control room in the local council offices, where sits the security officer who alerted him to the incident in the first place. It is a cramped and airless place, the windows of which are occluded by permanently drawn blinds, and yet from it you can get an unrivalled view of King's Lynn. For into this room, along fibre-optic cables laid by British Telecom, flow pictures from 60 steerable video cameras, strategically located to enable a single operator – let us call him Roger – to monitor every major public space in the city, 24 hours a day, seven days a week, 365 days a year. [...]

At the back of the room are 14 monitors, each of which shows four separate images – 56 continuous views of King's Lynn. On Roger's desk there are eight monitors displaying selected quadrants from the 56 in full-screen glory. If he detects anything interesting, he selects it for the full-screen treatment. He can zoom, pan and focus from where he sits. As he does so the image shakes: it is a windy day outside, and the camera is clearly being buffeted by the gale. Because there is no sound, the vibrating image seems eerie. The view from another camera is strangely blurred, and then a vertical bar appears moving slowly right to left and one realises that it is raining out there and the bar is simply a wiper.

A call comes though on the radio. Roger picks up the handset and listens. Then he hits a switch, and pans and zooms on to a car aligned erratically in a car park. It becomes clear that the vehicle is parked outside the marked lines. Roger presses a button and a still photograph of the scene issues from a slot. The call was from an attendant at the car park who wishes to have evidence of a customer infringing the rules.

While we talk, Roger displays the abstracted concentration which one sometimes sees in children intent on video games. He is with us, and yet not with us. His fingers are constantly on the go, incessantly flicking from scene to scene. 'What's that?' he exclaims suddenly, zooming in on a weird-looking vehicle which appears to have half-mounted a pavement. It looks like a cross between a bomb-disposal robot and an expensive wheelbarrow. It is probably harmless, but if Roger thinks it isn't he can hit another switch and the image will come up on a monitor at the police station.

To the outsider, the overwhelming impression is of information overload. It's hard enough to pay attention to a single image on a television screen, let alone four different pictures. And yet Roger is scanning 14 monitors. How does he do it? Training and instinct mainly, plus local knowledge and common sense.

The great trick is to be able to ignore the routine and pick out the unusual or unexpected event. A man in a car park is seen bending down to pick up a piece of wire. An innocuous enough event, you might say. But he does not look for a rubbish bin, and instead heads off in the direction of a white Fiesta, followed by Roger's panning camera. The man then commences to force an entry to the Fiesta, watched by another chap who has just got out of a nearby car. Eventually the observer strolls off, and passes a policeman alerted by Roger without thinking to mention what he has just witnessed. In the end it turns out that what we have seen is a man who has locked himself out of his car. But it might have been otherwise.

The striking thing is the acuity of the images. The King's Lynn technology seems light years ahead of that in the Bootle shopping mall which captured

James Bulger being led to his death. One of the reasons for this is that the designers of the Lynn system plumped for black and white technology rather than colour because of its superior resolution and low-light performance. 'Which would you rather know', asks Mr Loftus, 'the colour of a suspect car or its registration number?' And, as if to demonstrate the point, Roger zooms in on two women getting into a car in some gloomy cavern. Even in the murk the numberplate is easily legible on screen.

A compilation tape of recent events makes the same point. In one sequence, a character whom the police (and Roger) have been tracking intermittently all night arrives back at his jeep shortly before two police cars turn up. When the cops examine the vehicle, however, their quarry is nowhere to be seen. What they have not spotted, though they are on the scene, is what Roger has spied from his electronic eyrie, namely that the fugitive is hiding beneath the jeep. Once this information is relayed by radio, the flashlights come out and the man is apprehended.

Most people are blithely unaware of the extent of video surveillance in modern Britain. They notice the cameras sometimes, perhaps, but generally think no more about them. The majority of Marks and Spencer customers, for example, are probably unaware of being monitored – though some may be puzzled at the placement of certain mirrors, which are actually designed to enable the security cameras to 'see' behind pillars. Indeed, it seems to be accepted wisdom among store detectives that anyone paying close attention to the cameras is probably a potential thief.

The James Bulger case alerted many people to the astonishing pervasiveness of video cameras on our streets: the image of that little lad, hand in hand with his killers, has etched itself on to our collective consciousness. Yet in a sense that image is misleading, because it understated the power of this technology. Even after computer enhancement, the Bootle pictures were blurred and indistinct, whereas it is quite possible to get sharp, easily recognisable images. And there is more to come, as the techniques of satellite reconnaissance find their way on to the high street. After all, if LandSat can pick out a Volkswagen parked in a San Jose driveway, what's to prevent the same technology picking you out in the street from a passport photograph?

It is the pervasiveness of video surveillance which is most surprising, though. If, in the last 24 hours, you have been shopping, taken a train, bought petrol, visited a post office, bank or building society, attended a football match, visited an off-licence or just strolled down the high street, then the chances are that your image has been recorded on several videotapes.

Next time you drive on a motorway (or indeed any major road) see if you can see something that looks like a group of roosting vultures atop a pole. You will find them every few miles, and almost always at junctions. They are video cameras, and they feed a continuous stream of images back to a police control room somewhere. Given a little time and effort, even the most discreet trip along the M25 could be reconstructed simply by knowing the approximate time of the journey and then examining the tapes from successive junctions – rather as Jamie Bulger's last walk was chronicled by security cameras along the route.

High street and town centre surveillance is, if anything, more intense and likely to become more so. A quick survey suggests that Airdrie, Birmingham, Bournemouth, Croydon, Glasgow, Hexham, Islington, Liverpool, Newcastle and Sunderland have followed King's Lynn's example. Even affluent Hampstead Garden Suburb is reported to be getting in on the act – though of course it will go private. It is said that more than 300 local authorities are considering or planning the introduction of video surveillance in their areas. And all of this is happening without so much as a by-your-leave: no debates in Parliament, no legislation and precious little in the way of public debate. In so far as it is commented upon at all, it is in the PR speeches of Home Office ministers as they unveil yet another urban scheme. 'This is a friendly eye in the sky', said one as he launched the Liverpool system. 'There is nothing sinister about it and the innocent have nothing to fear.'

When Home Office ministers assure us there is nothing sinister about one of their projects it is generally time to start counting the spoons. Liberty, formerly the National Council for Civil Liberties, has called on the Government to introduce legislation to ensure that the cameras are only used for crime detection. The populace, however, does not seemed alarmed. This may be, of course, because it has no idea how pervasive it is; or it may be because, taken incrementally, the arguments in favour appear so compelling. Worried about street crime and yobbery? Well, just get yourself some cameras. (Some pubs have already installed them in their toilets.) Want to make that multi-storey car park less terrifying at night? Just install some lighting and a few cameras.

Video surveillance seems to be the ultimate technical fix for street crime. If resources don't permit police forces to give people what they always say they want – more policemen on the beat – then they can at least give them this elevated Cyclops to watch over their property. When Sunderland installed 16 cameras in its city centre a senior local policeman said that it was 'equivalent to having 16 extra police officers on the beat 24 hours a day'.

Which, of course, is nonsense. Sixteen cameras are equivalent to 16 cameras, full stop. A bobby on the beat is not just a disembodied visual perception device. He or she is a human being entering into a relationship – however fraught – with the people of a neighbourhood. And a beat bobby has ears as well as eyes, and a memory and a functioning intellect capable of interpreting what people say and do in their own contexts. There is plenty of evidence that the video camera can *complement* the police officer on the street, but it would be crazy to suggest that it is an adequate substitute for him or her. The proponents of video policing are falling into the trap first spotted by Heidegger when he defined technology as a way of arranging the world so that one does not have to experience it.

The argument in favour of more surveillance always seems so reasonable: it reduces itself to the line 'the innocent have nothing to fear'. The same argument is made for the introduction of ID cards, but one only has to look beyond the basic principle at how such things would work in practice to see what the dangers are. If Britain has a compulsory ID card, then logically one has to create the offence of not having one or of failing to produce it on request to a police officer, giving the police yet more grounds to stop people on sight.

And, police officers being what they are in this country, you can guess who will be stopped most frequently and asked to produce their ID. Much the same applies to video surveillance. It will be – indeed already is being – used as a means of anticipating trouble. 'See that crowd of boisterous teenagers over there on camera nine? Let's get someone down there before they get out of hand.' Or: 'What's that guy with dreadlocks going into Watches of Switzerland for?' The technology will become a way of singling out those who do not 'belong' in a particular environment, and of taking pre-emptive action to exclude them.

But its most sinister effect in the longer term will be to curtail our privacy. There will be fewer hiding places in urban society. The blessed anonymity which city life bestows on citizens will be much reduced. And those who fled the twitching net curtains of village life will find themselves being observed by an altogether beadier eye than that of the local postmistress.

Marshall McLuhan used to talk about how television would bring about a global village. But I don't think this is what he had in mind.

32

They're watching you

Martin Bright

Forty-nine workers at a Cable & Wireless call centre in Brighton – 10 per cent of the workforce – were called in to meetings with managers last month and told they were in big trouble.

They were informed that teleworkers at the centre had been hacking into the computers and upgrading the cable TV packages they had been given as staff perks. By short-circuiting the billing system, some people had apparently been giving themselves access to extra TV channels. And the management knew who they were.

Twenty people were sacked or suspended on the spot and the rest told they faced serious disciplinary action. It emerged that managers at the centre had been involved in an extraordinary six-week surveillance operation, keeping a constant watch on staff they suspected of fiddling the system. By tracing the use of personal computer passwords, downloading data that people thought they had deleted and listening in to phone calls, the company snoopers believed they had identified the perpetrators of thousands of pounds of theft.

The Cable & Wireless swoop is the latest evidence that bosses are increasingly resorting to 'Big Brother' tactics to spy on employees suspected of theft, fraud or Internet abuse.

We are a society that is fast becoming obsessed with watching and being watched. Britain now has around a million CCTV cameras. It is estimated that the average person in a major city could be filmed up to 300 times a day by CCTV cameras in shops, banks, places of work and, increasingly, the street itself.

Those with access to the Internet can secretly observe people cavorting by the side of a Las Vegas hotel swimming pool via a webcam, or watch a group of young women sharing a house who have agreed to let cable TV company Bravo film their every move.

SOURCE: From the *Observer* (29 August 1999).

One avant-garde musician known as Scanner has made a career out of sampling conversations on people's mobile phones using basic surveillance technology you can buy in the high street.

And last week it was revealed that a Croydon nursery was installing a webcam so that worried mums can watch their children from their work station.

But when it comes to being spied on ourselves, it's most likely to happen at work. With corporate fraud estimated to cost companies around 6 per cent of their annual turnover, the instinct to snoop is perhaps understandable, but unions are becoming worried that companies are beginning to invade people's privacy in a direct infringement of their human rights.

Last month an employment tribunal ruled that an IT firm was within its rights for sacking Lois Franxhi when she used office time to search for a holiday on the Internet.

The increased use of CCTV cameras, computer audits, the recording of phone calls and, in some cases, the hiring of undercover private detectives all adds to a growing sense that workers are being watched at all times. A report earlier this year from the Institute of Employment Rights found that the surveillance of workers was becoming increasingly prevalent. It has become 'more widespread, more continuous, more intense and more secretive', wrote the institute's director, Caroline Jones, in an open letter to her opposite number at the Institute of Personnel Development earlier this month.

'Secret surveillance should be unlawful,' Jones told the *Observer*. 'If the police ensnare you like this, it is called entrapment and they can't use the evidence. But if an employer does it, you can't stop them.' The Institute of Employment Rights has recommended that employees should always be informed when they are being watched and the procedures for that surveillance.

In the case of the Brighton call centre, the Communication Workers' Union was forced to back the company's right to protect itself from abuse by employees, but voiced workers' fears that the surveillance operation was far from foolproof.

'We fully understand that companies want to get a full day's work out of people', said Donald MacDonald of the CWU. 'But people are often being carpeted on the evidence of electronic auditing systems which are not very good.' The staff at the Brighton call centre say that the security on their computers was not strict and managers had often asked staff to divulge their passwords. It remains uncertain that all, if any, of the 49 were guilty of the fraud.

But there are signs that the tide is turning. Invoking the European Convention on Human Rights, telecommunications watchdog Oftel last week announced that companies which record their employees' phone calls must provide separate lines for personal calls. An increasing number of companies in the financial services sector routinely record their employees' calls for the purposes of training and quality control.

Now employment lawyers Eversheds have warned bosses to be extremely careful not to breach human rights legislation with their increasingly sophisticated surveillance techniques.

The Human Rights Act, which takes effect later this year, will ensure that all British law is compatible with the European Convention and enshrine the right to privacy in it.

The Data Protection Act, which comes into force in March of next year, will also ensure that the employee's consent is gained for the 'processing of personal data'.

Eversheds has identified six different types of office 'spook', who use different secret techniques to monitor their workforce.

The most common is the 'Listener', who simply monitors or records phone calls – this already happens in 40 per cent of US companies. The new Oftel guidance should limit this, but in practice each case will still have to be tested against European law.

The 'Watcher' monitors e-mails, usually simply to check how much company time is being taken up with personal correspondence. But in some cases employers go as far as monitoring the content of e-mails to check that commercial confidentiality is not being breached. The 'Psychic Watcher' records the number of keystrokes made by employees, working in typing pools and newspaper offices.

The 'Rematerialiser' finds computer documents employees thought they had deleted and the 'Poltergeist' looks through workers' desks. But the 'Brooding Presence', the ever-present CCTV camera, is identified as being used increasingly by bosses to snoop on workers.

In each case, Eversheds says employers now have to balance the genuine desire to monitor the behaviour of workers – bullying campaigns conducted by e-mail is the example they use – against people's rights to privacy.

Wherever possible, the lawyers agree with the unions that surveillance should only happen with the agreement of the workforce.

Partner Owen Warnock said: 'We advise employers to develop a clear policy on electronic monitoring. It can be used positively to stop harassment, fraud and theft, but they should really tell employees that they are doing it.'

Clearly, the more concerned employers become about the implications of the new Human Rights Act, the better it is for Eversheds' business.

But Sarah Veale, employment rights policy officer at the TUC, agrees that the new legislation will have an effect: 'Eversheds are certainly over-egging it, but the Human Rights Act will guarantee you privacy in the workplace.

'We need to achieve a balance between the legitimate observation and interfering with people's lives. Employers have a right to see people working, but they should know that people work better when they are trusted.'

There is ample evidence that, in some cases, the balance is not being struck. It hasn't gone as far as Japan, where some firms have toilet bowls that automatically test for drugs and then film the people who have a negative result using CCTV cameras installed inside the cubicle.

The new legislation is yet to be tested, but it is thought that the installation of any cameras in toilets or changing rooms will be outlawed.

Unions and human rights organisations are also keen to see an end to the practice of hiring private detectives to pose as workers, thought to be carried out by at least one major British company.

In this low-tech but extremely effective form of surveillance, the detectives report office gossip and dissent back to the management or, in some cases, are hired on specific cases where fraud is suspected.

In one instance, private detectives are believed to have set up bogus accounts when call centre staff were believed to be passing on commercially sensitive information about clients.

In Brighton, the case of the 49 workers 'caught' stealing extra cable TV channels remains unproven and the Communication Workers' Union is fighting their cases. Cable & Wireless has issued a statement denying workers' claims that the surveillance was an elaborate set-up to avoid paying redundancy.

Staff at the centre admit that the fraud was going on, but say that the company's snooping has been a vastly expensive exercise in proving nothing.

Unions and lawyers agree that that bosses may eventually be forced to trust their workers because of the practical difficulties of getting surveillance evidence to stick rather than a concern for their basic human rights. [...]

STUDY QUESTIONS

1   Think back to Box's argument (Reading 7) that crime is an ideological construct which serves the interests of the powerful and targets the powerless. What evidence for this proposition is there in the two newspaper articles that you have just read?
2   An article in *The Independent* (29 September 1997), headlined *'If you're black or pretty, Big Brother's watching you'*, claims that many operators of CCTV are 'bigots who often watch people for no good reason'. The report claims that black people are two-and-a-half times more likely to be watched than white people, and that few women are observed other than for voyeuristic reasons. The author of the study on which *The Independent based* its story (Clive Norris; see *Further Reading*) further claims that, while the technology is now sophisticated enough to focus in on a car's expired tax disc from several hundred metres away, it is not the offences of relatively affluent and older motorists that are the concern of CCTV operators, but the activities of poorer working-class and ethnic-minority youth. What are the criminological implications of these findings? What are the consequences of selective targeting of some social groups over others?
3   Urban spaces have long been recognized as sites of difference and diversity. What challenges or threats do surveillance technologies pose to the rich cultural mix that our cities have traditionally fostered?

FURTHER READING

Clive Norris's research on CCTV is written up in Norris, C. and Armstrong, G. (1999) *The Maximum Surveillance Society: The Rise of CCTV*, Oxford: Berg; and in Coleman, C. and Norris, C. (2000) *Introducing Criminology*, Cullompton: Willan. In addition, there have been several recent and innovative contributions to the study of surveillance and social-control. Peter Manning examines the omnipresence of surveillance and social-control technologies, and their use in the workplace, medicine and the police, in his essay 'Reflections: the visual as a mode of social control' in J. Ferrell and N. Websdale (eds) (1999) *Making Trouble: Cultural Constructions of Crime, Deviance and Control*, New York: Aldine de Gruyter. The use of CCTV in the workplace is the subject of McCahill, M. and Norris, C. (1999) 'Watching the workers: crime, CCTV and the workplace', in P. Davies, P. Francis and V. Jupp (eds) *Invisible Crimes: Their Victims and their Regulation*, Basingstoke: Macmillan. Gary Marx further extends conventional thinking about the omnipresence of surveillance motifs in our culture (including popular music, film, advertisements, cartoons and art) in 'Electric eye in the sky: some reflections on the new surveillance and popular culture', chapter 6 in J. Ferrell and C. R. Sanders (eds) (1995) *Cultural Criminology*, Boston, MA: Northeastern University Press. For a discussion of the commodification of privacy, see chapter 10, 'Disinformocracy' in Rheingold, H. (1994) *The Virtual Community: Surfing the Internet*, London: Minerva.

33

Land of the free

Gary Younge

Stanley Cohen's vision of social control that we have seen illustrated in the previous readings has been hugely influential within sociological criminology, but it has also come in for criticism for underplaying the alternatives to custody which have had some success over the past thirty years or so. Among the alternatives that courts in England and Wales have at their disposal when sentencing guilty offenders are: the discharge, the suspended sentence, the community service order, the probation order, and the fine (variants of which can be found in most other Western countries). However, despite the existence of alternatives, the continuing rise in the numbers of people sentenced to prison cannot be denied, and is a continuing concern for criminologists in the UK, the USA and many European countries. The prison population of England and Wales is expected to reach 75,200 in 2005 (rising from a figure of 39,000 in 1970) and, despite an intensive prison-building programme, many British prisons remain overcrowded. Some countries in Europe, notably those of Scandinavia, have, however, taken a rather more progressive view of the problem, and the reading that follows outlines alternatives to conventional forms of punishment and incarceration. Gary Younge focuses specifically on sentencing policies in Finland, the country with the lowest prison population in Europe. He traces the historical and political developments that have led to this admirable state of affairs (noting that they have had no discernible negative impact on crime rates) from a situation, thirty years ago, when Finland's prison population was among the highest in Europe. The reading highlights two concomitant developments that have changed the penal landscape in Finland. First, there has been a broad policy of decriminalization and minimizing the use and length of sentencing. Secondly, there has been a programme of significant prison reform, so that where custody *is* used, prisoners are unlikely to experience confinement in the way that it was described by Cohen and Taylor in Reading 28. But, even in the relatively liberal climate of Scandinavia, there is a growing tension between

SOURCE: From the *Guardian* (2 February 2001).

reformers' calls for humane and rehabilitative punishments and public expectations about what prisons should be like. The reading closes on a somewhat foreboding note that prison reformists and abolitionists in the UK, central Europe and the USA may find depressingly familiar.

In room 31 of Helsinki district courts, Tuomo Tapani-Salo is in trouble. Three years ago, on a ferry trip from Sweden, he was found with a bag full of cigarettes, alcohol and perfume stolen from the ship's duty-free shop. The short, barrel-shaped skinhead insists he was carrying the bag for a friend, Johannes. Johannes cannot be prosecuted because he was under 15 at the time. But he is in court to back up Tuomo's story, wearing two black eyes and army fatigues, courtesy of his national service.

Outside you could be in any courthouse in Britain. Anxious parents in their frayed Sunday best, the accused affecting studied nonchalance, bored policemen in uniform and lawyers carrying battered briefcases; all wait, whisper and walk in expectant circles on polished floors that smell of cheap disinfectant.

But inside, the room is a bare setting of wooden panelling and fluorescent glare. No emblem, crest or Latin scripture is embossed on the wall laying claim to the higher ideals of truth and justice. Just the sign of a cellphone inside a red circle with a red line through it – a sign of the times in a country where there are more mobiles than people.

Tuomo stands to hear the verdict. Not guilty, says the judge, and he and Johannes head out for a smoke with a smile. Next door, in room 32, six people have been tried. Two for possession of drugs, three for violent assault and one on 17 different charges ranging from possession of an illegal firearm to twice driving under the influence of drugs. Only the latter goes to prison, for an eight-month stretch. The rest are fined.

Seven cases, six guilty verdicts; one imprisoned, six walk free. Another morning in the Finnish judicial system – a country with the lowest prison population in the European Union. Here they have made it a point of principle to keep criminals out of prison, unless they are believed to pose a risk to society. 'I don't believe longer prison sentences help our real safety,' says Markku Salminen, general director of the Finnish prison administration. 'If you put someone in prison, then it is almost certain that they'll be released and go back again. Prison is like university – the university of crime.'

This, the Finns believe, is particularly true of the young, who are only incarcerated for the harshest crimes.

This liberal approach can produce what looks like very illiberal results. Rapists can sometimes walk out of a Finnish court with a conditional sentence – depending on the circumstances in which the crime was committed, and whether it was a first offence.

It wasn't always like this. As recently as the 70s, Finland had one of the highest prison populations in western Europe. But since then the number of prisoners has been falling dramatically, to just below the rest of Scandinavia, even as the rates and patterns of crime have kept in line with its Nordic neighbours.

The move to cut the prison population began not with politicians but academics during the late 60s. Inspired by the radicalism of the age, intellectuals insisted that criminal policy should be part of an overall social policy, related to employment and educational opportunities, and proclaimed that there was no evidence of a link between long prison sentences and less crime. 'The outcome of all this was a criminal political ideology – humane neo-classicism – which stressed both legal safeguards against coercive care and the objective of less repressive measures in general,' says the head of the national research institute of legal policy in Finland, Tappio Lappi-Seppälä. 'Instead of direct or simple deterrence, the theory speaks of indirect general prevention or – more often – the moral-creating and value-shaping effect of punishment.'

Gradually but consistently these abstract principles began to be translated into action by a mixture of decriminalising some offences (such as public drunkenness), relaxing sentencing on others, and reducing the minimum prison sentence from four months in 1976 to just 14 days in 1989.

The most dramatic changes were in the sanctions for two specific crimes – drink-driving and theft. During the mid-70s, judges were allowed greater scope to impose conditional sentences and fines instead of imprisonment. In the 90s community service also became a popular punishment for both, leaving only repeat offenders and rare cases ending up behind bars. The results, in terms of prison population, were startling. In 1971, 38 per cent of those sentenced for theft went to jail; in 1991, it was 11 per cent. Similarly, in 1971, 70 per cent of drink-drivers were sentenced to prison; in 1981, it was 12 per cent. There was no commensurate increase in rates of theft or drink-driving.

Remarkably, given the high and permanent profile that law and order has attained in British political culture, this ideologically inspired sea-change was introduced without any political comment or interference. So while crime has been extensively theorised, it has not been politicised for electoral advantage. 'Finnish criminal policy is exceptionally expert-oriented,' says Lappi-Seppälä. 'In a small country like this, reforms have been prepared and conducted by a relatively small group of experts. So far, Finnish politicians have been able to resist the temptation of low-level populism on this issue.'

At a recycling depot in the industrial area of the city, Jarmo Laihonen is savouring his finest hour. Last spring he was kicked out of his house after a drunken row with his wife. He decided to drive the short distance to his girl-friend's house and was stopped by the police for drink-driving. He was sentenced to 170 hours community service, which he serves eight hours a week in two, four-hour stints, hauling old furniture and electrical goods around the shop floor. This is hour 169. When he finishes later today he will be a free man.

'I was relieved when I was sentenced to community service,' he says. 'I've been to prison a few times before and it isn't useful for me. Many of my friends think it was too soft a sentence but they don't know what it's like. I think this will be my last time; where crime is concerned.'

If Jarmo succeeds, it will be against the odds. Whatever community service in Finland does achieve, it does not stop people getting into trouble. Three-quarters of those given community service, which usually involves menial work or helping the disabled or the elderly, reoffend, compared with 80 per cent who are released from prison. Maija Kukkonen, head of the probation service, says the rate is high but does not denote a failure of the system. 'So long as the rate is lower than those who are released from prison, or even if it was the same, then I would say it is a success. Because so long as they are on community service, they are still with their family, they can keep their house and job, pay their taxes and they remain in society. When people come out of prison, they often have nothing.'

Not everyone is convinced. As he begins the Wednesday night police patrol through central Helsinki, Markku Salminen says that without the threat of prison, it is difficult to enforce the law. But five hours into his shift, there does not seem to be that much law to enforce: he has yelled at a jay walker, and dealt with one parking incident, a women who could not turn off her car alarm, a man who would not pay his restaurant bill, and an elderly couple who have been terrorised by their violent son (who hit his father over the head with his shoe).

Finland remains a relatively safe country. Polls show that police are regarded as more trustworthy than priests. And they have earned it. The detection rate for murder is around 96 per cent, compared with 26 per cent in America. It is this, not prison, that prevents crime, says Salminen, who used to be a detective. 'People never think about what kind of punishment they are going to receive when they commit a crime. They worry about getting caught.'

Ronja Siren was dealing in drugs, guns and explosives, in a gang of 50, when she was caught. Sitting in the Hämeenlinna closed prison, where she is serving a nine-year sentence, she says she uses the gym as a physical outlet for the emotional stress of being separated from her two young children and husband, who is also in prison. 'The gym is very important to me. I go there every evening that I can. If I am going to get myself out of this situation, it will be down to myself,' she says.

The regime in Hämeenlinna, just over 60 miles from Helsinki, is strict but not oppressive. Prisoners are locked up from 10 at night to six in the morning, when they must slop out the buckets they use for toilets. Most have televisions and videos in their rooms and, on each wing, there is a communal area where they can eat and relax. But the rest of the time there is a range of work and study activities which they can do if they wish.

Siren's offence shows just how crime patterns in the region are changing. With Russia and Estonia now opened up, Finland, like the rest of Scandinavia, has become vulnerable to drugs smuggling and small-scale mafia activity, which has prompted both a rise in foreign prisoners and a more hardened, desperate type of criminal.

For with more serious crime comes stiffer sentences, which means the average time spent in prison is growing. Last year, for the first time in a long time, the prison population increased by 8 per cent.

Moreover, by adding heroin and amphetamine to the nation's favourite drug, alcohol, a growing number of drug-abusing inmates have created a sub-culture in prison which is demanding a more repressive response from guards. 'Prisoners trade drugs, which leads to a debt system where one prisoner owes another money or cigarettes which can then lead to violence,' says Anna-Kaarina

Grönholm, the governor of Helsinki prison. 'So we have to continually have checks, urine tests and raids, which does change the atmosphere within a prison.' Those with serious drug or alcohol dependency are also less likely to be suitable for community service, thereby compounding the likelihood of them going to jail.

In the nearby open prison of Vanaja, the atmosphere is more relaxed but the sanctions for transgression more severe. Prisoners here are free to come and go as they please, so long as they check in at night, and have access to a sauna, skis and a tennis court. Some work at sewing, weaving or gardening within the grounds. Others commute to colleges in the area. One woman, convicted of white-collar crime, drives the 60 miles to Helsinki every day to a regular job and is monitored with the use of a special kind of mobile phone. They are paid a wage or grant from which they pay taxes. Most are being prepared for release, and any breach of the rules would put them back in the closed prison.

Hessu, 70, who killed his wife 10 years ago, came to Vanaja recently after a spell in a closed prison, and works in the library. 'It's not hard to get used to here because you can freely come and go so I feel like I'm half-way to civilian life already,' says the former merchant seaman.

But there is evidence that the consensus that produces this comfort may be showing signs of strain. The expert-led approach to prison policy has partly been able to work because it has been shielded from the popular scrutiny. When it was formulated Finns had just a couple of state television channels and an exclusively broadsheet print media, and were primarily preoccupied with Russian foreign policy. Now the Finns are members of the EU, there are several cable channels and two vibrant tabloids. So perception of crime has increased, even when crime has not; between 1992 and 2000, the purchase of burglar alarms almost trebled, and special windows and door protection rose nine fold.

Moreover, the political consensus which produced it was underpinned by an economic cohesion that no longer exists, with some families already into a second generation which has not known work. The time may be ripe for a populist demagogic attack on perceived leniency.

The fragility was shown a few years ago when a paedophile and murderer, Yamu, was up for release. With a culture where tabloids could now set the agenda, the prospect of his release sparked great public interest. On the website of one of the red-top papers were two questions.

The first: 'Do you think Yamu should be released?'

The second: 'Do you think our prison sentencing is tough enough?'

STUDY QUESTIONS

1 What does this reading tell us about the deployment of resources within the criminal justice system in Finland? How are resources re-allocated in ways that ensure that crime does not significantly increase, despite the reduced threat of imprisonment for offenders?
2 Could a similar approach to punishment work in the UK? What factors recommend it for investigation in the UK, and what factors might militate against it working here?

3   What alternatives to custody already exist in the UK? How successful are they perceived to be by politicians, the public and by penal reformists?
4   What are the social and cultural processes that now threaten Finland's remarkable achievements in penal reform? What conclusions can be drawn in relation to the UK's policies on prisons and punishment?

FURTHER READING

For a critique of 'alternatives' to custody which includes a comprehensive discussion of why such alternatives have failed to produce a drop in the proportionate use of custody, see Vass, A.A. (1990) *Alternatives to Prison: Punishment, Custody, and the Community*, London: Sage. For a more positive analysis of the value of non-custodial penal measures, which charts recent legal and social developments, and makes a case for community punishments being more central to criminological inquiry, see Worrall, A. (1997) *Punishment in the Community: The Future of Criminal Justice*, Harlow: Longman. For an analysis of both non-custodial penalties and the role of the probation service, see Newburn, T. (1995) *Crime and Criminal Justice Policy*, Harlow: Longman. All daily newspapers now have their own websites on which to browse the archives and find articles like Readings 31–33. The best, in our view, is the site of the *Guardian* and *Observer* newspapers (www.guardianunlimited.co.uk).

34

New ways to break the law: cybercrime and the politics of hacking

Douglas Thomas

The readings that have preceded this final extract have moved our attention beyond a narrow criminological concern with crime and justice to a broader focus on the complexities of social control and social order. They have posed a number of important questions about the nature of power in society. As CCTV cameras become ever more ubiquitous, as databases continue to hold increasingly sensitive information collated from a range of personal sources, and as politicians continue to debate the ethics of a national DNA database, the calls for greater protection for people's civil liberties will grow. Yet, as the final reading in this volume demonstrates, power can sometimes be inverted, and nowhere is this potential more evident than in the sphere of new information and communication technologies, particularly the Internet. It would, of course, be foolish to overstate their democratizing capabilities: access to computer technologies is still restricted by cost and other social factors (the 'average' Internet user is male, educated and wealthy, according to Lax, in Gauntlett, 2000; see *Further Reading*) and it should not be forgotten that some of the insidious electronic surveillance techniques described by Martin Bright (Reading 32) are possible precisely because of the challenges to privacy that each new technological advancement brings with it. However, as the title of this final reading suggests, computer technologies are introducing new ways to break the law, and for some – in this case, hackers – this means turning the tables on powerful organisations, including the police and the military. Moreover, the case of hacking further demonstrates that crime and crime control can no longer be conceived in conventional ways. Just as the readings elsewhere in Part V demonstrate that advances in technology

SOURCE: From *Web. Studies: Rewiring Media Studies for the Digital Age*, ed. D. Gauntlett (London: Arnold, 2000), pp. 202–11.

have resulted in the principles of imprisonment being stretched beyond physically defined spaces to encompass whole communities, Douglas Thomas's piece illustrates how hackers are able to commit crimes via computer networks in spaces that cannot be defined by reference to physical boundaries. One doesn't need to be imprisoned to be subjected to confinement, surveillance, regulation and control. Similarly, one doesn't need to be in a physical location to commit crimes such as trespass and theft.

As cyberspace becomes an increasingly central part of everyday life, it opens new opportunities and presents new challenges to our senses of security and community. In particular, issues of online behaviour involving the law are an important consideration as cyberspace comes to play an increasingly central role in communication, commerce, and the sharing of data and information. Traditionally the law has been able to identify and control social behaviours with threats of surveillance and punishment. Virtual crime, or 'cybercrime', presents a new set of challenges, however. Unlike crimes in the physical world, crimes committed online are difficult to monitor and divorced from the body. Crimes such as trespassing are called into question when there is no actual physical area being trespassed upon, and no physical body performing the trespass.

This chapter examines the subculture of computer hackers in an effort to better understand how issues of cybercrime and community can be critically examined. Hackers, as a subculture, have been at the forefront of such challenges and explorations, often confounding the structure and nature of law, and in the process using various forms of transgression to form new communities, both online and in the real world. In analysing this subculture, I examine representations of hackers, both through culture and their own self-image, provide a brief history of hackers and hacking, detail several ways in which hackers have invented 'new ways to break the law', and, finally, explore the political debates surrounding hackers and hacker culture.

WHO ARE HACKERS?

The popular media has undoubtedly played a major role in how the public views the image of the hacker. Films such as *WarGames*, *Hackers* and *The Net*, have shown us an array of kids who find themselves in over their heads, struggling to save themselves (and often the world) from destruction. In books, and the mass media, hackers are often framed in terms of their crimes, from the most trivial to the grandiose.[1] These films preach to us the dangers of technology and warn us of its ability to threaten out existence (*WarGames*), cause ecological disaster (*Hackers*) and destroy our identities (*The Net*). The books give us tales of international espionage, gang warfare, and threats to national security. As one might expect, the realities of hacking are somewhat less grandiose, most likely involving free phone calls, rearranged Web pages, and pranks.

Hackers, as a rule, are boys – predominately white, suburban boys – who are generally between the ages of 14 and 20. The 'grand old men' of the scene are often in their twenties. Hacker culture exemplifies what Anthony Rotundo (1998) has described as 'boy culture', that moment of adolescence characterized by the testing of the boundaries of adult authority and the expression of independence. Accordingly, it is not surprising to see hackers and hacker culture as a resistant subculture that challenges mainstream culture and expresses itself through oppositional codes and by challenging adult, primarily male, authority.

While the popular image of hackers as 'criminals' is widespread, the types of crime they usually commit are relatively benign. There are two unspoken rules of hacker culture: first, never act maliciously (acts that damage or destroy data); second, never hack for financial gain. These rules are born from a recognition that is part practical (damage and financial gain will get you arrested) and part ethical (hackers claim that their exploits are for exploration and knowledge, not to cause problems or make money). To most hackers, damaging a system or getting paid to hack would be like visiting a museum in order to destroy paintings or sell them to the highest bidder. On a more practical level, they are also the primary offences for which hackers are arrested.

Stories that involve damage or financial gain are also those most frequently reported in the mainstream press. As a result, the primary image of the hacker in the popular imagination is that of the criminal. Extreme cases, such as that of Kevin Lee Poulsen, a hacker accused of espionage (charges that were eventually dropped), make for sensational news items and grab public attention. Therefore most public perception of who hackers are and what they do is shrouded in a cloak of mystery and criminality. Hackers, however, see themselves as upholding a staunch ethic, functioning as watchdogs against industry abuses and as pioneers, exploring the frontiers of the digital age. While the popular press and media construct hackers as criminals, hackers see themselves quite differently. As Loyd Blankenship (1985) wrote in 'The conscience of a hacker' (often cited as 'The hacker manifesto'):[2]

> We make use of a service already existing without paying for what could be dirt-cheap if it wasn't run by profiteering gluttons, and you call us criminals. We explore … and you call us criminals. We seek after knowledge … and you call us criminals. We exist without skin color, without nationality, without religious bias … and you call us criminals. You build atomic bombs, you wage wars, you murder, cheat, and lie to us and try to make us believe it's for our own good, yet we're the criminals. Yes, I am a criminal. My crime is that of curiosity. My crime is that of judging people by what they say and think, not what they look like. My crime is that of outsmarting you, something that you will never forgive me for.

This contrast between media images and hackers' self-perceptions can best be understood by examining the historical and political contexts that gave rise to hackers and hacking. Hackers' self-image can be traced back to the origins of the movement, starting with students at major research universities in the 1950s and 1960s. As Steven Levy defined them, hackers were defined by their adherence to an ethic, a code of beliefs that was predicated on access to computers, freedom of information, the mistrust of authority, judgement of others based on skill and performance, and the belief that computers could be used for constructive social change (Levy, 1984: 39–50). This first generation of hackers often had to resort to unusual means to solve problems, and were fond of practical jokes and pranks. Thus, the history of hackers and hacking is invariably connected to the ethics and traditions of the first generation.

A BRIEF HISTORY OF HACKING: OLD SCHOOL AND NEW SCHOOL

Hackers are often divided into two groups: 'old school' hackers and 'new school' hackers. The old school refers to the hackers of the 1960s and 1970s who are generally credited with the birth of the computer revolution, and subscribed to an ethic of 'free access to technology' and a free and open exchange of information. These hackers are the 'ancestors' of the new school hackers, the hackers of the 1980s and 1990s, generally stereotyped as 'hi-tech hoodlums' or computer terrorists. Historically, however, the two groups are linked in a number of ways, not the least of which is the fact that the hackers of the 1980s and 1990s have taken up the old school ethic, demanding free access to information. Further problematizing the dichotomy is the fact that many old school hackers have become Silicon Valley industry giants and, to the new school hackers' mind-set, have become rich by betraying their own principles of openness, freedom and exchange. Accordingly, the new school hackers see themselves as upholding the old school ethic and find themselves in conflict with many 'old schoolers' now turned corporate.

In the 1980s, hackers entered the public imagination in the form of David Lightman, the protagonist from the hacker thriller *WarGames* (1983), who would inspire a whole generation of youths to become hackers, and later, in 1988, in the form of Robert Morris, an old school hacker who unleashed the internet worm (a self-replicating virus), bringing the entire network to a standstill. These two figures would have significant influence in shaping hacker culture and in popular media representations of it. In the wake of these public spectacles would emerge the new school, a generation of youths who would be positioned both as heroes (like Lightman in *WarGames*) and villains (like Morris) and who would find little or no institutional or government support as the old school had two decades earlier.

The new school emerged in an atmosphere of ambivalence, where hacking and hackers had been seen and celebrated as both the origins of the new computerized world and as the greatest threat to it. New school hackers responded by constituting a culture around questions of technology, to better understand cultural attitudes towards technology and their own relationship to it.

The old school of hacking is perhaps best known for one of its basic tenets: 'information wants to be free'. It seems odd, then, that the new school of hackers, who follow many of the traditions of their older predecessors would be so staunchly supportive of something like cryptography. Cryptography is, essentially, the study of secrets – how to secure information and prevent others from seeing what you would like to keep secret. Such a principle appears to violate what Steven Levy described as the 'hacker ethic' in his 1984, book *Hackers: Heroes of the Computer Revolution*. But that was 1984, and hacking isn't what it used to be.

When one speaks of hackers, then, one is *either* referring to the valorized heroes who made personal computing a reality, or one is talking about the new generation of kids who break into computer systems, alter Web pages, or shut down systems with DoS (Denial of Service) attacks. As outlined above, these two types of hacker divide roughly into two groups: the 'old school' and the 'new school'.

On the surface, there appear to be tremendous differences between old school and new school hackers. Old school hackers were students at MIT, Harvard and Cornell in the 1950s, 1960s and 1970s, and were members of computer hobby clubs. New school hackers are kids of the 1980s and 1990s, raised on *WarGames, Hackers* and *The Net*. The differences between the two groups are, apparently, pronounced: old school hackers were the founders of many of the start-up companies that made the computer revolution possible; new school hackers were the founders of hacker groups such as the Legion of Doom and Masters of Deception, and would endure visits from the Secret Service and the FBI, and spend time in jail. But just below that surface, the line between the two begins to blur. Hacking hasn't changed all that much, but the context in which it occurs most definitely has.

The story of the Apple computer is often cited as one of the great old school hacker 'success stories'. Steve Wozniak and Steve Jobs still get a lot of mileage out of the story of how they built and sold 'blue boxes' (devices that enabled one to make free long-distance phone calls) in their Berkeley dorms. Old school hackers, like Wozniak and Jobs, were adventurers, explorers and innovators. When old school hackers ran into a problem, they 'hacked' their way around it. The result, usually an elegant piece of computer code or a new hardware device or configuration, would be proof of their status. These hackers were idealists of the first order, preaching their gospel – 'information wants to be free'. They were also naive. The fact the DARPA (the Department of Defense's Advanced Research Projects Agency) funded almost all of their research (including the internet) and that such research would go towards making better bombs, missiles and guidance systems during the Vietnam War, for example, is usually excised from the nostalgic account.

If you ask almost any of these old school hackers about the hackers of today their first response will be this: 'These kids today, they're not hackers. They break into systems, copy software, break copy protection, and generally violate the principles that inspired the hacker ethic of the 60s and 70s.' And, on the surface, they are right. But if we compare the two contexts – the 50s, 60s and 70s with the 80s and 90s – two things becomes clear: first, the context that enabled these old school hackers to experiment and innovate no longer exists; second, the loss of the environment is the direct result of those old school hackers violating their own most deeply held principles. In short, the old school went corporate. The first thing Jobs and Wozniak did, for example, was make the Apple proprietary (which may well lead to Apple's ultimate demise). They took the hacker ethic, 'information wants to be free' and turned it on its head. Others followed suit. The only person not to sell out was Bill Gates – he was corporate from the very beginning. Information wants to be free, but old school hackers wanted to be rich.

The 'new school' emerged in the wake of the incorporation and commodification of the computer (the PC in particular). New schoolers had tools that the old school never did, namely the PC, but no place to go and no government grants to build networks. They did, however, have modems, which opened up a whole new world of networked communication. The new school hackers didn't have to own any big machines to explore them, they just had to find them, connect to them and play. Innovation gave way to curiosity. But in most cases, exploration was met with obstacles. These hackers grew up in a world where the creed 'information wants to be free' didn't make much sense. That battle had been fought and lost; and it had been lost (or perhaps more appropriately 'surrendered') by the people that started it in the first place, the old school hackers. Hacking had given way to corporate secrets. Where the old school had lived in a world that threatened to become secret, new school hackers grew up in a world that *was* full of secrets: PIN numbers, house alarm codes, phone access codes, voicemail codes, passwords, credit card numbers and the like.

In a world in which secrets govern everything from financial transactions to reading e-mail to defining one's identity, secrecy becomes a way of life. Secrecy is power – government power, bank power, police power. But secrets can be broken or revealed, rendering them worthless. Power can be maintained through the creation of secrets and, therefore, can be stripped away in the revelation of secrets. Accordingly, for the new school hackers, there are dual concerns: breaking secrets and keeping secrets. If you are going to be a hacker, you had better know how to do both. There is an irony at work here, and new school hackers will be the first to admit it – you need to keep your secrets safe (especially your identity) if you are going to be successful at breaking others'. If it is true that the battle for freedom of information has been fought and lost, then the new school hackers are truly following in their predecessors' footsteps. If information still wants to be free, then it is new school hackers who will liberate it. What the old school hackers don't see, and don't understand, is that the ideals they one preached are still alive and well in the next generation.

What cryptography and security are about today is keeping secrets safe in a climate where privacy and security are threatened on a daily basis, and software and systems that don't take security seriously are prime targets for hackers to make this point clear. The hackers of today are no more malicious, deviant, or criminal that their counterparts of 20 and 30 years ago. In fact they share the same curiosity and desire to learn that inspired a revolution. The difference is that new school hackers have to live in the world that the old school made for them and, more often than not, they have to hack their way out of it.

NEW DIGITAL CRIME

New school hackers have invented a set of new crimes for the digital age and law enforcement has been slow to respond. One of the primary problems of identifying hackers' crimes is that they happen for the most part in a virtual space, a space which the law itself has trouble understanding. As a result, when hackers are arrested and charged with crimes, they rarely find themselves charged with violating newer laws specifically designed to combat cybercrime (such as electronic trespassing). Instead, hackers are most frequently hit with serious charges of conventional fraud.

Even as the law had difficulty dealing with them, hackers are continually inventing new ways to break the law. These crimes, often categorized as fraud, fall into three categories: social engineering, getting root and hacktivism.

'Social engineering', as hackers refer to it, is the process of obtaining information through interacting with people, often posing as a helpless neophyte or computer expert. The idea behind social engineering is that hackers can gain knowledge and learn secrets by taking advantage of social relationships of trust and by exploiting a common discomfort that many people feel with technology. A common social engineering trick, for example, is to pose as a computer security expect, telling an unsuspecting user that their computer account is in jeopardy. In order to 'test' the account, the hacker will ask the user for his or her account information and password. The more urgent the hacker can make the request seem, the more pressure he or she can generate on the unsuspecting user. The result is that by posing as someone with expertise or power, hackers can gain incredible amounts of information simply by asking for it.

The success of social engineering attacks rests on two related issues. First, that small, but vital, pieces of information are major gatekeepers to access. For example, the only way that computers are able to validate a user's identity is through secrecy. The very concept of a password is based on a shared secret. The computer asks the user 'what is your password?', and the user's ability to answer that question – to, in effect, share that secret with the computer – is the only way in which it can validate the user's identity. Unlike the physical world, where we have bodies, sights, and sounds to confirm information, the computer relies exclusively on secrecy and information to validate identity. As a result, knowing and sharing a secret is performing an identity. The second reason that social engineering attacks succeed is based on a general sense of discomfort with computers. According to one computer hacker, 'if you ask a person if they are having trouble with their computer, 95 per cent of the time they will say yes, even if there is nothing wrong.' This sense of discomfort makes users less careful with information such as passwords. To complicate matters, many systems force users to choose passwords that are difficult for hackers to guess, with unintended consequences. While such programs do result in more secure passwords, they also make them more difficult to remember and use and many users end up writing them down, often in obvious places for easy access. In a surprising number of cases, a routine tour of a company office will reveal a number of Post-it® notes stuck to monitors with user names and passwords in plain sight.

To the hacker, information is access. Even things like company phone books, carelessly discarded in the waste bin, can be a treasure-trove of information, allowing a hacker to impersonate anyone in the organization, complete with title, phone number and office information. A discarded memo may provide a cover story for a phone call to a secretary: 'I needed to get into Sarah's account for the X11 project. She left me the password, but I can't seem to find it. You wouldn't happen to know it would you?'

Social engineering in many ways defies the representation of the hacker as a 'hi-tech' wizard. It is, however, far and away the most common means of access to information and hackers rely on it extensively. As one hacker commented, 'Sure I could spend 3 days straight trying to break in, but why waste the time?' With one phone call, a hacker can get the same information and pursue more interesting areas of exploration.

Once a hacker is inside, the goal of hacking changes. On every system there is a privileged account, usually referred to as the 'root' account. This account gives the hackers complete control over the system, the ability to read (and alter) files and even to shut down the system should he or she choose to do so. Apart from exercising a degree of control over the system, root access allows the hacker to do something else – cover his or her tracks. By becoming the root user, the hacker can erase any log or trace of his or her presence on the system, making it appear as if he or she had never gained access at all. Doing so greatly reduces the risk of getting caught and allows the hacker to continue his or her explorations from a new starting point, so even if they are traced back to their point of origin, there is still a buffer between the hacker and the place from which they are hacking.

Root access also allows a hacker to take advantage of other system flaws in order to create trojan horses or backdoors in the system. In the event that the hacker is discovered and shut out of the system, these programs can leave other entrances that will allow the hacker back in at will. Root access, then, provides a large degree of control over the system and is the ultimate end point for exploration.

Apart from exploration, there has been a new set of activities which hackers have taken up under the banner of 'hacktivism'. Hacktivism is the idea that computer hacking can be applied to activist goals and produce social and political change in the world. Often done as a form of protest, hackers frequently break into computer Web servers and rearrange Web pages to display social or political messages. Those messages have ranged in scope from attacks on a furrier's website where the page was replaced with an anti-fur message and images of animals in traps, to defacement of political party Web pages in the UK, to calls for the liberation of East Timor. In 1998, the website for the *New York Times* was hacked in protest at the imprisonment of computer hacker Kevin Mitnick. Some 3 years earlier, Mitnick had been arrested in North Carolina, where *NYT* reporter John Markoff had been part of the investigation and had written extensively about the pursuit of Mitnick. The *Times* was forced to shut down its website for nearly 8 hours over the weekend that the Starr report was released and when traffic was anticipated to be at an all-time high.

The hack of the *NYT* website was the first instance where a major media website lost revenue as a result of a hack which claimed that its coverage had been unfair (the hacked website accused Markoff of unethical and criminal behaviour in the apprehension of Mitnick). Mitnick's case further served to radicalize an entire generation of hackers, prompting them to protest publicly against his arrest and prosecution, through means both legal and illegal. Hackers created a 'Free Kevin' movement which included media interviews, a public awareness campaign and several high-profile events, one of which included a plane sky-writing 'Free Kevin' over one of the protests. To understand the importance of hacktivism, we must return to the split between the 'old school' and the 'new school'.

THE POLITICS OF HACKING

Over the past few years there has been a decided shift in the way hackers think about the world. Born from an idealistic model of personal, individual achievement, the very idea of hacking has always been a singular and isolated phenomenon. In the early days, hackers rarely worked in groups or teams, preferring to 'hand off' programming solutions to one another in the process of what they called 'bumming code'. Each time a program was handed off, it would be improved slightly and then passed along to the next hacker, and so on. Hackers of the 1980s and 1990s, who began to form loosely knit groups such as the Cult of the Dead Cow, the Legion of Doom and Masters of Deception, practised a similar ethic: hackers would learn from one another, but generally the understanding was 'everyone for themselves' – especially whenever someone got arrested!

That ethic, which began with the hackers of the 1960s and 1970s, is beginning to dissolve in the face of politics. Old school hackers are often disgusted by the antics of their progeny. Indeed, many old timers insist that the hackers of today are unworthy of the moniker 'hacker' and prefer to terminologically reduce them, calling them 'crackers' instead – the idea being that 'crackers' are petty crooks, as opposed to 'hackers', who see themselves as more sophisticated explorers. That distinction denies too much history, too many connections, and is often nothing more than a nostalgic, and very convenient, revision of their own histories. The earliest hackers did most of the things for which they criticize today's hackers. They stole (the Homebrew Computer Club was famous for pirating code); they regularly engaged in telephone fraud and used all sorts of hacks to avoid paying for things (best represented by the hacker journal *TAP*, which taught people how to steal everything from phone service to electrical power); and they had no problem with breaking and entering or hacking a system if it meant more time on the mainframe (see Sterling, 1992). They also tended to forget a lot of things. Who paid for all those computers at Harvard, Cornell and MIT? Who funded ARPAnet? Could it be the same folks who were busily napalming indigenous persons halfway around the globe? And why were those computer labs such a potential target for anti-war protesters in the 1960s that they needed bullet-proof Plexiglas to shield them? The old school history is not as simple as it sometimes appears. Yes, they were the geniuses who gave us the first PCs, but along the way they tended to be implicated in a lot of nasty business, to most of which they were all too willing to turn a blind eye.

I don't mean to suggest that old school hackers were not hackers, only that they weren't all that different from the new schoolers they like to brand 'criminals', 'crackers' and the like. Where the old school seems to come off as (at best) forgetful, the new school has shown a new kind of commitment, something that is virtually unthinkable to the hackers of yesteryear. The hackers of the late 1990s are becoming *political*. There is a new move to group action, political involvement and intervention.

Recently, seven members of the Boston hacker collective, the L0pht, testified on Capitol Hill before the Senate Governmental Affairs Committee. As fellow hacker Peter the Great described it in his write-up of the testimony:

> Mudge gave a short, elegant statement which set the tone for the rest of the day's talks. He expressed his hope for an end to the mutual animosity that has long existed between the hacker community and the government and his sincere desire that the ensuing dialogue would pave the way towards civility and further collaboration between the two sides. This was a beautiful moment. It was as if a firm hand of friendship was being extended from the hacker community to the senate. I was moved, truly.

This is a gesture that would have been virtually unthinkable only a few years ago.

Even more dramatic is the fact that the hacker collective Cult of the Dead Cow [cDc] has a *policy on China*. In part, that policy was used in its justification for the release of Back Orifice, a computer security program that exploits vulnerabilities in Windows 95 and 98 operating systems. According to the cDc, Microsoft's decision to choose profit over human rights in supporting trade with China implicates it in the politics of oppression. The cDc has been working to support a group of Chinese dissidents, the Hong Kong Blondes, who are learning to use encryption and hacking techniques to stage interventions in Chinese Governmental affairs to protest Chinese human rights violations.

Most recently, in the USA, hackers have begun to band together in an effort to raise public awareness about the imprisonment of Kevin Mitnick, the aforementioned hacker facing a 25-count federal indictment who has been incarcerated without a hearing and has had the evidence to be brought against him withheld from discovery. In response to Miramax's decision to film Mitnick's story, hackers have banded together, launching a full-scale protest (among other things) in front of Miramax's offices in New York. The campaign also includes letter-writing initiatives, the distribution of 'FREE KEVIN' bumper stickers, websites, T-shirts, and even an online ribbon campaign.

Computers have begun to affect us in undeniably political ways. The globalization of technology, coupled with the power that the computer industry wields, makes the hacking of today an essentially political act. Some of the effects can be seen in the highly politicized trial of Kevin Mitnick and in the efforts to pass the WIPO treaty, US legislation that makes hacking (even legal experimentation) a criminal act.

The differences between old school and new school hackers are not as great as they might appear or as they are often made out to be. If there are differences, they reside in the fact that hackers today are stepping up and taking a kind of political responsibility that was altogether alien to their predecessors.

The future of hacking goes hand in hand with the future of technology. Today's hackers share not only a common ancestry with the 'old school' hackers, but also a common set of values and ideas. What has changed is the context in which hackers perform. The distinction made between the old school and the new school of hackers overlooks the many similarities between these two groups, not the least of which is the desire to see new uses for technology that help raise awareness of both the problems and possibilities that such technology presents.

NOTES

1   See, for example, Paul Mungo and Bryan Clough, *Approaching Zero: The Extraordinary World of Hackers, Phreakers, Virus Writers, and Keyboard Criminals*, New York: Random House, 1992; Katie Hafner and John Markoff, *Cyberpunk: Outlaws and Hackers on the Computer Frontier*, New York: Simon and Schuster, 1991; Clifford Stoll, *The Cuckoo's Egg*, New York: Simon and Schuster, 1989; Jonathan Littman, *The Watchman: The Twisted Life and Crimes of Serial Hacker Kevin Poulsen*, Boston: Little, Brown and Company, 1997; Jonathan Littman, *The Fugitive Game*, Boston: Little, Brown and Company, 1996.
2   This essay, originally published in the hacker underground journal *Phrack*, has taken on a life of its own. Often cited now as 'The hacker manifesto', it has appeared on countless websites and T-shirts, and has even made an appearance in the MGM film *Hackers*.

REFERENCES

Blankenship, L. (1985) 'The conscience of a hacker', *Phrack*, 1 (7), Phile 3.
Levy, S. (1984) *Hackers: Heroes of the Computer Revolution*. New York: Dell.
Rotundo, A. (1998) 'Boy culture' in H. Jenkins (ed.) *The children's culture Reader*. New York: New York University Press, pp. 337–62.
Sterling, B. (1992) *The Hacker Crackdown: Law and Disorder on the Electronic Frontier*. New York: Bantam.

STUDY QUESTIONS

1   In your own words outline what you think are the similarities and differences between hacking and trespass or theft.
2   What 'new ways to break the law' have emerged as a result of advancements in new information and communication technologies? What have been the responses of politicians to these developments?
3   Make a list of the positive and negative implications of new technologies in terms of both personal autonomy and social control. Are these benefits and disadvantages equally experienced by all?
4   Criminology has arguably been rather slow to recognize the importance of new media in generating new forms of criminal activity. The development and expansion of the Internet, for example, has led to increases in human trafficking, cyber-prostitution, paedophile rings, and many other forms of crime and

exploitation. What, in your opinion, are the most important issues facing criminologists in the early part of the twenty-first century? How do the issues that you have identified compare with those highlighted by South and by Hudson (Readings 29 and 30)?

FURTHER READING

Rheingold, H. (1994) *The Virtual Community: Surfing the Internet*, London: Minerva, is a relatively early examination of the ways in which the Internet is transforming communication, relationships and culture in modern life, and chapter 9, 'Electronic frontiers and online activists' pre-empts some of the comments made by Thomas in the reading concerning the uses of the Internet in forming communities (criminal and non-criminal) that are not limited by physical location and boundaries. For a discussion of the exploitation of women via the Internet, see Gillespie, T. (1999) 'Virtual violence? Pornography and violence against women on the Internet' in J. Radford, M. Friedberg and L. Harne (eds) *Women, Violence and Strategies for Action: Feminist Research, Policy and Practice*, Buckingham: Open University Press. The book from which Reading 34 was taken, Gauntlett, D. (ed.) (2000) *Web.Studies*, London: Arnold, is an equally innovative but more recent collection. Several contributors write about crime and deviance in relation to the Net, many of them arguing that traditional understandings of what constitutes 'deviance', 'exploitation', 'protest' and so forth are being reformulated in the light of the changing relations of power and control that new technologies precipitate. The chapter by Stephen Lax, 'The Internet and democracy', is of particular relevance. Another recent contribution is the overview of cybercrime provided by Wall, D. (1999) 'Cybercrimes: new wine, no bottles?' in P. Davies, P. Francis and V. Jupp (eds) *Invisible Crimes: Their Victims and their Regulation*, Basingstoke: Macmillan.

Author Index

Subject Index